THE NEW SHELL GUIDE TO
BRITAIN

Contributors

John R. Allen
Felix Barker
M. W. Barley
Alan Brack
Adrian Bell
Phyllis Bentley
Geoffrey Boumphrey
Bruce Campbell
Derek Chapman
Sid Chaplin
Charles Coles
Neil Cossons

Phil Drabble
C. J. O. Evans
Cuthbert Graham
J. S. Grant
Geoffrey Grigson
Marie Hartley
W. G. Hoskins
Jack House
Joan Ingilby
Roger Kain
Robert Kemp
K. J. Lace

Charles Lines
Alun Llewellyn
R. M. Lockley
Moray McLaren
Angus MacVicar
Alan Mattingly
John Montgomery
Frank Morley
John Moore
Sir Jasper More
Clifford Musgrave
Richard Reid

Michael Robbins
George Scott-Moncrieff
Frank Singleton
Martin Skinner
Harry Soan
George Speaight
Marguerite Steen
Wilfred Taylor
Jean Ware
J. Wentworth Day
Ellen Wilson

Also revised for this edition by:

Alan Brack
Anthony Brode
Vera Burden
Roy Christian

John Dawson
Paul Fincham
Alan Jenkins
Roger Kain

Charles Lines
Alun Llewellyn
Donald Macnie
Sir Jasper More

David Verey
Ellen Wilson

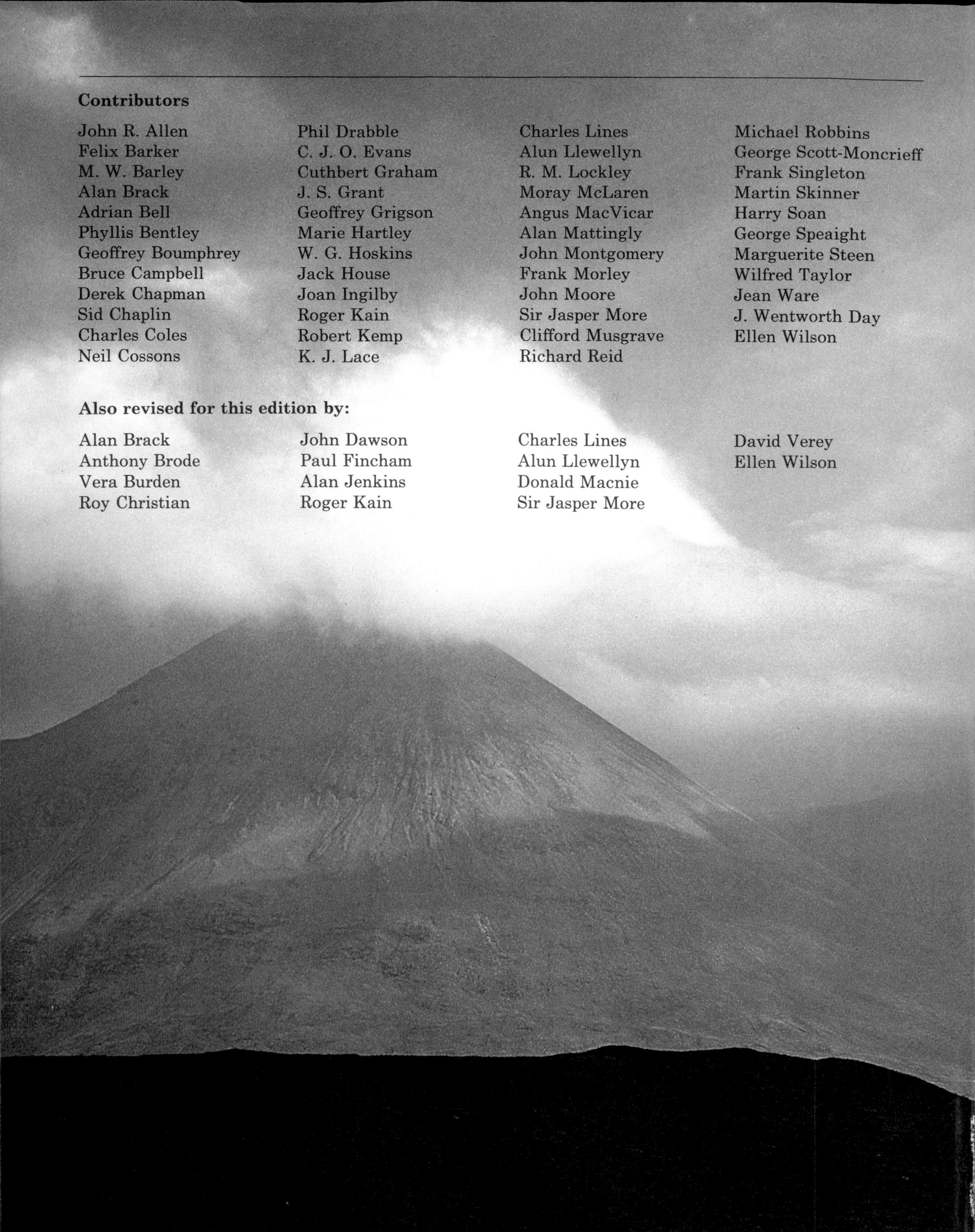

THE NEW SHELL GUIDE TO
BRITAIN

Introduction by
JOHN HILLABY

Edited by
GEOFFREY BOUMPHREY

Revised Edition by
GEORGE SPEAIGHT

EBURY PRESS, LONDON
in association with The Rainbird Publishing Group Ltd

The Shell Guide to Britain was first published in Great Britain
in 1964 by Ebury Press
National Magazine House
72 Broadwick Street, London W1V 2BP
in association with
The Rainbird Publishing Group Ltd
27 Wrights Lane, London W8 5TZ
who designed and produced the book

This fully revised edition published 1985 by Ebury Press
in association with The Rainbird Publishing Group Ltd

Reprinted 1987

ISBN 0 85223 410 4

House Editor: Georgina Evans
Designer: Yvonne Dedman
Indexer: Tony Raven
Cartographer: Lovell Johns Limited
Maps © Universal Mapping Limited

Text set by Servis Filmsetting Ltd, Longsight, Manchester, England
Illustrations originated by Bridge Graphics Ltd, Hull, England
Printed and bound by Kyodo-Shing Loong, Singapore

The name Shell and the Shell emblem are registered trademarks

Shell U.K. Ltd would point out that the contributors' views
are not necessarily those of this company.

The information contained in this book is believed correct at the time of
printing. While every care has been taken to ensure that the information
is accurate, the publishers and Shell can accept no responsibility for any
errors or omissions or for changes in the details given.

Endpapers: Britain's hedgerows

Title page: Cuillin Hills, Isle of Skye (see page 394)

CONTENTS

EDITOR'S FOREWORD

The series of guidebooks carrying the Shell name is now famous. England, Scotland, Wales, Ireland and France have all been described in an editorial pattern that has proved useful and popular: detailed gazetteers to places of interest are preceded by general introductory articles on history, architecture, landscape and similar topics. Some of these guidebooks are no longer in print but others have been revised, and the time has now come to bring out a revised edition of the very first of the Shell Guides, that to Britain.

Here the problem is different, for one set of introductory articles would be utterly inadequate to encompass the rich diversity of farmland and hillside, of town and country, of culture and tradition, that can be found within the island of Britain (Ireland is not covered in this volume). Indeed, the wider the field that has to be covered, the more one is driven to study the detail if one is to make sense of the whole: and it is only by knowing Britain as an island of three races and of innumerable small communities – each with its own character and fiercely held loyalties – that the nature of the country as a whole can be understood and appreciated.

So it was that the planners of this Guide to Britain thought of it from the first as a collection of guides to the historic counties of England, Wales and Scotland. Each county – or, exceptionally, two adjacent counties – was provided with an Introduction, written by someone deeply versed in the past and present of that part of Britain; and these Introductions were designed not just to highlight the tourist sights and beauty spots of their areas but to convey something of the atmosphere of each region. Following these introductions came gazetteers to the chief places of interest in each county; these were inevitably very brief and must be regarded as pointers rather than exhaustive descriptions, guiding the reader to places worth visiting, for some of which more detailed descriptions may be sought later.

No fundamental change has been made to this arrangement in the revised edition, but the revised county and regional boundaries (and sometimes nomenclatures) introduced in England and Wales in 1974 and in Scotland in 1975 have been taken into account. There are some who regret the disappearance of old historic names and of once-familiar territorial areas, and an attempt has been made to retain these names in the body of the text; but it cannot be denied that in some cases – for instance, the great urban conglomerations of Merseyside, West Midlands, or Tyne and Wear – the new counties recognize the reality of contemporary life in Britain today; this remains true whatever changes may be introduced in the structure of local government. Moreover, however non-Celts may stumble linguistically in pronouncing Clwyd instead of Denbigh, the new names of the Welsh counties are, in fact, names from an older Wales, that are now suitably revived in the Wales of today. Britain is a living and developing community of peoples, and this Guide attempts to reflect both its past and its present.

In the course of this revision every entry in the gazetteers has been examined and up-dated where necessary, and many new entries have been added. The introductions are largely timeless in character, but here, too, revisions have been made where appropriate. In the case of articles by authors who have since died, revisions have been limited to the correction of basic points of fact; where more extensive revision has been necessary, the name of the reviser has been coupled with that of the original author.

Grateful thanks are extended to George Dowse, Christopher Jennings, the Cumbria Tourist Board, the East Midlands Tourist Board, the Isle of Man Tourist Board, the London Tourist Board, the Northumbria Tourist Board, the North West Tourist Board, the Scottish Tourist Board, the South East England Tourist Board, Bet Davies at the Wales Tourist Board, the West Country Tourist Board, and the Yorkshire and Humberside Tourist Board for their help in supplying literature and updating the entries.

GEORGE SPEAIGHT

Editorial Notes and Abbreviations

No printed book, designed to last for several years, can take account of changes in the regulations for the many houses and gardens that are open to the public. An indication has been given as to which places are normally open, and between which months, but exact details of times, dates and charges should be sought from one or other of the annual guides that are published for this purpose.

The abbreviation NT indicates a property owned by the National Trust; membership of this body (details from 42 Queen Anne's Gate, London SW1H 9AS) gives admission to many of its properties. Likewise NTS indicates a property of the National Trust for Scotland. The abbreviation AM indicates an ancient monument or historic building in the care of the Department of the Environment. *See also* note regarding Scotland on page 337.

Among gazetteer entries, all of which are of some interest, * indicates a place – in the judgment of the compiler – of special interest, and ** a place of outstanding importance.

Places printed in **bold type** in the text of the Gazetteers will be found to have separate entries in the Guide under their own names. *Italic type* indicates a place near by.

Each gazetteer entry has a map reference. For example **Bristol** has a reference of 7H1; this means Bristol will be found on page 7 of the map section. The letter H indicates the grid line running along the bottom of the page and the number 1 refers to the grid line down the side of the page. Bristol will be found at the point where the letter and figure intersect.

The areas of local government represent the situation in the autumn of 1984.

INTRODUCTION

BY
JOHN HILLABY

My job is simply to raise the curtain on the great variety show of Britain and then, with a respectful bow to the company, leave them to their task of describing how the superb changes of scenery are related, one to another. However, like any strolling player, I cannot resist the temptation to mingle with the cast for a moment, adding a few words by way of a prologue. This is far from easy since the contributors are all scholars and writers of eminence – not least that one who just over 30 years ago taught us that our visible landscapes are in themselves an expression of centuries of history. That said we may swing forward – as this splendid compilation does – from Cornwall and the Isles of Scilly to the outermost Highlands and islands.

A bold transect from the southwest to the north is much to the fancy of those of us engaged in long-distance walking since we can look forward each day to the sun on our backs and not in our eyes. Moreover, it enables us to tackle the hills with progressive confidence because the Welsh borderlands are higher than the West Country; the Peak District is higher still, but less strenuous by far than the broken jaws of the Pennines and the sheer grandeur of the Scottish mountains. Another good reason for walkers and motorists alike to explore, perhaps even to traverse that southwest to northeast diagonal is that to one side, to the south and east, are mostly the milky shires of Saxon Britain but to the north and the west of that line are the refuges of the Celts.

As dedicated walkers can be almost as boring as reformed alcoholics I merely suggest that for part of your journeying – wherever it is – you should get to grips with the physical feel of the land. The feet rasp in entirely different ways on grits, sandstones and shales; they sense the elasticity of turf-covered limestones and peaty moorland; clays feel different too in a way that cannot easily be put into words. But there is an unmistakable ring about fire-born rock. In short, walking is a way of making love to the land, enabling it to return that affection.

On one point, however, I am on wholly indisputable ground. It is that when faced by the build and shape of a magnificent vista or, say, an age-mellowed market town, a cathedral perhaps, or an isolated burial mound, or even the curve of a village street, if you don't know what you are looking at you can't be expected to look at it for very long. It is a matter of decipherment. But how many books would you need to cover the whole country? Here is one that will serve for all, a well-established guide which is a library of reference and delight.

The introductory essays, especially those placed ahead of the vastly different counties and regions, have been prepared by experts so familiar with what they are writing about that they can, like illustrators, strip whole landscapes down to their essentials. It is here we can browse with profit, prepared for the details of individual places – such places as Rosedale Abbey. Midway between the once-great port of Whitby and York in North Yorkshire lies this little village with which I am on more intimate terms than any other. Here some 8,000 years ago the Mesolithic people colonized Yorkshire. By contrast, London where I spend most of my time, is not really an old city, at least not on the scale of Rome.

The rolling South Downs – which look as if they have risen from the sea – were literally shoved up into their present shape when the Alps arose around Lake Geneva and generated forces that pummelled our soft chalk. At the point where these ancient tracks such as the Downs and the Ridgeway meet, our forebears built Stonehenge, the biggest prehistoric temple in Europe. Likewise too, the moraines, drumlins and eskers, the stuff left behind by the glaciers of long ago, provided the Scots with ready-made golf-courses. Geography is everywhere. How fortunate we are in Britain to be within easy reach of the cream of it.

THE ARCHITECTURE OF BRITAIN

RICHARD REID

Architecture is always imported. The traditional buildings found in our countryside, however, have, metaphorically speaking, grown out of their surroundings. While architecture exists in both town and country, the cottage, and what the cottage represents, is the rustic and rural. As architecture shaped the towns so the cottage moulded the village.

Anglo-Saxon Britain was virgin country. For the few major structures that were built, materials were readily quarried from Roman ruins. By 1066, however, England had become a land of villages. Gradually the woodlands were reduced as small denes were cleared and cattle brought to graze. Many of the early villages were built from huts erected by squatters on common pasture or in a clearing in thickly wooded country.

After the Norman Conquest England was divided into 'manors'. The wealthier Norman landowners possessed several manors. Although such a landlord would probably have his own castle, he would invariably spend time in each of his manors and therefore build himself a manor house in each one. Most of the servants were quartered in the Great House, but for the farm labourers connected with the manor simple cottages were built near by.

Great changes occurred following the Black Death in 1348 which killed one-third of England's population of $3\frac{3}{4}$ million. Labour shortages increased the cost of labour. Some villages were gradually abandoned because landlords were unable to maintain traditional animal husbandry without the necessary labour. They switched to pastoral farming and converted the open arable fields into large enclosures of pasture for cattle and sheep.

The story of the cottage really begins in the 16th century when a man could build a house on the commonland if he raised the roof over his head and had a fire burning in his grate between sunset and sunrise. These houses were built either of wattle and daub or mud, and roofed with a thatching of straw or reed, or turves of growing grass or moss.

The timber-framed 15th-century Guildhall at Hadleigh, Suffolk (see also page 220)

The architectural style and character of the village were shaped by a complex series of factors as diverse as the building types with which the village itself was composed. The major influencing factor was the very nature of the village itself. There were feudal villages such as Penshurst and Chilham, in Kent, or Audley End, in Essex, where the whole way of life was bound up with that of the great mansion or Hall. The village almshouses and schools were usually provided by the local lord, as were the cottages and shops. Throughout were the tell-tale signs of such authority – the coat of arms on the inn; gates and monumental boundary walls of the great house; family memorials and chapels in the church – each detail symbolic of the feudal ensemble of served and servant.

In other villages, growing up in the shadow of great religious establishments, both building and daily life went hand in hand with religious observance. Abbeys and priories were the major architectural set pieces. Schools, hospitals, inns, mills and workers' cottages, all the elements associated with both their business and charity work as well as those necessary to sustain everyday monastic life, grew up around them.

By the 18th century there was another type of 'closed village', the model village. A product of 'emparking' or the need to accommodate an expanding agricultural labour force or, in the late 19th century, an industrial community, such villages were the creation of the landowning classes. Under the sole ownership of one man, they were a product of a particular vision, social or architectural, designed not by local builders but by architects. As a result, a range of pattern books catering for escapist tendencies was produced extolling the virtues of one style or another.

But it was in the traditional village, a product of centuries of gradual development and growth, self-contained and localized within parishes and manors, that vernacular building was largely shaped.

While architectural fashions were as important as comfort in the local manor house, the village builders were more practical men for whom utility was of primary concern. For them the major constraints concerned the particular use of the building, which

Rural labourers lived in one-room cottages with an attic in the 16th and 17th centuries

Village identity was moulded by the houses of the working class; the first of the cottage rows or semi-detached houses built 1812–16

gave them form; the level of technological expertise, which gave them shape and space; the availability of building materials, which gave them style.

The central feature was the church. Pre-eminent in size and position, it played a real and active part in medieval village life, and it was around the church that the village grew, almost as if to reinforce those early ties. This was the major piece of architecture in the village. A lych-gate often marked the entrance to the churchyard.

The next most important piece of architecture was the manor house. Unlike the major houses of the day, comfort and privacy were of greater importance in houses of more modest size. Their architecture was usually more restrained, but experiments in planning, the positioning of hearths or stairs, were more obviously in evidence. Once the centres of village government, the detail and organization of their façades and internal spatial arrangements express quite clearly the development in domestic architecture – such as the use of shutters to windows, the advent of mullioned lights, the use of wooden frames and sashes, the development of fireplace design with the inclusion of hoods, flues and chimneys.

The church and manor house, the major architectural set pieces, provided the necessary nucleus around which the village grew. Subtly, the manor house was mirrored in less sophisticated buildings such as the parsonage or the substantial houses of the rising middle class – the bailiffs and stewards; the wool merchants of the Cotswolds and East Anglia; the ironmasters of the Weald; doctors and tradesmen, and the prosperous farmers.

These buildings, marked by the ornamentation of architectural fashion, the shape and detail of windows, the elegance of entrance porticoes, the classical lines of cornice or balustrading, provided the necessary coherence, but it was the collective fabric of small cottages and terrace housing, the houses of the working class, that moulded and shaped the village identity. There were the retail stores and workshops of butchers and bakers, wheelwrights and blacksmiths. There were houses, in Kent and East Anglia, where, from the 13th century onwards, many

Flemish weavers set up looms, producing the broadcloth of Biddenden or the kerseymere of Kersey. Pebmarsh, Essex, still has a silk mill and Smarden, Kent, its medieval cloth factory.

Many villages had watermills, used for producing the West Country cloth or providing power for the ironmasters of the Kentish Weald, while windmills helped the Dutchmen drain the Fens. There were numerous other buildings too: old granaries and wool stores, oast-houses and the great tithe barns of the medieval parsons such as those at Bradford-on-Avon, Wiltshire, and Middle Littleton, in Hereford and Worcester.

But despite the multiplicity of use, the village was welded tightly together by the distinctive character of the region – each building shaped and styled from the local material available.

A characteristic feature of Dartmoor is the traditional longhouse. Built on the Moor from the 13th century onwards, they are long and narrow and were invariably built down a gentle slope. The family lived at the upper end while the cattle were housed at the lower end so that the slurry could be drained down the hill. They were generally constructed in local granite. By the late 16th century the living quarters and byre became separated by a cross passage.

Timber-framed buildings are rare in the West Country, much of the timber having been used for roof and floor joists while the bulk was earmarked for shipbuilding. Many houses were built of unquarried stone with walls often 2 feet or more in thickness. Typical of the region, especially Devon, from the late

Cob-walling, or sometimes stone as shown here, and thatch roof were common in Dorset circa 1700

In Somerset ranges of adjoining houses with gabled dormers were planned in the 17th century

Characteristic of the Cotswold houses are the gabled dormer windows with stone slate verges or carved finials (see opposite) and stone mullions

16th century, are the cob-built cottages. Consisting of a mix of mud bound with straw or stubble, the walls were built up in layers over several months. The cob walls projected an inch or so over a low stone base; the corners were rounded to avoid cracking.

Typical features of Cornwall and Dartmoor are tall, tapering chimneys and of Devon, from the 17th century, the built-in bread oven and the smoking oven.

The prosperity of the Cotswolds' cloth industry in the late 16th and 17th centuries is reflected in the beautiful limestone manor houses, market halls and cottages in the area. Regional features are gabled dormers flush with the façades of the house, carved finials, copings, decorative kneelers or stone-slate verges. Walls were built of random rubble with larger stones being used for window dressings and quoins. Most windows had moulded stone mullions and usually a drip moulding above windows and doors.

Further east, in the Middle Ages, Kent, Sussex and Surrey were covered by an unbroken forest with soil rich in iron ore. Indigenous oaks were used in the construction of ships and many fine towns and villages. These developments coupled with the clearances for agriculture so denuded the forests that a law was passed in the reign of Elizabeth I rationing the felling of oaks with the result that much timber for building was imported. The late 16th century was a time of stability and prosperity resulting in the building of many fine timber houses. Notable is the yeoman farmer's house, consisting of a lofty central hall flanked by storeyed ends. Many examples survive in the North and South Downs, and the Weald.

The wide choice of building material has created a remarkable wealth of village architecture in the southeast. During the 16th century the tiling of roofs began to replace thatching, while the old wattle and daub panels, the waterproof envelope between the timber framing, were replaced by an infill of brick nogging, laid either horizontally or in diagonals.

Throughout Surrey, East and West Sussex and Kent, tile hanging is a characteristic feature. A luxury before the 17th century, it quickly became the norm. Elaborate patterns were achieved by mixing

plain tiles with decoratively shaped tiles. Another regional feature is the use of mathematical tiles. Introduced here in the mid-18th century, it was conceived as an inexpensive way to make a timber-frame building more fashionable while avoiding the brick taxes. The tile was shaped to simulate a brick, but it was nailed to wood lathing.

The Romans had used river clay for bricks, but it was not until the 13th century that river clay was used once more, and then mainly in the low-lying areas around London and the eastern counties. In the 16th century it was imported and therefore expensive and was used primarily in larger houses.

Weatherboarding, used to protect windmills and watermills in Essex since the 15th century, was adopted for use on cottages and smaller houses by the end of the 18th century. Generally it consisted of a covering of overlapping horizontal boards of oak or elm, pegged to timber-framing.

During the Middle Ages the East Anglian peasant was as prosperous as his counterpart in the southeast, having successfully exploited the manufacturing revolution created by the Flemish weavers. Great wool churches were built by prosperous clothiers as were the fine wood and plaster houses lining the streets of Sudbury, Bildeston, Boxford and Kersey.

Building, especially of cottages, reached its peak between 1580 and 1630. Characteristic here in the east is the use of flint. Complete façades were faced in pebbles, and doors and windows were squared off with brickwork. In Norfolk there are many thatched roofs, some with elaborate patterns created by the laying

In Essex weatherboarding was not used for houses until light-weight timber frames were available

Norfolk's trading links led to a Flemish influence: bricks, pantiled roofs and tumbled gables with diagonal coarsing to the brickwork are common

and cutting of reeds. Additional decorative treatment includes the use of hazel spars at ridges, eaves and verge. In Suffolk many half-timbered houses have ornamental plasterwork known as pargeting, which consists of raised or incised relief work. First used by the Elizabethans, it increased in popularity but became out of fashion when brick-built houses gradually superseded half-timbering.

The use of pantiled roofs and the characteristic curved gable were products of commercial ties with the Low Countries. Dutch communities flourished in East Anglian towns and many merchant ships returning across the North Sea came laden with Dutch bricks and tiles. Because of the severe winds, gables were invariably taken up above the level of the roof to prevent thatch or tile being lifted. Where there was no coping or covering to the top of the parapet wall the brickwork 'tumbled in' at the gable end.

Characteristic of the borderlands of East Wales are storeyed houses not dissimilar to the black-and-white houses of the West Midlands. The timbers are generally large and square, and the panels between filled with wattle daubed with clay. A feature of west Dyfed are huge square or cone-shaped chimneys projecting out from the gable end of the houses. In Powys houses sometimes have a rush thatch roof with a turf-ridge, while in north Dyfed thatched roofs are often laid in decorative patterns. Further north, many cottages were built of unquarried stone generally of dry-stone construction with walls over 2 feet thick, plastered or

whitewashed and roofed in thatch or stone slates. Cob walling is also typical. Farmhouses here are quite utilitarian in design although robust in construction. The three-unit type of building consisting of barn, byre and farmhouse built in one single range is also characteristic here.

The vast tracts of woodland and forest in the Midlands encouraged the development of fine timber buildings, their panels filled with brick nogging or wattle and daub. Frames braced by arches are a feature. In the West Midlands the more important buildings of the 15th century were built of small framing. While the majority of smaller houses, particularly in Hereford and Worcester, continued to use the traditional cruck frame.

Cruck frames in small medieval buildings were split tree trunks shaped to join at their apex which supported a horizontal pole carrying the rafters

Small framing, typical of the West Midlands, became more economic and increased in the 17th and 18th centuries for smaller dwellings

The cottagers of west Dyfed built large fireplaces, often with two or three ovens, and chimneys modelled on those of more aristocratic castles

By the 17th century cottages further north were still built of timber but now comprised of several rooms on one storey and an attic

Another feature also of the Welsh borderlands is the black-and-white houses, often called 'magpie' houses. They are distinguished by a rich fretwork of black, ornamental braces against whitewashed clay panels. While brick and stone were used in the south-east in the 16th century, elaborate timber-frame buildings continued to be built in the Midlands well into the 17th century. But at this time cottages began to create more rooms like those further south.

The box-framed houses with darkened timbers and white painted walls typical of Cheshire are rarer further north. In Derbyshire and Staffordshire cottages have large ashlar door jambs and window frames made of stones bonded into rubble walls. Windows are unmoulded and gables are seldom taken above the shallow roofs of heavy, stone slates. Ornamentation was sparse.

In the industrial North and the Moors, most houses are built of red sandstone or of millstone grit from the Pennines. They are austere and utilitarian. Chimneys are usually square, with short, rounded stacks. In areas such as Humberside, where walls were built of limestone or millstone rubble, sandstone was used as a dressing for openings and quoins. In the uplands stone slates cover the roofs.

Characteristic of the Lake District from the 18th century was a long range of buildings consisting of a central farmhouse often rendered in a thick coat of rough cast and limewashed. Flanking it were farm buildings of dry-stone walling. Staircases were often added in a projecting outshut at the rear. Many houses here have thick rubble walls with an earth core. In parts of the Solway plain houses were built of 2-foot thick walls of clay bound with chopped straw. Thatch roofing was later replaced by sandstone flags.

In the early 18th century many houses in Scotland were built of clay, the roof load being carried on cruck trusses standing on stone footings. Good examples are found in Dumfries and Galloway. In rural areas the longhouse tradition of byre, stable and living quarters under one roof was the norm. Typical of the Strathclyde Region is the Dalriadic type of black house. A small, gabled cottage, its main characteristic feature is the carrying of the thatch roof over the gable ends to form overhanging eaves. The thatching itself is secured by ropes.

Scotland: a black house of the Dalriadic type built to beat the weather, it has overhanging eaves of thatch secured by stone weights

A feature of the seaports of Fife is houses built of harled rubble with a sandstone dressing to corners and openings. Many houses have stone forestairs. Roofs are generally covered with pantiles. The gable ends are stepped, termed crow-step.

Typical of the Scottish Highlands and islands is the Skye type of black house with byre and living quarters under one roof and an open, central hearth. It has a hipped-end roof of thatch with overhanging eaves. There is also a variation on the Dalriadic type of house with gabled ends above the level of the thatch. The horizontal ropes tying the thatch are lashed to the gable walls by pins. Stone weights generally hold down the vertical ropes. Stone walls are over 2 feet thick and openings are small and sparse formed with large stone lintels.

In the districts of Moray and Banff in Grampian many houses are built of clay, mixed with sand and straw, and large stones. A characteristic of the east-coast towns of Scotland of the 17th century are roll-moulded surrounds to openings, crow-stepped gables and angle turrets. Numerous mid-18th-century houses were built of blocks of peat, stone and broom.

Further north are the Hebridean black houses consisting of a long oblong divided into three rooms – byre, kitchen and sleeping quarters. Entry was through the byre. On the Isle of Lewis two or three buildings abut the side of the main house. The walls are 4–8 feet in thickness – a large cavity wall of boulders with a central core filled with stones, gravel or earth. The corners are round. The roof is set on the inside of the wall leaving the characteristic exposed broad ledge encircling the house. The rain water discharges into the central core creating a damp blanket designed to prevent the strong winds penetrating the dry-stone wall. The roof itself was originally thatched with heather and weighted down with boulders.

While the availability of materials dictated the structural systems, status and wealth could alter these. In the 16th century when brick and stone were expensive, they were found only in the great houses and mansions. The poor lived in rudimentary timber buildings. Even in the stone uplands, stone-built houses were rare, except among the gentry. With the development of cheap, speedy transport and the invention of the Hoffmann Kiln in 1858, which mechanized brick production, all this was to change. Soon houses and cottages could be built more rapidly and cheaply. But with the preponderance of Victorian red brick, the distinctive character of particular localities was gradually diluted. Old and well-tried craftsmanship was replaced by mass-produced work assembled by semi-skilled labour. And as the building by-laws of 1875 took effect, the remaining irregularities were ironed out as one began to see similar working-class housing everywhere and regional styles lost to modern housing.

OPEN AIR MUSEUMS

NEIL COSSONS

There are probably more museums per head of the population in Britain than in any country in the world. These museums represent over two centuries of steady growth and development although it is only in the last 20 years or so that museum visiting has become a widespread educational and leisure activity. Today more than 60 million people each year explore with delight the treasures of Britain's museums which range from some of the greatest collections in the world to tiny local history galleries run entirely by volunteers. The British Museum, the National Gallery, the Victoria and Albert and Science Museums, the Natural History Museum – these are major institutions of international standing and their fine collections attract many millions of visitors. Outside London are the great provincial museums of Birmingham, Liverpool, Manchester, Glasgow, Edinburgh and Cardiff, and many more municipal museums whose collections, often built up over more than a century, are increasingly becoming appreciated both by scholars and the public at large. The face of all these museums has changed radically in recent years; they have been revitalized and brought to life by new galleries and displays in which their riches are displayed.

But besides the renaissance among traditional museums there has been a boom in the creation of new ones, in part a reflection of the growing popular interest in archeology and history, in part the result of an awakening concern about the environment and its conservation. The last 20 years have seen numerous preservation groups and civic societies established; bodies of people anxious about the protection of hedgerows, wildlife habitats, endangered species or historic town centres and who are prepared to do something about them. At the same time the advancing threshold of public taste and attitude has resulted in a recognition that sites and landscapes that were hitherto disregarded are a valid part of the national estate, that the remains of the Industrial Revolution and later periods are important and that

Coalbrookdale Furnace and Museum or Iron at the Ironbridge Gorge Museum (see also pages 172–5)

something should be done to save at least the most important of them. All this has taken place during a period in which people have enjoyed increased leisure and mobility. In other words their opportunity not only to visit and gain enlightenment from museums but also to participate in their activities or even their running has been significantly enlarged.

In almost every respect museums have benefited from the new environmental movement for museums have always collected and represented, in an archival sense, the roots of a landscape's origins and history. But in one vital respect the traditional museum – seen as a building housing a collection of objects – could not satisfy the new demands for preservation and conservation. The physical constraints of buildings or site and sometimes financial ones as well have prevented many existing museums from active participation in certain types of preservation. Some have gone outside their walls to embrace wholeheartedly the landscape around them, either directly or by working with other bodies but, more often, new museums have been set up to do the job. Many of the museums of the last 20 years are outdoors; they attempt to preserve large objects like buildings, ships or steam pumping engines, and they provide a quality of visitor experience which is often impossible in the traditional urban museum. The very term 'museum' which for many years has been used in a derogatory sense has been reinterpreted in the last 20 years so that today museums of all types hold an important place not only in preserving the national heritage but in presenting it in an enlightened manner to a growing public.

The concept of the open air museum is not new. It has its origins in Scandinavia in the latter part of the 19th century when, with the encouragement of the King of Sweden, the great social historian Artur Hazelius (1833–1901) started to collect buildings for preservation in a 'folk park' called Skansen, then on the outskirts of Stockholm. The impetus came from a realization that rural communities were changing, or disappearing altogether, in the face of industrialization and the urbanization that goes with it, so Skansen like the hundreds of folk museums that have carried its ideas across northern Europe to the Black Sea, is primarily a museum of the countryside and its people, of rural communities, their traditions and social customs, reflected in buildings and their contents. In addition the Scandinavian open air museum was conceived as a place where folk music, art and other rural customs might be kept alive; in other words as a setting for activities.

The open air museum, in its formative years, was very much a product of the folk movement and was restricted to those countries where a consciousness of 'folk' and all that it represented in terms of material culture was strongest. Thus there are no open air folk museums as such in Latin countries while in Britain, for perhaps quite different reasons, the open air folk museum did not develop until relatively recently and then only in certain areas. Britain was the first country in the world to undergo the processes of industrialization on anything like a large scale and as birthplace of the Industrial Revolution, England in particular and Wales and Scotland to a lesser extent have undergone the enormous social and landscape changes resulting from industrialization for longer than any other countries. The impact of the Industrial Revolution on the landscape of England, both urban and rural, coupled with major changes in land tenure and agricultural husbandry that went with it resulted in the demise of the peasant culture which survived much later in many European countries. Indeed, many would argue that the roots of much of our cultural expression today lie in early industrial communities. Thus by the time Hazelius was contemplating Skansen the opportunity and even the need to create a similar museum in Britain had largely disappeared. The exceptions however were notable and significant for in rural Wales, Northern Ireland, the Isle of Man and more recently in Scotland – in 'Celtic' Britain, areas perhaps less affected by the cataclysmic effects of two centuries of pervasive industrial activity – open air folk museums have been set up.

The first of these was the **Cregneish Folk Museum** opened by the Manx Museum and National Trust in 1938 with the preservation of a single crofter's cottage. Cregneish is unusual in that the buildings are being preserved *in situ* in order to retain and present what was left of an ancient Celtic farming settlement. Some houses in the village are still occupied as dwellings but others have been restored to their original thatched condition and include Harry Kelly's cottage, the Karran farmstead, a turner's shop, weaver's shed and smithy. Harry Kelly died in 1934 but his family had lived in the village for over 300 years and his two-roomed cottage is furnished as he left it. The Karran farmstead, the centre of a 30-acre croft, has also been restored while the last handloom in the village, in use until 1939 for making woollen cloth for clothes and bedcovers, is preserved

Pendean, a farmhouse from Midhurst, at the Weald and Downland Open Air Museum, Singleton (see also page 92)

preserved in the weaver's shed. A flock of the island's indigenous breed of sheep, the Loghtan, is maintained in the museum and the Trust sells knitting wool from it. Cregneish is open from mid-May until the end of September every day of the week.

The **Welsh Folk Museum** at St Fagan's near Cardiff, accords more with the pattern established at Skansen for here buildings from all over Wales have been assembled on a 100-acre site adjacent to St Fagan's Castle, the former home of the Earls of

Plymouth. The castle itself, dating from 1570, has been preserved and holds fine collections of furniture and pictures including portraits of the Plymouth family who lived there from 1730 until shortly before the opening of the museum in 1948. Nearly 20 buildings form the open air museum proper including various types of farmhouses and associated agricultural buildings, a toll-house, Unitarian chapel, smithy, a tannery, and a woollen mill. The latter, Esgair Moel mill, stood some 2 miles east of Llanwrtyd, between Builth Wells and Llandovery. Today it is in regular use, its waterwheel powering carding engines, to open out and disentangle the wool

fibres, and an 80-spindle spinning mule. Dyeing and weaving can also be seen and the museum sells a range of traditional Welsh bedspreads.

St Fagan's has important social history collections, only a small proportion of which appear in the reconstructed buildings. Galleries of Material Culture, Costume, Agriculture and Agricultural Vehicles occupy a museum building at the entrance to the site where the social and cultural life of Wales over a period of several hundred years is illustrated. There are regular demonstrations by a wood turner, blacksmith and other craftsmen. The museum is open throughout the year.

In Scotland, at the **Auchindrain Museum of Country Life** near Inveraray, Strathclyde, a crofting settlement is being preserved *in situ*. With more than 20 buildings in various stages of restoration, and a few of them furnished, Auchindrain represents the way of life of a communal-tenancy settlement, owned by the Campbells, which was farmed well into the 20th century. There are some 20 acres of 'infield' which were once surrounded by several square miles of rough grazing. The arable land has been reclaimed for cropping in the traditional manner and appropriate breeds of animals and poultry are reared.

Although Auchindrain attempts to present the way of life of a complete agricultural community there are of course numerous farm museums which, while undoubtedly outdoors are not normally classed as open air museums. Some preserve farm buildings, most preserve machinery, but all are there primarily to present and in most cases actively demonstrate traditional methods of agricultural husbandry. At **Acton Scott** near Church Stretton in Shropshire, for example, 22 acres and the buildings of the Home Farm of Acton Scott Hall are worked in the manner of a typical local farm before the coming of the internal combustion engine. Horses are used extensively, and livestock includes cattle, sheep, pigs and poultry of breeds rarely seen today. Most of the fields are under grass but a four-course rotation of winter and spring corn, grass or clover leys and root or forage crops is demonstrated. Cows are still hand milked, although regulations insist that the milk is fed to farm animals, and there are regular demonstrations of butter and cheese making. Acton Scott Working Farm Museum, Wenlock Lodge, is open from late March to the end of September. Several other farm museums, with varying amounts of active demonstration, include **Shugborough Park Farm**, part of the Staffordshire County Museum, 6 miles east of Stafford, **Manor Farm Museum** at Cogges near Witney in Oxfordshire, **Easton Farm Park** north of Wickham Market in Suffolk and the **Norfolk Rural Life Museum** at Gressenhall, East Dereham, Norfolk.

Although the classic open air folk museum involves the reconstruction of buildings to form part of a broad social picture there are two open air museums in England which use buildings for a different purpose. The **Weald and Downland Open Air Museum** at Singleton, West Sussex and the **Avoncroft Museum of Buildings** in Hereford and Worcester are museums of buildings and set out to preserve and interpret examples of the history of building technology which in the case of both museums is closely related to the landscapes from which their exhibits come. Thus at Singleton the visitor can see more than 20 vernacular buildings drawn from the broad sweep of southeastern England stretching from the Solent to East Kent and northwards to the Thames. Here, in an assiduously scholarly manner, the minute detail of building design and construction is presented. The visitor has access to the structures of buildings and can understand how they were put together in a way which would be quite impossible from studying buildings still in use with all their modern additions and alterations. Sometimes open air museums are accused of destroying the landscape by detaching buildings from their true settings and reconstructing them in wholly artificial surroundings but both the Weald and Downland Open Air Museum and Avoncroft only move buildings which would otherwise be destroyed. Both museums have active policies of helping people who wish to preserve buildings *in situ* and there can be no doubt that the reconstructions which they carry out on their respective sites together with the enormous amount of research that this entails place them in a unique position to provide this type of expert advice. Besides being 'archives of fine buildings' these museums are of surprisingly popular interest, set in the most beautiful of surroundings, and they provide a first-class day out for the whole family.

In both museums timber-framed buildings predominate. At Singleton the museum's introductory displays are housed in a magnificent thatched and aisled barn from Hambrook, Sussex. There is a 15th-century hall from Boarhunt, Hampshire, a 16th-century farmhouse from Midhurst and, perhaps most spectacular of all, Bayleaf, a Wealden house of the early 15th century from Chiddingstone, Kent. Elsewhere brick and flint construction can be seen and smaller exhibits include a windpump from Pevensey, East Sussex, a saw-pit shed and a pugmill house which originally contained a horse-worked mill for tempering clay to a workable consistency. The Weald and Downland Museum is open from the beginning of April to the end of September daily. *See* pages 18–19.

At the Avoncroft Museum of Buildings near Bromsgrove, buildings and the crafts associated with their construction derive in the main from the West Midlands. There is a granary from Temple Broughton, Hereford and Worcester, a cruck barn from Cholstry, Hereford and Worcester, and Danzey Green windmill from Warwickshire, restored and in regular operation. There are brick buildings too, including a chain-maker's forge and an octagonal counting house from Bromsgrove. One of the delights of Avoncroft is that building reconstruction is always being carried out so that many of the traditional craft skills of the building trade can be seen. The museum is open from early March to late November every day.

Just as Skansen attempted nearly a century ago to catch and rekindle the dying embers of Sweden's rural heritage, since the 1950s in Britain increasing efforts have been made to preserve the remains of early industrialization in the face of change. Surprisingly much still survives of the early Industrial Revolution period of the 18th century although increasingly, in the face of urban renewal and industrial revitalization, these remains are disappearing. At Beamish in County Durham an open air museum – the **North of England Open Air Museum** – attempts to preserve elements of the social and industrial history of the region on a 250-acre site near Stanley. Here whole groups of buildings are being reconstructed in order to reflect the culture of the industrial northeast. Beamish colliery has been reconstructed complete with winding engine, headstocks and coal screens. Railway sidings with chaldron wagons serve the mine and a row of miners' cottages nearby illustrates the living conditions of mining families at the turn of the century and later. A Gateshead tram links a growing town, complete with Co-operative shop, to other parts of the site. Beamish is very much an industrial folk museum and its enormous collections, a small sample of which can be seen on exhibition in the museum's headquarters in Beamish Hall, will eventually fill many more buildings on the site. The museum at Beamish is open daily throughout the year.

A museum with very similar objectives, the **Black Country Museum**, is being developed at Dudley in the West Midlands. Here shops, a coal mine, chain shop and pub, the Jug & Bottle, have been reconstructed on a canalside site near the entrance to Dudley tunnel. The Black Country Museum is open from April to October every day except Saturdays.

The nature of industrial landscapes and the structures they contain – factories, mills, blast furnaces, canals, railways and so on – present peculiar problems of preservation and extend the concept of the musum to its limits. An example of this can be seen in the **Ironbridge Gorge Museum** in Telford, Shropshire, where a whole valley, some 3 miles long and half a mile wide, forms the framework for a new type of open air museum. Here sites are preserved *in situ* and the visitor, using a ticket which gives access to the various elements of the museum, travels through the network by foot or in a car or coach.

The essential importance of Ironbridge derives from the events that took place there during the 18th and early 19th centuries, events that were fundamental to the development of Britain as the world's first industrial nation. Today this section of the valley of the River Severn is still rich in the remains of those momentous times. In Coalbrookdale at the west end of the Gorge is preserved the blast furnace where in 1709 iron was first smelted using coke as a fuel instead of the traditional charcoal. Nearby, occupying the Great Warehouse, is the Museum of Iron containing an outstanding collection illustrating the development of ironmaking technology, while overlooking the site are the houses of ironmasters and the cottages of their employees, all preserved by the museum to reflect the history of this pioneer ironmaking community. At the point where Coalbrookdale meets the main valley of the Severn a wharf and warehouse have been preserved, the latter used as an interpretive centre to tell the story of this extraordinary district through the eyes of previous visitors who for five generations have been visiting the Ironbridge Gorge. A few hundred yards downstream is the Iron Bridge itself, the first civil engineering work in the world to be built of iron, its 200 feet spanning the Severn in 1779. (*See also* page 173.)

Downstream again are further blast furnaces, at Bedlam – in total five iron furnaces are preserved in the museum complex. Half a mile down river is Coalport, a new town of the late 18th century, where the museum has reopened the old china factory. Here fine Coalport China was made from the early 19th century down to 1926. Now a museum of the people, products and processes of china-making occupies the old workshops and bottle ovens. Overlooking Coalport, on a 50-acre site to the north, stands **Blists Hill Open Air Museum** where buildings and machines which cannot be preserved *in situ* are being reconstructed to illustrate the social and industrial history – in a living sense – of the East Shropshire Coalfield a century or so ago. A toll-house, miner's cottage and mission church have been rebuilt while in the industrial town developing at the north end of the museum a colliery winding engine is in everyday operation raising and lowering a cage in a mine shaft, and there is a working sawmill, printer's, cobbler's and candle-maker's. Future exhibits will include a working foundry and an ironworks where wrought iron will be manufactured.

Ironbridge is open every day of the year and like the others in this new generation of open air museums it is there to serve a demanding public, a public looking for thought-provoking and stimulating leisure activities. Many of its visitors come as schoolchildren or students for specifically educational purposes but frequently it is these young people who, having discovered what an open air museum has to offer, bring their parents so that *their* image of a museum can be reconditioned and brought up to date.

WALKING IN BRITAIN

ALAN MATTINGLY

A motoring friend of mine, whose life seems to be centred on the intricate wonders of camshafts and carburetters, sometimes obliges me to concede that you *can* see quite a lot of countryside through the window of a car. Indeed, there are now so many 'scenic drives' and 'car-parks-with-viewpoint' that the visitor to the countryside may feel deprived if their view is not framed in a car windscreen.

But ramblers know better. If we ran the tourist boards, we would have slogans like 'See Britain Better – Get Out and Walk' posted in car parks and picnic sites throughout the land. (But sited discreetly, of course, so as to blend with the surroundings.)

The advantages of walking over driving are many. First, you can often get much higher on foot than by car. The views, therefore, are a lot better – longer, more rewarding, more breathtaking (and not just on account of the steep climb). Also, for motorists like me who regard the car as, at best, a grudgingly-acknowledged convenience and, at worst, a temperamental device capable of great malevolence towards its owner, there is a wry satisfaction to be gained from looking down on your vehicle parked hundreds of feet below, knowing you have just accomplished something it never could.

Then, too, the only way of finding peace and quiet in the countryside is by setting off on foot along a trackway or footpath. However, this does *not* mean having to set off for the remotest corners of the Scottish moors or the Welsh mountains with a heavy backpack and several days' rations. You can feel far from the madding crowd without actually being so. The New Forest in Hampshire, for example, is extremely popular with motorists and campers in the summer months, but the chances are that, 15 minutes after setting out on foot into the forest from a roadside car park, you will have only the birds and the squirrels for company and will feel that you have stepped into a timeless landscape of forest and heath that is utterly detached from the bustle and noise of the 20th century.

A walker can experience spectacular views away from urban civilization: the route to Scafell, Cumbria

Walking is an exercise that offers the chance of studying wild plants and animals; of marvelling at the variety of colours, scents and patterns that make up the landscapes, waterscapes and skyscapes of the countryside; and of locating the ancient earthworks, dotted about the Ordnance Survey (OS) maps and that can only be tracked down on foot. In short, walking can add a new dimension to your exploration of the British countryside.

First Steps

But what of the practicalities? Where can you walk? What are your rights on private land? What should you wear and take with you?

Most land in Britain is in private ownership – the public has no general right to walk in the countryside. This even applies to common land and to designated areas such as national parks. The principal means of access is along public rights of way, of which there are well over 100,000 miles in England and Wales alone. OS maps afford the most comprehensive, accurate and easily obtainable information about these rights of way, although many bookshops and information centres now stock other maps and guides to paths in particular areas.

Long-distance paths are based on public rights of way and are generally well-signposted and properly maintained. The guides to the official long-distance paths published by HMSO are of an excellent quality and contain extracts from the relevant OS maps.

Most land owned by the National Trust is open to the public as is land managed by the Forestry Commission. Many local authorities own or manage areas of countryside for the purpose of public access. In Surrey, for instance, there are many wooded hills and sandy heaths preserved as public open space. Some common land is open to the public as a right (although by no means all). In the Lake District, much of the central fells are common land open to the public for access on foot. In a strictly limited number of other upland areas – notably in the Peak District – land is subject to access agreements, which allow people to walk on the hills on all but a few days in the year when shooting is in progress.

On top of this rather complex pattern of legal access rights, there is in practice a good deal of *de facto* access to mountain and moorland country throughout Britain, especially in Scotland. In other words, there is much open country that you have no right to walk over, but where it is most unlikely that you will be challenged and turned back. (This is not to say, however, that such a situation is satisfactory. In parts of Wales such as the Aran Mountains, for example, you may still today be stopped by a local farmer. The Ramblers' Association has for many years been pressing for a general right of access on foot to all open country in Britain.)

The answer to the question of what you should *wear* when out walking will depend very much on where you are walking and when. If walking along green lanes in Kent in summer, light clothes, training shoes and a lightweight nylon cagoule (anorak) carried in case of a shower will certainly suffice. But if setting out on the Pennines on a windy autumn day, a strong pair of walking boots and plenty of warm and rainproof clothing are essential. In general, wear what you feel most comfortable in but always assume that the weather is likely to turn worse rather than better. The well-equipped rambler with stout walking boots, long woollen socks, tough-wearing breeches, anorak, rucksack and bobble hat, may seem a caricature, but (except in hot, dry weather) is really very comfortably and adequately clad for a country walk. However, don't be compelled to follow this pattern. For example, wellington boots may be better than walking boots for muddy conditions in relatively flat country – but make sure they fit tightly and don't expect them to keep your feet warm in very cold weather. And if you prefer to wear a long duffle coat because it warms the parts most anoraks don't reach, that's fine too – but expect a bit of bother getting over stiles and fences. In general, if you pay attention to keeping your hands, head and feet warm, brisk walking will soon raise the temperature of the rest of your body. A shower or two causes no long-term discomfort, but heavy rain or snow can present serious problems of body cooling. So make sure you have some protection against the worst that the weather is likely to throw at you during the day.

As for other things to carry with you, the most important items will be a map and a compass. Of course you may prefer to walk with a group or go on a guided walk, in which case you can leave the navigation to the leader. Otherwise, an ability to read a map and use a compass, not only add to the interest and enjoyment of a walk, but are often essential if you are to arrive safely at the chosen destination.

Walking is thirsty work, so carry some liquid refreshment with you. Do this even if you plan to make a time-honoured lunchtime pub stop, because if the walk takes longer than you allow for and you arrive after closing time, you will be glad of the contingency arrangement. The same applies to food. Take a whistle if you are going on the hills and a torch if there is the slightest chance that you won't return before nightfall. For carrying all this gear, you will quickly find that a rucksack is much more comfortable than a duffle bag and is out of all comparison better than a plastic bag from the supermarket.

Conventional wisdom has it that an average walking pace is 3 miles per hour plus an extra hour for every 1,500 feet of ascent. However, a relaxed rambling pace – particularly in the first hour or so after lunch – is more like a mile in 25 or 30 minutes, allowing for stops to admire the scenery and study the map. Again, you will soon come to judge your own walking pace, but for heaven's sake don't try to turn a country walk into a route march – it ruins the whole experience.

Walking does, of course, have its problems – paths can often be blocked, or ploughed, shooting may be taking place at a location uncomfortably close to your route, and you may even have the misfortune to find a bull standing astride your footpath. While it would be wrong to pretend that such problems do not exist (although the Ramblers' Association is struggling valiantly to overcome them, often with some success), don't let them put you off. In your early days of country walking, keep to the more popular and more clearly defined routes – canal towpaths perhaps, or sections of long-distance paths. You will find that your confidence and ability quickly grow and that you will soon be able to explore less frequented countryside and to tackle some of its endearing little dilemmas like bulls and shooting parties.

The Best of Britain's Walking Country

A map of long-distance paths, national parks and areas of outstanding natural beauty in England and Wales and national scenic areas in Scotland provides a snapshot of what many people would regard as the best walking routes and walking areas in Britain. However, there is such an abundance of riches that in almost every rural parish in the land, one can find attractive and delightful walks of unique quality.

Any selection of walking regions is therefore subjective and inadequate, but I have chosen below a 'Top 10' list of areas that range from the picturesque to the highly dramatic and which are all excellent and worth travelling many miles to sample. The list is arranged in no order of merit, but for the sake of convenience, we begin in the southeast and work westwards and northwards, ending in Scotland.

One of the most popular walking areas with ramblers from London is centred on the wooded greensand summit of Leith Hill, near Dorking. From here there is a famous view southwards across the green and peaceful patchwork quilt landscape of southeast England. In these **Surrey Hills** are little scenic gems that are the quintessence of the English countryside, such as Friday Street, a minute village tucked in a deep wooded valley behind Leith Hill; and St Martha's Church, an old and charming building perched on top of a steep, sandy hill. Londoners are very lucky to have such countryside near by.

In a journey from London to Bristol, one crosses the great range of hills known as the **Cotswolds**. The warm, brown rocks from which these hills have been shaped are reflected in the region's soils, stone walls and many beautiful old buildings. The most prominent landscape feature in the Cotswolds is the west-facing escarpment, which is followed from Chipping Campden to Bath by the Cotswold Way, an 'unofficial' long-distance path that has been mapped and waymarked by The Ramblers' Association. The escarpment is particularly striking around Cleeve Hill, an area of high open common near Cheltenham whose cliff-like western slopes overlook the Vale of Gloucester and the Forest of Dean in the far distance.

From Bristol to Brecon in mid-Wales takes less than two hours by car these days, but it is a journey that takes one into completely different country. This quiet rural market town lies beneath the towering mountains of the **Brecon Beacons** – a most imposing range of glaciated valleys and summits carved out of dark red sandstone rocks. A walk along the main ridge, culminating in the summit of Pen y Fan is tough. But it is also immensely rewarding.

Lying to the south of the Bristol Channel is the **Exmoor** National Park. Here, the colourful heather and grass moors reach their highest point at Dunkery Beacon. This summit is best gained from the village of Horner, where paths lead through lovely National Trust woodland up to the high ground. From the top, there is a superb view of West Somerset.

Returning to Wales, special mention deserves to be made of the coastline of **Pembrokeshire** in west Dyfed, which is so outstanding that it has merited the accolades of a national park *and* a long-distance path. From Tenby to Cardigan, the Coast Path runs along the tops of great cliffs; dives and climbs as steep valleys and coombes cut into the coastline; and occasionally levels out to cross broad sandy beaches and wind-blown sand dunes. Flowers in profusion cling to the thin soils above the cliffs and sea birds whirl and swoop in this paradise for naturalists.

The first of the long-distance paths to be opened in this country was the **Pennine Way**, running along the spine of England from Derbyshire to Scotland. It is a tremendous walk, and one of its many highlights comes near Malham in North Yorkshire. The Way passes close to the amphitheatre-like cliffs of Malham Cove, crosses the moor to Fountains Fell and then ascends Pen-y-ghent – the mountain with a famous lion-like profile. Giant potholes, bare limestone pavements and deep ravines such as Gordale Scar are some of the features that mark this very distinct Pennine landscape.

Lying to the east of the Pennines, on the other side of the Vale of York, is the **North York Moors** National Park. Here, there is more splendid walking country. The seasonal colours of this area are well worth special visits. In the early autumn, the heather in bloom is as bright and as colourful as any you will find in this country. And in the spring, there is the spectacular appearance of the wild daffodils in Farndale along an 8-mile stretch of the valley floor. It is one of the most joyful sights that a walker can experience.

To the west of the Pennines is the **Lake District** – a land of high fells, mountain tarns, great lakes and woodlands that is without peer in the English countryside. A first-time ascent of any of the major summits, such as Scafell, Helvellyn or Skiddaw, is a real adventure; but one that can be accomplished comfortably in one day by anyone who is reasonably fit and well equipped. However, perhaps the most rewarding walks are those that link ridge-top and lake-side paths and reveal several of the incomparable aspects of this national park. For example, one can plot a marvellous walk from the head of the Buttermere valley, along the open ridge that divides Buttermere from Ennerdale and then down to lower ground along the shore of Buttermere lake itself.

North of the border in Scotland, the walker is faced with a wealth of excellent areas to choose from. One of the most popular is the **Isle of Arran**, which is easily reached from Glasgow by steamer. Noted for its plants and birds, the island also contains some very exciting granite mountain country. The highest point is on Goat Fell, 2,900 feet above the coastal town of Brodick. The mountain ridges in the country around Goat Fell offer some very exhilarating walking with extensive views across islands and lochs.

The highest point above sea level in Britain is the summit of **Ben Nevis** (4,406 feet). This huge, brooding mountain towers above the surrounding moors and valleys. But, despite its daunting appearance, it can be climbed comfortably in one day. A path leads from Fort William to the summit, from where, on a clear day, there is perhaps the best panoramic view in the country. It is one of a vast and magnificent mountain wilderness. And it is a scene that could not be more different from the enchanting wooded hills of Surrey, where this rapid tour began. It is a contrast which reflects the great variety and beauty to be found in the countryside of Britain if one is prepared to step out of the car and explore it on foot.

(For further information about walking in Britain readers are invited to write to The Ramblers' Association at 1–5 Wandsworth Road, London SW8 2LJ. The Association publishes a number of fact sheets, guides and books on all aspects of walking. It also welcomes enquiries from those interested in joining the Association. You can ask for a publications list and leaflet about the Association and should send a stamped addressed envelope when writing.)

THE WILDLIFE OF BRITAIN

BRUCE CAMPBELL

Two things have profoundly affected the wildlife of Britain as we see it today: our position as an island group off the western coast of the Eurasian land mass and the enormous influence of man on so relatively small an area over several thousand years.

Our island status means that a number of plants and animals, which are quite common just across the Channel, are unknown in Britain, having failed to colonize it after the retreat of the ice and the disappearance of the land bridge to the Continent. But our isolation has lasted sufficiently long for a few creatures to have evolved distinctive characters, separating them from the parent populations in Europe. They are called 'endemic subspecies', and some of them, most notably the Scottish crossbill of the old Caledonian pine forests, are now even regarded as true species.

Our insular position on the edge of the Continent also makes us an obvious stopping place for huge numbers of birds on their migrations, especially in autumn, when for a few weeks favoured estuaries are crowded with shorebirds. As well, we 'catch' rare wanderers both from eastern Eurasia, for example on Fair Isle between Orkney and Shetland, where there is a custom-built bird observatory, and from across the Atlantic, notably on the Isles of Scilly.

On the comparatively limited native flora and fauna of Britain was imposed the hand of man, who seems, even in the Stone Age, to have been able to clear areas of primeval woodland and convert them to grazing land for his stock. Improved tools enabled him to make greater and greater inroads on the natural habitat, until it is now true to say that only on the remotest islands is the situation unaffected by man. The other last stronghold, the hill tops, has been conquered; people can ascend in numbers on to the plateau of the Scottish Cairngorm hills, to leave their litter among the arctic-alpine plants.

So what we now have are a number of habitats, modified by man, but occupied by native kinds of plants and animals and by an increasing number of species introduced by man. These have made themselves thoroughly at home, usually but not necessarily, close to habitations and cultivated fields.

This hybrid situation is not a matter for despair: it is full of beauty and interest – that Oxford's great 'lung', Port Meadow, has been used for grazing probably for a thousand years makes it as impressive as any ancient monument.

Modern means of transport have made it relatively easy to explore Britain by land or sea. Nowhere on the mainland is more than a few hours from a hot bath. Some of the islands still pose visiting problems, but few seasons pass without an expedition landing even on remote North Rona, off the northwest coast of Scotland, with its great breeding colony of grey seals.

Although most people will do their 'exploring' by car, there is something to be said for a train ride to give a good general idea of the changing landscapes of Britain. Regarded very broadly, the country south and east of a line from the Severn estuary to the Humber is 'lowland', made up of younger rocks, notably chalk and limestone. Soils derived from these formations have a far greater variety of plants – and hence also of animals – than the older, harder rocks of 'highland' Britain, which, however, has the more spectacular scenery.

A spring journey from southern England to the Scottish Highlands shows how comparatively quickly one type of countryside merges into another. Each type is now of a pattern imposed by man, ranging from the completely built-up manscape, through suburbs, to farmland of fields and hedgerows in which small areas of woodland and wetland survive, the semi-natural relics of the ancient 'wildwood' and of the great marshes and fens which once filled the river valleys. The conditions of southern farmland are changing all the time. Agriculture today demands larger fields in which massive equipment can operate, and this means the removal of hedgerows; while the havoc of Dutch elm disease has done away with the characteristic hedgerow tree, and it remains to be seen what the outburst of new planting of other species of tree along roadsides and in groups will achieve.

Kittiwakes nesting beside flowering thrift and sea campion – they are one of Britain's most populous seabirds

Britain's landscape is largely a pattern imposed by man – fields in Wensleydale

In southern and Midland river valleys, gravel extraction has led to the creation of gravel pits. Some become permanent lakes and important habitats for wildlife, as do the increasing number of new reservoirs, often covering large acreages and with areas specially set aside as nature reserves.

As the traveller proceeds north, whether by train or car, he will notice that wayside trees gradually become less tall, that rough grazings increase and marshy areas become more extensive. Then come the hills, stone walls begin to replace hedges and dark plantations of conifers cover the slopes. This is not an uninterrupted process: 'southern' pockets appear in northern valleys even north of Inverness, after the traverse of some of the finest highland scenery in Europe. Ultimately lie the rock-bound coasts and islands where one of our most important wildlife 'resources', our seabird colonies, survive a continuing series of threats. But Britain has over half the world population of the gannet, the largest seabird in

the country, and estimates run into half a million pairs for the number of smaller kinds like the guillemot, puffin and kittiwake (*see* page 26).

Another world begins at the tide-line. The examination of the shore line, and especially of rock pools, was one of the chief interests of amateur naturalists in the 19th century and many a child has had its first glimpse of the meaning of habitat divisions by playing among the inter-tidal zones. The coming of the aqualung and wet suit has meant that we can extend this exploration out to sea. But it is essential to be trained in modern diving technique before venturing offshore. After a period of often unrestricted collecting, for example of starfish and sea urchins, saner counsels have prevailed and, under the Wildlife and Countryside Act of 1982, provision is made for underwater nature reserves.

Bird spotting can enliven a train journey, or amuse the passengers in a car. The kestrel has become known as the 'motorway bird' because of the numbers seen hovering over the broad grass verges in which their prey, principally field voles, live. In parts of western Britain another bird of prey, the buzzard (sometimes mistaken for an eagle), may be seen perched on a post or soaring overhead on broad wings. Even quite small birds with characteristic outlines, like the swift and swallow, can be identified from a moving vehicle, but often there are tantalizing sightings which cannot be defined.

Massive intrusion of the car into the countryside can lead to the attrition of semi-natural habitats and to the disappearance of the shyer animals. On the other hand, the car makes an effective 'hide' and allows far better views than can be obtained by an observer on foot – one of the best ways to get on terms with the wildlife of woodlands is to park in a clearing and sit quietly. Unfortunately this is often not possible without trespassing or obstructing passage and the motorist may have to settle for recognized parking places and take to his feet.

The Royal Society for Nature Conservation (The Green, Nettleham, Lincoln LN2 2NR) has recently published *A Nature Reserves Handbook*. This describes 363 of some 1,400 nature reserves now managed by the 46 local trusts for nature conservation which cover the United Kingdom. The book is only available to members of trusts, but every sympathizer should join one, and a donation will confer membership of a chosen trust and bring a copy of the book, which is an open sesame to so many choice areas. There are reserves in every English and Welsh county, in all the Scottish regions, and in the Isle of Man. They range from the $\frac{3}{4}$ acre of Drake Street Meadow in Hereford and Worcester with its 75 kinds of plant, 'whose beauty can be appreciated merely by leaning over the gate', and an acre of moorland marsh at Rhos-y-fforest near Aberystwyth with 135 kinds of flowering plant, to the 14,600 acres of Ben More Coigach, near Loch Broom in the West Highlands, with red and roe deer, pine marten, wild cat, otter and badger, as well as some spectacular birds. There is also a long stretch of the Devil's Ditch near Newmarket, one of the last stations of the famous pasque flower; and 6 miles of foreshore along the Cornish side of the Tamar estuary, winter home of some of the British avocets, the emblem of the Royal Society for the Protection of Birds (RSPB).

While many trust reserves are of national importance, the 184 areas called National Nature Reserves have been designated by the Nature Conservancy Council, the government agency responsible for wildlife conservation. Most of the reserves of the RSPB, are also of great importance, such as Minsmere in Suffolk, one of the breeding places of the avocet, an area of diverse habitats, so well managed that birds and visitors can almost rub shoulders without any ill effect.

The seven centres of the Wildfowl Trust, although best known for their collection of ducks, geese, swans and flamingos from all over the world, are also important reserves for wild birds. Other bodies with a strong interest in wildlife conservation are the Forestry Commission, Britain's largest landowner, the two National Trusts (England, Wales and N. Ireland; and Scotland), the rapidly expanding Woodland Trust; and there are a number of areas controlled by private bodies and even individuals.

Although between them these reserves provide some protection and encouragement for great rarities and for communities of plants and animals whose hold in this country is precarious – southern heathland is a good example – their total area is only a tiny fraction of Britain and the survival of our wildlife depends very much on what happens on the four-fifths which is devoted to farming of some kind. It is by walking the splendid network of public footpaths traversing the farmland that most people can get to know the commoner plants and animals.

Some 20 years ago the Nature Trail concept was introduced from North America and rapidly became popular. In essence it is a walk of a mile or more, punctuated by points of interest. These are designated by numbers referred to on a guide sheet or leaflet, usually available in a dispenser on the spot. There are now so many trails in operation, set up by a variety of agencies, that no national list has been published for some years. But the Nature Conservancy Council (19 Belgrave Square, London SW1) notes in its lists of National Nature Reserves those with nature trails; and the National Trust has recently published a list of nature walks on its properties. A most encouraging development has been the publication by the Royal Association for Disability and Rehabilitation (25 Mortimer Street, London W1N 8AB) of an access guide to Nature Reserves of England, Scotland and Wales for the disabled.

Altogether, it is not too difficult to find out how to visit good places for wildlife, especially for birds. Several books have been devoted to the subject, with detailed notes as to access. But the best course for a beginner is to join one of the many national and local natural history societies, most of which conduct excursions and field trips. On these the more experienced members are ready to help the novices. This fraternity of naturalists is one of the features of the British scene, and in recent years there has also been a notable growth of wildlife tours led by experts.

Finally, there has been an attempt to bring non-native animals to Britain by the establishment of safari or wildlife parks. While they are no substitute for a visit to East Africa or other areas still rich in wildlife, the best of these have a valuable educational side. Details may be found in the *International Zoo Year Book*, published by the Zoological Society of London. Incidentally, their broad acres often contain an interesting native population of plants and animals, thus exemplifying the wonderful adaptability which has enabled our wildlife to withstand so many vicissitudes.

THE YEAR IN BRITAIN

GEORGE SPEAIGHT

In addition to the places in this guide that are, as it were, permanently on view, there are a host of annual events that enliven the calendar both for residents and for visitors to Britain. The visitor with a special interest might well time his visit to take account of these. Some of the more important of these events, both nationally and locally, are listed in the following calendar.

Some of them are Festivals devoted to the Arts, with music, plays and exhibitions. Pre-eminent among these is the Edinburgh Festival, whose fame has attracted a Fringe of events much larger than the official programme; but there is also the Bath Festival, with an emphasis on chamber music; the Aldeburgh Festival, still bearing the imprint of Benjamin Britten who helped to found it; the York Festival, with performances of the medieval mystery plays; and many others, some of which are less known like the Cambridge Poetry Festival and the Cheltenham Literary Festival.

Among festivals devoted entirely to music there is the Three Choirs Festival, held in alternate years in three cathedral cities of the southwest; the Cheltenham Music Festival, with an emphasis on contemporary composers; and many festivals in Wales, of which those at Fishguard and St David's are particularly important. The Eisteddfods, both international and national, were originally meetings of Welsh bards and minstrels but now embrace all forms of art. Among purely theatrical festival seasons, outstanding are those at Stratford-upon-Avon, devoted largely to the works of Shakespeare; at Chichester, in a purpose-built theatre of interesting design; and at Glyndebourne, where small-scale opera is presented in an elegant setting in the grounds of a Tudor manor house in the Sussex Downs.

During the summer most regions of Britain stage Agricultural Shows, and these are full of interest for the general visitor. The ones listed in the Calendar represent only some of the better known. Sheepdog trials are held in many sheep-rearing areas, with dog

Regatta time at Henley-on-Thames: the 1-mile course begins at Temple Island (see also page 149)

and shepherd working in a fascinating partnership. And rallies of steam-driven engines, originally intended to drive agricultural threshing machines and now lovingly restored to their original glory, provide a striking attraction today.

Then there are the surviving folk festivals, like the Viking-inspired Up-Helly-Aa in the Shetlands, the Hobby Horse dances in Somerset and Cornwall, the Mumming Plays in Yorkshire, the Dressing of Wells with flower designs of biblical scenes that are a feature of Derbyshire villages; and the more recent events of public celebration that have become folk festivals of our own day, like the Illuminations at Blackpool or the Miners' Gala at Durham. And all the time the traditional fairs are renewing themselves with more and more thrilling rides, while preserving the spirit of the past with coconut shies and roundabouts, as at the Goose Fair in Nottingham or St Giles' in the streets of Oxford.

Finally, there are Sports. The visitor may be drawn to sports that are particularly associated with a specific region. In England he will think of cricket, whether on county grounds for games stretching over three days or even longer or on any village green for a Saturday afternoon. In Wales rugby football is the national passion; in Scotland perhaps golf or curling, but certainly the Highland Games; in Cumbria and Northumberland interesting local sports have developed among the peaks and fells. In England in general, horses, whether for racing or in shows, still exercise a fascination upon millions who have never ridden one; and one has only to mention the names of Wimbledon, Wembley, Henley and Cowes to summon up the peaks of achievement in tennis, soccer, rowing and sailing.

In addition to all these events, created by the British for themselves, there are the great state occasions. No other country can stage these better, and even if every year cannot produce a coronation or a royal wedding, every year does witness the Lord Mayor of London riding through the streets of the City in his painted coach, or the Queen riding on horseback down The Mall to review her guards in Trooping the Colour.

CALENDAR

The following list should be regarded as no more than a general guide. Dates and locales are subject to change and some events may be discontinued. Intending visitors should check with the tourist authorities listed on page 408 for exact details in any particular year.

JANUARY

1st week	International Boat Show. London, Earls Court
3rd week	Rugby Union International Matches begin, played at London, Twickenham; Cardiff, Cardiff Arms Park; and Edinburgh, Murrayfield
4th week	Up-Helly-Aa Festival. Lerwick, Shetland

FEBRUARY

2nd week	Cruft's Dog Show. London, Earls Court
mid	Scottish Curling Championship. Perth, Tayside
Shrove Tuesday	Pancake race through the streets of Olney, Bucks

MARCH

mid	Shakespeare Theatre Season opens at Stratford-upon-Avon, Warks, running until the end of the year
	Oxford versus Cambridge Boat Race. London, Thames, Putney to Mortlake
	Horse racing, steeple chase, Cheltenham Gold Cup. Cheltenham, Glos
3rd week	Festival of Choirs. Cardiff
4th week	Horse racing, steeple chase, the Grand National. Aintree, Liverpool, Merseyside

APRIL

Good Friday	Pace Egg Play, a traditional mumming play performed in the villages of the Calder Valley, West Yorks
Easter Monday	Easter Parade. London, Battersea Park
2nd week	Poetry Festival. Cambridge
	Badminton Horse Trials. Badminton, Avon
	Morpeth Gathering of Northumbrian speech, song, arts, music and athletics
3rd week	Yorkshire Three Peaks Fell Race. Settle, North Yorks
	(23) Shakespeare Birthday Celebrations. Stratford-upon-Avon, Warks
4th week	St Andrews Golf Week. St Andrews, Fife
	Pitlochry Theatre Festival opens, running till September. Tayside
	London Marathon, long-distance foot race for all comers – some years held in May

MAY

1st week	(1) Hobby Horse Dance Festivals at Minehead, Somerset; Padstow, Cornwall
	Chichester Theatre Festival opens, running till September. West Sussex
	Horse racing. Newmarket, Suffolk
	Shetland Folk Festival. Lerwick
	Spring Flower Parade. Spalding, Lincs
2nd week	(8) Helston Furry Dance, Cornwall
mid	Brighton Festival, East Sussex
3rd week	F.A. Cup Final. London, Wembley
	Malvern Festival, Hereford and Worcester
	St David's Cathedral Bach Festival. St David's, Dyfed
4th week	Bath Festival, Avon
	Glyndebourne Opera Festival opens, running till August. East Sussex
	Chelsea Flower Show. London, Royal Hospital Grounds
	Royal Academy Summer Exhibition. London
	Orkney Folk Festival

JUNE

1st week	Beating the Retreat, London, Horse Guards Parade. Also in May and June at Edinburgh Castle
	Royal Bath and West Agricultural Show. Shepton Mallet, Somerset
	Dickens Festival. Rochester, Kent
2nd week	Horse racing, the Derby. Epsom, Surrey
	International TT Motorcycle Races. Isle of Man
	Aldeburgh Festival, Suffolk
	York Festival. North Yorks
	Three Counties Agricultural Show. Malvern, Hereford and Worcester
mid	Ayr Burns Festival. Strathclyde
	Llandaff Festival of Music. South Glam
	Cricket. First test match against visiting eleven. London, Lords
	(16) Trooping the Colour. London, Horse Guards Parade
	Aberdeen Highland Games. Grampion
	Sailing. Round the Island Race. Isle of Wight
	Royal Highland Agricultural Show. Edinburgh
3rd week	Horse racing, Royal Ascot. Ascot, Berks
	Pre-Wimbledon Women's International Tennis Tournament. Eastbourne, East Sussex

4th week	Lawn Tennis Championships. London, Wimbledon
	Royal Regatta. Henley-on-Thames, Oxon
	Wells dressing. Bakewell, Derby

JULY

1st week	Highland Games. Dundee, Tayside, and elsewhere during the summer
	Royal International Agricultural Show. National Agricultural Centre, Stoneleigh, Kenilworth, Warks
	International Musical Eisteddfod. Llangollen, Clwyd
	Great Glen Sheepdog Trials. Fort Augustus, Highland
mid	Polo, British Open Championship. Cowdray Park, Midhurst, West Sussex
	International Music Festival. Cheltenham, Glos
	Wells dressing. Buxton, Derby
	Royal Tournament. London, Earls Court
	City of London Festival
	Durham Miners' Gala
3rd week	Kings Lynn Festival, Norfolk
	Henry Wood Promenade Concert Season opens – till September. London, Albert Hall
	British Grand Prix. Brands Hatch, Kent
	Celtic Folk Festival. Dolgellau, Gwyn
4th week	Folk Song Festival. Cambridge
	Royal Welsh Agricultural Show. Builth Wells, Powys
	Fishguard Music Festival. Fishguard, Dyfed

AUGUST

1st week	Horse racing. Goodwood, West Sussex
	Highland Games. Strathallan, Bridge of Allan, Central, and elsewhere
	Royal National Eisteddfod of Wales
	Canterbury Cricket Week. Kent
	Sailing. Cowes Week. Isle of Wight
mid	Welsh National Sheepdog Trials. Llangedwyn, near Oswestry, Shropshire
	Edinburgh International Festival and Military Tattoo opens
3rd week	Three Choirs Festival. Worcester, Hereford or Gloucester
	Lincolnshire Steam Spectacular. Grange de Lings, Lincoln
	Vale of Rydal Sheepdog Trials. Rydal Park, Ambleside, Cumbria
	Grasmere Sports. Grasmere, Cumbria
4th week	Navy Days. Portsmouth, Hants

SEPTEMBER

1st week	Blackpool Illuminations. Blackpool, Lancs, till mid-October
	Royal Highland Gathering. Braemar, Grampian
	Cricket. Final of NatWest limited-over competition. London, Lords
	Highland Games. Pitlochry, Tayside, and elsewhere
	Great Working of Steam Engines. Stourpaine Bushes, near Blandford Forum, Dorset
mid	Horse racing, St Leger. Doncaster, South Yorks
	Thamesday. London, South Bank
	Carriage Driving Championships. Windsor Great Park, Berks
	Burghley Horse Trials. Near Stamford, Lincs
	St Giles' Fair. Oxford
4th week	North Wales Music Festival. St Asaph, Clwyd

OCTOBER

1st week	Horse of the Year Show. London, Wembley
	Goose Fair. Nottingham
mid	Cheltenham Festival of Literature. Cheltenham, Glos
3rd week	International Motor Show. National Exhibition Centre, Birmingham
4th week	International Curling Tournament. Ayr, Strathclyde

NOVEMBER

1st week	London to Brighton RAC Veteran Car Run
	(5) Guy Fawkes Night Firework Displays everywhere, especially at Lewes, East Sussex, and Aberdeen, Grampian
2nd week	Lord Mayor's Procession. London
3rd week	Festival of Music. Cardiff

DECEMBER

1st week	Royal Smithfield Show. London, Earls Court
mid	International Show Jumping Championships. London, Olympia
4th week	(24) Midnight Christmas services in many churches
	(31) New Year's Eve Celebrations, traditionally centred on Trafalgar Square, London
	(31) The Allendale Baal Fire. Northumbria
	(31) Hogmanay celebrations in Scotland

ENGLAND

PREFACE TO ENGLAND

GEORGE SPEAIGHT

The Scots and the Welsh are entitled to object to the titles of the 'Histories of England' on our book shelves. They are really histories of Britain. But England does have an identity of its own. We speak correctly of the British Empire and British grit; but we also speak correctly of English literature and an English sense of humour. England may simply be regarded as the largest partner among the three nations that constitute the island of Britain; but it should also be regarded as that part of the island occupied by the Romans, colonized by the Angles and Saxons, and invaded by the Normans; that accepted Christianity as brought by St Augustine, and later developed its own particular form of Christian ethos and worship; and that carries in its language, in the shape of its fields, and in the design of its buildings the marks of this rich ancestry.

Merely to listen to the language, with its mixture of Anglo-Saxon monosyllables and Latin-derived polysyllables, is to understand something of the heritage that has come to us from the men who spoke in the language of *Beowulf* and the men who spoke in the Norman French of William the Conqueror's knights. When we speak of *house* or *cow* or *sheep* we are echoing the tongue of the Saxons who tended the animals in the fields; but when we speak of *mansion* or *beef* or *mutton* we are echoing the language of the Normans who ate their meat in their castles.

The sounds of England are redolent of our heritage. Take a seat in a theatre to hear a play by Shakespeare or an opera by Gilbert and Sullivan; step into a cathedral for Evensong to hear the language of Cranmer and the Authorized Version, or the music of Tallis and Byrd; hear the *Messiah* sung by a choir larger than Handel ever dreamed of, or the brass band of a northern colliery. These are English sounds.

And what we hear with our ears we can see, too, with our eyes. Travel with this guide in your hand, and see the rare Anglo-Saxon village church, as at Escomb in Durham; the great Norman cathedral, as at Norwich; and the soaring glory of Early English

Previous page: A typical English village, Hambledon, Buckinghamshire, nestles into a valley in the Chiltern Hills

Gothic, as at Salisbury. This last can be matched across the Channel, though seldom so tenderly cared for, but nowhere else in the world can you see fan vaulting like that of Henry VII's chapel in Westminster Abbey in London, or the sober classical baroque of St Paul's Cathedral. Nowhere else in the world can you see anything to match the grandiloquence of the Tudor nabobs, as at Hatfield House; or the assurance of Queen Anne's nobility, as at Blenheim Palace; or – more essentially English in character – the quiet dignity of innumerable manor houses as they stand at the end of their drives among the meadows.

Other countries may have produced scholars as learned as the English, but where else has learning been partnered with gracious surroundings to match the quads at Oxford or the Backs at Cambridge? Other countries have their formal gardens, but where else has Nature been tamed and led by the hand, as it were, as at Stourhead or at Sissinghurst? Where else has the community of country dwellers been so perfectly reflected as in the grouping of church and Hall and cottages around the village green as in the traditional English village? Granted that England is no picture-postcard land, that there were country slums in the past, that the Nonconformist chapel on the edge of the village hints at spiritual conflicts, that the village shop and post office may be in danger of closing, that the bus no longer runs to the nearest town, that many residents are weekenders, granted all that and accepting it as part of the development of our history, the English village remains one of the supreme creations of civilized living.

If all this sounds too neat and perfect, throw in the odd maverick eccentricity. England is the land of follies. Whether these are grottoes, as at Skipton or at Woburn, or towers, as at Wentworth Woodhouse or at Faringdon, Greek temples as at Stowe, Chinese pagodas as at Kew, or Gothic gateways and bogus ruins almost anywhere, whatever they may be in their mad irrelevance, they provide the spice that saves the English scene from becoming bland and pretty.

The Englishman is by nature a countryman, and his dream (and her dream too) is to retire to a cottage in the country and tend his garden. Yet most of the

English live in towns, and have done so for the past 300 years. England was the land of the Industrial Revolution, and that is part of our history too. You can find it in the canals winding their way across the Midlands and sneaking into towns by the backyards, on which you can hire a boat and journey through an England in which time seems to have stood still. You can find it in the railways, which still provide an excellent service on the InterCity routes that were cut out and embanked a century ago. You can find it in the docks of London, now searching for a new life after the ships have left them; in the mills of Yorkshire, standing up like fortresses among the dales; in the salt workings of Cheshire; and in the rows of terrace houses in the inner cities that sometimes present a sad face of decay, but which at other times blossom with the fresh paint of new, young house owners who are revitalizing whole streets as fashion ebbs and flows.

The English genius does not, on the whole, show itself at its best in towns; but there are glorious exceptions to a general level of mediocrity: the squares of London, each with its own private garden in the middle for residents; the crescents of Bath, the Rows of Chester, the Pantiles of Tunbridge Wells, the arcades of Leeds, the Inns of London's legal quarter, the close of many cathedrals, the tree-lined streets of the garden cities, the pedestrian precincts of the New Towns. Each of these, in periods from the medieval to our own day, is an example of how to live and work in a town in conditions of grace and dignity.

And if one thinks of public monuments, there can be few buildings in history that have created so universal an icon of Democracy as the Houses of Parliament at Westminster. In the same way the spirit of Civic Pride is powerfully conveyed by the Town Hall in Birmingham, of Scholarship by the

In the 18th century many hill figures were cut on chalk hills. The horse at Cherhill, Wiltshire, was made in 1780

John Rylands Library in Manchester, and of Drama by the Theatre Royal in Newcastle upon Tyne. The provincial towns and cities of England are proud of their inheritance, and visitors with eyes to see (and the aid of this book) will find much to admire in them.

Finally, there is the land itself from which all this has sprung. England may lack the dramatic scenery of its sister nations, but in its modest, almost domestic scale there is no more beautiful landscape on earth. And no landscape has inspired better poetry. Whether it is Kipling writing of the 'blunt, bow-headed, whale-backed Downs', or Matthew Arnold of 'all the live murmur of a summer's day'; Edward Thomas conjuring up the platform of a deserted railway station:

> *And willow, willow-herb, and grass*
> *And meadowsweet, and haycocks dry,*
> *No whit less still and lovely fair*
> *than the high cloudlets in the sky*

or Wordsworth in the Vale of Esthwaite:

> *The solid mountains shone, bright as the clouds,*
> *Grain-tinctured, drenched in empyrean light;*
> *And in the meadows and the lower grounds*
> *Was all the sweetness of a common dawn –*
> *Dews, vapours, and the melody of birds.*

John Clare could summon up the spirit of the Fens:

> *Wandering by the river's edge,*
> *I love to rustle through the sedge*
> *And through the woods of reed to tear*
> *Almost as high as bushes are*

and Rupert Brooke that of the flat lands of Cambridgeshire:

> *Ah, God! to see the branches stir*
> *Across the moon at Granchester!*
> *To smell the thrilling-sweet and rotten*
> *Unforgettable, unforgotten*
> *River-smell, and hear the breeze*
> *Sobbing in the little trees.*

And in every age innumerable modest rhymesters have been moved by this land of England to pen their halting tribute to its beauty, like one George Derbyshire, a parish clerk of Dunstable in about 1850, as he stood on a spur of the Chiltern Hills:

> *How ample to the wandering eyes*
> *The variegated prospect lies;*
> *There pleasant villages are seen,*
> *And shady groves that intervene,*
> *The green wood waves upon the hill,*
> *And softly winds the silver rill,*
> *While many a steepled dome appears*
> *Grown reverend in the vale of years;*
> *Embower'd in shade there seem to reign*
> *The guardian spirits of the plain.*

CORNWALL
AND THE ISLES OF SCILLY

AN INTRODUCTION BY
GEOFFREY GRIGSON

Until the railway came to the far west and crossed the Tamar into Cornwall by Brunel's tall Saltash bridge of 1859 (which now has the modern road bridge as neighbour), Cornwall was a most isolated county. For centuries the Tamar, twisting in a narrow valley, then widening into a tidal estuary, had kept Cornwall and Devonshire, Cornwall and the rest of England, considerably apart. There was not a bridge below the narrow medieval New Bridge at Gunnislake miles up from the sea. So Cornwall retained its antiquities, its small, rather secretive fishing ports, its little Tudor and Jacobean manor houses, its holy wells and wayside or churchyard crosses, its Celtic sentiments and its dialect – English indeed, but peppered with words surviving from the old Cornish language.

Cornwall, whatever a very patriotic Cornishman may allege, is not at all purely Cornish. The English fought their way over the Tamar more than eleven centuries ago. When the visitor crosses out of Devonshire into Cornwall (a name which began on English lips as a term for the Cornish people, meaning the Welshmen of the land of Kernow), the signpost names which greet him will be fairly divided at first between the English and the Cornish languages. If he enters, not by the 20th-century bridge at Saltash, but by the 14th-century bridge I have mentioned at Gunnislake, the steep climb from the Tamar, past the chimney-stacks of abandoned mines, will set him under the heather-heights of Hingston Down, which was where King Egbert defeated the Cornish, with Viking allies, as long ago as 838, and so opened their country to English settlers. It is over a thousand years now since Cornish was regularly spoken in the east of the county. Still, the Anglo-Cornish on the Cornish side of the Tamar did not have so much to do with the English people on the Devonshire and Dartmoor side; and as you drive west you quickly see more Cornish place-names written up, beginning with *pen-* (head or end), *tre-* (farm), *lan-* (church), etc. The first town of some size on the road from Gunnislake is Liskeard, as Cornish as could be, meaning the *lis-*, the court or capital, of a Cornish king, a petty one but still Cornish, whose name was Cerruyt. The road continues along the moorland spine of Cornwall, it comes to Bodmin, Cornish for the 'House of the Monks', it makes for Cornish-named town after town – Truro, Redruth, Camborne, Penzance (which means 'Holy Headland') – passing signposts with the names of unfamiliar saints, such as St Mabyn, St Breock, St Wenn, St Columb, St Enoder, St Piran, St Erth, St Ives, and so on, all holy men or women of the British Christianity of 1,300 and 1,400 years ago, which continued, in Wales, in Cornwall and across the water in Brittany, when the newly arrived English were still pagans, their worship centring around such fierce deities as Woden.

Cornwall is astonishingly full of entertaining and rewarding things to see, and for the holiday-maker this favourite of all the holiday counties of England divides into four, Cornwall of the seaside, Cornwall of the granite moors, the ferny luxuriant Cornwall tucked out of the wind along tidal creeks and wooded combes, and the Cornwall of small villages and small fields and deep lanes and isolated lichen-rough churches, which often seem to grow out of hill flanks in the most intimate and natural way.

The Coast
Cornwall of the seaside is exceedingly various. The long peninsula of the county has a rougher side and a gentler side, and it slopes from one to the other. Down the coast on the northern rougher side, from the Devon border to Land's End, you have the Atlantic, the considerable intermittent savagery of abrupt headlands and high cliffs, and small difficult harbours. Make an Atlantic northern journey from Morwenstow to Boscastle and Tintagel, and on, till you reach St Agnes and the Reskajeage cliffs and Cape Cornwall and Land's End, if you like the sight and sound of long rollers and the sentiment of land and rock resisting the sea (and if you like surf-bathing – but watch out, for the undertow can be dangerous in places). Make a southern journey along the milder, less aggressively resistant Channel coast – Looe, Talland, Polperro, Fowey and its river or estuary, Mevagissey, the many inlets of the oak-banked complex of the Fal, and so round the Lizard to the sub-tropical shelter of Mount's Bay and Penzance – if you

In 1044 monks founded a monastery on St Michael's Mount but by 1425 it had become a royal fortress

like colour, fertility, mildness of air, coves of sand, bland little grey harbours, unruffled inland tide-waters, and a sense of comfort and enclosure, spiced with the recurrent wilderness of rock, and wind-rounded gorse and blackthorn.

Opposites in combination are one of the marks of this county. If it is rough and rocky, with rocks which vary from the bluntness of granite to red and purple slates, it has also its extraordinary exuberance of vegetation and flower-colour (bluebells, primroses, foxgloves especially) out of the wind, and under the shelter of the rock. If it seems – and is – remote, as well as rough and primitive, it is a county also where the valleys and hills crowd together, and where you may have half a dozen or more parish churches within a few square miles. If hills break out, they emerge from an unusually close pattern or embroidery of small earth- and stone-hedged fields, medieval or still older in origin, irregular in outline and fitted closely to the swell and curve of the land.

Cornish Buildings
Neither churches nor mansions nor towns are architecturally of great merit. Cornwall is no treasure-county of the arts; and as far as buildings go, the great pleasure afforded by Cornwall is that house

or church or village or small town – or railway viaduct – seldom does violence to its landscape.

This is even true of the relics of Cornwall's indus-trial period of the late 18th and early 19th centuries. The engine-houses of the abandoned mines of West Cornwall, on the moors, along the cliffs, or in the valleys, are stony outgrowths of Cornwall no less than its churches or low white cottages, or the small ruined lime-kilns often to be found on the creeks and above the beaches. Yet internally many of the rather low almost cave-like parish churches – for instance Lanteglos-by-Fowey, Talland, Lanreath, Blisland, Morwenstow – are very full of the flavour of a late medieval, Tudor and Jacobean past which liked colour and image and symbol, and provided them liberally in its own provincial way.

Several of the small Cornish houses or small mansions on show are eloquent of the wakeful, grasping, alert time in Cornwall after the Reforma-tion, when the Cornish gentry were building up estates, and were busy, in this Atlantic county, with maritime speculation and the chancy profits of a New World. No one should miss two of the National Trust houses, Cotehele, on the Tamar, which has the strongest early Tudor feeling, furniture, tapestries and all, of a Cornwall just leaving the Middle Ages, and Lanhydrock, built a hundred years later by a Puritan who was one of the wealthiest merchants of Cornwall, and one of its principal Cromwellians.

Both are rather squat granitic houses. Near Cotehele, the little 15th-century building of Dupath Well, with water running through it, gives one a feeling of a Cornwall as old as its saints, and older still.

The Towns

The best of the Cornish towns, for different reasons, I believe to be Launceston in the far east, Truro in the west, and Penzance in the far west. Those who come into Cornwall by the A30 from Okehampton too often rush uphill and bypass Launceston, which is a town of many eras, compact, encircled with green views, and satisfying for church, Norman castle ruins, Georgian houses, and an uncommon look of having missed – so far, and for lack of funds – the nastiness of 20th-century town commerce. Truro, the cathedral town of the county, is made satisfying by its clean Georgian look, its surrounding hills, its runnels of fresh water along the edge of the streets, and its luck in having a small, almost entirely delightful museum and art gallery. Penzance speaks still of the discovery of the pleasures of the seaside early in the 19th century, a town of terraces, villas and gardens with bedding-out and tender shrubs on one side, and of an overcrowded main street on the other – a town, too, with an antiquarian bookshop specializing in books on Cornwall and the Isles of Scilly. Both Penzance and Truro are in debt to the fortunes made out of tin and copper in the era of Cornish shaft mining. The geological museum at Penzance and the geological collections in the museum at Truro are full of strange crystals brought up from the dark galleries of the mines.

Across Mount's Bay from Penzance, St Michael's Mount (an island at high water) is the noblest and most exciting of the National Trust properties in Cornwall. Capped now with a mansion and a chapel, which survive from a medieval priory, there is not much doubt that this was the 'certain island lying off the coast of Britain called Ictis', where the merchants of the Mediterranean bought ingots of tin from the Cornish, some 2,000 years ago.

The Moors

Cornwall of the granite moors is not quite as attractive as it is supposed to be – at any rate in the eastern Cornwall of Bodmin Moor, of which the best part is the extreme western edge, Sharp Tor, Twelve Men's Moor, and Hawkstor Downs: these give, from their great height, a huge hollow view of the valleys of the Lynher and the Tamar and the myriad, many-coloured, tiny fields of every farm between Bodmin Moor and Devonshire's Dartmoor. But then Penwith, the Land's End district, once the end of the known world, is also granite moorland and in right conditions one of the most emotive stretches of Britain, brilliant in sea-light, and spattered with neolithic tombs and with the forts and villages of prehistoric tinners, and ruined 19th-century mines – including the engine-

Land's End's dramatic sheer cliffs are made of granite slabs cut by deep vertical crevices

houses of Botallack mine, like cliff castles one after another down to the crumping volume of the Atlantic, which swells roundly forward and swells roundly back from the rock with a dull weight.

Scillonia

The Isles of Scilly (never to be called the Scilly Isles, by the way) are Cornwall extended, across more than 20 miles of ocean. But that is only true of the stuff they are made of: they are knobbly, low, hard little islands of granite, softened between the rock by an abundance of blown sand. But in spirit and in look they are different altogether from Cornwall or anywhere else in or round the British Isles. The light of the islands is more brilliant, the surface pattern of small bulb plots protected by the tallest grey-green pittosporum hedges makes a landscape of its own. But this is the pattern only of a fold or a flat here and there between wastes of green or ochre or dark red fern and slabby uplifts of granite, under a vast concave of surrounding sky, inside a blue, white-edged surround of limitless ocean.

St Mary's is the metropolitan island, longest, most 'developed', with the conveniences of its small town, but the least attractive scenery. Of the other islands that are inhabited – Bryher, Tresco, St Agnes and St

Martin's – each has an individuality, and independence. Each is a pocket of freedom from the pressures and limited views of mainland living; Tresco (with its beautiful sub-tropical abbey gardens and 13th-century ruins of a Benedictine priory) the most urbane, Bryher the most ragged and broken, St Agnes the most oceanic, St Martin's offering the greatest variety of beach and scenery. The necessary warning is that these are islands for the extrovert visitor who enjoys walking, air, light, colour, slightly chilly oceanic bathing, natural history, history, and archeology – any or all of these. Others, who may be less adventurous, often condemn these islands as deserts with nothing to do.

GAZETTEER

Altarnun   2D3
Fine, spacious, grey-stone moorland church, Norman font, rood-screen, carved bench-ends. Pack-horse bridge. The village centre is a happy blend of substantial and humble buildings, emphasizing and underscoring the gradual, organic growth of this village over a long period of time.

Bodmin Moor   2D3/E3
Some 100sq m of moorland much over 800ft above sea level. Highest points, with rewarding views, are Brown Willy (1,375ft) and Rough Tor (1,312ft), both N of the main road. Source of the rivers Camel and Fowey. Earlier inhabitants left numerous stone monuments. *Bolventor* is a good starting-point for walks to Brown Willy, etc., and also to Dozmary Pool.

Boscastle   2D4
A narrow cleft winding between high wild cliffs, almost blocked by stone piers. Impressive even on a calm day, terrific in a gale. The main part of the village is in the steep woods behind the little harbour. **St Juliot** Church, 1m E of the village, was restored under the supervision of Thomas Hardy; Boscastle is 'Castle Boterel' in his novel *A Pair of Blue Eyes* (1873).

Bude   2D4
Originally a small seaport town which has now grown into a thriving seaside resort. Renowned for its long sandy beaches and excellent surfing. A 3m cliff walk S of the town.

Cawsand   2E2
Pretty coastal village. 4m N is *Antony House* (NT) built in 1710-21. A very fine house of its period.

Chysauster   2B2
Excavated remains (AM) of an Iron Age village of farmers and tin smelters. The houses have lost their roofs and the upper part of their walls but their shape is clear. Roger's Tower, an early 19th-c 'folly', stands on the higher ground of an Iron Age hill fort; excellent panoramas of Mount's Bay from Chysauster.

Cotehele House*   2E3
A very remarkable early Tudor manor house (NT) set above the Tamar. Worth a special visit for its enclosed courtyard, hall, chapel, furniture, delft, tapestries, etc. Beautiful gardens on many levels and a picturesque group of 18th- and 19th-c buildings, a mill and a shipping museum at Cotehele Quay. House, gardens and mill open April–end Oct.

Duloe   2E2
Hill-crest village inland from **Looe**, notable for its church, its holy well (St Cuby), and its stone circle.

Dupath Well   2E3
Not far from **Cotehele**. Medieval holy well enclosed in a pinnacled 15th-c granite building. Probably visited by sufferers from skin diseases.

Falmouth   2C2
A combination of seaside resort and active seaport. Excellent buildings of early 19th c, especially the Customs House, and late 18th c. The long main street running parallel to the river contains most of the historically interesting buildings in the town; there are also some well-kept gardens. On the lofty headland projecting into the broad estuary of the River Fal, Henry VIII built *Pendennis Castle* (AM) (approach via Castle Drive) with another opposite at **St Mawes** to complete the defences of this magnificent natural harbour. The wooded creeks of the Fal estuary are best appreciated from one of the several boat trips available in season. *See also* **Glendurgan Gardens**.

Fowey*   2D2
Pronounced 'Foy'. A maze of narrow streets on the steep W bank of the estuary providing exquisite creek and river scenery. Quays upstream busy with the export of china clay (used for making pottery, paper, paint, chemicals, etc.); elsewhere pleasure-boats of all kinds. There is a good view of the town from *Polruan* reached by ferry.

Glendurgan Gardens   2C1
Among the finest gardens open to the public in Cornwall (NT). There are superb shrubs – rhododendrons, camellias, magnolias, embothriums and others such as tree ferns and bananas which thrive in the mild climate of this region.

Helford River   2C1
Popular centre for yachting, fishing and creek exploring. Helford is a pretty village with rows of white cottages on either side of a narrow creek. There is a pedestrian ferry across the river to Helford Passage and the only practicable way to explore Frenchman's Creek is also by boat. *Gweek* at the head of the Helford River has a seal sanctuary.

Helston   2B1
Attractive old town with good Georgian and Regency buildings. Celebrated for the Furry (or Floral) Dance which takes place annually on 8 May. Flambards Victorian village and Cornwall Aero Park display life-size village and full-size jets etc. Near by are Godolphin House and the Poldark Mining Museum.

Lamorna Cove   2B1
Celebrated picturesque cove 'discovered' by 19th-c artists. A small brook winds by the road down a wooded valley to the strip of turf above the boulder-strewn beach.

Land's End　　　　　　　　　　　2A1
Some 290m from London and 870m from **John O'Groats**, England ends with a hotel, comprehensive exhibitions ('Land's End Heritage' and 'Man at Sea'), craft centre, workshops, souvenir shops, snack bars and acres of threadbare grass. (*See also* page 40.)

Lanhydrock House　　　　　　　　2D3
At *Bodmin*. Secluded mansion of Lord Robartes, Cornish parliamentarian leader in the Civil War. Much of the original 17th-c building was destroyed by fire in 1881 and has been rebuilt but the exquisite Long Gallery ceiling (*c.*1650) survived and is one of the outstanding features of this house (NT). Open April–end Oct.

Lanreath　　　　　　　　　　　　2D2
A 15th-c church, with rood-screen, carved bench-ends, and monuments, facing a pretty green, flanked on one side by inn and cottages, on the other by early 17th-c manor house. Also a mill and museum.

Lanyon Quoit　　　　　　　　　　2B2
Chamber (NT) of a New Stone Age long barrow: a granite slab 18in thick, 8ft 9in wide and over 17ft long, balanced on three upright slabs.

Launcells　　　　　　　　　　　　2E4
Church with wonderful collection of 60 carved bench-ends, and medieval tiles. Holy well.

Launceston　　　　　　　　　　　2E3
Built on a steep hill with fine views of the surrounding country. Up and down streets, early Tudor church crusted with granite carvings, early medieval remains of a castle (AM) with a Norman mound; pretty 18th-c houses. Launceston was the county seat until 1838.

Linkinhorne　　　　　　　　　　　2E3
St Melor's Well is 15th-c. Fine granite church. The three Bronze Age circles of the Hurlers are near by.

The Lizard　　　　　　　　　　　2C1
Most southerly point on England's mainland, a breezy moorland peninsula some 300ft above sea level, dropping down to many-hued rocks, golden sands, flowers and coves: *Poldhu, Mullion, Kynance*, etc. In 1901 Marconi received the first trans-atlantic wireless signals at Poldhu, and in 1962 the first television pictures from America via Telstar satellite were received on Goonhilly Downs.

Looe, East and **West**　　　　　　2E2
Two valleys unite in a narrow estuary dividing the twin fishing towns. East Looe has a pier and a sandy shore; a modern bridge connects the two towns. Good centre for deep-sea fishing and for exploring E. Cornwall. The tide journey up the West Looe River to *Watergate* is a time-honoured pleasure. *Woolly* monkey sanctuary 2m NE.

Lostwithiel　　　　　　　　　　　2D3
Here, 5m above the mouth of the River Fowey is the first bridge, built in the 15th c. Former capital of Cornwall and centre of tin trade. *Restormel Castle* (AM), 1m N, a moated castle, mainly 13th-c, was used by Parliamentarians in the Civil War. The castle is in the beautiful Glynn Valley.

Luxulyan Valley　　　　　　　　　2D2
One of the most beautiful of the many deep, wooded valleys of Cornwall. Follow the signs to Luxulyan Valley from *St Blazey* – the road passes under the giant granite viaduct built by Joseph Treffry in 1839 to carry a railway from his famous Luxulyan granite quarries.

Mevagissey　　　　　　　　　　　2D2
Steep, narrow streets, pier-sheltered harbour; once a delightful village but its charm is now overlain by tourism. Good model railway museum. Fine coastal scenery.

Morvah★　　　　　　　　　　　　2A2
Here is the remarkable Chun Castle, a ring fort with granite walls dating from about 250 BC and occupied till about AD 500. Probably a fort of tin-miners and smelters.

Morwenstow　　　　　　　　　　2D4
Lonely clifftop church with Norman pillars and carvings, and vicarage built by the poet R.S. Hawker (1803–75); the cliffs are among the highest in Cornwall.

Mount Edgcumbe　　　　　　　　2E2
Facing Plymouth Sound. Sea-girt grounds open to public; mansion burned out in World War II and now rebuilt after the same style. Magnificent views of the Sound.

Mousehole　　　　　　　　　　　2B1
Charmingly apt name for this pleasant fishing village crowded round its near-circular harbour. At one time the focus of W. Cornwall's most important fishery, it has not been affected by tourism too much.

Mylor　　　　　　　　　　　　　2C2
Beautifully situated partly Norman church with rood-screen and very tall Cornish wheel-headed cross of the Middle Ages. A tombstone in the churchyard tells its story with exemplary brevity: 'His foot it slip And he did fall, Help help he cried and that was all.'

Newquay　　　　　　　　　　　　2C3
A town built on cliffs. Its sandy bays, 'pirate' caves and surf-bathing have made it one of the most popular resorts in N. Cornwall, far removed from its days as a fishing village when, from the Huer's House on the headland, the lookout watched for shoals of pilchard. 3m W is *Holywell Bay* with its holy well and a magnificent stretch of sands and caves.

Padstow　　　　　　　　　　　　2C3
Charming small Cornish harbour town with a number of narrow, unspoiled streets. The May Day Hobby Horse Festival is one of the oldest dance festivals in Europe. Tropical Bird and Butterfly Gardens – open daily.

Penzance　　　　　　　　　　　　2B1
Terminus of the old Great Western Railway; busy shopping, marketing and holiday centre of the **Land's End** peninsula, sheltered and sunny, with pretty terraces and villas. Penzance developed as a Regency watering-place and winter resort. The flamboyant façade of the Egyptian House *c.*1830 in Chapel Street is well worth seeing. It has been restored by the Landmark Trust and part of its ground floor is now a NT shop. Sub-tropical plants abound in the town's parks and gardens. 2m W is *Trengwainton Garden* (NT) with magnificent shrubs, especially rhododendrons. 10m SW at **Porthcurno** is the open air Minack Theatre.

Polperro　　　　　　　　　　　　2D2
Chapel Rock on the W side of the harbour provides a good gull's-eye view of this diminutive, picturesque fishing-port crammed into a rocky gulf. Land of Legend and Model

Polperro: originally a smuggling village, it lies in a ravine and has a very narrow harbour mouth

Village depicts history of county. The cliffs each side of the estuary are NT. Within easy reach are some interesting churches: *Lansallos, Lanteglos-by-Fowey, Talland, Pelynt.*

Porthcurno   2A1
Even if you cannot attend a performance, the open air Minack Theatre cut in the granite cliffs some 200ft above the sea is worth visiting.

Port Isaac   2D3
A fishing village that is a piece of pure Cornwall: steep, narrow streets lined with thick-walled cottages arranged tier upon tier down the slope to the harbour where there are fishing boats and lobster pots. It is best, however, to park in the car park at the top of the village and walk down.

Rame Head   2E2
The most easterly headland of Cornwall, with panoramic views of Plymouth Sound and the coastline from Cornwall's **Lizard** Point to Devon's Bolt Head. Do not be deceived by the long crescent of Whitesand Bay immediately to the W: it can be a death-trap for bathers.

Reskajeage Cliffs   2B2
Between Navax Point and Portreath. A stretch of cliffs forming an extraordinary series of sharp, grim triangles.

Roche Rock   2D2
About 4m N of **St Austell**. Granite outcrop in the china-clay district capped with the hermit's cell and chapel of St Michael, built 1409.

St Agnes   2C2
A holiday village with a good beach, surf bathing and leisure park, surrounded by old tin mines, some on the cliff edge. Rugged, most remarkable cliff scenery especially at St Agnes Beacon (NT).

St Austell   2D2
The 'capital' of the china-clay mining industry; approached along the main road from the E, the spoil heaps stand up like white mountains behind the town. The clay is used in papermaking, in paints, cosmetics and medicines as well as for porcelain. 2m N the open air museum, *Wheal Martyn*, illustrates clay-mining industry.

St Buryan   2A1
Fine 15th-c church with notable rood-screen. Not far away are three Bronze Age monuments (*c.*1600–1000 BC), the stone circles of Boscawen-Un and the Merry Maidens, and the standing stones called The Pipers.

St Cleer   2E3
Church with noble granite tower. St Cleer's holy well, under a little granite building of the 15th c close by. In this parish is Trevethy Quoit, very fine chamber of a Neolithic tomb (*c.*2000–1600 BC).

St Clether   2D3
2½m N of **Altarnun**. 15th-c holy well and baptistery, beautifully set in the valley of the Inney.

St Germans   2E2
A priory church with a deep-set Norman porch between two massive towers. Port Eliot mansion, with parts designed by Sir John Soane, adjoins, on the site of the priory buildings.

St Ives   2B2

The art centre of W. Cornwall. The Penwith Gallery in Back Road West has a good collection of modern abstract paintings; the Barbara Hepworth Museum and Sculpture Gardens in Back Street trace the development of her work; the St Ives Society of Arts Gallery is in Norway Square. The harbour is often crowded with boats, the 'old town' is riddled with courts and alleys. Most new developments have been quite sensitively done. There are cliffs and sandy bays near by and, of course, the sparkling brilliance of light and colour. Very busy in season.

St Juliot   2D4

E of **Boscastle**. Thomas Hardy met his future wife here in 1870 when he came to restore the church and some of his best poems – all love poems – were written about the 'shagged and shaly Atlantic' scenery of the parish which was 'West Endelstow' in his novel, *A Pair of Blue Eyes*.

St Just in Roseland   2C2

The simple church of St Just is set in what must be one of the most beautiful churchyards in the country. It is sited at the head of a side inlet of the sea and is in effect a sheltered cliff face further protected by great pine tress. Tender plants and shrubs flourish and the churchyard is particularly attractive in spring, a season which occurs very early here.

St Mawes   2C2

A small boating and fishing resort on the E side of the Fal estuary opposite **Falmouth**. Henry VIII's castle (AM) looks across to *Pendennis Castle* on the other side.

St Michael's Mount★   2B1

Probably the 'island of Ictis' from which Mediterranean merchants obtained tin during the 1st century BC. A priory on the Mount belonged to the Breton abbey of Mt St Michel. The priory buildings were transformed into the mansion of the St Aubyn family, which with the rest of the Mount now belongs to the NT. The castle dates from the 14th c. Access by boat or, at low tide, by causeway from which a steep path leads to the battlements with a fine view towards **Land's End** and **The Lizard**. (*See also* page 39.)

St Neot★   2D3

In a wooded valley on a tributary of the Fowey, a church justly celebrated for its 15 stained-glass windows of the 15th and 16th c. St Neot's holy well is just outside the village.

St Piran's Oratory   2C2

1½m N of *Perranporth*. A tiny Celtic church of the 6th or 7th c, encased in a modern, concrete shelter, among ragwort-yellow sandhills which overwhelmed it in the 11th c. Once a pilgrimage centre where the head, body, bell and staff of St Piran, patron saint of the tin trade were preserved.

Saltash   2E2/3

Here are two notable bridges spanning the Tamar estuary: one built for the railway by Brunel, opened in 1859 and still going strong; the other, the new suspension bridge opened in 1962 to provide a much-needed additional road link between Devon and Cornwall. Cornishmen are reputed (by Devonshire men) to leave their tails in the cloakroom of Saltash station when they cross to Devon.

Scilly, Isles of   Inset 2

An Atlantic archipelago of granite rocks, sandy islets and islands, which form the most delectable of all the holiday areas of Cornwall. Five islands are inhabited. Hugh Town is the small capital and chief settlement of the largest island, St Mary's. The 'Off Islands', reached by launch, are St Martin's (the most beautiful), Tresco (notable for the sub-tropical gardens of Tresco Abbey, and the 17th-c Cromwell's Castle (AM)), Bryher, St Agnes (lighthouse of 1680). The Elizabethan fort of Star Castle (1593–4) above Hugh Town is the most remarkable building in the Islands. Remains of little Celtic monastery on St Helen's. The small daffodil fields are cleared of their crops between early winter and early spring. Helicopters (several flights a day) cross from **Penzance** to St Mary's and also Tresco in about 20 mins.

Sennen   2A1

The westernmost village in England, on Whitesand Bay just NE of **Land's End**.

Tintagel   2D4

It has little to offer other than the legends of King Arthur, Merlin, King Mark, Tristan and Iseult. The 12th–14th-c remains of the castle (AM) are magnificently perched on black shaly cliffs and a projecting spur of rock. Excavations have shown that the castle was preceded by a Celtic monastery. The Old Post Office (NT) is 14th-c. The village has suffered a little from tourism. But the coastline N and W is superb and much is protected by NT ownership.

Trecarrel   2E3

4m S of **Launceston** is the 16th-c manor house and chapel of Sir Henry Trecarrel, builder of Launceston church.

Trelissick   2C2

These NT gardens, 4m S of **Truro**, contain many shrubs that cannot be grown in England outside S. Cornwall. The house, which is not open to the public, has an elegant, porticoed façade from the 1820s.

Trerice   2C2

An Elizabethan manor house owned by the NT about 3m SE of **Newquay**. It has beautiful E and S façades and the North Wing is now open to visitors.

Trevelgue Head   2C3

1m NE of **Newquay**. Sea-cut promontory massively defended by ditches and banks, forming a 'tin-traders' cliff-fort, of the 3rd c BC to post-Roman era.

Truro   2C2

Administrative centre of Cornwall. Has dignity, charm and good Georgian buildings. The cathedral, *c*.1880 incorporating part of 16th-c church but not completed until the 20th c, with its three spires, splendidly dominates the town. The museum (in River Street) has a collection of pictures and drawings that is full of pleasant surprises. The river trip down to **Falmouth** is well worth doing. Guided tours at the Pottery and Old Kiln Museum. 6m E is *Probus Gardens and Rural Studies Centre* – unique garden with apiary. Also at *Trewithen* are 20 acres of gardens with camellias, rhododendrons and magnolias etc.

Zennor   2B2

A village set in a hollow in the windswept Penwith peninsula. The landscape around is a piece of pure Penwith, with small irregular pasture fields bounded by dry-stone walls and dotted with gorse bushes. It has that treeless, upland flavour. The cliff scenery in this part of Cornwall is awe-inspiring and a magnificent stretch can be reached by taking the easy, level path left of the church and behind the Tinners' Arms to Zennor Head (NT).

DEVON

AN INTRODUCTION BY
W. G. HOSKINS

The special quality of Devon is apparent immediately we cross the county border from the east, indeed a few miles before we get to the actual boundary. Coming from Bristol and the Midlands, we cross the River Parrett at Bridgwater in western Somerset and the landscape changes at once. Gone are the compact villages, clustered about their stately perpendicular churches: in their place we see white farmsteads scattered about the hillsides, and in the combes off the main road an occasional whitewashed cob-built hamlet of three or four farms. Its rather plain 15th-century church, buried among tall trees, stands either on its own or beside 'the barton' – the West Country name for the principal farm of the parish. These bartons are invariably of great antiquity. They were the 'home farms' of the Norman lords when Domesday Book was compiled, and they can be traced back without a break to Anglo-Saxon times. On most of them the farming has gone on continuously for well over a thousand years. In certain richer parts it is likely that there has been no break for 2,000 years or more, from the Iron Age onwards.

Coming down from London on the A303 or A30, or on the A35 from Bournemouth and Dorchester, we see ahead the massive dark wall of the Blackdown Hills, the geographical frontier of the southwest, the former Celtic kingdom of Dumnonia. Together, the Blackdowns and the River Parrett marked off this ancient British Kingdom, and they still bring a sudden change in the landscape, in human settlement, in dialect, even in the colour of the cows. We enter the lush pastoral west by steep climbs followed by sudden drops into green combes.

But Devon is by no means all lush green pastures and red cliffs or soil: the New Red Sandstones, so beloved of railway advertisements, underlie about one-seventh of the county, mostly in the east and round Exeter. For the rest the geographical range is vast, from the crumbling chalk at Beer Head to the granite of Dartmoor and – that most ancient of all rocks – the Pre-Cambrian of the extreme south, round Bolt Head and Prawle Point. Slate formations of various ages cover a good deal of the South Hams and the northern parts of Devon, giving dramatic and

tormented coasts north and south. The cliffs of North Devon, from Hartland Point southwards, are considered by some to offer the most magnificent coastal scenery in the whole of England and Wales. The ancient rocks of Bolt and Prawle give hardly less dramatic cliff scenery.

Between the uplands of Dartmoor and Exmoor stretches a broad expanse of Devon which hardly sees a tourist. Though its yellow clay has always given a poorer living than the rich soils of much of the county, the area has a scenic quality and a charm of its own. Here are small forgotten hamlets on the upper reaches of rivers like the Taw and the Torridge which are better known in their estuaries. Their small parish churches, built in the local brown dunstone, are redolent of the past life of yeoman farmers and backwood squires whose modest memorials, from the 16th to the 19th centuries, hang on the plain walls or grace the floors in beautifully engraved floor-slabs. You can meander quietly round these places day after day, on winding roads between high hedges.

Hills and Valleys

Both the geography and the topography of Devon are broken up and rather complicated. The core of the county is the granite mass of Dartmoor, a plateau with an average elevation of some 1,200 feet, rising in two places (High Willhays and Yes Tor) to just over 2,000 feet above sea level. Some hundred or more jagged tors break the skyline, the rocks which form their summits denuded of soil by centuries of wind and rain. Heather covers their upper slopes, giving way lower down to rough grazing, crossed here and there by stone walls or little streams, and lower still to fields of pasture or the more treacherous green of bogs. Exmoor is a gentler moor altogether, rising to 1,705 feet at Dunkery Beacon (which is in Somerset). Outside the two moors, many hills rise to 800 or 900 feet and command magnificent views, the finest perhaps from Haldon, the range just to the west of Exeter, and from the hill forts of Woodbury, Cadbury or Posbury – but it is idle to choose between so many that are equally fine. Of the valleys, the Exe is the

least known, despite its pastoral beauty throughout its entire length; while the river trip up the Dart, from Dartmouth to Totnes, is a memorable experience. Most of the river valleys are well wooded: all are beautiful.

Architecture

Everything is on a small scale in Devon. There are really no great country houses. Most typical are the little medieval manor houses that can be found all over the county. There are, indeed, important houses like Powderham Castle and Castle Hill, but it is houses like Wear Giffard, Little Hempston and Higher Hareston (which take some finding even on a large-scale map) that are the true Devon at this social level. Many of these manor houses are now farmhouses, generally well cared for as far as a working life permits.

Of the churches, Exeter Cathedral is supreme. On the site of a Saxon abbey, founded in 670, it is not very impressive externally, except for its Norman towers; but internally it is perhaps the most harmonious of all the English cathedrals. Monastic ruins are few and disappointing in Devon, though the rebuilt abbey at

Knightshayes Court, a beautiful Victorian house, which stands in a large woodland garden

Buckfast (completed in 1938), also on a Saxon site, is worth a pilgrimage. Of castles, Totnes is the best, small but perfect. Exeter's ruined castle possesses a fine Norman gatehouse; otherwise there is little to compare with castles elsewhere.

Though I have suggested that the parish churches of Devon are generally small and often plain, their great glory is in their woodwork. Probably no other county can show such glorious rood-screens and such a wealth of late medieval bench-ends. The former cloth towns, such as Totnes, Crediton, Ottery St Mary, Cullompton and Tiverton, have, of course, more splendid churches, worthy to stand beside parish churches anywhere; but it is the smaller churches that are possibly more appealing, more profoundly characteristic of old Devon: churches above all which because of poverty escaped Victorian 'restoration' and survived to be rescued more gently. Such are Honeychurch (as appealing as its name), Molland, Ashton, Torbryan (a delightful building all through), Hittisleigh and a score of others. As most of the Devon churches were rebuilt in the great days of the cloth trade and tin-mining in the 15th and 16th centuries, one can become a little tired of Perpendicular Gothic; but their charm lies in less obvious features – in their medieval woodwork, the engraved floor-slabs commemorating local families, or simply in their quiet green churchyard settings.

Apart from the many Elizabethan farmhouses, there are few buildings of a later date worth travelling far to see – though one may always meet with the odd surprise such as Victorian Knighthayes Court near Tiverton. Devon can show very little good Georgian architecture. As for the 20th century, the new Plymouth will stimulate some as much as it depresses others. To me, the rebuilt Exeter is dull but not all would agree with me.

Archeology
Archeologically, the granite upland of Dartmoor is one of the richest regions in Britain. It was used as a vast summer pasturage during the New Stone Age; but from the Bronze Age (c.1900 BC) until the end of the Iron Age (c. AD 250), when the climate deteriorated, mixed farming took the place of the earlier nomadic, pastoral life. Dating from this period we have several hundred hut-circles (i.e. the foundations of pre-historic farmsteads), stone avenues, stone circles, cattle pounds and burial chambers.

From the 12th century onwards, with the discovery of the richest deposits of tin in Europe, Dartmoor was reoccupied. There survive many monuments of this period also, such as the 'blowing houses' where the tin ore was smelted on the spot. Farmers followed the tin-workers, building their houses of granite as their Bronze Age ancestors had done some 3,000 years earlier. The remains of these medieval peasant houses may be seen in various parts of the Moor, notably at Challacombe, near the prehistoric village of Grimspound. A complete medieval village found near Hound Tor has been excavated, and seems to consist of a number of houses abandoned at the time of the Black Death. Among other medieval monuments on the Moor are the famous Clapper Bridge at Postbridge, once thought to be prehistoric but now believed to be early medieval, and the numerous wayside crosses, like Bennett's Cross and Marchant's Cross, which marked the way across the Moor in the 13th century.

Of the Roman period, when Dartmoor was a silent wilderness, the most important survival is the City of Exeter. First settled some two or three hundred years before the Romans came, it became the tribal capital of the Dumnonii, and is still the mother-city of the southwest. It was walled round by the Romans in about AD 200, and some of the original Roman walls may still be seen. In the countryside there are numerous hill forts of the period immediately before the coming of the Romans. The grandest of these is

Hembury, which was first occupied in the New Stone Age and was finally abandoned when the Romans took over Exeter. Cadbury and Woodbury are other notable Iron Age hill forts near Exeter.

Kent's Cavern in Torquay is unique. In this cave was found the earliest evidence of man in Britain, dating back perhaps 25,000 years – long before our own species *homo sapiens* had appeared on the earth. It is now open to the public.

Flora and Fauna
The flower most characteristic of Devon is the primrose. Begin looking for them in late February in the deeper lanes, but remember that the removal of wild primrose roots is an offence against the county by-laws. The other notable plant is the whortleberry, which fruits on the rougher hills and moor in late summer. Flowers bloom all the year round – I have seen over 20 different kinds of wild flower in the Tamar valley on Boxing Day.

Of the fauna, the most distinctive are the wild red deer of Exmoor, where they have lived for centuries and are still hunted, and the Dartmoor ponies. These attractive little animals are no longer entirely wild: they all belong to someone and are periodically rounded up and sold no longer as pit ponies, but now mainly as pets for children. Devon is a great county for riding of this harmless and pleasant kind. The Dartmoor ponies are the lineal descendants of the 'wild horses' referred to in Saxon times as roaming these moorlands. They were themselves the descendants of the small horses domesticated by the Iron Age people more than 2,000 years ago. They can be easily tamed today, and therefore cannot be called true wild horses.

In the world of birds, the noble buzzard is a common sight anywhere in the rougher parts of Devon away from traffic – above all, in wooded combes. Peregrine falcons are common on the north coast of Devon, and the estuaries in winter are full of migrant birds that are rare elsewhere – especially, perhaps, the Exe estuary with its ample mudflats and sandbanks.

Specialities for the Gourmet
Devonshire cream is a delicacy which has been made for many centuries. The best cream should have a thick yellow crust and be firm enough to hold a spoon upright. Probably because of an ancient addiction to clotted cream, Devon, unlike its neighbours Dorset and Somerset, has no special cheeses – a curious deficiency in a county that makes so much excellent butter. Half a dozen rivers produce fine salmon, usually served on local menus under the river names – Torridge salmon, Exe salmon and so on. On a lower level, fresh mackerel, caught off the south Devon coast and cooked the same day, is a much underrated dish, at its best about midsummer. Devon spring lamb is a real delicacy. In the realm of drink, there used to

be much beautiful cider made (and much 'rough' stuff too); but with the spread of bottled brands it is becoming rare. With luck you will find village inns that are still supplied from neighbouring farms. Quality varies, but the best is a genuine '*vin du pays*'. This genuine cider seems a harmless enough drink, but it goes to the knees very quickly. Cider on a close Devonshire afternoon in some deep combe must be one of the most powerful sleeping draughts known to science. As a restorative, Brixham crab or lobster may be recommended for supper, or scallops freshly caught at Budleigh Salterton. Euphoria, a sense of well-being, is common in Devonshire – and this perhaps accounts for the outstanding kindliness with which the Devonians greet and treat strangers fortunate enough to cross their borders.

GAZETTEER

Appledore   2E5
On the corner where the Torridge and Taw rivers unite. Pleasant fishing village with cobbled streets, Georgian cottages, quay, a stony beach, boating and boat-building, and fishing.

Arlington Court   2F5
An early 19th-c house near *Kentisbury* now owned by the NT and open to the public. Neither very big nor very grand outside but a fine central hall and staircase inside and model ship, shell, snuff-box and other collections on display. There are nature trails laid out in the woods and by the lake.

Ashburton   2G3
An important town in the heyday of tin-mining. The church has an extremely fine tower. Robert Herrick (1591–1674) was the vicar of near-by *Dean Prior*, but there is no gravestone to mark his burial place in the churchyard there.

Axminster   3H4/I4
Famous for the carpets that originated and are still made here – see the original factory near the church. Handsome Georgian and other houses.

Bampton   2G5
A little market town among wooded hills on a tributary of the Exe. A great sight here is the annual Fair for Exmoor ponies in late Oct.

Barnstaple*   2F5
The late medieval bridge (restored and widened) spans the Taw at the head of its estuary. Engaging little town with a long history reflected in some of its buildings. Note the colonnaded house crowned with a statue of Queen Anne: this was the exchange of the Barnstaple Merchant Venturers. Note also the twisted spire of St Peter's Church. The covered pannier market behind the Guildhall is still lively with stalls on Fridays. 7m NE at *Bratton Fleming* are the Exmoor Bird Gardens.

Beer   3H4
No longer a simple fishing village in an opening of the cliffs, but still a friendly place for boating, fishing and bathing from its shingle beach. Exhibition of model and miniature railways. Pleasure garden overlooking Lyme Bay. The Beer quarries have provided the stone for many famous buildings.

Berry Pomeroy   2G3
1½m E of **Totnes**. Ruins of a 13th-c castle (AM) partly converted in the 16th and 17th c into a handsome mansion. By 1701 it was described as a ruin; tradition speaks of lightning and fire being the cause.

Bicton Gardens   3H3/4
At *East Budleigh*. Magnificent gardens laid out in the 18th c to designs by le Nôtre who landscaped Versailles for Louis XIV. Also a fine collection of coniferous trees, conservatories, a rural and transport museum, and miniature railway. The 18th-c house is now an agricultural college.

Bideford*   2E5
A prosperous port in the days of sail, when it carried on a considerable trade with America. Charles Kingsley wrote part of *Westward Ho!* in a room in the Royal Hotel, and such adventurers as Sir Richard Grenville bestrode its quay. An ancient 24-arch bridge spans the Torridge, linking Bideford proper with 'East-the-Water', and the town is beautified with many good houses built by the shipowners of old. Pannier market and Craft Centre.

Bovey Tracey   2G3
Pleasant town set beside the little Bovey river, though the scene is somewhat spoiled by the clay workings. In the church note the coloured 15th-c screen and pulpit. One of the Tracey family was involved in Becket's murder, but also built Bovey church. At Parke Rare Breeds Farm are dairy cows, cattle, sheep, poultry and a pets corner.

Branscombe   3H4
Village of stone and cob cottages among broken cliff-top hills, with paths leading down to the beach. Beautiful church with an unusual three-decker pulpit, box pews and an imposing tower.

Braunton Burrows   2E5
This extensive area of sand dunes is botanically important and part is a National Nature Reserve; access by foot is permitted over the whole of the Reserve. To the N is *Croyde Bay*, a pretty village with a Gem Rock and Shell Museum. Sandy beach for surfing.

Brixham   2G2
Active fishing port looking out across Tor Bay and well protected from SW gales. Beside the inner harbour with its fish quay is a large outer harbour protected by a stone mole. The British Fisheries Museum illustrates the industry from the 12th c. A statue of William of Orange on the quay commemorates his landing here in 1688. The Rev. H. F. Lyte composed the words of 'Abide With Me' at Berry Head House.

Broadhembury   3H4
One of Devon's best 'cob and thatch' villages. High above the present settlement is the Iron Age *Hembury Fort*; on clear days the views from here are superb and stretch away to the Haldon Hills and beyond to **Dartmoor**.

Buckfastleigh 2F3

The main attraction of this old town is *Buckfast Abbey* just to the N. This is a modern rebuilding on the site of a pre-Conquest abbey. It was the work of the Benedictine monks, who also produce honey for sale to visitors.

Buckland Abbey 2F3

13th-c monastery granted by Henry VIII to Sir Richard Grenville, grandfather of the hero of *The Revenge*, who also lived here. Sir Francis Drake bought it on his return from his circumnavigation of the world. Now a naval and Devon folk museum (NT), with Grenville and Drake relics.

Budleigh Salterton 3H3

Seaside town of fairly recent growth, but with some attractive Georgian houses from the time when it was a 'fashionable' resort. Arts Centre and Museum in 18th-c house. Near by, *East Budleigh* is a typical pretty Devon village; its church has interesting bench-ends. A farmhouse at *Hayes Barton* was the birthplace of Sir Walter Raleigh, and in the church is the Raleigh pew.

Clovelly★ 2E5

One of the more picturesque villages in Devon. The street descends 400ft in a few hundred yards, and vehicles are not admitted. On either side are flower-decked cottages; at the foot, a stone 16th-c jetty protects a tiny harbour.

Crediton 2G4

Busy little town in 'Red Devon' whose church is large enough for a cathedral. The See of Devon and Cornwall was here in 909–1050, when it moved to **Exeter**.

Dartmouth: the Butterwalk, built in the 1630s when dairy goods were sold in the arcade

Dartington Hall 2G3

The centre of a successful scheme for utilizing the resources of a large old estate. The Hall is partly 14th-c and partly Elizabethan. Around it are scientifically run farms, sawmills and workshops, and here too is the well-known co-educational school. You can drive into the estate, walk in the gardens, see inside the Hall if it is not in use and buy Dartington products, including glass from the N. Devon factory at Torrington, in the shop at Shinner's Bridge.

Dartmoor★ 2F3

A great elevated mass of granite, 200sq m in extent, which fills most of the western part of S. Devon. Much heathery moorland, a walker's paradise, interspersed with valleys and streams, with rocky outcrops known as Tors. Highest point: High Willhays, 2,038ft. The boggy northern part is the source of most of Devon's rivers; access here is restricted by the Army. Stone monuments (mainly Bronze Age) abound – such as *Grimspound* Ancient Village, and *Scorhill* Stone Circle near Chagford. Botanists and ornithologists will not be idle here. The Wildlife Park at *Sparkwell* has over 100 species of birds and animals. National Park information centres are open every day from Easter to mid-Oct. They are at *New Bridge* (on the B3357 near Holne); *Postbridge* (on the B3212); *Steps Bridge* (on the B3212 near Dunsford); and **Tavistock** (town centre).

Dartmouth★ 2G2

Its long and honourable history is mostly concerned with voyages and exploration. Dartmouth ships and men have taken part in nearly every naval battle for centuries. Stroll in the arcaded Butterwalk; and for one of the finest painted rood-screens in Devon visit St Saviour's Church. N of the town is the famous Royal Naval College. S is Darmouth Castle (AM), the outcome of an offer by Edward IV to pay the

burgesses £30 a year 'for ever' if they built a defensive new 'towre with a cheyne sufficient in lengthe and strengthe to stretch a travers the mouth of the haven'. Colourful market. Also Newcomen engine house.

Dawlish 2G3
Seaside resort 2m S of the long sandy tract known as Dawlish Warren at the mouth of the River Exe. A stream ripples quietly through the town. Sandy beach, good bathing, picturesque red cliffs.

Devonport 2E2
The Royal Naval Dockyard, parts of which may be visited, faces the part of the Tamar estuary known as the Hamoaze. Good views of the waterway from Mount Wise, where there is a monument to Captain Scott, born here in 1868. *See also* **Plymouth**.

Doone Valley 2F5
For many, Lorna Doone is as much a reality here as King Arthur is at **Tintagel**. An interesting exercise is to try to follow the topography of R. D. Blackmore in his novel.

Drewsteignton 2F4
On the edge of Dartmoor National Park; S and SW of here there is some spectactular scenery. *Fingle Bridge*, $\frac{3}{4}$m SE, is a well-known beauty spot. About 1m SW of the village, *Castle Drogo*, a granite castle built between 1910 and 1930 is one of the most remarkable works of the architect Sir Edwin Lutyens. It stands at over 900ft overlooking the wooded gorge of the river Teign with beautiful views of **Dartmoor**. It is owned by the NT and the house, gardens, and grounds are open to the public.

Exeter* 2G4
Ancient city with a variety of buildings – medieval, Regency and modern – the last-named mostly as a result of heavy bombing raids in 1942 (many churches and nearly 2,000 other buildings were damaged or destroyed). The choir screen in the cathedral can hardly be missed, but note also the bishop's throne, the little minstrels' gallery in the N wall of the nave, and the various chapels. See the 15th-c Guildhall (the oldest municipal building in England), the Tuckers' Hall, St Nicholas' Priory with a Norman crypt, and the remains of Rougemont Castle (Norman). Visit also the city's medieval passages which run underneath the main streets, the Cathedral Close and see the fine, classical terraces of Southernhay. The Museum and Art Gallery shows pictures by Devon artists. Exeter University is in its own estate of 250 acres on the N side of the city. The Maritime Museum with over 100 boats afloat is the biggest collection of its kind in the world.

Exmouth 2G3
Exeter's seaside resort with good sands and a working harbour with ferries across the Exe to *Starcross*. There are good public gardens and walks but it is not the most architecturally distinguished of resorts (cf. **Sidmouth**).

Hartland 2E5
Hartland 'Town' was an important borough with a portreeve, a town hall and a charter dated 1285. Today it is a pleasant village 2m inland from Hartland Point. Here, however, is none of the softness usually associated with Devon scenery, but harsh black cliffs rising 300ft above the waves, which in storms whip spray over the top. On a plateau below the cliffs, but still 120ft above the sea, is the lighthouse. *Stoke*, $1\frac{1}{2}$m W, has a church tower 128ft high.

Honiton 2G4
It is good to be able to record that lace is still made here and has been since Elizabeth I's reign, though not on the scale which made Honiton famous in the 19th c when Queen Victoria wore a wedding veil of Honiton lace. Annual fair in July which dates from *c*.1250.

Ilfracombe 2F6
The oldest and most unusual of the N. Devon holiday resorts, built in and among small hills, its beaches reached by tunnels in the rocks. Steamer and other trips from the ancient harbour; cliff walks, concerts and all modern amenities. 1m SE is *Chambercombe Manor*, mainly 16th-c. Open at set times.

Killerton House 2G4
House and gardens owned by the NT 2m N of *Broadclyst*. The gardens are particularly beautiful in spring while the mainly 18th-c house contains the Paulise de Bush collection of costumes which is displayed in a series of rooms furnished in different periods of the 18th–20th c. The house is open in the spring and summer and the gardens during daylight hours throughout the year.

Kingsbridge 2F2
Busy town at the head of the tidal estuary extending up from **Salcombe**. The centre of the prosperous farming area known as the South Hams. Local 'sons': William Cookworthy, porcelain manufacturer (see the Cookworthy Porcelain Museum), and Dr John Wolcot, satirist ('Peter Pindar'). Note the arcade known as The Shambles.

Knightshayes Court 2G5
2m N of **Tiverton**. The building of this house, the home of the Heathcoat Amorys, was begun in 1870 and it is a rare survivor of the work of the Victorian architect, William Burges. Today it contains Sir John Amory's fine collection of old masters. The house has a richly decorated exterior and stands in a large garden on the E of the Exe valley overlooking Tiverton. There are fine specimen trees, rare shrubs, formal terraces, spring bulbs and summer-flowering borders. Both house and garden are owned by the NT and are open to the public. (*See also* page 46.)

Lundy 2D6
Some 11m NW of Hartland Point. The island is a huge mass of granite $3\frac{1}{2}$m long, about $\frac{1}{2}$m wide and bounded by cliffs rising almost sheer for about 400ft. Lobsters are caught, seals breed on the rocks, and the island itself is a naturalists' paradise. Bird life is strictly preserved. The island was sold to the NT in 1969 who now lease it to the Landmark Trust.

Lydford Gorge 2E3/F3
Where the River Lyd emerges from the 2m of deep-cleft gorge is a fine waterfall (NT). Also *Lydford Castle* (AM), a 12th-c stone keep once used as a prison.

Lynton and **Lynmouth** 2F6
Motorists approaching Lynmouth from the E should take the warning notices of steep descent seriously. Lynton is on the cliff top some 400ft above the point where the East and West Lyn rivers join to flow into the sea by Lynmouth harbour. Much of Lynmouth is new, following the flood disaster of 1952 (the River Lyn takes its name, significantly, from the Old English word *Llynn*, a torrent), but Lynton

Lynmouth: it became a popular resort in the 18th century having previously been a centre for the herring industry

retains something of a Victorian air. The twin towns are joined by a water-operated cliff railway. The river and coastal scenery is some of Britain's finest. *Watersmeet,* where the East Lyn and one of its tributaries unite, is extremely popular with the House used as a NT shop.

Mortehoe *see* **Woolacombe**

Okehampton Castle 2F4
Built after the Norman Conquest, it was the home of the Courtenays until they moved to **Powderham**. Castle (AM) dismantled in 16th c.

Ottery St Mary★ 3H4
Small market town with a great church dating partly from the 14th c and bearing a striking resemblance to Exeter Cathedral. The bells are a notable feature; so too are the unusual medieval clock and the minstrels' gallery. S.T. Coleridge, author of *Kubla Khan* and *The Ancient Mariner,* grew up in the town. *Cadhay* is 1m NW – a handsome Tudor house open at stated times.

Plymouth★ 2E2
The site is an excellent natural harbour – a broad tongue of land, its coast fretted by creeks and coves, looking out on to the estuary of five rivers. It is an old town but reconstruction after damage in World War II has been on such a scale that the City Centre, for example, has a completely new look with a modern shopping centre. In 1982 the new Theatre Royal was opened. However, one can still enjoy the Hoe, where tradition has it that Drake played out his game of bowls; old houses such as the Elizabethan House in New Street; the aquaria of the Royal Marine Biological laboratory in the cliffs below; and Sutton Pool, departure-point of the *Mayflower* with the old buildings of the Barbican which survived World War II. On the Hoe, too, is Smeaton's Tower, upper part of the previous Eddystone Lighthouse, now removed, visible (in clear weather) 14m to seaward. *See also* **Devonport** and **Saltram House**.

Powderham Castle 2G3
About ½m E of *Kenton*, this has been the seat of the Courtenay family (Earls of Devon) since 1390 and is open daily in summer. The mainly 18th- and 19th-c exterior is not especially beautiful but the house has a fine site with estuary views and is splendidly decorated and furnished.

Princetown 2F3
Nearly 1,400ft above the sea, it is one of the highest towns in England. The grim prison was built in the early 1800s to house prisoners of the Napoleonic Wars.

Salcombe★ 2F2
The little town clings to the steep hillside overlooking the winding estuary which enters the sea between *Bolt Head* and *Prawle Point.* Sheltered yacht haven, sandy beach, good bathing, sub-tropical vegetation. *Sharpitor Gardens* (NT) are 1½m SW. Magnificent views. The house contains the Overbeck Museum of ship-models and other relics.

Saltram House 2F2
3½m E of **Plymouth**. A George II mansion and a garden with an orangery all set in a landscaped park. There is magnificent plasterwork and decoration inside; two rooms were designed by Robert Adam and all is furnished in fine period style. There is an important collection of paintings by Sir Joshua Reynolds. The unique Great Kitchen (access from outside the house) should not be missed (NT).

Sheepstor 2F3
The view from the Tor (1,010ft) ranges over the village and Burrator reservoir, whence **Plymouth** draws water. Sir James Brooke ('Rajah Brooke of Sarawak') lived for some years in the village and is buried in the churchyard.

Sidmouth 3H4
Fashionable in the early 19th c, it lies where the River Sid cuts through the high cliffs to the sea. A sheltered spot, with eucalyptus trees and other sub-tropical vegetation and splendid Regency buildings. In the first week of August it hosts an International Folk Song and Dance Festival.

Sticklepath 2F4
Motorists hurrying past on the A30 miss the Finch Foundry, an engineering works powered by water-wheels, a form of power used for over 100 years. Open to the public.

Stoke Gabriel 2G2
Quiet creeks of the River Dart, spreading trees, an old watermill, and a Regency mansion by Nash which was the home of John Davis, the navigator. A fascinating blend of historical association and beauty.

Tavistock 2E3
A town built around an abbey which was demolished after the Dissolution and later a centre of tin, copper and arsenic mining and woollen industries. Tavistock has many signs of its former prosperity, particularly that of its greatest landowners, the Dukes of Bedford who used revenues from their Devon Great Consols mine to embellish the centre of the town in the 19th c. 3½m SW is the restored mineral port of *Morwellham* which evokes most effectively the industrial past of the Tamar River.

Teignmouth 2G3
Built on the broad spit of land where the River Teign joins the sea, Teignmouth has the advantage of a river aspect as well as a sea front, the town extending some way up the valley. A resort with good beaches and sporting facilities. Fine public gardens. The bridge across the river to *Shaldon* is said to be one of the longest of its kind in the country. The narrow streets of Shaldon have some nice late Georgian and Regency cottages.

Tiverton 2G4
Prosperity founded first on wool and then on lace has endowed Tiverton with an unusual number of good buildings. The church has a fine tower and S porch; the organ by 'Father' Smith is in a case attributed to Grinling Gibbons; see too the well-carved Greenway chapel. The castle built 1106 has a clock collection in the round tower. Blundell's school (NT) (founded 1604) occupies new buildings at *Horsdon*, 1m out of town; the altar in the chapel was designed by Eric Gill. 4m S is the pretty village of *Bickleigh* with its 15th-c castle and also the Mill Craft Centre and Farm. *See also* **Knightshayes Court**.

Torbay 2G2/3
New County Borough created April 1968 (now a District Authority) comprising the three towns of *Torquay, Paignton* and **Brixham**. Sands, harbours, parks. Except for the remains of 14th-c Torre Abbey hardly a building pre-dates the Napoleonic Wars, when houses were built for officers and their families awaiting orders. The design and siting of these 'villas' are one of the engaging features of the older part of the town, which has now spread far inland. The climate has aided the growth of many trees not seen

elsewhere in England. Contrasting with the more modern town is the 'old-world' suburb of *Cockington*, with its well-known forge.

Kent's Cavern, Ilsham Road, consists of two parallel caves with stalactites and flood-lighting. It is of outstanding archeological interest owing to the discovery there in the 19th c of remains of people who may have been among the very earliest inhabitants of Britain. Some of the remains are now in the Torbay Museum. Visit the Zoo; Festival Theatre and Torbay Aircraft Museum with aircraft and model railway and a garden dedicated to Kenneth More. *Torre Abbey* has a tithe barn and monastic buildings converted into a house in the 18th c. About 1¾m W of Cockington is *Compton Castle* (NT), the best example of a medieval fortified manor house in Devon; it is open to the public.

Totnes*   2G3
At the head of the Dart estuary, with gated, winding streets, narrow and steep, the ruins of a Norman castle (AM), a 17th-c Guildhall with a colonnaded front and a church with the finest stone screen in Devon. It was an important wool town and is still a busy shopping centre for the South Hams.

Widecombe-in-the-Moor: the granite outcrops of Dartmoor overlook the village

(*See also* **Berry Pomeroy**.) Totnes is a conservation showpiece and is one of the British Council for Archeology's Top 40 'Gem Towns'.

Westward Ho!   2E5
An open-air resort overlooking Bideford Bay, with golf, bathing and a pebble ridge some 2m long and 20ft high. Beyond the ridge are remains of a submerged forest.

Widecombe-in-the-Moor   2F3
A once pretty stone and-thatch Dartmoor village which has suffered from the popularity of the well-known song. But it has a fine church with a magnificent granite tower and a Church House of *c*.1500 (NT).

Woolacombe and Mortehoe   2E5/6
This stretch of coast is an area of particular beauty (much is owned by the NT). 3m of golden sand and surf stretch between these twin villages.

SOMERSET

AN INTRODUCTION BY
W. G. HOSKINS

Somerset has everything to offer the visitor except a decent coastline. Towards the extreme west, it is true, from Minehead to Porlock, the great hog-backed cliffs fall from the moorland 1,000 feet above into a wrinkled, crawling sea far below; for the rest, there are but few oases (like Brean Down) between the long spoiled stretches.

Inland, Somerset has a serene natural beauty – a beauty enhanced by man's activities during the past 2,000 years. I call to mind those wonderful Perpendicular church towers in and around the Vale of Taunton, a group that would be outstanding in any country; the massive stone barns almost everywhere, which speak of centuries of rich farming; the miles of willow-lined Levels under rain-washed skies in the middle of the county; the little stone-built towns like Somerton and Shepton Mallet, and lively, brick-built Taunton itself, the county town. And from another world, the grey fragments of the ancient abbey of Glastonbury, the earliest site of the Christian faith in England, even if one does not accept the legend of Joseph of Arimathea having come here just after the Crucifixion to construct 'with twisted twigs' the very first Christian church in Britain. Whatever one thinks of this story, first written down in the 12th century, Glastonbury is holy ground where saints have trod.

Geology and Scenery

To understand even a little geology is to appreciate vastly more the colour and the shape of the manmade landscape in Somerset: for example, the little lilac-coloured town of Somerton, the many golden country houses, the little towns built of the local Blue Lias stone, and the great houses of Ham Hill stone from near Montacute. And the natural landscape takes on meaning, too – especially the hills of Somerset: Mendip, Quantock, Exmoor, Brendon, and Polden, and the strange isolated hummocks like Brent Knoll and Glastonbury Tor that rise suddenly from the Levels to a height of 400 feet or so.

The Levels themselves, so much more attractive than this dull word would suggest, were once under the sea, which laid down sands and silts and slowly raised the land above the waters. Silt and peat now overlie the old sea-bed. Man came into this landscape later, from the 7th century onwards (though he was living on the hills round the margins thousands of years before) and completed the process of drainage. Indeed, it was the monasteries which created this landscape. So we have the miles of ditches, some broad and straight and some narrow and winding (these are the oldest), known locally as *rhines*, with willow-lined roads running along the top of ancient causeways or along medieval embankments, giving those sharp bends for no apparent reason today, a few brick houses here and there (often showing signs of subsidence as the peat shrinks), and occasional stone-built villages clustered on the summits of old islands that rose some 20–30 feet above the Levels. The higher hills are outliers of Lias limestones and shales that often give terraces on the hillsides. The lower gentler islands, so easily missed in a car, are much more important from the human standpoint, for they were better suited for the siting of early villages than the abrupt Lias hills. Sedgemoor's villages, for example, stand on islands of the so-called Burtle Beds, rising only 30–50 feet above the winter floods.

Across the middle of the Levels run the Polden Hills, a long backbone of the Lias again, rarely more than 300 feet above sea level, but giving wonderful views in all directions. Along the northern edge of the Levels runs the long flat-topped upland of the Mendips (averaging about 800 feet but rising to 1,068 feet at Blackdown), formed of the grey Carboniferous Limestone. This plateau, rather dull country on the top (though here were the Roman and medieval lead mines), is most striking along its broken edges, where ancient streams cut into the rock and then disappeared underground, leaving us with the magnificent dry gorge of Cheddar in the south, and Burrington Combe in the north. Cheddar is painfully overcrowded during the summer, when the northern edge is perhaps better worth visiting.

Coming back to the Levels again, the western horizon is bounded by the rolling, almost down-like profile of the Quantocks (1,260 feet at their highest point). This is broken into by deep, wooded combes,

The Quantock Hills viewed from the hill above the pretty hamlet of Cothelstone

especially on the eastern side, rising to miles of heather-covered upland from which can be seen the distant Welsh mountains on a good day. Beyond the Quantocks, to the west, lie the long smooth curves of Exmoor (1,705 feet at Dunkery Beacon), a quiet land of ravens, curlew, wild red deer, and (in late summer) whortleberries. This is the country of *Lorna Doone*. Southwestwards the greensand escarpment of the Blackdown Hills closes the horizon, the old frontier of the Celtic kingdom of Dumnonia. South and eastwards from the Levels lies a very tumbled kind of country, small hills and hidden valleys – the oolitic limestone country that gives some of the best building stones, such as the famous Ham Hill, quarried in Roman times and since.

Industries

Somerset has a large and growing tourist industry – today, perhaps, even more important than farming in terms of money turnover. Apart from this and farming, Somerset has no large-scale industries. Brick and tile-making in and around Bridgwater used to be important but is now declining. Of the large centuries-old woollen industry little remains except old mills at Frome, Wellington and Wiveliscombe. Printing, clothing and footwear have tended to take over here. The glove trade is important in and around Yeovil, and the Mendip quarries make Somerset the fourth largest producer of limestone in England. On the Somerset Levels, the ancient industry of peat-cutting has been taken over in a big way for garden use rather than as fuel. Basket-making on Sedgemoor is locally very important, and the withy-beds are very beautiful in winter.

Flora and Fauna

With its many soils, Somerset has a wide range of wild-life – best brought out, perhaps, by looking at the various Nature Reserves. That on Bridgwater Bay (6,076 acres) is notable for its population of wildfowl and waders. The Stert Island area here, to which access is prohibited, is now visited by such rare birds as the avocet and the spoonbill. On Steep Holm, an island in the Bristol Channel, is a reserve mainly for the study of the large herring-gull colonies. The Nature Reserve at Rodney Stoke (86 acres), on the south escarpment of the Mendips, is the best surviving example of a characteristic Mendip ashwood. Shapwick Heath (484 acres) in the Levels was made into a Nature Reserve in 1961. It contains some of the last remnants of the raised bogs which once covered most of central Somerset. There is a wide range of distinctive fauna and flora (e.g. the rare Royal Fern). The peat deposits, where they remain uncut, give a wonderful opportunity for studying changes in vegetation, climate and human activity from about 4000 BC.

Of the larger fauna, the red deer and the semi-wild ponies of Exmoor are the most noticeable. The ponies are the descendants of wild horses first domesticated by the Celtic population before the Romans came. The red deer, which are hunted, are probably of the same ancient origin. Exmoor is a National Park, administered by both Devon and Somerset. It is gentler by far than Dartmoor, but archeologically less rewarding.

Archeology

From this standpoint, Somerset is one of the most fascinating regions of Britain. The peat diggings of central Somerset have produced evidence of human occupation from the Neolithic, the Bronze and Iron Ages, and the Romano-British period, including clear traces of timber causeways built in the late Bronze Age between the Polden Hills and the islands in the Levels as the climate grew wetter. Neolithic trackways have also been found in the peat. In the Old Stone Age, in the late Iron Age, and in Roman times, Somerset was one of the great cultural centres of Britain, and continued to be during historic times in such places as Glastonbury (Dark Age and Medieval). In the Old Stone Age (Palaeolithic) the Mendips with their deep dry caves were the homes of the Magdalenian hunters. The caves at Cheddar and Wookey, though much commercialized, should therefore be visited. Many other caves along the north and west sides of the Mendips were important during this period. In the succeeding Bronze Age we leave the caves for the high dry uplands like Exmoor, the Quantocks, the Brendons, and the Mendip top, where numerous barrows and occasional stone circles tell of this period. In the Iron Age that followed, the lake villages of Glastonbury and Meare show a high level

Glastonbury Abbey: the kitchens, containing a museum, and the 14th-century Abbot's Barn are still intact

of culture again – Glastonbury in particular was 'a great Celtic emporium' at this time. Of this, little trace now remains; but the massive hill forts of the period are well seen at Cadbury and Hamdon. Cadbury Castle is becoming an increasingly important site for the Arthurian controversy, and is now considered to be possibly the legendary Camelot.

Architecture

Somerset was rich in monasteries. Glastonbury, the richest and oldest of them all, is perhaps the most evocative; but more substantial remains are to be found at Cleeve Abbey (near Watchet) and at Muchelney in the Levels, both well worth a long visit. Somerset is poor in castles, but rich in country houses, probably for the same reasons that led the Romano-British to build so many villas in this serene countryside. The Elizabethan period was, of course, the great age for building country houses, though Barrington Court is earlier (begun c.1514) and Lytes Cary (a highly attractive house) has considerable medieval remains. Montacute is the best of the country houses (built c.1588–1600), large but not ostentatious (most Elizabethan country houses were vulgar, the typical expression of the New Rich). This was the great age also for the rebuilding of the ordinary houses in towns and countryside. Somerset contains an extraordinary number of beautiful stone-built villages with farmhouses and cottages dating from the 16th to the 18th century. Most of the parish churches were rebuilt during the 15th century and the early 16th, and are rather monotonously Perpendicular in style. But they are usually far statelier and richer than their Devonshire counterparts, their great glory being their towers – spires are rare. In the towns the outstanding features are the medieval Vicars' Close at Wells (1348), Wells Cathedral itself (a superb example of English 13th-century Gothic), Shepton Mallet for its early 18th-century merchants' houses, and Taunton for many things, including the historic County Cricket Ground – where Jack Hobbs equalled and then surpassed W. G. Grace's record number of centuries in 1926.

GAZETTEER

Athelney   3I5
The legend of King Alfred and the cakes is better remembered than the great battle he was planning while taking refuge here in 878 – the battle in which (at Ethandune in Wiltshire) he put an end to the domination of the Danes. Nothing remains of the abbey he built at Athelney to celebrate the victory, but there is a monument on the little hill called the Mump.

Brent Knoll   3I6
From the Iron Age hill fort (NT) at the summit of this little isolated hill are excellent views across the vast flatness of the Somerset Levels. There are public footpaths leading to the top from Brent Knoll and East Brent villages.

Bridgwater   3H5
Important, sprawling town in which the A38, A39 and A372 meet for the crossing of the River Parrett. Admiral Blake was born here in 1599; his house is now a museum. 5m N is *Bridgwater Bay*, a National Nature Reserve. 8m W is Coleridge Cottage (NT) at *Nether Stowey*.

Bruton   3J5
Pleasant little town on the River Brue. Note the old packhorse bridge and, ½m S, the remains of a little 16th-c dovecot (NT) which belonged to a 12th-c abbey now in ruins.

Burnham-on-Sea   3H6
A small, mainly red-brick resort with championship golf-course and huge sandy beaches on Bridgwater Bay; a walk here provides excellent views S past Hinckley Point nuclear power station to the **Quantock Hills** and N over sand dunes and ribbon development to *Brean Down*, a NT bird sanctuary with hill fort and field system.

Cadbury Castle★   3J5
An Iron Age hill fort with fine views over typical Somerset tree-scattered vales.

Castle Cary   3J5
'Capital' of Caryland – an old yellow-stone town, the home of good cheddar cheese. Note the little 'pepper-box' lock-up and the remains of the Norman castle. Conservation area.

Chard   3I4
John Stringfellow, first to make (and fly) a power-driven aeroplane (1848, in the **Science Museum**, London), was born here, as was Margaret Bondfield, the first British woman Cabinet minister. The mile-long main street has a stately, pillared Guildhall and many attractive buildings, some in mellow Ham stone. There is a wildlife park and heavy horse centre at **Cricket St Thomas**.

Cheddar   3I6
A little cheese is still made here, but the place is best known for its caves, though any romantic leanings are soon dispelled by the sight and sound of the booths and shops around the entrances at the foot of the gorge. Flood-lighting and other effects cannot, however, entirely disguise the beauty of stalactite and stalagmite. How much of the Mendip limestone is riddled with similar, still silent, caverns, excavated by underground rivers? Do not omit to explore the upper gorge, hardly appreciated by those who go no further than the caves. Motor Museum, nature trails and stock car track.

Cleeve Abbey *see* **Watchet**

Crewkerne   3I4
Attractively planned around a central market place, with good stone buildings. In the SE corner of the church is a chamber once thought to have been an anchorite's cell – more probably a shrine. 3m S are *Clapton Court Gardens*, in a beautiful setting. Open daily except Sat.

Cricket St Thomas   3I4
A beautiful 1,000-acre estate S of Windwhistle Ridge (A30 E of **Chard**) part of which has been stocked with exotic animals and birds and opened to the public. A recent addition to the park is the National Heavy Horse Centre. The fine Ham-stone house (1804) is the work of the architect Sir John Soane.

Culbone★   2G6
Near **Porlock**. One of England's smallest churches (about 35ft by 12ft) lies hidden in a wooded combe. Cars cannot come near. All is quiet. The Bristol Channel lies below. In one of the farmhouses above the church Coleridge wrote *Kubla Khan*.

Downside Abbey   3J6
The abbey was founded by English Benedictine monks expelled from Douai in 1793. The Gothic church was consecrated in 1935. Here too is the well-known Roman Catholic boys' school.

Dunster▲   2G6
Notable are the wide main street, the picturesque 17th-c yarn market, and the ancient inhabited castle (NT) rising impressively in the background. In the church note the 14-bay rood-screen, 11ft high and beautifully carved.

Exmoor   2F6/G6
Over 250sq m of wild moorland scored with deep valleys; highest point Dunkery Beacon (1,705ft). Most of it is in

Somerset, but a small portion is in Devon. Much of Exmoor is now a National Park with information centres at *Combe Martin*, **Lynmouth**, *County Gate* and *Dulverton*. The Dulverton centre is the only one open throughout the year and it is also the National Park headquarters. (*See also* **Tarr Steps**.) Though its 'official ' title is Exmoor Forest, it is mainly open heather and grass country, with red deer and small shaggy ponies roaming at large, numerous sheep, and a great variety of birds, rare plants and flowers. The National Trust has also done much to protect the wild life.

Farleigh Hungerford   3J6
A ruined castle (AM) built *c*.1383. Notable chapel and tower.

Frome   3J6
Once one of the busiest wool towns in the West Country, Frome (pronounced 'Froom') is now busy with printing and other industries. See Cheap Street – narrow and with a runnel of water down the middle. In the area of town known as Trinity, one of the earliest estates of industrial workers' houses remaining in the country is being carefully restored. Most of the buildings date from the 17th c, streets are being pedestrianized and a few new buildings sympathetically inserted. *See also* **Norton St Philip**.

Glastonbury★★   3I5
Before exploring the town it is well to clear one's mind of the legends concerning Joseph of Arimathea, King Arthur and Guinevere. The Abbey ruins are sufficiently rewarding. They are all that is left of a famous shrine of the Middle Ages, 'an house meet for the King's Majesty and no one else'. Founded in Celtic times; suppressed by Henry VIII in 1539; bought by the Church of England in 1908 and vested in trustees, under whom intelligent excavations have taken place. (*See also* page 56.) A landmark from afar is Glastonbury Tor (525ft) crowned by a 14th-c tower marking the site of a chapel destroyed by a landslide in 1271. Somerset Rural Life Museum is in a tithe barn at Abbey Farm.

Hinton St George   3I4
The church is notable for the many monuments (showing appropriate contemporary costumes) of the Poulett family – notables of Tudor and medieval times. A lovely Ham-stone main street.

Ilminster   3I4/5
Stone-built town: conspicuous church with the tombs of Nicholas and Dorothy Wadham, founders of Wadham College, Oxford. The best parts are S of the A303. 3m NE is *Barrington Court* (NT), 16th-c with Renaissance features.

Kilve   3H5
At the foot of the **Quantocks**. One of the best points to observe the beds of oil-bearing shale which extend for more than 10m. As one looks up the Severn estuary from here, the nuclear power station at Hinkley Point can be seen, towering above the natural scenery.

Lytes Cary   3I5
Some 2½m NE of *Ilchester*, visit the manor house with 14th-c chapel and 15th-c Great Hall (NT).

Mendip Hills   3I6/J6
A typical limestone range which subterranean rivers have over the centuries riddled with caves, potholes, gorges (besides **Cheddar** visit also Ebbor Gorge, S of **Priddy**); they extend some 30m NW from the valley of the Frome almost to the Bristol Channel. Average height over 600ft, highest

point Blackdown (1,068ft). Wide views over **Sedgemoor** to the **Quantocks** from the steep western escarpment. Everywhere there is evidence of ancient lead mines.

Minehead   2G6
Most westerly of Somerset resorts, lying at the foot of the wooded hill culminating in Selworthy Beacon (1,104ft). Splendid walking country around. Sands and sheltered gardens; steamers connect with Bristol Channel ports. Minehead can now be reached from **Taunton** by the West Somerset Railway Company's reopened Taunton–Minehead line; some services are by steam.

Montacute House★   3I5
Tudor domestic architecture at its best produced this immense mansion with its formal Early Jacobean gardens (NT). Fine Long Gallery with portraits on loan from **National Portrait Gallery**, London. Open April–end Oct. In the village see the old-world square of Ham Hill stone houses called The Borough. Also *Ham Hill Camp* near by, an Iron Age and Roman hill fort.

Muchelney Abbey   3I5
2m S of *Langport*. A Benedictine abbey founded *c*.697. The ruins (AM) are mostly 16th-c. The Priest's House is NT.

Montacute House: it was built during 1588–1601 for Sir Edward Phelips, Speaker of the House of Commons

Norton St Philip   3J6
The partly 15th-c George Inn – stone-built ground floor and two storeys of timber and plaster – was once a guest house for Hinton Charterhouse Priory (now in ruins). At the foot of the church tower is the tomb of two ladies described by Pepys as having 'two bodies upwards and one stomach'. Next door is the Old Malthouse (now private) and the Brewhouse, converted into a Craft Centre for local craftsmen and women and open May–Sept. 2½m SE at *Rode* are the Tropical Bird Gardens in 17 acres of grounds.

Nunney   3J6
Impressive ruins (AM) of a moated castle built in 1373.

Porlock   2G6
Modern cars make less of the notorious hill on the **Lynmouth** road than did their forerunners; but it is still a long pull up, and many people prefer the toll road. The Ship Inn in Porlock village has associations with the poets Coleridge and Southey. Porlock Weir, 1¼m NW, is a small natural harbour with wooded cliffs overlooking Porlock Bay. From here you can walk to **Culbone** 3m W.

Priddy   3I6
Scattered village on the **Mendips** with entrances to mysterious caves and channels known only to pot-holers. Hurdles stacked on the wide village green are held to carry the right to hold the 600-year-old Sheep Fair.

Quantock Hills★   3H5
About 12m of superb wooded undulating upland extending to the sea from between **Taunton** and **Bridgwater**. Fringed by pretty villages. *Nether Stowey* and *Alfoxton* have associations with Wordsworth; at *Stowey* the NT cares for the cottage where Coleridge lived from 1797 to 1800 and wrote *The Ancient Mariner*. There is a visitors' centre for the Quantocks at Fyne Court, *Broomfield*. (*See* page 55.)

Sedgemoor   3I5
Extending SW from the **Mendips** to **Taunton** and **Ilminster**, this great low-lying area with its dykes and pumping stations is more like the Lincolnshire Fens than the popular conception of Somerset. Great crops of withies are cut, cured and made into basket-ware. Here is the site of the battle of Sedgemoor (1685), where the rebellious Duke of Monmouth and his followers were routed in a terrible hand to-hand struggle, the last battle to be fought on English soil. *See also* **Athelney**.

Selworthy
2G6

NT village in Exmoor National Park. Thatched cottages, 14th-c barn and village green make a pretty village.

Shepton Mallet
3J6

Ancient sheep-market town on a hill, once famous for cloth and stockings. Note the excellent hexagonal market cross, c.1500 (rebuilt 1841). This small town has become famous in recent years for its output of champagne-perry. Home of Bath and West Show.

Tarr Steps
2G5

About 4m NW of *Dulverton*. Ancient bridge across the River Barle, formed by huge stone slabs. Some of them weigh nearly 5 tons, yet such was the force of the water during the great storm in 1952 that they were washed away and the bridge had to be rebuilt; it was repaired again in 1980. It is not known when the bridge was originally constructed but most, if not all, of the stones are certainly of local origin.

Taunton
3H5

The county town of Somerset and the bustling, prosperous centre of a thriving agricultural area. Its other industries range from the printing of Admiralty charts to wickerwork and the making of church organs. Note the fine tower of St Mary's Church. Good museum in the remains of the ancient castle, in the Great Hall of which Judge Jeffreys held his 'Bloody Assize' over the survivors of the battle of **Sedgemoor**. There is an Information Bureau in the Public Library opposite the Municipal Buildings in Corporation

Tarr Steps on Exmoor: these once formed a packhorse bridge 180 feet long with 17 spans

Street. 3m N is *Hestercombe House* with gardens designed by Lutyens and Jekyll, restored to original planting. Taunton Racecourse is SE. 9m NW in *Tolland* is *Gaulden Manor* situated in a beautiful valley. Open summer months occasionally.

Trull
3H5

In the church the pulpit, rood-screen and bench-ends are excellently carved – though not all by 'Simon Warman, maker of thys worke Ano Dni 1560', who did the linen panelling in the N aisle.

Watchet
3H6

A little town with a harbour and cliffs containing vari-coloured strata of gypseous alabaster. The harbour, although relatively dormant for many years, has been given a new lease of life. 3m SW at Old Cleeve are the well-preserved ruins of 12th-c *Cleeve Abbey* (AM) with its fine refectory. It is open to the public daily throughout the year. 5m S at *Monksilver* is *Combe Sydenham*, an Elizabethan house recently restored. Gardens and medieval fishponds. Open during the summer at set times.

Wellington
3H5

The conspicuous monument (NT) on the highest point of the *Blackdown Hills* to the S commemorates the great Duke of Wellington who took his title from the town. New sports centre in town and swimming pool.

Wells★★
3I6

A city within a city, for inside the municipal boundary is the ecclesiastical city, enclosed by walls and containing the Cathedral, Chapter House, Bishop's Palace, and Deanery. The Cathedral W front is famous for its array of carved figures; notable inside are the inverted arches (installed in 1337 when the tower foundations began to give way), the Chapter House and the humorously carved pillar capitals in the S transept. The swans at the Bishop's Palace ring the bell when they are ready for lunch. The Vicars' Close is an outwardly little-altered street of 14th-c priests' houses.

Wookey★
3I6

Here the River Axe issues from the **Mendips** by way of Wookey Hole, into which the general public can penetrate for some way. The museum displays objects found in the caves proving that they were occupied in prehistoric times. Also a Fairground Collection and Madame Tussaud's store-room. Less spectacular than **Cheddar**, the Glen is quieter and prettier than the Gorge. The handmade-paper mills (1610, oldest in England) are commendably unobtrusive.

Yeovil
3I5

The glove-making industry here is at least 350 years old. More recent are the Westland aircraft works (occupying in part the site of a Roman settlement inhabited as late as 367). Yeovil is the main centre of industrial employment and the fastest growing urban area in S. Somerset. 2m SW is *Brympton d'Evercy*, an attractive village with a 16th–17th-c house, cider museum and gardens. Open Easter–end Sept. 5m NW is *Tintinhull House* (NT). Fine 17th-c house with Ham-stone front. *See also* **Montacute House**.

Yeovilton
3I5

Within the Royal Navy Air Station (now bypassed by the A303) is the excellent Fleet Air Arm Museum of war planes; it also has Concorde 002, the British prototype. There is an enclosure where you can watch the planes of today, like the Harrier 'jump jet' taking off and landing.

AVON

AN INTRODUCTION BY
ROGER KAIN

On 1 April 1974, a completely revised structure of local government for England and Wales came into force; one of the new names to appear on the administrative map was the County of Avon which subsumes the City of Bristol and parts of southern Gloucestershire and northern Somerset. One of the smallest of present-day counties, Avon is essentially urban in character. With the exception of the Avon Gorge and the Gordano valley it is not possessed of spectacular natural beauty. Much is low land flanking the Severn estuary where resorts such as Weston-super-Mare enjoy extensive beaches, if not picturesque surroundings. The southern boundary of the county skirts the edge of Somerset's Mendip Hills and likewise the main extent of the Cotswolds lie over the border in Gloucestershire. Some flavour of these can, however, be sensed in the east of Avon near Bath, Chipping Sodbury and Great Badminton.

Relics of Avon's industrial past are to be found in the old Bristol coalfield, especially around Radstock, while its fame for 19th-century transport engineering is due to structures such as I. K. Brunel's Clifton Suspension Bridge over the Avon (1836–64), his Great Western Railway station at Bristol Temple Meads (c.1840) and his *Great Britain*, the world's first ocean-going, propeller-driven, iron ship now restored and on display in Bristol's redundant city-centre docks. The modern petro-chemical establishments at the new port complex of Avonmouth and the British Aerospace works at Filton are evidence of the county's continuing industrial prosperity today.

In the days of sail, Bristol was one of the country's chief cities; Bristol-based ships reached every part of the known world and bequeathed the expression 'all ship-shape and Bristol fashion' to the English language. The prosperity of Bristol as a port and commercial centre increased through the 18th century and by its end the wealthy were moving out of the city centre to fast growing and fashionable suburbs like Clifton. The elegant Regency terraces record the taste of many Bristol citizens, impart a classical flavour to the city, and confirm that, although Bristol was located in the provinces, in the early 19th century it was far from 'provincial' in outlook.

Avon, then, is an urban county and undoubtedly the jewel among its towns from a tourist's point of view is the City of Bath. As Aquae Sulis it had been a thriving spa centre in Roman times and by the 18th century it was *the* arbiter of spa fashion in England. As a city, it underwent what amounted to a complete metamorphosis in the course of that century. The formalized pattern of living organized by Richard 'Beau' Nash was reflected in the provision of physical facilities at the spa: the baths and pump rooms were accompanied by assembly rooms, parades, libraries, theatres and terraces of houses laid out in a series of squares and crescents so that in sum it presents, next to London and Edinburgh, some of the finest expressions of classical architecture and town planning in Britain. Today it is one of the architectural and urban conservation showpieces of Europe.

Clifton Suspension Bridge, completed in 1864, crosses the Avon Gorge at 245 feet above high-water level

GAZETTEER

Aust   7H2

Eastern end of the suspension bridge that carries the M4 motorway across the Severn and into Wales. The brightly coloured, early Jurassic age strata of the cliffs are well worth a special note.

Badminton*   7I2

The Palladian mansion (*c.*1680), seat of the Dukes of Beaufort, was altered by William Kent *c.*1740. A noted hunting centre and scene of the annual Three Day Event Horse Trials in April. Beaufort monuments in the church.

Bath★★   3J6

The medicinal waters of Bath have been used at least since it was the Roman city of Aquae Sulis. It reached its zenith of prosperity around the year 1790 at which time it was the most fashionable summer watering place in England. Throughout the 18th-c landowners and their architects while not actually working to some grand design, were conscious of extending the city in a harmonious and uniform

Bath: the Roman Baths fell into ruins when the legions departed, until 1879 when they were rediscovered

manner. Landowners like the Gays and Pulteneys and architects like John Wood, father and son, carried, so it is said, Bath triumphant through the 18th c. The work of John Wood the Elder must have first place in any discussion of the building of Bath as it should in the wider context of English town planning. It was he who in the second quarter of the 18th c introduced the grand manner of uniform building to Bath and England; this is best exemplified by Queen's Square (1728–35) and the King's Circus (now carefully restored) which was begun in 1754, the year of his death. His son extended this monumental sequence with the superb Royal Crescent. This was begun in 1767, took about eight years to finish and has been described as the finest achievement of English urban architecture. If that is something of an overstatement, it is certainly the most dramatic building in Bath and one of the great set-pieces of European architecture. Smollett, Fielding, Jane Austen and Dickens (Pickwick said the waters tasted like 'warm flat-irons') have all given us pictures of Bath at various periods. The Pump Room, near the Abbey, is still a favourite meeting place. Analysis of the water has been undertaken to identify harmful bacteria but from 1985 visitors are able to drink the waters again. The Pump Room, Roman Baths and Roman Baths Museum can also be visited. The Assembly Rooms, reopened in 1963 after the repair of bomb damage, are NT. Here also, is the Museum of Costume, founded by Doris Langley Moore in 1963. The excellent Theatre Royal (opened 1805) was restored during 1981–2. There is an Information Bureau near the Abbey. National Centre of Photography has exhibitions in the Octagon, its headquarters. Bath Races are held at Lansdown Racecourse. *See also* **Claverton Manor**.

Bristol★   7H1
From 1373 until 1974 Bristol was a county in its own right; it is a city with a long history of maritime adventure and commerce. The boat basin by the city centre marks the position of the harbour around which Bristol grew up. As ships became larger, deeper docks have been built at the mouth of the river at *Avonmouth*. The old city-centre docks are now being converted to recreational use; some of the 19th-c warehouses are being refurbished and provide, for example, a home for an industrial museum and arts complex on Narrow Quay, and also the home of Brunel's SS *Great Britain* in the Great Western Dock (open daily). To understand Bristol fully go first to these old docks and then see the soaring St Mary Redcliffe Church, the restored cathedral, the museum and art gallery adjoining the university and facing the Cabot tower which celebrates Cabot's discovery of North America in 1497. In front of the exchange are four short pillars called *nails* on which merchants conducted cash transactions; hence the expression 'paying on the nail'. Notable also is the 18th-c Theatre Royal. See too the Roman Catholic Cathedral (1973). At *Clifton* NW of the city, the Avon Gorge is spanned by Brunel's spectacular suspension bridge (*see* page 61). 4m N is Blaise Castle House Museum at *Henbury*, displaying West Country rural life and with a hamlet of thatched cottages.

Burrington Combe★   3I6
One of the major gorges of the **Mendips**; only the lower part is properly in Avon. Sheltering from a storm, Augustus Toplady here wrote the hymn 'Rock of Ages'.

Chipping Sodbury   7I2
Georgian brick houses mingle with Cotswold stone cottages. The fine, mainly 15th c parish church ('restored' in 1869) has a high tower with pinnacles; the similarly pinnacled pulpit is entered through a hole in one of the nave pillars. *Dodington Park*, 2m SE, was landscaped by Lancelot Capability Brown; the present house by James Wyatt is in splendid early Regency style. There are also a Carriage Museum, British model soldier exhibition, children's farm, and nature trails. It is open during summer months. 8m S is *Dyrham Park* (NT) – *see* **Pucklechurch**. *See also* **Horton Court**.

Claverton Manor   3J6
2½m SE of **Bath**, this house was built by Sir Jeffry Wyatville in 1820. It is now the American Museum in Britain and contains furniture and paintings illustrating American domestic life from the 17th to 19th c.

Clevedon   7H1
This resort has long been fashionable by reason of its proximity to **Bristol** and has good examples of Victorian seaside resort architecture. Poets Walk Nature Trail. 1½m E on the Bristol road is *Clevedon Court* (NT), a 14th-c manor house and the home of the Elton family who built much of Clevedon town. It was once partly fortified and includes a 12th-c tower and a 13th-c hall. Open to the public during the summer. **Cadbury Castle** is 3m E.

Compton Martin   3I6
Some of the best Norman architecture surviving in the West Country is incorporated in the parish church. To the N are the two Bristol reservoirs of *Blagdon* and *Chew*. Fishing permits can be obtained from Woodford Lodge, Chew Stoke and Blagdon Lodge on the S bank of Blagdon.

Horton Court   7I2
3m NE of **Chipping Sodbury**, this is a Cotswold manor house (NT) with a 12th-c Norman Hall and many Renaissance features which add to its architectural importance.

Pucklechurch   7I1
About 2½m E of the village is the NT house of *Dyrham Park*. This was built in the 17th c for William Blathwayt, one of William III's ministers of state, and the rooms have been little changed since they were furnished by him. The house is set in beautiful grounds which are open all the year.

Stanton Drew   3J6
Three prehistoric stone circles in a field E of the village. About 1½m N is Maesknoll, a hill with good views of the **Wansdyke** (*see* in Wilts) – the old earth wall that stretched from Portishead to **Salisbury Plain**, Wilts.

Weston-super-Mare   3I6
A resort which grew very quickly in the 19th c; it was to some extent planned with wide sea-front roads, pavements and gardens. At low tide the sea retreats far, exposing mud, but this, so it is said, gives off the ozone which is claimed to make the air here so healthy. *Steep Holm*, a tiny island offshore is managed as a nature reserve by the Kenneth Allsop Memorial Island Trust. Coastal walk N to *Worlebury Hill*, the site of an Iron Age camp, has superb views.

DORSET

AN INTRODUCTION BY
GEOFFREY BOUMPHREY

It is often claimed that the British Isles hold a wider variety of scenery for their size than can be found anywhere else in the world. Whether this be true or not, there can be little doubt that no county of Britain offers a richer diversity than Dorset. High uplands rising in places to 900 feet, bare for many miles save for the earthworks of prehistoric man, or, in contrast, richly wooded; lush vales of arable and pasture land threaded with quiet streams; sombre heaths where the sandy soil is hidden (or not) by heather and bracken, scrub oak or silver birch; and a long coastline that in itself offers a variety from sandy beaches or shingle banks to high golden cliffs or cliffs of grey limestone scalloped out into caves and arches or delicious coves – could more be asked of an area only 50 miles from east to west and averaging about half that distance from north to south?

The Rock Beneath

As with the British Isles in general, it is the great variety of geological formations occurring close together that gives Dorset so wide a range of scene. Truly, it is the rock beneath that paints the landscape. Four main types are responsible, though with many subdivisions and interpenetrations which make the coastline in particular a geologist's paradise.

First the chalk. Originating in Wiltshire in the uplands of Salisbury Plain and the Marlborough Downs, a dominating ridge crosses the county diagonally from the northeast, near Shaftesbury, to the southwest, near Bridport. From this point another narrower ridge doubles back due east and reaches the coastline between Swanage and Poole Harbour.

In the triangle which lies between the two ridges of chalk, its points at Studland, Dorchester and Cranborne, lie the sands, occupying about one-quarter of the county, to the chalk's one-half.

Third are the limestones. These lie along the coast between the chalk and the sea, forming the 'Isle of Purbeck' (Purbeck stone), the Isle of Portland off Weymouth (Portland stone of building fame) and a wonderfully spectacular line of cliffs. At the western end of the county they form the southern extremity of the great belt of building stone that runs northeastwards across England, through Bath, the Cotswolds, Northamptonshire (as ironstone) and Lincolnshire.

Finally come the clays, one-quarter of the county in extent, lying chiefly in the west, northwest and north. It is these – as in the Vales of Marshwood and Blackmoor – which constitute the richest farmlands in the county, growing first-class wheat and barley (and immense oak trees) and no doubt justifying the claim that 'Dorset butter is the best in the world'.

Local Industry

Happily, from the point of view of the visitor or tourist, large-scale industry has made little mark on Dorset, though prospecting for oil could cast a question mark over the future. Quarrying for stone is primarily carried out on the Isle of Portland, which has its own strange beauty, as the work of certain modern artists testifies.

Rope-making has left a not unwelcome mark on Bridport in the great width of the main streets which allowed each or any house to have its own rope-walk. The only more recent incursion of industry into the county is that of the Atomic Energy Establishment at Winfrith Heath, half-way between Wareham and Dorchester. Set low down in country which, as its name suggests, is on the relatively barren sands, its presence is unobtrusive enough.

Thomas Hardy's 'Wessex'

And so today Dorset still looks much as it must have looked two or three centuries ago, or as Thomas Hardy describes it so incomparably well in his novels. There are many ways to approach it, and none better, perhaps, than through his writing. *Under the Greenwood Tree* or *Far from the Madding Crowd* will make a good enough introduction, if you don't already know him; but, if you want something weightier, read *Tess of the D'Urbervilles*, one of the few novels in any language comparable with the Greek tragedies. No one, after reading these books, can fail to see Dorset with clearer vision, to perceive a greater depth in its beauties. The faint disguises of Hardy's place-names are easily pierced: for his 'Shaston' is Shaftesbury,

Dorset's magnificent coast is epitomized by the sweep of this sandy beach near Lulworth

Dorchester becomes 'Casterbridge', and for 'Egdon' see Puddletown Heath.

If pilgrimages appeal to you, Hardy's birthplace, his school, his home, and old Stinsford Church where his heart is buried, all lie within a radius of a very few miles. The Hardy Monument, by the way, a tall column prominent for many miles on a hill top near Portesham, commemorates not the novelist and poet but the Admiral who was present at the death of Nelson. Thomas Hardy's memorial statue by Eric Kennington stands (or rather sits) in the county capital, Dorchester.

The Archeological Record

Should your tastes extend further into the past, there is a far older Dorset than Hardy's to be explored. In no other county are the traces of Roman and pre-Roman habitation more abundantly evident, and in no other county, I think, do they lie in such lovely settings.

When the Romans came, they found a country uninhabited for the most part in the low-lying districts where we live today. It was on the downs and uplands where the light shallow soil was easily tilled, that the Ancient Britons preferred to live. The Romans, and still more the Saxons who followed them, were the first to tackle the heavier soil and tougher trees and undergrowth of the valleys. As civilization moved downhill, it left almost untouched the evidence of earlier days; and it is these which we can still see and wonder at today. Ignorance of at least a glimmering of their significance robs the traveller of half the interest and joy in his journeyings and keeps him from some of the loveliest parts of Dorset.

If you drive down on the A354, the main road from London after Salisbury, you cross the county boundary about 10 miles beyond Sarum. At this point you are on the old Roman road that ran almost straight (as Roman roads did) from Old Sarum to Dorchester. On your left is to be seen a high embankment with a broad ditch on the near side. This is the Bokerly Dyke. It runs for miles; and excavation has proved that it was dug and raised right across (and thus must be later than) the Roman road. So it was probably dug as a defence against raiders from the east, culminating in the Saxons, who eventually drove the Britons westwards as far as Cornwall and Wales after the fall of the Roman power. A mile and a half further on, the modern road bends slightly to the right; but if you look you will see clearly the line of the old road running dead straight ahead over the downs to the distant skyline. Next, on the left of your road, in the angle between the new and the old, you will come to the finest group of round barrows or tumuli in the country. These circular mounds of earth, often with a ditch round them, are the graves and monuments of important Britons. They are anything up to 4,000 years old or older. It may be wondered whether later stone monuments – even cathedrals – will last so long.

A mile southwest of Dorchester lies Maiden Castle, the largest hill-top camp in Britain. Three and sometimes four lines of ramparts up to 60 feet high surround the great oval of 900 by 400 yards – and all this dug with red deer antlers for picks and their shoulder-blades for shovels. The site was originally inhabited as far back as the New Stone Age, say 10,000 years ago; but the last great fortifications were raised against the impending Roman invasion. When the Romans did take it by storm in AD 45, little wonder that they decided to rehouse the surviving tribesmen on a less easily defended site at Durnovaria, today's Dorchester. A visit to the County Museum will add much to the interest of 'the Maiden'.

Special to Dorset

The gourmet will like to know that many of the villages and towns along the coast make something of a speciality of lobsters. Afterwards, he may eat Dorset's own cheese, Blue Vinny, a close rival to Stilton. Nothing goes better with it, of course, than Dorset butter spread generously on Dorset knobs. These are like very miniature cottage loaves, but crisp right through. Other specialities of the county include the indigenous Dorset Horn Sheep – horn-rimmed spectacles indeed, and on both sexes! And where is the equal of the Swannery at Abbotsbury? There you will see over 500 birds living on the placid waters of the Fleet, the narrow 8-mile-long lagoon that lies between the Chesil Bank and the mainland.

Castle and minster and ancient church – these are listed in the Gazetteer which follows. What cannot be given is the beauty of the countryside itself, of the thatched roofs (and thatched walls), of the stone in the houses and cottages, grey-white to the east, sun-drenched gold in the west of the county: for this, and much else, only Dorset can bestow.

GAZETTEER

Abbotsbury   3J3
Famous for its Swannery, this village of stone and thatch lies near the western end of the Fleet, the narrow lagoon that runs for some 8m between the **Chesil Bank** and the mainland. There are the ruins of a Benedictine Abbey (AM) and a noble 15th-c tithe barn 276ft long. On a hill-top between village and sea stands the chapel of St Catherine (patron saint of spinsters) of the same date (AM). It has a remarkable stone roof. Garden-lovers should not miss the Sub-tropical Gardens★, approached from the **Bridport** road, especially in magnolia and camellia time (earlier here than usual). Open March–Oct.

Affpuddle   3J4
In the valley of the River Puddle – also called the Piddle or Trent. The church, close to the mill, has a 13th-c chancel, a Norman font, and rare Early Renaissance carved pulpit.

Badbury Rings★   3K4
One of the most impressive Iron Age camps. Tree-crowned and sombre, it stands beside the disused Roman road from Old Sarum to **Dorchester**, which here makes a bend. Legend associates it with King Arthur, who is said to have won his last great victory over the Saxons near by, in the battle of Mons Badonicus, where he also received his death-wound.

Batcombe   3J4
3m NW of **Cerne Abbas**. The rebuilt church retains its 15th-c tower and stone screen. The font is 12th-c. On Batcombe Down, worth the climb for the view alone, stands the carved Cross-in-Hand pillar, mentioned in Hardy's *Tess*.

Beaminster   3I4
As a result of wars and fires, this ancient market town looks younger than it is. The church has a fine Tudor tower, with carvings of the Virgin, the Crucifixion, the Resurrection and the Ascension. Two notable Tudor manor houses in the neighbourhood are *Mapperton* and *Parnham*. The latter, home of the John Makepeace furniture workshop, is open April–end Oct.

Bere Regis   3K4
Its name shows that this ancient place held a royal residence in Saxon times. The church is of particular interest, with a splendidly carved and painted roof. It contains the tombs of the Turbervilles, a name associated with Hardy's *Tess*. *Cloud's Hill* (NT), T. E. Lawrence's cottage, is 3½m SW, open April–end Sept.

Blandford Forum   3K4
Handsome market town on the Stour. Apart from the Almshouses and the Old House, there are few antiquities, since fire almost wiped out the old town in 1731; but many fine 18th-c houses prove the quality of two local architects, the Bastard brothers. Their stately church contains a canopied mayor's chair and other contemporary fittings. Bryanston House, now a public school, is 1m NW of the town. Among numerous pre-Roman earthworks in the neighbourhood, *Pimperne Barrow*, dating from the New Stone Age, has been rated the finest earthen long barrow in the country.

Bournemouth   3L4
Now a town of hotels and language schools set among the pines, it was 150 years ago little more than a group of fishermen's huts clustering around the mouth of a chine. Its pier, opened in 1880, has been recently restored. The Russell-Cotes Museum has some splendid Victorian paintings and is well worth visiting for the building alone, and there is a Shelley museum at *Boscombe*. Bournemouth still does not seem entirely at home in Dorset, into which it was thrust in

1974, though the wild Hampshire moorland here is 'typical Hardy country'. *Hengistbury Head* has a nature trail and is the best viewpoint in the area. *See* **Christchurch.**

Bradford Abbas   3J4
A village on the River Yeo with one of the great churches of Dorset. Wyke Farm, to the E, is a moated house with a splendid medieval tithe barn.

Bridport   3I4
Pleasant old rope-making town, with a wide street of fine red-brick houses; produced cables for the Royal Navy from time immemorial until recent years, and net-making is still carried on. Near West Bay, in magnificent country.

Broadwindsor   3I4
Two landmarks look down on this village: *Lewesdon Hill* (894ft, NT) and *Pilsdon Pen* (908ft, NT). The latter, the highest point in the county, has a fine view. The church (Norman and Perpendicular) has a 12th-c font and a Jacobean pulpit. 5m W, near **Chard**, stands **Forde Abbey**, founded by the Cistercians in 1138. Among later additions it has a Tudor entrance-tower and work by Inigo Jones.

Cerne Abbas★★   3J4
The 180ft figure of the celebrated Cerne Giant (NT), Britain's most uninhibited monument, is cut in the chalk of the hill side above this charming village. It was probably associated with ancient fertility rites, and is thought to have been cut during the period of Roman occupation. Among the ruins of the Abbey are a fine gatehouse, a guest house, and a tithe barn. Opposite the church (mainly Perpendicular) is a most lovely row of overhung Tudor cottages and a Georgian house with a shell porch. At *Minterne*, 2m N, is a wild shrub garden specializing in rhododendrons.

Charminster   3J4
2m N of **Dorchester**, has a church of 12th-c origin, re-fashioned in the 18th. Its fine tower, of Ham Hill stone, dates from the 18th c. Wolfeton House, a Tudor manor, is open to the public on occasion, but only by appointment.

Charmouth   3I4
Attractive resort with Regency houses, little altered since Jane Austen described the 'sweet retired bay' in *Persuasion*. Good displays at Barney's Fossil and Country Life Exhibition. Coastline E is called *Golden Cap* (NT).

Chesil Bank   3J3
A remarkable pebble ridge extending about 10m, from **Portland** to **Abbotsbury**, and in a lesser form for another 7m to a point near **Bridport**. Unique in its formation, the bank is composed of graduated pebbles. It is one of the most dangerous beaches in Europe.

Christchurch   3L4
Built where two rivers, the Avon and Stour, meet before flowing into Christchurch Harbour, the settlement was known originally as Twynham. The priory – now the parish church – is all that remains of an Augustinian foundation dissolved by Henry VIII. it has a massive Norman nave and remarkable chantries, carvings and rood-screen. Norman remains near by include a roofless castle hall and the two-arched bridge over the Avon. Red House Museum housed in a fine Georgian building has local natural history exhibits and a costume gallery. See Britain in a day at Tucktonia Leisure Park with its 4-acre animated model of Great Britain – said to be the largest model landscape in the world.

Corfe Castle: once a spectacular fortress, it was largely demolished after Cromwell seized it in 1646

N of the harbour are *Standpit Marshes*, a nature reserve, and 2m walk towards **Bournemouth** leads to *Hengistbury Head* with fine views. *Mudeford* to the E and *Highcliffe* are holiday resorts.

Corfe Castle★   3K3
The gaunt ruins of the Norman castle (AM) stand splendidly above the town, with its old stone houses and inns. The church suffered badly in the Civil War, but its fine 15th-c tower survives. The Town Hall Museum is open daily. The Purbeck Hills run E to **Swanage** and W to Worbarrow Bay, above which rise the earthworks of *Flower Barrow Camp*, an Iron Age hill-top fortress that is worthy of its magnificent natural setting. 2m NW of Corfe is the famous *Blue Pool*, the largest of many small lakes that fill the old clay pits on Wareham Heath. 5m SW is *Smedmore*, an 18th-c manor house with a collection of antique dolls.

Cranborne   3K4
Small village with a great church built in the 13th c, near the borders of Wiltshire and the disafforested Royal Forest of **Cranborne Chase** (*see* entry in Wilts). The fine Jacobean manor house has Renaissance loggias and a brick gatehouse. It was often visited by James I and Charles I when they hunted on the Chase. In Saxon times the Hundred Court assembled on Castle Hill, a fortified mound 1m S.

Dorchester★   3J4
Founded by the Romans, the city is surrounded by traces of far earlier habitation, notably the forts of Poundbury and Maumbury Rings (*see also* **Maiden Castle**). The County Museum contains many Roman and pre-Roman finds and much else of Dorset interest, including a Hardy Memorial Room. There is also the Dorset Regiment Military Museum (open daily). Max Gate, which Hardy built and where he spent the last years of his life, lies off the **Wareham** road, about 1m out. The cottage where he was born (NT) is at *Higher Bockhampton*, 3m NE. The lodgings of the notorious Judge Jeffreys, the old Grammar School, and the Old Crown Court, where the Tolpuddle Martyrs were sentenced in 1834, are all of interest.

Eggardon Hill 3I4
Its 50 acres of unimproved downland (NT) include a magnificent example of an Iron Age promontory camp, and breathtaking views.

Forde Abbey 3I4
5m S of **Chard**. Fine 12th-c Cistercian monastery in 15-acre garden on banks of River Axe (open May–Sept.).

Lulworth Cove★ 3K3
An almost land-locked bay, is as beautiful as it is interesting geologically even to those who are not geologists. Along the cliffs to the W lie the 40ft rock arch of Durdle Door and the chasm of Stair Hole. E, the Fossil Forest of petrified tree-stumps slopes down to the sea; beyond that are the stratified rocks of Worbarrow Bay. Inland, the village of *East Lulworth* has thatched cottages and the shell of a 16th-c castle, gutted by fire in 1929. Roads are sometimes closed when the military firing range is in use (times advertised in *Dorset Echo* and *Bournemouth Echo*), but there is always access to both East and West Lulworth. *See also* page 65.

Lyme Regis 3I4
Seaside town of charm and distinction with a quay 600ft long known as the Cobb, where the Duke of Monmouth made a landing in 1685 and Louisa Musgrove (in Jane Austen's *Persuasion*) jumped and fell. There are almshouses dated 1549 and handsome Georgian houses. The cliffs are of great geological interest.

Maiden Castle★ 3J4
2m SW of **Dorchester** rise the 60ft ramparts of the greatest of Britain's prehistoric forts. The vast scale of its quadruple walls and the intricacy of the two entrances make this site as impressive as any medieval fortification (AM).

Milton Abbas★ 3J4
An 18th-c model village (now rated as the prettiest in England) of thatched cottages on a wide street, built by the 1st Earl of Dorchester to replace a small market town which marred the privacy of his own newly built home. Milton Abbey, with its ancient Abbot's Hall, is now a school – open Easter and summer holidays. In the beautiful Abbey Church, which dates from the 14th c, should be noted in particular the vaulting of the tower, the sacrament house, the altar screen and a unique Gothic pyx. On a hill E of the Abbey stands the small St Catherine's Chapel. 4m SW is *Bingham's Melcombe*, a great Tudor house with ancient bowling-green and yew hedge. *Bulbarrow Hill*, 4m NNW, gives one of the most extensive views in the county.

Poole 3K4
A port and a resort, with much character and much history. The old town is 14th-c: almshouses, an old postern gate, and some admirable 18th-c buildings including the Guildhall and the Custom House. The almost land-locked harbour is ideal for sailing; its shores, with many beautiful creeks and inlets, measure nearly 100 miles. Near the entrance lies *Brownsea Island* (NT), a wild-life sanctuary. *Compton Acres Gardens* (open April–end Oct.) on the Canford Cliffs road, contain remarkable statuary in marble and bronze. At Yaffle Hill, *Broadstone*, are 6 acres of gardens with many rare trees and shrubs.

Portland 3J3
A high rocky peninsula, with the naval harbour and breakwater to the N, **Chesil Bank** to the W, and Portland Bill with its lighthouse (*see* page 70 and **Weymouth**) and

Pulpit Rock on the southern point. Both coast and interior of the 'Isle' are full of interest. Portland Castle (AM) was built by Henry VIII, on the site of a Saxon castle. Since the 18th c the fine oolitic stone has been extensively quarried for building purposes; Wren used it for St Paul's Cathedral. Interesting also is Avice's Cottage, given to Portland by Dr Marie Stopes; now home of the Portland Museum.

Puddletown 3J4
To E and W of the village are splendid manor houses: *Athelhampton Hall* (open April–Oct.) is 15th-c; Waterston Manor is Jacobean. There is a great church (mainly Perpendicular) with a splendid nave roof, a Jacobean gallery, and a tumbler-shaped early Norman font.

Shaftesbury★ 3K5
Busy market town with a great past, splendidly placed above the Blackmoor Vale. The Abbey was founded by King Alfred, who made his daughter the first Abbess. There are a few remains of the Abbey, a few old houses, and the picturesque cobbled Gold Hill. St Peter's Church has a remarkable crypt and a finely vaulted porch. The Historical Society's excellent Museum is in Gold Hill. 2m SE, Zigzag Hill climbs the downs with views of **Cranborne** Chase.

Sherborne 3J5
Historic town on the northern border, once the capital of Wessex, with houses that date from the 15th c and a magnificent Abbey Church (Norman to 15th-c) notable for its fan vaulting, choir and chapels. In its tower hangs 'Great Tom', the tenor bell, gift of Cardinal Wolsey. The adjacent school occupies part of the former Abbey building: it was founded in the 8th c. The beautiful 14th-c Abbey Conduit stands at the foot of Cheap Street. The Sherborne Castle of today was built in part by Sir Walter Raleigh, to whom Elizabeth I gave the estate. The mansion has been continuously occupied by the Digby family since 1617. Open Easter Sat.–end Sept. There are still remains of the original Norman castle (AM) to be seen in a park at the E of the town. 2½m W is *Worldwide Butterflies* with an indoor jungle and free-flying butterflies. Also here is *Lullingstone Silk Farm*.

Stinsford 3J4
2m E of **Dorchester**. This village is the 'Mellstock' of Thomas Hardy's novels, and in the ancient church there is a Hardy memorial window. His heart is buried in the churchyard, beside the grave of his first wife and near many of his ancestors. His ashes are in **Westminster Abbey**, London. Kingston Maurward, a fine Elizabethan manor house, stands in the grounds of a later mansion.

Studland 3K3
Seaside village of great charm, as yet almost unspoiled. It has a sandy beach and good bathing. Its church is 'a singularly perfect and unaltered specimen of Norman style'. There is a fine walk to **Swanage** over Ballard Down. In the opposite direction, on the way to *Poole Haven* are two massive upright stones, the Agglestone and the Puckstone, and the lake called Little Sea – a very lovely landscape.

Sturminster Newton 3J5
An old market town of stone buildings, standing on a great loop of the River Stour. A fine bridge of six arches unites Sturminster with Newton, and carries a 'transportation tablet'. The birthplace of the Dorset poet William Barnes.

Sturminster Newton: the Old Mill was built in the 17th century but is still in working order

Portland Bill: the red and white lighthouse, built in 1906, replaced the original which is now a bird observatory

Swanage   3K3
A pleasant resort in a beautiful position, with sandy beach, rugged cliffs, and good anchorage for yachts. The town is for the most part modern, but there are some old stone houses, notably near the mill pond, overlooked by the 13th-c tower of the church. Tithe Barn Museum and Art Centre holds exhibitions. Anvil Point Lighthouse and Lifeboat House at Peveril Point are open to the public.

Tarrant Hinton   3K4
The beautifully placed 13th-c church has a Norman font and piscina and a remarkable 16th-c Easter sepulchre. 2m to the N are the ruins of *Eastbury House*, designed by Vanbrugh. 2m to the NE stands *Chettle House*, a good example of 18th-c Baroque work. *Tarrant Rushton*, to the S, has a very unusual church, shaped like an equal-armed cross, dating from the 12th c.

Toller Fratrum and Toller Porcorum   3I4/J4
Two villages 1m apart in the valley of the River Hooke, at the foot of the fortified **Eggardon Hill**. The 'Brethren' of the first name are the Knights Hospitallers of St John, who had granaries here; the fine manor house, with twisted chimneys and heraldic beasts, stands on the site of their ancient home. The church, dedicated to Basil the Great, has an early Norman font. The second village, 'Toller of the Pigs' (which were once bred here), has an interesting church with a 13th-c chancel arch and a Roman capital as pedestal of the font.

Tolpuddle   3J4
Hamlet that became famous when, in 1834, six agricultural labourers were condemned to transportation for the crime of asking for a wage increase. The 'Tolpuddle Martyrs' are commemorated by the 'Martyrs' Tree' (NT).

Wareham   3K4
A delightful old town near the mouth of the River Frome, almost surrounded by pre-Roman earthworks. The small restored Saxon church of St Martin has a figure of T. E. Lawrence in Arab dress sculptured by Eric Kennington. St Mary's Church contains a unique six-sided lead font, and the marble coffin of Edward the Martyr. 3m S stands *Creech Grange*, a Tudor manor in wooded gardens. *Morden Bog* to the N and *Arne Heath* to the E are nature reserves of great beauty.

Weymouth   3J3
Finely placed on Weymouth Bay, the modern resort, grown up round the old seaport and the 18th-c watering-place, still retains memories of its past. There are some charming Georgian houses, and fine portraits in the Guildhall. No. 3, Trinity Street, composed of converted Tudor cottages, is completely furnished with objects of the 17th c. George III lived at Gloucester House (now a hotel); his likeness on horseback is cut in the turf of the downs behind the town, and his statue presides on the sea front. There are good sands and bathing, fishing and sailing. The ruins of Sandsfoot Castle, a blockhouse built by Henry VIII, stand on the cliff overlooking Portland Harbour. The Sea Life Centre is the largest marine life display in Britain (opened 1983). *See also* **Portland**.

Wimborne Minster★   3K4
This venerable town in the valley of the River Stour is dominated by its great Minster. The lantern formed by the partly Norman central tower is of particular interest; so are the chained library, the 14th-c Astronomical Clock, and many fine monuments and tombs. 2m NW stands *Kingston Lacy*, home of the Bankes family for over 300 years. It is a magnificent house and has been recently acquired by the NT.

Wimborne St Giles   3K4
The church, restored and enlarged in 1908, is still an excellent example of Georgian architecture. St Giles's House, the home of the Earls of Shaftesbury, is mainly 17th-c, incorporating late 16th-c work. There is an 18th-c Shell Grotto in the grounds; and in the kitchen garden, it is claimed, was grown the first cabbage to be raised in England.

Wool   3K3
Beside the handsome 15th-c bridge over the Frome stands Woolbridge – the 'Wellbridge House' of Hardy's *Tess* and one of Dorset's most perfect manor houses. The ruins of the 12th-c *Bindon Abbey* lie to the E. 6m to the W is *Woodsford Castle*, now a farm, with ancient tower and a fine thatched roof. The large military camp of *Bovington* has a museum of armoured fighting vehicles – open daily.

Worth Matravers   3K3
Quarrying and lobster fishing occupy the inhabitants of this village on the Purbeck Downs, the site of the first radar station. There is much fine Norman work in the church, particularly the chancel arch. 2m of rough road lead SW to *St Alban's* (or Aldhelm's) *Head*, with a Norman chapel and a magnificent view.

WILTSHIRE

AN INTRODUCTION BY
GEOFFREY GRIGSON

Wiltshire is one of the lonelier counties, its towns rather few and small, except for industrial Swindon in the north and cathedral-city Salisbury in the south, its villages, or most of them, widely scattered. It is not much of a railway county, or for that matter much of a road county. In spite of Swindon with its railway works (and Railway Museum) the trains speed across anxious to get elsewhere, and the Great West Road has been replaced by the M4 motorway. Once the county's famous highway, in a hurry to link London to Bath in Avon, it was indifferent to most of the Wiltshire towns and gave no more than the quickest glimpse, along downland stretches west of Marlborough, of the county's ancient past.

The prime things in Wiltshire are few, yet remarkable and famous. They are Stonehenge, Avebury, Salisbury Cathedral, Wilton House and Stourhead Gardens, its water meadows and farming, all of which have a special relation to the heart of Wiltshire loneliness, in other words to Salisbury Plain.

Stonehenge
In the Middle Ages (which did not bother to take any notice of Avebury with its earthworks, its great ditch, and its stones) Stonehenge was already listed among the Wonders of Britain. All by itself in the wide sheep-walks and cornfields of Salisbury Plain, yet mysterious and suggestive, small in such immensity, yet made up of gigantic stones, Stonehenge has been for England the chief symbol of remotest and most enigmatic antiquity as has its smaller forerunner, Woodhenge. Poets, novelists, painters, and romantic mystifiers have been to Stonehenge, and have drawn after them the archeologists and the preservers. But today there are fences around Stonehenge, it has a ticket office and a car park, and one can see on the horizon one of those great military establishments which occupy too much of the loneliness of Wiltshire. The reputation of this monument has always been a solemn one. People imagined it – as we still imagine it – to have been a 'temple' of some kind (though it is as likely to have been the stockaded 'palace' or HQ or seat of government of a New Stone Age and then Bronze Age kingdom).

The poet William Wordsworth, when he was young, in 1793, watched the fleet off Portsmouth, preparing for the French Wars. Very soon after, depressed by the thought of a war which would be long and full of misery, he spent two days travelling on foot over Salisbury Plain, where the sight of the tall trilithons and the fallen stones of grey Stonehenge and of the prehistoric barrows or burial mounds of the dead round about, made him think all the more of past and present and the disasters of war – and caused him to write a poem, which contains, incidentally, one of the best of all descriptions of the Plain, where roads (but nowadays they are tarred) 'their bare white lines extend'. The forlorn wanderer of Wordsworth's stanzas came to Stonehenge in the night (which is a good time for a visit, by the way, if there happens to be a moon). He had crossed the Plain as the light failed, looking back first to the thin spire of Salisbury Cathedral. He found no house, or hut, or human being,

could only hear
Winds rustling over plots of unripe grain,
Or whistling thro' thin grass along the
unfurrowed plain.

It rained, it grew dark, and the Wanderer at last found shelter in Stonehenge, which Wordsworth in the poem called an 'inmate of lonesome Nature's endless year' – which it certainly is.

Stonehenge, then, is the necessary thing above all things which must be visited in this county. It should be at the head of the tourist's programme – and when he reaches it, he can meditate upon one fact established firmly by modern archeological research, that the grey Stonehenge is some 3,800 years old.

Avebury
Item Two in the explorers' programme will probably be – since they are so close to Stonehenge – either Salisbury itself, or Old Sarum, which is the fortified site of the first cathedral, on what is now the suburban fringe of the city. But out of order, let us have a first look at Avebury (which is hardly less wonderful and no less enigmatic than Stonehenge), even though it lies north of the Plain, across the Vale

of Pewsey in the Swindon sector of the county. Avebury was perhaps an earlier chalkland capital which was deserted for Stonehenge. Its neighbourhood is rich with an extraordinary medley of objects. Here you have a museum, a manor house, an ancient church, an ancient village half in, half out of the huge circle of rampart, ditch and massive squat stones. Here, as well, you have a winding avenue of stones, and the unexplained enormous mound of Silbury, as well as the camp or corral on Windmill Hill, which was the home, some 5,000 years ago, of some of the first herding and corn-growing people of Britain. Here too is the West Kennet Long Barrow, a damp Neolithic family tomb which has been excavated and restored, some of the stones of which are smooth with the polishing of stone axes.

Sarsens (the Avebury circles and most of Stonehenge are made of sarsens) lie on the Marlborough Downs above Avebury; and the A4 (by which you approach Avebury from London) is in part, hereabouts, that ancient highway of the Romans which began in London with the straight line of Oxford Street. Between Avebury and Devizes the main road cuts across a striding, strongly defined length of Wansdyke (i.e. Woden's Dyke), which the West Saxons probably built, more than 1,000 years ago, to check the Mercians who pushed hard against them from the north. Also between Avebury and Calne, one of the finest of Wiltshire's stud of White Horses is cut clear into the chalky hillside. A few miles the other way, another White Horse extends on the chalk and harebell slope of Hackpen Hill. All in all, Avebury is the best centre in Wiltshire – and one of the best centres in any county of Great Britain – for a combination of walks, distances, huge skies, and a superabundant quantity of ancient monuments. Its genuine rurality is unimpaired.

Salisbury

Salisbury is Wiltshire of the valleys – a meadow city where three chalk streams, the Nadder, the upper part of the Avon, and the Bourne, join into one, after draining the chalk country of Salisbury Plain. The city is below the Plain and yet its product – a 13th-century successor to the original Old Salisbury or Old

Salisbury Cathedral, an Early English building begun in 1220, has the highest spire, at 404 feet, in England

Sarum (Sarum is the medieval Latin – and conveniently shorter – form of Salisbury). Old Sarum was built within the multiple ramparts of an Iron Age hill fort on the border of the Plain, in a position the 13th-century ecclesiastics of the first cathedral found too windy and waterless. So Salisbury is the natural capital of the ancient sheep wealth, wool wealth and corn wealth of the great open lands extending to the north, northeast, west and southwest. As Wiltshire's county town (though not its administrative capital, which is Trowbridge, a town without much to offer to the visitor), Salisbury is also successor to Wilton, once the aboriginal capital of the Wiltshire English, 3 miles upstream on the little River Wylye, which joins the Nadder. 'Wilton' means the farm settlement on the Wylye; Wylye in turn means the tricky or twisty river, and Wiltshire means the Shire of Wilton; and Wiltshire people, more than 1,000 years ago, were the *Wilsaetan*, or the Wylye dwellers.

Salisbury contradicts the common idea that medieval cities were jumbles without plan. It was planned, alongside the new cathedral, on a grid system of intersecting streets, roughly parallel. Traffic still follows the old grid in part, but a new inner ring road relieves traffic congestion. The cathedral still stands by itself in the middle in its own river-meadow precinct or close, where the foundation stones were laid on an April day in 1220. Most cathedrals are a mixture of the different medieval styles and centuries. Nearly all of Salisbury Cathedral was built between 1220 and 1280. Early in the next century the great spire was built and can be seen from many points of Salisbury Plain.

This small city flourishes, and looks a credit to the civilization of England, with good shops (including a fine secondhand bookshop near the principal gate into the Close), good buildings, a good museum, and good markets. It is a town of entry, not only to the Plain, but to the serene intricate system of chalk valleys with their valley villages along the banks of chalk-streams, which are clear, and white in the early summer with the crowded flowers of water-crowfoot, rare nowadays.

Wilton and Stourhead
Wilton House, upstream at Wilton, bedded between two shoulders or flanks of Salisbury Plain, I have mentioned as another of the prime things of the county. As mansions go, Wilton House is not over-large or super-grand. But, for its 17th-century architecture (Inigo Jones), its extraordinary pictures (Van Dyck, Rembrandt, Lucas van Leyden, etc.), its grounds, and its associations with many of the greater Elizabethan and Jacobean writers, Wilton is as much a national shrine and a European treasure-house as unique Stonehenge is a national and European antiquity, or Salisbury Cathedral a national and European master-work of medieval art and piety.

Westward beyond the source of the Wylye, on the border of Wiltshire, there is yet another beautiful and peculiar attraction of European and national importance, in the shape of the 18th-century landscape gardens, with temples, grotto, and lakes, attached to the mansion of Stourhead (National Trust). Not only on the edge of the county, but on the extreme edge of Wiltshire chalkland, which is visible from the portico, Stourhead is the last of a westward-extending line of mansions all of which are rooted in the ancient wealth of Salisbury Plain.

Towns and Villages
So much for the greater things of Wiltshire, which few other counties can rival. The best of the small towns and the prettiest villages of the county, with few exceptions, are to be found west and southwest of the Plain, bordering Somerset, Gloucestershire and Dorset. Here the building influence of Bath, in the next county, extended into Wiltshire. Here, instead of soft chalk, good building-stone was available for wall and roof, and in the westward valleys of Wiltshire streams run fast enough to turn the cloth mills which earned very considerable wealth.

Bradford-on-Avon, which has a concentration of seemly houses of the 17th and 18th centuries (as well as its Saxon church), was such a clothiers' town. Malmesbury, which, with Devizes, I prefer to all the smaller Wiltshire towns, had the benefit of water, clothiers and building stone, and carried over a tradition of well-being or self-importance from the great abbey of Benedictine monks, part of whose church survives, with its involved and elongated Romanesque carvings, in the porch, of angels and apostles. Clothiers, too, gave its stony character to the small town of Corsham, where one of them in the church has a memorial blandly remarking:

> *The labouring poor he never did contemn,*
> *And God enriched him by the means of them.*

Castle Combe, which has been voted England's prettiest village (it is pretty, but not that pretty, by any means), lies by a mill-swift stream in a deep stony valley, a cloth-centre once of a smaller kind. Other stony villages of note are Sherston, Biddestone, Lacock (with its abbey), and Steeple Ashton, with a clothiers' church, factory and manor house.

Contrariwise it is the chalk, the chalk escarpments and the valley views they afford, which give Wiltshire much of its more select scenery, away from its better villages. For example, not much in the south or west of England surpasses the downland chalk near Baydon, in the northeast of Wiltshire, or the views of the Pewsey Vale from the chalk spurs of Martinsell Hill, which is an outlier of the Marlborough Downs, or the lofty and lonely country around Haydown Hill on the border of Hampshire, northwest of Hampshire's Andover.

GAZETTEER

Adam's Grave 3K6
Neolithic long barrow overlooking the **Pewsey Vale**, above the village of *Alton Priors*. Area of lofty, breezy downland, crossed by **Wansdyke**.

Avebury** 7J1
The village is built in and out of the great companion-piece to **Stonehenge**. The Avebury monument (AM) is a complex of circular rampart and ditch, stone circle and small interior circles, carefully (though not completely) excavated and restored. The stones are lumpier and dumpier than those of Stonehenge; and Avebury presumably had a similar function, religious or secular or the two combined, at a somewhat earlier date in the New Stone Age (late 3rd millennium to early 2nd millennium BC). Near to Avebury are the **Marlborough Downs**; and among other things to see are the museum, in the grounds of the Elizabethan manor house (open April–Oct.), the great barn housing the Rural Life Museum, the church (partly Saxon); the huge artificial prehistoric mound of *Silbury* (AM); the *West Kennet* Long Barrow, a chamber-tomb alongside Silbury, an underground aisle of huge sarsens (AM); the early Neolithic camp of *Windmill Hill* (AM), which has given its name to the earliest culture of Neolithic settlers, *c*.3000 BC.

Bemerton 3L5
The parson-poet George Herbert (1593–1633) lies buried near the altar under a stone marked with his initials in Bemerton Old Church. The church of 1860 is the Church of England's memorial to Herbert.

Biddestone* 7I1
One of the prettiest stone-built villages of N.W. Wiltshire.

Bowood* 7J1
2m W of *Calne*. 18th-c mansion designed by the Adams, in a magnificent park, with lake by Capability Brown. The house is the home of the Earl of Shelburne. The original Big House was demolished in 1955 leaving the present building, Robert Adam's library, laboratory, chapel, exhibition rooms with displays of Indiana and Victoriana. Gardens with arboretum and fine rhododendrons. Open April–end Sept.

Bradford-on-Avon* 3J6
Ancient, sunny, stone-built town mostly on a steep slope. Notable things: Saxon church with carved angles (10th-c); medieval church house for church feasts, etc.; medieval hermitage; stone bridge (14th–17th-c) with bridge chapel, later used as lock-up; tithe barn (14th-c) (AM); John Hall's almshouses (1700). This decorous grey-gold town owes much to its neighbour **Bath** (Avon). *Great Chalfield Manor*, 2½m NE, is a moated 15th-c house (NT) – skilfully restored. 3m E is *The Courts* (NT) at *Holt* with a fine garden.

Bremhill 7J1
Hill-top village. Wick Hill with Maud Heath's statue is joined to *Chippenham* by her Causeway, endowed in 15th c to provide a dry passage to market.

Avebury: the sarsen stones and earthworks form the largest stone circle in Europe and pre-date Stonehenge

Bromham   3K6
Church with noble medieval Baynton chapel and the grave of the Irish poet Tom Moore.

Castle Combe   7I2
Medieval clothiers' village in a deep valley with a 15th-c market-cross, stone houses and cottages beside a placid trout-stream, small bridges, and a church surmounted by a good tower. *Doctor Doolittle* was filmed here. Motor-racing circuit is close by.

Castle Eaton   7K2
NE of *Cricklade*. Lonely and charming small church on grassy bank of the Thames.

Cley Hill   3K6
Lofty isolated chalk hill. Notable landscape feature (NT).

Corsham   7I1
Handsome little 17th–18th-c clothiers' town in Bath stone (extensive subterranean quarries). Good church, and alongside it Corsham Court, a fine 16th–18th-c house with gardens laid out by Capability Brown and completed by Repton. The house has a fine collection of old masters. Open at set times throughout the year. 5m NE near *Chippenham* is *Sheldon Manor*, dating from 1282 one of the oldest houses in the county. 15th-c chapel, gardens, stable barn all on the site of a medieval village. Open April–end Sept. at set times.

Cranborne Chase   3K5
In the SW corner of Wiltshire, a medieval hunting-ground extending into Dorset and notable for downland scenery and prehistoric antiquities – barrows, earthworks, etc. *See also* **Cranborne** in Dorset.

Devizes★   3K6
This small town has seemly 18th-c houses, a wide market place, churches (St Mary's, St John's) notable for light-enclosing 15th-c architecture; the admirable museum of the Wiltshire Archaeological and Natural History Society; and a series of locks by which the disused Kennet and Avon Canal climbs into the **Pewsey Vale** – the Caen Hill flight has been repaired and the Wharf Museum opened in the town in 1983. The Bear Inn contains mementoes of Sir Thomas Lawrence, whose father was landlord ('Gentlemen, here's my son. Will you have him recite from the poets or take your portraits?'). The local name for Wiltshiremen, 'Yellow bellies', derives from the Pond. The point where chalk and clay meet outside Devizes gave rise to the expression 'as different as chalk from cheese'. *Roundway Down* above Devizes is the remarkable downland site of the Civil War battle in 1643, near the Iron Age camp (c.250 BC) of Oliver's Castle. Also a Countryside Trail open all year. 2m S is *Broadleas*, a beautiful garden often open March–Oct.

Dinton▲   3K5
Has an unusual conglomeration of NT houses, largest of which is Philipps House (open April–end Sept.).

Edington   3K6
Large, light-filled 14th-c church surviving from a priory of the brethren known as the Bonshommes, or Boni Homines. It is well placed under the chalky flank of **Salisbury Plain**.

Everleigh   3L6
Salisbury Plain village with an isolated Gothic revival church of 1813 of considerable beauty. Note 17th-c brass and poem tenderly commemorating a former incumbent's wife.

Fonthill★   3K5
William Beckford, writer, dilettante and millionaire, demolished his father's mansion and built the great 'Gothic' fantasy of Fonthill Abbey (1796–1800), of which only a cloister fragment remains at Fonthill Gifford. From Fonthill Bishop the public road passes under the huge classical gate which led to the old mansion, then along the ornamental lake over romantic artificial caverns opening into a grove of yews.

Froxfield   3L6
At *Littlecote House* the remains of an extensive Roman villa dating from the 1st to the 5th c, with magnificent mosaic, add to the interest of the house. A large Tudor manor (c.1500) it is notable for plasterwork, panelling, paintings, furniture, and Cromwellian armour displayed in the Great Hall. Open April–Sept. Also near by is a replica Wild West town of the 1880s.

Great Yews and Grims Ditch (or Grimsdyke)   3L5
Near *Homington*, 2½m SSW of **Salisbury**. A remarkable, eerie yew wood of some 80 acres, in a downland neighbourhood of Neolithic and Bronze Age Barrows. The double rampart of Grims Ditch (which forms the N boundary of Great Yews) is part of the fence of a prehistoric ranch or tribal area, built c.800 BC.

Haydown Hill   3L6
On the Hampshire border, near *Tidcombe*, encircled by a great bend of Roman road running NW from **Winchester**, and crowned (833ft above sea level) by the Iron Age *Fosbury Camp*. Hereabouts is some of the best Wiltshire scenery of chalk combe and down.

Heddington   3K6
3m S of *Calne* it is a village in itself of little note, below shapely downland escarpment of exceptional attraction: Kings Play Hill, Beacon Hill, with disused section of old Bath Road, and the Roundway battle site of 1643 (*see also* **Devizes**).

Inglesham   7K2
Lonely Thames-side church, with box-pews; minute, simple and beautiful. William Morris helped to preserve it.

Lacock★   3K6
Village and abbey both belong to the NT. Much of the village is late medieval. The abbey housed a community of Augustinian canonesses 1232–1538. Cloister, sacristy, chapter house, warming-house, lavatory, kitchen, barn, etc remain. It was the last abbey to be dissolved after the Reformation when it was converted to a house. The well-designed Fox Talbot Museum commemorates the pioneer photographer who produced the first negative – a one-inch square depicting a mullioned window of the abbey which was then (1835) his country home. Open March–end Oct.

Longleat★   3J6
The mansion of the Marquesses of Bath, an architecturally important Elizabethan building (1559–78), beautifully set in grounds landscaped by Capability Brown in the 18th c and now relandscaped to incorporate a safari park and facilities for visitors including juke-boxes in the old stables, plastic grass and boat trips. Special events for gardeners – rhododendrons, fuchsias, roses etc. Open daily. Near by is beautiful Heaven's Gate, a ½m walk through woodlands with rhododendrons and azaleas leading to a park commanding a lovely view of Longleat and the valley below.

Lydiard Tregoze   **7J2**
3m W of *Swindon*. Isolated church (with numerous coloured monuments) and 18th-c mansion of the Bolingbrokes, approached by a tree tunnel – open to the public.

Malmesbury   **7J2**
A hill-top town, designated an Outstanding Conservation Area, which grew up around the precincts of a major Benedictine Abbey founded in 7th-c but only the 12th-c part of the abbey church remains. The Romanesque carvings of the Twelve Apostles., etc, in the porch, are one of the major works of early medieval art surviving in Great Britain. King Athelstan was buried in the earlier abbey church, 941. Churchyard stone with verses to victims of a circus tiger. Late medieval market-cross. Town prospered from the weaving industry and has many old buildings of interest. The Athelstan Museum displays local antiquities. A few miles SW are several pretty villages including *Sherston*, *Luckington* and *Easton Grey★*.

Marlborough   **7K1**
Small town on the old Bath road, 'capital' of a downland area. Remarkable 16th- to early 19th-c main street, partly arcaded; good bookshops, antique shops, autumn fair, and market. The nucleus of the famous public school is a mellow brick building which was once a coaching inn. To the SE of the town is **Savernake Forest**.

Marlborough Downs   **7K1**
Continuation on N side of the **Pewsey Vale** of the chalk downland of **Salisbury Plain**. Areas on either side of A4 have sarsen stones still *in situ*. Good walking, mushrooms, etc. *See* **Marlborough, Avebury, Adam's Grave, Martinsell.**

Martinsell (St Martin's Hill)   **3L6**
4m SW of **Marlborough** above the village of *Oare* and the **Pewsey Vale**. Remarkable scenic perch, 964ft above sea level, capped by an Iron Age camp. A smooth spur projects entrancingly into the Vale.

Mere   **3J5**
Grey, stony little town on the county border, under **Salisbury Plain**, and directly below the mound of a (long-destroyed) castle. Roomy, rewarding church. Otherwise the best building is the Ship Inn, a 17th-c mansion with an earlier-timbered dining-room and elaborate 18th-c curling iron work upholding the inn sign.

Old Sarum★   **3L5**
The original site of **Salisbury** (New Sarum) on a hill between Salisbury and **Salisbury Plain**, 2m from the city centre. Fortified in the Iron Age, later the site of a Norman Castle and of a cathedral built by St Osmund, nephew of William the Conqueror. Lack of water, the windy exposed position and the insolence of the castle soldiery led to the decision to build a new cathedral and city by the river (AM).

Pewsey, Vale of   **3K6/L6**
Sheltered, fertile greenland vale, between **Salisbury Plain** and **Marlborough Downs**, traversed by the railway and the Kennet and Avon Canal.

The Ridgeway   **7K2**
Ancient 'green road' keeping for the most part to high, dry chalkland, crossing the county NE into Berkshire and Oxfordshire; a trackway for earlier inhabitants, Neolithic, Bronze Age, etc. making for the north and east. A good stretch will be found left and right of the **Marlborough–Wootton Bassett** road, on Hackpen Hill, its course marked here by beech clumps.

Salisbury★★   **3L5**
Wiltshire's most pleasant and civilized town, laid out on a grid plan by Bishop Poore in the 13th c, alongside his great cathedral (*see* page 72), mostly built 1220–80. The spire (404ft) was added in the 14th c, on foundations insufficient for so great a tonnage – the worry and pride of the cathedral authorities ever since (note weight-buckled columns at the crossing). The 13th-c cloisters added after 1260 are a masterpiece of serenity. See in the cathedral library Anglo-Saxon manuscripts and Sir Christopher Wren's report on the spire. Pleasures of the city include the clear waters of the Avon, the 15th-c painting of the Last Judgement in St Thomas's Church, 15th-c hall of John Hall (cinema foyer), the Salisbury Museum, Mompesson House (NT) in the Close; several good bookshops, antique stalls in the market on Tuesdays and Saturdays, good restaurants, a modern shopping precinct, an enterprising theatre, and a thriving arts centre in a former church (St Edmund's). Salisbury Races are held at the racecourse 3m W. At *Redlynch*, 6m SW, Newhouse is a Y-shaped building – Jacobean with Georgian wings. Open May–Sept. Heale House Garden, 4m N in *Woodford*, covers 5 acres and includes a water garden with Japanese tea house and bridge. Open Easter–end Sept.

Salisbury Plain   **3K6**
A great undulating area of chalk extending westward from *Amesbury* for some 20m at an average height of 400–500ft; highest point 755ft just above *Westbury*. Much of it is now under cultivation – or used as Ministry of Defence firing ranges often closed to the public – but the scarcity of streams and villages, with the numerous earthworks and barrows, distinguish it from any other part of England. *See also* **Stonehenge**.

Savernake Forest   **3L6**
A royal deer forest reputed to be the only English forest which is the property of a subject. Beautiful, with its 8 paths meeting in the centre of a beech forest. The part bordering the Old Bath Road (A4) conveys only a hint of the former magnificence of the older trees and glades, especially oak and beech. Celebrated for woodland fungi.

Silbury *see* **Avebury**

Steeple Ashton   **3K6**
Cloth-trade village of stone houses. Noble late 15th-c church, 17th-c market-cross, and stone round-house or lock-up for those who broke the peace.

Stonehenge★★   **3L6**
Remote in **Salisbury Plain**, the major prehistoric monument – and mystery – of Britain (AM). It began as a bank and ditch without stones, *c.*1850 BC. Later in Neolithic times stones were transported from Wales and incorporated in a complex of standing sarsen stones from Wiltshire. About 1600–1500 BC, in the Bronze Age, Stonehenge was grandly remodelled with taller uprights and cross-stones, regularly fashioned and combined. The function of Stonehenge (*see also* **Avebury**) was probably religious, though it may also have formed a royal 'palace', the power-centre of the farming and herding communities of the surrounding chalkland. Bronze Age barrows are particularly numerous and impressive in the Stonehenge neighbourhood. 4m NW is *Woodhenge* near Durrington – rings of ancient timber posts.

Stourhead Gardens: laid out by Henry Hoare in the 18th century, with rare trees, shrubs and rhododendrons

Stourhead** 3J5

In *Stourton*. The mansion and landscaped gardens of Stourhead are interesting NT properties of exceptional importance, created by a member of the Hoare family (of Hoare's Bank). The 18th-c mansion (open April–end Sept.) is notable for furniture, pictures, library and position, facing the last slopes of the Wiltshire chalk country. In a valley below, the gardens are an exquisite pictorial composition embracing village, parish church, medieval cross from Bristol, artificial lakes, classical temples, a grotto and splendid banks of foliage. Brought into being 1730–80, and the finest surviving example of the English landscape garden. Best seen in autumn. Do not miss King Alfred's Tower (1766) above the gardens, a prospect tower raised as a memorial to King Alfred and a tribute (from a banker) to constitutional monarchy. Gardens open daily.

Swindon 7K2

Industrial and railway workshop town which expanded first in Victorian times and again – under the curious name of Thamesdown – since World War II and it is now one of the fastest growing towns in Europe. Good Railway Museum, opened in 1962, with locomotives, drawings, relics of Brunel, etc. alongside the original model village set up for the craftsmen of the railway workshops.

Wansdyke 3K6

An intermittent 60m bank and ditch, once reaching from the Bristol Channel near Portishead to the E of **Savernake Forest**. Possibly a West Saxon defensive work against the Mercians but perhaps of earlier date. A good section crosses the downs and the main road (A361) between Beckhampton and **Devizes**. The name means 'Woden's Dyke', as if only the great god Woden could build himself so vast a work.

Wardour Castle 3K5

SW of *Tisbury*. Wardour Old Castle, once seat of the great Arundel family, was split by mines when besieged in the Civil War. Cedar trees and a romantic grotto (AM). The new 'castle' near by is a classic mansion (now a girls' school) by James Paine (1768).

West Dean 3L5

Neglected fragment of a church, replete with an unusual, colourful collection of memorials to members of the Evelyn and Pierrepoint families.

White Horses 3K6/7J1/3L6/7J1/7J1/3L6

Wiltshire 'white horses' cut into chalk scarps will be found at *Bratton*, 2½m NE of Westbury, ancient but recut 1741; *Cherhill*, 1780 (*see* page 37); **Marlborough**, 1804; *Milk Hill*, N of Alton Priors, 1812; *Hackpen Hill* near Broad Hinton, 1838; *Broad Town*, NW of Broad Hinton, now faint, 1864; *Pewsey*, 1937; and SW of Marlborough–Broad Hinton road, 18th- or 19th-c, only visible after ploughing.

Wilton House** 3L5

Seat of the Earls of Pembroke. Many of the greatest Elizabethan poets were entertained here by the Countess of Pembroke, sister of Sir Philip Sidney. A considerable portion of the house is among the few surviving works which Inigo Jones (1573–1652) designed. He was responsible for the Double Cube Room, for which Van Dyck painted the huge portraits. The visitor sees other fine paintings, e.g. by Rembrandt, Lucas van Leyden and Honthorst (Prince Rupert). The contents of this not very large mansion reach a level of taste which few other aristocratic families attained in the decoration of their homes. The riverside park (good trees, mossy statues) is peaceful and in keeping.

Visitors are welcomed in the celebrated carpet factory in the small town of *Wilton* outside the walls. Once the capital of Saxon Wessex, it also has a Gothic church.

HAMPSHIRE AND THE ISLE OF WIGHT

AN INTRODUCTION BY
CHARLES COLES

There are four distinct Hampshires. Much of the county consists of chalk uplands, typified by sheep and skylarks, moving cloud-shadows and tiny flowers, Celtic barrows and seas of barley. This is my favourite country. I lived in a chalk village for ten years, and when I moved a mere 5 miles across the river to the New Forest, friends came to wish me a very final goodbye. They assured me that I was moving to quite another world with different people. This was true. There is a very different feeling about the Forest. Physically the deeply wooded, silent parts are very beautiful, with their historic oases of very old oak and beech, interlaced by peaty brown streams. There are also wildernesses of holly and honeysuckle, silvery beams and dark yews.

Different again are the tranquil green water-meadows, where the last of the drowners and eelpot men still work, and where the finest dry-fly fishing and some of the best coarse angling in the country are to be found. This is also the sketchbook Hampshire of thatched cottages, prize dahlias and Norman churches – intimate and welcoming but not peculiar to Hampshire. Incidentally, the county was always noted for anglers: Izaak Walton retired to the 'silver streams' of the Meon, and Charles Kingsley used to fish the Itchen.

Lastly there are the 'vilainous heaths' of Cobbett (where I spent part of my boyhood) – the sandy wastelands of the northeast, with their counterpart in the form of the lonely acid moors and bogs of the southwest. On a bleak overcast day, when the horizon is bare except for a group of Scots pines and a row of telegraph poles, and when the over-all colour of the vegetation is brownish, the sandy tracks grey and the cotton-grass a dirty white, the landscape has a melancholy about it. But this same heath country has another face, and also produces miles and miles of vivid mauves and purples and heady golden gorse. It's a question of timing!

Beneath the Surface

Hampshire is a splendid county for 'bones and stones'. Geologically, the most obvious feature is the chalk. The South Downs cross the border near Butser Hill and range northwest to the far side of Winchester. The limestone at Binstead and Bembridge, which provided the material for several famous buildings (such as Winchester Cathedral), is important; the multi-coloured cliffs at Alum Bay are not – but in a thousand attics there must be a host of forgotten jam-jars full of those coloured sands, collected by holiday children of the past.

People and Places

After Vespasian's capture of the Isle of Wight in AD 43, Hampshire quickly became romanized. Of Silchester – the 'lost city of Calleva' – much is to be seen in Reading Museum. Apart from its walls, the once-great city has now returned to its grave under the green grass.

It was after the Romans that Hampshire really came into its own, with Winchester as King Alfred's Wessex capital. There is still a good deal of Saxon work to be seen in some of the village churches today, and the many -worthies, -bournes and -hams in Hampshire speak of Saxon settlements. Of Norman times we have many solid reminders, castles at Odiham and Winchester – where there is also beautiful Norman work in the cathedral and in Henry de Blois' Hospital of St Cross (c.1133).

The old capital city still retains a dignity and a beauty: the suburbs do not intrude. View it first from St Giles Hill – the site of that famous, boisterous Fair of the Middle Ages – and look over the Cathedral and the many other centuries-old buildings, with the great chalk downs away to the east. Then enter by the medieval gate to the town itself for a closer look at (dare I say it?) the town where English history started. And English schooling, too, for there you will find the illustrious College, founded in 1387 by William of Wykeham, of 'manners makyth man' fame. It might almost be claimed as the birthplace of English weather too, for St Swithun was a Bishop of Winchester in Saxon times. At his own request his body had been buried outside the Cathedral, 'where the rain of heaven might fall upon him'; but (according to the popular legend) Authority decided that the grave should be transferred to a more appropriate place near the altar. The moment they tried to move the body it started to rain, and operations were delayed for forty days while the rains continued. Authority was slow to take the hint!

The New Forest scene deserves leisurely exploration, though it is traversed by roads of tempting excellence. The story that William the Conqueror ruined scores of villages and churches to enlarge his hunting preserve is incorrect: research has shown that they just weren't there to destroy. And there is also a theory that William Rufus was more likely done away with by ritual murder than accidentally killed by Walter Tyrell's arrow. Great Hampshire names are the Duke of Wellington (of Stratfield Saye) and Nelson, whom one always associates with Portsmouth. To see the surgeon's cabin on *Victory*'s orlop deck – painted red to disguise the bloodstains – is a macabre reminder of conditions at sea 150 years ago. The whole ship is very much alive, and yet full of ghosts: not just a place to visit on a wet afternoon. A gentler ghost may be felt to haunt Jane Austen's home at Chawton, now a museum.

After Winchester, Southampton has probably played the greatest part in the county's history. It claims to be the 'Gateway of England': it was certainly once the gateway to the New World, for it was from this port that the Pilgrim Fathers set sail for America. From here (as from Lymington or Portsmouth) you can cross with your car to the Isle of Wight, or from Southsea you can skim across to Ryde in a spray-shrouded hovercraft.

The Isle of Wight

The Garden Island is small, only 22 miles from one side to the other and 13 miles from north to south. I know it almost better from seaward than inland – the loom of the great St Catherine's light on the dark horizon having many times welcomed me home after a wet night in the Channel. Indeed the island looks almost at its best from seaward: the coastal scenery, the deep chines, the trees down to the water's edge – and at the right time of the year the wild fuchsias, hydrangeas and rhododendrons are surely at their loveliest when seen across the water. The little towns and villages too: Ventnor terraced up the steep hillside almost Italian fashion; Sandown and Shanklin looking cosy behind their bright sands.

In some obscure way the island is unlike Hampshire, possibly because the inhabitants regard us 'overners' from the mainland as not belonging. In places a Victorian atmosphere still pervades.

Cowes Week takes place during the first week in August. If you are prepared to walk you can still be alone or nearly so even in holiday time, and you will get some spectacular views – St Boniface Down, or the cliffs above the Needles. This is the place from which to watch the round-the-island race, often with over a hundred yachts taking part. With a fleet of striped spinnakers bellying out over a sparkling sea this race is as picturesque as any in the world.

Beyond Alum Bay, on the Isle of Wight, past The Needles and Tennyson Down, are Freshwater and Compton Bays

A great deal of history has been buried or built on the island since the Romans first invaded it. The villa at Brading is one of the best preserved in the whole country. In Carisbrooke Castle, built as a Norman fortress, the betrayed King Charles was imprisoned before his execution. There are also several fine old manor houses. Osborne House, the seaside home of Queen Victoria, is where she died. To this day there *is* something final about it, as though it marks the end of an era of island remoteness and the start of a new period of fashion and popularity.

Hampshire Occupations

Though light industry increases all the time, Hampshire is still predominantly an agricultural county, and I hope you will admire the work of the skilled thatchers and hurdlemakers. Some old iron-works still remain. Coastal industries include a petrochemical complex but the Royal Navy provides the main interest – with the Army in evidence at Aldershot and the R.A.F. at Farnborough.

Hampshire claims Hambledon as the birthplace of modern 'crickett'. This famous club was started in the mid-18th century, and so skilled were the players that they used to play and often beat the All-England XI. In 1778 they played them for 1,000 guineas, and in 1783 for 'eleven pairs of white corded dimity breeches and eleven handsome pink striped waistcoats'. Mr Thomas Lord, the proprietor of the original Lord's Cricket Ground in London, which was opened in 1797, is buried not far away at West Meon.

Natural History

In the home county of that famous naturalist, Gilbert White of Selborne, there is a rich variety of wild life. Most species of deer, including Sika, are to be found in the New Forest: if you get up early enough you will probably see them, and at rutting time you will smell them and hear them. The New Forest ponies are to be seen all over the area. These are not wild; they are all privately owned. The owners of certain properties in the Forest have the right of free grazing for their animals. The New Forest pony is a distinct breed, a hardy one that can survive the weather and the sparse herbage; it can be of any colour, but not piebald or skewbald. Unauthorized feeding of any of the animals in the New Forest is forbidden. The Forest is still a good centre for the bug-hunter – White Admirals, and some of the less common fritillaries and hairstreaks are to be seen. If a pinpoint of greenish light stares at you from near the ground, it will be a glow-worm.

Food and Drink

The day of the once famous 'Hampshire Hog' – when pork and pudding were the farm worker's staple diet – is virtually over, though the commoners' pigs are still turned out to free-range in the Forest during the pannage months, the season of beech-nuts and acorns. The Romans, who first brought the vine to Hampshire, would have been amused to know that grapes are still grown and wine made regularly from at least four successful vineyards in this area.

GAZETTEER

Alresford   3M5
Pleasant small 18th-c town. Mary Mitford, author of *Our Village*, was born here and Admiral Rodney was buried in the church at Old Alresford. The Mid-Hants Railway known as the Watercress Line has its HQ at the station and is run by volunteers at weekends March–Oct.

Alton   4C8
Busy little town on the route of the **Pilgrims' Way**. Good Georgian buildings, a handsome church (note S door with marks of bullets fired by Parliamentary troops in 1643), the Curtis Museum specializing in agricultural implements and the Allen Gallery housing a collection of ceramics. Hopfields all round, and a brewery. 4m N is *Lasham*, where gliders ride serenely in the air. At *Froyle* near by is a splendid wooden waterwheel plant.

Alum Bay, Isle of W   4L4
Notable for its cliffs of many-hued sands, its view of the line of chalk rocks called *The Needles* and the lighthouse on the end. Has a museum of clocks – open Easter–Oct.

Andover   3M6
An old town now overtaken by development. A good centre, however, for visiting the area. 6m W at *Middle Wallop* is the

Museum of Army Flying. 2m E is *Finkley Down Farm*, a country park with farm animals and an agricultural museum. Open April–Sept. 4m W near *Weyhill* is a Hawk Conservancy with birds of prey from all over the world. Open Easter–Oct. *See also* **Stockbridge**.

Avington   3M5
Both the little brick church (built *c*.1770), with its original pews, gallery and pulpit, and the neighbouring mansion of Avington Park have associations with Shelley.

Basing   4D8
2m E of **Basingstoke**. Under the 5th Marquess of Winchester, Basing House (now a ruin) withstood a long siege before yielding finally to Cromwell himself (1645). Note the 16th-c dovecot, and the magnificent tithe barn.

Basingstoke   4D8
Fast-growing town with extensive shopping centre. Worth noting are the Willis Museum and Art Gallery (open Tues.–Sat.), and the Viables Craft Centre in Harrow Way, with demonstrations by craftsmen in a rural setting (open Tues.–

Lyndhurst: near by at Swan Green Tudor cottages surround the green where a New Forest pony roams

Sun. afternoons). *See also* **Sherborne St John** and **Stratfield Saye**. The Basingstoke Canal is currently being restored except for the Basingstoke end which has been largely built over.

Beaulieu* 3M4
Separated by a road from the river are the remains of the Cistercian abbey founded by King John in 1204. The Great Gatehouse forms part of Palace House, which is now the residence of Lord Montagu of Beaulieu; the Refectory is the parish church (note reader's pulpit). Beside these ancient buildings is Lord Montagu's National Motor Museum founded in 1952 and exhibiting several hundred veteran and vintage cars and also motor-cycles. 2m S is picturesque **Buckler's Hard**.

Bembridge, Isle of W 3N4
A yachting centre at the mouth of Brading Haven, home of the famous 'Redwings'. There is a windmill (NT) open to visitors, and at Bembridge School an important collection of Ruskin's manuscripts and drawings.

Bonchurch, Isle of W *see* Ventnor

Brading, Isle of W 3M4
Once a sea port, now a quiet inland town, but has a good church containing monuments of the Oglander family. See stocks under old town hall and the bull ring at near-by crossroads. To the S is a Roman villa with well-preserved pavements and hypocausts (under-floor heating) and a small museum. Also Morton Manor dating back to 13th c. Open at set times. One of Britain's finest collections of dolls is at the Lilliput Museum. The famous wax museum is in the 11th-c Rectory Mansion.

Breamore 3L5
The pre-Conquest church in this Avon valley village (pronounced 'Bremmer') still has an inscription over an arch in Anglo-Saxon lettering. On the downs above the village is the Miz-Maze, a medieval labyrinth cut in the turf. In the grounds of Breamore House (Elizabethan, partly rebuilt after a fire in 1856) is a countryside museum specializing in agricultural vehicles – open April–Sept.

Buckler's Hard* 3M4
Where New Forest oak was turned into 'wooden walls of old England'. Three of Nelson's ships at Trafalgar were built on the slipway here: details may be found in the Maritime Museum. The present-day charm of the place rests in the old shipwrights' brick-built cottages and the delightful setting beside the Beaulieu River popular with yachtsmen. The tiny church can accommodate a congregation of perhaps 30 people at a squeeze. *See also* **Beaulieu**.

Burghclere 3M6
The Sandham Memorial Chapel (NT) (just N of *Highclere* station) was built in 1927 in memory of a soldier who died in World War I. It is filled with wall paintings of wartime scenes by Stanley Spencer.

Carisbrooke, Isle of W 3M4
The Castle** is the most interesting building in the Isle of Wight, its keep one of the most perfect of Norman shells. Fine machicolated gatehouse with inner doors dating from 1470. Charles I was imprisoned here 1647–8 shortly before his execution; there is a museum of island history, including objects associated with Charles I. In the Well House (AM) is a donkey-wheel for drawing water.

Chawton 4C8
The house in which Jane Austen spent her last eight years, and wrote *Emma* and *Persuasion*, is now a museum. She died in **Winchester**, and is buried in the Cathedral there.

Corhampton 3M5
Set in the quiet Meon valley with an 11th-c Saxon church containing wall paintings and its original stone altar.

Cowes, Isle of W 3M4
The main part of the town is on the W side of the Medina river. Here are Cowes Castle (headquarters of the Royal Yacht Squadron) and the principal boatyards and moorings. Cowes Week in August is one of the great events of the yachting world. Regular steamer and hydrofoil connection with **Southampton**. Trips round the Island, etc.

Freshwater, Isle of W 3L4
The little River Yar rises so close to the S coast that it almost turns this corner of the Isle of Wight into another island. Hills rise steeply on either side of the valley. Tennyson Down, to the W is crowned by a tall monument commemorating the poet who spent many years at Farringford House. Splendid walk W from the cross to the point looking down on *The Needles*. N is **Alum Bay**. (*See also* page 79.)

Hamble 3M4
Popular yachting centre near the mouth of the River Hamble.

Hambledon 4B8
The cradle of cricket. The Hambledon Club was founded in 1760; see the memorial on Broadhalfpenny Down opposite the Bat and Ball inn.

Hartley Wintney 4D8
Note West Green House – which is a charming early 18th-c house (NT). Open April–end Sept.

Laverstoke 3M6
Henri Portal, a Huguenot refugee, built Laverstoke Mill on the River Test in 1719 to expand his paper-making business and from 1724 for over 200 years the family firm made bank-notes here for the Bank of England.

Lymington 3L4
An ancient borough enjoying a new lease of life as a yachting centre. Past the moorings and down the fairway ferryboats take cars and passengers to **Yarmouth** on the Isle of Wight. Near by is *Hurst Castle* (AM) built by Henry VIII – walk from *Milford* or ferry from *Keyhaven*.

Lyndhurst 3L4
The 'capital' of the **New Forest** it retains a royal hunting lodge now known as the Queen's House. In the adjoining Verderers' Hall may be seen the 'expedition stirrup': if a dog was too big to get through, its claws would be maimed ('expeditated') to prevent its chasing the king's deer. The Victorian church has William Morris windows and a fresco by Lord Leighton depicting the Wise and Foolish Virgins. Which of the ladies, if any, were based on local girls is still a matter of debate. In the churchyard is the grave of Alice Liddell, original of Lewis Carroll's *Alice in Wonderland*. (*See also* page 81.)

Mattingley 4D8
2m N of *Hook* is an unusual and delightful little 15th-c half-timbered church.

Mottisfont
3L5

A Test Valley village dominated by a so-called Abbey (NT), a 12th-c Augustinian priory converted into a mansion. *Trompe l'œil* painting by Rex Whistler in drawing room. Garden with double plane tree and early varieties of rose.

Netley
3M4

Among trees and unalluring recent buildings are remains of a beautiful Cistercian abbey (AM) founded (1239) by monks from **Beaulieu**. Most of the vast Victorian military hospital on Southampton Water has been demolished, and the site is now part of The Royal Victoria Country Park.

New Forest
3L4/M4

Between Southampton Water and the Hampshire Avon lie over 100sq m of what William the Conqueror made into a royal hunting preserve. Oaks and beeches survive the planting by the Forestry Commission of regimented conifers. As well as woodlands there are considerable areas of open heathland rising in places to 400ft with views extending to the Isle of Wight. Numerous ponies roam the Forest and though the main roads are now fenced motorists should remember that animals have priority – including cattle and (at acorn-fall) pigs. Summer camping only, by permits from the Queen's House, **Lyndhurst**, or major camp-sites. Road signs announcing Forest Full sometimes erected at bank holidays refer to these sites. At *Ashurst* is the New Forest Butterfly Farm now open May–Oct. At *Brook* is the Rufus Stone where it is said William Rufus met his death in 1100. (*See also* page 81.)

Newport, Isle of W
3M4

The capital of the Isle of Wight, at the head of the navigable part of the Medina river. Meeting-place of most of the island's main roads and a busy market town. The church has a good Marochetti monument to Charles I's daughter (who died in captivity at **Carisbrooke**) and a medallion of the Prince Consort. Small Roman villa in Avondale Road. 3m SE is *Arreton Manor*, a 17th-c manor house with Pomeroy Museum and National Wireless Museum.

Odiham
4D8

A pleasant town with Georgian houses and other old buildings. Note the old pest-house in the churchyard of the 14th-c church. 1m W are the Norman remains of Odiham Castle.

Osborne House, Isle of W
3M4

Long the home of Queen Victoria, who died here in 1901. A building in the Palladian style, designed by Thomas Cubitt and the Prince Consort. Part of it was used as a Naval College in World War I (King George VI was trained there); one wing was a convalescent home for officers and civil servants. Visitors (Easter Mon.–mid Oct.) can see the State Apartments – a notable excursion into 'Victoriana', which is continued in *Whippingham* Church, also of the Prince Consort's designing (AM). At Barton Manor are gardens originally laid out by the Queen and Prince Consort. Open May–Sept.

Petersfield
4C8

This town became prosperous with the medieval wool trade. Later it was a coaching stop on the London Portsmouth road. Today it is a peaceful market town with many fine old buildings, particularly in Sheep Street, Dragon Street and College Street. The surrounding area is also attractive with wooded hills to the N and open downland to the S forming part of the *Queen Elizabeth Country Park* with a prehistoric farm, displays and crafts. *Butser Hill*, 3m SW, rises to 889ft.

Portchester Castle★
4B8

A castle (AM) within a castle; Henry II built his inside the walls of one built by the Romans to protect the Saxon shore. Also within the Roman walls is a 12th-c church.

Portsmouth and Southsea
4B8

'Pompey' to the Royal Navy, and formerly England's chief naval base, it is still an important naval port. Every corner is redolent of the sea. The great sight is Nelson's *Victory*★, in dry dock near the entrance to the Royal Dockyard and close to the Royal Naval Museum. Also in dry dock here is the *Mary Rose*, Henry VIII's warship raised from the seabed in 1982. A permanent display of relics from the ship opened in June 1984 near the entrance to the Royal Dockyard. The cathedral of St Thomas of Canterbury is 12th-c while the Royal Garrison Church (AM) dates from the 13th c. Other noteworthy attractions include the City Museum, the D-Day Memorial (and in Southsea is the D-Day Museum which opened in June 1984), Buckingham House, the Royal Marines Museum, the Natural Science Museum and Aquarium, and Fort Widley. E of the city is *Southsea*, a resort with sandy beaches, an amusement complex, gardens, and promenade to view the constant coming and going of shipping of all kinds through the harbour mouth – including submarines from HMS *Dolphin* at *Gosport*. Here too is the HMS *Alliance* Submarines Museum and to the N of Gosport is *Fort Brockhurst* (AM).

Ringwood
3L4

Market town at W edge of the New Forest. Fishing in the River Avon.

Rockbourne
3L5

Remains of a Roman villa. Open daily Easter—Sept.

Romsey
3L5

An old-fashioned market town probably once a Roman settlement. Its varied architecture includes handsome examples of Tudor, Georgian and Regency buildings. Romsey is notable for its Abbey Church★ founded in the 10th c, but mainly a Norman building with typically massive piers and many remarkable details. Note the Saxon crucifix in the S choir aisle – a relic of the nunnery of which the church was a part. The Abbey Church was the burial place of Lord Mountbatten. King John's House near by is 13th-c, note the medieval graffiti, and has been restored. *Broadlands* was first opened to the public by Earl Mountbatten of Burma, whose wife was a descendant of a previous owner, Lord Palmerston. Capability Brown is partly responsible for the present appearance of the grounds and house of 16th-c origins. Open April–Sept. Also near are **Mottisfont Abbey** and the Hillier Arboretum. *See also* **Winchester**.

Ryde, Isle of W
3M4

The island's port of entry from **Portsmouth** with a ½m pier which is also the beginning of the only surviving length of railway, now linking the holiday resorts of Ryde itself, **Sandown** and **Shanklin**. *Quarr Abbey* is near by.

Sandown, Isle of W
3M3

A holiday resort now almost contiguous with **Shanklin**. There is a geological museum at the Public Library. Inland are an airport and the island's principal golf-course.

Selborne
4C8

Quiet, unspoiled village made famous by the parson naturalist Gilbert White (1720–93), who spent most of his life here as curate. His home, Wakes (named after its original farmer-owner), is now a museum: also open to the public is the garden which figures largely in his writings. Behind it is 'The Zigzag' leading up to Selborne Hanger, which is partly NT property – along with two tiny wooded valleys, the Long Lythe and the Short Lythe, on the other side of the single winding village street.

Shalfleet, Isle of W   3M4
The squat rectangular tower of the church is so wide as to be almost a cube. The walls are 5ft thick, and it may have originated as a place of refuge. Note Norman carving over inner doorway. British Sports Car Exhibition open at set times.

Shanklin, Isle of W   3M3
The wooded Chine and the Old Village with its thatched cottages distinguish this resort from others on the Island. Good sands and a cliff lift. S towards **Ventnor** the downs rise to nearly 800ft.

Sherborne St John   4D8
The Vyne (NT): beautiful Tudor mansion with diaper brickwork, and later alterations. Oak gallery and chapel date from *c.* 1510. Palladian portico (believed first in England) from 1650: 'Theatric' staircase from 1764. Charles II, Queen Anne, and Chippendale furniture. Open April–Oct.

Shorwell, Isle of W   3M3
Attractive village among the downs. Over N door of church is a good 15th-c wall painting of St Christopher. Note Elizabethan pulpit, brasses, and the chained Cranmer and Vinegar Bibles.

Silchester★   4D8
The high Roman walls of the Roman town Calleva Atrebatum still stand – over a mile in circumference – but of the town they once enclosed there is now no sign. Its ruins were excavated, and the important finds removed for safe keeping in **Reading** Museum, Berks.

Southampton★   3M4
The Romans had a military port (Clausentum, now Bitterne Manor) here at the mouth of the Itchen and the Saxons a trading centre (Hamwih, later Hampton) on the opposite bank. Later the port imported wine from Gascony and medieval merchants prospered on the contents of galleys from Florence and Venice. A brief time as a spa followed by industrial development and the so-called double tides (a prolonged period of high water) led to its supremacy as a transatlantic port. Although it is very much a modern city, with shops in the main street (Above Bar), rebuilt after bombing in World War II, it has managed to retain a great deal of its medieval past. The city walls, especially the stretch along the Western Esplanade called the Arcades, while not complete are among some of the finest in Britain. Also worth noting are the Bargate and a number of merchants' houses. There are several good museums including the new Spitfire Museum in Albert Road South, and a well-endowed art gallery in the civic centre should not be missed. A memorial marks the departure, via **Plymouth**, of the Pilgrim Fathers in 1620. Southampton Water provides an ever-changing scene of shipping ranging from oil tankers and dredgers to cruise liners and car ferries. Harbour cruises are available. Guided walks are arranged throughout the year around the old parts of the city and there are bus tours during the summer months. Annual international boat show in Sept. At *Eling*, near Totton, is a restored tide mill.

Southsea *see* **Portsmouth**

Steventon   3M6
The village in which Jane Austen was born in 1775. Unfortunately nothing remains of the rectory in which she spent her first 26 years and where she wrote *Pride and Prejudice* and *Northanger Abbey*.

Stockbridge   3M5
Noted for the trout fishing in the River Test. A notice in Welsh over a private house advertising 'Worthwhile grass, pleasant pasture, good beer and comfortable shelter' recalls its days as one of many inns catering for cattle drovers bound for the fairs and markets of Surrey and Kent. Near by is the Iron Age fort of *Danebury Ring*.

Stratfield Saye   4D8
The mansion and estate were given by the nation to the Duke of Wellington in gratitude for the victory at Waterloo. Open mid-April–end Sept. The lofty monument on Heckfield Heath at the entrance to the park is capped by a statue by Marochetti. Part of the estate (entrance 2½m away on the A32) is now open, as the *Wellington Country Park* with many attractions for children and also the National Dairy Museum, March–Oct.; weekends only in winter months.

Tichborne   3M5
2m S of New **Alresford** it was originally 'At Itchenbourne' – the river rises near by. In Henry II's time the bedridden Lady Tichborne begged from her husband, for charity, the revenue from as much land as she could crawl round: the field is still called The Crawls. Today local women receive flour from the annual Tichborne Dole, but the family's finances never recovered from a Victorian lawsuit over the inheritance.

Titchfield   3M4
Taking materials from the 13th-c church of the abbey dispossessed at the Dissolution, the Earl of Southampton built the huge Tudor mansion called Place House which was much demolished in the 18th c to reveal the original stonework of the abbey (AM).

Ventnor, Isle of W   3M3
A terraced resort with a Victorian and Edwardian flavour, built at the foot of the steep slopes of *St Boniface Down★*, which rises behind it to 785ft, the highest point in the Isle of Wight. Good winter climate; pier, sands, and multivision stereo show guide to the island. E is *Bonchurch*, where A. C. Swinburne (1837–1909) is buried; beyond is the Landslip, a tumbled mass of chalk and limestone through which the road makes its picturesque way. 4m N is *Appuldurcombe House* near Wroxhall.

Whitchurch   3M6
Town on River Test with a silk mill open to the public. N of the town are *Beacon Hill* and *Watership Down* in the chalk hills which form the Wayfarers Walk.

Winchester★★   3M5
Parliaments have met here regularly, kings have been crowned and kings buried. For long the city was the kingdom's joint capital with London. Winchester has had a cathedral since the 7th c; curfew has rung nightly since the time of William the Conqueror. Extensive excavations have produced new evidence of 2nd-c Roman Winchester and of the Saxon forerunners of the present inspired Cathedral built by the Normans. The remains of Canute are among

Winchester: At Cheyney Court, in the Close, the bishops held courts for the area called the Soke

those in the mortuary chests on the screens enclosing the choir of the cathedral. Among more modern graves are those of Izaak Walton and Jane Austen. Graceful ironwork abounds throughout this most beautiful of all English cathedrals. Note well the chantry of William of Wykeham to whom the splendid nave is due, as also Winchester College and New College, Oxford. Of Winchester's historic castle only the Great Hall remains; the so-called Round Table of King Arthur is of Tudor design but tests suggest it may be 13th-c. The endowment of the Hospital of St Cross almshouses (c 1133) provides for a 'wayfarers' dole' of bread and beer to all comers – so long as the daily ration lasts. The

city has a modern shopping centre with a pedestrian precinct, several military museums, two art galleries and museums. Also an 18th-c mill (NT), and a zoological park 7m S at *Marwell*. At *Ampfield* 9m SW is the Hillier Arboretum a remarkable collection of trees and shrubs. To the W is *Farley Hill*, an open country park.

Yarmouth, Isle of W   3M4
Southern terminal of the car ferry from **Lymington**; its harbour a popular sailing centre. A busy little place with an air of the past. Remains of a Henry VIII castle (AM); a quaint little town hall rebuilt 1763 and a church with a curious statue whose body represents Louis XIV of France and the head Sir Robert Holmes (d. 1692), who captured New York from the Dutch.

EAST AND WEST SUSSEX

AN INTRODUCTION BY
CLIFFORD MUSGRAVE

The fame of Sussex owes much to one distinctive kind of scenery: the South Downs with their whale-back shapes, grass-covered slopes and exhilarating air. Yet these Downs are but the backbone of a county that in a length of some 70 miles, with a width of 20–30, possesses a variety of scenery that must satisfy every type of personality or mood. The county is no less rich and diverse in its wealth of historical associations, and in its splendid heritage of the works of man, as seen in its towns and buildings. Sussex offers not only the delights of numerous small ancient towns and villages, but also the glittering attractions of large modern resorts, culminating in the cosmopolitan sophistication of a town where a legendary monarch created a fabulous pleasure-palace.

Divided for many years for administrative purposes into East and West Sussex, this separation became more distinct in 1974, when many of the powers of the county boroughs of Brighton, Eastbourne and Hastings, particularly for education, police, health, planning and libraries, were transferred to the two county councils, and the county boroughs were relegated to the status of boroughs.

The Structure of Sussex

As elsewhere in Britain, the rapid changes of geological formation that occur within a small distance give the county its delightful variety of scenery. Three principal formations, the chalk, the sands and the clay, create the distinctive character of Sussex. The great rampart of the Downs is but a remnant of the immense dome of chalk, 3,000 feet high, that was formed ages ago when primeval cataclysms thrust upwards. The character of Sussex scenery has changed radically in recent years. The destruction of thousands of elm trees by Dutch elm disease has had a lamentable effect, but the landscape has been opened up to many new and interesting vistas.

Ancient Sussex

In prehistoric times the dense forests of the Weald left only the shores of Sussex and the open hill-tops free for human habitation. On the principal summits of the Downs are still to be seen the remains of the hill camps that were built in a chain throughout the county by the Bronze Age farming people of the 'Windmill Hill' culture about 2000 BC. In the Iron Age they were fortified, and eventually became a final defence against the Romans.

The largest and finest of the hill camps is at Cissbury, near Worthing, which was a centre of the Neolithic flint industry supplied by the flint mines within the camp boundary. Other surviving works of ancient man in Sussex are the round barrows, long barrows and cultivation terraces, and the downland trackways that stretch from the coast westwards inland towards Stonehenge. One of the principal Roman roads of England, the Stane Street, runs through Sussex from Regnum (Chichester) to London over Bignor Hill, near which lies one of the finest Roman villas in the country, Bignor Villa, with its wonderful mosaic pavements of Medusa, Venus and the Four Seasons. The Roman Palace at Fishbourne, near Chichester, is also worth visiting. Found accidentally in 1960, the site was uncovered and purchased by the Sussex Archaeological Society and opened to the public in 1968.

When the Normans came, they used the great natural divisions of the county as the basis for parcelling out Sussex into six areas of government, the six 'Rapes', each with its strip of coastland, a portion of downland for grazing flocks and herds, a river, a stretch of cleared and cultivated Wealden land, and on the north an area of wild forest for hunting and for the feeding of hogs. Each of the Rapes – Chichester, Arundel, Bramber, Lewes, Pevensey and Hastings – was dominated by its castle, not only for protection, but also to hold the country in subjection.

Pevensey Castle, first built by the Romans to protect Sussex against the Saxons, and later enlarged and strengthened by the Normans, still stands. Not far away, at Battle, the Saxon Kingdom itself under Harold was destroyed by William the Conqueror.

Arundel Castle, with its Norman gates, barbican and keep, second only to Windsor in the romanticism of its castellated skyline, is the greatest of Sussex castles. Bodiam, standing foursquare in its lily-

The South Downs Way, a long-distance path, passes by Chanctonbury Ring, an Iron Age site amid a beech wood

covered moat, is of the 14th century. Herstmonceux was one of the first great castellated houses of brick. Lewes Castle commemorates Simon de Montfort's victory which gave us the beginnings of Parliament.

In the 14th century some prosperity came to Sussex from the sheep-farming that flourished on the downland grass. Because of this new wealth several of the ancient Saxon manors were developed into great estates in Tudor times, as at Parham in the west and Firle in the east. Medieval piety brought European culture and fine ecclesiastical foundations to Sussex. Battle Abbey, with its beautiful 14th-century gatehouse, commemorates the Battle of Hastings; Michelham Priory, moated on an island in meadows near Hailsham, shows us with its ancient buildings and restored rooms the life of an Augustinian priory. Medieval wall-paintings in the churches of West Chiltington and Hardham still testify to the arts of painting that were disseminated with other learning and culture through Sussex from the great Cluniac priory at Lewes, founded by the Conqueror's sister Gundrada and destroyed by Henry VIII. Bayham Abbey and Boxgrove Priory have impressive remains of similar religious establishments; Wilmington Priory is on a smaller scale.

Hundreds of fascinating village churches and the austerely magnificent Chichester Cathedral, with its ancient Saxon stone-carvings, tell us of past religious life, and continue into our own day the Christian tradition that was brought to Sussex, not from Canterbury by St Augustine, but from the sea by the wandering Bishop Wilfrid, who taught the starving pagan South Saxons the art of fishing.

Industries Ancient and New

Museums at Brighton, Hastings, Worthing and Lewes preserve many remarkable treasures of past ages, together with relics of the bygone agricultural and social life of the county. They are rich in examples of the Sussex ironwork that was the chief industry of the county from Roman times until the 17th and 18th centuries when the industry moved north to the coal mines. The first English cannon was cast at Buxted in 1543; but the most enduring traces of this vast industry are to be found in the names that commemorate the iron-workings – Iron Hill, Smoke Alley, Furnace Wood and Mine-Pit Copse.

An important and extensive nature reserve has been formed by the National Trust in the valley of the River Cuckmere, with a downland museum at Exceat. At Singleton the Weald and Downland Open Air Museum preserves over 20 important examples of domestic buildings from medieval times. *See* pages 18–20.

Such ancient crafts as the making of wattle-fencing and trug-baskets, those long shallow baskets of bentwood, are still carried on in the villages. An old craft that has developed with the times is that of the blacksmith, whose work of shoeing horses has now almost completely vanished. Instead he has turned to the making of decorative ironwork for garden gates, sign-brackets, balcony and staircase railings, and even iron jewelry on a tiny, delicate scale. Around the principal towns, highly advanced modern electrical, electronic, engineering and other light industries have become established, while inland the town of Crawley is a vast centre of modern industries, with a huge population of residents that has overspilled into the neighbouring countryside and towns for recreation, shopping and entertainment.

Around the western harbour towns, boat-building reflects the world-wide interest in this industry. Shoreham harbour has been enormously improved in recent years and is visited every day by cargo boats from Holland, Scandinavia, Germany and Russia, chiefly carrying timber and vegetables. Newhaven remains an important cross-Channel port.

Sussex Houses

As in so many other respects, Sussex is rich in the variety and beauty of its houses, ranging from the small manor houses of the Middle Ages like Brede and Great Dixter, to fine Elizabethan houses like Glynde Place, Parham Park and Danny Park, and to the great houses of the years of William and Mary and the Georges: Uppark with its gloriously decorated rooms and furniture of several successive periods of style; noble Petworth with its paintings by Turner and carved room by Grinling Gibbons; Firle Place near Lewes, a splendid gem of Georgian decoration, with fine pictures and furniture; and at Brighton a past royal residence, the exotic Royal Pavilion, built by the Prince Regent in oriental style as a monument to Britain's connections with the Far East, and with its original decorations and furniture restored. In these houses are some of the most splendid rooms in the country, and many works of art.

The Arts

As befits a county that was given urban sophistication by the patronage of an art-loving monarch, King George IV, the arts have always held a high place in the life of Sussex. Brighton's Theatre Royal is famous for the large number of successful plays it puts on before London production, and Chichester's revolutionary Festival Theatre, a 'theatre-in-the-round', brings fresh vitality into the world of drama. The superb productions of opera, especially of Mozart, performed each year in the opera-house near Lewes make the name of Glyndebourne as famous as Salzburg and Bayreuth. The Dome at Brighton presents a season of symphony concerts and recitals every year by famous orchestras and soloists from all over the world.

The Art Galleries and Museums of Sussex are treasure-houses of works of art: Brighton with its collection of Old Master paintings and modern paintings, silver, porcelain, miniatures, jewelry, and the astonishing Willett Collection of pottery; Worthing and Hastings with their local collections and lively programmes of art exhibitions; Eastbourne, specializing in the work of modern artists. As in so many other respects, in Sussex the arts have immense vitality and offer a wide range of interests to the visitor on an intimate and informal level as well as on a grand scale. Simplicity and sophistication, grandeur and intimacy, these are the qualities that enhance the life of Sussex, no less than its scenery, and ensure the enjoyment of a world of delight for all who visit it.

GAZETTEER

Alfriston, East Sx   4B5
Snugly placed in the valley of the Cuckmere, a village with smuggling traditions. The Star Inn is a good example of 16th-c half-timbered work (the ferocious lion on the corner was a ship's figurehead). The 14th-c Clergy House (acquired by NT in 1896) is half-timbered with a very fine thatched roof. Alfriston Church is so large that it has been called 'the cathedral of the Downs'. *Lullington*, across the river, has a church reputed to be the smallest in England; it is, however, only part of a once larger building. Drusillas Zoo Park is at *Berwick* and at Drusillas Corner is The English Wine Centre with cellars in an old Sussex barn and a Rural Cider Museum. Open by prior arrangement.

Amberley, West Sx   4B7
A village that apparently never knew a planning scheme: well-kept brick-and-flint and thatched cottages lining a handful of winding lanes leading to the Norman church and the lofty remains of a 14th-c castle (the garden is sometimes open). This looks out on to Amberley Wild Brooks – luscious pasture in summer, but often a lake in winter.

Ardingly, West Sx   4C5
Near by is *Wakehurst Place* (NT) with an important collection of exotic trees, shrubs and plants with a picturesque stream linking several lakes. Managed by the Royal Botanic Gardens, **Kew**, London. Open daily.

Arundel,★ West Sx   4B7
Though originally built about 20 years after the Battle of
Hastings, much of the Duke of Norfolk's castle is restored
(he and his family now live in a modern house in the park),
but from across the wide curve of the River Arun it still
presents the vision of an authentic medieval stronghold.
Adding to the richness of the scene is the Roman Catholic
cathedral of St Philip Neri, built in the 19th c in French
Gothic style. Adjoining is Arundel parish church (14th-c),
with a dividing wall separating the E end (known as the
Fitzalan chapel) from the nave and aisles which serve for the
parish church. Castle and chapel open April–Oct. daily
except Sat. The castle park has magnificent beech trees and
the picturesque Swanbourne Lake. Lovely walks along the
river; rowing boats are available. Also near by is the
Wildfowl Trust Reserve (open all year). The town has a
Museum and Heritage Centre, a Toy and Military Museum
and a Museum of Curiosity.

Ashburnham, East Sx   4B4
3m W of **Battle**. The chancel and side chapels of the church
were built after the Restoration by John Ashburnham, who
attended Charles I in his flight from Oxford to Scotland,
when Parliamentary forces closed in on the town, and at his
execution. Garments worn by the King in his last hours are
preserved at Ashburnham.

Ashdown Forest, East Sx   4C5
W of *Crowborough* and N of *Uckfield*. Splendid walking
country on the Wealden ridges, thousands of acres of lofty
undulating heath and woodland interspersed with lovely
streams and ponds. Highest point, Crowborough Beacon

(792ft). Despite the name, ash trees are in a minority; oaks,
Scots pines, hazel and sweet chestnuts predominate.

Battle,★ East Sx   4B4
Before the famous battle of 1066 (which was fought, not at
Hastings, but just to the SW of the Abbey Gate here)
William of Normandy vowed he would build an abbey should
the day be his. Here, now part of a school, are the remains of
the abbey (AM) he built on the historic slope, with the high
altar over the actual place where King Harold fell. The
grounds are open to the public every weekday. The town has
some teashops, and good antique and book shops.

Beachy Head *see* **Eastbourne** and **Cissbury Ring**

Bexhill, East Sx   4B4
Notable in the annals of road transport as the site of the first
public motor racecourse in Britain (half a mile long!), laid
out by Earl de la Warr when he was developing Bexhill as a
holiday resort.

Bignor Hill,★ West Sx   4B7
Near here are the important remains of a Roman villa with
some of the best mosaics outside Italy. Open March–Oct.

Bodiam Castle,★★ East Sx   4C4
A 14th-c stronghold, reflecting its imposing walls among the
water-lilies in the surrounding moat. Perhaps the most
romantic castle ruin in the whole of England (NT). Open

*Bodiam Castle: built in 1386 to protect the land from
French invaders sailing up the River Rother*

daily April–Oct., less frequently in winter. In one tower an audio-visual presentation describes life in a medieval castle.

Bosham, West Sx 4B7
A popular centre for artists and yachting enthusiasts near the head of a creek in **Chichester** harbour. The village is old enough for its Saxon church to figure in the Bayeux tapestry; remains dug up by the chancel arch in 1865 may well be those of Canute's little daughter.

Boxgrove, West Sx 4B7
Beautiful remains of an 11th-c Benedictine Priory.

Bramber, West Sx 4B6
Where the Adur cuts through the Downs, with remains of a well-placed Norman castle (NT) open throughout the year. Potter's Museum of Curiosity, in which stuffed animals are arranged in tableaux such as the Kittens' Croquet Party, has now removed to **Arundel**. Note St Mary's, the finest 15th-c timber-framed house in Sussex, housing the National Butterfly Museum. Open April–Oct. daily, Nov.–March at weekends.

Brede, East Sx 4B4
Peter Pan's Captain Hook lived here – or at least his real-life original. He was J. W. Mahler, who became rector after retiring from a life of piracy on the high seas. It was while staying at Brede that Barrie heard the story of Mahler and of his blackmailer Smith, who figured as 'Smee'. Brede Place is notable.

Brighton,★ East Sx 4B6
In 1724 Brighton was 'a poor fishing town'. But when Dr Russell taught the medicinal value of sea-bathing and the Prince Regent brought the Court here to relax, the small town was set on the way to becoming the great popular resort we know. Fine Regency terraces still defy the encroachment of modern hotels and blocks of flats. The unique Royal Pavilion was built for the Prince Regent (George IV) by Henry Holland (1787) and completed by John Nash after the style of the Moghul palaces of India. The State apartments are decorated in the Chinese manner. The Pavilion is open daily throughout the year. Exhibitions and concerts are held here. The Great Kitchen with its equipment is fascinating. On Palace Pier Pavilion is the National Museum of Penny Slot Machines. Open April–Oct. daily, Nov.–March Sun. The destroyer, HMS *Cavalier*, with its Museum has been towed from **Southampton**.

On the Downs near *Falmer*, NE of the town, is the University of Sussex, and heading the list of very good schools is Roedean College for girls. *Hove*, closely adjoining Brighton, not only keeps its curiously sedate air but jealously retains its identity as a separate borough.

Burwash, East Sx 4C4
An attractive tile-hung village. ½m S is *Bateman's* (NT), a Jacobean ironmaster's house and Rudyard Kipling's home 1902–36. Its 33 acres of garden were designed by himself. A museum of mementoes of his stories, almost as he left it at his death, it is open most afternoons (not Fridays) March–Sept. Also here is a restored watermill which grinds flour for sale in the NT shop. Here is one of the oldest working water-driven turbines in the world.

Camber Castle, East Sx 4B3
One of the best examples of Henry VIII's coastal defence castles built when French invasion threatened. The extent of the coastal changes hereabout can be gauged from the fact that originally the castle was close to the shore (*see also* **Winchelsea**). This is a favourite spot for bird-watchers.

Chanctonbury Ring,★ West Sx 4B6
This ring of beeches is a well-loved landmark from many distant spots. Conversely the view from the Ring is equally extensive. The trees were planted in 1760 around a small Iron Age camp. They are 779ft above the sea. Near by is a 19th-c 'dewpond'. (*See also* page 87.)

Chichester,★ West Sx 4B7
The Romans founded it (calling it Regnum) at the intersection of two important roads, a point now marked by the beautiful 16th-c Butter Cross. The site of the Roman amphitheatre is at the E end of the town. The Normans built the cathedral on the site of a Saxon church; two sculptures in the N choir aisle are almost certainly Saxon work. Note the striking picture by Graham Sutherland, the cope designed by John Piper and modern glass by Christopher Webb in the N aisle. In St Martin's Square is the almshouse known as St Mary's Hospital, a lovely 13th-c building which stands almost as built. The 15th-c church of St Andrew's contains the grave of the poet William Collins, who died here in madness in 1759; and in the medieval Guildhall William Blake, the great artist and poet, was tried for high treason in 1804 – and acquitted. A modern structure of more than usual interest is the theatre built in 1962 for the Festival. Chichester 'harbour' is an extensive inlet from the sea reaching from Chichester across to *Hayling Island*; a wonderful stretch of water for small-boat sailing, full of delightful creeks and protected from the sea swell by a

Chichester: the 277-foot-high cathedral spire forms an impressive background to the Deanery gates

narrow entrance with a sand 'bar'. 2m W at *Fishbourne*★ is the Roman Palace, the largest Roman building in Britain. There is also an extensive museum.

Cissbury Ring,★ West Sx   4B6
Remarkable example of a prehistoric hill fort, on the Downs above the village of *Findon* to the NE of **Worthing.** The shafts of Neolithic flint mines are still visible. The ramparts were built about 300 BC and the fort was occupied until 50 BC. Views to the Isle of Wight and *Beachy Head.*

Ditchling Beacon,★ East Sx   4B5/6
At 813ft, it crowns the downs NNE of **Brighton.** The view is superb; worth choosing a clear day for the visit.

Eastbourne, East Sx   4B4
A former fishing village which became popular during the threatened Napoleonic invasion, when officers 'standing by' sent for their families. Later, the Duke of Devonshire took a hand; the western part of the town is a mark of his enlightened ideas about town planning – wide, tree-lined roads with houses set in good gardens. Between this and the parish church (12th-c) is a wide gulf filled with buildings of every style. Eastbourne makes a feature of good music and beautifully kept gardens; it also has the Towner Art Gallery, a new leisure centre and a good shopping centre. In Grand Parade is the Lifeboat Museum. Walks along the 3m promenade and up the hill to the dizzy summit of *Beachy Head.*

Exceat, East Sx   4B5
At Exceat Barn near *Seaford* is a new exhibition called *The Living World* – displays butterflies, ants, snails, scorpions, spiders, stick insects and mantids. Open daily.

Fishbourne *see* **Chichester**

Glynde *see* **Lewes**

Glyndebourne, East Sx   4B5
In 1934 John Christie courageously established a summer festival of music at his lovely part-Tudor manor house, adjoining which he built an opera house. The Glyndebourne opera season is now famous the world over.

Goodwood, West Sx   4B7
In this lovely undulating stretch of parkland lies Goodwood House, the home of the Duke of Richmond and Gordon, with its splendid array of pictures, French furniture (mostly Louis XV), porcelain and tapestries. The 18th-c mansion in Sussex flintwork is open May–Oct. on set days. Here too is the racecourse which brings enormous crowds to the annual meeting in July. In recent years Goodwood has become the scene of some of the most important events in the motor-racing calendar.

Hastings, East Sx   4B4
At the E end of the long front are the tarred net-lofts and red-tiled cottages of the old fishing town. In Rock-a-Nore Road is the Fisherman's Museum. Open April–Sept. (not Fridays).Above, on West Hill, are the remains of the Norman castle, built to protect the ancient harbour by virtue of which Hastings became a Cinque Port. St Clement's Caves, once used for smuggling and some 3 acres in extent, are entered from near the castle. The Old Town nestles between West Hill and East Hill, its narrow streets containing many fine old houses, two Perpendicular churches, St Clement's and All Saints', and the Stables Theatre (c.1700), etc. From East Hill is a lovely walk along

the cliffs. The Hastings Museum and Art Gallery has a good collection of Sussex ironwork, prehistoric relics – and birds. The Model Village in White Rock Gardens is open in the summer. At West Hill are caves once used for smuggling.

Herstmonceux Castle, East Sx   4B4
Brick-built in the 15th c and set within a wide moat, this picturesque castle is now the home of the Royal Greenwich Observatory, moved to the clearer atmosphere from London. The Newton Telescope and the beautiful gardens are open in summer. *See also* **Old Royal Observatory**, London.

Horsham, West Sx   4C6
From the centre of this picturesque old town the quiet tree lined Causeway leads to the museum (large collection of riding and driving bits for horses) and the church. Among monuments in the church is one commemorating P. B. Shelley, who was born at Field Place. This house (c.1325) is not open to the public, but the gardens may be visited at advertised times. Many of the older buildings in the town are roofed with slabs ('Horsham slabs') of stone quarried in the neighbourhood. 2m SW is *Christ's Hospital*, the famous 'Bluecoat' boys' school.

Hove, East Sx *see* **Brighton**

Hurstpierpoint, West Sx   4B6
On the road to Hassocks is *Danny*, a late Elizabethan house with a Queen Anne wing. In the imposing Great Hall is a plaque commemorating a 1918 War Cabinet meeting here at which Lloyd George drew up terms of an Armistice with Germany. The house is open at stated times. 2m S of the village is *New Timber Place*, a 17th-c house with a moat. Its hall contains some remarkable wall paintings. Open occasionally May–Aug.

Lancing, West Sx   4B6
The cathedral-like chapel of the College, well seen from the coast road near **Worthing,** is a splendid example of modern Gothic architecture begun in 1868. The interior is equally fine, with canopied stalls from **Eton** (Berks), and paintings by Rubens, etc. The College is a public school for boys, founded in 1848. The chapel is open to visitors.

Leonardslee, West Sx   4C6
At *Lower Beeding*. A valley garden with lakes (old hammer ponds), famous for rhododendrons, camellias, magnolias and azaleas. Open on stated days in spring when it is a blaze of colour, especially Camellia Weekend in April.

Lewes, East Sx   4B5
Built in a gap through the South Downs made by the River Ouse and with a Norman castle built to defend that gap. A town for leisurely wandering. Southeastward Mount Caburn rises steeply to 490ft; westward is Mount Harry (639ft) with the racecourse. In Barbican House, by the Castle Gateway, is the museum of the Sussex Archaeological Society. See Anne of Cleves' interesting house at Southover and the tomb of Gundrada, William the Conqueror's daughter, in the church across the way. In the old tilting ground attached to the castle is a rare (intentionally) undulating bowling green. 4m SE of the town is *Glynde Place*, an early Elizabethan house noted for its panelled Long Gallery with collections of portraits, bronzes, needlework and documents, also a pottery and an aviary. Open on certain days in spring and summer. Also near by is *Firle Place* with a fine collection of old masters, china, porcelain and furniture. Open at set times.

Lullington, East Sx *see* **Alfriston**

Michelham Priory, East Sx   4B5
At *Upper Dicker* 4m W of Hailsham is an Augustinian priory founded 1229 with a 14th-c gatehouse. It is surrounded by one of the largest moats (1m round) in England, formed by a diversion of the River Cuckmere. The Priory contains displays of furniture, tapestries, stained glass, Sussex ironwork and a picture gallery. In the grounds are old farm vehicles, a craft shop and an old mill which was restored in the 1970s and now grinds local wheat. House and grounds open daily April–Oct.

Midhurst, West Sx   4B7
The name is apt, for on every hand are lovely woods. Midhurst has few outstanding buildings but a number of very attractive 16th–17th-c houses including the Angel Hotel named thus by the Pilgrim Fathers who sheltered there during their journey to **Southampton** where they embarked for America. Note Elizabeth House, its half-timbering revealed by removal of plaster some years ago. The road to **Petworth** undulates through the beautiful park of *Cowdray*. Near the famous polo grounds are the ruins of the splendid 15th-c mansion burned down in the 18th c (some say because of a curse on the Browne family to whom it belonged). The present Cowdray Hall was built in the 19th c.

Northiam, East Sx   4C4
A large village with a rich variety of old houses and a village green with a venerable oak tree associated with Elizabeth I. The Sussex novelist Sheila Kaye-Smith lived here and built a local chapel. In Main Street is the Perigoe Workshop Museum exhibiting items of local interest. Open April–Sept. To the N is *Great Dixter*, a conversion by Lutyens (1911) of a 15th-c timber-framed barn brought from Benenden, Kent. The lovely gardens, planted by Nathaniel Lloyd and his wife, are noted for clematis, topiary, yews and are of horticultural interest. House and gardens are open on certain afternoons April–Oct.

Nymans, West Sx   4C6
At *Handcross*, Nymans (NT) has been called 'one of the great gardens of the Sussex Weald', with 30 acres of rare and beautiful plants, shrubs and trees from all over the world, including conifers, magnolias and camellias in 570 acres of woods and farmland. Open four afternoons a week, April–Oct.

Petworth, West Sx   4B7
A compact little town at the gates of Petworth House★, the home of Lord Leconfield, who in 1947 conveyed it to the NT. This magnificent house, mainly late 17th-c with 320ft long W front, stands in a 738-acre deer park with a 13th-c chapel, and contains many Van Dycks and Turners and a carving by Grinling Gibbons. Turner stayed here and painted several of his well-known pictures. The park, 14m round, is open daily all the year, the house on advertised days April–Oct. There are also 'connoisseurs' days'. Facilities for disabled.

Pevensey, East Sx   4B4
Here, as at **Portchester** in Hampshire, the Normans built a castle inside a Roman one. Both were for the protection of a harbour (now silted up and built over by Pevensey village) which served as beach-head for the respective invading armies. Here was fought the savage battle in 961 when the Saxons attacked the castle 'and slew all that dwelt therein, nor was there a Briton left'. William the Conqueror landed at Pevensey in 1066 before advancing to attack King Harold

at Senlac, some 9m to the NE and now the site of the present abbey at **Battle**.

Pulborough, West Sx   4B7
A small town on the River Arun, it is a popular fishing centre. *Parham Park* is a splendid privately-owned Elizabethan mansion with historic paintings spanning three centuries, furniture and needlework. In the grounds, an old walled garden (4 acres) and a tiny family church. Gardens open at set times Easter–Oct.

Rodmell, West Sx   4B5
4m S of **Lewes** is *Monks House* (NT), a 17th-c farmhouse with garden and studio, home of Virginia and Leonard Woolf from 1919 until his death in 1969. Open at stated times in the summer. Near by is Breaky Bottom Vineyard with cottage and barn. Guided tours available by prior arrangement.

Rye,★ East Sx   4C3
In its original form the name meant 'island', and the town still rises impressively out of the surrounding flat marshlands which have more than once been submerged by the sea. Rye is certainly 'quaint' and 'picturesque' with its steep, cobbled streets, but it also has a solid background of good and historic building and its story goes back to medieval times. Before the sea receded it was an important Cinque Port. After seeing the church with its famous clock and its many monuments, and Mermaid Street, and Lamb House where the American writer Henry James lived, find the Gun Garden outside the Ypres Tower (a museum of local and Cinque Port history) and enjoy the views of Rye Harbour.

Selsey Bill, West Sx   4A7
It is not nearly so pointed as maps would suggest, but it is at the tip of a peninsula with good sandy beaches. Terns and other sea birds nest in *Pagham* harbour on the E; on the W is *Bracklesham* with its beds of fossils.

Sheffield Park Gardens, East Sx   4C5
Near *Uckfield*, ½m from Sheffield Park station (Bluebell Line). 100 acres (NT) with five lakes laid out in 18th-c by Capability Brown with many mature trees, rare shrubs and water lilies. Beautiful all the year round but especially in autumn colours. Open most days in spring and summer. The Wings Haven Bird Sanctuary is also here.

Shoreham by Sea, West Sx   4B6
The silting-up of the mouth of the Adur has produced a canal-like waterway nearly 2m long, the water in which is now warmed by the effluent from the power-station built on the narrow bank which divides it from the sea. Great activity here, with boats of all kinds. Marlipins Museum has much of local interest and there is a fine Norman church. This is *New* Shoreham; the original port and town were at *Old* Shoreham, upstream, until silting blocked the river.

Singleton, West Sx   4B7
Here is the *Weald and Downland Open Air Museum* (*see* introductory essay on Open Air Museums, pages 18–20). Special events and exhibitions. Open April–Oct. daily; Nov.–March set days. At Old Station House is the office of Chilsdown Vineyard. Tours of 13-acre vineyard, winery and press with talk daily May–end Sept. At *West Dean* are gardens with old specimen trees, a pergola, a Garden History exhibition and shop. Open April–Sept.

South Downs Way
Long-distance path from Beachy Head to Hampshire border.

Wilmington Priory: the 13th-century ruins have a Tudor crypt and now house an agricultural museum

South Harting, West Sx   4B8
Uppark (NT), a late 17th-c house with 18th-c wallpapers and furnishings, a Queen Anne's dolls' house and Victorian kitchen quarters (where H. G. Wells' mother was a housemaid) and garden landscaped by Repton. Open at advertised times.

Steyning, West Sx   4B6
Old-fashioned little town beside the Adur with a number of very attractive buildings including a Norman church and a market hall with an interesting clock tower.

Westdean, East Sx   4B5
The church has some good 17th-c monuments. Near by is *Charleston Manor*, an ancient manor house of Norman, Tudor and Georgian construction, with a tithe barn and large gardens of romantic beauty. Strongly associated with the Bloomsbury Group, the house is open on certain days in April–Oct. Gardens open daily in summer.

Wilmington,★ East Sx   4B5
The 'Long Man', whose portrait is cut in the steep chalk side of Windover Hill above the village, is possibly a relative of the **Cerne Abbas** giant in Dorset, but he is larger (over 200ft tall). First recorded in 1764, he is of uncertain age and origin. In the village are the remains of the 13th-c priory now an agricultural museum. Open March–Oct.

Winchelsea,★ East Sx   4B3
14th-c town-planning with some very nice flint-and-brick building and a splendid church. The old town down by the shore was engulfed by the sea in 1287, but three of the original gateways survived: one of them is the Strand Gate at the top of the hill leading up from the **Rye** road. Only the E end was completed of the huge church originally conceived, but even so it is large and impressive. Note the famous Alard tombs. The town never recovered from repeated French raids in the 14th c and except during the holiday season still justifies the description of 'a town in a trance'. There is a museum in the town hall.

Worthing, West Sx   4B6
Holiday and residential borough where glasshouses produce vast quantities of tomatoes and grapes. Repertory theatre, concert hall, sports centre, golf-courses, pier, good library, excellent local art gallery and museum, and a Museum of Sussex Folklore, and easy access to the Downs. In Broadwater cemetery are the graves of naturalists, Richard Jefferies and W. H. Hudson. *See also* **Cissbury Ring**.

KENT

AN INTRODUCTION BY
DEREK CHAPMAN

An unimaginable time ago Kent lay buried under the sea. For millions of years generations of microscopic shellfish lived and died, leaving their hard outer cases to form a charnel-house of lime superimposed on the sea-bed layers of sand and clay. With the shrinking of the earth's crust, giant pressures from north and south heaved the whole mass of rock into an arch; and when the sea went down, the topping of calcium shells was revealed as a vast whaleback of chalk rising to half a mile high at its loftiest point. From the exposed uplands rivers emerged; abetted by the weathering forces of frost and rain they began their long process of demolition. The chalk, now reduced at its highest to under 1,000 feet, remains today as two east–west ridges of beautiful hills: on the one hand the South Downs of neighbouring Sussex; on the other the North Downs, which run westward across Surrey into a corner of Hampshire, and eastward from Westerham through the full length of Kent until, laid bare as the white cliffs of Dover, they tower high above the seaborne traveller from France.

The North Downs are broken at three points by north-bound rivers. Near Sevenoaks the Darent has quite worn through them on its way to Dartford; the Medway breaches them near Maidstone; further east, from Ashford to Canterbury, the Stour flows abrasively through the Wye gap. Although every year there is still slow but steady reclamation of ancient wild downland yet higher up its flanks, there are some areas of indigenous springy turf, sympathetic to walk on. From a hundred vantage points they provide some of the most breath-taking views of England: at the eastern end the sea and the Channel traffic, coming close to the shore to avoid the Goodwin Sands, and across the water, on a fine day, the town of Calais clearly visible through binoculars; northward the age-old accretions of silt and saltings which have made the low-lying fringes of the Thames estuary and the mouth of the Medway; and southward – the Weald of Kent.

The Weald, which occupies half of Kent, was originally a vast forest, the Andredsweald of the Anglo-Saxons. Though exploited for 2,000 years by piecemeal clearing for timber and farming, wealden

scenery is still heavily wooded. The locals distinguish between the High Weald and the Low, the former being the sandstone hills that run high into Goudhurst and Cranbrook, the latter the wealden clay lowland. The High Weald is a garden where everything grows; the Low Weald is quieter, heavier, colder and sleepier country.

Between the Weald and the sea, south of the Tenterden–Hythe road, lies the flat, secretive country of Romney Marsh, an area that became part of Kent, almost as an afterthought, when the Romans first built its defending sea-wall. It is a fascinating triangle of fertile flats, precariously separated from the sea by a system of drains and embankments; the land seldom rises more than 12 feet above sea level. The sunsets, when good, are incomparable. In spring and summer the remaining grass fields are dense with grazing sheep and the large rich areas of arable carry heavy crops of corn, potatoes and oil seed rape. When the cold winter winds sweep in from the sea and drive the sheep to more sheltered pastures inland, the Marsh settles down to brood over its smuggling past. The Marsh men are a race on their own.

Local Industries and Activities

In Kent the main industry is farming and the farmers produce everything from potatoes to the native Kent (or Romney Marsh) long-woolled sheep – a hardy, adaptable breed that has colonized most of the world's sheep farms. On Thanet they grow barley of fine malting quality, and rather boast about it, while some of the pastures in the marshland fatten more lambs to the acre than any in Britain. Sheep grazing in a cherry orchard, a group of cowled oast-houses set among hop-fields – these are the characteristic views of Kent. Orchards are everywhere: to view them in their greatest profusion, start from Tonbridge or Maidstone. Cherries, apples and pears are abundant. The hop gardens are found mostly in three areas: around Maidstone; between Paddock Wood and Ashford; and between Faversham and Canterbury.

Of the mineral resources the most improbable is coal, mined in the east of the county. The lower greensand, such as prevails in the Maidstone district, yields the attractive building stone called Kentish Rag, used in the construction of churches in all periods. Bethersden marble also ranks with ragstone for church building. The chalk and mud vales of the lower Thames and Medway are quarried for making cement; the gault clay is made into bricks as it has been since Roman times near Wye.

Archeology and Early History

The high plateaux of the Downs in west Kent have yielded examples of man's oldest known handiwork, the roughly worked flints known as eoliths. Signs of Old Stone Age occupation are abundant in the river valleys, while Mesolithic (6000 BC) dwelling pits have been excavated at Sevenoaks, Ightham, and East Malling. In the Medway gap there are several New Stone Age tombs, the most famous being Kit's Coty House, near Aylesford. These same tomb-builders – centuries before Chaucer – trod out the Pilgrims' Way, which runs along the foot of the Downs.

The Roman occupation of Britain began in Kent, and the earliest Roman road, Watling Street, linking Canterbury with London is still in use. At Richborough a fortified Roman township (still impressive) guarded what was then the coast, from the time of Claudius, in AD 43, until the legions departed.

The succeeding ages were to give Britain to the Angles and Saxons. It is said that the first Saxon invaders, Hengist and Horsa, landed at Ebbsfleet in 449 and founded the Kingdom of Kent, its extent roughly matching the present county boundaries. But Kent was largely inhabited by Jutes from the lower Rhine, who established themselves first in the north coastal zone, and presently spread out as far as the Medway. The distinction between the Kentish Men, born on the London side of the river, and the Men of Kent, born on the east and south side, may stem from the differences between Saxon and Jute.

The Jutes introduced customs and laws very different from those in the neighbouring kingdoms of Wessex and Mercia, the most striking being gavelkind, whereby on a man's death his property was divided equally among all his sons. Gavelkind made for more but smaller farms and for a large middle class of Kentish yeomen rather than a few rich and powerful landlords. Today you may note a prevalence of isolated farmsteads and an indefinable yeomanness about the Kentish men.

Towns and Buildings

Canterbury, of course, with its Cathedral founded in 597 is *the* tourist attraction in Kent, perhaps the most visited city in Britain outside London. It flourished in Roman times (below Butchery Lane you may see a display of mosaic tiles), and the prominent knoll known as Dane John is a 1st-century burial ground. The medieval city walls survive in parts; and the west gateway has hardly altered for 600 years.

Canterbury Cathedral, beside the 18th-century city walls, is the mother church of the Anglican Communion

In contrast to the hushed Gothic air of Canterbury, Tunbridge Wells has an 18th-century sensibility. The discovery of health-giving springs persuaded the 'quality' to summer out of London and to cure all those ills the Restoration flesh was heir to. By 1750 a town had arisen; socially it rivalled Bath, from which spa it lured for a time the uncrowned king, Beau Nash, to advise upon fashions and modes of merry-making. In the Pantiles, a raised walk with shops, trees and quiet, you may sample the waters if your taste runs that way – for black bile, alias melancholia, the traditional dose is 20 pints at a sitting.

Of the original Cinque Ports that for centuries commanded the narrow seas and, in fact, maintained the navy, all but Hastings lie in Kent. The office of Lord Warden of the Cinque Ports continues to survive as a gift of the crown bestowed upon distinguished men, and with it the right to reside in Walmer Castle. The present Warden is the Queen Mother.

Dover, the chief Cinque Port, is now the only one with a harbour. The great keep of its castle, which gives as fine a view of an approaching enemy as ever it did, goes back to 1180 and compares in size and strength with the Tower of London. Sandwich, today, is 2 miles from the seashore it once commanded. Some of its houses have a Flemish look, influenced by the refugees who fled from the Netherlands in Elizabethan times and brought with them their skill in weaving. New Romney, too, is now an inland town, the old port lying well within the Marsh. Its church is

exceptionally fine, with an impressive pinnacled Norman tower. The main street presents an array of Tudor and Georgian fronts. Finally, Hythe: it remains on the sea, although the old town on the hill is farther from the beach than when it supplied eleven ships, as against neighbour Folkestone's four, to meet the Armada.

Folkestone owes its prosperity to the holiday-maker. As a seaside resort it retains pretensions to fashion, despite the excursions and incursions of trippers to France. The old town and the harbour have not yet lost all their fishing-village character. On the north coast, Margate and Ramsgate both speak for themselves, not wholly in measured tones. Herne Bay is rather less extrovert, Birchington residential. Broadstairs, the farthest east, radiates the same charm that attracted Charles Dickens. He frequently stayed there and for a time settled in Bleak House overlooking the harbour. Even now, at the height of the season, you may encounter the ghost of an Edwardian nanny searching the beach for her vanished charges.

The Dover Road traveller, soon after shaking off London, finds himself in the curious complex of Medway towns, one leading into another. The most pauseworthy, Rochester, straddles the Medway. Augustine, in 604, founded a bishopric there. The cathedral, a Norman foundation, took the place of the early church. Although the cathedral and the castle are major attractions, Rochester is full of smaller but history-rich houses and inns, many of them associated with Dickens. On the north side of Rochester, Strood is manifestly industrial; to the east, Chatham and Gillingham speak, in the passing tense, of docks and shipbuilding.

Kent can show castles, or fortified houses, of every period and in every state of preservation, from the primarily Norman keep of Dover Castle to the coastal Martello towers, part of a chain constructed during the Napoleonic Wars. Stately homes include Knole, Leeds Castle, Hever and Penshurst Place. Ightham Mote, which dates from about 1340, is a splendid example of a moated manor house.

Most villages contain one or two timber-framed houses, particularly in the wooded wealden area. Brick with infillings of flint is more typical of the Downland country, where flints are found among the chalk. Elsewhere, indeed almost everywhere, the weatherboarded cottage, with its horizontally lapped whitewashed clapboards, is very characteristic.

Flora and Fauna
Of Great Britain's 50 species of wild orchid, over half can be found in Kent. A similar richness extends to wild flowers in general, especially in the valley of the Medway. Blean Woods, north of Canterbury, harbour endless varieties of birds, insects and fungi. The tree-lover should visit the Forestry Commission's national pinetum at Bedgebury near Goudhurst.

Many migratory birds and butterflies halt in Kent, if only to rest their wings. The Foreland area is a favourite landing-place for bird visitors in the spring whereas butterfly immigrants seem to prefer the cliffs further round the coast at Folkestone.

GAZETTEER

Appledore 4C3
As attractive as its name, a peaceful wide-streeted village of good cottages and houses looking out over Romney Marsh from its slight eminence above the Royal Military Canal. There is a good 14th-c church with fine stained glass and Flemish wood-carving; the church was partially burned in one of those 14th-c raids by French marauders.

Aylesford* 4D4
Notwithstanding Aylesford's paper-making activities, the picturesque old village remains beside its restored 14th-c bridge over the Medway – its peace, too, mercifully restored since the building of the Maidstone bypass and M20. Since 1949 Carmelite monks and sisters have returned to the Friary which their order inhabited as long ago as 1284. On the hills around are some ancient monuments, the best being *Kit's Coty House**, 1½m NE, remains of a Neolithic burial chamber, the earliest prehistoric monument in S.E. England (AM). 1m upstream, from Aylesford, beautiful by the river, stands the restored Norman castle of *Allington**, now occupied by Carmelites (White Friars), noted for pottery,

A Jacobean staircase at Knole is just one of 52. The house contains magnificent furnishings and tapestries

but open to the public. It is also a retreat house for up to 20 guests, and is used as a Christian Centre for conferences. It holds interesting events such as its 'Mammoth Medieval Market'.

Barfreston▲ 4D2
About 4m E of *Barham*. The church is a rare and exquisite specimen of Norman architecture, rich with carving and moulding. Notice especially the S doorway, and the church bell in the yew tree.

Biddenden 4C4
Two sisters who were joined together at birth and lived to the age of 34 provide the village legend. More interesting are the many ancient weavers' cottages lining the street, the old Cloth Hall and the 14th–15th-c church with its unusual collection of portrait brasses. At Biddenden Vineyards, 3m outside the village, tours are available on weekdays.

Bigbury 4D3
2m W of **Canterbury**. Iron Age settlement on the brow of a hill overlooking Canterbury. Here, too, Britons tried unavailingly to defend themselves against the onslaught of Roman legions in 54 BC.

Biggin Hill 4D5
Famous RAF airfield in the Battle of Britain. Some of the aircraft are exhibited beside the road.

Boughton Monchelsea 4D4
The centre of Kentish ragstone quarrying. Boughton Monchelsea Place, a ragstone castellated 16th-c mansion (much altered) in an 89-acre deer park, was the home of Sir Thomas Wyatt, executed in 1554 for his revolt against Mary I. The house contains a costume collection, tapestries, furniture and stained glass windows. Open Easter–Oct. on stated days.

Broadstairs 4D2
Smallest and most individual of the *Thanet* coast resorts. Sandy bay below gardened cliffs overlooked by Georgian houses and sheltered by the same old pier that pleased Dickens. Although he lived here, there is no evidence that the Bleak House on the cliff is the one of which he wrote (open summer afternoons). Dickens House Museum, in Victoria Parade, is open at set times. In High Street is the Crampton Tower Railway Museum (open at set times).

Canterbury★★ 4D3
Busy centre of prosperous farming country, a town rich in history going back to pre-Roman days, but above all dominated by its famous and venerable cathedral. When St Augustine arrived here in 597 he found Christian worship already being conducted in St Martin's Church (which though restored is perhaps the oldest in England so used). King Ethelbert followed his conversion by a gift of land, on which Augustine founded a monastery outside the city walls and the Cathedral within. The early bishops were buried at St Augustine's (AM), which was then more important than the cathedral, but after the murder (1170) and subsequent enshrinement of Becket the pre-eminence of the cathedral became absolute. Parts of St Augustine's are used as a missionary college. Excavations have revealed the graves of early bishops and the church of St Pancras, once a pagan place of worship. The cathedral (*see* page 95), basically 11th-c, was much altered in the 15th c. One striking feature is the way in which the choir is raised above the nave and the altar above the choir. Do not miss the site of Becket's murder, the Black Prince's Tomb, the Norman crypt, the beautiful stained glass, and the grounds of King's School. The city's 14th-c West Gate has a good museum. Of its 11th-c castle only the keep remains. In a vault in St Dunstan's Church lies the severed head of Sir Thomas More. The Roman Pavement is a museum with mosaic floor and hypocaust (open daily). The earliest feature of Canterbury is the mound called the Dane John, originally a burial mound, fortified later by the Normans and now the centre of a park. Kent Cricket Week, held in July/August, is famous. The University of Kent is based on the outskirts of the city. The zoo park at *Bekesbourne*, 4m E, is worth a visit. 2m NE is **Fordwich**, once Canterbury's port.

Charing 4D3
Good timbered houses and remains of a palace of the Archbishop of Canterbury where Henry VII and Henry VIII were entertained.

Chartwell *see* **Westerham**

Chiddingstone 4C5
Picturesque village with 16th–17th-c timber buildings (NT) and attractive groups of oast houses. The 19th-c mansion known as Chiddingstone Castle has a collection of Stuart and other relics, including Ancient Egyptian, Japanese and Buddhist art. Also a newly restored Georgian barrel organ. Open to the public at advertised times. Near by is a 'chiding stone' which was originally used for the arraignment of scolding wives.

Chilham 4D3
Round the spacious square at the top of the village are gracious timbered houses, an old inn, a richly monumented 15th-c church, and the imposing gateway to the present castle (really a Jacobean manor) built in 1616 by Inigo Jones. It is the seat of Viscount Massereene and Ferrard. Among the beech trees in the park are the keep of a Norman castle and the largest and oldest heronry in England. Capability Brown's gardens are open at stated times. Other attractions include Petland, a Bird of Prey Centre, and the grounds are used for the displays and tournaments of the British Jousting Centre.

The Cinque Ports 4C2/D2/C3/C2/B4
A defence system of fortified ports built up during the Middle Ages to protect SE. England against raiders and invaders from the Continent. In return for certain customs and other privileges (often abused by smugglers), the ports provided men and ships when required by the King. The original Cinque Ports were **Dover**, **Sandwich**, Romney (now **New Romney**), **Hythe**, and **Hastings**.

Cobham 4D4
A name well known to readers of *Pickwick*: the Leather Bottle Inn has Dickens relics. *Owletts*, a 17th-c brick mansion (NT), is open to the public on certain days in spring and summer. The church has a celebrated collection of medieval brasses. Cobham Hall, a large Elizabethan mansion, has work by Inigo Jones and the Adams brothers. Since 1962 it has been an international girls' school. Open to the public at advertised times during school holidays.

Cranbrook 4C4
Former cloth-weaving town of painted weatherboard houses, with a splendid windmill said to be the largest working mill in England. In the 15th-c church is a baptistery for total immersion, and a room over the S porch was used as a prison during the Marian persecution. In Carriers Road is the local history museum.

Deal 4D2
For centuries a naval dockyard, Deal has no sheltered harbour; stores have always had to be carried off in small sailing or rowing boats. Deal therefore has a maritime tradition strengthened by the reputation of its pilots – and lifeboatmen (the treacherous Goodwin Sands lie only a few miles off shore here). Deal is a good place for fishing and golf. Deal and *Walmer* Castles (AM) (Deal open all year; Walmer closed Mon. and when Warden in residence) were built by Henry VIII to protect the Downs when invasion was feared: Walmer Castle is the official residence of the Lord Warden of the Cinque Ports.

Dover★ 4C2
Thousands of years ago the famous White Cliffs were part of a much higher ridge of chalk which continued across to the cliffs of Calais (clearly visible on a fine day). Ancient past and bustling present mingle in this busiest of cross-Channel ports, once chief of the medieval Cinque Ports. To guide

Deal: a stretch of sandy beach north of the holiday resort famous for its castle built in the 1530s

their legionaries across the water the Romans (who called the place Dubris) built a pharos, or lighthouse; much of it still stands in the Castle precincts. The great Norman castle* (AM, open weekdays and Sun. afternoons) is grimly impressive on its steep height overlooking town and sea, especially when floodlit at night. Near the eastern dock German shellfire from Calais during World War II laid waste an area now occupied by modern blocks of flats and a hotel. The Roman Painted House in New Street, discovered fairly recently, has remarkable wall paintings – the oldest in Britain. Open April–Oct.

Dungeness 4B3
A vast sheet of shingle, deposited by the swift Channel tides and still growing seaward. Once a place of melancholy solitude and a famous bird sanctuary, it is now dominated by the huge nuclear power station visible for miles along the coast. There is also a modern lighthouse of revolutionary design, tall and slender, with an automatic light and a fog signal booming from 60 loudspeakers. The old lighthouse still stands close by. The shore here descends very steeply, and bathing is *most dangerous*. The famous miniature railway, the Romney, Hythe and Dymchurch, is still in operation at the time of writing. *See* **Hythe**.

Ebbsfleet, Pegwell Bay 4D2
A full-scale model of a Viking ship (sailed over from Norway in 1949) commemorates the landing of Hengist and Horsa in 449. Landing here a century and a half later St Augustine brought the first great Christian missionary effort to Kent. It is now a hovercraft port.

Faversham* 4D3
The attractive town centre lies N of the A2 road. Abbey Street, with an array of timber-framed houses, leads to the site of the abbey where King Stephen was buried. Arden's House still survives, once belonging to a town mayor whose murder in 1550 inspired the Elizabethan melodrama *Arden of Faversham*. The church is notable for its crown spire (1797) and medieval aisled transepts, 100ft long. In Westbrook Walk are the Chart Gunpowder Mills, once part of the Royal Gunpowder Factory. They supplied Nelson and Wellington and are the only ones of their kind to survive in Britain. Recently restored they are open March–Nov. on Sun. and Bank Holiday afternoons.

Folkestone 4C2
The parish church, well placed on the cliffs, stands between the old town down by the harbour (whence steamers and car ferries sail for Boulogne) and the more modern hotel and shopping area with an excellent indoor sports centre, Arts Centre, museum and art gallery. The Leas is the finest seacoast promenade in England, with views to the French coast. E of the harbour the cliffs have fallen away to form the Warren, a great place for fossils and flowers. 5m N is St John's Chapel (AM) at *Swingfield*, built at the time of the Crusades. Visit *Port Lympne Zoo Park* and Gardens 8m W (*see* **Lympne**). Folkestone Races are held at *Westenhanger*.

Fordwich 4D2
NE of **Canterbury**, it is a picturesque cul-de-sac, once the port of Canterbury. On the N end of the tiny timbered Town Hall (Tudor) is the crane from which nagging wives were dipped in the River Stour. The church is partly Norman.

Godinton Park 4C3
NW of *Ashford* off the A20. A Stuart mansion (1628) with unusual curved gables; inside, fine Jacobean panelling,

carving, portraits and furniture. 18th-c gardens have fine examples of topiary. Open most afternoons, June–Sept.

Godmersham 4D3
S of **Chilham**. Jane Austen often stayed here when her brother owned the Georgian house known as Godmersham Park. A 12th-c bas relief of Thomas à Becket in the church is the earliest known.

Goudhurst 4C4
Attractive hill-top village with a duck-graced pond and a wide view over undulating acres of orchards and hop gardens. In the 15th-c church are excellent monuments to the Culpepers, once a force in this land. 2m S at *Bedgebury* is the beautifully laid out Pinetum, planted when the one at Kew began to succumb to London smoke and fumes. Open daily throughout the year.

Gravesend 4E4
Busy Thames-side town. The famous Red Indian princess Pocahontas lies buried in St George's Church. She died in 1617, her statue in the present churchyard is a replica of that in Jamestown. There are also two memorial windows to her in the church. At *Milton* chantry (AM) priests prayed here in 14th c and the building housed the chapel of a leper hospital. Open April–Sept.

Groombridge 4C5
SW of **Tunbridge Wells** it has a large triangular green rising to a long row of brick and tiled cottages; larger houses looking on. The whole delightful. Do not miss the moated manor house (17th-c) with gardens designed by John Evelyn (open to the public in summer), or the curious clock in the church.

Hever 4C5
SE of *Edenbridge*. Henry VIII met Anne Boleyn at the moated 14th–15th-c castle where she had spent much of her girlhood. Has everything a castle should have (even a small torture chamber). Magnificent Italian gardens with Roman sculptures collected (1903) by the 1st Lord Astor, an American who became a British citizen. Open to visitors regularly on stated occasions.

Hythe 4C3
Pleasant little shopping town set back from its shingle beach. Under the partly Norman church is a crypt stacked with bones and skulls. Hythe was one of the original Cinque Ports, but like **Sandwich** and Romney it has seen its harbour turn to dry land. Through the town runs the Royal Military Canal, a 'moat' built during the Napoleonic invasion scare and running all the way to **Rye**; it now provides boating and fishing. Hythe is the terminus of the world's smallest-gauge public railway (all stations to **Dungeness**). About ½m N is the fine restored Norman castle of *Saltwood*, whence on a winter's evening in 1170 rode four knights on their way to murder Thomas à Becket in Canterbury Cathedral (*see* **Canterbury**); it is now a private home, but the grounds are open at certain times.

Ightham* 4D5
The 14th-c moated manor house known as Ightham Mote is one of the few extant specimens of its kind. Lovely gardens. Open set days in summer. On *Oldbury Hill*, to the SW of the village, is a large prehistoric hill fort and the site of Stone Age rock shelters (NT).

Kit's Coty House *see* **Aylesford**

Knole *see* **Sevenoaks**

Lamberhurst   4C4
Village of timbered houses, once a centre of the iron industry. 2m W are the remains of Bayham Abbey, and just to the SE the lakeside ruin of *Scotney Castle* (NT). The Old Castle and Gardens are open at stated times in summer. So is the Owl House, a 16th-c tile-hung half-timbered cottage with smuggling associations and woodland gardens (at their best in spring). Lamberhurst Vineyards (32 acres) at Ridge Farm have a Vineyard Trail and shop open all year.

Leeds Castle★   4D4
Through the trees beside the A20 romantic glimpses may be had of the magnificent 9th–14th-c castle on its islands in the lake, said to be one of the loveliest castles in the world. It is open to the public at stated times and has facilities for the disabled. There is a unique collection (dating from the Middle Ages) in the Dog Collar Museum in the gatehouse.

Lenham   4D4
The 13th–15th-c church is notable for its woodwork.

Lullingstone   4D5
Excavated remains of a Roman villa★ with a fine mosaic floor (AM). The Tudor mansion known as Lullingstone Castle (open Wednesday afternoons in summer) was long the centre of a silk-growing enterprise; the silk for the Queen's wedding dress was produced here, but the silk farm is now at **Sherborne** in Dorset.

Lydd   4C3
The airport (Ferryfield) is now used chiefly for private aircraft. The Anglo-French cable by which electric power is exchanged comes ashore at **Dungeness** and at Lydd is fed into the British grid system. Lydd gave its name to the explosive lyddite, first developed at the military research depot here. The spacious 14th-c church with its massive tower is justly called 'The Cathedral of the Marshes'.

Lyminge   4C3
The chancel of the present church is part of an earlier church built about 975 which incorporated Roman materials. The massive tower was added in the 16th c.

Lympne   4C3
In Roman days, before the sea receded, this was a port. The fortress which guarded it fell into ruins after a landslip; its remains, known as Studfall Castle, are still to be seen at the foot of the hill. From Lympne the Roman 'Stone Street' ran (and most of it still runs) straight to **Canterbury** along a ridge of the Downs with long views of weald and sea. The airport (renamed Ashford Airport) is now used for freight and private light aircraft. Lympne Castle includes part of a 15th-c moated manor. It is open at set times in the summer. *Port Lympne House* is a handsome 20th-c house with zoo park, gardens and art gallery. Open daily.

Maidstone   4D4
Capital and chief market town of Kent, straddling the River Medway. It is today a major commercial centre with a good shopping area. It has an indoor sports centre, a theatre and other leisure facilities. Local industries: timber, paper, cement, beer. Alongside the 14th-c church is the Archbishop's Palace, once belonging to the Archbishops of Canterbury; it has a fine panelled banqueting hall. Opposite, is the new County Court, and in the old stable here, is the Tyrwhitt-Drake Museum of Carriages (open daily). The Maidstone Museum and Art Gallery (now renovated), in the former Chillington Manor in St Faith's Street, has good art, natural history and archeological collections.

New Romney   4C3
One of the original Cinque Ports, it replaced Old Romney (still there, 2m farther inland, with its 13th-c timber-roofed church) when the sea receded. But a violent storm in 1287 altered the course of the River Rother and left even the new town without access to the sea (now 1m away at *Littlestone* with its excellent sands). New Romney's church is largely Norman, with a fine tower and nave.

Penshurst   4C5
In the gracious 14th-c mansion of Penshurst Place★ Sir Philip Sidney was born in 1554; it has been the home of the Sidney family for over 400 years, and now belongs to a descendant, Lord de l'Isle and Dudley. One of the great

Leeds Castle: the Castle of the Queens of Medieval England was given to the nation in 1976

showplaces of England. The house has magnificent gardens with a wonderful collection of sundials, and other attractions such as a venture playground, toy museum, countryside exhibition and nature trail. Open April–Oct.

Pilgrims' Way see entry in Surrey

Reculver   4D2
The still visible remains of a Roman fort (AM) and the western wall of an ancient church. Early 19th-c prints show the twin towers still surmounted by tall spires; these went long ago, but the towers were so useful as a navigational guide to Thames shipping that they were taken over by Trinity House; they are now in the care of the Department of the Environment (AM).

Richborough★   4D2
Quietly impressive ruins of the huge fort (AM) built by the Romans to protect their harbour (since silted up by the River Stour) and the entry to what was then a wide navigable channel (also silted up) cutting behind the island of Thanet to Reculver. Acres of ground are enclosed by stout walls still bonded by Roman mortar, and remains of the amphitheatre are visible. Good museum.

Rochester   4D4
Since Roman days Rochester has been a place of great strategic import. Here Watling Street crosses the Medway and here the Medway opens out to a wonderful natural harbour. In 604 Augustine founded the third English bishopric here. On the site of his church the Normans raised a cathedral; they also built a great castle (AM). The remains of these two buildings are still the principal historic features of the town. Rochester has many Dickens associations – not to be missed at Eastgate is the Dickens Centre with tableaux and exhibits of Dickens' life and times. Open daily. His home, Gad's Hill Place, is on the NW outskirts. It is now a school and may be visited by arrangement.

Romney Marsh see **Introduction**

Sandwich   4D2
A town of ancient ghosts: ghosts of the days when it was an important Cinque Port and fishing and smuggling thrived. Now the nearest sea is 1½m away. Rebuilding and street-widening have changed the town's face, but the huge echoing churches still tell their vivid story. The Royal St George is one of England's finest golf-courses.

Scotney Castle see **Lamberhurst**

Sevenoaks   4D5
Pleasant dormitory town on greensand hills 400–500ft above sea level. Beside Sevenoaks School (founded 1432) is an entrance to the great deer park of Knole★ (NT), one of England's largest and finest private mansions (365 rooms) in a 1,000-acre deer park. Built 1456, enlarged in the early 17th c, it still belongs to the Sackville family. Valuable collection of pictures, furniture, etc. Park open daily, house open on stated days April–Sept. (See also page 96.)

Sissinghurst   4C4
The 15th–16th-c Castle (NT) is partly open to the public. The famous gardens★ created by Vita Sackville-West and her husband Sir Harold Nicolson are open almost daily in summer. Less well-known but very attractive are Sissinghurst Place Gardens, around ruins of a house burned down in 1948. Gardens open daily in summer.

Tenterden   4C4
Attractive town with old buildings and an unusually wide green-verged main street. The church, 'Queen of the Weald', has a notable shingled tower from which it is said one can sometimes see the French coast. William Caxton, first English printer, was born here in 1422. The Unitarian Meeting House has a painting of Benjamin Franklin attending a service here in 1774. Ellen Terry, the actress, spent her last years at Smallhythe Place (NT), 2m S. This half-timbered house (c.1480) contains mementoes of her and of other famous stage personalities. Open most days in spring and summer. Near by at Spots Farm are the 10 acres of Tenterden Vineyards. Open June–Sept.

Tonbridge   4D5
The bridge spans the Medway, a busy point guarded since Norman times by a castle of which the gatehouse is the best remnant. The well-known public school for boys dates from 1553. Tonbridge, a busy shopping and market town with many fine old buildings, has become less of a bottle-neck since the A21 London–**Hastings** road bypassed it.

Tunbridge Wells   4C5
This busy residential town has expanded enormously since it became a fashionable 18th-c spa centred round its chalybeate spring. Then, as now, the tree-shaded, colonnaded promenade known as the Pantiles★ (where the waters may still be taken) was the gem of the town. There are scenic walks at the High Rocks with rocks and grottoes.

Walmer see **Deal**

Westerham   4D5
General Wolfe, who led the British against the French at Quebec in 1759, spent his early years in the square brick house known as Quebec House (NT) (open on stated days). He is commemorated by a monument on the small village green. Not far to the S is Chartwell (NT), home of the late Sir Winston Churchill, whose pictures, maps, documents and uniforms may be seen, also gardens and lake with black swans. House and gardens are open at stated times (long queues in summer). Squerryes Court, SW of the town, is a 17th-c mansion with notable furnishings and paintings. Open March–Oct.

Whitstable   4D3
The world-famous oyster beds have been in continuous cultivation for at least 2,000 years. Old houses, harbour for small yachts, modern jetty for small cargo ships. The **Canterbury**–Whitstable railway, laid by George Stephenson, was the first passenger line to be opened (1830); the engine which pulled the first train, the Invicta, still stands by the SE gate of Canterbury's city wall.

Wrotham   4D4
Splendid view of the Weald from the picnic area at the top of the hill. The conspicuous mast is the BBC's VHF transmitter. The attractive village has an interesting 13th–15th-c church with a collection of brasses.

Wye   4D3
Quiet little town under the Downs. Fine old oak beams and good modern glass in the church; an attractive Georgian mill house by the bridge. Wye is well known for its Agricultural College (offshoot of London University) with an agricultural museum at Brook 2m S. Open at set times. On the Downs is a crown dug in the chalk by students to celebrate Edward VII's coronation.

SURREY

AN INTRODUCTION BY
JOHN MONTGOMERY

Although one of the smallest counties in England, Surrey has a high population, and the number is increasing rapidly. Guildford alone has doubled its population since 1900, but the big towns are not typical of the county. For although large farming areas near the sprawling metropolis of London have fallen victim to suburban ribbon development, there still remain beyond the fringe of hastily built housing estates and semi-detached 'bypass Tudor' villas many wild, unspoiled acres of pine and heather, white chalk downs, fertile valleys and rich woodlands. The county owes much of its reputation to its wealth of trees, covering over 12 per cent of its soil, the remains of the great Forest of Windsor which was once 100 miles in circumference.

The 'Cockney's back yard', Surrey has been called; but it is really a neat green back garden. Thomas Fuller compared it in the 17th century to 'a cynamon tree, whose bark is far better than the body thereof. For the skirts and borders bounding this shire are rich and fruitful, while the ground in the inward parts thereof is very hungry and barren, though, by reason of the clear air and clean waves, it is full of many gentile habitations.'

The county is about 38 miles across at its greatest length, with a maximum breadth of 25 miles. In the north there is a low-lying belt of clay along the Thames valley; in the west there are the Bagshot Beds, a relaxing area of pine and fern, to the south lies the rich clay soil of the garden lands of the Weald. But perhaps the best-known feature is the long chalk ridge of the North Downs, crossing the middle of the county from east to west, and narrowing into the Hog's Back. The hills predominate: on their heights, particularly at Leith Hill, Box Hill, the Hog's Back, Newlands Corner and other vantage points, motorists picnic and survey the pleasant views of the wooded weald.

The rivers are small, nearly all flowing northwards into the Thames. The most attractive of the Surrey streams is the Mole, which starts in West Sussex and curves and bends its way through rich meadows and lush waterfields to cut the North Downs between Dorking and Leatherhead before joining the Thames

opposite Hampton Court Palace. At Burford Bridge near Dorking it appears to burrow underground. Perhaps no stream in England has been honoured by so many poets. Spenser wrote of it in his *Faerie Queene*:

*Mole, that like a nousling mole doth make
His way still underground, till Thames he overtake.*

Milton called it 'sullen Mole, that runneth underneath', and Pope, in his *Windsor Forest*, mentions the 'sullen Mole, that hides his diving flood'.

Things to See
From the motorists' point of view there is much to see. One can go to Wisley for the R.H.S. Gardens, to Epsom Downs where the Derby is run, or further afield westwards to Blackdown, the highest point in the south after Leith Hill. Here, about $2\frac{1}{2}$ miles south of Haslemere, is an extensive, unforgettable view

Above Guildford on the Pilgrims' Way is the pilgrims' chapel of St Martha (see pages 25 and 104)

across the Weald. On a fine day the South Downs are clearly visible, a long bare ridge extending to Mount Harry above Lewes, some 35 miles away, with the crown of trees on Chanctonbury Ring standing out clear against the sky, and 'green Sussex fading into blue, with one gray glimpse of sea' visible through the Arun Gap.

Haslemere itself is between 500 and 600 feet above sea level, as high as Newlands Corner. Although not so picturesque as Farnham, it has some attractive red 17th-century houses, with weather-tiled gables and tall chimneys. A window by Burne-Jones in the church is dedicated to the memory of Tennyson, who lived at Aldworth on Blackdown. And at near-by Hindhead you will be 895 feet above sea level when you stand on Gibbet Hill, where three men were hanged in chains for the murder in 1786 of an unknown sailor on the old Portsmouth road.

Travelling for pleasure around the county is best in April, May or October, when the hotels and inns are less full and the roads not so congested. At these times the countryside is at its richest, the lanes and banks and hedgerows are bedecked with wild flowers, the views from the hills are more clear, and the narrow side roads, which the wise motorist will prefer, are less crowded. From Box Hill one looks across the Mole stream to the long lime avenue of Betchworth Park and the spire of Brockham Green, one of the most attractive of villages: Dorking town is to the right, with Leith Hill behind it, and a glimpse of blue heather shows us where Hindhead lies far to the west. Nearer, to the east, is the spire of Reigate church and the tree-crested summit of Priory Park. Far beyond, southwards, is green Ashdown Forest. One of the most popular views in the south of England, this noble prospect has changed little with the passing years.

The gardens at Polesden Lacey, near Dorking, are magnificent. In the grounds of Esher Place you will find the oldest tulip tree in the country, planted in 1685. At Albury, with the near-by silent pool, the gardens were made by John Evelyn, the diarist, the cedars planted from seeds brought from Lebanon; and at Pain's Hill, Cobham (where Matthew Arnold lived), there stands the largest cedar in England. But if you seek a fine expanse of water, where there is yachting, you should visit the great pond at Frensham, surrounded by woods and heather. And for tea in delightful surroundings you cannot do better than go to Shere, with its gabled cottages and a stream running through the village. On the way back to London is the pilgrims' chapel of St Martha (*see* page 103) on the hills above Guildford, with the Tillingbourne valley below, and the modern cathedral near by begun in 1936.

Cobbett thought Guildford 'the prettiest, and taken altogether the most agreeable and happy-looking town that I ever saw in my life'. Today it is a far busier place than in Cobbett's day; but its High Street, rising steeply from the river, is still picturesque with many historic buildings. At the top, the Abbot's Hospital, founded as an almshouse in 1619, confronts the old Grammar School of a century earlier; and in many of the surrounding streets quaint gabled houses survive to remind us of an older England.

In Godalming, a small town hall (now a museum), with graceful clock tower and copper cupola, sits squarely in the middle of the High Street. It slows down the traffic; but since it was built in 1814 all attempts to have it removed have failed. In the little church at Stoke d'Abernon, on the north bank of the Mole between Leatherhead and Cobham, are the oldest brasses in England. One commemorates the death of Sir John d'Abernon in 1277, and the other bears the name of his son, who died in 1327. If you have time, stay to admire the view (now interrupted by the M25 motorway) from the churchyard across the stream, over a broad stretch of meadow grassland. And at Cobham you will again meet the Mole beside a silent water mill.

The county is rich in ancient buildings, all within easy reach of London by car. There are Norman walls at Guildford castle, overlooking the grey and red slates of the town; Farnham castle, although ruined by Cromwell, has a keep which dates partly from Henry III, and round it a deer park, lawns, and a cricket ground, with old cedars. Compton Church contains the oldest piece of Norman woodwork in the land – but for the rest I must refer you to the Gazetteer.

Many great names have lived and stayed in Surrey: George Meredith at Box Hill, Tennyson and George Eliot and George Macdonald at Haslemere, Jonathan Swift at Moor Park near Farnham, Lewis Carroll at Guildford (where you can see the house in which he died), also P. G. Wodehouse, whose Guildford birthplace was marked by a plaque in 1981, Cobbett at Farnham, Lord Howard of Effingham who lies at Reigate, and (it is believed) Sir Walter Raleigh who is buried, headless, at Beddington.

There are many famous hostelries in the county, such as the Bush, which Thackeray described in *The Virginians* as having stood in Farnham town for 300 years; or the Burford Bridge Hotel, near Dorking, where Nelson, Keats and Stevenson stayed. But perhaps more typical of the county are the small village inns, many unspoiled by the centuries; often near by you will find a village pond, a blacksmith's forge, a cricket ground or a green, some timbered cottages with neat gardens, and perhaps an old post office and a cattle pound. Here is the true Surrey, unspoiled by the chain stores and multiple shops of the suburban towns and near by London. England is constantly changing; but many of us hope that the backwaters of this beautiful county will remain unspoiled for future generations to enjoy.

GAZETTEER

Abinger Hammer 4C6
The stream once worked the hammer-mill when the village was a centre of the iron industry – hence the name. The figure of a working blacksmith on the clock projecting over the road is a further reminder of Abinger's industrial past. A motte and pit-dwelling indicate early inhabitation. The watercress beds, for which the village is noted, are fed by underground springs.

Albury★ 4C7
The mansion, remodelled by Pugin, contains a valuable collection of paintings, clocks and some notable chimney-pieces. Note the 63 chimneys, all different. The Yew Walk is very fine. Albury old church has Saxon and Norman work.

Betchworth 4D6
W of **Reigate** it is one of the most attractive villages on the winding Mole, with a venerable barn and a church with a font carved by Eric Kennington.

Bisley 4D7
The ranges of the National Rifle Association are the scene of important international shooting competitions. Prizes worth more than £10,000 are awarded during the annual meeting in July.

Bletchingley 4D6
Pleasant old houses border the wide street. The church has a sturdy Norman tower but is mostly 15th-c. In the wall of the S chapel note the 'Hermit's Hole' and then (by contrast) turn to the huge Clayton monument. There are some remains of Bletchingley Castle.

Burford Bridge 4D6
N of **Dorking** under *Box Hill*. The Mole, the bridge and the trees make a background to memories of Keats (who completed *Endymion* here) and Nelson (here the night before he left for Trafalgar). This is the most popular approach to Box Hill.

Burstow 4C6
A little church with an unusual tower of timber. It is partly 12th-c and has an interesting memorial to John Flamsteed, the royal astronomer who died in 1719 and was rector here from 1684. *See also* **Old Royal Observatory** London.

Camberley 4D7
The centre of an important military training area. Here is the Royal Staff College. The Royal Military College, Sand-hurst, is ½m N. See the very moving War Memorial chapel. The National Army Museum, opened in 1960, has a wonderful collection of pictures, models, weapons, uniforms, etc. *See also* **National Army Museum**, London.

Chaldon 4D6
The church has a well-preserved medieval painting of St Michael weighing souls in the balance while a demon leans heavily on the scales and rampant devils pitch-fork the bad souls into hell. In its day no doubt more effective than the most violent of sermons.

Charlwood 4C6
The church has a very fine 15th-c screen, also traces of medieval wall paintings.

Chiddingfold 4C7
Picturesque old houses border the green of this large village surrounded by beautiful countryside. Near by in an area of some 2,000 acres over 80,000 oaks have been planted in a State forest. The Crown Inn dates from the 14th c and is one of the oldest inns in England. Chiddingfold was once a centre of glass-making: see examples in the church, where there are also examples of modern glass.

Clandon Park★ 4D7
In the village of *West Clandon*. This Palladian mansion (NT), c.1733, was built by the Venetian architect Giacomo Leoni for the 2nd Lord Onslow. Superb 18th-c interior with important collections of furniture, pictures and Chinese porcelain; and the Museum of the Queen's Royal Surrey Regiments. Capability Brown laid out the grounds which contain a Maori house. Open April–Oct. at set times. *See also* **Hatchlands** in *East Clandon*.

Cobham 4D6
Church Cobham and Street Cobham stand beside the Mole with its old watermill. There are several good houses in the neighbourhood. Cedar House (15th-c) (NT) may be seen on application: note the fine open timbered roof of the Great Hall. Pain's Hill mansion stands in magnificent gardens laid out in the 18th c and noted for their fine cedars. On Chatley Heath is a five-storey tower, part of a chain of semaphore stations by which messages were sent from London to **Portsmouth** (in less than a minute) in pre-telegraph days.

Compton 4C7
NW of **Godalming** it has a unique 12th-c chapel built over the vaulted sanctuary of the church. The Norman screen is among the oldest woodwork in England. Limnerslease, a little to the N, was long the home of G. F. Watts, the Victorian portraitist, painter and sculptor. Some of his works are in the Watts Picture Gallery behind the Pottery which he and his wife established.

Crowhurst 4C5
A yew tree beside the church is over 30ft in girth. It is still growing, although the trunk is so hollow that a dozen people are said to have gathered round a table inside it. Note the striking gatehouse of Crowhurst Place, a moated mansion dating from the 15th c.

Dorking 4D6
At the S end of the gap worn through the North Downs by the River Mole, with *Box Hill* rising to 596ft to the N and **Leith Hill**, 965ft high, to the S. Excellent centre for walking. George Meredith's grave is in the cemetery. At one time Dorking was noted for its edible snails.

Egham 4D7
The 17th-c church of St John the Baptist contains memorials and replicas of the Surety Barons' coat-of-arms – the barons who confronted King John with Magna Carta at **Runny-mede**. There is also a fine Georgian pulpit.

Epsom 4D6
Epsom salts are named after the same mineral spring which brought the town 18th-c fame as a spa. Nowadays it is the racecourse on Epsom Downs which brings the crowds, to see the Derby and the Oaks.

Esher
4D6

The wide street retains a countryfied air and pleasant Georgian buildings. In the former parish church note the handsome chamber pew with fireplaces and the high pews at the back for servants. Cardinal Wolsey once lived in the 15th-c gatehouse in the grounds of Esher Place.

Farnham
4C7

A busy little market town with many attractive Georgian buildings and literary associations. William Cobbett is buried in the church (he was born in the house which was the Jolly Farmer inn and is now called the William Cobbett); Waverley Abbey, 2m E, provided Sir Walter Scott with a title for his novels; and at Moor Park Swift wrote *The Battle of the Books* and met Stella. The 12th-c Farnham Castle, for centuries the home of the Bishops of Winchester, is now the residence of the Bishop of Guildford; parts are open to the public (AM). Willmer House (1718), with richly-moulded brickwork, and fine panelling and carving inside, has a museum of local antiquities and 18th-c furniture, clocks and costumes. Open most days. Near by at *Tilford* is the Old Kiln Agricultural Museum with an arboretum. Open April–Sept. at set times. At *Holt Pound* is Birdworld and Underwater World – over 1,000 birds, a seashore walk, aquarium, tropical house, and a new penguin enclosure in 6½ acres of garden and parkland. Open daily.

Feathercombe
4C7

Gardens with flowering trees and shrubs, a heath garden and wide views. Open on first and last Sun. in May.

Frensham Ponds
4C7

Popular lakes for sailing and fishing. The larger of the two ponds covers over 100 acres. Under the tower in the church is a great cauldron, nearly 3ft across, probably used at wedding feasts.

Friday Street *see* Leith Hill

Godalming
4C7

'The most considerable town in the county' – that is how Godalming was described in 1749 when it was an important centre of the clothing industry. Many good old houses remain from those times. The old town hall, with its clock and cupola, was built in 1814 by public subscription; it is now a museum. Godalming's history goes back a long way – at least as far as King Alfred. Charterhouse School is 1m N, and 3m SE is *Winkworth Arboretum* (NT), with rare trees and shrubs in 95 acres of hillside, two lakes and many wild birds. Open all the year; especially fine in spring (azaleas and bluebells).

Guildford*
4D7

Well placed in the valley of the River Wey, with a steep main street beautified by the half-timbered Guildhall with its projecting clock (note the nice ironwork and also the buttresses upholding the little balcony, carved like ships' figureheads). On the other side of the street are the remains of the Castle built by Henry II and for a time used as a jail: the Keep crowns a knoll probably raised by the Romans. Lewis Carroll died in the house called 'The Chestnuts' near the Castle in 1898. The Yvonne Arnaud Theatre on the bank of the River Wey, was completed in 1965. The modern Guildford Cathedral stands on Stag Hill, NW of the town. The foundation stone was laid in 1936, but owing to World War II consecration did not take place until 1962; Sir Edward Maufe's design, a simplified treatment of Gothic, was accepted as long ago as 1932.

Haslemere
4C7

Beautifully placed among wooded hills close to **Hindhead**. Well known for the July Musical Festival founded by Arnold Dolmetsch in 1925 and featuring ancient music played on old-time instruments. There is a fascinating Education Museum, founded in 1888 and since copied elsewhere. *Aldworth*, 2m E, was built by Tennyson; he died here in 1892.

Hatchlands
4D7

In *East Clandon* is a noble, if severe, red-brick mansion (NT) built in 1758 for Admiral Boscawen. Splendid interior, mostly by Robert Adam, recently refurbished. Open April–Sept. on stated days. *See also* **Clandon Park**.

Hindhead
4C7

'The most villainous spot God ever made' – so wrote William Cobbett. But he must surely have been unlucky with his weather, for Hindhead (800ft up) is one of southern England's finest viewpoints, surrounded by woods and heathlands, much of which is protected by the NT. 1m or so to the SW are the well-known ponds of Waggoners' Wells. The highest point in the area is *Gibbet Hill* (895ft) above the deep hollow of the *Devil's Punch Bowl*. Note the sombre inscription on the Sailor's Stone close at hand.

Leith Hill★★
4C6

The highest (965ft) of a series of hills among some of the choicest scenery in Surrey and with wonderful views over the Weald. This is the highest point in SE England. From the top of the tower (1,029ft up) 13 counties can be seen on a clear day. Large areas of this lovely countryside are now cared for by the NT. About 2m NNW is the hamlet of *Friday Street*, a row of brick-built cottages with ample gardens.

Limpsfield
4D5

A peaceful village almost lost among the modern residential areas. It looks out from the greens and hills to the North Downs above Titsey Hill and has a fine common. In the churchyard are the graves of Frederick Delius, the composer, and Sir J. Arthur Thomson, the scientist.

Loseley House
4C7

1½m N of **Godalming** this historic Elizabethan house (1562) built by Sir William More (kinsman of Sir Thomas) is still the home of the More-Molyneux family. Fine panelling, ceilings, tapestries and furniture dating back to Tudor times. Open on stated days.

Mickleham
4D6

A quiet village on the NW slopes of *Box Hill*, with high chalk hills on either side and lovely woods by the River Mole.

North Downs
4D5/7

This chalk range runs through the county from W to E, starting with the narrow ridge of the *Hog's Back* near **Guildford** and gradually widening and rising until at the Kentish border it nears the 900ft mark. Its steep southern escarpment is largely covered with yew, box, juniper and beech trees. Two rivers have breached this green wall: the Wey, which provided Guildford with its valley situation; and the Mole, amid fine wooded scenery along the A24.

Nutfield
4D6

E of Redhill on the A25. Note the extensive workings of the 'fuller's earth' beds beside the road. Once mainly used in connection with cloth-making, 'fuller's earth' is now an important ingredient in the refining of oil.

Outwood
4C6
Here is one of the best-preserved windmills in England. Built 1665, restored 1961–2. Its tall companion, once beautiful in its decay, sadly collapsed in 1960.

Pilgrims' Way
4D5/6
It is commonly supposed that pilgrims from **Winchester** to **Canterbury** used this ancient track. Possibly they did, but it was certainly not they who first trod it out. Note how it avoids steep gradients and keeps mostly to the sunny southern slopes of the Downs, well above the low ground which in former days was often soggy with marshland. Much of it is now clearly marked by NT signposts.

Polesden Lacey★
4D6
A Regency villa (NT) near *Great Bookham* remodelled after 1906 by Mrs Ronald Greville the Edwardian hostess. Fine paintings, furniture, porcelain, silver. Set in grounds with magnificent views. Open-air theatre in July. Garden open all the year; house daily April–Oct., and at stated times in winter.

Reigate
4D6
An ancient town which has become a popular residential and commuting area. Of the Norman castle there are only a few ruins and a subterranean excavation known as the Baron's Cave. St Mary Magdalene's Church has a valuable library of about 2,000 volumes and the tomb of Lord Howard of Effingham (1536–1624), 'Admyrall of Englande, Generall of Queen Elizabeth's Royale Navey at Sea against the Spanyards invinsable Navey'. From the **Pilgrims' Way** on Colley Hill panoramic views extend to the South Downs.

Runnymede★
4D7
The riverside meadows near **Egham**, where King John affixed his seal to Magna Carta in 1215 were given to the NT in 1931. Memorial buildings and kiosks designed by Sir Edwin Lutyens. The Magna Carta Memorial itself, was the

Polesden Lacey: set among extensive grounds, it has a fine rose garden and lovely views across the North Downs

gift of the American Bar Association. Not far away is the John F. Kennedy Memorial. Among the trees on Cooper's Hill to the S is the Air Forces Memorial, designed by Sir Edward Maufe and unveiled in 1953.

Shere
4C6
Beautiful old village with a Norman church, among wooded hills and now mercifully preserved from the roar of traffic by a bypass. Visit the Silent Pool, 1m W.

Stoke d'Abernon
4D6
The church has Saxon and Norman work employing Roman materials and good medieval and Renaissance glass. The brass effigy of Sir John d'Abernon (1277) is the earliest in England.

Wisley Gardens★
4D7
Easily accessible from the A3 near *Ripley*, the famous 300-acre show gardens of the Royal Horticultural Society; at their best in spring and autumn. Large gift shop. Open daily (except Sun. mornings).

Witley Common Information Centre
4C7
Near **Godalming** it is a 'must' for students of natural history. Amid pinewoods, an exhibition and audio-visual programme explaining all you see on the Common (NT), flora and fauna and how to spot them on three guided nature trails. Open most days in summer, weekends in winter.

Wotton
4C6
At the foot of the long rise to **Leith Hill**, and now used as a Fire Service College, is Wotton House, where John Evelyn, the diarist, was born and died; the house is the old home of the Evelyn family, whose tombs are in the 13th-c church. Note wooden belfry on early Norman tower.

LONDON:
THE OUTER RING

AN INTRODUCTION BY
MICHAEL ROBBINS

The outer ring of London is taken here as being those parts of the county of Greater London that lie outside the North and South Circular Roads. The northern one was built in the 1930s as a new ring road; the southern one is little more than a collection of signposts in existing streets, so the boundary has no relation to history or administrative areas, but it is useful. Outside it lie the fringes of London which, though not part of the original city, have been strongly under its influence for the past three centuries at least. These areas were detached, at different times, from the counties of Middlesex, Essex, Kent and Surrey and incorporated in the expanding mass of London. They have no common history, except that none of the areas could escape the economic pull of London, and in 1965 they were pulled into the new county of Greater London.

The ancient and famous county of Middlesex disappeared completely from the administrative map, though it is still used in postal addresses and will no doubt go on being a name to respect so long as cricket is played in England. It used to be a kind of outer shield wrapped around London from the Thames at Staines to the Lea near Waltham Cross, providing for

Sion Road, Twickenham, is an attractive Georgian terrace built in 1721

London's inner areas first hunting-forests, then corn, later hay, and finally, houses and services (schools, waterworks, playing fields, and airports). Most importantly for today's visitor, it provided the royal palace at Hampton Court and innumerable country houses, from the grandeurs of Syon, Osterley, Canons and Trent Park to more modest riverside seats along the Thames bank, like Horace Walpole's Strawberry Hill at Twickenham, and sequestered villages from there round to Enfield.

Today the western sector bears most heavily the imprint of London's outward wave of settlement between the wars: 'semi-detached London', it has been called, when electric railways and motor buses made shy villages like Ruislip and Stanmore accessible and the pink-brick houses seem very desirable. The historic sites are numerous and not all completely submerged: Syon and Osterley, aristocratic park-girt mansions; Harrow Church and School on their Hill, one of the earliest continuously inhabited settlements; the ancient market town of Uxbridge with its most modern of town halls.

The northern sector, its boundary tidied in 1965 by taking in Barnet and Hadley from Hertfordshire, is, for the London area, broken and hilly. Here are Mill Hill, with its school and old village, looking down on Colindale with the RAF Museum; Barnet, an old market with Great North Road inns; Enfield Chase, tamed and prim now but with traces of its thickets still detectable; along the eastern edge, the marshy industrial valley of the Lea, now being slowly transformed into a more or less continuous river park.

Across the Lea to the east is what used to be called 'Metropolitan Essex', with tracts of Epping Forest terminating the sea of brick with a green fringe, and on the Thames-side flatlands the lower parts of Dockland and the rambling 'cottage estate' of the old London County Council's Becontree and Dagenham housing.

Over the Thames, on the Kentish side, lies Woolwich, once famous for its dockyard, arsenal, and military establishments, with Thamesmead, a bold attempt to create a town on soggy land, where the Greater London Council raised the Thames Barrier to prevent London being flooded. The southeastern suburbs, Bexley and Bromley, run up to the chalk heights of the North Downs. Due south of London's centre are Dulwich, with 'village', college, and picture gallery; the Crystal Palace grounds, on a commanding ridge; and Croydon, once a market town linked with the archbishopric of Canterbury, now a commercial centre of skyscraping office blocks.

The southwest is characterized for the traveller by a string of commons and parks: Clapham, Wandsworth, Tooting Bec, Mitcham, Putney, Wimbledon, Richmond (the largest and most various), Old Deer Park, and the Royal Botanic Gardens at Kew, with a former royal palace, a pagoda, and remarkable 19th-century glass houses. Richmond and Kingston are riverside towns on the stretch of the Thames that presents the view that Scott's character Jeanie Deans admired and Constable and Turner loved to paint. Royalty found this sector agreeable to live in: as well as Kew, there were palaces at Richmond, Hampton Court on the Middlesex side and Nonsuch (just over

the Surrey border at Ewell). Wimbledon is the home of international lawn tennis, with a good museum; and Twickenham the home of Rugby football.

Hampton Court is perhaps the best place in London's outer ring to leave the traveller. With its mellow buildings dating from Wolsey's time and William and Mary's, its formal and informal gardens and water, its collections of paintings and furniture, its great hall and kitchen and royal tennis court, its adjacent Home Park and Bushey Park, it is a place that enshrines one example of English development over four and a half centuries. Another example is shown by all the tracts in between the places mentioned here – the modest, sometimes ugly, places where people live, in houses of varying degrees of status and attractiveness. They are there because London's inhabitants have tried to combine the advantages of city life with more open layout and purer air than the city itself can afford. These are the outer suburbs, the sprawling result of Londoners' demands to have the best of both worlds.

GAZETTEER

Brentford 4E6
Often called the county town, this is a busy built-up area. It retains the Butts, a former archery ground. Boston Manor (1622) is notable for interior decoration and allegorical subjects executed in plaster on walls and ceilings. In a disused church in the High Street there is an unusual Musical Museum of pianolas and other forms of automatic music, and near by at the old water works powerful Victorian steam engines have been restored to working order and can be seen at weekends. *See also* **Syon House**.

Bushey Park 4D6
Great park adjoining **Hampton Court** and begun in 1689; it was intended by William III to rival Le Nôtre's work at Versailles. The imposing avenue of chestnuts is interspersed with lime trees. In the circular pond, the bronze 'Diana Fountain' is thought to be a statue of Venus bought in Italy by Charles I for the Privy Garden in Hampton Court. Bushey House, rebuilt in the early 18th c, was converted for use by the National Physical Laboratory for scientific and industrial research.

Cranford 4E6
The church of St Dunstan, standing isolated in the parkland of a great house that has been demolished, has notable monuments, the chief of which is that of Sir Roger Aston and his wife, executed in 'alabaster, tuche, rance and black and white marble' by William Cure, Master Mason to James I.

Edmonton 4E6
In this busy town, Lamb's Cottage, where Charles and Mary lived, still exists near All Saints' Church, their burial place.

Enfield 4E6
Picturesque and varied cottages in Gentleman's Row have been preserved in a town of very fast growth. Charles Lamb stayed for a time at No. 85. A modern house to the S has an

annexe that contains detail from Enfield Palace, including a fireplace of about 1552 carved with Ionic and Corinthian columns and the Royal Arms.

Ham House★ 4D6
Near the village of *Petersham*, it is one of the largest Stuart houses in England and remains almost unaltered from the time it came into the possession of the Earls of Dysart in the 17th c and in the 1670s by Lauderdale who redecorated the house. It contains a wealth of fine paintings and tapestries and late Stuart furniture. The grounds have been restored to their original 17th-c plan and include a knot garden of intricate design. Polo is played on most Sundays in the adjoining field. The house is NT but administered by the **Victoria and Albert Museum**. Open daily except Mon.

Hampton Court★★ 4D6
When Cardinal Wolsey began building in 1514, he declared that his residence must surpass all others. In 1529 he gave it to Henry VIII, who added the Great Hall and Chapel. At the direction of William III, Sir Christopher Wren designed Fountain Court, the S side of Clock Court and a new orangery. This was to be the Versailles of William and Mary. George II was the last king to live here, and nowadays much of the Palace is allotted 'by grace and favour' to widows and dependants of distinguished servants of the Crown. The historic buildings, which give an insight into the domesticities of Tudor times, and the state apartments with their incomparable collection of pictures and tapestries, are open to the public. So too are the delightful orangeries and the Great Vinery. The extensive grounds, mainly modelled on the work of the French landscape gardener, Le Nôtre, have intimate corners, such as the vestiges of Henry VIII's Privy Garden and a reconstruction of a Tudor knot garden. The Maze, in that part of the grounds known as the Wilderness, has a fascination of its own. There is a 'real' tennis court. Open daily at varying times.

Harrow*   4E6
The lead spire of St Mary's Church on Harrow Hill (400ft) draws attention to the famous public school, rival of **Eton**. It was founded in the late 16th c by John Lyon, a yeoman of the hamlet of Preston, Middx, after obtaining a charter from Queen Elizabeth. The Old School (1611) is the earliest part, still in use. The panelling of the Fourth Form Room is scored with the names of past pupils, including Sheridan, Byron, Palmerston, Trollope and Winston Churchill.

Hendon   4E6
Home of the RAF Museum on the former Hendon airfield. The Museum covers all aspects of the history of the RAF with over 40 aircraft on display. In 1979, the Battle of Britain Museum was opened and in 1983 the Bomber Command Museum. Open all year. The church at Hendon contains a square arcaded Norman fort and Sir Stamford Raffles's (founder of Singapore) tomb.

Kew   4E6
It is not always appreciated that the beautiful and world-famous Botanical Gardens** (nearly 300 acres, open all year) have a severely practical purpose. But for Kew, which supplied the seeds, there might have been no rubber plantations in Malaya and Ceylon (as they were then), or quinine in India. There is a Pagoda erected in 1761 by Sir William Chambers. Kew Palace has relics of George III. Open April–Sept. Gainsborough and Zoffany are buried on Kew Green. *Strand-on-the-Green*, just below Kew Bridge, has an unspoiled row of 18th-c Thames-side houses.

Kingston-upon-Thames   4D6
The Coronation Stone on which Saxon kings were crowned is still preserved – in the open, near the Market Place. Lovekyn's Chapel and the parish church date from the 14th c. Clattern Bridge crossing the Hogsmill River dates back to the 12th c. But Kingston today is an extremely busy shopping and residential suburb with many boating interests. Across the River Thames, begins the greenery of **Hampton Court** Park.

Osterley Park   4E6
The original great house was built by Sir Thomas Gresham, the Elizabethan banker. Another banker, Robert Child, commissioned Robert Adam to reconstruct it. The result is the remarkable double portico that, contrary to other neo-classical practice, serves as an entry to the central court-yard and gives lightness to the structure. Much of the furniture was designed by Robert Adam and the house is administered by the **Victoria and Albert Museum**. Lord Jersey presented Osterley Park to the NT in 1949. It is open all year, except Mon.

Richmond**   4D6
New buildings and the conversion of old buildings have not destroyed the flavour of this Thames-side borough, which has been a Londoners' pleasure resort at least since the 18th c. It stands between two good open spaces – **Kew** Gardens and the Old Deer Park to the N, and on the S the fine extent of Richmond Park, reached by Richmond Hill, with delightful views down to the Thames. In the Park stands the Palladian White Lodge (1727), originally a Royal residence, now part of the Royal Ballet School. Some rooms open to the public during August. The park is a magnificent extent (2,350 acres) of turf and trees and bracken, with herds of

Kew Palace (or the Dutch House) built in 1631, the Royal Family lived here for over a century

deer, ponds and streams high above the 18th-c bridge spanning the river. In the summer the river is gay with pleasure-boats. The gem of the town is Richmond Green, bordered by 17th–18th-c buildings. Near by are the remains of Richmond Palace and 1½m S, the splendid 17th-c **Ham House**. *Asgill House*, a villa with original Palladian Georgian design, facing the Thames was designed by Sir Robert Taylor.

Stanmore   4E6
The ruined church of St John stands with the newer one in the same churchyard. See the monuments to the two John Wolstenholmes (1639 and 1669), and the figure of an angel standing over the grave of W. S. Gilbert. In Whitchurch Lane the church of St Lawrence was rebuilt by the Duke of Chandos in 1715. Its baroque architecture and interior decoration are considered unique among parish churches.

Strawberry Hill   4D6
The eccentric 'Gothick Castle' that grew out of a 'little plaything house' acquired in 1747 by Horace Walpole, who died there 50 years later. It has been enlarged and renovated since its occupation by St Mary's Training College for Roman Catholic Teachers. Open on set days by appointment.

Syon House, Isleworth   4E6
The property of the Duke of Northumberland, it was rebuilt by Robert Adam in the middle of the 18th c on the site of a Brigittine nunnery founded in 1415 and granted to Protector Somerset at the dissolution of the monasteries. Lady Jane Grey was living here when she was called to the throne in 1553. The façade, surmounted by the lead Northumberland Lion taken from the family's former town house in London, is seen at its best from **Kew** Gardens on the Surrey side of the Thames. The 1st Duke was, according to Adam, 'a person of extensive knowledge and correct taste'. They worked together to build and decorate a house of noble beauty, full of art treasures, and surrounded by parkland and a garden designed by Capability Brown. The house is open on set days April–Oct. Syon Park is open daily and houses the Heritage Motor Museum, the Butterfly House and one of the largest garden centres in England.

Twickenham   4D6
Fashionable 18th-c riverside village that has retained its residential quality despite rapid growth. Several houses once occupied by famous people have been turned to other uses: York House, where the two last Stuart queens were born, is now municipal offices; the Octagon Room surviving from Orleans House now an art gallery; Kneller Hall now the Royal Military School of Music. Sandycombe Lodge was the home of the painter Turner; Tennyson once lived in Montpelier Row as did Walter de la Mare. Pope's Grove and Grotto Road are reminders of Pope's villa, demolished 1807; *Marble Hill House*, open all year, is a fine example of a Palladian villa. 1m N is the famous Rugby football ground. (*See also* page 108.)

Welsh Harp   4E6
The Brent Reservoir, a great stretch of water constructed in the 19th c to supply the Regent's Canal. Part of the lake and its shores is conserved for public recreation. It is now a yachting centre.

Wembley   4E6
The stadium, built for the Exhibition of 1924, is the scene of the F.A. Cup Finals and the autumn Horse of the Year Show; the 11th Olympic Games were held here in 1948.

INNER LONDON

AN INTRODUCTION BY
FELIX BARKER

A first visit to a large city is exciting, but also rather intimidating. Confronted with a place as bewildering as London, the stranger has good reason to worry about what to see and what he needs to know.

The approach through faceless suburbs from airport or docks can be uninspiring, but once the glum outskirts are breached, the visitor's interest quickens as famous places and buildings come into view. The leafy glory of Hyde Park and the Serpentine glistening in the sunlight make a quick conquest. Turning down The Mall, there is a glimpse of Big Ben towering above the roofs of Westminster. The eye is dazzled by the creamy splendour of Nash's Carlton House Terrace.

Few can resist the thrill of their first sight of St Paul's, silhouetted above the City skyline, and there is magic in the floodlit portico of the British Museum looking by night as impressive as a Greek temple.

Even more subtle responses may be evoked by an elegant Georgian square strewn with leaves on a damp autumn evening; by lamplight reflected in a wet street; or by mist swirling over the river at Chelsea in a passable imitation of a Whistler nocturne.

But, before he becomes too besotted by London's varying moods, the visitor needs one or two guidelines and a map spread out in front of him. He is looking at a sprawling city through the centre of which the Thames winds from west to east. As they say about Egypt and the Nile, London is the 'gift' of the Thames. For centuries, goods flowed from all over the world into the Port of London carried on the tides of the river. The modern commercial centre has grown up exactly in the place where, 2,000 years ago, the invading Romans first crossed the Thames. Here they built the embryonic city, a square mile in size, surrounded by a defensive wall. That city today covers an overall area of 616 square miles and has a population of about 7,000,000 people.

Originally, London was just the City. Westminster was an outlying district where the early kings had their palace and monks built a great abbey. The West End, the now fashionable district of shops and entertainment, consisted, right up to Tudor times of meadows crossed by rough lanes. All this has now become Inner London, looking on a map like a jagged jigsaw made up of 14 variously shaped boroughs. Some of their old individual flavour is retained by districts such as Whitehall (Government offices), Mayfair (fine residential houses), Soho (small foreign shops and restaurants) and Bloomsbury (where London University and the British Museum preside over the academic world).

In the league table of capitals, London is very old. Though an infant compared with Rome, and 100 years the junior of Paris, 'the most noble city', as a medieval monk called London, is older than Moscow or Berlin and probably the senior of Prague and Vienna. Quite a remarkable amount of the past survives despite a number of disasters: the sacking of the 7th-century Roman city by the formidable rebel queen, Boadicea; the Great Fire of 1666 when five-sixths of the old City was destroyed; and the German bombing in the 1940s which left 164 acres round St Paul's in ruins.

Before setting out on a detailed journey to discover historic London, the complete newcomer may well want a masterview. He cannot do better than follow the advice of Mr Gladstone. The best way to see London, declared, the Victorian Prime Minister, was from the top of a bus. For this, London Transport provides special help with a 20-mile circular tour.

From the top of the bus there will be brief glimpses of places to be seen. There is no gainsaying the 'sights'. They must be earnestly tackled, guidebook in hand. The Tower of London will do its sombre best to conjure up scenes of torture, imprisonment and execution, and certainly deserves a visit, if only for the massive White Tower. This multi-purpose Norman stronghold has apartments (for royal refuge in time of danger), council chamber, dungeons, storerooms and an exceptionally fine chapel. Obviously time must be set aside for Westminster Abbey where England has crowned all her kings and queens since William the Conquerer, and one cannot leave without gazing at the miraculous fan-vaulted ceiling of the Henry VII Chapel.

No one in his right mind is going to miss Wren's St Paul's Cathedral, that burst of architectural splendour on Ludgate Hill, and while in the City it would

Tower Bridge has a hydraulically operated road between the Victorian Gothic towers to let ships through

be criminal not to slip into one or two of the architect's surviving churches. St Stephens Walbrook is perhaps the finest but may be locked.

So famous a landmark as the Houses of Parliament and Big Ben can hardly be ignored. But they can be viewed quite adequately from the outside unless the visitor has a penchant for Victorian Gothic ornamentation or is curious to see members of Parliament going about the nation's business. Westminster Hall, created in the late 14th century by Richard II, is the finest hall of its kind in Europe.

Another magnet for tourists is Buckingham Palace. Though you can't approach nearer than the railings, pageantry is on daily tap in the form of the Changing of the Guard. If the Royal Standard is flying the Queen is at home, but unlikely to be visible as her apartments face on to the high-walled garden at the back. Really, it would not be too lazy to visit all these sights on a coach tour especially if the visitor needs extra time to search for more unusual manifestations of London's personality.

Individual quests can be rewarding if undertaken on foot and with a curiosity that leads to exploration.

In narrow alleyways and neglected courtyards may, perhaps, be found London's unadvertised soul.

One informal tour could well start at the Mansion House and continue by way of Cheapside, to Guildhall, the administrative centre of the City. From here it is only a step across London Wall to the Barbican where historic ruins and modern architecture live cheek by jowl in apparent amity. In Southwark, a search may be made for the site of Shakespeare's Globe and, going down passageways with names like Bear Garden Alley, Bankside is reached and ale taken at the Anchor Tavern. To wander south off Fleet Street is to enter the dusty legal world of the Inns of Court with glimpses of lawyers preparing briefs behind the windows of their chambers.

The trick is always to abandon the main thoroughfare for the interesting side street, and if possible to get lost. After a glance at the strange 'pepper-pot' building devised by Nash opposite Charing Cross, desert the Strand, and, going north, wander by devious routes to Covent Garden. The area surrounding what used to be the market has been restored to a fair semblance of the way it looked in the 17th century. If, then, the Strand is crossed to the south, the visitor's reward is to find himself in streets lined with gracious Georgian houses. Many of these are the work of the Adam brothers who developed this area, created their masterpiece in the now demolished Adelphi Terrace, and left their highly individual mark on the Royal Society of Arts.

In Mayfair the maze of little streets off Shepherd Market are worth exploring, and an alleyway off Knightsbridge leads past some delightful small houses in Old Barrack Yard to the Grenadier pub in Wilton Mews. The spirit of old London lives on in all these byways.

Anyone interested in tracing how a city grows and spreads must go outside the City and Westminster in search of London's lost villages. Some are so completely swallowed up that they have almost totally sacrificed their rural identities. Only the postman and the ratepayer is certain where Westminster ends and Kensington and Chelsea begin. Unlike Thackeray we do not think of Clapham as a pretty suburb. Hackney is no longer separated from the City, as it was in the 18th century, by fields and watercress beds. When Dr Johnson went to stay with the Thrales at Streatham he was going well into the country. The huge population growth in the 50 years after 1801 – it more than doubled – led to building which linked the little villages and fused them into what is now Inner London.

Some places have survived on the perimeter. Hampstead triumphantly maintains its entity. Like adjoining Highgate, it keeps a rural flavour largely thanks to the heath. A wide open common also helps to preserve Blackheath as a place very much like a village. Pleasantly sandwiched between the Thames and the park, Greenwich manages to keep alive its personality as a historic riverside town. Putney is nearly as lucky, and Dulwich, too, retaining its village flavour due, in part, to the college playing fields.

Is there a single place to which a visitor can be directed in order to obtain one abiding memory of London's beauty? The middle of Waterloo Bridge has a good claim. From here may be enjoyed the finest panorama that the city has to offer. To the left, and just about as far as the eye can see, is that stately essay in Gothic Revival architecture, the Houses of Parliament. In the other direction, dominating the City despite encroaching skyscrapers, is St Paul's.

Between these extremes, along the north side of the river, is Old Scotland Yard (the former police headquarters) designed like a Scottish castle; the pinnacled Whitehall Court (where Bernard Shaw lived); the 17th-century York Watergate (set now in fine gardens); the Savoy Hotel (from which Monet painted the Thames); Somerset House (an 18th-century building of classical grandeur); and the lawns of the Temple (ancient centre of legal London).

Even this does not exhaust the view. Turn round and face the south bank. In the distance to the west, behind a Tudor gatehouse, is Lambeth Palace, official London home of the Archbishop of Canterbury, though obscured by County Hall from which Greater London is administered; then comes a group of modern buildings whose large concrete surfaces contrast with carved Portland stone on the other side of the river. Here is the Royal Festival Hall, heritage of the 1951 Festival of Britain, backed by the tall Shell building; the Queen Elizabeth Hall for music and the Hayward Gallery for art; and, most assertive of all, the massive National Theatre, opened in 1966, the 20th century's architectural challenge to 18th-century Somerset House across the river.

This sweeping panorama of London seen in golden sunshine late on a summer afternoon, or just as the lights begin to twinkle in the gathering dusk, is something no one will quickly forget.

GAZETTEER

ANCIENT MONUMENTS AND HISTORIC BUILDINGS

The Banqueting Hall, * Whitehall, SW1   15I5
Sole fragment of Charles I's proposed Palace of Whitehall, designed by Inigo Jones in 1625 and with a superb ceiling painted by Rubens. The weathercock at the N end of the roof was believed to have been put there by James II in 1686 to see whether the wind favoured the Prince of Orange's arrival. Charles I stepped to his execution from one of the windows of the Hall. Open daily except Mon. afternoon. May be closed at short notice if required for government function.

Carlyle's House, Chelsea, SW3   14E1
An authentic early-18th-c Chelsea house (NT). Robert Tait's paintings of 1857 introduce the visitor to the Carlyles and there are sketches and photographs of scenes associated with them. The furniture in the little rooms was used by the Carlyles. Open daily except Mon. and Tues.

Guildhall, Gresham Street, EC2   15L7
17th-c hall, the setting for the Lord Mayor's banquet and other City of London ceremonial; it houses the famous wooden figures of Gog and Magog, replaced after their destruction in World War II. Also in the precinct is the museum of the Worshipful Company of Clockmakers, where rare and beautiful watches and longcase clocks are exhibited in a gallery. Open Mon.–Sat. but subject to closures for State and special occasions.

Horse Guards Parade, off Whitehall, SW1   15I5
Open space used for the ceremony of Trooping the Colour in June held on the Queen's official birthday. Its entrance in Whitehall is guarded by two mounted troopers, either from the Life Guards (red tunics and white plumes) or the Royal Horse Guards (blue with red plumes). The changing of the Guard ceremony here takes place on horseback and can be observed daily at 11 a.m. (at 10 a.m. on Sun.).

House of Lords: the sumptuous neo-Gothic chamber was
begun in 1840 after the Palace of Westminster burned down

Houses of Parliament,* Westminster, SW1   **15I4**
19th-c masterpiece of the Gothic Revival. The structure
includes the House of Commons (rebuilt after bombing), the
House of Lords (with sumptuous Victorian decorations), Big
Ben (the bell whose chimes are famous round the world,
housed in the clock on the great N tower), the Victoria Tower
(at the other end of the building), **Westminster Hall** and
the dwellings of various parliamentary officials. Debates
are in progress if a flag flies on the Victoria Tower by day or
a light shines above Big Ben by night; the public may be
admitted to the debates by prior application to an M.P. or
Peer or by queuing for the public gallery. Also guided tours
on Sat.

Marlborough House, Pall Mall, SW1   **15H5**
Begun by Wren in 1710 as a town house for the Duke of
Marlborough, the fine frescoes on the walls depict his
victories. The House has at various times been the home of
members of the Royal Family, including Edward VII as
Prince of Wales and Queen Mary; it is now the Commonwealth Conference Centre. Open weekdays by arrangement.

Royal Naval College,* Greenwich, SE10   **4E5**
Originally built as a palace for Charles II, then used as a
home for aged, disabled seamen, it has been a training centre
for naval officers for over 100 years. There is a fine Painted
Hall, used for dining, and a chapel. Open May–Sept. Near by
is the *Cutty Sark*, the last tea clipper, in dry dock, and Sir

Francis Chichester's *Gipsy Moth IV*. The river trip from
Westminster is a popular approach to this impressive site.
Behind the College is the **National Maritime Museum**,
Greenwich Park and *Blackheath*, surrounded by fine 18th-c
houses.

Somerset House, Strand, WC2   **15J6**
Palladian building erected by Sir William Chambers in 1776.
It is mainly occupied by government offices but the collection of the **Courtauld Institute** is to be installed in the fine
rooms here.

Tower Bridge, by the Tower of London, E1   **15N5**
Built in 1886–94 in Gothic style, its two bascules can open to
allow ships to pass upstream to the Pool of London.
Although ships seldom use the Pool these days, the
mechanism is tested on Sun. mornings between 8 and 9 and is
open to public view daily. High level walkways enclosed in
glass, with displays showing the history of the bridge, give a
splendid view across London. Just upstream is HMS *Belfast*,
a World War II cruiser now a naval museum that is open to
the public.

Tower of London,* Tower Hill, EC3   **15N6**
Built by William the Conqueror, it has been a royal palace,
an armoury, a prison, and even a zoo. Its stones are steeped
in British history. It is guarded by the Yeoman Warders also
known as Beefeaters, and its most popular exhibits are the
Crown Jewels. A new attraction, the Wall Walk, allowing
visitors to walk between the towers, gives a good idea of the
strategic role of the Tower in the past. Open daily.

Westminster Hall,★ Parliament Square, SW1   **15I4**
The oldest building within the **Houses of Parliament**, built
in the 11th c, with a superb 14th-c hammer-beam roof. It has
been the scene of many famous state trials, including those
of Warren Hastings, Guy Fawkes, Charles I and St Thomas
More. Not open to the public.

CHURCHES

All Saints', Margaret Street, W1   **15H7**
Designed by Butterfield, 1849. A good example of Victorian
Gothic Revival, and famous for its Anglo-Gothic style of
worship.

Brompton Oratory, Brompton Road, SW3   **14E3**
A large Roman Catholic church, built 1884 in the Italian
baroque style. The interior which has a very wide nave is
decorated with marble and statues. Good choir and music.

St Bartholomew-the-Great, Smithfield, EC1   **15L7**
The City's oldest church, dating from the 12th c, with 14th-c
additions. Regular lunchtime concerts and recitals.

St Bride's, Fleet Street, EC4   **15K6**
One of Wren's finest churches, rebuilt after the Great Fire, it
was wrecked by bombing, but the outer walls and spire
remained. It has been impressively restored.

St Clement Danes, Strand, WC2   **15J6**
Built by Wren in 1680, gutted by bombs and restored, it is the
church of the RAF.

St Etheldreda's, Ely Place, EC1   **15K7**
The only pre-Reformation church in London in Roman
Catholic ownership, dating from the 13th c. It escaped
destruction in the Great Fire by a sudden change in the
direction of the wind.

St Martin-in-the Fields, Trafalgar Square, WC2   **15I6**
Built 1720 by James Gibbs, with a striking elliptical ceiling
to the nave, and a general Grecian style of architecture. This
church has always been noted for its vigorous social and
pastoral apostolate. Regular lunchtime concerts on Mon.
and Tues.

St Mary-le-Bow, Cheapside, EC2   **15L6**
It used to be said that a true Cockney had to be born within
hearing of Bow bells. This is yet another Wren church that
was largely destroyed. The exterior has now been restored to
its original design and the interior has been adapted to suit
the needs of the 20th c, making it more splendid than ever.

St Paul's Cathedral,★★ Ludgate Hill, EC4   **15L6**
Christopher Wren's masterpiece. Fine carvings by Grinling
Gibbons in the choir stalls and organ case. This is one of the
great buildings of Europe. The Whispering Gallery provides
an unusual acoustic effect, as well as offering a superb view
of the interior, and the marble floor pattern.

St Stephen's, Walbrook, EC4   **15M6**
Rebuilt by Wren in 1672. The dome represents, on a smaller
scale, Wren's original design for St Paul's.

Southwark Cathedral,
Borough High Street, SE1   **15M5**
A large parish church, with Shakespearean associations,
this was raised to cathedral status for the new Anglican
diocese of Southwark in the 20th c.

*St Paul's Cathedral: the 'Parish Church of the British
Commonwealth', built by Wren, it is the third on the site*

Westminster Abbey,★★ SW1   **15I4**
A pure example of Early English architecture, with the
superb Perpendicular Henry VII chapel at the E end. The
interior of this great church is somewhat encumbered with
monuments to famous Britons, some of which however are
of great interest in themselves including the tomb of the
Unknown Warrior. Here and in **St Paul's Cathedral**
Anglican worship is performed to its highest standard with
fine choirs and a dignified liturgy. Off the cloisters is a
fascinating collection of wax funerary effigies.

Westminster Cathedral,
Victoria Street, SW1   **15H3**
The cathedral church of the Roman Catholic Archbishop of
Westminster. It was built in 1895 in an adapted Byzantine
style. Although flawed in detail, it is generally considered a
masterpiece of austere simplicity. The choir is famous and
the standard of music very high.

MONUMENTS

Albert Memorial,
Kensington Palace Gardens, W8   **14D4**
An elaborate memorial to the greatly loved consort of Queen
Victoria. The prince is depicted holding a catalogue of the
Great Exhibition of 1851. On the steps are marble groups
representing the four continents, and around the plinth are
marble reliefs of the world's greatest artists and architects.

Cleopatra's Needle, Victoria Embankment, SW1   **15I5**
This granite obelisk was originally erected c.1500 BC with
two others at Heliopolis. It was brought from Egypt in 1878.
Another stands in Central Park, New York, U.S.A.

Marble Arch, W2   14E6
Designed by Nash, it was erected in 1828 as an entrance to **Buckingham Palace**, and as a memorial of the Napoleonic War. It was moved to its present site as an entrance to Hyde Park in 1851. In 1908 the park railings were moved back to allow the Arch to stand in isolation.

Monument, The, Fish Street Hill, EC3   15M6
This was designed by Wren to commemorate the Great Fire of London; it stands on the spot where the fire began in 1666. It originally carried an inscription, since erased, blaming Roman Catholics for having started the fire. A spiral staircase of 311 steps leads to the top.

Nelson's Column, Trafalgar Square, SW1   15I5
This monument was finally completed in 1867, 62 years after the death of Admiral Nelson. His statue is 17ft tall. The lions at the base were designed by Landseer.

MUSEUMS AND ART GALLERIES

Apsley House, Piccadilly, W1   14F4/5
The Duke of Wellington lived in this house after the Napoleonic Wars. It is now a Wellington Museum, displaying some fine paintings, magnificent dinner services, and souvenirs of the Iron Duke. Open daily except Mon. and Fri.

Bethnal Green Museum of Childhood,
Cambridge Heath Road, EC2   4E5
It houses a very interesting display of toys, dolls and puppets. Also on view is a collection of wedding dresses and fine art. Open daily except Fri.

British Museum,★★ Bloomsbury, WC1   15I7
One of the world's great museums, with superb collections in almost every type of antique art. Outstanding exhibits include the Elgin Marbles from the Parthenon in Athens, Assyrian sculptures from Nineveh, the Rosetta Stone that led to the decipherment of Egyptian hieroglyphics, the Ibert Collection of clocks, and among the manuscripts the Codex Sinaiticus of the Bible and Magna Carta. Open daily.

Cabinet War Rooms, Westminster, SW1   15I5
This intriguing maze under Horse Guards is now open to the public with the map room, the cabinet room and Churchill's bedroom, as they were in 1945. Entrance from Clive Steps, King Charles Street. Open daily except Mon.

Commonwealth Institute,
Kensington High Street, W8   14A4
A modern building with displays of the life and culture of the lands that make up the British Commonwealth. Exhibits by each Commonwealth government. Open daily.

Courtauld Institute Gallery,
Woburn Square, WC1   15H8
This small museum, forming part of the University of London, houses the collection of French Impressionist and Post-Impressionist paintings – many bequeathed by Samuel Courtauld. The Courtauld Collection is due to transfer to **Somerset House.** Open daily.

Dickens' House, Bloomsbury, WC1   15J8
A Georgian terrace house, it seems to be the only house (in London) of the many houses Dickens lived in, to have survived. There are portraits of Dickens and original drawings, pages of original manuscripts of his books are on view and many other personal relics. Open daily except Sun.

Dulwich College Picture Gallery, SE21   4E5
Oldest public picture gallery in Britain. Contains works by Rembrandt, Rubens, Watteau, Gainsborough, Van Dyck, Canaletto and Murillo. Open daily except Mon.

Geffrye Museum, Kingsland Road, E2   4E5
A row of 17th-c almshouses converted into a museum of everyday life with an interesting collection of woodwork and furniture displayed in a series of period rooms from Elizabethan times to the 20th c. Open daily except Mon.

Geological Museum, Exhibition Road, SW7   14D3
Minerals of every kind, including precious stones and a fragment of the moon, are excellently displayed. Open daily.

Hayward Gallery, South Bank, SE1   15J5
Leased to the Arts Council for exhibitions. Open daily.

Horniman Museum, London Road, SE23   4E5
An important collection of ethnographical objects from primitive cultures, and the finest collection of musical instruments in the country. Open daily.

Imperial War Museum, Lambeth Road, SE1   15K4
Opened in 1920, it has collections of many kinds, with models and original objects, devoted to the two World Wars and the Falklands Islands conflict. Open daily.

Keats' House, Hampstead, NW3   4E6
Half Regency house and half museum, former home of the poet. Manuscripts and relics have been preserved, recalling his time. Open all year.

Kenwood House, Hampstead Heath, NW3   4E6
An 18th-c house, in a magnificent setting of woods and lake. Good concerts in summer. A fine collection of paintings and furniture (the Iveagh Bequest). Open daily except Tues.

London Dungeon, Tooley Street, SE1   15M5
Re-created scenes of medieval torture. Open daily.

London Toy and Model Museum,
Craven Hill, W2   14C6
A fairly new museum with displays of tin soldiers, model railways, toy cars, boats and planes dating from 1850 and a reconstructed Victorian nursery. Open daily except Mon.

London Transport Museum,
Covent Garden, WC2   15I6
A display of the buses, trams and tubes that have given London its public transport system. Open daily.

Museum of London,★★ London Wall, EC2   15L7
The story of the development of London is told in fascinating displays and reconstructed rooms of many periods. The Lord Mayor's coach is on view here. Note Great Fire of London model. Open daily except Mon.

Museum of Mankind,★ Burlington Gardens, W1   14G6
The ethnographical branch of the **British Museum,** with a superb collection of masks and tribal deities from many parts of the earth. Open daily.

National Army Museum,
Royal Hospital Road, SW3   14F2
Weapons, medals, uniforms, pictures and models tell the story of the British army from the 15th c. There is a new gallery 'From Flanders to the Falklands'. Open daily.

National Gallery,★★ Trafalgar Square, WC2   **15I5**
One of the finest collections of western European paintings anywhere in the world. Open daily.

National Maritime Museum, Greenwich, SE10   **4E5**
Paintings, models and mementoes of the Royal Navy and of British naval achievements superbly displayed. Open daily.

National Portrait Gallery,
St Martin's Place, WC2   **15I6**
Includes portraits of British kings and Queens from Tudors to the present day together with Prime Ministers and other important people. Open daily.

National Postal Museum,
King Edward Street, EC1   **15L7**
Houses a complete collection of British stamps and a large selection of foreign stamps. Open daily except weekends.

Natural History Museum,★ Cromwell Road, SW7   **14D3**
Animal, vegetable and mineral sciences are displayed here in all their richness. Open daily.

Old Royal Observatory, Greenwich, SE10   **4E5**
The work of the Observatory has almost exclusively been related to navigation, and it is now part of the **National Maritime Museum.** Flamsteed House, designed by Wren, has 17th-c living-rooms furnished as in the first Astronomer Royal, John Flamsteed's days. (*See also* **Burstow,** Surrey.) There are reproductions of his instruments in the Observatory and the planetarium gives shows to the public. The day-to-day work of the Observatory is now carried out at **Herstmonceaux Castle,** Sussex. Open daily.

Public Records Office Museum,
Chancery Lane, WC2   **15J7**
Displays include Domesday Book. Open Mon.–Fri.

Pollock's Toy Museum, Scala Street, W1   **15H7**
A small private museum of dolls, toy theatres, and all objects of childhood. Open daily except Sun.

Queen's Gallery, Buckingham Palace Road, SW1   **14G4**
Changing exhibitions of paintings from the royal collection. Open daily except Mon.

Royal Academy of Arts, Piccadilly, W1   **15H5**
Burlington House, now the home of the Royal Academy, was originally built in 1665. The annual Summer Exhibition shows contemporary works of painting, sculpture, architecture, and engraving not previously exhibited. Important temporary exhibitions are staged here. Open daily.

Science Museum,★ Exhibition Road, SW7   **14D3**
The application of scientific invention in every sphere of human activity. The Wellcome Collection shows medicinal methods through the ages to the present day. A new gallery also of telecommunications. The working models are a never-failing attraction to children. Open daily.

Serpentine Gallery, Kensington Gardens, W2   **14D5**
The gallery holds contemporary art exhibitions in the summer. Built by Henry Tanner 1908, it was once a tea house.

Sir John Soane's Museum,
Lincoln's Inn Fields, WC2   **15J7**
The private house and antiquarian collection of the early 19th-c architect. Open daily except Mon., Sun. and Aug.

Tate Gallery,★ Millbank, SW1   **15I3**
This has two distinct sections: paintings by British artists from 1500 to the present day, including important rooms devoted to Blake and Turner – a new extension, the Clore Gallery to house Turner's paintings open 1985; and modern painting and other types of art by artists of all nationalities. Open daily

Telecom Technology Showcase,
Queen Victoria Street, EC4   **15K6**
A new and imaginative museum displaying the story of telecommunications and its future. Many exhibits can be operated by the visitor.

Victoria and Albert Museum,★★
Cromwell Road, SW7   **14D3**
The greatest collection of fine and decorative art in the world, with wonderful examples of applied art in sculpture, furniture, metalwork, tapestry, jewelry, and every form of handwork. A newly opened gallery, the Henry Cole Wing provides space for permanent and changing exhibitions and paintings. The Theatre Museum is planned to move to Covent Garden in 1986. Open daily except Fri.

Wallace Collection, Manchester Square, W1   **14F7**
Superb examples of French 18th-c furniture, Dutch paintings, and Renaissance armour, all collected by three generations of the Marquesses of Hertford. The collection is unalterable, with nothing permitted to be added or loaned elsewhere. Open daily.

PALACES AND ROYAL RESIDENCES

Buckingham Palace, The Mall, SW1   **14G4**
The London home of the monarch since the beginning of the reign of Queen Victoria. It is not open to the public. The façade that one sees behind the forecourt was built in 1913. A view of the gardens and of the older part of the building may be obtained from the top of a bus going down Grosvenor Place. The Changing of the Guard takes place every morning at 11.30. When the monarch is in residence the Royal Standard flies from the flagpole. The **Royal Mews** and the **Queen's Gallery** are at the S side of the palace. Near by is Clarence House, the home of the Queen Mother.

Kensington Palace, Kensington Gardens, W8   **14C5**
This was a royal residence 1689–1760. Princess Victoria was born here, and was living here as a girl of 18 when she learned she had become queen. The State Apartments are open to the public, and contain many interesting royal mementoes, including the young princess's own doll's house. A new museum opened in 1984 exhibits 300 years of Court dress displayed in what were Queen Victoria's apartments. Open daily.

Royal Mews, Buckingham Gate, SW1   **14G4**
Coaches, carriages and motor cars used by royalty in the past and at the present day, including the state coach used for coronations. The Queen's horses can also be seen when not being used for State and ceremonial occasions. Open to the public Wed. and Thurs. afternoons.

St James's Palace, Pall Mall, SW1   **15H5**
This was the official royal residence 1698–1861, and is still used by the royal family, partly for residence and partly for administration. Architecturally it has grown over the centuries, the oldest parts going back to the reign of Henry VIII. It is not normally open to the public.

THEATRES, CONCERT HALLS AND EXHIBITIONS

Barbican Centre, Silk Street, EC2   15L7
This area of the City was devastated in air raids during
World War II. It has now been rebuilt on an entirely new
plan, with tall towers for residential flats, the **Museum of
London**, and the Barbican Centre, with a major concert hall,
a theatre for the Royal Shakespeare Company, a small
studio theatre, a cinema and an art gallery.

London Coliseum, St Martin's Lane, WC2   15I6
Home of the English National Opera Company.

Madame Tussaud's, Marylebone Road, NW1   14F7
This exhibition of waxworks has long been popular with
visitors to London. It was founded by an émigré from the
French Revolution, and displays models of many important
people of the past and present as well as some very effective
tableaux. The building also incorporates a Planetarium.
Open daily.

*The National Theatre, designed by Sir Denys Lasdun, has
three theatres – the Olivier, Lyttleton and Cottesloe*

Mermaid Theatre, Puddle Dock, EC4   15K6
This theatre was the first to be built in London after World
War II, and set a pattern for a new style with its open stage,
plain brick walls, and generous foyer that has been widely
copied elsewhere.

National Theatre, South Bank, SE1   15J5
Finally opened in 1976 after over 100 years' campaigning,
this complex includes three different theatres and a large
foyer in which small-scale free entertainments are given
daily. An important collection of theatrical paintings is
hung on the walls.

Old Vic Theatre, Waterloo Road, SE1   15K4/5
Opened in 1818, this was a popular place for lurid melo-
dramas. In 1880 it was taken over as a place of culture and
modest entertainment for the poor residents of the district;
from 1914 under the direction of Lilian Baylis it became the
home of Shakespeare, and later opera and ballet, at modest
prices. Many actors who were later to achieve worldwide
fame appeared here, and it eventually housed the National
Theatre company before its own building was completed. It
has now been completely refurbished.

Royal Albert Hall, Kensington Road, SW7 **14D4**
London's largest concert hall, holding 8,000 people, it was built in 1867. The Proms, a popular series of summer concerts, are held here.

Royal Festival Hall, South Bank, SE1 **15J5**
Built as a permanent feature of the 1951 Festival of Britain, this concert hall is now linked with two other smaller ones to provide the centre of London's musical life. Within the same group of buildings is the Hayward Gallery for temporary art exhibitions and the National Film Theatre (members only) for special film shows. Part of the complex, the Festival Pier, London's first new pier for many years, gives passengers shelter under a glass dome and will be used both for charter and scheduled services.

Royal Opera House, Covent Garden, WC2 **15I6**
This magnificent theatre was built in 1858 on a site that had held several previous theatres from 1732. It is now the national home of the Royal Ballet and Opera staging performances of the very highest standard. It is famous for its 'crush bar', foyer and grand staircase and its auditorium seats 2,158 people.

Sadler's Wells Theatre, Islington, EC1 **15K9**
Rebuilt in 1931, it is now an opera and ballet centre. The building replaces an earlier theatre where Grimaldi played in 1781–1805 and where Samuel Phelps produced 34 of Shakespeare's plays in 1844–64.

SPECIAL INTEREST

Bank of England, Threadneedle Street, EC2 **15M6**
Open to visitors on application to the Information Division with a letter of introduction from a bank. The 'Old Lady of Threadneedle Street' is sculpted on the pediment of the building. Originally built in the 18th c the bank was rebuilt in 1925–39. It received its Royal Charter in 1694 when it financed the French wars.

City Halls and Inns of Court. There are 84 Livery Companies in the City, many of them very old and established to maintain trade standards at a high level. Each Company maintains a Hall, some of which are fine examples of architecture. They are not normally open to the public except during the City of London Festival in July, but visitors with a special interest should write to the Company's Clerk. The Inns of Court are four legal communities, dating from about 1300, to one of which every barrister who qualifies to practice in England and Wales must belong. Each Inn consists of a Hall, where the members may dine, and a group of Chambers, where they work. The Halls are not normally open to the public, but anyone may wander round the courts, which form oases of peace amid the bustle of the streets outside. The four Inns are Middle Temple, Outer Temple, Lincoln's Inn, and Gray's Inn.

Law Courts 15J6. Criminal cases are tried at the *Old Bailey* and civil cases at the *Royal Courts of Justice* in the Strand. The public are admitted, but seating capacity is limited. The magistrates' courts, of which the most central is at *Bow Street*, try minor offences, and an hour spent in the public gallery here can give a revealing picture of the murkier side of London life.

London Diamond Centre, Hanover Street, W1 **14G6**
Some of the world's most famous diamonds, diamond cutting and goldsmiths can be seen at work. Open Mon.–Fri.

London International Financial Futures Exchange, Royal Exchange, EC2 **15M6**
Visitors gallery for viewing dealers buying and selling financial commodities. Open at set times Mon.–Fri.

Stock Exchange, Old Broad Street, EC2 **15M7**
The floor can be viewed from a spectators' gallery. Open Mon.–Fri. 10 a.m.—3.15 p.m.

GENERAL INTEREST

Inns and Public Houses. There is no better place to savour the typical atmosphere of the different London 'villages' than in a local pub. A few pubs with special associations may be noted: *The George* (NT), Southwark, is a galleried inn with a Dickensian atmosphere; *The Sherlock Holmes*, Northumberland Street, has many mementoes on its walls and a reconstruction of the great detective's Baker Street room upstairs; *Ye Olde Cheshire Cheese*, off Fleet Street, has associations with Dr Johnson (whose own house – open to the public – is in Gough Square nearby) and a traditional menu; *The Prospect of Whitby*, Wapping, is a riverside pub with a balcony on the Thames; *The King's Head*, Islington, is one of several pubs that incorporate small theatres (prices here are still quoted in pre-decimal currency).

Covent Garden: the market buildings around the Piazza have been restored and house shops, boutiques and cafés

Markets. Vegetables used to be sold in *Covent Garden* but this has now been converted into an attractive shopping precinct; fish used to be sold at *Billingsgate*, but this wholesale market has also now moved further out; meat is still sold at *Smithfield* where the scene early in the morning is a busy one. Antique markets have blossomed in recent years: best is the *New Caledonian Market*, the dealers' market, in Bermondsey Square, held very early on Fri. mornings. The largest is on Sat. morning in *Portobello Road* and there is another thriving one in *Camden Passage,* Islington. A popular street market for goods of every description is *Petticoat Lane* on a Sun. morning. *Carnaby Street* acquired a reputation for trendy clothes in the 'swinging 'sixties' and is still a tourists' attraction, but the smartest shops for young fashion are now in the *King's Road, Chelsea* or *Covent Garden.*

Squares. A typical feature of 18th- and 19th-c town planning was the building of houses round a square with a communal garden in the middle for the residents. Good examples of such squares are St James's Square, Bloomsbury Square, Bedford Square, Cavendish Square, Woburn Square, Berkeley Square and Fitzroy Square, and there are many more that are to be found in almost all districts. At the back of the big houses in the square, stables were built for the owners' coaches and horses, with accommodation for the grooms above; today these Mews are now mostly converted into smart flats.

Tours of London. London Transport runs a popular sightseeing bus tour, with pick-up points at Grosvenor Gardens, Victoria, Piccadilly Circus and Marble Arch. Other companies also organize tours. Another excellent trip is by boat from Westminster or the Embankment, down the river to *Greenwich* (throughout the year) or up the river to *Kew* or *Richmond* (summer only).

PARKS AND OPEN SPACES

London is fortunate in containing a superb stretch of parkland in its centre. From Birdcage Walk to Notting Hill you can walk for an hour on grass almost all the way and hardly meet a motor car. This stretch of open country has been preserved for us today by monarchs in the past, who used it for hunting or recreation. It is made up from four parks, each of which has its own distinct character. *St James's Park* was a promenade for the Court; the wildfowl on the lake are of great interest. *Green Park* offers an informal display of paintings on its Piccadilly railings on Sundays. *Hyde Park* has horseriding in the Row, swimming and boating in the Serpentine, and free speech on every subject under the sun at Speakers' Corner. *Kensington Gardens* has model boating on the Round Pond, kite flying, statues of Peter Pan and Physical Energy, an Italian Garden with fountains and a sunken garden ablaze with tulips, puppet shows in August, and **Kensington Palace.**

Hidden away behind brick walls by the Thames, the *Chelsea Physic Garden* in Swan Walk has a great selection of plants and excellent research and teaching facilities. Each spring *Battersea Park* hosts an Easter Parade. During the summer months regular band concerts are held in these parks.

On the South Bank, near County Hall, are the new *Jubilee Gardens.*

A little further from the centre to the north is *Regent's Park*, with its lake for waterfowl and boating, an Open Air Theatre holding summer performances of Shakespeare, Queen Mary's Rose Garden, the Central London Mosque, and round its edges the superb terraces of houses designed by Nash as part of the Prince Regent's ambitious exercise in town planning. The *Zoological Gardens* (London Zoo), also in the park – one of the great zoos of the world – have a deservedly famous collection of animals. There is a branch at Whipsnade in Bedfordshire (*see* **Luton**), where animals can be kept in natural surroundings. The Regent's Canal passes through the zoo. Band concerts in the summer.

To the west is *Holland Park* surrounding Holland House, once a centre of intellectual life in the 18th and 19th centuries and now housing a Youth Hostel.

Further to the north lies *Hampstead Heath*, a huge stretch of rolling country with wonderful views of London on the plain below; to the east lies *Blackheath*, ringed by fine 18th-century houses; to the west are the grounds of *Chiswick House*, built by Lord Burlington as the first example of Palladian architecture in Britain; and to the south *Clapham Common*, which offers a welcome relief to the somewhat decaying areas of the inner city that surround it together with the open spaces of *Putney Heath* and *Wimbledon Common.*

SPORT

Association Football. The Cup Final and international matches are played at the *Wembley Stadium*. There are 12 London clubs in the four League divisions; leading clubs are Arsenal with its ground at Highbury, Chelsea at Stamford Bridge, and Tottenham Hotspur at White Hart Lane.

Rugby Football. International matches are played at **Twickenham**. There are club grounds at Blackheath, **Richmond**, and Roehampton.

Cricket. *Lord's* is the headquarters of the MCC and the home ground for Middlesex; the *Oval* has a more popular character and is the home ground for Surrey.

Tennis. The tournament at *Wimbledon* held for a fortnight in June and those at *Queen's* just before the championship are the high spots of London's social and sporting life. Tickets for the Centre Court at Wimbledon are hard to obtain, but during the first week of the tournament there is plenty to see on the outer courts.

ESSEX

AN INTRODUCTION BY
K. J. LACE

'This shire is moste fatt, fruitfull and full of profitable things exceding (as far as I can finde) anie other shire for the general commodities and plentie.' So wrote John Norden in 1594: and he might well say the same of Essex today, although he would find it difficult to recognize the county as the place he visited four centuries ago. Essex was perhaps the last of the Home Counties to suffer 'development'; but since 1800, when London began to spread over the county boundary, and in particular during the last 70 years, the southern part of the county has seen the spread of 'Metropolitan Essex'. The expansion of London is now, however, 'cabined, cribbed, confined' by the Green Belt, and building beyond this barrier is being allowed only in a planned and orderly fashion. The plans include the exciting experiment of the New Towns of Harlow and Basildon, and the expansion of places which appear to have changed but little since Norden reported on them. The reorganization of London local government made 'Metropolitan Essex' a reality. Outside this area, however, there remains the Essex of field and river, coast and marsh, village greens and inns: a county rich in history and full of varied scene and interest.

Essex has, perhaps, the most rapidly rising population of any in England. Almost a quarter of its area is covered with houses. In the southwest and along the Thames, the sprawl of London has engulfed the countryside. Here the county is populous, flourishing, busy with the work of great new industries – motor engineering, board mills, cement, shoes, oil, sugar, medicines – which have been established along the north bank of the river. The new towns of Harlow and Basildon, planned and built since World War II, are bright and colourful with their modern architecture, green lawns and spacious squares. North of the Green Belt the county is less changed, and here the smaller towns, Ongar, Halstead, Thaxted, Saffron Walden, Epping and Dunmow still look to a rural economy for their support. Among the closely cultivated farmlands only the electricity wires, the television aerials and motorway embankments suggest that any change has come to the villages in the last 200 years.

Chelmsford, in the centre of the county, shows the meeting of industrial and rural Essex in bustling harmony. Here you may see a heron fly ponderously over the centre of the town, and the martins still nest under the eaves within a few yards of the busy High Street. In the northeast the fashion of holidays by the sea has encouraged the development of the coastal resorts at Clacton, Frinton, Walton and Dovercourt.

No part of Essex rises above 500 feet. In the coastal plain the roads meander through a tree-lined land of large fields, with unexpected glimpses of silver water or the white sails of small boats where the creeks run farther inland than seems possible. North of the A12 the wayfarer, expecting Essex to be flat, will take pleasure in the wooded vistas of the undulating countryside, and will hardly find a level stretch of road between Saffron Walden and Colchester, Chelmsford or Stansted.

Along the roads, especially in the north, the weatherboarded cottages and timber-framed farmhouses fit quietly and appropriately into the wooded landscape. In the narrow streets of the market towns, and in the villages, such houses and inns lend charm and dignity to the scene. These characteristically English buildings of the 15th and 16th centuries, built when oak, ash and elm (John Norden's 'three building trees') were plentiful, and stone expensive and hard to come by, are indigenous, well-built, gracefully proportioned and show the use of local materials to the best advantage. Many of the houses have external beams of oak, weathered to a silvery grey by the passing years, and tastefully carved with floral designs or sometimes, as at Felsted, with the builder's name. The thickness of the plaster applied externally to these half-timbered houses encouraged the decoration of the walls with elaborate patterns or ornaments in high relief. This process, which has shown signs of revival in recent years, known as pargeting, may still be seen in its original form on some larger buildings and on many cottages.

Land and Water
The county lies, as it were, on a great saucer of chalk, its rim exposed in the Saffron Walden area, which

In rural Saffron Walden, the façade of the former Sun Inn is a fine example of pargeting plasterwork

conveniently acts as a reservoir for water. Into this saucer at various times have been deposited alluvial and glacial sediments and gravel. First, in a tropical heat the great bed of London clay was laid down. This is exposed in the south and east of the county, and yields fossils of tapir, turtle, shark and the seeds of exotic trees. Next, after a startling change of climate, glacial boulder-clay was left by the retreating ice-cap in a great triangle in the north and west of the county. Today this maintains the great wheat belt of Essex, growing some of the finest wheat in England on a stretch of country which runs northeastwards across the county for almost 20 miles. On these soils thrives a vigorous farming community, modern in outlook and methods. In the southwest is a great deposit of Valley Gravels. Among these are the remains of elephant, mammoth and elk. At one point, the number of bones is so large as to suggest that the carcasses of thousands of these beasts were deposited together in a backwater of some great prehistoric river. Along the coast and river estuaries are found alluvial deposits which form the low coastal plain and marshlands. Almost 300 miles of wall and dyke now defend these from the relentless attack of the sea, since in the last 2,000 years the level of the coast has

sunk some 12 or 13 feet and is still sinking. In this unending battle between land and water both sides may claim their victories. The parish church at Walton was engulfed in 1798 and is now deep beneath the sea. In 1953, Foulness Island was evacuated along an ancient road, running parallel to the coast. This is still usable at certain states of the tide, but is now half a mile off-shore. The great tide of 1953 was the latest and most disastrous of many occasions when the sea defences of the county have been breached. On the other hand, the draining of marsh and island at various points along the coast and estuaries has yielded many valuable acres for the use of man since Charles I brought Cornelius Vermuyden from Holland to build the walls which encircle and protect Canvey Island. In spite of the length of the coastline, only at Tilbury, Shellhaven and Harwich is there a sufficient depth of water to allow the establishment of ports for larger ocean-going vessels. In the past, however, the deep indentations of the Thames, Crouch, Blackwater, Colne and Stour, with their creeks and inlets, brought trade, both legal and illegal, to the shores of Essex; and the smaller ports – Leigh, Tollesbury, Maldon, Colchester, Brightlingsea and Manningtree – grew up along the coast. Only yesterday the survivors of the once great fleets of ships – Essex bawleys and Thames barges – plied their trade in this last stronghold of sail.

Plants and Birds

Within 10 miles of Charing Cross, reaching down a green finger from rural Essex into London-over-the-border, is the marvel of Epping Forest. Here, over 5,500 acres of the old Royal Forest, remnants of which also remain at Hainault and Hatfield, were preserved by an Act of Parliament in 1878 (after half the area had been rescued from illegal enclosure) for public use for ever. Travelling north, the wayfarer is startled by the dramatic change of scene as he emerges from the fringe of London suburbs straight into the glory of heaths and woodlands which press to the edge of the Cambridge road, stretching unbroken from Woodford to Epping Town itself. Its glades, ponds, wooded valleys and open hilltops are the homes of a great variety of trees, plants, birds, fungi and insects – everything, in fact, of interest to the naturalist.

In the wide marshlands and deep estuaries on the other side of the county the naturalist will also find much to engross his interest. Here Essex is indeed a maritime county. Its creeks and inlets are alive with the movement and colour of a host of wading birds: the knot, dunlin and turnstone on the shallows, tern and cormorant over the waves, and, in due season, the Brent geese winging from the north to the saltings, now overshadowed by the Bradwell atomic power station. A swannery, which rivals that at Abbotsford in Dorset, with hundreds of birds, exists on the estuary of the River Stour, an inland sea 10 miles in length from Harwich to Manningtree, between the green fields of Essex and Suffolk

The Special Flavour

Essex, no less than any other county, has its special points of appeal: its busy yachting centres on the Crouch, Blackwater and Colne; its communities of artists and writers; the 'cathedral' church at Thaxted; rare wild flowers, the Bardfield oxlip, butterfly orchid and leopard's bane; its groups of villages – the Easters, the Lavers, the Tolleshunts; oysters at Colchester; the colours of its miles of wheat at harvest. These things give the county some of its special flavour. But more than these are the contrasts which are, perhaps, nowhere so clearly drawn. The turmoil of the industrial south, and the rural quiet of the countryside, the closely cultivated farms, and the wide desolation of the marshes; the narrow, enclosing streets of the towns, and the wide sweep of the open skies; the buildings which have weathered the centuries, and the modern splendour of the new towns; thatched cottage and tower block; the bustle of the roads, and the quiet reaches of the great rivers; the small industries of weaving, lace-making, thatching, boat-building – and the modern mechanization of the Thames Valley. This is the true flavour of Essex. In its diversities lies its essential charm.

GAZETTEER

Ashingdon   4E4

Of great antiquity but much enlarged by recent building. Scaldhurst Farm is widely accepted as the site of Canute's defeat of Edmund Ironside at the Battle of Assandune. St Andrew's Church, reputed to be founded by Canute (1020) in memory of his victory, was restored from a ruinous state, 1949. In the 14th c a shrine of the Virgin was reputed to cure barrenness: pilgrims crawled on their knees from Goldencross at the foot of the hill to the church, 1m away. The idea that marriage at Ashingdon was lucky survived long.

Audley End House★   4G5

Though smaller than the 'palace' built (1603) on the ruins of a Benedictine monastery by the 1st Earl of Suffolk, the present mansion (AM) remains a splendid example of 17th-c architecture, with chapel, library and pictures. Vanbrugh, Adam and Biagio Rebecca are among those who worked on the house, and Capability Brown landscaped the park. Fine Tudor brickwork in the stables at one entrance. The house is open to the public April–early Oct.

Basildon   4E4

One of eight New Towns planned, after 1945, to take some of London's overspill population and industry, it already has a population of over 140,000. Originally seven parishes, with five medieval and two Victorian churches, one of the latter now converted to a house. The town's main feature is the traffic-free square, whose surrounding buildings, statues, fountains and lively market place make a welcoming impression on visitors. Further S, on the Thames estuary, *Tilbury Fort* (AM) is the scene of Elizabeth I's famous review at the time of the Spanish Armada, 1588.

Boreham   4F4

Parts of the church, with battlemented tower, are Norman and the S chapel has a 16th-c triple monument to three Earls of Sussex. Boreham House, with dignified façade (1728) is now Ford's Tractor Division training-centre. New Hall, 1½m W, now a convent, was once part of a sumptuous mansion, built for Henry VIII, whose arms are in the chapel.

Bradwell-on-Sea   4F3

A tiny village, with a sand and shingle beach at the quay, and a nuclear power station of 1957. Bradwell Lodge (open April–Sept.) is a 16th-c house with an Adam wing. A footpath leads E to the Saxon chapel of St Peter's-on-the-Wall, a small barn-like building, composed of materials from the Roman fort that once stood here. This is all that remains of the much greater church originally built by St Cedd in the 7th c. *Bradwell Waterside*, the neighbouring village, has a Bird Observatory.

Brightlingsea   4F3

Attractive little town, a centre for yachting enthusiasts, boatbuilding and oyster cultivation. There is a notable timbered Tudor house, Jacobes, some of whose owners have brasses in the church, with fine flint and flushwork tower of the 1490s.

Burnham-on-Crouch   4E3
With pebbly beach and oyster beds, it is a centre for yachtsmen and river craft, and abounds with a variety of wild fowl.

Castle Hedingham   4G4
The village is dominated by the keep (1140) one of the most impressive in England, reached by a Tudor bridge across the encircling ditch. The church has a brick tower of 1616, but the bulk of the fabric is late-Norman, including the original S door (open May–Sept.). Station, now part of the Colne Valley Railway, has displays of locomotives.

Chelmsford   4F4
An important thoroughfare town from Roman times, it hums with the rush of traffic. Essex's county town, with a handsome Shire Hall (1791) and some good domestic buildings of the 18th and 19th c. The cathedral, until 1914 the parish church, was much restored after 1800, but the S porch with an upper chamber is earlier work, and there are interesting monuments and memorials. Marconi developed his electronic industry here and at *Writtle*, 2m W, home of the Essex Institute of Agriculture, where the church has many brasses and a famous marble monument by Nicholas Stone, 1629.

Chignal Smealey   4F4
In the absence of local stone, many Essex churches contain an unusual amount of flint and brickwork, but the little Tudor church here is unique in being entirely constructed of brick, including the font.

Chipping Ongar *see* **Ongar**

Clacton-on-Sea   4F3
Developed as a seaside resort in the 1870s: Royal Hotel 1872, pier 1873, promenade 1889. Now a flourishing holiday centre, with amusement park and a rash of caravans and chalets at the S (*Jaywick*) end.

Coggeshall   4F4
A leading Essex clothing town in the Middle Ages, and still the centre of the area's economic life. There has been some unattractive building lately, but Paycocke's House (NT) redeems this: a fine half-timbered merchant's house, *c*.1500, whose richly-carved interior matches the façade of five bays, oriel windows and carved figures. Open April–Sept. *Little Coggeshall*, just S, had a Cistercian abbey, fragments of which have been built into a house. Near by, an interesting group of farm buildings includes a barn whose timbers are thought to be 12th-c.

Colchester   4G3
The first Roman city in Britain was founded here. It fell to Boadicea (archeology has provided startling evidence) but was rebuilt, and still has much of its Roman walls and the Balkerne Gate, the London exit. The Normans built a castle here, using the vaults of a Roman temple for foundations. The keep remains, housing a remarkable collection of Roman and other material. Hollytrees, a house of 1718, is a museum of costume and social history. Redundant churches have provided premises for two more museums. Colchester was besieged in the Civil War. Bullet holes in the Siege House, and the ruins of St Botolph's Norman priory survive from this episode. Bourne Mill (NT), a converted fishing lodge of 1591, is a beautiful building, once more in working order and open to summer visitors. Of the modern buildings, the Mercury Theatre (1972) is one of the best. The Colchester

nurseries (roses) are noted. *Stanway*, on the W side of the town, has a very good zoo. To the E, the University of Essex has grown up at *Wivenhoe* (in a park often painted by Constable). Its tall towers are now a familiar feature of the landscape. (*See also* page 126.) 5m SW, *Fingringhoe*, on the W bank of the Colne, has a nature reserve and Interpretative Centre: a good place to discover the beauty and wildness of an Essex marsh at any time of the year.

Copford   4F3
In the opinion of Professor Tristram, the medieval wall paintings in the Norman apse of the church 'rank among the finest examples of English workmanship'.

Cressing   4F4
In the 12th c, one of the two communities of the Knights Hospitallers in the county. Here, unlike **Little Maplestead**'s, the church has long disappeared, but two of the old barns – for wheat and barley – are among the finest in the country: radio-carbon tests suggest the barley barn's timbers to be 11th-c. The tiled roofs are still supported by the original oak timbers; the older of the two dates from 1480.

Danbury   4F4
From its elevated site, between **Chelmsford** and **Maldon**, there are good views of the Blackwater estuary. Church, rebuilt after 1941 bombing, has three 13th-c oak effigies of knights. The Armoury Museum, local and natural history, is open in summer. Danbury Country Park has 39 acres of lakes, exotic trees and shrubs.

Dedham   4G3
Dedham Vale was declared an Area of Outstanding Natural Beauty in 1970. The noble church tower is familiar from many of Constable's pictures. He was at school here. Another artist, Sir Alfred Munnings, lived at Dedham. His home, Castle House, is open to the public mid-May–Oct., with his studio and a number of works. The village has some handsome houses. The owner of Shermans (*c*.1730) (NT, but not open) was an ancestor of the general of American Civil War fame. Modern pews in the church commemorate man's landing on the moon in 1969. At the Heavy Horse Centre, Suffolk Punches and other horses are paraded, also displays and demonstrations. Open April–Oct.

Epping   4F5
In spite of London's sprawl and the M11 motorway, Epping retains the atmosphere of a market town. The forest, nearly 6,000 acres (and once much larger), was bought for the public in 1882. There is a Conservation Centre at *High Beach*, and at *Chingford* Elizabeth I's Hunting Lodge has a display relating to the forest's history and wildlife.

Feering   4F4
The church, mainly of beautiful early-Tudor red brick with silver and black diapering, has for its reredos a painting by Constable, who used to stay here, and whose rector had baptized him; also a Florentine crucifix, and a Virgin and Child in Nottingham alabaster.

Finchingfield*   4G4
The grouping of church and cottages, above the pond, has made this one of England's most photographed villages. The former guildhall is now a museum (open Easter–Sept.). Spains Hall, an Elizabethan manor house in beautiful gardens, is open May–Aug. 3m NE, *Toppesfield* has the Museum of the Working Horse: forge, wheelwright's and harness-maker's shops, farm implements. Open May–Oct.

Frinton-on-Sea★ 4F2
The adjoining resorts of Frinton and *Walton-on-the-Naze* are celebrated for their beaches, golf and fishing. Frinton, the more 'select', was developed in the late-Victorian period. Its church has Burne-Jones glass. Walton developed earlier. Its red crag cliffs contain fossils, its backwaters, where oysters are cultivated, are a series of little harbours leading towards **Harwich**.

Great Bardfield 4G4
Many artists have made their homes here. The church has fine window tracery, and a 14th-c stone rood-screen. 3m SE, *Great Saling Hall* has an arboretum and a William and Mary walled garden, open in summer.

Great Leighs 4F4
One of the finest of the half-dozen Essex round flint towers. Part of the church is late 10th-c. N wall of chancel has a good Easter sepulchre. At *Hartford End*, Little Leighs or Leez Priory has fine gardens and Tudor buildings, open in summer.

Great Waltham 4F4
With *Little Waltham*, twin parishes just N of **Chelmsford**. Attractive village, with a handsome 18th-c house, Langleys, beautifully maintained in its park. The church, much restored, has fine monuments including one of 1703, telling a story of shipwreck, battle and death at sea. 3m NW, all that remains at *Pleshey* of Geoffrey de Mandeville's 11th-c castle are vast earthworks and a brick arch spanning the moat.

Greensted 4G3
There are other wooden churches in Essex, but Greensted-juxta-Ongar is unique. The nave consists entirely of rough-hewn oak, secured with wooden pins, and the tower is weatherboarded, its spire covered with wooden shingles.

Hadleigh 4E4
The ruins of the 13th-c castle (AM) are familiar from Constable's painting. The little Norman church has an almost contemporary glass-painting of St Thomas à Becket. *Rayleigh*, just N, has a tower windmill with local history exhibits, open most of the year.

Halstead 4G4
Courtaulds silk manufactory set up here in 1826 in a still handsome weatherboarded mill. There are Bourchier monuments and brasses in St Andrew's Church. At near-by *Gosfield*, a Courtauld village, the Hall (open in summer) is Tudor, built round a courtyard and with a fine long gallery and a brick Tudor court. It was Louis XVIII's first English home 1807–09.

Harlow 4F5
Like **Basildon**, Harlow, conceived 1947, is another New Town just W of M11. It was planned to develop beside, not around, the existing settlement, with its good 16th–17th- and 18th-c houses, and a church with a number of brasses. The Civic Centre has on display objects unearthed during building. The new area has at its heart a large pedestrian precinct, with market square to N, civic buildings to S. The station is considered an especially good example of railway architecture. Three main housing areas, each with its own amenities and facilities, and all using sculpture, mosaic and glass in enterprising ways. There is a museum of local history and another of veteran bicycles of 1819–1960. On the S boundary, Parndon Wood Reserve has nature trails, observation hides and a study centre.

The Colne flows through rich farming country, heath and woodland before reaching Wivenhoe (see page 125)

Harwich 4G2
A town of much interest and character, overlooking the mouth of the Orwell and Stour rivers, principal port of departure for the Continent (from Parkeston Quay). Many 16th–18th-c houses, including the red-brick Guildhall with an eccentric Gothic door. Fine views of the whole harbour from the Redoubt, an 1808 fort, now a lively museum. The Low Lighthouse, painted by Constable, is a maritime museum. Both open Sun. Easter–Oct. *Dovercourt*, near by, is a small seaside resort, with a good beach.

Hempstead 4G5
William Harvey, the discoverer of the circulation of blood, lived here and is buried in the church. The parish register records the baptism of Dick Turpin, 1705.

High Easter 4F5
In the neighbourhood are a number of moated, timber-framed farmhouses with brick chimneys. The church has a brick clerestory and fine S porch; the nave's oak roof is carved with representations of gates, commemorating Sir Geoffrey Gate who restored it in the 15th c.

Ingatestone 4F4
Bypassed by the A12. The church, as at neighbouring *Fryerning*, has a splendid 15th-c diapered brick tower, and there are interesting monuments to the Petre family, who lived at Ingatestone Hall and entertained Elizabeth I there. Most of the house is used by the Essex Records Office (open in summer), and excellent exhibitions of local history are regularly mounted there.

Lawford 4G3
The Hall, an Elizabethan house of 1583, has been given a Georgian front. The church has fine carvings and a Waldegrave monument of 1584. 1m E, *Mistley* still has the twin towers (AM) Robert Adam designed in 1776 for an earlier church there, as part of a masterplan for a spa, which came to nothing.

Layer Marney 4F3
The eight-storeyed gatehouse of a Marney mansion never completed, Layer Marney Towers, is open in summer, providing superb views of the surrounding countryside. The magnificent towers are 16th-c and built in brick but diaper patterned in blue. The Marney tombs in the church are scarcely less remarkable. 2m E, *Abberton Wildfowl Reservoir* has a picnic area and public observation post.

Little Maplestead 4G4
The round church here was the last of four built in England by the Knights Hospitallers (*see* **Cressing**), but was severely restored in 1851, like the one at **Cambridge**. Its circular nave is 29ft diameter. *Great Maplestead*'s Norman church remains more impressive.

Maldon 4F4
Site of a battle against the Danes in 991, now a busy port and yachting resort at the head of the Blackwater estuary, with its islands and mud flats and flocks of wild fowl, *Northey Island* (NT), where the Danes had their camp, is a nature reserve with restricted access. The public library, entered through a medieval church tower, was designed 1704 by Dr Plume, who retained the upper room for his own collection of books. All Saints' Church is unique for its 13th-c triangular tower. 1m W, the fine chapter house and other remains of *Beeleigh Abbey* are incorporated in a handsome private house, sometimes open to the public.

Margaretting 4F4
The church has a timber porch, and its tower is built on ten vast wooden posts. There is a 15th-c Jesse window, the tree winding its way round medallion portraits to reach the Madonna and Child.

Newport 4G5

One of Essex's most attractive villages, with a number of fine timbered buildings. Crown House, with excellent pargeting, and Monk's Barn, with brick-nogging and carvings, are especially noteworthy. The church has a 13th-c chest in use as an altar, its lid painted as the reredos. 2m S, *Mole Hall Wildlife Park* at *Widdington* has a large and varied collection of birds and animals.

Ongar 4F5

Only a 50ft mound remains of the castle at *Chipping Ongar*. The Norman church has a good E window and *art nouveau* angels in its aisle roof. David Livingstone trained as a missionary in 1838–9, in the congregational church. *High Ongar*'s church has a fine Norman doorway.

Saffron Walden* 4G5

A beautiful and ancient town as seen by the extensive earthworks to W and S, and the discovery of a large Saxon burial ground, and still of much charm. Of the many pargeted houses, the former Sun Inn (NT) displays perhaps the best example of this type of plasterwork in Essex (*see* page 123). Little remains of the 12th-c castle, but the museum on Castle Hill is of great interest; and near by is the so-called Maze, a series of curious circular excavations of unknown origin. The old Grammar School was the headquarters in 1941–5 of the 65th Fighter Wing of the U.S.A.A.F. The Victorian Corn Exchange has successfully become a library and Arts Centre. The church, which is spacious and well-proportioned, is mainly 15th-c though much restored, and with a spire added 1831.

St Osyth 4F3

A pleasant old village where Osyth, Queen of the Saxons, was murdered by the Danes *c*.870. An Augustinian priory

Waltham Abbey: much was destroyed in the Reformation but the fine Norman nave survives

was built here in the 12th c, on the site of an earlier nunnery established by St Osyth, daughter of E. Anglia's first christian king, in the 7th c. The remains are incorporated in the present beautiful house. The gardens and the richly patterned flint gatehouse, with twin towers and posterns, are open in summer. Another tower gives fine views of the neighbouring creeks and marshland, with Martello towers, but also many acres of caravans. There is a good boating-lake on the creek. ½m SE, St Clair's is one of the best surviving 14th-c aisled hall houses.

Southend-on-Sea 4E4

With adjoining *Leigh-on-Sea*, *Prittlewell* and *Westcliff*, which it has swallowed, Southend now stretches 7m along the Thames estuary. It is still a popular seaside resort, providing every kind of entertainment and sports facility. The illuminations are especially famous. Belfairs Park has a nature reserve. There are three museums of local and social history, as well as one of historic aircraft; and many parks and gardens, including the Cliff Gardens and Shrubbery. Appropriately, Southend Airport is increasingly important for cross-Channel services.

Steeple Bumpstead 4G4

Moyns Park is a fine example of an Elizabethan moated house, and the village has a half-timbered guildhall of 1592. The church has several very fine monuments.

Thaxted 4G5

The stone church of this small and pretty town is very fine indeed, and has been restored well: airy and light interior. The tall spire is echoed by John Webb's Windmill (1805) now a museum. The town has Tudor and Georgian houses, in one of which Gustav Holst was living while composing his 'Planets' suite. The most remarkable building is the 15th-c Guildhall, on wooden pillars, whose open ground floor was once a market hall. 2m SW, *Horham Hall*, a fine Tudor house, visited by Elizabeth I in 1571 and 1578, may now be visited in summer.

Tilbury Fort 4E4

Charles II commissioned this defensive fort (AM), which took 13 years to build. Entry is across two restored bridges.

Waltham Abbey 4F5

The nave of the great abbey's church remains in use. The body of King Harold was buried here after the battle of Hastings and a slab of Purbeck marble is said to be from his vanished tomb. E end of the church was rebuilt in the 19th c, with work by William Burges, Poynter and Burne-Jones. Hayes Hill Farm is a working farm, with guided tours, and demonstrations at summer weekends.

Walton-on-the-Naze *see* Frinton-on-Sea

Wimbish 4G5

The restored 12th-c church has glass and a screen of the 14th c, and a curious brass, dated 1347. Tiptofts, a moated farmhouse, dating from 1300, has a unique aisled hall.

Witham 4F4

This ancient town greatly expanded in the 1970s, and a bypass allows its Georgian character once more to be appreciated: there are three old coaching inns and some good houses. The fine 13th–15th-c church has become a youth centre. 2m NW, *Faulkbourne Hall* is a splendid Tudor house, with much of its brickwork still intact. *Tiptree*, 4m E, is noted for its jam industry.

HERTFORDSHIRE

AN INTRODUCTION BY
MICHAEL ROBBINS

Hertfordshire, which used to go with Middlesex as London's northern Home Counties, remains as a kind of buffer between London and the eastern Midlands: a part of the great chalk basin of the lower Thames valley, exposed on the Chiltern ridge running from Tring through Hitchin to Royston, overlaid with London clay in the south and east. Seventy years ago, the words 'Home Counties' conveyed a picture of undulating countryside, leafy lanes, cheerful cottages, and well-kept big houses, their own local that is, agricultural – activities sustained by the spending of money made in the metropolis. Today they are more often thought of as mere obstacles which tiresomely separate the city dweller from countrysides farther away, where ancient peace and the like are not disturbed by suburban nastiness. They get dismissed with a sneer-word, 'subtopia' – a word as barbarous as the evil it was devised to describe: the mess of brick, concrete, wires, and gaudy lights that creeps like an eczema outwards from the great cities along the highways and into the green lanes and little towns that many people choose to regard as the *real* England. Hertfordshire is afflicted with this disease along the great traffic routes; but it does retain much natural and much manmade beauty, which is there to be sought out.

The traffic routes are dictated by the gaps of the Chiltern escarpment near Tring, Luton, and Hitchin, all used by railway as well as road (at Tring by the Grand Union Canal as well). South of this ridge is broken country, wooded with a pleasing variety of scene and the occasional deeper cuts made by river valleys which have caused railways to throw up viaducts – the noble work at Welwyn is all to cross the trifling Mimram stream. Nearer to London is the clay plain, where the Colne flows sluggishly southwest of St Albans and the Lea winds out past Hertford and Ware. Here are Hertfordshire's finest monuments – the abbey of St Albans, the country houses of Hatfield, Gorhambury, Moor Park, Knebworth, Brocket.

Over 960,000 people lived in Hertfordshire at the 1971 census; 70 years before, there had been just over 250,000. In the decade 1951–61 the increase was $36\frac{1}{2}$

per cent – more than any other county. This has meant very rapid change: development, migration and settlement at top speed. The garden cities at Letchworth (1903) and Welwyn (1920) made inroads into Hertfordshire acres which were curtain raisers to the New Towns of the 1950s that dumped three virtually new communities of 60,000 people each at Hemel Hempstead, Stevenage, and Hatfield/Welwyn Garden City.

So Hertfordshire, the smallest but two of the remaining historic counties, is the scene for a prime example of 20th-century England's series of attempts to accommodate its inhabitants in decent homes, with access to country scenes and pursuits. Enough remains from earlier ages to show a continuity of

St Albans Abbey, dedicated to Alban, a Roman soldier who was executed on the site, became a cathedral in 1877

development that, though here and there precarious, has never been quite disrupted. These New Towns, which have been called 'bland' by progressive designers (who would presumably prefer brutality), respect their old centres; enough small houses of the 18th century remain to make walking in the older parts of St Albans, Hitchin, Hatfield, Hertford, and Ware comparatively pleasurable; there are good brick-built houses of the 16th and 17th centuries and scores of moated manors or farms. Perpendicular churches abound, many with a thin spire, the 'Hertfordshire spike'; the abbey of St Albans is noteworthy for its historical development, even if its visual qualities do not make it outstanding among English cathedrals; Verulamium's Roman site has largely uncovered the only *municipium* of Roman Britain: there were Iron Age camps at Wheathampstead, Verulamium, and Welwyn. Hertfordshire is as good a county as any for the traveller (or the resident) who will peel away the successive layers of time in his imagination so as to perceive the historic process from the evidence before his eyes.

GAZETTEER

Aldbury   4F7
Picturesque village below steep escarpment. Manor house, farm, the green with stocks (AM) are gathered by the pond. Novelist Mrs Humphry Ward (1892–1920) lived at Stocks and is buried in the churchyard.

Ashridge Park   4F7
Originally a monastery for 20 Bonhommes from Normandy, it was later made into a home for the children of Henry VIII. Elizabeth was arrested here on the order of her sister Mary I. In the following century, the place was allowed to decay, but in 1808 the 7th Earl of Bridgewater commissioned Wyatt to rebuild. It is now Ashridge Management College. The gardens are open weekends April–Oct. The common and woodland of the Ashridge estate (NT), which extends N to **Ivinghoe Beacon** (Bucks), is a popular beauty spot. The Park was landscaped by Capability Brown, the gardens by Humphry Repton. A monument was erected in 1832 to the memory of the 3rd Duke of Bridgewater 'father of inland navigation'. There are 172 steps to the top but it is worth the climb for it commands a good view.

Ayot St Lawrence   4F6
Shaw's Corner (NT), the home of George Bernard Shaw (1856–1950), is kept by the NT exactly as it was in his lifetime. Open Feb.–Nov.

Baldock   4G6
The 17th-c almshouses in the main street have been endowed with funds to maintain them 'to the worldes end'. The church has a 15th-c rood-screen extending in three parts across the nave and aisles, and a typical 'Hertfordshire spike'. John Smith, who is buried here, became Rector after three years deciphering the shorthand of Samuel Pepys's diary, which had lain in Magdalene College, **Cambridge**, for nearly a century. Important excavations of a large early Roman settlement.

Berkhamsted   4F7
Earthworks and a little masonry are all that remain of the 11th-c castle presented by William the Conqueror to his brother. Here stayed Thomas à Becket, Piers Gaveston, Chaucer and three of Henry VIII's wives. King John of France was also imprisoned here. The castle (AM) is open daily. The 17th-c grammar school, N of the churchyard and greatly enlarged, is famous. Novelist Graham Greene was a pupil here. William Cowper (1731–1800), poet and hymn-writer, was born in the old rectory, which has been superseded by a more modern one.

Bishop's Stortford   4F5
A mound in the public gardens is all that is left of the 11th-c castle of Bishop Maurice of London, who was entrusted by William the Conqueror with the security of a ford over the Stort. The church has medieval woodwork. Cecil Rhodes (1853–1902) was born in the old vicarage in South Street. He is commemorated by the Rhodes Centre and Commonwealth Museum.

Chorleywood   4E7
Developed into a pleasant residential area around an attractive large common. William Penn (founder of Pennsylvania) and his wife married at King John's Farm 1672 (*see* **Rickmansworth** and **Jordans** (Bucks).

Elstree   4E6
The first British film studios were built here in 1913 at a time when a clear atmosphere for outdoor photography had to be found near London.

Gorhambury   4F6
2¾m NW of **St Albans**. A fine avenue leads from near St Michael's Church in St Albans to the 18th-c house of the present Lord Verulam; adjoining this we find the remains of the Elizabethan house of his ancestor, Francis Bacon. Open May–Sept. He is buried in the chancel of St Michael's. A statue shows him in a characteristic pose: *sic sedebat* – thus he used to sit.

Haileybury College   4F6
2½m SE of **Hertford** is the famous public school founded in 1862. It occupies buildings originally designed for candidates studying to enter the East India Company. In 1942 Haileybury was amalgamated with the Imperial Service College. Earl Attlee (1883–1967) was a pupil there.

Harpenden   4F6
The flint tower of the church dates from the 15th c. When Sir John Lawes inherited Rothamsted Manor in the early 19th c, he devoted all his resources to agricultural research. His work continues as Rothamsted Experimental Station which faces the common.

Hatfield House★   4F6
The Palace of Hatfield was originally the home of the Bishops of Ely, built of beautiful brick at a time in the 15th c

Berkhamsted: the Grand Union Canal runs parallel to the High Street

Hatfield House: seat of the Cecils. Its clock tower rises above the Great Hall which extends over two floors

when stone was unfashionable. Here the children of Henry VIII spent much of their time. The house was given to his sister Elizabeth by Edward VI. Soon after the Queen's death, Robert Cecil accepted it in exchange for his own manor, Theobalds (*see* **Waltham Cross**), which James I coveted, and immediately began to build the great Jacobean house which he did not live to occupy. One of the most splendid in the country, built in the shape of an E, it still belongs to the head of the family, the Marquess of Salisbury. The park and the gardens are as memorable as the house and palace with their state rooms, priceless collections, paintings and relics of Elizabeth I. Open April–Oct.

Hemel Hempstead   4F7
At confluence of rivers Gade and Bulbourne. Henry VIII granted it the dignity of a Bailiwick. Careful planning has ensured it is one of the best of the New Towns, with striking modern architecture, a fine water garden, yet retaining the character of its older quarters. *Piccotts End*, ¾m N, has remarkable 15th-c murals in a house believed to have been a Pilgrims' hospice. Open March–Nov.

Hertford   4F6
The county town stands at the point where two smaller rivers meet the Lea. The town centre has a Victorian Corn Exchange. The castle (AM) dates from 905, and was visited by almost every English Monarch from William I to James I.

A few walls and a rebuilt gatehouse remain. The grounds are used as a public park. On the road to **Ware** are the interesting buildings of Christ's Hospital School with a 17th-c gateway, now exclusively a girls' school.

Hitchin   4G6
The market town dates back to Belgic times and was the site of a monastery in the time of Offa. The museum, containing displays of local history collections, natural history and tropical fish, costume and Victoriana and the Regimental Museum of the Hertfordshire Yeomanry, and the art gallery in Paynes Park are of interest (open all year). The Tues. and Sat. markets are outstanding attractions.

Knebworth   4F6
Bulwer Lytton, the 1st Baron (1803–73), wrote many of his novels in the 16th-c family home, which was partly demolished and rebuilt into its present fantastic design. The house contains relics of this politician-novelist, as well as admirable paintings and furniture. House and adjoining country park with bird garden, garden centre and children's adventure playground are open April–Oct. The church of SS Mary and Thomas in the park was built in the 12th c and has many family memorials in the 18th-c Lytton Chapel.

Lemsford   4F6
The 18th-c Brocket Hall was the home of Lord Melbourne and his wife, Lady Caroline Lamb. He engaged Richard Wood to landscape the gardens. The Lea was widened to form a lake and bridged in stone by James Paine.

Letchworth 4G6

The first English Garden City. It was developed by Ebenezer Howard in 1903 as a result of a campaign for better housing conditions that he conducted in his own paper, *Tomorrow*. His terms of reference, the allotting of zones for industrial, civic and residential usage, have been followed in later New Towns. The Letchworth Garden City Museum contains the original offices of the architects of the Garden City and displays explaining the concept and development of the city.

Little Gaddesden Manor 4F7

16th-c with stone mullioned windows, Elizabethan fire-places and wall paintings. Limited opening in summer.

Moor Park 4E6

This historic house belonged to Cardinal Wolsey but underwent a transformation in the 18th c, when it was rebuilt in the Palladian style by Giacomo Leoni, with a grand portico and splendid ceilings and doorways. It is now a golf club. Open to the public on Mon.

Rickmansworth 4E7

Edging the Chilterns at meeting of rivers Colne, Chess and Gade, the town's municipal offices occupy Basing House, former residence of William Penn, founder of Pennsylvania, and his wife Guliclma Springett (*see* **Chorleywood** and **Jordans**). Numerous lakes, the *Grand Union Canal* and an Aquadrome provide for water sports and pleasant walks.

St Albans* 4F6

The walls of the Roman city of Verulamium enclosed an area of 200 acres, much of which has been excavated. The Saxons changed its name to St Albans in honour of the first English martyr, who was beaten and beheaded in the 3rd c for succouring the Christian priest who converted him. A great Benedictine abbey was founded in 793 and rebuilt after the Norman Conquest. Cardinal Wolsey was its 38th abbot.

The nave of the cathedral is 275½ft long, a record for a medieval building. Flint, brick and stone taken from the old Roman city are still visible in its walls. Much of the cathedral has been restored, notably by Lord Grimthorpe, who in the 19th c spent £140,000 of his private fortune on the work. The magnificent stone screen, dating from the 15th c, was shattered during the Reformation, but its stone fragments have been patiently fitted together again. The same is true of the saint's shrine, reconstructed from 2,000 pieces. Note especially the 13th-c iron grille on the S side of the saint's chapel, and the vaulting of the presbytery. (*See also* page 129.)

The museum is comprehensive. It houses beautiful sections of mosaic, coins found on site, pottery and many other articles that demonstrate the continuous life of the city. A visit is recommended as a preliminary to the Roman remains, which include part of the Roman wall and its bastions, the foundations of the London Gate, a mosaic pavement, and the hypocaust that stored hot air for private baths. The theatre is impressive.

Salisbury Hall 4F6

5m S of **St Albans**. Fine moated 17th-c mansion with many historical associations. Charles II remodelled it in 1668 for Nell Gwynn and Sir Winston Churchill spent part of his childhood there. Prototype of the de Havilland Mosquito is on view. Limited opening Easter–Sept.

Stevenage 4G6

Of ancient origin it is, today, clearly a 20th-c New Town with sculpture by Henry Moore, and a church with a bell-tower resembling a rocket. Stevenage Museum contains, among others, exhibits on the natural history of the town and its surrounding villages.

Tring 4F7

The parish records go back to 1566 and contain the names of George Washington's ancestors. In Tring Park, Lord Rothschild's Zoological Museum, bequeathed to the **British Museum**, London, in 1938, shows thousands of rare birds, fish, reptiles and insects. An ornithological research centre adjoins the museum. N of the town the *Grand Union Canal* reservoirs are excellent for bird-watching and coarse fishing – four reservoirs, in part of a national nature reserve. Tring Church is 13th–14th-c.

Waltham Cross 4F5

Although a traffic-congested town, the Eleanor Cross, one of three remaining crosses, erected by Edward I in 1294 in memory of his wife on her funeral journey to **Westminster Abbey**, has survived but Waltham House where the novelist A. Trollope lived has not. At the entrance to *Theobalds Park*, site of Robert Cecil's house (*see* **Hatfield**), stands Wren's Temple Bar. Originally in Fleet Street, London (1672), it was moved here in 1878.

Ware 4F5

The turning point of John Gilpin in Cowper's poem. The church of St Mary has a magnificent 14th-c font with beautiful sculptured figures of the saints. The Great Bed of Ware – mentioned in the plays of Shakespeare, Ben Jonson and Farquhar – came from Ware Park, and is now in the **Victoria and Albert Museum**, London.

Welwyn Garden City 4F6

The second great development (1920) by Ebenezer Howard, who promoted the company that chose **Letchworth** as a pilot plan. Out of his pioneering grew the Town and Country Planning Acts. A charming 16th-c brick house, *Queen Hoo Hall*, near *Tewin*, 3½m NE, has contemporary murals.

Wheathampstead 4F6

Birthplace of John of Wheathampstead, the 15th-c abbot who founded the library of the Abbey of **St Albans**. Among noteworthy monuments in the church are brasses of his parents, Hugh and Margaret Bostock and a statue of A. G. B. Cherry-Garrard (1886–1959), the arctic explorer. This village was greatly loved by Charles Lamb.

BUCKINGHAMSHIRE

AN INTRODUCTION BY
FRANK MORLEY

Topographically, Buckinghamshire is like a lettuce that has bolted. There is the compact, leafy region of South Bucks, rising gradually to the Chiltern Hills; towards the north the Chilterns present a steep escarpment, after which the county bolts away across the Vale of Aylesbury to Northamptonshire.

Each half of the county has its own characteristics, but they are rarely spectacular. Geological forces in this region were gentle. The traverse escarpment of the Chilterns as a physical feature is not so startling as the Cotswold Edge. The chalk barrier is rather to be compared with the downs of Berkshire or Sussex, but with a difference – other downs tend to be bald, but the Chilterns exhibit a splendid growth of beechwoods which becomes thin only as the hills draw northeast towards Dunstable. So thick are the beechwoods (and lovely at any time of year) that even when crossing the escarpment there are not apt to be wide views; although here and there (as at Coombe Hill) one may see the flat vale to the north, spread out like the chess-board country of *Alice Through the Looking Glass*.

North of the Chilterns, Buckinghamshire is a land of many little rivers, a low-lying clay plain riddled with small streams and marshes; in the main a sparsely populated agricultural land. South of the Chilterns the plateau, sloping down towards London, alters from chalk to clay with flints; what characterizes South Bucks is thus light, hungry soil scored by dry valleys, with a comparative absence of rivers. There are only five streams to be counted from west to east: Hamble, Wye, Misbourne, Chess and Colne. All these streams flow southwards to join the Thames, which forms, from Henley Reach in the west to Dorney Reach in the east, a southern boundary of the county.

The few river courses of South Bucks thus run from north to south, and they have scored deeply into the dry plateau, leaving sharp ridges between, so that in early days east–west traffic must have been difficult. Along the northern edge of the Chilterns there was the east–west Icknield Way, and to the south of the area there might be transport on the Thames, but the main routes were, and are, up and down the few river valleys. Although much of the Icknield Way has been motorized, the short sections which remain as green tracks, often bordered by travellers' joy and the wayfaring tree, form part of the excellent network of public footpaths and bridleways for which the Chiltern region is renowned. Since 1973, some have been linked, between Ivinghoe and the Thames at Goring, to form a 44-mile stretch of the Ridgeway long-distance path.

The Past

The archeological features of Buckinghamshire contain nothing so breathtaking as some of the monuments of the West Country; there is no Avebury, Stonehenge or Maiden Castle. A specialist may see a mound; to the layman, even when it is pointed out, it is only a mound. Nevertheless, the flints which are a curse to the gardener in South Bucks were to the prehistoric weapon-maker as valuable as diamonds. In the British Museum in London are treasures from South Bucks representative of all the early periods. In addition to prehistoric tools and pottery, urns (and a pigmy cup), and weapons, there are the exquisite blue-and-white marbled 1st-century glass bowl and other objects from the Radnage Roman burial. Here, too, are the princely trappings from the famous grave of an Anglo-Saxon chieftain at Taplow. There is no relic of a Roman city, such as Silchester near Reading, but evidence of Roman habitation is provided by the villas excavated at Latimer, Hambleden and High Wycombe. Thought to be a prehistoric boundary, Grim's Ditch runs across the Chilterns, being best seen near Great Hampden. While on the north-facing escarpment at both Whiteleaf and Bledlow there is a large white cross of unknown origin cut into the chalk.

The wealth of Buckinghamshire may not reside in spectacular topography or important ancient remains, but there is no county that can excel it for small beauties. Forget the past that is very far away, forget the long distances, and be prepared to look for little things; then you will find much in small compass to reward the sight and stir the memory. The Thames – Buckinghamshire cannot claim much of it, but what

Burnham Beeches, Buckinghamshire's glory. The county name may derive from 'buccan' meaning beech

it claims is good: Marlow and Medmenham and the pleasant lazy meadows of Hambleden are on the Buckinghamshire bank, and no one would dispute the beauty of the wooded Cliveden reach.

At Cliveden one remembers George Villiers, the powerful Duke of Buckingham, in the time of Charles II, who started the building of the original house; in more recent times the Astors and the 'Cliveden Set'. Medmenham, where the Hellfire Club met in the Abbey, is a reminder of Sir Francis Dashwood, the eccentric 18th-century landowner who built the church surmounted by its conspicuous golden ball, and the curious Mausoleum, on West Wycombe Hill. But it is away from the riverside that the real heart of Buckinghamshire is to be discovered. More characteristic of the county was the life represented by such small villages as Turville and Little Missenden, rural retreats little changed by the passage of time.

It is impossible in a short space to treat adequately the variety of villages, churches and houses to be seen in North Bucks, but it is hoped the Gazetteer which follows will draw you through the Chilterns and north beyond Aylesbury to Buckingham, to churches such as Stewkley and Wing, to villages such as Dinton and Olney (Cowper's Olney).

Famous People

Mention of Cowper reminds me not to neglect all of the notables who have had particular associations with the county. Close as it is to industrial Slough (now within the county of Berkshire) the church at Stoke Poges strives to retain the atmosphere in which Gray composed the *Elegy*. At Chalfont St Giles Milton's Cottage attracts visitors, and it was from near-by Beaconsfield that we first heard of *The Innocence of Father Brown*, for here it was that G. K. Chesterton lived for the latter part of his life. His contemporary, the typographer and artist Eric Gill, lived and worked at Piggotts, near Speen. It was at Marlow, at Albion House in West Street, that the Shelleys dwelt briefly: Mary working away at her story *Frankenstein*, Shelley at *The Revolt of Islam*. He and Thomas Love Peacock explored much of the surrounding countryside on foot; still the best way to see it today. Back in Beaconsfield a prominent obelisk in the churchyard remembers Waller, poet and politician, while a simple plaque within the church commemorates Edmund Burke.

Undoubtedly one of the great houses of the county is, to use Pope's phrase, 'the paradise of Stowe', now a public school; rococo state rooms distinguish the home of the Verneys at Claydon, while Disraeli's Hughenden Manor is known for its Victorian embellishments. It was in the Victorian era that the Rothschilds invaded Buckinghamshire, building lavish mansions as at Waddesdon and Ascott.

Character

The people of South Bucks have a reputation for independence. Defiance of authority would seem to have been typical from the beginning. As an 'islanded' region it was a natural underground for rebels. All of Buckinghamshire was of course much fought over in the Civil Wars. John Hampden (a statue of him stands at Aylesbury) recorded his refusal to pay King Charles' ship-money levy at Great Kimble church. In later religious struggles Lollards and Quakers were among the independent spirits who risked their lives for the sake of their beliefs. William Penn (buried not in the State of Pennsylvania but at the small Friends' Meeting House at Jordans) must have had trouble assisting some of his 'scrupulous' followers in this county of churches. What is now sometimes called the Penn country was also gypsy country: broom handles and wood for the Windsor chairs made at High Wycombe were traditionally scrounged by the 'diddicoys'. But the 'bodger's' pole-lathe is no longer heard in the beechwoods.

No longer does the lacemaker sit at her cottage door, do women earn a pittance from straw-plaiting, or Aylesbury breed its once famous ducks. Modern Buckinghamshire has, nevertheless, retained its rural character. Apart from the popular beauty spots such as Coombe Hill, Ivinghoe Beacon, Marlow and Brill, there are quiet unspoiled villages, The Lee, Fingest, Chenies, Latimer and Bradenham to name but a few. The county continues, despite its fast growing population, to defend itself stubbornly against encroachment on its green belt. The contemporary venture of the New City of Milton Keynes, although developing fast, is still in its infancy.

Seek out the beechwoods, Buckinghamshire's supreme glory, and find a tranquil refuge from the noise and stress of modern life. See farmland (well farmed too) and a countryside where, if they are looked for at the right time, there are violets, primroses, bluebells, blackthorn hedges, and wild cherry; a county not of great dimension but, when you know your way around, a county of great beauty.

GAZETTEER

Amersham   4E7
A charming old town in the Misbourne valley with a modern suburb on the hills N. The spacious main street is bordered by a lovely sequence of 17th- and 18th-c buildings with a town hall on arches and attractive small almshouses. A monument on the hill commemorates Lollards and other martyrs burned at the stake during the Marian persecutions. The museum is open at set times.

Aylesbury   4F7
The county town was expanded in the 1960s and forfeited many of its older buildings. The medieval core is best seen near the church which has a beautiful 12th-c archetypal font, four misericords in the choir stalls and a rare 15th-c vestment press. The King's Head (NT) dates from the 15th c and has original mullioned windows and armorial glass. The County Museum has archeological and local collections.

Beaconsfield   4E7
Here the London–**Oxford** Road (A40) becomes a fine wide street between mellow Georgian red-brick buildings. The 17th-c church has a great pinnacled tower and memorials to Edmund Burke and Edmund Waller the poet. The half-timbered rectory dates from 1543. G. K. Chesterton lived at Overroads, Grove Road, in 1909–35. Bekonscot Model Village is near by. Open all year.

Bradenham   4E7
NT village among the beech-clad hills NW of **High Wycombe**. The manor house (not open to the public) was the home of Isaac Disraeli, and here his son Benjamin (*see* **Hughenden Manor**) spent his youth. The church has the oldest door (1100) in the county, and two bells made by Michael de Wymbis in 1300 which are among the oldest in England.

Brill   4F8
Noted for its hill-top post-mill dating from the 17th c. At one time the village had pretensions to being a spa; there are several good 15th–17th-c buildings. 2m W is the conspicuous 14th-c Boarstall Tower (NT), the remnant gatehouse of a fortified and moated house long in possession of the Aubrey family. The 18th-c Boarstall Duck Decoy (NT) is in working order and set amid 13 acres of natural woodland. Open April–Aug.

Buckingham   4G8
The swan atop the clock tower of the town hall is the county emblem and a reminder that Buckingham was the county town until superseded by **Aylesbury**. In the wide market place is a squat castle-shaped erection that was at one time used as a jail. Close by is a chantry (NT) built by the Normans, rebuilt and restored; in Henry VI's reign it became the Royal Latin School. A splendid beech avenue leads from the town to **Stowe**.

Burnham Beeches   4E7
3 miles E of **Maidenhead** (Berks), it is famed for its ancient beeches. A large area of beautiful woodland and heath bought for the public by the City of London Corporation in

1879. To this was added the 215 acres of Dorney Wood, given to the NT during World War II, with house and contents, by Lord Courtauld-Thomson as a residence for a Secretary of State or Minister of the Crown. (*See* page 135).

Chalfont St Giles 4E7
Beyond the pond is the cottage to which Milton fled in 1665 to escape the plague ravaging London. Here he finished *Paradise Lost*, began *Paradise Regained*. There is a small museum. The cottage is open Feb.–Oct. The fine 14th-c church has wall paintings and brasses. In Newland Park the *Chiltern Open Air Museum* reflects 500 years of life in the Chilterns, and is open April–Sept.

Chenies 4E7
Stylish 19th-c Bedford estate cottages around the green overlook the Chess valley. In the flint church the Bedford Chapel has a magnificent collection of funeral monuments. The adjoining manor house, early home of the Russell family, was visited by Henry VIII and Elizabeth I. Of note are the elaborately patterned Tudor chimneys, the ancient well and the Physic Garden. Open April–Oct.

Chequers 4F7
The owner of the original 13th-c house was Henry de Scaccario (i.e. of the Exchequer), hence the name. The present Tudor building and the surrounding estate were presented to the nation during World War I by Lord Lee of Fareham as a country residence for successive Prime Ministers.

Claydon House: it consists of the surviving wing of a larger mansion. An elaborate alcove in the Chinese Room

Chicheley 4G7
Chicheley Hall, an early Georgian house with fine panelling, naval pictures and mementoes of Admiral Lord Beatty. Open Easter–Sept.

Claydon House★ 4F8
1½m E of *Steeple Claydon*. A mid-18th-c house, home of the Verneys, containing series of fine rococo state rooms. Museum with mementoes of Florence Nightingale (NT). Open April–Oct.

Cliveden★ 4E7
Beautifully wooded estate on the cliffs looking across the Thames to **Maidenhead**. With the mansion, home of Lady Nancy Astor the first woman MP, it was presented to the NT in 1942 by Lord Astor. The grounds are open all year, but only part of the house (which is let to tenants) can be visited in April–Oct.

Denham 4F8
An unspoiled old-fashioned village, complete with pond, which has figured in many films made by the huge Denham studios. Denham Place is a 17th-c house with notable original friezes and ceilings.

Dinton 4F8
The ruin beside the **Aylesbury** road is mock-ancient, having been built to display the splendid ammonites inset among the flints. Dinton, a pleasant village among farms, has stocks and a whipping-post on its green and a good Tudor manor house. Excellent Norman door to church. *Nether Winchendon House* is 2m W. A Tudor manor house with late 18th-c additions. Limited opening April–Oct.

Fawley   4E8
3m N of **Henley-on-Thames** (Oxon). Beautifully set among beech- and yew-clad hills, with good 17th-c farms and cottages and a church with carving by Grinling Gibbons. Fawley Court (now a school) 2m S, was built in 1684 in Wren style, and has 18th-c additions. Open at set times.

Fingest*   4E8
Tiny village of Saxon origin in a hollow of the Chilterns. It is dominated by the great Norman tower of the church. Equally unusual is the twin saddle-back roof probably added in the 17th c.

Great Missenden *see* **Missenden**

Haddenham   4F8
Although largely surrounded by new estates the attractive village with several ponds, a large green, and a church with curious carvings and some 15th-c glass, has been preserved.

Hambleden   4E8
About 1m N of the lovely combination of locks and weirs on the Thames between **Marlow** and **Henley-on-Thames** (Oxon). A typical Buckinghamshire village among the hills, with cottages and the 17th-c manor house in brick and flint. (*See* pages 34–5.) A curiosity in the church is a panel said to have been part of Cardinal Wolsey's bed. A Roman villa was excavated in 1912 and relics are on exhibition in **Aylesbury** Museum. At *Mill End* near by is a picturesque timbered mill and mill house.

Hampden   4F7
John Hampden, who in 1636 refused to pay the tax known as Ship Money, is buried in the church at *Great Hampden* which adjoins the house in which he lived. Across the valley is *Little Hampden*, with a tiny church with a half-timbered porch, a Saxon altar and faded wall paintings.

Hanslope   4G8
The tower and spire are the tallest in the county. They are seen from afar, but only on closer approach does one become aware of the church attached.

High Wycombe   4E7
One of the largest towns in the county. Bypassed by the M40 it is still not without traffic problems. In proportion to its width this must be one of the longest towns in Britain, the A40 and the River Wye running side by side through the valley for over 2m. Note the octagonal market hall with its lantern, and the excellent Guildhall raised on arches and surmounted by a good cupola. Furniture-making founded on the local beechwoods still flourishes here, but Wycombe today is the home of many and various industries. Wycombe Chair Museum, in Priory Avenue illustrates the history of the local craft. *See also* **Hughenden Manor**.

Hughenden Manor*   4E7
1½m N of **High Wycombe**, the home of Benjamin Disraeli, who died here in 1881. Open April–Oct. (see also **Bradenham**). The house (NT) contains much of his furniture, books, etc. His insignia as Knight of the Garter was brought from **Windsor** (Berks) and placed over the chancel arch in Hughenden Church, and his grave is in the churchyard.

Ivinghoe   4F7
The village from which Scott took the title for his novel *Ivanhoe*. The church has an interesting roof and good carving on the pillars in the nave. The view from the Beacon

(750ft) above the village includes a large NT acreage of the Chiltern Hills, the historic landmark of the ancient *Pitstone Windmill* (NT), and the lion carved in the chalk hill to the E marking the site of *Whipsnade Zoo* (open all year). The Beacon marks one end of the **Ridgeway** path (*see* in Berks).

Jordans*   4E7
The simple red-brick Quaker Meeting House (1688) among the beechwoods had early associations with William Penn, who returned after founding Pennsylvania and was buried here beside members of his family. Open Wed.–Sun. (*See also* **Chorleywood** and **Rickmansworth**, Herts.) The Mayflower Barn, at Old Jordan's Farm, is believed to incorporate beams from the *Mayflower* in which the Pilgrim Fathers sailed to America in 1620. Open daily.

Latimer   4E7
It is a picturesque hamlet in the best part of the Chess Valley with a pretty waterfall by a bridge. Paths round the pump on the tiny village green are paved with local Roman tiles.

Long Crendon   4F8
A village of notable buildings, large and small. The 14th-c Courthouse now belongs to the NT. The manor house, dating from the 15th c, has a fine timbered hall.

Ludgershall   4F8
Note amusing carvings on the pier capitals in the church, the fine roof and the tomb of Anne Englische and her daughter and a child – all in Tudor costume. *Wotton House* is 2m SE. Built 1704 for Sir Richard Grenville, it was partially rebuilt by Soane after a fire in 1820. Gardens landscaped by Bridgeman. Open June–Sept.

Marlow   4E7
The wide, pleasant High Street leads to Tierney Clark's graceful suspension bridge over the Thames, beside the Compleat Angler Hotel, which provides a good view of the tumbling weir downstream and of **Bisham Abbey** upstream on the Berkshire bank. On the N side of West Street is the house in which P. B. Shelley lived. In the church is a monument to Sir Miles Hobart (1682) who courageously locked the King's Messengers out of the House of Commons and was subsequently killed in a carriage accident (depicted on the monument). The many distinguished 17th- and 18th-c buildings include the NT's Marlow Place, and Remnantz where the Royal Military College started in 1799.

Medmenham   4E7
Thames-side village among trees below steep chalk hills. The church has a chancel 'arch' formed of kingpost tie-beams with curved braces. The village became notorious in the 18th c for the curious activities of the Hellfire Club which held its meetings in the ruined Abbey here (*see also* **West Wycombe**). On the escarpment to the N is Lodge Farm (NT), a 17th-c house of flint with red-brick dressings.

Mentmore Towers   4F7
SE of **Wing**, a magnificent mansion designed by Sir Joseph Paxton for Baron Meyer de Rothschild. Currently the seat of The World Government of the Age of Enlightenment – Great Britain. Limited opening April–Oct.

Milton Keynes New Town   4G7
Planned with foresight, its design includes tree-lined walks, green open spaces and plant displays. Gathered under one roof is the largest shopping centre in Europe with an extensive and comprehensive range of services.

Stowe: the grounds were laid out by Capability Brown and Kent. An ornamental Palladian bridge spans a lake

Missenden   4E7/F7
Great Missenden, in the Misbourne valley, has a narrow main street lined with small 16th-, 17th- and 18th-c buildings. The 19th-c neo-Gothic Abbey, on the site of a 12th-c abbey founded for the Black Canons, is an adult college. *Little Missenden★*, 1½m SE, is a lovely unspoiled village watered by the Misbourne. Dating from the 10th c the church has remarkable 13th- and 14th-c murals.

Olney   4G7
The first of the annual Shrove Tuesday pancake races is said to have been run in 1445. The *Olney Hymns* were written here by William Cowper (1731–1800) and John Newton, the former slave-trader who saw the error of his ways and became pastor of Olney. The 18th-c brick house in Market Place, is the Cowper–Newton Museum.

Stewkley   4F7
Village on a hill-crest some 500ft up, with the finest Norman church★ in Buckinghamshire. Note especially the W doorway and the chancel arch with its intricate carving.

Stoke Poges   4E7
The scene which inspired Thomas Gray (1716–71) to write his *Elegy Written in a Country Churchyard* would seem to have changed little since his day, despite the proximity of Slough. The NT now cares for Wyatt's monument to the poet, buried in the churchyard. In the church is the 'Bicycle Window', of a man riding a form of hobby-horse.

Stowe★   4G8
The public school for boys occupies the former seat of the Dukes of Buckingham, whose title became extinct in 1889. It is a magnificent mansion in Vanbrugh's best style, with details by Robert Adam. The exquisite parkland was laid out by William Kent, Capability Brown and others (the house itself is not open to the public). The 13th-c church in the grounds is the only vestige of the village left after it was removed when the park was made in 1713. Grounds open Easter and summer vacations.

Turville   4E8
'Picture-postcard' village in deep valley with brick and timbered cottages grouped about the small Norman church and overlooked by the Cobstone windmill.

Waddesdon★   4F8
The great manor house on the edge of the village was bequeathed to the NT in 1957 by James de Rothschild, together with its magnificent collection of French furniture, paintings, porcelain and books, second only to that in the **Wallace Collection**, London. Open April–Oct.

Wendover   4F7
1½m W of this attractive little town is one of the highest points in the Chilterns, *Coombe Hill* (NT), 852ft above sea level, with wonderful views towards **Aylesbury** and **Thame** (Oxon)and over the woods surrounding **Chequers**.

West Wycombe★   4E7
2m NW of **High Wycombe**. The village, threatened with demolition in 1929, is now owned by the NT. Good 17th- and 18th-c buildings border the main road. On the hill above is the church, crowned by the famous golden ball, and the curious mausoleum, both built in the 18th c by Sir Francis Dashwood of Hellfire Club fame (*see* **Medmenham**). Caves in the hill are open to the public. W is Dashwood's Palladian house *West Wycombe Park* (NT). Exquisite landscaping by Humphry Repton. Open June–Aug.

Wing   4F7
The village church is largely Saxon and contains five monuments to the Dormer family. *Ascott★* (NT), ½m to the E, houses the fine Anthony de Rothschild collection of French and Chippendale furniture, paintings and oriental porcelain. Open April–Sept. *See also* **Mentmore Towers**.

Winslow   4G8
Neat village with thatched cottages and a church with an unusually large porch. The 18th-c George inn in the market square has an elaborate wrought-iron balcony from **Claydon House**. Winslow Hall, with its imposing façade, contains tapestries and baroque wall paintings, and was designed by Wren in 1700. Open July–Sept.

BERKSHIRE

AN INTRODUCTION BY
GEOFFREY BOUMPHREY

The Royal County of Berkshire has lost almost a third of its area to Oxfordshire under the 1974 boundary revisions, but what remains has much of interest.

In the southwest corner Inkpen Beacon and Walbury Camp at almost 1,000 feet are the highest chalk downs in England. Combe Gibbet still stands near by – what a marvellous view must have been his last for many a poor devil, doomed to dangle from the gibbet till he rotted away.

Although the southern borders of the county are composed of poor sands or gravel, capable of growing little but silver birch and bracken, in this part man (rich man especially) has done much to improve upon Nature. Virginia Water was made for the Duke of Cumberland in the middle of the 18th century; and an artificial landscape of great beauty was created round the lake by the planting of carefully considered clumps of beeches, oaks and other trees. A little later George IV, while Prince of Wales, did much to improve Windsor Great Park, and had many thousands of conifers planted on the waste land near Sunninghill and Ascot. From the late 18th century onwards many grand mansions were built in the district, their gardens elaborately landscaped. With the coming of the railways more and more rich people built houses in the 'toe' of Berkshire, so near to London and the land of so little use for anything else, and therefore (at that time) so cheap. Mention the racecourse at Ascot laid out for Queen Anne in 1711, with later golf-courses and country clubs – and the description will serve well enough for the present day. A more recent addition is the creation of the Savill Gardens in Windsor Great Park, which draw keen gardeners like a magnet.

At Aldermaston the Kennet Valley from Reading joins us; with it the Bath road and the main line from Paddington to Taunton. The Bath road: what memories the words conjure up! – of nobility and gentry making their slow way by coach or carriage to the Bath of Beau Nash and Jane Austen – and of highwaymen on Maidenhead Thicket. Nowadays the sprawl of factories and new housing beside it reaches almost to Newbury. To the south of the river, broad stretches of heather and bracken or extensive pinewoods tell of poor, acid soil. But by the side of the stream the water-meadows are lush, and rising from the north bank towards the Downs are clays which, if not ideal farming land, can be fertile enough, though even here tracts of bracken tell of the sand beneath. Northeastwards from Newbury the hills are covered with lovely dingled woods which persist until the land drops steeply down to Pangbourne and Streatley.

The River

The Thames forms the northeast boundary of the county. It is along this stretch between Streatley and Pangbourne that the Chiltern Hills of Oxfordshire most nearly approach their fellow chalk of the Berkshire Downs. The Goring Gap, as it is called, is a most beautiful stretch of river – quiet meadows with poplars and willows by the river, and the woods on the Berkshire side rising almost precipitously 600 feet to the Downs, balanced by their Oxfordshire fellows. But the river valley is almost uninterruptedly lovely all the way down to Windsor, if you except an odd half mile or so past Reading. And so, for the most part, are the villages along it – Sonning, Wargrave, Hurley, Cookham (where the Stanley Spencer Gallery is well worth a visit), Bray, and the rest. Riverside architecture of the turn of the century is in a taste which I, personally, have not acquired; but where the houses may not be thought beautiful, the settings almost always are. It was along these tree-hung reaches that fashionable Victorian and Edwardian society used to take its pleasure at summer weekends, the men in flannel blazers and straw boaters, the ladies in more elaborate creations. Today the river is still busy enough, though the screw-propeller has largely replaced the oar, the paddle and the punt pole.

Building Materials

Berkshire is mainly a county of brick buildings. But to see what the 17th and 18th centuries could do with brick you have only to note the warm and intimate beauty of little towns like Hungerford and Newbury. In the villages, farms and scattered cottages, other local materials are put to fitting and almost always picturesque use: thatch in place of lichen-gilded tiles; chalk, either cob or block, for walls, combined perhaps with a few sarsen stones brought from the Downs where the Ice Age left them stranded; flints, dressed or not, with mellow brick, maybe, round doors and windows; timber-framed buildings, their panels filled in with almost any combination of these materials or with wattle-and-daub. Imagine villages built of such homely materials, set low in the fold of some valley by a willow-hung stream with watercress beds. Add a thatched wall or two – its chalk laced, quite possibly, with the horns of oxen that once tilled the fields around. This is the kind of scene you may come upon in almost any part of Berkshire once you leave the main roads.

Farm and Factory

Much of the county is still grass, farm or woodland, though industry has spread and is spreading. Reading's industries include brewing, insurance, electronics and foodstuffs among other activities. There was a time in the Middle Ages when the Berkshire Downs and the Cotswolds supplied most of the wool on which England's wealth was founded; and the county grew fat on the various processes concerned with turning it into cloth. Today one sees more arable farming than sheep on the Downs. When the gold of the harvest has been erased by the plough, the fields are still no less beautiful, the soil shading in colour from coffee to cream as the chalk lies deeper or less deep. The importance of pig-keeping to the county is proved by the fame of the snub-nosed, black Berkshire breed. Racehorse training is a major industry. All over the Downs you may come across their 'gallops', neatly marked out, and (if you and your car are not in a hurry) very beautiful a string of them can look on their way to or from exercise.

Wild Flowers

On the Downs, too, you may find the rare purple pasque-flower (*anemone pulsatilla*). Another wild flower in which Berkshire claims a priority interest is the tall snowdrop-like Loddon lily, so called because it can be found in early summer beside the River Loddon. By this stream lies Swallowfield, on the Reading–Basingstoke road, where the authoress Mary Mitford is buried. If you would learn what life in the county was like 150 years ago, read *Our Village*. I should be very happy to think that my picture of Berkshire today was half as vivid as hers.

GAZETTEER

Aldermaston 3M6
The proximity of the Atomic Weapons Research Establishment has not yet spoiled this village of peace and quiet in the Kennet valley, with its pleasant brick and tiled cottages and its church with medieval wall paintings. It was here that the William pear was first grown. Near by is Ufton Court, a good Tudor gabled mansion with priests' holes.

Aldworth★ 7L2
Elizabeth I turned aside to view the effigied tombs of the de la Beche family under elaborate crocketed canopies in the church. Note also the magnificent yew in the churchyard.

Ascot 4D7
The most fashionable racecourse in Britain. Royal Ascot Week (June) is famous all over the world.

Avington 3M6
Ignored by the traffic of the A4 this little cedared hamlet, set by a Kennet weir 2m E of **Hungerford** is worth visiting for its unspoiled Norman church.

Basildon Park 7L2
Between **Pangbourne** and *Streatley*, a classical 18th-c house (NT) in a beautiful setting overlooking the Thames valley. Notable for its unusual octagon room, the Anglo-Indian room, and a decorative shell room; fine garden. Open April–Oct.

Bisham Abbey 4E7
Among lawns beside the Thames is the Elizabethan mansion occupied by the Central Council of Physical Recreation. It was built by Sir Philip Hoby, whose family are commemorated by fine monuments in the church. Note steps in the river bank for those attending service by boat.

Bracknell 4D7
One of the New Towns on the A329 between **Wokingham** and **Ascot**, covering the former villages of Bracknell and Easthampstead. Begun in 1952, it is the home of the Meteorological Office, the Royal Air Force Staff College and many international computer and high technology companies.

Bradfield 7L1
The public school, founded in 1850 with an 18th-c manor house as nucleus, is famous for its open-air Greek theatre.

Bray 4E7
Remembered for Simon Alwyn, who would always be vicar 'whatsoever king may reign' rather than give up his living. His pleasant Thames-side village has been much expanded. 1½m W is the beautiful Elizabethan *Ockwells Manor*, with its original window-glass.

Combe 3L6/M6
Of all the odd clauses in a lease, surely the oddest is that of the farm given the responsibility of maintaining in good order the gallows on the hill between *Inkpen* and *Walbury Hill*.

Cookham★ 4E7
The river scenery is not excelled anywhere else on the Thames; the lock gardens are as gay as any. Cookham has

been the home of many artists from Fred Walker to Stanley Spencer (whose Gallery is here – open daily Easter–Oct., and weekends Nov.–Easter). At *Cookham Dean*, 2m W, Kenneth Grahame wrote *The Wind in the Willows*.

East Ilsley   7L2
Famous for training racehorses, strings of which may be seen on the Downs. Before horses Ilsley was deeply involved in sheep – it is said that as many as 80,000 were gathered in one day.

Eton   4E7
The college founded by Henry VI in 1440 is the most famous school in England. Mellow red-brick buildings and a splendid greystone chapel. The 4th of June is Eton's great day, with a procession of boats on the river, followed by fireworks.

Hungerford   7K1
Here the Kennet runs close beside the road. Hungerford treasures a horn alleged to have belonged to John of Gaunt; also some good Georgian buildings. The wide main street full of antique shops runs S from the A4 and the M4 keeps well to the N. A favourite centre for anglers. A picturesque ceremony is held every Hocktide (the first Tuesday after Easter) to elect the Constable in whom the government and manor of Hungerford are vested for the year. In this a bellman and two tutti-men (tithe-men) with decorated poles play a prominent part. Near **Froxfield** (Wilts) to the W is *Littlecote House*.

Hurley   4E7
Here the Thames is divided by several islands and the backwaters are among the prettiest on the river. A picturesque 16th-c timbered inn, remains of a 13th-c monastery and a Norman or possibly pre-Conquest church (restored) are other attractions.

Lambourn   7K2
Famous for its racehorse training stables. A little old town with a grand medieval church and some good buildings. At *Seven Barrows*, 2m N, are some 20 round barrows of various types and a chambered long barrow.

Maidenhead   4E7
Busy residential town and popular boating centre, its 18th-c river bridge now saved from through-traffic by the M4. Brunel's railway bridge is the setting of Turner's painting 'Rain, Steam and Speed'. 2m upstream beyond *Boulter's Lock*, the famous house of **Cliveden** stands high above the river on the Buckinghamshire bank (NT).

Newbury   3M6
A cheerful-looking old town with a narrow balustraded 18th-c bridge over the Kennet. Its importance as a cloth-making town was established in the 16th c by John Winchcombe or Smallwood (Jack o' Newbury), part of whose house still survives, as does his memorial brass in the tower of St Nicholas's Church which he built. Newbury's prosperity has continued – as proved by the choice of charming 16th-, 17th- and 18th-c buildings still to be seen, including many almshouses. The ancient Cloth Hall, with overhanging upper storey, is now a museum. The town has a good theatre, a wide range of shops and a country park at *Snelsmore*. The racecourse is beautifully sited E of the town. 2m S is Sandleford Priory (1781), built by James Wyatt for Mrs Elizabeth Montagu, the original 'blue-stocking'. N of Newbury is *Donnington Castle* (AM) built in 1385. Ruins are

open daily. Below Donnington is *Bagnor*, famous for its Watermill Theatre.

Padworth   3M6
A village E of **Aldermaston**. The little church here is almost pure Norman, the interior being 'overwhelmingly grand', despite its size.

Pangbourne   4E8
A boating village where the Thames is joined by the Pang. Pangbourne College was founded in 1917 to train boys to become officers in the Merchant Service, but it is now a public school. The town is linked to *Whitchurch* by an iron toll-bridge. At *Lower Basildon*, Basildon House overlooks the Thames Valley between Pangbourne and *Streatley* across the river from *Goring* in Oxon. It has a park and the 18th-c house (NT) has an octagon room, plasterwork, pictures, etc. Open April–end Oct. at set times.

Reading   4D8
At the junction of the rivers Kennet and Thames. It is difficult to recognize in the bustling industrial town of today the Reading whose Abbey first echoed to the lovely sounds of 'sumer is icumen in', written by a monk in the 13th c and inscribed on a stone tablet in the Abbey chapter house; the Abbey itself was so despoiled at the Dissolution that the few remains hardly help the imagination. Reading has played its part in history. Here Edward IV defied Warwick 'the King-maker' and announced his marriage to Elizabeth Woodville. It was the birthplace of Archbishop Laud (1593). Jane Austen went to school in the abbey gatehouse. Here the imprisoned Oscar Wilde wrote *De Profundis* and *The Ballad of Reading Gaol*. Life in Roman times is fascinatingly portrayed in Reading Museum★ by the many objects found when **Silchester** (Hants) was excavated. Life in more recent days is admirably recorded in the Museum of Rural Life at the University, also here are the Ure Museum of Greek Archeology and the Cole Museum of Zoology.

The Ridgeway   7K2/L2
Men and cattle have walked this way along the top of what are still, despite the 1974 boundary revisions, known as the Berkshire Downs at least since the Bronze Age and it is still a glorious route, floored with resilient turf and with far-spreading views on each side. It crosses the old county W above the *Goring Gap* where tracks from three river-crossings unite, to near *Ashbury*, from where, in Wiltshire, it turns southwards to **Avebury**, **Stonehenge**, and beyond. Every 9 or 10m (a convenient day's drive for cattle) are enclosures or camps: *Lowbury Camp* (Roman), *Segsbury Camp* and *Uffington Castle* (Iron Age), and others.

Sandhurst   4D7
In the Royal Military College here is to be found The National Army Museum although part of it is now in its modern building in Chelsea, London (*see* entry).

Shottesbrooke   4E7
The village has 'one of the most celebrated Decorated churches in the country'.

Wickham   7L1
The late Saxons who built the tower of the flint church (largely for defence, it seems) would have been surprised to see that the roof of the N aisle is apparently supported by huge elephants' heads, coloured and gilded – an unusual feature in any English church. The whole interior is a perfect example of the early Victorian Gothic Revival.

Windsor   4E7

Thames-side town dominated by the royal castle★★, and with **Eton** close at hand on the other side of the bridge; in between, the river with its boats and swans. The town hall was completed by Wren, though he inserted the internal pillars (which do not in fact support the upper floor) against his will. The town has an exhibition of the Queen's horses and carriages, the Household Cavalry Museum, and at the railway station, built by Brunel and now restored to its original splendour, is a remarkable display of Queen Victoria's Diamond Jubilee mounted by Madame Tussaud's. There is also a 10m Royal Heritage bus tour.

Kings and queens have lived in the castle since the 11th c. William the Conqueror founded it – but none of his original building survives, though the Round Tower crowns the original Norman mound. The present structure contains work of every age from medieval to the early 19th c. St George's Chapel is a magnificent example of 15th-c work, ablaze with banners of the Knights of the Garter. Henry VI, Edward IV, Henry VIII, Charles I and all monarchs from

Windsor Castle, founded over 900 years ago, is the largest inhabited castle in the world covering a 13-acre site

George III to George VI are buried here. The State Apartments have valuable pictures, furniture and gifts and trophies presented to successive monarchs. In St George's Hall hang the banners and coats of arms of the Knights of the Garter since the Order was founded by Edward III in 1348. The Home Park and the Great Park extend S as far as *Virginia Water*. There are regular meetings at the racecourse and Windsor Safari Park is open daily.

Old Windsor, about 1½m SE, was a seat of Saxon kings long before William the Conqueror arrived in Britain. Remains have been found of a building which may have been Edward the Confessor's palace.

Wokingham   4D7

Flourishing market town on A329, 2m E of **Reading**. Attractive blending of old and new, with modern town centre surrounded by half-timbered cottages.

OXFORDSHIRE

AN INTRODUCTION BY
MARTYN SKINNER AND GEOFFREY BOUMPHREY

Even with the acquisition of much Royal Berkshire territory to that county's irreparable loss, many people think of Oxfordshire only in connection with Oxford and the Thames, and picture its landscape as one of the watermeadows, willows and a spire in the background. And although one of its chief characteristics is in fact variety, there is some justification for this restricted view, since the county is centred on the basin of the Thames; and the river, fed by several tributaries, including the Evenlode, the Windrush, the Cherwell, the Ock and the Thame, forms its southern boundary for many miles. Nor is the flat country confined to the neighbourhood of the Thames. The great Oxfordshire plain, formed largely of clay, spreads north towards Bicester and east to where the steep scarp of the Chilterns extends its striking horizon. To the west of this plain the Cotswolds rise less conspicuously (their steep side is in Gloucestershire) and blend in the northwest with the ironstone area round Banbury. It is these three ranges of hills – chalk, limestone and ironstone – that bring such variety, and give Oxford its one undeniable advantage over Cambridge: a surrounding countryside of singular interest and character.

The Thames Valley

Indeed, an undergraduate at Oxford who wished to spend a day exploring the county would have the choice – without leaving the county – of four regions, each quite different from the other, and each with a distinctive scenery and architecture of its own. Even if he kept to the river he would find contrast enough: the Thames at Henley, where a magnificent, wide, straight reach forms 'the finest regatta course in the world', being very different from what Matthew Arnold called 'the stripling Thames at Bablock Hythe', winding through rather remote, flat country of willowed fields, grey humped bridges, and occasional pleasant pubs beside them. In this part are Kelmscot, where William Morris devised the Kelmscott Chaucer, and Bampton, where Morris dancing is still performed in the village street.

In some ways the Thames gives the county a kind of substitute coastline. Regatta Week at Henley and

Eights Week at Oxford are great social as well as sporting events; and the increased popularity of boating, due to the development of the cabin cruiser, has given places like Goring and Henley the status of holiday resorts. It is in the Goring Gap, where the river cuts through the chalk, and the Chilterns and Berkshire Downs rise steeply on either side, that the scenery is most spectacular. Here, if anywhere, history and geography mingle. It is one of the great thoroughfares and crossroads in the south of England, the only railway-worthy gap between London and Bath, and the point where those ancient roads, the Icknield Way and the Ridgeway, join and intersect the Thames.

The Oxfordshire Chilterns

The Romans were not a people to neglect so strategic an area, and no doubt they made good use of the Icknield Way. Where it crosses a farm near Goring a field is still called the Vineyards, supposed relic of their attempt to grow grapes (it faces southeast as a vineyard should). A little farther north the Way intersects Grim's Dyke (or Ditch), 'the most mysterious and elusive earthwork of any of its kind in England', and skirts a hill named after St Birinus, the Apostle of Wessex, who converted its king, Cynegils, in 634, and founded the See of Dorchester.

The Chilterns are typical chalk country: valleys without streams, steep grassy banks sprinkled with juniper and spindle, beechwoods with flinty floors and the occasional yew, thin-soiled fields that gleam white in March. Estate records show that some of the beechwoods are centuries old, their management based on a system of selective felling and regeneration. In them the chair-bodgers and the tent peg-makers pitched their cabins (piled high with shavings on three sides) and worked their treadle lathes, a craft now extinct like many of the rare flora that used to be found on the hills, and in some cases perhaps still are.

The Oxfordshire Cotswolds

What a contrast the Cotswolds are after the flint and brick buildings and white soil. (And how pleasant to be beside a stream after the dry chalk.) Drystone walls instead of hedges, grey limestone houses and barns with Stonesfield slates that attract moss and lichen – take away the villages and the farms and the unique quality of the Cotswold landscape would be lost. Sheep harmonize with the grey stone of the walls; and when wool was a national staple, the Cotswolds were prosperous: the size of the Cotswold sheep, the largest of the native breeds, was evidence of the demand for large fleeces and family joints.

The Oxfordshire Stone

In the northwest corner of the county the presence of ironstone becomes apparent as the honey-coloured stone replaces the grey. The character of the countryside alters too, as the high, walled wolds become more wooded and broken. The countryside around Wroxton Abbey (the old home of the Norths now belonging to the Fairleigh Dickinson University) has witnessed opencast ironstone mining on a large scale. Even the area round Great Tew was threatened; but local opposition was successful – fortunately, because it is one of the finest parts of the county.

Great Tew, cottages steeply embowered in trees (and where fortunately, at the time of writing, restoration is in progress); Burford, a single-streeted masterpiece of grey stone; Ewelme, incomparably grouped round its fine flint church; Dorchester, with its willowed abbey, and curving bridge and street that wind like the Thames beside it – each of these four contrasting villages seems to sum up its own region. A county that contains such diversity is rich indeed.

Country Houses, Towns and Churches

Like its villages, Oxfordshire's country houses are representative: Broughton of the north, Cotswold Chastleton unchanged for centuries, Chiltern Stonor and Mapledurham by the Thames. There are many others, notably Blenheim Palace, Oxford's Versailles, where Winston Churchill was born. During the Civil Wars the county was the Royalist stronghold, and many of its mansions took knocks from Cromwell's artillery. Rycote, near Thame, was the scene of a battle. Its enormous house was burned down in the 18th century, leaving only a tower, an exquisite chapel and a ghost behind. Rousham has a unique William Kent garden, and the grounds of Pusey House are quite outstanding.

Little-known Shirburn Castle, near Watlington, is still completely moated. Compton Beauchamp, between Wantage and Ashbury, is linked with *Tom Brown's Schooldays*. Garsington Manor, near Oxford, is remembered as the home of Lady Ottoline Morrell, who made the Italian garden and gathered a literary coterie around her.

The county's smaller towns are most of them famous for something: Witney for blankets, Banbury for its cross and its cakes (apart from marmalade and lardy cakes, the only item for the gourmet the county

offers), Woodstock for Blenheim, Henley for its Regatta and Thame for having the largest one-day show in England. Faringdon can boast perhaps England's last 'folly' (of the architectural kind) and a gracious country house where once pigeons dyed in bright colours flew fascinatingly in the sunshine. Wallingford is still charming.

Its churches are many of them noted for their spires and it has been suggested that this may be because Oxford Cathedral had one of the earliest spires in England. Witney, Burford, Cassington, Bampton, Shipton and Broadwell are examples. In the north, the churches of Bloxham, Adderbury and King's Sutton (just over the border in Northants) are locally proverbial as typifying length, strength and beauty.

The Downs

The best scenery in Oxfordshire lies in what are still called the Berkshire Downs, the area south and west of the Thames that once lay in Berkshire. The county border now runs near the crest of the hills, but this area cannot be considered on a strict administrative basis, for its peculiar charm lies in the contrast between the lushness of the river valley and the austere beauty of the Downs. Along the northern crest of these runs a road as old as any in Britain, the Ridgeway, making for Avebury and Stonehenge (though their ancient monuments had not been reared when early Britons first trod its turf). Thyme-scented, lark-haunted, it can still be followed, 100 yards and more wide in places, right across the county from Streatley to Ashbury – a 20-mile walk or ride that takes one as near to heaven as seems likely on this earth. For the motorist I would recommend as the most beautiful road in the county the one that runs north of and parallel to the Ridgeway, along the foot of the Downs – especially the section westwards from Wantage. The modelling of the little green valleys round which the road twists and turns in miniature alpine fashion is quite perfect. Northwards you look right across the breadth of the Vale of White Horse to the hills beyond, and, on the nearer side, to the thatched roofs of farms and villages half-hidden by trees. The climax of both scenery and interest is reached at the White Horse itself, believed to date from about 100 BC. Here you can drive your car almost to the top; and it is imperative that you park it and climb to the summit of 856 feet. Below you is the huge ribbed bowl of the Manger, and the flat-topped Dragon Hill on which St George is said to have fought and killed the monster; as proof, you can still see that no grass grows where its blood once trickled down. The Horse itself is better seen from the Vale below (though it is said if you stand on its eye, it should bring you luck); but while you are up here you must look southwards and get a just idea of the vastness and beauty of the Downs. Then you will have tasted the full flavour of the Berkshire Downs.

Off the Beaten Track

Oxfordshire has its remote places and minor curiosities. Otmoor, for instance, that strange inland marsh north of Oxford – an obvious place for a bird sanctuary (it became a bombing range instead). Or Wychwood, once a medieval royal forest, equally atmospheric. Or what has been called the Flora Thompson country, the uplands where the hamlet of Juniper Hill is the *Lark Rise* of a book that has become a classic as a description of a cottage childhood in the Victorian countryside. Typical local curiosities are the Rollright Stones in the north of the county; the monument at Chalgrove to John Hampden, killed in the battle there; a Roman well with a Jacobean well-head in a farmyard at Headington; the Maharajah's Well at Stoke Row near Henley, presented to the village by the Maharajah of Benares to requite an obligation to the local squire; the ruins of Godstow Nunnery, associated with Fair Rosamund; or – in Oxford itself and hardly off the beaten track – the queer circle of classic heads at the base of the Sheldonian Theatre, once described as 'a collection of Bernard Shaws'.

Oxford – the University

It is a varied list, and brings us back to Oxford itself, as any consideration of the county must. Historically Oxford was of great importance in the 17th century, when Charles I made it an alternative capital and started it off as a home of lost causes. Few cities are so packed with ancient and notable buildings – its very railway station is unique as being on the site of an ancient abbey. And in spite of cars and Cowley it is still possible to get an idea of the city as it once was: either from the National Trust property on Boar's Hill, where the distant view resembles one of those engravings by Hoefnagle or Farington still to be found in its own print-shops; or from the top of the Sheldonian Theatre, an amazing roofscape of domes, spires, towers and pinnacles; or early on a Sunday or Bank Holiday morning, from the end of the High Street itself, a majestic curve of colleges, 'Europe's loveliest street'. Trees play a great part in the Oxford landscape: 'Towery city and branchy between towers'

remains a true and vivid description. Another feature is the gardens – what other city (except possibly Cambridge) can rival these? Apart from the noted University buildings (*see also* page 151), the finest architecture, both old and modern, is to be found in the many colleges, of which University is the oldest, Christ Church the largest and Magdalen the loveliest. The last of these alone would be worth visiting England to see.

Oxford: the City

Oxford is a well-known city in its own right, and has given its name to a car, a marmalade and a religious movement. In the 20th century, a Mr W. Morris set up a bicycle shop in one of its suburbs and it developed into a large industrial centre. Although the industrial area is well away from the old city, the increase of population and traffic has affected the city's character. It is difficult, as one waits to cross the traffic procession in the High Street, to imagine that not many decades ago grass grew in the cobbles where now the vibration of wheels threatens the fabric of the colleges.

As might be expected in so venerable a place, curious customs have survived. Every year the city's bounds are beaten; and each May Day morning the college choir sings from Magdalen Tower, listened to by a crowd on the bridge beneath. For two days in September the wide street of St Giles is given over to an annual Fair, to the dislocation of local traffic.

Oxfordshire has no Hardy (few counties have), though Oxford is mentioned as Christminster in his novels. Through Oxford it has been associated with many literary names: Johnson endured the University: Gibbon rejected it; it rejected Shelley. Perhaps the literary names most closely associated with Oxfordshire are those of Robert Bridges and Matthew Arnold (but John Buchan and J.R.R. Tolkien must not be forgotten) and on Oxford itself, Arnold has certainly the final word:

> *That sweet city with her dreaming spires,*
> *She needs not June for beauty's heightening,*
> *Lovely all times she lies, lovely tonight!*

GAZETTEER

Abingdon*   7L2

The perfect approach is on the A415 from **Dorchester** – just meadows, the old bridge with boat-houses, and across the river the tall spire of St Helen's Church drawing the old town round it. Abingdon is so full of good things that they can only be listed: the superb Charles II County Hall (Abingdon was once the county town of Berkshire); St Helen's and St Nicholas' Churches, with the beautiful graveyard at the W end of the former, bounded by

almshouses of 1446, 1707 and 1797; the Prior's House (*c.*1250) and the Guest House (*c.*1400), their interiors accurately restored; East St Helen's Street; the Tompkins almshouses (1733) in Ock Street, and many other medieval–Georgian buildings. Of the Abbey (AD 573), little remains but a 15th-c gateway and some rebuilt fragments. The Checker (counting house) is 13th-c and the Long Gallery, with its beamed roof, is not to be missed. The old Gaol built 1805–11, is now an arts and leisure centre.

Adderbury 7L4
On the hills above the Cherwell, 3m S of **Banbury**, a village of thatched cottages and fine 17th-c houses. The early 15th-c church* is noted for its spire and its carved stonework; corbels, capitals and roof bosses are elaborately decorated with human figures, flowers and grotesques.

Ardington 7L2
12m S of **Oxford** and 2½m E of **Wantage**. A model village developed in the 19th c. Today Home Farm is a crafts centre and pottery. Ardington House is early 18th-c in grey brick with red facings. The hall has an exceptional staircase, and there are fine cedars. Open May–Sept., by appointment only.

Ashbury 7K2
2¼m S, and 3½ N of **Lambourn**, Berks, is *Ashdown House* (NT), built by the Earl of Craven in the late 17th c, with mansard roof and cupola. There are portraits associated with Elizabeth of Bohemia, a box parterre and lawns. Hall, staircase, roof and grounds open May–Sept. at set times.

Bampton 7K2
Quiet little town in the upper reaches of the Thames Valley. Noted centre of Morris Dancing. The Elizabethan manor house was formerly used by the deans of Exeter. The partly Norman church has a Saxon chancel arch.

Banbury 7L4
The present Banbury Cross at the bottom of the hill on the A41 is a Victorian replacement of the original Cross of the nursery rhyme, which was destroyed by Puritans in 1602. A century later the church, too, was destroyed, to be replaced by the present 18th-c Palladian building. There is a good museum. Banbury cakes are still available. The town has a busy and important cattle-market. 6m SE is **Aynhoe Park**, Northants, and 7m NE is **Sulgrave Manor**, Northants. *See also* **Adderbury, Broughton** and **Upton House**, Warks.

Bicester 7L3
The old town, with its market square, has grown enormously in recent years. The church, neighboured by some good stone houses, has a typical small Saxon arch and some Norman work, but is mainly 14th-c. 1½m S is the site of the Roman town of Alchester.

Black Bourton 7K3
So called because it once belonged to the Black Canons of Osney Abbey. The church has a splendid series of 13th-c wall paintings* which have been restored.

Blenheim Palace* *see* **Woodstock**

Blewbury 7L2
Lovely downland village, with good 17th–18th-c houses, gardens and orchards with thatched chalk walls. Memories of the miserly Rev. Morgan-Jones who figures in *Our Mutual Friend* as 'Blackberry Jones'.

Bloxham* 7L4
The 198ft church spire of this hill-top village makes a beautiful landmark for miles around. In the church, which is mostly 13th-c with later additions, note the painted screen, and the humorous carvings over the W door.

Broughton* 7L4
The moated castle (open at set times), mainly 14th-c, with 15th-c gatehouse, has been the seat of the Fiennes family (Lords Saye and Sele) for over 500 years. It was begun by Thomas Broughton, while Sir John completed the original manor house here in 1306. Sir Thomas's effigy is in the church. In the chancel is a monument to William Fiennes, one of the founders of Connecticut in the 17th c.

Broughton Castle: relics of the Civil War belonging to the 8th Lord Saye and Sele are displayed within

Buckland   7K2
Buckland House is a former home of the Throckmortons (see **Coughton Court**, Warks), designed by John Wood, the younger, of **Bath** (Avon), in the 18th c, and well extended in recent times. There is a fine church in the village.

Burford   7K3
Numerous variations of the Cotswold building theme border the lovely street leading down to the bridge over the Windrush. The exterior of the fine 13th–15th-c church was defaced during the Civil War, when it was used as a temporary prison (see inscription scratched on the font). The interior with its chapels and monuments contains all the history of Burford. A busy little town, built on the wealth of the wool industry, beautiful – and mercifully unspoiled. Local museum in the Tolsey. S on the A361 near *Kencot* is the *Cotswold Wild Life Park*, with many attractions for the family. Open daily. At *Filkins* near by is the Swinford Museum (domestic articles, a lock-up, and mantrap). Open daily by appointment.

Buscot   7K2
Here is the second lock on the Thames and a good stone village. The church has glass by Burne-Jones and a painted pulpit, but Buscot is best known as a centre of agricultural experiment in the 19th c. The house and grounds of Buscot Park (NT) are open at set times.

Chalgrove   4E8
Picturesque cottages survive, but modern development has substantially altered the village's character. An obelisk, ½m away, commemorates the battle (1643) at which John Hampden was fatally wounded.

Charlbury   7K3
In the Evenlode Valley, looking over to the remaining parts of Wychwood Forest. A pleasant, stone-built little town: note 17th-c Lee Place (a private residence) and the splendid wistaria covering houses near the church. Museum (key from shop opposite). 2m NE is *Ditchley Park*, at *Enstone*, an imposing 18th-c mansion (open occasionally). *See also* **North Leigh**.

Chastleton★   7K3
Lovely secluded village with a great manor house built in Cotswold stone, *c.*1610 by a **Witney** wool merchant. The manor was once owned by Robert Catesby, a conspirator in the Gunpowder Plot. A long gallery, portraits and a topiary garden are among features of the fine house which is open all year except on Wed.

Chinnor   4F8
On the *Icknield Way* at the foot of the Chilterns. There are cement works but the village is pleasant enough with its moated manor house. The church has pictures wrongly ascribed to Sir James Thornhill, 14th-c glass and brasses.

Chipping Norton   7K3
An old wool town, still making tweeds, overlooking a tributary of the Evenlode. Stone-built 18th-c houses and 17th-c almshouses.

Chislehampton   7L2
Here is a Georgian church of a beautiful and rare simplicity with box-pews, panelled pulpit and reader's desk. A narrow many-arched bridge crosses the Thames. Chislehampton House, 1768, was designed by Samuel Dowbiggin, and is his only known work.

Churchill   7K3
Warren Hastings was born here (1732). So was William Smith (1769), the pioneer geologist who produced the first geological map of England. The church tower is a deliberate copy of that of Magdalen College, **Oxford**.

Clifton Hampden   7L2
The bridge over the Thames was designed by Sir George Gilbert Scott the Elder; the church was restored by him and he built the gabled manor house and local school. The village of mellow red brick and thatch and the Barley Mow Inn provided the background to one of the uproarious incidents in *Three Men in a Boat*. John Masefield, the poet, lived here for almost 30 years.

Cornwell   7K3
Typical Cotswold stream-threaded village, thoroughly restored by Clough Williams-Ellis. The fine mansion with its formal gardens is well seen from the road.

Cropredy   7L4
Rivers and streams were important features in the Civil War: here is another of the bridges where Royalists and Parliamentarians fought it out (1644). In the 14th-c church are fragments of a wall painting, a very rare Pre-Reformation lectern, and the churchyard has some exceptionally good tombstones.

Cumnor   7L3
Scott's version (in *Kenilworth*) of the death of Amy Robsart departs somewhat from the facts, and in any case Cumnor Place is no more. Cumnor Church, however, is worth seeing, especially the very fine spiral wooden staircase in the tower. Stones in the churchyard wall show where the house was.

Cuddesdon   7L3
Well-situated village with a Theological College. The Bishop of Oxford's palace was burned down some years ago.

Deddington   7L4
Village of honey-coloured stone with a remarkable number of large old houses. Only earthworks (open daily) remain of the castle in which Piers Gaveston was arrested by Warwick. The tower of the 14th-c church fell down in the 17th c and was rebuilt.

Dorchester★   7L2
A cathedral city from 634 to 707, now a charming village on the Thames with a variety of good buildings and a huge Abbey church (12th–13th-c) with many treasures. Do not miss the fine Jesse window in the chancel. *Wittenham Clumps* are conspicuous across the river. *Dykes Hills*, Iron Age double earthworks, are near by.

East Hendred   7L2
An unusually beautiful and well-kept village of 16th- and 17th-c cottages, timber-framed and brick or chalk. It has a disused 15th-c stone chapel or shrine, the Chapel of Jesus of Bethlehem (open Easter–Sept. Sun. afternoons, Oct.–Easter first Sun. in month). The Priest's House of the same date is near by. The church possesses one of the earliest clocks (1525) still in use. To compensate for the lack of face and hands, this strikes all the quarters and, on occasion, plays a hymn.

Elsfield   7L3
Hill village with views over **Oxford**. Long the home of John Buchan, who is buried in the churchyard.

Enstone
7K3

On one side of the sharp valley of the River Glyme is *Neat Enstone*; on the other, *Church Enstone*. Here is a fine tithe barn built by the Abbot of Winchcombe in 1382. The church has chained books and coloured effigies.

Ewelme★
4E8

One of the best villages in Oxfordshire. The 15th-c church has the tomb of Alice, Duchess of Suffolk, a granddaughter of Geoffrey Chaucer. Jerome K. Jerome is buried in the churchyard; he lived in a farmhouse nearby. Watercress is grown here.

Faringdon
7K2

This remote little market town has what is probably the last 'folly' to have been built in England – the stone tower built in 1936 among and overtopping the clump of firs on Folly Hill is the Faringdon Folly. It was built by Lord Berners of Faringdon House (1780) and is a considerable landmark. The grounds of the house are open occasionally. All Saints' Church has many fine features.

Great Coxwell
7K2

The cathedral-like tithe barn★ (NT), built by the monks of Beaulieu in the 13th c, is considered by many the finest in England. William Morris often took guests to admire it. Open daily.

Great Milton
4F8

The 14th-c church has a fine relief of Sir Ambrose Dormer encamped at Calais, a splendid four-poster Dormer monument and good brasses. *Little Milton* near by is a lovely village of thatched stone houses.

Great Tew
7K3

An early 19th-c model village, with thatched cottages in a lovely setting. Restoration has been taking place.

Harwell
7L2

The nuclear research station is out of sight of this picturesque little village. The church is noteworthy for a number of quaint and even comic 14th-c stone carvings. At *Didcot*, 2m NW, is the Didcot Railway Centre. Open Easter–Oct. *See* **Milton**.

Henley-on-Thames★
4E8

Beautifully situated among wooded hills, with a picturesque 18th-c bridge over a wide curve of the Thames, and many good-looking Georgian and older houses. The annual regatta, held in the first week of July, makes a gay and fashionable scene along the straight mile of river on the downstream side of the bridge (*see* page 30). Near by is the boathouse of the Leander Club. The church has monuments to many people notable in their day and still remembered; the tower is a prominent feature of the town. *Greys Court* (NT), 3½m NW, is 16th-c with delightful grounds, medieval ruins, rare donkey-wheel, and a maze. Open April–Sept. at set times. The stretch of Thames between *Goring* and Henley is of outstanding natural beauty.

Iffley★
7L2

2 m SE of **Oxford** is one of the finest Norman churches in England. It was built in 1170 and has rich stone carving, an imposing W doorway and chancel.

Great Coxwell Barn: 'the finest piece of architecture in England, as beautiful as a cathedral' (William Morris)

Kelmscot 7K2

From 1871 to 1896 Kelmscott Manor was the home of William Morris, poet, printer, designer and social reformer. His printing press at Hammersmith was named after it. His tomb is in the churchyard here. The house is now owned by the Society of Antiquaries of London. Open at set times.

Kingston Bagpuize 7K2

Kingston House★ is a charming Charles II manor house with good panelling and gardens of flowering shrubs, bulbs and woodland. Open Easter–June at set times. *See also* **Pusey House Gardens**.

Kingston Lisle 7K2

4m W of **Wantage** on the B4507. Kingston Lisle Park is a 17th-c house with an 1812 interior, including a remarkable 'flying' staircase. Open at set times. The Blowing Stone is a perforated sarsen that used to stand on the **Ridgeway** (*see* in Berks). A strong and sustained blast down one of the holes can produce a horn-like note. Legend says that Alfred the Great used to sound it as an alarm to gather his chiefs against the Danes.

Long Wittenham 7L2

A straggly village much of which was burned down in 1868. It has an interesting church with a pretty porch. Many old cruck-framed cottages in the village. The site of the village cross was once the market place. Pendon Museum of Miniature Landscape and Transport is open weekend afternoons.

Mapledurham House★ 4E8

4m N of **Reading**, off the A4074. The late Elizabethan home of the Blounts and Eystons has fine ceilings, a private chapel, paintings and recusant associations, with a lovely situation by the Thames. Open Easter–Sept. weekend afternoons. The estate has a restored 15th-c watermill. Boat trips can be made to House and Mill from Caversham Bridge, Reading.

Milton 7L2

In the village 4m S of **Abingdon** Milton Manor is a 17th-c house with Georgian wings and a 'Gothick' chapel and library. Many charming collections of artefacts. There is a walled garden. The parish church is near by. Open Easter–Oct. weekend afternoons.

Minster Lovell 7K3

Attractive old village on the River Windrush with a fine central-towered 14th-c church, dovecot and the ruins of a 15th-c manor house, Minster Lovell Hall (AM). Open all year.

North Leigh 7K3

The village with its disused windmill is on a hill; the old church at the foot of the slope has a collection of beautifully wrought coffin plates. A short distance to the NE are the remains of a Roman villa (AM). Open April–Sept.

Oxford★★ 7L3

One of Europe's most important and ancient universities and, historically and architecturally, Britain's second most interesting city. A busy administrative, marketing and shopping centre, its streets almost invariably crowded. The city is best seen on foot.

The earliest colleges – University, Balliol, and Merton – were founded in the 13th c. The largest is Christ Church, whose chapel is the ancient cathedral – the smallest in England. Christ Church also has the largest quad, Tom Quad, and the bell in Tom Tower tolls every evening. Nearly every college has its lawned quadrangle (open most afternoons), its chapel and its hall to which visitors are admitted at stated times, and many of them have valuable collections of pictures and books. Almost every college is of considerable architectural importance, including the most modern, notably St Anne's and St Catherine's. Of the old colleges the loveliest is Magdalen with a great variety of architecture. It has a bell tower 144ft high and its Hall has a fine Jacobean screen. The catalogue of notable buildings goes on: the Bodleian Library containing over 3 million books (Duke Humphry's Room, 1480); the Radcliffe Camera reading room (Gibbs, 1737); the Sheldonian Theatre (the University's ceremonial hall, where degrees are bestowed, designed by Wren); the Ashmolean Museum of Art and Archaeology (the first public museum to be opened in Europe), and the University Museum which is devoted to natural history. The 17th-c Botanic Garden is the oldest of its kind in Britain. The Museum of Modern Art in Pembroke Street should not be missed. Other attractions include several museums, among them the British Telecom Museum (open by appointment), a brass-rubbing centre, numerous bookshops, and also an excellent theatre where Richard Burton began his career.

At Magdalen Bridge and Folly Bridge punts may be hired for the exploration of the tree-embowered Cherwell; below Folly Bridge college boats are usually at practice. Torpids is held in late Feb. and Eights Week in late May. Carfax Tower at 74ft affords panoramic views of the city (open in the summer). Tourist Information Centre is in St Aldate's. And beyond this wonderland of beauty is the great hive at *Cowley* founded by Lord Nuffield, donor of one of Oxford's newest colleges. *See also* **Iffley**.

Pusey House Gardens 7K2

5m E of **Faringdon**, off the A420, and SW of **Kingston Bagpuize**. These exceptionally beautiful gardens, with herbaceous borders, lovely trees, shrubs, roses and water, cover 15 acres of land. Open April–Oct. at set times.

Radley 7L2

The 18th-c mansion, Radley Hall, was the original nucleus of Radley College, the public school founded in 1847. The little village church is sumptuously furnished with carved oak and contains wonderful heraldic glass of the 15th and 16th c.

Rollright Stones 7K3

Famous prehistoric stone circle, less impressive than the larger circles in Wiltshire at **Stonehenge** and **Avebury**, but set high up on a ridge commanding wide views over Warwickshire (AM).

Rousham House★ 7L3

12m N of **Oxford**, off the A423, and near the grey-stone walled village of *Steeple Aston* is one of England's finest Jacobean mansions. It was the home of the Cottrell-Dormers. It has a remarkable landscape garden by William Kent. House open April–Sept. at set times, gardens daily.

Shipton-under-Wychwood 7K3

Many good houses, built in the days when 'sheep towns' and wool markets meant prosperity. Note Shipton Court (1603, but much restored) and the Shaven Crown inn with its Tudor archway.

Oxford: a city of college domes, quads, towers, spires and mellow buildings – a cultural heritage in itself

South Newington   7K4
Where the Swere stream runs out from the hills, a village church with wall paintings long concealed (and preserved) under layers of whitewash.

Sparsholt   7K2
This little village is worth visiting for itself alone, as well as for the three 14th-c carved wooden effigies in the church which is of great interest.

Stanton Harcourt   7L3
Delightful village among water meadows of the upper Thames Valley. The great house of the Harcourts was pulled down in 1780 but the tower, gatehouse and huge kitchen are open at set times. In the tower Pope worked on his translation of the *Iliad*. There are Harcourt monuments in the church and a 13th-c screen.

Steventon   7L2
A series of beautiful 17th-c houses (NT) of brick and plaster, all half-timbered, can be seen from the mile-long, roughly paved causeway.

Stonor Park   4E8
On the B480, 5m N of **Henley-on-Thames**. The ancestral home of the Stonors with portraits, fine furniture, and private chapel, is in an exceptionally beautiful park setting. Open Easter–Sept. at set times.

Swinbrook   7K3
A church so small that effigies of the Fettiplace family, depicted reclining on their sides, are arranged bunk-fashion against the wall. Note the 'woolpack' gravestones in the churchyard, long rounded stones representing the woolpacks which once meant such prosperity to the Cotswolds. Nancy Mitford is buried here. Lovely riverside views.

Taynton   7K3
Taynton stone has gone into many good buildings, including St Paul's Cathedral in London, the New Bodleian Library at Oxford, Blenheim Palace, and St George's Chapel, Windsor (*see* entries), but no industry now disturbs the peace of this little village beside the Windrush.

Thame   4F8
Very attractive market town with a wholly successful mixture of architectural periods and an unusually wide street designed for markets and fairs. Beside the river is the imposing church. John Hampden was but one of many famous men educated at Thame School. He died in the Greyhound inn from wounds received at the battle of Chalgrove (*see* entry). The fine old Spread Eagle inn was made famous by John Fothergill's *Innkeeper's Diary*. 3m W is *Rycote Chapel* (AM). The mansion is no more but the chapel, founded in 1449, survives.

Uffington   7K2
A little village of chalk-and-thatch cottages, with a fine stately church dating from *c*.1150. The village and district are well described in *Tom Brown's Schooldays*. See **Wayland Smith's Cave** and **The White Horse**.

Wallingford   7L2
A charming old riverside town, its best approach by the many-arched bridge. Its fine 17th-c Town Hall in the market square is raised on Tuscan pillars and houses a collection of fine portraits. There are many beautiful Georgian buildings and in Lamb Arcade an antiques and crafts market has been developed in such a building. But its history goes back still further (it has held a Charter for over eight centuries). Here, in 1066, William the Conqueror crossed the Thames to take London in the rear; here, to its castle, fled Queen Maud when she escaped from Oxford Castle one icy night in 1142. Wallingford, on the side of King Charles in the Civil War, was the last town to surrender. Of these old times only ancient earthworks and a few fragments of the Castle remain today. Agatha Christie lived here in a house called Winterbrooke.

Wantage   7K2
The statue of King Alfred the Great in the market place commemorates his birth here in 849. The town museum's collection is now displayed in the new purpose-built Vale and Downland Museum Centre in Church Street. Here also are displays about the landscape of the Vale of the White Horse and local life from primeval settlements to the 20th c. A silver plate in the 13th-c church is reputed to have belonged to Peter the Great.

Watlington   7L2
Charming small 17th–18th-c town built around its market hall. 1m NE *Shirburn Castle*, originally 14th-c, has corner towers, and an all-embracing moat and a drawbridge; it is not open to the public.

Wayland Smith's Cave   7K2
Near **Uffington**. Here if you leave your horse overnight, with a coin, legend tells that you will find it shod in the morning. The 'cave' is actually a cromlech, the exposed stones of a long barrow (now restored). In Scandinavian mythology, Wayland the Smith has a white horse – and this barrow, most beautifully sited in a clump of beeches by the **Ridgeway** (Berks), is only 1m or so from the **Uffington** White Horse. But it is 1,000–2,000 years older (AM).

The White Horse★   7K2
Probably the oldest and certainly the most famous of its kind, this gigantic figure (NT), 374ft from nose to tail, is carved out high up on the chalk flank of the downs near **Uffington**. Since at least the 12th c it has given its name to the broad vale it overlooks, and from time immemorial its periodic 'scouring' has been an occasion for local junketing, well described by Thomas Hughes in *The Scouring of the White Horse*. Its style – beaked muzzle and two legs completely detached – is far more impressive than any naturalistic representation could be, and the design is, in fact, very like one to be found on certain British coins of the late Iron Age. Possibly it represents the totem animal of the Celtic tribe living in *Uffington Castle* just above. The ribbed dry-valley just to the W is known as The Manger, and near by stands the flat-topped *Dragon Hill*, on which St George is reputed to have slain the dragon (the Horse?). The White Horse and its surroundings are best seen when the sun is low in the sky and viewed from *Longcot* in the vale. Near by is **Kingston Lisle**.

Witney   7K3
Blankets have been made here for centuries and they still provide the main industry. The best part of the town is above the many-gabled 17th-c Butter Cross and the Town Hall. Here good stone buildings stand back behind wide grass verges, the vista being closed by the very fine church. Note the old Blanket Hall and the 17th-c former Grammar School. 1m E is Manor Farm Museum, a working museum of local farming through the centuries. Open April–Sept. *See also* **North Leigh**.

Woodstock 7L3

Small town on the edge of the Cotswolds, long famous for gloves. Many good stone houses, some built when Woodstock still had a royal palace (demolished when neighbouring Blenheim was built). The Black Prince was born here. Today the town is charming with old inns, tea shops, and a museum in Fletcher's House has excellent displays.

On the very edge of the town lies the great park of *Blenheim Palace*★, the imposing pile (covering 3 acres) given to the Duke of Marlborough for his victories in the Low Countries, including Blenheim (1704). Vanbrugh designed it with Hawksmoor's help, and the 2,500-acre park with its Great Lake owes much to Capability Brown. Furniture, portraits, carving by Grinling Gibbons, ceiling painted by Thornhill depicting the battle, tapestries depicting Marlborough's campaigns, and in the chapel the marble tomb of the Duke and Duchess. Palace open March–Oct., Park daily.

Blenheim Palace: a vast national monument and a celebration of the Duke of Marlborough's victories

Wytham 7L3

A charming Oxfordshire-style stone village looking across river-meadows to *Godstow Nunnery* and sheltered from the W by rising woods. The E window in the church is said to have come from the chamber in Cumnor Place (*see* **Cumnor**), now demolished, in which Amy Robsart spent her last night. *Wytham Woods* were much used by Sir Charles Elton for his studies of animals. The woods were bequeathed to **Oxford** University.

Yarnton 7L3

The splendid Tudor manor house, built about 1611 by Sir Thomas Spencer, was partly pulled down and used as a farmhouse before it was restored in 1897. The parish church has Spencer monuments and medieval glass.

GLOUCESTERSHIRE

AN INTRODUCTION BY
JOHN MOORE

In the sense of landscape there are three Gloucestershires: Cotswold, Severn Vale and Forest of Dean. Each of these is as different from the others as chalk is from cheese. The whale-backed oolitic Cotswold Hills present an unspoiled skyline 50 miles long, from Chipping Campden in the north down to the extreme south of the county (and indeed to Bath in Avon). The Severn Vale, whence you can look up at this heart-lifting sight, goes down from Tewkesbury – where the river is joined by Shakespeare's Avon – to the City of Gloucester. Beyond are the tidal reaches of the great river, with the Vale of Berkeley on the left bank and on the right the coal-bearing, oak-wooded Forest of Dean, bounded on its west side by the swift tumbling Wye. A fourth part, sometimes called the Bristol quarter, has now become part of the county of Avon.

The Cotswolds
The image of Gloucestershire which perhaps most readily comes to mind is one of 'galloping country' – stone walls dividing the great sweeping sheep-pastures of short-cropped fescue grass, trout-streams, and what Belloc called:

> The hundred little towns of stone
> Forgotten in the Western Wold.

It was a sheep-country in Shakespeare's day also, and Shallow asked a Cotswold man's question when he said, 'How a score of ewes, now, Cousin Silence?' meaning how much were they fetching at market. Indeed, long before then the Cotswolds were producing the fleeces which enriched the 15th-century wool-merchants, who spent part of their great wealth in building the handsome churches which tower over the little towns – such as Chipping Campden's, the lordly burial place of William Grevel, or Fairford's, paid for out of the fortune earned by Cotswold sheep for John Tame. As a lavish extra, he gave it some of the best stained glass in England, including the famous West Window with its lively picture of the Eternal Pit, into which the host of the damned (all noticeably women) are being pitchforked and prodded by cheerful imps with animal faces. Cirencester and Northleach have fine churches too,

and the country towns of Stow-on-the-Wold ('where the Devil caught cold') and Moreton-in-Marsh, such villages as Bourton and Bibury, indeed almost all the hamlets and habitations in the heart of the Cotswolds, look as if they had grown naturally out of the ground, like the trees; and in a sense so they have, as the old over-grown stone-quarries bear witness.

The trout-streams, such as the Coln, the Evenlode, and the sweetly named Windrush, go briskly but never turbulently between the gently sloping hills. As well as the trout, they contain a plentiful supply of crayfish. Myriads of mayflies dance over them in early June. The 'monkey-flower', *mimulus*, grows freely along their banks. The meadows and pastures show some rarer flowers: butterfly-orchids, even man-orchids, fritillaries, and the slaty-violet *anemone pulsatilla* or pasque-flower; lilies-of-the-valley, herb Paris and Solomon's seal are found in the woods. Buzzards have become common, quail are seen by the partridge-shooters now and then, and the garganey teal has nested by these Cotswold streams. The very rare large blue butterfly still survives, though precariously, in one or two colonies; but the localities are necessarily kept secret.

Close under the Cotswolds lie the towns of Cirencester and Cheltenham. Ciren, as the locals call it (*not* 'Cisiter'), was the Roman town of Corinium, where the two great roads, the Icknield Way and Ermine Street, joined the Fosse Way. The Roman villa among the beechwoods at Chedworth, not far from Cirencester, was found by accident when a keeper was digging out his ferret that had killed a rabbit in a burrow, and was 'lying up'. More than 50 of these luxurious villas, with tessellated floors and elaborate heating systems, are known to have existed in Gloucestershire, which is rich in Roman relics.

Cheltenham possesses almost as much good Georgian building as Bath; but it is scattered over the large town instead of being concentrated in one small area. The 'garden-town', with its tree-lined Promenade and beautiful parks, used to be famous for

Upper Slaughter is a Cotswold village on a tributary of the River Windrush

peppery retired colonels; they are no more, and light industry, which they would have deplored, keeps Cheltenham busy and prosperous. Its annual Cricket Week brings to mind memories of W. G. Grace and Gilbert Jessop, whose famous swipe once smashed the clock-face in Cheltenham College pavilion.

The Severn Vale

From the flat river-meadows around Tewkesbury you lift up your eyes unto the hills whichever way you turn: to Cotswold or to Malvern. A Gloucestershire poet, F. W. Harvey, wrote in the trenches during World War I of his homesick longing:

> *To see above the Severn plain*
> *Unscabbarded against the sky*
> *The blue high blade of Cotswold lie,*
> *The giant clouds go royally*
> *By jagged Malvern with a train*
> *Of shadows . . .*

The vale itself is not beautiful; at best it is ordinary pastoral England, a green and pleasant land; but it offers you, at sunrise or at sunset, some heartening horizons.

The 7-mile drive from Cheltenham to Tewkesbury takes you back, architecturally, from Georgian to Tudor. The black-and-white half-timbered buildings in the High Street mostly date from the late 1500s. In a jumble of back streets and alleys (now mostly tidied up and modernized) the old and new join together to form a remarkable hotchpotch. Over all stands the tower of one of the finest churches in Britain, the tremendous Norman abbey. Here, among the tombs and the memorials of Despencers, Warwicks and De Clares, of a knight that fell at Agincourt and of a baron who witnessed the signing of Magna Carta, there lie in a dark, damp, and appropriately sinister vault the remains of that Duke of Clarence who is supposed to have been drowned in a butt of Malmsey wine. His bones, in a glass case, are confusedly mixed up with those of his lady.

The River Severn, roaring over Tewkesbury Weir, flows down through a quiet pastoral landscape to the city of Gloucester:

> *The men that live in West England*
> *They see the Severn strong,*
> *A-rolling on rough waters brown*
> *Light aspen leaves along.*

These rough waters brown, upon the first floods of autumn, carry with them the silver-coated eels on the first stage of their journey to their breeding-place in the far-off Sargasso Sea; the fishermen string wicker traps called 'putcheons' across the river and count their catch sometimes in hundredweights. In the early spring another generation of eels, no thicker than bootlaces, the tiny, wriggling gelatinous fry that have drifted and swum 3,000 miles from that

breeding-place, swarm upriver by the million million, and themselves are caught in nets of cheese-cloth stretched on frames of withy. They are locally regarded as a delicacy, fried in bacon fat or jellied into 'elver-cakes'. Double Gloucester cheese would go well with them, to make a Gloucestershire midday meal. The Severn salmon provide another harvest for the fishermen; so in a very small way do the curious lamperns, from a surfeit of which Henry I is reputed to have died. The city of Gloucester, by ancient custom, makes them into a pie for the monarch, on the occasion of a Coronation. Porpoises and sturgeons (which are another royal prerogative) have been known to swim up the Severn upon its tides, which are very powerful and produce the inrush of waters known as the Bore. This noisy wave, which races through the winding narrows below Gloucester, is caused by a tide which may have risen as much as 18 feet in an hour and a half. When there is a big Bore the wave is 7 feet high, and it travels at 15 knots. Stonebench is a favourite place from which to watch it when there is a high spring tide.

The upper estuary would be difficult to navigate, because of its shifting sands; but a ship canal 17 miles long, from Gloucester to Sharpness, gives passage to vessels of up to 1,000 tons burden. The canal passes through a countryside somewhat reminiscent of Holland: flat grassland grazed mainly by black-and-white Friesian cattle, and veined with little watercourses which are frequently criss-crossed by narrow lanes having humpback bridges. This Berkeley Vale, some 50,000 acres of it, is very thinly populated, and in winter there are more geese than people there. The Severn Wildfowl Trust has its headquarters at Slimbridge and in some seasons as many as 6,000 whitefronts feed upon the foreshore area quaintly called the Dumbles.

Dr Jenner practised in Berkeley Vale; and here on 14 May 1790 he inoculated a farm labourer's son, James Phipps, with lymph taken from a cowpox pustule on the hand of a dairymaid, Susan Nelmes; six weeks later he inoculated the boy a second time, but with smallpox. James did not develop the disease and so demonstrated for the first time the advantages of vaccination. Jenner was also a pleasant minor poet, as well as a first-rate naturalist who anticipated some of Darwin's discoveries by a century.

The Forest

About twenty million trees, many of them fine oaks, grow in the Royal Forest of Dean, which Michael Drayton in about 1600 called 'The Queen of Forests all'. Deep down under the roots of the trees is a coalfield of some 22,000 acres. The 'tips' rise up in the neighbourhood of the collieries, neat little manmade hills, and provide vantage points from which you can look down on some of the most magnificent woodland scenery in Britain. The older of these tips are pleasantly overgrown with birch-scrub and broom, and the whole area is unique in being the only coalfield which has been exploited and yet remains beautiful. Scattered among the oaks are ancient hollies, the largest in England, some of them 40 feet high. Groves of birches, daffodil-fields on the Forest fringe, plantations of conifers, here and there an open heath, tall bracken, and the abundant foxgloves which are said to be at their best on St Swithun's day, make a varied landscape in a forest which offers you about 2,000 miles of woodland path for your walking.

About half the forest is fenced; the other half is grazed by the foresters' sheep, an ancient privilege rather than a right of common. The 'ship-badgers', as these commoners call themselves – presumably because, as shepherds, they 'badger' the sheep – may own 200 sheep or only one cherished ewe. They also have the privilege of letting their pigs feed among the Queen's oaks when the acorns fall – called the 'right of pannage' upon 'the open and unenclosed woods and woody lands of our Lady the Queen'.

These and other rights they guard jealously. Old customs and old trades are cherished in this ancient forest – where charcoal-burning and iron-mining have been practised since prehistoric times. The Foresters are very different both in speech and manners from the Gloucestershire people who live upon the hills; as different as their rough, tough hard-living sheep are from the fat deep-fleeced flocks on Cotswold. The Forest of Dean accent has a lilt in it which perhaps comes from Wales, across the river which forms the boundary of Gloucestershire on the western side, the turbulent, beautiful, half-Welsh River Wye.

GAZETTEER

Arlington Mill *see* **Bibury**

Barnsley   7J3
Barnsley House Garden near **Cirencester** is an old garden redesigned since 1962. It has 18th-c summer houses. Plants for sale. House of 1697 is not open. Gardens open every Wed. and other set times.

Batsford Park Arboretum *see* **Moreton-in-Marsh**

Belas Knap *see* **Winchcombe**

Berkeley*   7I2
The splendid castle is a 12th-c feudal stronghold on rising ground looking out over the Severn. Built of vari-coloured stones and set among lovely gardens; a place of winding stairways and arched doorways with a magnificent 62ft Great Hall. Within these walls Edward II was hideously murdered in 1327. The castle has been occupied by the Berkeley family continuously since the 12th c. Terraced gardens and deer park with fallow and red deer. Open April–Sept. except Mon. The Wildfowl Trust is on the estate 5m away at **Slimbridge**. In the parish church (which has a detached tower) is the grave of Edward Jenner (1749–1823) who introduced vaccination, while in the town is the Jenner Museum.

Beverstone   7I2
2m W of **Tetbury**. A neat village with 13th-c castle.

Bibury*   7J3
Stone cottages and the Swan hotel look out across the rippling Coln to the NT row of late 14th-c cottages known as Arlington Row, and a fairer scene would be hard to find. Lean on the bridge and watch the trout in the current below, or go a little way along the Quenington road for the view of the Court Hotel against a background of wooded hills. Arlington Mill (Cotswold Country Museum) is a very attractive 17th-c corn mill. Open March–Oct. daily, and winter weekends. Bibury also has a trout farm – open summer months.

Bisley   7J3
Village of excellent stone houses and a 14th-c church. The near-by house of Lypiatt Park had connections with the Gunpowder Plot.

Blockley   7K4
3m S of **Chipping Campden**. A village of old silk mills.

Bourton-on-the-Hill*   7K4
Picturesque village of bow-windowed stone cottages. The manor house has a fine tithe barn. 1m or so S is the Indian style mansion of *Sezincote*, which was the inspiration for the Pavilion at **Brighton** (Sussex). Open at set times.

Bourton-on-the-Water*   7K3
The Windrush flows between lawns alongside the main street and is crossed by graceful stone bridges. All around are good Cotswold houses, and at one end is an old mill. Behind the New Inn is a model of the village constructed from local stone. Birdland attracts many visitors. Bourton Motor Museum in an 18th-c watermill; Cotswold Perfumery; and Notgrove Long Barrow 4m W the excavated remains of a Neolithic burial chamber. 5m NW of Bourton at *Guiting Power* is the Cotswold Farm Park, a rare breed survival centre with pets corner, cart rides and cart-horse centre. Open May–Sept.

Chavenage   7I2
Near **Tetbury**. An Elizabethan Cotswold manor with Cromwellian associations. Open May–Sept. at set times.

Chedworth*   7J3
On the N of Chedworth Wood, just off the Fosse Way near Fosse Bridge, are the comprehensive remains of a large Roman villa (with mosaic pavements) dating from between AD 180 and 380 (NT). Lilies-of-the-valley abound in the woods.

Cheltenham*   7J3
Well cared-for Regency buildings, wide streets, and a wealth of trees preserve the character of this beautiful town despite

the pressure of modern commerce. No shopping street in England can compare with the Promenade for beauty. Cheltenham developed as a spa during the 18th c (the waters are still dispensed at the Town Hall), but it is as a residential and educational centre, with festivals of music and literature etc., that it is best known today. Its industries include the design and assembly of jet aircraft, the manufacture of air-venting equipment and thermostatic mixing valves. It has two famous public schools. Also the Holst Birthplace Museum, town museum and a pump room. St Mary's Church has a fine rose window. Excellent centre for exploring the Cotswolds. The famous steeplechase racecourse is at Prestbury Park to the N.

Chipping Campden*   7J4/K4
Home of some of the wealthiest of the 14th–15th-c Cotswold wool merchants. Many excellent buildings (note especially William Grevel's house) and an arched market hall. Good brasses in the fine church, and near by a row of almshouses in typical Cotswold style. In one of the oldest buildings is the Woolstaplers Hall Museum. 4m NE is **Hidcote Manor**.

Cirencester*   7J2
The feature of the town is the elaborate three-storeyed 16th-c porch in front of the parish church. The church has a good tower, and fan vaulting in St Catherine's Chapel, and magnificent 16th-c nave. There are many well-preserved old buildings in the town which has a good modern shopping centre. Cotswold District Council offices in Trinity Road. Cirencester was the Roman Corinium, and excavations have revealed the layout of the entire town. See the excellent modernized Corinium Museum which has full-scale reconstructions of a Roman kitchen and dining-room. Earl Bathurst's 3,000-acre Cirencester Park near *Coates* has a notable 5m avenue of chestnuts, several follies and a polo park (the house itself is not open to the public). *See also* **Barnsley**.

Dean, Forest of   7H3/I3
Extends roughly N and E of **Chepstow**, Gwent. One of the few true forests remaining in England; an extensive hilly area of oak and birch between the Wye and the Severn, with excellent views from some of the high points. For centuries coal and iron have been worked, but the pits were mostly small and in recent years all have been closed. The Speech House Hotel, in *West Dean* in the centre of the Forest, was once the Verderer's Court. Dean Hall Garden in *Little Dean* is open April–Sept. except Thurs. and Sun.

Deerhurst   7I3
Tiny village among the fields, worth visiting for its church*, one of the most complete Saxon buildings in England, though aisles and other features are Norman.

Didmarton   7I2
Redundant medieval church with 18th-c furnishings in care of the Redundant Churches Fund. Worcester Lodge, a folly on the **Badminton** estate in Avon, can be seen from the A433 near the village.

Dursley   7I2
The 18th-c market house, raised on pillars, gives no hint of the industries tucked away down the hill. Good old houses are solid evidence of the town's former cloth-making prosperity, but they are now crowded out by the rapid spread of new building. *Stancombe Park*, between Dursley and **Wotton-under-Edge**, has an elaborate 19th-c formal garden. Open occasionally or by appointment.

Elkstone   7J3
Cotswold village with an unusually good little Norman church. Note the dovecot over the E end.

Elmore *see* **Severn Bore**

Fairford   7K2
Famous for the 28 windows of its church*, filled with late 15th-c glass illustrating Biblical themes. The glass was made especially for these windows when the church (except the tower) was rebuilt by the rich wool-merchant John Tame.

Frocester   7I2
A small village under the Cotswolds, with a good Elizabethan manor house and a splendid 13th-c tithe barn 60yd long and 36ft high, reputed to be the largest in England. From Frocester Hill, 1m SW, magnificent views over the Severn valley.

Gloucester   7I3
For centuries the city has guarded the lowest crossing of the Severn and the routes into Wales. It was the Roman fortified town of Glevum, the British Caer Glowe; the Normans walled it and built a castle (destroyed in the 17th c). The glory of the city is the Cathedral** built mainly in the 12th c as a monastic church but refounded by Henry VIII as a cathedral. The pillars of the nave have been standing there for nearly 900 years. Note especially 14th-c glass in E window, largest in England, and (15th-c) in the Lady Chapel. The cloisters display the earliest fan vaulting in England. The library has 10th-c books. In Northgate Street is the 15th-c New Inn with its galleried courtyard, and in Ladybellegate Street is Blackfriars (AM) founded in 1239. The friary buildings were altered in the 16th c. Open April–Sept. Gloucester is one of the centres of the Three Choirs Festival. The modern city is a busy inland port and has much light engineering industry. Archeological excavations during redevelopment of the city have revealed the site of a Roman forum and evidence of two Roman occupations. The finds are in the City Museum. Other museums are the Folk Museum, a regimental museum and the Beatrix Potter Centre – the house of the Tailor of Gloucester.

Hailes Abbey   7J3
2m NE of **Winchcombe**. Little but ruins marking the ground plan remain. This once great 13th-c Cistercian foundation was the burial place of Richard Earl of Cornwall, King of the Romans (1209–72), and drew pilgrims to see a phial said to contain Holy Blood. An excellent museum preserves relics of the abbey (NT and AM). Open daily.

Hidcote Manor   7K4
At *Hidcote Bartrim*, 4m NE of **Chipping Campden**. A 17th-c Cotswold house with one of the most celebrated gardens in England (NT). Open April–Oct. *See also* **Kiftsgate Court**.

Kiftsgate Court   7K4
Opposite **Hidcote Manor** Gardens. Famous for its roses. Open April–Sept. at set times.

Lechlade   7K2
Where the River Leach joins the Thames the counties of Gloucestershire, Oxfordshire and Wiltshire meet. A charming little place with quiet Georgian houses; it has clearly changed little over the years. The 15th-c church is an interesting example of Perpendicular architecture and its spire dominates the Thames for several miles. There are many gazebos and summer houses in Lechlade.

Hidcote Garden: high on the Cotswolds and home of 'Hidcote' hypericum, verbena and lavender, it dates from 1905

Lydney Park 7I2
In the town of Lydney, the park known as Camp Hill has a woodland garden and Roman remains. Open most Sun.

Minchinhampton 7I2
Pretty little town with beautiful church and many 17th–18th-c buildings. Once a staging post for the London coach. Large common and land owned by NT, with superb views.

Moreton-in-Marsh 7K4
Not 'Marsh' but 'March' gives the true meaning of the name, march being used in the sense of 'boundary'. Moreton's old curfew bell is still in its tower overlooking the Fosse Way. 1m W is *Batsford Park Arboretum*, open daily April–Oct.

Nailsworth 7I2
Among wooded Cotswold hills and steep winding roads (the 'ladder' is a famous hill-climb test) leading to the widespread commons with views in all directions.

Northleach 7J3
Stone-built little town, once an important centre of the Cotswold wool trade. The church★, with its splendid carved S porch, is one of the finest of those built by the old wool merchants. Among the brasses are some portraying the kind of sheep which produced the Cotswold Golden Fleece. The Cotswold Countryside Collection is a new museum run by the Cotswold District Council in the old prison, showing the Lloyd-Baker collection of farm carts.

Painswick 7I3
Hillside town with a remarkable number of good stone buildings dating from the heyday of the wool trade. Its Court House, 16th c, has notable fireplace and panelling. Open at set times. The churchyard is famous for its collection of 99 clipped yews. Splendid views from Painswick Beacon, 2m N. Painswick House, a fine Palladian house, is open to the public on Sat. and Sun. afternoons in summer.

Prinknash Abbey 7I3
About 4m SE of **Gloucester**. Benedictine monks (who until 1924 lived on an island off the Welsh coast near **Tenby**, Dyfed) have built an immense new abbey (1972). Pottery factory, monastery garden and Abbey Church are open daily. In the grounds is a bird park. Beautiful views.

Rodmarton Manor 7J2
An Arts and Crafts Centre. Gardens open by appointment.

St Briavels 7H2
In a wooded valley with a small, restored, partly 12th-c castle, with two round towers at the gatehouse. Views down the valley towards the **Forest of Dean**.

Severn Bore★
A phenomenon which occurs at certain high-water spring tides when the waters of the Bristol Channel surge up and roll back the waters of the Severn. The best views of it are at *Stonebench* and in the neighbourhood of *Elmore*, some 3m downstream from **Gloucester**.

Sezincote *see* **Bourton-on-the-Hill**

Slimbridge 7I2
4m E of *Sharpness*. The Severn Wild Fowl Trust founded here by Peter Scott (and open to visitors) protects the largest and most varied collection of wild waterfowl in the world in 73 acres with observation towers overlooking saltmarshes. The nave in the church has 12th-c carved arcades.

Snowshill Manor 7J4
3m S of **Broadway**. A Cotswold manor (NT) mostly 17th- and 18th-c. Famous magpie collection of artefacts. Attractive garden. Open April–Oct.

Stancombe Park *see* **Dursley**

Stanton★ 7J4
A single street of 16th–17th-c houses and barns, with a partly Norman church. One of Cotswold's loveliest villages, restored with skill and restraint.

Stanway 7J4
Village with tithe barn and church worth noting. It also has a stately manor house with a superb gatehouse, and behind the house itself a folly constructed in 1750. Open occasionally in the summer.

Stow-on-the-Wold 7K3
Small hill-top town at the conjunction of 8 roads (the Fosse Way is one of them); it is not surprising that it was once an important market town. Hence the large market place in which the great annual sheep fairs were held. Good village cross. In the church is a large painting of the Crucifixion by Gaspar de Craeyer (1582–1669). 1m away is *Abbotswood*, a house and garden designed by Lutyens. Open occasionally.

Stroud 7I3
A famous manufacturing centre of the cloth trade, especially in the late 18th c. It is now a bustling modern town, which has somehow lost its way.

Sudeley Castle *see* **Winchcombe**

Tetbury   7J2
Quiet, dignified houses, an Elizabethan market hall mounted on pillars, and a church with an unusual arrangement of numbered box pews. There is also a redundant church, St Saviour's in the care of the Redundant Churches Fund, with a 19th-c Tractarian layout by S. W. Daukes. 3m S *Hodges Barn* has 8 acres of garden open by appointment. In *Doughton* is *Highgrove House*, the private home of the Prince and Princess of Wales.

Tewkesbury★   7I4
Old-fashioned town of timbered houses, venerable inns, and above all a splendid Norman abbey church to which a series of chantries and chapels were added in the 14th c. Museum of local history. Here the rivers Severn and Avon unite, and Tewkesbury is a popular sailing and boating centre. Parts of the bridge over the River Avon are over 750 years old. Near by at **Deerhurst** is Odda's Chapel, built in 1056.

Uley   7I2
An old weaving village in a valley among steep wooded hills. The 14th-c *Owlpen* manor house, 1m E, with its clipped yews is one of the most picturesque of all the smaller Cotswold manors. Above the village is the prehistoric long barrow known as *Hetty Pegler's Tump* (AM), with splendid views across the Severn Valley into Wales.

Upper Slaughter   7K3
Delightful village and home of the early 19th-c diarist, F. E. Witts, the Cotswold parson, who lived in what is now the Lords of the Manor Hotel. (*See* page 155.)

Westbury-on-Severn   7I3
By the church is Westbury Court Garden (NT). Pavilion, canals and Dutch garden. Open April–Oct.

Westonbirt   7I2
The well-known girls' school is in an Italian mansion built by Lewis Vulliamy for R. S. Holford. The arboretum is one of the best in England: a rarity is an avenue of tulip trees.

Tewkesbury: a maze of half-timbered buildings and alleyways, with an ancient mill and a Norman abbey

Winchcombe★   7J3
Attractive little grey-stone town in the Cotswolds. A Benedictine abbey, founded *c.* 800 by Kenulf of Mercia, was rebuilt, and then dissolved and razed by Henry VIII. Two stone coffins in the 15th-c church are said to be those of Kenulf and his son. One of the altar cloths was the work of Catherine of Aragon. Near by is *Sudeley Castle*. Sir Thomas Seymour, lately married Catherine Parr, who died here and is buried in the chapel. Attractions include the Emma Dent Museum, a collection of toys, paintings, Charles I's four-poster bed. In the grounds are waterfowl and a children's fortress. Open March–end Oct.

On a hilltop to the S of Winchcombe, and nearly 1,000ft above sea level, is the famous long barrow of *Belas Knap★*, a Stone Age burial mound with a false portal, masked by dry walling at one end, with burial chambers opening in the sides (AM). *See also* **Hailes Abbey**.

Woodchester   7I2
The Roman villa covering 26 acres, one of the largest Roman villa sites in Britain, is generally kept covered with earth for preservation. There is a mosaic pavement under the old churchyard. *See also* **Wotton-under-Edge**.

Wotton-under-Edge   7I2
Old market and cloth town on the western escarpment of the Cotswolds with widespread views over the Severn. The church organ which Handel played came from **St Martin-in-the-Fields,** London. Bradley Court is Elizabethan with a beautiful garden remade by the owners since 1970 with grotto. There is a replica of the mosaic floor at **Woodchester** Roman Villa in Rowland Hill Tabernacle. Open March–Oct. 1m S of Wotton, Kingswood Abbey Gatehouse (15th-c) is all that remains of the abbey. Open daily. 1½m E of Wotton is *Newark Park* (NT), a 16th-c house remodelled by James Wyatt and surrounded by some 643 acres of woodland and agricultural land.

HEREFORD AND WORCESTER

AN INTRODUCTION BY
HARRY SOAN AND JOHN MOORE

These two old counties, lying between the Midlands and Wales, now form one administrative area, but as they are divided in the south by the Malvern Hills and in the north, for a short distance, by the River Teme, it is convenient to treat them, topographically, as two distinct geographical areas.

Hereford

Most of the soil of Hereford is rich red earth derived from Old Red Sandstone. The more resistant form of this rock is responsible for its hills and for the Black Mountains on its southwestern border. Here and there, chiefly by the Malvern Hills on the eastern border, are sandstones and shales of Cambrian and Silurian rocks.

The Hereford rivers are Wye, Lugg, Teme, Frome, Arrow, Monnow and Dore – lovely names all of them. The Wye offers salmon; all have trout and some grayling. The principal towns are Hereford, the cathedral city, Ross, from which to explore the beauties of the Wye Valley, Leominster, Ledbury and Bromyard, with their many superb black-and-white timbered houses and inns, and Kington, set amid hills in the valley of the Arrow. Each of them a place to stay in and enjoy slowly, like good wine.

Hereford's history is a long one. At Dorstone, a fine long barrow, misleadingly called Arthur's Stone, takes us back to the New Stone Age. Near Ross-on-Wye, King Arthur's Cave tells of even earlier habitation. The Iron Age comes alive for us in the camp on the Hereford Beacon, at the southern end of the Malvern Hills. The Romans have left evidence of a small town at Kenchester. The scanty ruins of Clifford Castle, reputedly the birthplace of Fair Rosamund in about 1140, remind us of the Normans, and the Middle Ages speak in the impressive pile of Goodrich Castle, once the strongest on the Welsh border. Saxons, Angles, Normans, English, Welsh, York and Lancaster, Cavalier and Roundhead all fought their battles in this troubled area, so peaceful today.

But all these bare facts, filled in with detail and mulled with imagination, can produce no picture or experience comparable with Hereford as it is today.

The farmers are as hard-headed as farmers anywhere. They don't farm to beautify the countryside; yet that is what they achieve. To see this red earth ploughed in autumn and spring, with jackdaws, rooks, seagulls and pied wagtails following the plough is a sight that, fortunately, leaves most people wordless. The native breed of white-faced Hereford cattle, whose colour is predominantly that of the soil which nourishes them, seen in early morning on the silver dew-sheen of a green pasture or standing in the water of a quiet stretch of the Wye with swallows and martins flighting around them like black lightning, is a microcosm of the beauty of all the earth. Of these cattle, famous wherever beef is grown, you can but adapt the lines of the psalm and say, 'Their line is gone out through all the earth and their blood to the end of the world'. Sadly they are now giving way to interlopers like Charollais and Limousins.

In the fields round Ledbury there are wild daffodils in spring; daffodils so small and lovely as to make the cultivated kinds seem gross and vulgar by comparison and quite properly hidden away in gardens. Round Ledbury, too, are the hop-yards behind tall, wind-breaking hedges. In spring a vast mileage of twine to support the vines is set up by men who look as though they are playing a complicated string game.

Despite the fact that the country is so well farmed, it is yet a land of trees: lone trees, thin coppices, and denser masses like Capler Wood hanging above the Wye near Fownhope. In autumn, when the corn stubbles are weathering and sunlight is a pale gold haze and Michaelmas daisies and dahlias are everywhere in cottage gardens, and leaves are spinning and drifting from the trees – in autumn in Hereford there is beauty almost beyond enduring. Oak leaves turning brown as slowly and surely as loaves in an oven, and other leaves floating on many an unnamed brook like fragments of beaten gold and the deep rich red of wild cherry and orchard pear leaves lying on the yellowing grass like spilled wine – these are not sights so much as experiences no man should die without savouring.

The villages and lone farmhouses have nearly all one thing in common, something that writes the word 'home' wherever men work and eat and sleep and when it is all over go at last to rest in the parish churchyard. This is the apple orchard. So many farms have one, covering a handy paddock by the house; the bulk of them cider fruit, many of unknown age; trees that time and neglect and the itching flanks of cattle have twisted and bent and that heavy bearing and gales have broken. Cider today is one of Hereford's principal industries.

Worcester

Three rivers impose their personalities upon the Worcester scene: the strong Severn and its tributaries, the swift-running temperamental Teme and the slow meandering Avon. We may thus divide the area into three watersheds, and find a distinctive character in each. But this arrangement leaves out the most populous part of Worcester, the wealthiest and the most unprepossessing. This extends from Kidderminster in the west – affectionately known to its inhabitants as 'Kiddie', and famous all the world over for its carpets – to Redditch in the east, equally famous for fishing-tackle; and from Bromsgrove in the south to the outskirts of Birmingham in the north. The hills of Clent and Lickey provide some good walks still, and among the ling there you seem a long way from the second biggest city in Britain. Seeking the open country, people who live and work in the Birmingham area, in West Midlands, turn west towards Bewdley on the Severn (the birthplace and home of a Prime Minister, Earl Baldwin) and to the Wyre Forest lying beyond it, against the Shropshire border. Wyre consists mainly of birchscrub mixed with oak, hazel and buckthorn; the rock beneath is Old Red Sandstone. From the naturalist's point of view it is interesting, as one of the very few localities in England where the big terracotta moth called the Kentish Glory still survives. The caterpillars feed in companies on the birch trees, and the moths fly swift as swallows over the heaths in the early April sun.

The Severn goes down through a dairy-farming land by way of Stourport, Holt and Hallow. It grows deeper, wider and more murmurous as it comes in sight of Worcester's cathedral tower. In some of these reaches above the city the angler has a chance of catching a salmon. Below Worcester, for some reason which has never been satisfactorily explained, the salmon won't take; and the banks are lined every weekend with coarse-fishermen from the industrial Midlands.

Worcester, with its noble cathedral (overlooking one of the most delightful cricket grounds in England), has the air of a country town, but possesses some old and new industries. Among other things it makes the famous Worcester porcelain and the equally famous Worcestershire sauce. Its battle, on 3 September 1651, was Cromwell's 'crowning mercy', and the Faithful City saw the King's downfall and the

Worcester's Cathedral lies beside the River Severn in this county town of Hereford and Worcester

triumph of the hated Roundheads. It has always had a great reputation for loyalty to our Kings; as it happens, the worst of them, King John, is buried in its cathedral. In the remarkable effigy upon his tomb you meet him, as it were, at close quarters; and are dismayed, even horrified, by what Sir Arthur Bryant described as his 'sly, vulpine face, and deceptive geniality'.

In flood-time the brown Severn runs brick-red, tomato-soup colour for a little way below Powick, where the Teme comes into it out of the red sandstone country to the west. This sandstone is rather soft, so that the Teme has cut itself a deep channel; and wears away a little more every flood. It is a river of moods, up-and-down very quickly. The gently rippled pools, dimpled with the rises of grayling, may be changed within an hour to raging torrents in which no human swimmer could survive.

The Teme Valley, from Ludlow and Tenbury Wells to the junction with the Severn, is a vivid place of bright red soil and the lushest green grass. In summer everything is colourful here: purple loosestrife and yellow skull-cap along the river banks, the river itself speckled with water-crowfoot as a lawn is with daisies, buttercups decking out every May meadow as a Field of the Cloth of Gold. If you care for the humbler and rarer plants you can find twayblade and butterfly orchis and the two scarce ferns, the adder's tongue and the quaint delicate moonwort.

This is cherry country, such as A. E. Housman wrote about, and in fact there are more of the orchards in Worcester than there are in the Shropshire-lad district above Tenbury Wells. But Teme-side farming is more mixed than most, and the orchards, of damson and apple as well as cherry, alternate with pastures and hayfields, patches of soft fruit, corn and hops. The hop-yards lie along the Teme and to the west of it, towards Bromyard. The old, large, half-timbered farmhouses give to this land an air of graciousness and prosperity; and indeed it is a rich countryside, where a man may successfully grow almost anything he has a mind to, from Clun sheep to cider-apples – or even cricket-bat willows, which are successfully grown in meadows beside the Teme.

Shakespeare's Avon (and therefore to some of us a Sacred River, like Alph in *Kubla Khan!*) enters the county near Priors Salford, close to its junction with the Arrow. The willows hang over it, the yellow flags process beside it, and except at flood-time it goes slowly upon its meandering way. Chub, perch, roach and bream are the fishes which give sport to the anglers in these favourite stretches between Bidford and Evesham town.

The country round Evesham is flat, almost treeless, and is given over to market-gardening. The black earth grows the best asparagus in the world; and the tawny asparagus-fern or 'bower' in early autumn imparts its brightness to what is otherwise one of the bleakest landscapes in the Midlands. The fields, denuded of hedgerow timber and nowadays, indeed, of hedgerows too, are not so much fields as vegetable-factories.

There are, however, belts of plum orchards to alleviate this dismal spectacle. The Vale of Evesham is almost as famous for its Pershore plums as it is for asparagus. About three springs in five, the blossom comes before the leaf; and then on 'blossom Sunday', which sometimes happily coincides with Eastertide, the motorists drive out from the towns to tour the orchard districts, where the black boughs are dressed with the delicate white petals like a late sprinkle of snow. Alas, the blossom lasts not much longer than an April snow! One day the Vale seems to wear its bridal gown; next day the myriad petals, blown by a chill wind, put you in mind of confetti on the day after the wedding.

The plum-picking, generally in August, is almost as busy a time in these parts as the Teme-side hop-picking in September. Yellow egg-plums, Prolifics, purple Pershores and Victorias are reckoned by the ton and sent by train and lorry all over Britain. When the harvest is over there is only time for the briefest of holidays before the market-gardeners are busy picking their sprouts.

The Avon flows discursively as good talk, devious, leisurely, catching Evesham in a big loop like a bight in the middle of a rope. In this noose poor Simon de Montfort was caught too, when he unwisely chose to stand and fight against the Lord Edward, son of Henry III, and Gilbert De Clare on 4 August 1265. There he died as bravely as he had lived. It was the last battle of the Barons' War; as decisive as Cromwell's victory at Worcester and the Yorkists' at Tewkesbury – both places within 15 miles of Evesham. So within a little triangle of country much history has been made.

To the east of Evesham is some stone-walled country, which in spirit seems to belong to Gloucestershire; with Broadway somewhat self-consciously beautiful, amid inspiriting north Cotswold slopes. But even here some of the big fields which used to pasture sheep, and which in war-time grew corn, have been turned over to market-gardening; and, close to Campden, sprouts by the 100 acre disfigure a landscape that was surely destined for grander things.

By way of Cropthorne (where at Craycombe House Francis Brett Young wrote his later novels), the Avon with many twists and turns flows down to Pershore, an old-fashioned town, contented among its plum-orchards. South of Pershore the river, still wriggling like an eel, passes through farmland and more market-gardens down to Eckington and under the beautiful Eckington Bridge to the foot of Bredon Hill. You can, on a clear day see several counties from the top of Bredon Hill. It is an outlying piece of the Cotswolds, formed of the same oolitic rock, in which the skeletons of ichthyosaurs have been found. Delightful villages, some built of the local stone, some black-and-white half-timbered, stand in a ring about its lower slopes. A tour of the narrow lanes which run right round the hill is well worth making. Close to the summit there was an Iron Age fort, which seems to have been the scene of a great fight or massacre. The hill is 991 feet high, but a Folly built at the very top adds the necessary 9 feet to make up the 1,000.

This Folly gives you a splendid view over the plain of Malvern. You look down on the Avon easing itself round the lower slopes of the hill and traipsing lazily through the enormous meadows or 'hams' which are still held in common: the owners of other land in the adjacent village have a right to pasture cattle on the ham's aftermath.

Across the plain, which is 15 miles wide, rises the magnificent ridge of the Malverns: 'old as the hills' is the word, for this pre-Cambrian rock is more than 500 million years old. The highest hill, the Worcester Beacon, is 1,395 feet. You can walk south from its summit by a tremendous saddleback 9 miles long until you reach the British Camp or Hereford Beacon (1,114 feet). From the trenches and parapets running round the British Camp a platoon could still hold the

hill against a battalion: it must have been a formidable fortress, guarding the pass over the hills. South of it, at the end of the range, is the quaintly named Ragged Stone Hill, which possesses a Midsummer Night's legend: you must take care to walk clear of the stone's shadow when the sun first strikes it at first light on Midsummer morning, or some fearful fate will befall!

Malvern, tucked under the ridge, sheltered from west winds but denied the late afternoon sun, is known for its schools and its waters, for the good stained glass in its priory church, and for its annual Festival, which before World War II was given over chiefly to performing the plays of George Bernard Shaw. Indeed, the town was almost a second home to him; and each summer he was to be seen, lanky, bearded and prophetic, striding over those tall bare hills, from which according to his mood a man may look west towards the wildness of Wales, or eastwards upon the assured agricultural landscape of Worcester, with its air of custom and continuity. Almost smug, you might say – but remember that these fields have been cultivated continuously for more than 1,000, possibly for nearly 2,000, years. The local place names, pretty thick on the map, are sometimes Celtic, often Saxon: occasionally a bit of both. The Romans came, the Saxons, the Normans; the fields were ploughed in turn by sweating men with the plough, by the heaving oxen, by the heavy-hoofed horses, with wooden share, with the sharp steel; by Celt, Saxon, Frenchman, serf, peasant, by the servants of monks and lords, by tenant-farmers and owner-farmers, by German and Italian prisoners-of-war. This land is the very heart of England. Our conflicts and our battles, our king-making and king-breaking, our conquests and our disasters, have never interrupted the rhythm of ploughing and planting for long. History has passed like the cloud-shadows which dapple the fields on a changeable day; but the grass and the corn have kept growing.

GAZETTEER

Abberley   7I5
Together with a 19th-c church, the ruins of a Norman one beside the rectory, and a 160ft clock tower, its distinctions are an unchanging charm and the Abberley Hills, rising in a curve to the S. 1m S, *Great Witley*, where there is a Georgian hundred-house (now a hotel), lies beneath Woodbury Hill (904ft), crowned with an ancient British camp. Here is an 18th-c church, with rich rococo decoration and Rysbrack's giant memorial to the family of the 1st Lord Foley (d.1732) who built it. He also built Witley Court (in the 19th c the Earl of Dudley spent £250,000 on enlarging it), which, in its 500-acre park, was burned down in 1937.

Abbey Dore*   7H3
Amid quiet orchards at the S end of the *Golden Valley* of the River Dore is a magnificent parish church, once part of a Cistercian abbey, founded in 1147, and restored by Viscount Scudamore in the early 17th c. The near-by Abbey Dore Court gardens are on view in summer.

Besford   7J4
The church has unusual 14th-c timber work. The W window is of oak, as also are the traceried windows in the bell-tower, which is timber-framed like the nave. The wainscoting here is made from old pews, but the roof-loft is a rare pre-Reformation example. Noteworthy too is an Elizabethan painted triptych.

Bewdley   7I5
Perched above the Severn, on the fringe of Wyre Forest, the town recalls by its heraldic anchor its one-time importance as a river harbour. Tudor and Jacobean houses and the predominantly Georgian character of the town as a whole bear witness to its days of prosperity. The original parish church, 1m S in the park of *Ribbesford House* (presented to George Herbert and his brothers by Charles I, but rebuilt in 1820), is remarkable for its Norman tympanum, the rare 14th-c oak arches of the S arcade, and a window by Burne-Jones and William Morris. Bewdley has its own worth-while museum in the Shambles on the S side of Load Street. E on the A456 is the West Midlands Safari Park. Open March–Nov. At Bewdley station the Severn Valley Railway runs steam trains to **Bridgnorth** (Shrops) in summer.

Birtsmorton   7I4
The Court is an admirable example of a 14th–15th-c manor house, with a timbered quadrangle; moated, and approached by a bridge and a massive turreted gateway. It was presented by Henry VI to Sir R. Nanfan, whose tutor here was Wolsey and who is buried in a tomb of Purbeck marble in the church. Waterfowl Sanctuary open all year.

Bosbury   7I4
A large village of character with a church of great interest and a splendid detached tower.

Bredon   7J4
Large, picturesque village on the Avon, at the foot of *Bredon Hill* (991ft) 3½m NE, at the top of which are fine views, Romano-British earthworks and a 200-year-old tower, Parson's Folly. In the village, timbered houses and a splendid tithe barn (NT) (burned, alas, in 1981) lie beside the river, and a slender 14th-c spire reaches 160ft. The nave and tower, with original vaulting, are Norman; note the canopied monument to the Reeds (1611), who founded the almshouses in the centre of the village.

Bretforton   7J4
Largest and most accessible of a 5m string of villages, all watered by Avon tributaries, all with gabled manor houses, timbered dovecots and cottages, and medieval churches. To the N, the three *Littletons*: South (manor rebuilt 1921, clipped yews, church with Norman door and old pews); and

Symonds Yat: an old pass, towering 400 feet above the River Wye which flows along the gorge below

Middle and North (lovely grouping of 14th-c manor, tithe barn, and a dovecot and the church, with fine Norman font, 16th-c pews, embattled Smith chapel over porch and monuments); and *Cleeve Prior* (broad streets, the Kings Arms, manor with great yew hedge). Bretforton itself has no fewer than six dovecots, of varied architecture, and the half-timbered Golden Fleece. To the S lie *Badsey* (a 17th-c monument in the restored church); and the loveliest of all, *Wickhamford* (many-gabled manor beside a stream, looking over lawn to the lake; church with Jacobean linenfold box pews, chancel-gates and altar-rails, and some fine canopied alabaster monuments).

Broadway   7J4
Considered the finest Cotswold village; its main street and its green are lined with stone cottages and great houses, among which are Abbots Grange (with chapel and hall), Tudor House and the Lygon Arms. The old church, not much used, has some Norman work and a rare palimpsest brass; the new one is 19th-c. The road to **Stow-on-the-Wold** winds up Fish Hill (1,024ft) with Beacon Tower and fine views at the top. 3m S is **Snowshill Manor** (NT) in Glos. Also S is Broadway Tower Country Park. The 55ft tower houses an observatory and exhibition and has a 19th-c barn.

Bromsgrove   7J5
An ancient industrial town, bypassed by the M5 but with an overspill from **Birmingham**, less than 15m N. Its old buildings include part of the grammar school; the Council House of mellow brick, Dutch gabled and mullioned; and near by, the church, approached by an ascent of many steps, with its 15th-c steeple rising to 200ft and, inside, Talbot monuments. Their ancient manor, with its Tudor chapel and Renaissance porch, stands at the end of a lane, 2m SW. The Perry Hall Hotel close by the church claims to be the family home of A. E. Housman of 'Shropshire Lad' fame. 2m S is *Avoncroft Museum of Buildings*, of interest to architects, and antiquarians. Granary, barn, mill, houses, etc. and crafts. Open March–Nov.

Bromyard   7I4
Small market town in the valley of the River Frome. Many good timber houses, especially the Falcon inn, and good wood carving in the Norman church. 2m E is *Lower Brockhampton Hall* (NT), open to the public in the summer.

Burton Court *see* **Eardisland**

Chaddesley Corbett   7I5
In its wide street of black-and-white cottages, the old Talbot inn faces the church (Norman arcade and font, and 18th-c tower and spire). 1m NW, *Harvington Hall* rambles many-gabled within its moat, opening to a lake. Tudor, with wall paintings and secret passages and hides, much modified in 18th c and since restored, the Hall is open most days.

Cleeve Prior *see* **Bretforton**

Colwall   7I4
On the slopes of the **Malvern Hills**. Elizabeth Barrett Browning spent her girlhood at Hope End (but the house no longer exists). On the hills SE is an Iron Age camp on **Hereford Beacon**.

Cotheridge   7I4
A double avenue of limes, ½m long and nearly 300 years old, leads to Court and church, which (largely 12th-c, with massive timber-framed tower, box-pews and altar-rails of

later period) faces the great house, Georgian, with remains of earlier gabled building.

Croft Castle★   7H5
5m NW of **Leominster**. Except for the years 1750–1923, this ancient Welsh border castle, with its four round corner towers in pink stone, has been inhabited by the Croft family since the Norman Conquest. It is now owned by the NT and is open in the summer months.

Cropthorne   7J4
Cottages and church (wall painting, Saxon cross recovered from chancel wall, and Dingley tombs) sloping to the Avon; and N across the river, past Charlton Hall, *Fladbury*, with its landing-stage, inn, water-mill and church, surrounded by yew trees and containing notable brasses. Also here is the Delamere Bird Garden. Open all year.

Dormston   7J4
2m W of *Inkberrow*. A tiny hamlet, in which Moat Farm, with its dovecots and lantern, and the fine church tower, make a delightful group of black-and-white.

Dorstone   6G4
A village at the N end of the *Golden Valley*. The church was founded by Richard de Brito, one of the knights who murdered Becket. A chalice found in his tomb when it was opened during restoration is now displayed in the church. Note the very good iron candelabra. A near-by prehistoric long barrow known as Arthur's Stone (AM) is yet another of the traditional graves of King Arthur.

Droitwich   7J5
Has a small town centre with a few old houses and three churches, of which one (RC) is noted for its modern mosaics; and four great houses within reach: *Hanbury Hall* (NT), 3½m E, is of the Wren period and open to the public; *Salwarpe Court*, 2½m SW, the 16th-c timber-framed home of the Talbots, is now a farmhouse; 1½m E stands brick-built, stone-mullioned *Westwood House*, Jacobean with a gatehouse; and 5m SE, Elizabethan *Huddington Court*, with latticed windows, twisted chimneys, swans on the moat and dovecots on the lawn. Droitwich was always famous for salt. In the 19th c it was taken over by John Corbett who developed it into a famous spa with brine baths and who built some very grandiloquent hotels. But the spa is now in decline and the town is becoming a commuter centre. Exhibitions on history of town at the Heritage Centre.

Eardisland   7H4
Pretty village with many lovely timbered buildings on the grassy banks of the River Arrow. Note especially the 14th-c Staick House and the 17th-c dovecot. Near the bridge is the whipping-post. *Burton Court*, 1m S, has a museum of costume and is open during summer months.

Eardisley   6G4
The partly Norman church is particularly interesting for its remarkably beautiful 12th-c font. Some good black-and-white in the village which is unusual among Hereford villages for having a regular street.

Eckington   7J4
Approached by a fine old bridge across the Avon, the village church has a Norman doorway and S arcade, an ancient dug-out chest and the Hanford tomb – Tudor husband and wife with their 13 children beneath a canopy. 2m E, on *Bredon Hill* (*see* **Bredon**), is Jacobean *Woollas Hall*.

Elmley Castle 7J4

No longer any sign of the castle, but a lovely village street, and a medieval church worth visiting for its 13th-c dragons, writhing beneath the eight carved sides of the font; and for its monuments, especially the sculptured figures of the Savage tomb.

Evesham 7J4

Built on both sides of the Avon, in the centre of the orchards of its Vale, the town has an air of elegance and prosperity. A few timber-framed, and more Georgian, buildings; and, at its heart, the precincts of the ruined abbey (AM) running to the river bank. Here, side by side, are two noble churches, both much rebuilt in the 16th c and since restored, both containing chantries with superb fan vaulting built by the last abbot, Clement Lichfield, who also completed the fine bell-tower just before the Dissolution swept away the remainder of his abbey. The Almonry, a 14th-c half-timbered building, houses the local museum. Open Easter–Sept.

Eye Manor see Leominster

Fladbury see Cropthorne

Goodrich★ 7H3

Picturesque village beside the Wye, with splendid remains of a 12th–14th-c castle (AM), long the home of the Talbots, Earls of Shrewsbury, but left a ruin after its capture by the Parliamentarians in the Civil War. In the church is panelling from the sham 'Gothic castle', Goodrich Court, pulled down in 1950.

Great Malvern see Malvern

Hartlebury 7I5

Though surrounded by much modern building, the village has an attractive centre dominated by the stately church (1830s). Its castle has for centuries been the residence of the Bishops of Worcester. The state apartments are on view occasionally in summer; but open almost daily is a wing of the castle that has been transformed into a county museum of the highest quality.

Hereford★ 7H4

Busy centre of a flourishing agricultural area: hop-yards, fruit orchards, cider factories, and recently imported industry. The Cathedral★ was begun in 1107, but the process of building and alteration has continued through the centuries; observe the noble tower, the impressive Norman pillars of the nave and the magnificent Gothic N transept. Among its treasures are the *Mappa Mundi* (13th-c), one of the oldest maps in the world; one of the world's finest collections of valuable chained books (another good collection is in All Saints' Church); and a recently installed display of church plate in the crypt. In centre of city note picturesque timbered 17th-c Old House, now a museum. Nell Gwynn is supposed to have been born in Hereford; David Garrick is known to have been. Sarah Siddons and the Kemble family lived here for a time. Nelson was a freeman of the city and is commemorated by a column. The Three Choirs music festival is held at Hereford every third year. In Hereford Museum are most of the finds excavated from the Roman town at **Kenchester**. Other museums include the Churchill Gardens Museum (costumes, furniture, paintings), the St John Coningsby Museum with 11th-c chapel and dining-room, a unique Museum of Cider, and Bulmers Railway Centre. 6m N is *Dinmore Manor*, a modernized preceptory of the Knights of St John of Jerusalem. Open afternoons. 1m S of the city is *Rotherwas Chapel* (AM). Of medieval origin it was enlarged by Pugin in the 19th c. Open Tues. April–Sept. 7m NW is the weir at *Swainshill*. Open at set times.

Hereford Beacon 7I4

Here, the **Malvern Hills** reach 1,114ft above sea level, and there is an extensive ancient British camp covering 44 acres. The citadel, about 50yd in circumference, consists of a thick stone wall covered with earth defended by a ditch.

Kenchester 7H4

The site of the important Roman *Castra Magna*, mosaics and other relics from which are in **Hereford** Museum. The Norman font in the church was made from a discarded pillar.

Kidderminster 7I5

Still making carpets as it has done for 200 years, still looking up to St Mary's on the hill above the River Stour. Much rebuilt in the 18th and 19th c, the church is noteworthy for its brasses and monuments, and as the place where Richard Baxter (d.1691), the Nonconformist preacher, had to build five galleries to accommodate his audiences. Art gallery and museum in Market Street.

Kilpeck★ 7H3

Here is one of the finest small Norman churches in Britain. Note especially the superb intricately carved S doorway, the huge Norman font under the gallery, the carvings in the chancel reminiscent of Celtic craftsmanship, and a curious Norman stoup.

Kilpeck Church: the carved doorway is just part of this perfectly preserved example of Norman architecture

Ledbury: half-timbered 16th-century buildings in cobbled Church Lane which adjoins the Market Place

Kington   6G4

Small market town close to the Welsh border, noted for its annual September show and autumn sheep sales. Interesting church with good Early English work. In the neighbourhood is a well-preserved section of **Offa's Dyke**. Just outside the town the fine gardens of *Hengest Croft* are open to the public in the summer months.

Ledbury   7I4

Old town on the western approach to the **Malvern Hills**. The 17th-c market house is still supported by its original oak posts. Beside it a narrow lane bordered with timbered buildings leads to the large church with its detached tower, tall spire and impressive monuments.

  Eastnor Castle, 1½m E, built *c.*1815, and occasionally open to the public in summer, contains good collections of pictures, armour and tapestries. The splendid park has many specimen trees, including one of the 12 mistletoe oaks growing in England.

Leominster   7H4

An old wool town among rivers, hop-yards and orchards. It has many lovely timbered buildings, including a sensational timber-framed Old Town Hall, and a church remarkable for having three naves built respectively in the 12th, 13th and 14th c. In the church is kept the ducking stool in which nagging women were placed before being dipped in the river. The Folk Museum opened in 1972 has fine local history displays. 5m NW is **Croft Castle**. *Berrington Hall*, 3m N, is a beautiful late Georgian house, often open on summer afternoons. *Eye Manor*, 4m N, with remarkable Renaissance

interior and contents, is open summer months in the afternoons. 4½m NW at Lucton is *Mortimer's Cross Mill* (AM). Built in the 18th c it worked until the 1940s. Open Thurs. April–Sept. 5m S is 14th-c *Dinmore Manor*.

Littletons, North, Middle and South *see* **Bretforton**

Lower Brockhampton *see* **Bromyard**

Madley   7H4

The large church has developed from a small Norman edifice into a fine example of various styles of Gothic. The Norman N transept now serves as the N porch. In the apsidal chancel is famous early stained glass. More early glass can be seen in the E window of the church at near-by *Eaton Bishop* where there is also Wormhill Farm Museum, open in summer.

Malvern, Great★   7I4

Inland resort and residential town, noted for its drama festival and public school, it is beautifully situated on the slopes of the **Malvern Hills**. Its chief beauty is the majestic priory church, the Norman arcades of the nave enclosed in a 15th-c building, with wonderful glass of the period, especially in the E window. The waters of Malvern Wells were discovered in the 1600s but today the spa is not of great importance. At *Little Malvern*, 3m S, the tower and choir of another priory church remain, also with good medieval glass. 2m NE, *Madresfield Court* stands behind its moat in a large park, with an avenue of trees 1m long.

Malvern Hills   7I4

The most impressive range in the county, extending for 9m, with superlative views★ (over ten counties, it is said, can be seen on a clear day) from the Worcester and **Hereford Beacon**s (1,395 and 1,114ft respectively).

Martley   7I4

A neat village, with a fine 300-year-old rectory and a grey-and-red sandstone church, visited for its well-preserved wall-paintings, largely 13th-c, but partly 15th-c. To the S, *Berrow Hill* rises 602ft, with views of the Teme Valley.

Much Marcle   7I4

Peaceful village near the Gloucestershire border, with a 13th–15th-c church rich in interesting monuments, and two fine old houses: Hellens, a manorial house begun in 1292 and with a dovecot dated 1641, occasionally open on summer afternoons, and Homme House, shown by appointment only.

Offa's Dyke   6G4

Sections of high earthen banks stretching from the Wye to the Dee, planned by King Offa of Mercia in the 8th c to mark the boundary between England and Wales where it was not marked by natural barriers of river and forest. Sections can be seen, for example, at **Kington**. Offa's Dyke Footpath stretches 168m from **Prestatyn** (Clwyd) to **Chepstow** (Gwent). *See also* entry in Clwyd.

Ombersley   7I5

An attractive place, with many elaborately timbered houses, including the pleasant King's Arms; the Court, an early 18th-c house, since refronted; and a notable church of the 1820s. At *Boreley*, is the BBC *Gardeners World* Garden. Open set times May–Oct.

Pembridge   7H4

Large village with picturesque timber houses and a church noted for its detached timber belfry.

Pershore   7J4
A medieval stone bridge of six arches crosses the Avon to this market town, with its 18th-c houses and two churches. The greater of the two is only a part of the mighty abbey church that once stood here, but what remains beneath the lantern tower is of rare beauty, especially the Norman arches that support the tower, the presbytery and the vaulted roof.

Pirton   7J4
Two contrasting qualities of black-and-white timbering are the simplicity of the church tower and, ½m away, the elaborate work of Pirton Court.

Ripple   7I4
An attractive village, grouped round the slender cross on the green. Its treasure is a set of misericords in the church, carved to show the activities of the months.

Ross-on-Wye*   7H3
Understandably a centre of tourist attraction at the height of summer owing to its spectacular position on a beautiful curve of the Wye; out of season, a delightful quiet market town centred round its arcaded market hall. Splendid views from The Prospect near the churchyard. 'The Man of Ross' praised by Pope in his essay *On the Use of Riches* was John Kyrle (1637–1724), man of vision and local philanthropist. *See also* **Goodrich**. 15m E at *Newent* is a Falconry Centre and Museum.

Rous Lench   7J4
A small but lovely village, the black-and-white cottages culminating in historic Lench Court, with its clipped yews and 7 acres of terraced gardens. The church too is impressive, with Norman work, canopied altar and one of its chapels that contains a series of Rous monuments.

Severn Stoke   7I4
A pleasant village by the river, with the folly known as Dunstall Castle near by, and one of Capability Brown's masterpieces 2m E at *Croome d'Abitot*. At Croome Court, former home of the Earls of Coventry, he not only laid out the grounds, with grottoes, statues and artificial lake, but is also said to have designed and built the mansion, with church and village to match.

Shelsley Walsh   7I5
Tiny hamlet in the Teme Valley, among hop fields and kilns. The court house is good Jacobean, timber-framed; the restored church noted for one of the finest chancel screens in the county and a rare wooden tomb (1596). At *Hanley William*, 3½m NW, standing considerably higher, the church has a timber turret, Norman font and pulpit hewn in one piece from the trunk of a tree and beautifully carved.

Shobdon   7H5
In the mid-18th c the 2nd Lord Bateman pulled down the old Norman church, built the present very remarkable rococo-Gothic church in its place, and re-erected parts of the original church as 'romantic' embellishments to the grounds of his own house, Shobdon Court, now demolished.

Spetchley Park *see* Worcester

Stourport-on-Severn   7I5
Nothing was here but a small hamlet until in 1766 James Brindley built his canal linking the Severn and the Trent. Within 30 years it had become a major inland port, complete with quays, warehouses and bridge, much of which can still be seen, though falling into disuse. Today iron and carpets are its staple industries. Sir George Gilbert Scott built the church in the 19th c; its Methodist chapel is noted for the richness of its marbles and alabaster; there is a fine public park; boat trips on the Severn; and at the outskirts, Old Mitton Mill which is mentioned in Domesday Book.

Strensham   7J4
The church of this tiny hamlet (birthplace of the poet Samuel Butler in 1612) looks out across the Avon to Bredon Hill (*see* **Bredon**). Noted for its painted gallery, two-decker pulpit and 14th–18th-c effigies of the Russells; some are brasses (including the oldest in the county), others marble.

Symond's Yat*   7H3
The word 'yat' means gate or pass. In this well-known beauty spot the Wye flows through a narrow gorge and describes a tremendous loop, taking 5m to encompass Huntsham Hill and curve back to near its own earlier course. About 3m downstream, in the Doward Hills above the river, is King Arthur's Cave in which were discovered relics of inhabitants of 20,000 years ago. (*See also* page 164.)

Tenbury Wells   7H5
A little market town, with pump room, hotels and excellent trout fishing in the Teme. **Burford**, 1m W – which though in Shrops, forms a 'suburb' of Tenbury – the church is noted for its monument and a fine Elizabethan triptych. Burford House Gardens and nurseries open regularly.

Weobley   7H4
Attractive old village, once a borough, with an unusual number of half-timbered houses. The Red Lion dates from the 13th c. The mainly 14th-c church has a splendid spire and several notable monuments. The Jacobean house called The Ley has fine timbers and a priest's hole.

Wickhamford *see* **Bretforton**

Worcester*   7I4
For centuries the Cathedral City, and today an industrial town with one of the Severn power stations, and celebrated for glove-making, china and Worcester sauce. The Royal Porcelain Works, founded in 1750, and the Dyson Perrins Museum, can be inspected on weekdays. Old Tudor timbered houses can be seen to advantage in New, Fish and Friar Streets. Among 18th-c buildings are Britannia House, the Berkeley Hospital, St Swithun's, four stately churches, and, exceedingly handsome, the Guildhall (designed by Thomas White, a pupil of Wren's), with statues of Charles I and Charles II on its façade.

The Edgar Tower leads to College Green, with the King's School (still using the monk's refectory), circular chapter house, cloisters and, overlooking the river, the cathedral. Originally Norman (the magnificent crypt remains) and much restored in the 19th c, the major part of the building dates from the 14th c. Its glory is the choir, with innumerable monuments, including Prince Arthur's delicately wrought chantry and King John's effigy and tomb. Near by, the Commandery is a Tudor house, built on the site of an earlier hospital of St Wulstan, and now a museum of local life. In the City Art Gallery is a collection of 28 paintings by David Cox. Once every three years the Three Choirs Festival is held in the cathedral. (*See* page 162.) *Spetchley Park*, 3m E, has a spectacular garden, open to the public Easter–Sept. except Sat. 3m W of Worcester at *Lower Broadheath* is Elgar's Birthplace Museum. Open all year.

SHROPSHIRE

AN INTRODUCTION BY
PHIL DRABBLE AND JASPER MORE

Shropshire is about 50 miles long and 40 miles wide and is roughly divided in half by the River Severn, which is the longest river in England and Wales. Its western boundary is the border between England and Wales, and memories of the raids and skirmishes, bloodshed and hates that have rattled round the marches through the centuries are still green – so much so that it can be taken as a slight to hint that a Shropshire man was born 'the wrong side of the border'. Looking down on all this turmoil, and on everything in history and pre-history that happened before, is Shropshire's most famous mountain, the Wrekin, whose volcanic rock is the oldest in England. The Watling Street runs just below it; but if you turn off and follow the lanes at its foot until you return to the Watling Street again, you will have seen peerless scenery – and covered a surprisingly long distance.

To the west of the county the hills lift range upon range into Wales; south of the Severn are the uplands of Shropshire, and to the north is the rich dairy and arable country which has made Shropshire farming famous. In the north of the county, too, lie the Shropshire meres, six huge sheets of water which are paradise for the naturalist and botanist. By contrast, the Long Mynd, towering above the Shrewsbury–Ludlow road, is quite out of context with the rest of the county. It is a heather-covered plateau of grit and shale, rising to 1,674 feet, almost as old as the rock of the Wrekin. The bleak, wild central area is shared by wild ponies and grouse, and to the west the hill falls suddenly away, so that the prevailing winds provide a constant surge of eddies and up-currents which account for its popularity as a centre for gliding.

Leaving the Long Mynd, the road from Church Stretton to Much Wenlock runs along the narrow spine of Wenlock Edge, famous for its views and its lime quarries. In parts the Edge is so narrow that it is possible to look out either side and see the country dissected beneath like a specimen on an anatomist's table. Much Wenlock, with its ancient priory and guildhall, welcomes travellers along the Edge with an unchanging, almost medieval, hospitality. The limestone core of the Edge is as much in contrast with the grit of Long Mynd as it is with the rugged glacial gorge at Ironbridge, or the rich red sandstone of basalt-capped Clee Hill.

The south of the county is as soft and beautiful as the northwest is wild. Lovely Corvedale, from Ludlow to Bridgnorth, is wooded and rich, good country for game, often resonant with crowing pheasants at dusk and brilliant with them at sunset.

History and Towns

Watling Street, entering Shropshire from Stafford-shire at Weston-under-Lizard, passes near Wroxeter, which is on the site of the Roman settlement of Uriconium, once the fourth Roman city in Britain. You can still see remnants of the original paving, of shops and of the lawcourt, the whole enclosed, originally, by a wall 2 miles long. There are, too, remnants of the baths (used also as brothels in those days), of the forum and of various workshops. A multitude of personal belongings have been dug up and are to be seen in the museum at Shrewsbury. The later history of Shropshire is inextricably interwoven with the history of Wales. Offa, King of the Mercians, built his dyke, in the 8th century, from the Dee to the Wye. A great deal of the earthworks, ditches and ramparts still remain and will be an irresistible attraction to anyone in tune with the romance of the past. The best stretch is in the Clun and Mainstone area. From Norman times onwards, a string of castles was built to keep the Welsh under control.

The county was as famous for men of God as for men of war. Much Wenlock Priory was founded by Mercian King Penda's granddaughter Milburga. It was destroyed by the Danes; but Lady Godiva restored it. Again it was destroyed – to be restored once more by the Norman Roger de Montgomery. The ruins are well worth visiting, as is the rest of the town with its unspoiled medieval buildings. There were other religious houses at Lilleshall and Haughmond; but the most famous of all is at Buildwas. Roger de Clinton, crusader and Bishop of Chester, built it 800 years ago; it is still a vast impressive monument to the religious fervour of olden times. The great pillars support seven pairs of the finest Norman arches in England, and the crypt and cloisters still remain. The abbot's

Below Wenlock Edge is Much Wenlock and its priory, founded in the 7th century and rebuilt by Lady Godiva

house has been made into a private riverside residence. Incongruously enough, the ruins of this peaceful riverside abbey are now dominated by a clinically functional power-station.

The county (renamed Salop in the 1974 county reorganization but now reverted to its old name) has always been centred round its county town of Shrewsbury. Always a great agricultural market, it was also for many centuries a prosperous market for Welsh wool and flax. A great railway centre in the late 19th century, the town has become in recent years the home of a number of engineering enterprises. It is a curious feature of the county that with the exception of Wellington all the other towns are situated almost on the county boundaries. Wellington, a small industrial town east of Shrewsbury, is being swallowed up into Telford, a new town planned on a scale which will challenge the long pre-eminence of Shrewsbury.

Industry

Thinking of the Clun Forest sheep that make such spectacles of the sales at Craven Arms, or of the rich dairying land to the north, on the Cheshire border, most people consider Shropshire an agricultural county. But the story of the Ironbridge Gorge is of the greatest interest either to the historian or to the student of the rise and fall of our prosperity. The town of Ironbridge clings to the steep banks of the gorge like grimy starlings clinging to a cliff. It got its name, as well as its prosperity, from the iron bridge which spans the river. This was built by the ironmaster Abraham Darby in 1779, the first bridge in the world to be made of iron, symbol of the prosperity that iron was to bring to this valley. It had to wait for the second Iron Age, the Industrial Revolution, to become rich. Wilkinson, another ironmaster so wrapt in his craft that even his coffin was of iron, confounded the sceptics by building a boat of iron – which to their amazement floated! At about the same time, the district became as famous for the delicacy of its Coalport China as for its heavier industry.

Success had come to Coalbrookdale; but success ate into the supply of raw materials, and prosperity faded. Since 1967, however, the scars of old enterprise are being covered by the new town of Telford, which will bring back prosperous industry.

Famous People

Shropshire has produced other famous characters. Clive of India, born near Market Drayton, later lived at Walcot Hall, near Lydbury North, with its wonderful parkland and lakes. He went to school at Market Drayton and his family home was Styche Hall at Moreton Say. Charles Darwin was born and educated in Shrewsbury. Mary Webb's novels fired popular imagination the more because of the vivid pictures of Shropshire life they contained. She lived, at various times, at Stanton and Pontesbury and Meole Brace and Leighton. But the writer who has perhaps done most to make Shropshire known to readers all over the world was a Worcestershire man – A. E. Housman, author of 'A Shropshire Lad'.

GAZETTEER

Acton Burnell   7H6
The rebuilt Georgian hall stands in a hilly park, with folly and two lakes; and, near by, is the ruined fortified manor house (AM), one of the oldest in England and visited by Edward I in 1283. It was built at the same time as the church by Robert Burnell, Bishop of Bath and Wells. To the S, *Langley Chapel* (early 17th-c, with period furnishings) stands close by the walls and gatehouse of Langley Hall.

Acton Scott *see* Church Stretton

Alberbury   6G6
Church (Norman to 15th-c, with saddle-back tower and magnificent roof). Loton Park, Carolean with additions; 2m SW, Braggington Manor, now a farm, is 17th-c; and, 2m S, the red sandstone tower of *Wattlesborough Castle* is incorporated in a farm, with moated garden.

Atcham 7H6
Small village in a bend of the Severn, with concrete bridge carrying main Holyhead road, alongside earlier one of 1768. The Mytton and Mermaid Inn was previously a dower-house. Across the river, 1m S, *Cronkhill* is a country house by John Nash. N of Atcham a drive leads to *Attingham Park* (NT), late 18th-c, with period plaster ceilings, in grounds improved by Humphry Repton. Open at set times.

Attingham Park *see* Atcham

Battlefield 7H7
Here, in 1403, Henry IV defeated Hotspur. So great was the slaughter that Robert Ive, rector of near-by *Albright Hussey*, built the church (1410) to commemorate the slain. Albright Hussey Manor (timber and brick of 16th and 17th c) still stands within its dry moat.

Benthall *see* Broseley

Bishop's Castle 6G5
Hilly borough in attractive Clun Forest (*see* **Clun**) country. The timbered 'House on Crotches' dates from 1573; the best 18th-c buildings are the town hall and the Castle Hotel (on the site of the vanished castle). Road to N leaves *Stiperstones* to the E and follows Hope Valley to *Minsterley*, 10m away, with attractive brick-and-stone church (1690), period pulpit and maids' garlands.

Bitterley 7H5
Pretty village at the foot of *Titterstone Clee Hill* with *Brown Clee Hill* 6m away NNE, both over 1,700ft and both crowned with ancient British camps; here are fine views over Hereford and Worcester to Radnor Forest. There is a churchyard cross, and the church has a Norman font, a Jacobean pulpit and monuments.

Boscobel House *see* Tong

Bridgnorth 7I6
Busy Low Town is connected with enchanting High Town by a funicular railway. The charm of the place lies in the medieval atmosphere that pervades its streets of black-and-white houses, well viewed from the funicular. Midland Motor Museum and Gardens are open daily at Stanmore Hall. The Severn Valley Railway is a preserved railway running 13m from Bridgnorth to **Bewdley** (Hereford and Worcester) – rolling stock etc on display. *Dudmaston Hall* (NT), 4m SE, is a large William and Mary house with good furniture and interesting relics of the Darby family. Open at stated times. *Upton Cressett*, 4m W, is an Elizabethan manor house recently restored. Open on occasional afternoons. 3¼m W is *Morville Hall* (NT), an Elizabethan house with later alterations which is open by appointment.

Bromfield 7H5
At the junction of the Onny and Teme rivers, with a broad waterfall beside the footpath through Oakly Park. There is the stone, timbered gatehouse of a former priory, the nave of whose church now serves the village. (Note the great entrance porch, and the 17th-c painted chancel ceiling.) Near the station is **Ludlow**'s racecourse.

Broseley 7I6
A fascinating survival of Shropshire's 18th-c industrial revolution. Some modern building and some dereliction but much of the original character survives. 2m W at *Benthall* is a well-restored late 17th-c church (box-pews and gallery)

and the magnificent Hall (NT) built in 1535 of grey stone with mullioned windows. Open Easter–Sept. on set days.

Buildwas 7I6
The ruins of the 12th-c abbey are now AM; the six chimneys of the power station stand in contrast. Beside the Severn are a lido and a camping ground.

Burford 7H5
Attractively situated in Teme Valley on Hereford and Worcester border, with 18th-c red-brick rectory and restored church noteworthy for 15th-c Cornwall monuments.

Chirbury 6G6
Charming brick-and-stone village, with half-timbered school and church surrounded by yews. *Corndon Hill* (1,640ft) is 3m E and **Powys** 2m in the other direction.

Church Stretton 7H6
The attractive village grouped around the parish church was developed in the late 19th c into an ambitious inland resort. The neighbouring country is superb. There is a nature trail at Old Rectory Wood. A 2m walk up lovely *Cardingmill Valley* leads to Robin Hood's Butts (1,461ft) at the top of *Long Mynd*. The Long Mynd is now vested in the NT; walkers can roam over 6,000 acres of moorland but it is wiser to keep to the paths. *Little Stretton*, 2m S, has a 16th-c black-and-white manor house and a modern black-and-white church. *Acton Scott*, 3m S, has a fine brick Elizabethan hall in an attractive park, part of which has been taken over by the County Council and opened as the Acton Scott Working Farm Museum. Open March–Oct.

Claverley 7I6
Half-timbered cottages and red sandstone church (Norman to Perpendicular, restored; with 13th-c wall paintings, two fonts and an alabaster tomb). 1m NE is moated *Ludstone Hall*, restored Jacobean with formal gardens.

Cleobury Mortimer 7I5
Charming little town of timbered and Georgian houses, with very little building since mid-19th c, except Sir George Gilbert Scott's restoration of the church. Fishing in the River Rea, walking in *Wyre Forest* to E or on *Clee Hill*, 6m W, which rises to over 1,600ft. *Mawley Hall*, 1m SE is a Georgian house with a magnificent interior. Open by appointment.

Clun 6G5
Market town, with stone bridge over River Clun, and Clun Forest (no trees, but mile upon mile of rounded hills up to 1,600ft, famous for sheep) to NW. Here are the ruins of the moated Norman castle once a stronghold in the Marches and still formidable; and the church, mainly of the same date, has later angels in the roof. 9m W, running N and S of *Newcastle*, there is a stretch of the famous **Offa's Dyke**.

Coalbrookdale *see* Ironbridge and Telford

Condover 7H6
Church originally Norman, but mainly 17th-c, pinkish stone with monuments from 1587 to 1868, one by G. F. Watts. Several old houses, but principally the fine Elizabethan hall, of the same stone as the church, gabled and mullioned, with a yew garden in the large park. Now a school for the

Telford: the world's first iron bridge, built in 1779, stretches 100 feet over the Gorge (see also pages 16 and 21)

blind, it may be seen by appointment in August. 3m SE, *Pitchford Hall* (16th-c), the outstanding timbered house of the county, was occupied by 13 generations of the Ottley family, the first having bought the estate in 1473 and the last dying there in 1807. The church, adjacent to the house, mainly 13th-c with 17th-c furnishings and, most impressive, an effigy of a medieval knight carved in oak.

Craven Arms 7H5
Famous among sheep farmers for its sales; but to others for the countryside roundabout and *Stokesay Castle* (AM), an example of a 13th-c fortified manor house, with well-preserved Elizabethan gatehouse. The church here, largely rebuilt after damage in the Civil War, has 17th-c furnishings, almost intact. Norton Camp is a Celtic camp on a wooded hill 2m SE. At *Onibury*, 2½m SSE, the interior of the little Norman church is attractively restored.

Diddlebury 7H5
In Corvedale, at foot of *Wenlock Edge* (*see* Introduction), it has a Georgian Hall with a park, and pre-Norman work in the church. 1¼m SW, Elsich Manor, timber and brick, has a moat. 3m E, 800ft up *Brown Clee*, the small *Heath Chapel*, lonely in a field, is perhaps the outstanding Norman structure in the county.

Ellesmere 7H7
All around are small lakes or 'meres'; the largest of them (113 acres), with boating and plenty of pike, comes right up to the town. Across it one glimpses rebuilt Oteley Park, with fallow deer that browse at the water's edge. At *St Martin's*, 3½m farther on, are Regency almshouses and one of the most remarkable churches in the county (13th-c with much later tower), because of its pews, gallery and three-decker pulpit, which still has its velvet hangings.

Haughmond Abbey *see* High Ercall

High Ercall 7H7
The last place except **Ludlow** to hold out against Parliament in the Civil War; the Hall (built 1608) was the Royalist HQ. In the course of the fighting, the church tower was badly damaged. The almshouses were built in 1694. 4m W, the **Shrewsbury** road passes the ruins of *Haughmond Abbey*, grey-green among ponds and woods. The Norman chapter house, with three fine arches, is complete; parts of the kitchen and the abbot's lodge also exist; and beyond stretches the great demesne of Sundorne Park, on the edge of its 60-acre lake.

Hodnet 7H7
Main-road village, with black-and-white houses. The church has Norman priest's door, octagonal tower, monuments and chained books. The Hall (fine gardens open to the public) was built in 1870 to house the large family of Bishop Heber ('From Greenland's Icy Mountains'). 2m NW at *Hawkstone* is an attractive landscaped park, with a Queen Anne mansion (now housing RC students), a folly, grotto and lake, as well as a hotel and golf-course.

Hopton Castle 6G5/7H5
Tiny half-timbered village, dominated by Norman keep of ruined castle beside a stream, with Hopton Titterhill rising 1,300ft behind.

Ironbridge 7I6
In the Severn gorge, famed as the world's first iron bridge. *See* account under **Telford** and pages 16, 21 and 173.

Kinlet 7I5
To N of Wyre Forest, its Hall (1729) stands in a fine park; as does the 14th-c church, with notable monuments.

Leebotwood 7H6
Picturesque Pound Inn and black-and-white houses on the slopes of Lawley Hill. The church, not to be missed, is on a hill ½m off main road; lit by clear glass, there are box-pews, gallery and double-decker pulpit, quite unspoiled. Similar furnishings also at 13th-c *Longnor* church, 2m N, where there is also a fine 17th-c brick house. *See also* **Condover**.

Lilleshall 7I7
Obelisk to 1st Duke of Sutherland (1833) on crag, and Leveson monument (1764) in restored 13th-c church. 12th-c abbey ruins (AM, open April–Sept.) (note carved Norman arch) crumbling by a stream 1m SE, at the edge of the park, where the modern Tudor Hall (Wyatville, 1830) is now a national recreation centre. E across the main road, 7m away, at *Preston-on-the-Weald Moors*, a fine brick-and-stone hospital, flanked by lodges, stands behind elegant iron gates at the end of an avenue of trees.

Llanyblodwell 6G7
Pretty little inn beside the rushing Tanat, much favoured by anglers; but everyone can enjoy the lovely scenery from the hills above it. The church, originally medieval, was largely rebuilt and redecorated by a 19th-c vicar and is a remarkable monument to Early Victorian taste. The Hall, now a farm, has an 18th-c garden house.

Longville-in-the-Dale 7H6
An Apedale village, with *Wilderhope Manor* (NT) higher up the slopes of *Wenlock Edge*, an early 17th-c stone house little altered and now a youth hostel. Open April–Sept. on Wed.

Ludlow★ 7H5
Shropshire's finest town. It was a planned town dating from the early 12th c surrounded by walls of slightly later date. On view to the public is the magnificent pink sandstone castle, for centuries the seat of the President of the Council of the Marches, now a splendid ruin with a marvellous viewpoint. Here Milton's *Comus* was performed in 1634; here also Butler's *Hudibras* was written. The church is one of the noblest parish churches in the country, with carved screen and stalls and a magnificent window. In the churchyard are the ashes of A. E. Housman, author of 'A Shropshire Lad'. The only surviving gate is Broad Gate leading to Broad Street, Ludlow's finest street lined with black-and-white and Georgian red-brick houses and terminated by the impressive Butter Cross of 1742. Other worthwhile views in High Street, Mill Street and Corve Street, notably the brown-and-white façade of the Feathers Hotel. 9m E are *Burford Gardens*, often open and famous for plants, shrubs, clematis etc.

Lydbury North 6G5
Pretty village below Clun Forest (*see* **Clun**). The church has battlemented tower, a 15th-c screen and loft, and Plowden and Walcot chapels. Elizabethan *Plowden Hall* with its own chapel and numerous hiding places, is 2m E. Across the dammed-up stream, in a great park, *Walcot*, an 18th-c house, was bought by Clive of India, a Shropshireman, for his retirement.

Market Drayton 7I7
The principal town of N. Shropshire. Some good black-and-white houses and notable late Georgian buildings such as the Corbet Arms Hotel.

Much Wenlock 7H6

An attractively situated little town on the NE tip of Wenlock Edge, with Georgian houses and inns, some half-timbered: notably Raynald's Mansion, with its galleries; Guildhall (movable stocks and panelled rooms); and Manor House (1577). The priory ruins (AM) are considerable, mainly Early English, with outstanding interlaced Norman arches and doorways. *See* Introduction.

Munslow 7H5

A pretty lane leads from the main road to a group of limestone cottages, with Georgian rectory and medieval church of the same material (16th-c glass and timbered porch). Beyond, Millichope Park is a classical Regency house, with a lake and grounds. 3m E, *Broncroft Castle*, local red sandstone, 14th-c with 19th-c additions, is still inhabited. *See also* **Diddlebury** near by. At *Aston Munslow*, 2m W, the medieval White House is often open in April–Oct. with its museum of buildings and country life.

Newport 7I7

A main-road town of E. Shropshire but very satisfactory in terms of townscape. Impressive parish church and a number of good red-brick Georgian buildings.

Oswestry 6G7

The town has notable buildings including the church of St Oswald, much Georgian red-brick and black-and-white buildings. N is *Old Oswestry*, a superb Iron Age hill fort covering 40 acres.

Preston Brockhurst 7H7

17th-c manor house. 2m W is Clive Hall, birthplace of William Wycherley; and, 2m SE, *Moreton Corbet* has ruins of a 16th-c castle (AM).

Shifnal 7I6

Attractive town, gradually losing to industrialization, but with a large and important parish church and fine houses in the neighbourhood: Haughton Hall (1718) beside its lake to NW; Aston Hall, classical 18th-c, in park to E. There is an Aerospace Museum at *RAF Cosford*.

Shipton 7H6

Lovely Corvedale village, church and cottages making a group with the fine Elizabethan manor and 18th-c stables.

Shrewsbury★ 7H6

Wonderfully situated, on a hill almost islanded by the Severn, which is crossed by two classic bridges (English and Welsh), and on its landward side is guarded by the castle (pink sandstone, notable for Telford's conversion to a private dwelling, now used by the Council). Its half timbered buildings are to be found everywhere. Among the most admirable are: Henry VII's house and the Unicorn in Wyle Cop; Council House gateway; Whitehall, with gatehouse and dovecot; Drapers' Guildhall; Ireland's, Owen's and Rowley's mansions. Outstanding of the 18th c is new St Chad's (1792), which looks out across the attractive park known as the Quarry and the river to Shrewsbury School, removed from the 1630 grammar school buildings (now public library). There are many Georgian town houses and the Lion Hotel, an old posting-house with decorated ball-room. A good museum is at Clive House on College Hill open daily except Sun. Percy Thrower, horticulturist, has a garden centre here. At Preston Montford Field Centre is a nature trail. *See also* **Atcham, Battlefield** and **Condover**, all near by.

Stokesay Castle *see* **Craven Arms**

Telford 7I6

Shropshire's New Town. Originally launched as Dawley in 1963 and greatly expanded in 1968 when the decision was taken to include everything from the *Ironbridge Gorge* to **Wellington** and *Oakengates*, an area of approx. 8m from N to S and 4m from E to W covering the old industrial area of E. Shropshire. Much reclamation of old workings, new roads, factory zones and housing estates. A main town centre near Malinslee and large town park running S. Noteworthy churches at Wellington and at *Madeley* by Telford, also the Elizabethan *Madeley Court*. A major attraction for visitors is the *Ironbridge Gorge Museum★*, in a 2m area of Ironbridge Gorge. It includes Darby's original furnace at *Coalbrookdale*, the Museum of Iron, the Severn Warehouse, the iron bridge (*see* **Ironbridge** and pages 16 and 21), and the Bedlam Furnaces. *Blists Hill* (*see also* page 21) is an area on which industrial buildings of every kind have been assembled. At the end of the gorge are the rehabilitated Coalport china works which closed in 1926.

Tong★ 7I6

Justifiably one of the show places of the county. Its church, with unusual spire, was converted to a collegiate foundation in 1410 by Elizabeth de Pembruge, whose effigy lies with her husband's near the choir-screen. These are only two from a remarkable collection of tombs (mostly of the Vernon family) that, together with the fan vaulting of the Golden Chantry and much fine timber-carving, make the place unique. *Boscobel House* (AM), Charles II's hiding place, is 4m E; and, beyond in Staffs, 18th-c *Chillington Hall* stands in its 1,000-acre park. Open in summer. 3m N, also in Staffs, is *Weston Park*, (1671). Home of the Earls of Bradford. Grounds laid out by Capability Brown. Open April–Sept.

Upton Cressett *see* **Bridgnorth**

Wellington 7I6

Incorporated into **Telford**, it has a parish church built in 1790 by George Steuart. To the S is the *Wrekin* (1,335ft) (*see also* Introduction).

Wenlock Priory *see* **Much Wenlock**

Whitchurch 7H7

Many Georgian houses and Higginson's Almshouse, founded in 1647. The majestic church was rebuilt in 1715; but, though there are noteworthy monuments, particularly the 15th-c Talbot tomb, much of the period beauty of the interior has been spoiled by restoration. To the SW stretches the primeval peat-bog known as *Fenn's Moss*, extending into *Whittington*. This village has romantic castle ruins where, beneath ivy-covered masonry swans frequent the water-filled moat; the turreted twin towers of the gatehouse are splendidly intact and house the local library.

Wilderhope Manor *see* **Longville-in-the-Dale**

Worfield 7I6

Half-timbered village, with a fine church (spired tower and screen, both Perpendicular). Davenport House, a brick-and-stone building of 1726–7, stands adjacent in a pleasant park.

Wroxeter 7H6

Here is a church with coloured effigies and 17th-c furnishings, and near by the excavated remains of Roman Viroconium (*see* Introduction).

WARWICKSHIRE

AN INTRODUCTION BY
JOHN MOORE AND CHARLES LINES

Some say the heart has been torn out of Warwickshire. That is an exaggeration, but it has lost much to a new, usurping county. Birmingham has gone (parts, one must admit, were once in Worcestershire or Staffordshire, and that not so very long ago). Coventry of the Three Spires has gone, too; so has Meriden, the supposed 'Centre of England', Solihull, Knowle, Temple Balsall, and not a little of the old Forest of Arden area. But it still has the noble county town of Warwick; Stratford, too, of course; castles and churches, simple or splendid, and many acres of fine, if not necessarily spectacular, farming land. There are still aristocratic, double-barrelled names, such as Baddesley Clinton, Wellesbourne Hastings and Wellesbourne Mountford, Temple Grafton, Wootton Wawen, Radford Semele – even Bishop's Itchington, though that sounds less aristocratic!

It has the tree-fringed Edge Hills and lovely Warmington on the Oxfordshire border, Cotswold Warwickshire with delectable Ilmington. There are great houses, too, such as Packington, Coughton, Compton Wynyates, Arbury, Alscot and Ragley, where ancestral families still live, and landscapes we owe to Capability Brown and those who employed him. Tragically, however, we shall never see again the elm, once the 'Warwickshire Weed', in its glory; its death has seriously marred the long, straight Fosseway, though that road, where Roman legions trod, has lost, too, the peace it enjoyed for centuries!

Shakespeare's Country

The great Forest of Arden originally covered most of the old county lying northwest of the Avon; a forest neither dark nor formidable if we may draw conclusions from *As You Like It*: 'Here shall you see no enemy but winter and rough weather.' Where the forest touched the River Avon at Stratford, Shakespeare was born, appropriately on St George's Day, 1564 and there, by a happy coincidence, if we can believe the legend, he died also upon St George's Day, in 1616. For sentimental as well as practical reasons, Stratford is the proper centre and starting-point for any tour of Warwickshire. Every year visitors from almost every land visit Shakespeare's birthplace in Henley Street, a delightful timber-framed house which was probably about 50 years old when he was but a little tiny boy there. Presumably most of these multitudinous pilgrims also visit the poet's grave in Holy Trinity Church beside the river; New Place, the home of his last years, has long gone, but there is the enchanting, if restored, garden; and Hall's Croft, the beautiful house of his son-in-law, the physician John Hall, whose famous casebook was called 'Selected Observations of English Bodies or Cures both Empiricall and Historicall, performed upon very eminent Persons in desperate diseases'. He left no account of Shakespeare's last illness: perhaps because he failed to cure it.

The Royal Shakespeare Theatre is a modern brick building, not always admired, rising sheer from the river-bank and delightfully reflected in the water, where its image may be rippled by occasional swans.

Anne Hathaway's cottage is not a cottage at all but the very handsome farmhouse (which belonged to Anne's yeoman father); here Shakespeare courted the girl, much older than he was, whom he married after a bit of a shemozzle by special licence when she was already three months gone with child. There is a footpath way to it from Stratford, and going along it you are certainly treading where Shakespeare trod. But whichever way you go from Stratford-upon-Avon you are following in his footsteps. They will lead you to the villages round about, to which he is supposed to have given their epithets in the old jingle – Piping Pebworth, Dancing Marston, Haunted Hillboro', Drunken Bidford and so on. The legend of Bidford's drunkenness rests upon a tale, probably apocryphal, of Shakespeare's drinking-bout there, a little time before he died. Michael Drayton, the Warwickshire poet who wrote *Poly-Olbion*, is said to have been his companion, in some versions of this story. Drayton loved his native Warwickshire and especially its River Avon: he was probably thinking of its alternating pools and swift shallow reaches when he wrote of 'Ev'ry pearl-pav'd ford and ev'ry blue-ey'd deep'.

Now the river has been made navigable again from Tewkesbury to Stratford, but, despite incessant traffic and the near-by Moat House International Hotel,

*The gatehouse to Charlecote Park is unaltered since
Shakespeare saw it as a young man*

it is not difficult to picture Shakespeare leaning upon
Clopton Bridge and watching the perch he described
as 'tawny finn'd fishes' in *Antony and Cleopatra*. He
certainly must have walked upstream along the river
bank to Charlecote, the home of the Lucy family
where he is supposed to have poached one of Sir
Thomas Lucy's deer, though it seems there were none
there at the time, and the incident could only have
taken place on some other Lucy property. This got
him into trouble (so the tale runs) for which he took
an immortal revenge, if indeed Sir Thomas, the local
magistrate, is portrayed as the doddering Justice
Shallow. The whole story is discounted by the scholars; but there are red and fallow deer in Charlecote
Park today.

Round about here the Avon runs the sweetest
course of any river I know, between its willows and its
water-meadows, by delightful old mills, and through
the villages which have grown up about them. Upstream lies Warwick with its most majestic castle –
'the fairest monument of ancient and chivalrous
splendour,' wrote Sir Walter Scott, 'which yet remains uninjured by time'. It is matched in splendour
by the church of St Mary, rebuilt many times, with a
tower magnificently looming over the whole ancient
town. Its Lady Chapel contains the marvellous tomb
of Richard Beauchamp. Elizabeth I's Leicester has
his monument here, and thousands of less famous
men are commemorated, elsewhere in the great
church, in the memorial to those of the Royal
Warwickshire Regiment killed during the World
Wars of the 20th century.

Warwick has been hailed as a splendid capital city
by an 18th-century poet, Richard Jago, in the following lines:

*Now WARWICK claims the promis'd Lay, supreme
In this her midland Realm! Precedence due,
And long maintain'd! For her kind Nature rais'd
The rocky Hill, a gentle Eminence,
For Health and Pleasure form'd! where her gay Tribes
Indulge the social Walk; once gloomy Haunt
Of solitary Monks! now beauteous Seat
Of rural Elegance! around whose Skirts
Parks, Meadows, Groves, their mingled Graces join,
And AVON pours his tributary Urn.*

Travellers in the 20th century, whether motorists on
the A46 or boaters on the Grand Union Canal, will
echo these sentiments.

Above Warwick is Leicester's own castle, Kenilworth. In 1575 the Queen made one of her progresses
thither and there were great junketings in her
honour, which cost her favourite £1,000 a day; a

minor item in the bill represented the cost of 38,400 gallons of beer. It is likely that young Shakespeare, then aged 11, may have had his first glimpse of the Queen there, and his first awe-struck sight of the great lords and ladies whom one day he would write about with such familiar ease.

Cotswold Country
Southwest of Stratford you approach the foothills of the Cotswolds. The river here is the Stour, which winds down off the hills through charming villages and hamlets, where you can sometimes see the greyish-brown stone from local quarries: Clifford Chambers, Atherstone-on-Stour, Preston-on-Stour – a perfect estate village – Newbold, Tredington, Honington and Shipston, the 'sheep's town' long famous for its fleece and its flocks.

The highroad from Shipston to Chipping Norton runs along a fine ridge from which you look down at good Cotswold country on either side. This is a borderland between four counties; the near-by Four Shires stone marks what used to be the meeting-point of Warwickshire, Worcestershire, Oxfordshire and Gloucestershire. It was a meeting-place for people too – horse-copers and hucksters used to foregather there, wrestlers and prize-fighters, with the crowds that cheered them on. Today only three counties meet at the Four Shires Stone; the bureaucrats have re-drawn the boundaries and from the neighbourly get-together of English counties Worcestershire has been excluded.

Villages near here include Long Compton, Little Compton and Compton Verney, and there is even Compton Scorpion, where Sir Thomas Overbury was born. But the most famous of the Comptons is, of course, Compton Wynyates, the seat of the Marquis of Northampton, tucked under the scarp of Edge Hill close to the Oxfordshire border. It is perhaps the most splendid of all the great houses in the West Midlands (but is only open by special arrangement). It was begun in 1480 by Edmund Compton, and finished in 1520 by his son William. It has had an exciting history: Henry VIII, Queen Elizabeth and James I, all stayed under its roof. James ennobled the second William Compton, making him Earl of Northampton; the second Earl naturally took the King's side in the Civil War: he and his three sons, all of whom were knighted, fought right on their home ground as it were, in the battle of Edgehill. That was in 1642; and the Earl was killed next year at Hopton Heath. In 1644 Compton Wynyates was taken by the Parliament troops after a brief siege, but the Northampton family got it back two years later by paying a fine of £20,000, and promising to fill in the moat and dismantle the fortifications.

The name Wynyates means 'wind gate' – a gap in the hills through which the wind blows. (In the old days they called the place less elegantly 'Compton-in-

the-Hole'.) The Tudor house is built of rosy-pink brick which glows most wonderfully in the sun, set off by the pitch-black timbers.

Rugby is a nice-looking market town with its tree-lined roads and striking churches, and is an important railway and engineering centre. Its great school has Butterfield's imposing chapel, and counts among its pupils Matthew Arnold, Arthur Hugh Clough, Rupert Brooke, Wyndham Lewis, C. L. Dodgson (Lewis Carroll), Thomas Hughes who wrote *Tom Brown's Schooldays*, and W. S. Landor, whose schooldays were terminated by his expulsion from Rugby School.

Atherstone, long famous for hats and its Shrovetide football and Bedworth are not tourist towns. Neither is Nuneaton, despite its George Eliot connections and certain reminders of its past. Leamington Spa, made 'Royal' by Queen Victoria, is. It has its considerable industries and supermarkets, but retains not only its spa but much Regency and early Victorian elegance. Among its fine stuccoed houses one in Clarendon Square was occupied by Prince Louis Napoleon, later the Emperor Napoleon III. The wide streets and many trees are features. Nathaniel Hawthorne, the American author, lived briefly in noble Lansdowne Crescent and near-by Lansdowne Circus, and writes delightfully of Leamington's gardens, and of Warwick and the villages he visited.

Although William Shakespeare overshadows all the other great folk of the Heart of England, one must not forget Warwickshire's 'second son', Sir William Dugdale, Garter King at Arms and antiquary. His home, near the attractive town of Coleshill, is still in the hands of his descendants, and there he wrote his *Antiquities of Warwickshire* of 1654. The fruit of intensive study and many journeys by mule over terrible roads, it is still indispensible to the historian.

Then there is Sir Francis Willoughby, the naturalist of Middleton Hall, near Tamworth (a town now wholly in Staffordshire); Michael Drayton and George Eliot have been duly mentioned; so has Richard Beauchamp and his marvellous Beauchamp Chapel, but not Sir Fulke Greville, statesman, poet and friend of Sir Philip Sidney. Richard Hayward, the eminent 18th-century sculptor, responsible for what is now the oldest-surviving public statue in North America – that of Lord Botetourt at Williamsburg, Virginia – lived at Weston Hall, Bulkington, and a word should be said for Henrietta, Lady Luxborough, discarded wife of a peer who, at Barrells Hall, Ullenhall, gathered round her a remarkable literary coterie in the same century. Nor must we forget, the eccentric Greek scholar, Dr Samuel Parr, minister of Hatton and chaplain to the unfortunate Queen Caroline, or Dr Henry Jephson, who did so much for the medical reputation of Leamington. But the list is endless, or certainly as long as the beauties of Warwickshire.

GAZETTEER

Alcester   7J4
A market town notable for the number and variety of its ancient houses. Early 16th-c buildings are a feature of Malt Mill Lane, and adjacent is a recent residential development of very pleasing character. 18th-c and earlier houses form a delightful setting for the parish church (Greville and Seymour monuments, one of the latter by Chantrey) and a town hall of 1618. There was a Roman settlement and an abbey, and the town has seen much enlargement in recent years. 1½m SW, *Ragley Hall* and its park are open from spring to autumn: this 17th- and 18th-c mansion contains pictures and period furniture, and there is superb plasterwork, especially in the Great Hall. Graham Rust's 'The Temptation', the largest country-house mural of the 20th c, was completed in March 1983. Playground, maze, nature trail etc. Open summer months. *See also* **Coughton Court**.

Arbury Hall★   7K6
Standing in a 300-acre park with a chain of lakes, the house, originally Elizabethan but transformed in the 18th c, is chiefly in 'Gothick' style. The stables are 17th-c, with a doorway ascribed to Wren. The house (open Easter–Sept.) is the Cheverel Manor described in *Scenes of Clerical Life* by George Eliot who was born at South Farm on the estate where her father was agent, and later lived at Griff House near by. *Astley*, adjoining one of the park entrances, has a remarkable church with 15th-c priests' stalls.

Baddesley Clinton★   7K5
¾m W of the A41, near *Chadwick End*. The moated manor house (NT), 15th-c with earlier and later work, is outstanding and open May–Sept. This former home of the Ferrers family contains heraldic glass and chimneypieces, panelling, pictures and tapestry. The near-by church has a tower erected by Nicholas Brome (d.1517), father-in-law of Sir Edward Ferrers, as an act of penance. Sarah Green organ and interesting glass.

Brinklow   7L5
Noteworthy by archeologists for one of the finest motte-and-bailey castles in the country. *Coombe Abbey* is the former home of the Earls of Craven and has associations with Elizabeth of Bohemia. The fine gardens are regularly open to the public and the house occasionally; the latter incorporates some remains of a Cistercian monastery.

Burton Dassett   7K4
Little remains of a once flourishing village, except one of the most attractive of Warwickshire churches, with Norman and later work, including remarkable carvings and wall paintings; and being built on a hillside, the altar is almost on a level with the capitals of the nave. The so-called beacon tower was probably a windmill. There are splendid views S to *Edge Hill* and W over the Avon valley.

Charlecote Park   7K4
4m E of **Stratford-upon-Avon** near *Wellesbourne*. Home of the Lucys since the 12th c. The present house is a much-altered and extended 16th-c mansion; its charming gatehouse (*see* page 177) is attributed to John of Padua. House and park, with herds of red and fallow deer and Spanish sheep, have been held by the NT since 1945. Open April–Oct. The Victorian church, near the main entrance, has Lucy effigies of Elizabethan and later date.

Coleshill   7K6
Situated on a steep hill, the town is dominated by the church, one of the most interesting in the county for its monuments. Near by the combined pillory, whipping-post and stocks may still be seen. 1½m E is *Maxstoke Castle*, a red sandstone structure dating from the 14th c, built on a square plan, with curtain-walls, angle-towers and parapets, and surrounded by a moat. The residential portions are of varied dates. The castle is open by arrangement. 2m S are the remains of a priory founded in 1342.

Compton Wynyates   7K4
Situated in a valley SW of *Edge Hill*, this Tudor mansion, scarcely changed since its completion in 1520, is one of the most beautiful in England. Built round a courtyard, of mellow brick with stone roof, twisted chimneys, gables with blackened timbers. It is no longer open to the public, except by special arrangement.

Coughton Court   7J5
2m N of **Alcester**. This, the home of the Throckmorton family for over 500 years, is now the property of the NT. Its outstanding feature is the battlemented gatehouse, dating from the early 16th c and there is fine timbering in the courtyard. The house contains many family portraits, tapestries and documents. It figured in the Gunpowder Plot of 1605, when the wives of the conspirators awaited its outcome although the head of the family was absent at the time. Open April–Oct. on set days. The parish church, just S of the house, has family tombs and interesting glass.

Henley-in-Arden   7J5
A charming market town in the heart of the one-time Forest of Arden, its single street lined with 15th–17th-c houses, many of them timber-framed. Adjoining the church is the 15th-c Guildhall. *Beaudesert* Church, on the other side of the River Alne, built at the end of the 12th c, contains much fine Norman work.

Kenilworth★   7K5
Standing on a mound, formerly surrounded by a lake, are the remains of the red sandstone castle (AM) described in Scott's novel. The oldest part is the keep, completed in about 1180; John of Gaunt built the Great Hall and State Apartments; while further additions, including the gatehouse, were made by Queen Elizabeth I's favourite, the Earl of Leicester, to whom she presented the castle. Castle open daily. The rich Norman work of the W doorway of the church was probably brought there from the abbey, whose remains may still be seen a little to the SW. There are many old cottages, some thatched.

Leamington Spa   7K5
Noted for its medicinal waters since the 18th c, the town is spaciously laid out with Regency and Victorian (see the Town Hall) buildings and tree-lined streets. There are fine public gardens. Both residential and industrial, its position and hotels make it an excellent touring centre. The town has a small, but interesting art gallery and museum, as well as good shops, and Jephson Gardens opposite the Royal Pump Room (1814). At *Newbold Comyn* is a 309-acre park with many recreational facilities including a golf course.

Maxstoke Castle and Priory *see* **Coleshill**

Merevale Abbey   7K6

W of *Atherstone* off the A5. The main surviving part of this Cistercian foundation is the large and beautiful 'chapel without the gates', still, from medieval times, serving as the parish church. The S chapel, with its E window, dating from about 1340 and filled with glass of the period, is noteworthy.

Packington Hall   7K5

Off the A45 W of **Meriden** (W. Midlands) is the seat of the Earls of Aylesford. It is a remarkable Italianate house chiefly 18th-c. The park also contains the Old Hall (late 17th-c and earlier) and a curious Georgian church by Bonomi, with an organ built to Handel's specifications. Not open to the public.

Packwood House★   7K5

1m E of *Hockley Heath* on the A34. A delightfully intimate Tudor and Carolean house (NT) with brick moulding, sundials, oak-panelled rooms and period furnishings. The gardens are charming, in particular the Yew Garden, said to symbolize the Sermon on the Mount. Set in beautiful countryside. Open May–Sept.

Polesworth   7K6

Of the Benedictine nunnery little remains except the 14th-c gatehouse and the nave of the church. An impressive monument in this is the sculptured effigy of an abbess, probably the only one still to be seen in England. *Pooley Hall*, NW of the village on the opposite side of the River Anker, has a fortified tower and a former chapel.

Ragley Hall *see* Alcester

Rugby   7L5

The town has important engineering works and good residential areas with many trees, but is best known for its school, made famous by the reforms of the 19th c. Its Head at that time, Dr Arnold, was described by one of his pupils, Thomas Hughes, in *Tom Brown's Schooldays*. There are fine churches and an attractive shopping precinct.

Shipston-on-Stour   7K4

A pleasant agricultural town in the Vale of Red Horse, midway between the two northern spurs of the Cotswolds. An unclassified road leads NW through the village of Ilmington to the highest point in the county, *Ilmington Down* (854ft), with a splendid view, including the isolated Meon Hill, crowned by Iron Age earthworks. 4m E of the town, at *Upper Brailes*, another unclassified road forks left to *Edge Hill* (705ft), some 6m NE, with its octagonal Gothic tower. In the little village of *Lower Brailes*, the church, so imposing that it is known as 'the Cathedral of the Feldon', should not be missed.

Stoneleigh   7K5

The village has a fine manor house, a church containing Norman works and the Leigh monuments, historic almshouses and a green surrounded by cottages. Stoneleigh Abbey, to the S, has an imposing early Georgian W front, by Smith of Warwick, and earlier work including the gatehouse of the original monastery. Open at set times. Near the Abbey are the National Agricultural Centre and the permanent site of the Royal Agricultural Society's Show.

Stratford-upon-Avon★★   7K4

Famous as the town where Shakespeare was born and to which he retired. His birthplace in Henley Street has been restored and contains many relics. Adjoining is the Shake-

speare Centre, opened in 1934 and since extended. The Guildhall has in its upper storey the grammar school where Shakespeare was probably educated. The Guild Chapel is charming. There are many historic buildings including Holy Trinity Church, notable in itself, where the poet was buried. Here are also his bust and the registers of his baptism and burial. Nash's House (now a museum) adjoins the garden of vanished New Place, where Shakespeare spent his retirement. The restored Knot Garden is particularly charming. The properties of the Shakespeare Trust (the Birthplace, Anne Hathaway's Cottage, Mary Arden's House, New Place and Hall Croft) are open all year. The Shakespeare Memorial Theatre, built in 1932 to replace the earlier theatre, presents productions by the Royal Shakespeare Company. There is a picture gallery and a museum here. A new theatre called the Swan is planned within the shell of the earlier Memorial Theatre. The Shakespeare Memorial is in the

Stratford-upon-Avon: the cottage at Shottery in which
Anne Hathaway lived before her marriage to Shakespeare

adjoining Bancroft Gardens beside the River Avon. The town
also has a motor museum specializing in the 1920s and 1930s.
Note also Harvard House (1596) where the mother of the
founder of Harvard University, U.S.A., lived. 7m SW are
Dorsington Manor Gardens, home of the Domestic Fowl
Trust. Pottery, arts centre, model railway. Open April–Sept.
except Mon.

Upton House   7K4
7m NW of **Banbury** (Oxon). This charming 17th-c mansion,
enlarged in 1927, stands high to the S of *Edge Hill*. Now
belonging to the NT, the house contains English china and
18th-c furniture, and one of the best private collections of
pictures in the country. Open April–Sept. on set days.

Warmington   7K4
Built round a green, with views to *Edge Hill* and across the
valley to the so-called beacon tower on the Burton Hills, it
has a fine Elizabethan manor, and a 14th-c church with one
very unusual feature: a priest's chamber, with its original
door, fireplace and sanitary accommodation built over a
chapel.

Warwick★★   7K5
Owes its distinctive character to having been largely
rebuilt, probably by the Smith brothers, after the great fire
in 1694. High Street, Jury Street, Church Street and
Northgate Street have delightful 18th-c work; the Court
House (Francis Smith) and the Shire Hall (Sanderson
Miller) are particularly handsome. Tudor architecture is
well represented by Mill Street, Oken's House (a Doll
Museum), Lord Leycester's Hospital (open daily except

Warwick: pretty cottages in Mill Street are overshadowed by England's finest medieval castle

Sun.), the Tudor House Hotel, while two medieval town gateways remain. Of the Collegiate Church of St Mary only the Norman crypt, the later chancel, chapter house, and medieval Beauchamp Chapel escaped the great fire. There are magnificent Warwick and Dudley tombs. Nave, transepts and tower were rebuilt to Sir William Wilson's designs. The castle, on a cliff above the River Avon, is one of the most imposing medieval fortresses in the country, and unlike its rival, **Kenilworth**, is admirably preserved. The State Apartments, with impressive armour on show, furniture, pictures, a Madame Tussaud waxwork display of 'A Royal Weekend Party – 1898' and the private apartments, extensive grounds and the Peacock Gardens are open daily. St John's House (Jacobean and later) and the Market Hall are museums. Attractive Warwick Racecourse is near by.

Wootton Wawen★ 7J5

Although the traffic is difficult here, this is a delightful village with Saxon work and a chained library in its exceptional church and late 17th-c Wootton Hall which is near a double weir on the River Alne.

Wroxall 7K5

On the A41 near Five Ways. Wroxall Abbey, now a school, is a grand Victorian house replacing that bought by Sir Christopher Wren and a Benedictine priory. (There never was an abbey.) A delightful medieval lady chapel survives in richly-wooded grounds which also have a serpentine wall doubtfully ascribed to Wren.

WEST MIDLANDS

AN INTRODUCTION BY
CHARLES LINES

Variety and contrast are words which spring to mind automatically when discussing the new county of West Midlands. Formed from contiguous slices of Warwickshire, Worcestershire and Staffordshire, and extending from Wolverhampton to Coventry, including Dudley, Halesowen and Stourbridge, but just omitting the small town of Coleshill, it boasts two great cities, three cathedrals, three universities and old-established schools, fashionable Solihull, and – surviving precariously in a Green Belt – rural areas to set against an enormous conurbation inhabited by diverse races.

Contrasts

Contrasts are indeed vast: late Georgian and Victorian dignity, and some good modern building in Birmingham's Edgbaston (which, close to the city centre, has a Capability Brown park) with tower blocks and miles of houses – Aston Hall splendid on the skyline – stretching towards Sutton Coldfield. The endless sprawl of the Black Country can be depressingly industrial, if greatly changed, since Queen Victoria is reputed (a doubtful story) to have ordered the lowering of the blinds of the royal train against belching chimneys and furnace fires! But, to the observant, even that landscape of strange shadows and factories under wide skies, with Lowry-like figures, has photogenic quality – bridges mirrored in manmade waterways that supplanted plodding pack horses, occasional church towers; a ruinous castle on a wooded hill, patches of green, even a linear park made from a railway line for the enjoyment of Wolverhampton folk and their neighbours.

Inevitably, one thinks of child labour of not so very long ago, men in mines, Black Country stories, Willenhall locks and Walsall leather, and the beauty of Bilston enamels. But there are great surprises, like those two houses at West Bromwich – one moated and going back to medieval times – the grand Victorian church at Wednesbury with the unique fighting-cock lectern, as well as the richness of Kempe glass. Kempe glass – Morris fabrics, too – at Wightwick Manor, which has bits of the Houses of Parliament next to green and gold yews.

Near to Knowle and Solihull are still a few villages – Barston, Bickenhill, Tanworth-in-Arden – where life does not seem to have changed over much for decades. There is countryside where a certain 'Edwardian Lady' (achieving immense fame long after a tragic death) walked and cycled in lanes then unpolluted by petrol fumes. There is Hampton-in-Arden to remind us of a once wild expanse – a light, legend has it, hung on the church tower to guide benighted strangers through the forest region.

With little between Birmingham Airport and Elmdon Church except the A45, once Telford's Holyhead Road, the airport – windswept, runways aglow – contrasts with the plastered Georgian-Gothic church, with epitaphs and enlarged for a population far bigger than it was when squires lived at the Hall next door. Planes now fly over ground where the Woodmen of Arden still ply long bows in their green tailcoats and Tyrolean hats, as they did two centuries ago. This is at Meriden, where the cross on the village green marks the so-called 'Centre of England', and inns once catered for such travellers as William Cobbett, the captious diarist John Byng and the young Princess Victoria. Near by, a motorway carves ruthlessly through the Green Belt; at Berkswell a picture-book church has cool Norman crypts, Thompson 'mice' on modern woodwork, and there are stocks, the odd thatched roof and a school not closed.

The Towns

Birmingham has advanced in the 20th century like an insatiable monster. It is mentioned in Domesday Book, when it was sold to a vassal of Baron Fitz Anscult of Dudley Castle, and was worth 20 shillings. The Conquerer's scribes did not have a great deal to record, but nonsense has been written about the town (it was not a city until late in the 19th century) as once 'near Solihull', or 'near Coleshill', as if they were far more important! In fact, it had its market by the 12th century, and by 1538 the antiquary Leland speaks of the many metalworkers beside the Rea though he missed the tanners and fullers. Its ancient hospital, or priory, was, of course, dissolved; its first King Edward's School was founded in Edward VI's reign.

In the wretched Civil War, the townsfolk's sympathies lay with Parliament, and 15,000 sword blades were made for what Royalist Sir Thomas Holte – out at Aston – would have called 'the rebels'. He suffered because of the Cromwellians; Birmingham suffered at Prince Rupert's hands and, before and after, from dreaded plague. Guns and cutlery were being made before the rebellion. William III encouraged not only arms manufacture, but that of shoe buckles. With Boulton, Murdoch and Watt we think of steam engines, but Boulton produced fine ormolu work that now sells for fantastic prices; John Taylor, a founder of Taylor and Lloyd's Bank, made buttons and enamels. Dozens of firms have their roots in the 19th century, whether producing jewelry, cocoa or the products of heavy engineering. Herbert Austin, with a tiny capital, started business at Longbridge in 1905.

Coventry – the phoenix city – has likewise grown enormously, and far beyond its almost vanished walls. The city where Lady Godiva rides eternally in Broadgate (the statue may perpetuate only a legend, and 'Peeping Tom' was certainly a later addition to the tale) has made, or makes, cloth, stained glass and beautiful tiles for churches, ribbons, watches, cycles, cars and aircraft; its James Starley, who has his own monument, earned fame with the bicycle.

It is, perhaps, unnecessary to emphasize its sufferings in World War II, like those of the Dresden it was later to befriend. Now shopping precincts and ringways – though destruction of the old had begun before the holocaust – replace narrow streets that John Byng found. The new cathedral, allied to the ruins of the old, has work by Epstein, John Piper (his 80-foot high window is superb) and Graham Sutherland, whose tapestry is not admired by all. The medieval mystery plays have been revived. A few Georgian town houses survive, as they do in Stourbridge and Dudley. There is the fine Herbert Art Gallery and Museum and a Museum of British Road Transport. There are theatres and a flourishing and exciting Arts Centre has been established at the University of Warwick which is in Coventry – off the beautiful road from the city to Kenilworth.

Culturally, in fact, the new county has much to offer, despite its critics. The City of Birmingham Symphony Orchestra is widely acclaimed; there are old-established choirs and new ones. There are delightful English portraits at Wolverhampton, amid a host of lovely things. Birmingham secured two of the Canaletto paintings from Warwick Castle; its libraries are rightly famed, and there is the 'new' Repertory Theatre; the refurbished Hippodrome can, and does, accommodate Grand Opera. Dudley has the quite remarkable and extensive Black Country Museum; Walsall a gallery with unexpected sculpture, drawings and paintings. Amateur theatre can achieve high standards.

Famous Names

One recalls famous names at random: the Chamberlains and Cadburys; William Withering and 'Digitalis'; poor, harried Joseph Priestley of oxygen fame; Sister Dora with her loving care of sick and injured at Walsall which saw the birth of Jerome K. Jerome; George Eliot in Coventry. W. H. Auden lived at Solihull and Harborne. Samuel Lines, farmer's boy and artist, who sired brilliant sons, came from Allesley to Birmingham which is also closely linked with Burne-Jones and David Cox. Controversial Bishop Barnes has a fascinating memorial window at Sutton Coldfield; the minor poet, William Shenstone, lies at Halesowen; the poet and dramatist, John Drinkwater, was closely associated with the old 'Rep' in Birmingham, founded by Sir Barry Jackson. Professor Tonks, who taught Augustus John, was born at Solihull, and, sadly, Samuel Johnson was refused a headmastership there. But let Wolverhampton have the last word – Button Gwinnett, one of those who signed the American Declaration of Independence, was married in St Peter's Church.

GAZETTEER

Aston Hall   7J6
2m N of **Birmingham** city centre. Now controlled by Birmingham City Museum and Art Gallery, this former home of the Holtes is one of the most splendid Jacobean mansions in the country, and contains a collection of English furniture and some valuable pictures. The near-by parish church, rebuilt, except for the tower and spire, in the 19th c, has important family monuments. Open April–Dec.

Berkswell   7K5
Near **Coventry**, but still surprisingly rural, it is an attractive village with a small museum of local life. The church of St John the Baptist is remarkable for its Norman chancel and two crypts with groined vaulting, as well as good old and new woodwork, and a timbered chamber over the 16th-c porch. There is a restored medieval cross in the exceptionally well-kept churchyard. Near by, is a well where early Christian converts are said to have been baptized, and the village green retains its stocks. Berkswell Hall stands in a park and has fine rhododendrons.

Bilston   7J6
It gives its name to the lovely enamels. The attractive St Leonard's Church was rebuilt in classical style by George IV's reign, by Francis Goodwin, but much altered by Ewan Christian in late Victorian times. The timber-framed Greyhound pub remains and a few interesting old houses. The museum and art gallery include local exhibits.

Birmingham   7J5

Large areas have undergone reconstruction since World War II, high-rise blocks drastically altering the face of the city, and the Inner Ring Road (Queensway) and the Aston Expressway linking this with the Gravelly Hill Interchange (Spaghetti Junction) have been made. A Middle Ring Road is under way. The impressive Rotunda by James A. Roberts dominates a reconstructed Bull Ring. Although there have been sad losses, Barry's King Edward's School in New Street (which went between the wars) among them, many reminders of the past, or not so distant past, remain, ranging from the early 16th-c Crown Inn, Deritend, to 19th-c buildings in the Colmore Row, Waterloo Street area, Philip Hardwick's Curzon Street Station and 'stately homes' in *Edgbaston*. The civic buildings in Victoria Square include the Council House (Yeoville Thomason, 1874–9) with noble reception rooms, and the Town Hall by Hansom and Welch (c.1834) with seating for 2,000 and one of the finest organs in the country; the latter building has been the centre of Birmingham's musical life since Mendelssohn conducted the first performance of 'Elijah' there in 1847. Adjacent is the magnificent new Central Library (over 1 million volumes) and the Museum and Art Gallery★, one of the best outside London, with impressive collections of old masters, Pre-Raphaelite paintings, watercolours, porcelain, jewelry, silver, and natural and local history galleries. The city is also responsible for the Museum of Science and Industry in Newhall Street; **Aston Hall**; Blakesley Hall, 6m SE at Yardley, a 16th-c timber-framed yeoman's farmhouse (open all year); Sarehole Mill at Hall Green, 18th-c (closed in winter); the remains of Weoley Castle at *Selly Oak*, 13th-c with a small museum (closed in winter); Selly Manor House and Minworth Greaves, both at *Bournville*. There is a Railway Museum at *Tyseley*. The Gas Street canal basin, part of the city's lengthy canal system, is a pretty area.

Other important cultural and artistic centres include the Birmingham and Midland Institute and Conference Centre,

now merged with the Birmingham Library (founded 1779); the well-reputed Birmingham Repertory Theatre; the Midlands Arts Centre for Young People at Cannon Hill Park; and the Barber Institute of Fine Arts at Edgbaston which is part of Birmingham University (not to be confused with the University of Aston in Birmingham) and has a fine concert hall and an expanding collection of pictures. Of the city's churches, the most memorable are St Philip's (now the Anglican Cathedral), built 1711–15, with later tower and extended chancel, and windows designed by Burne-Jones and executed by William Morris; St Paul's (1779 and later) with box-pews and octagonal spire; St Martin's, which, though rebuilt in the 19th c on the medieval site, contains tombs of the de Berminghams; St Chad's Roman Catholic Cathedral by Pugin; the early 20th-c Oratory Church at Edgbaston, and the 'village' churches of *Northfield*, *King's Norton* and *Yardley*. There are many parks; the old-established Botanical Gardens at Edgbaston have a handsome range of glasshouses and accommodation for functions; and Cannon Hill Nature Centre has a natural history museum (open all year except Tues.).

Coventry   7K5

Established under the protection of a Saxon convent in the 7th c, the fourth city in England and centre of the cloth weaving industry from the 14th c to the end of the 17th c, the city has become important for its coal-mining, car and other industries, now affected by recession. Despite bombing in World War II, various historic buildings have survived, including St Mary's Hall (AM), built in 1340–2 as the guildhall of the Merchant Guild and enlarged c.1400 for the Trinity Guild; something of the city wall; two of the original 12 gates; Bablake School; Bond's and Ford's Hospitals; part of the White Friars' monastery; and the Charterhouse. Of

Coventry: Bond's Hospital was founded in 1506 by a draper, for the care of 12 elderly poor men

the principal churches, two escaped disaster: Holy Trinity and St John the Baptist. The Cathedral Church of St Michael was completely destroyed, except for the 300ft steeple and some external walls. Here, the most controversial of modern cathedrals* has been completed to the design of Sir Basil Spence and with outstanding works by various artists including the altar tapestry by Graham Sutherland. In other respects, too, the city has led the work of postwar reconstruction by building the new shopping precincts, the Belgrade Theatre, the Herbert Art Gallery and Museum, and the Lanchester Polytechnic. The Museum of British Road Transport is another important addition. The new University of Warwick is within the city boundaries and has a notable Arts Centre. Reconstructed Roman fort at *Baginton*, 3m S, is open at set times.

Dudley 7J6
Famous for its castle of 11th-c foundation, and now housing a zoo. The town also has remnants of a priory, St Edmund's Church (early Georgian), St Thomas's Church (Regency), and Our Lady and St Thomas by Pugin. There is an art gallery and an excellent library and the fascinating Black Country Museum with reconstructed houses, shops, a pub, rolling-mill, etc. Near by at *Kingswinford* is the Broadfield House Glass Museum. Open all year except Sun.

Knowle 7K5
Now part of the Metropolitan Borough of **Solihull**. It has a parish church with exceptional Perpendicular work. There are misericords, a very fine chancel screen and a pulpit hourglass. Timbered buildings in the 'village' are the Guildhouse, Chester House (public library) and Milverton House, with charming Grimshaw Hall, ½m NE.

Meriden 7K5
Here a medieval cross and the Cyclists' War Memorial mark one of the many 'Centres of England'. It was once an important stopping-place for travellers between London and Ireland. It has grown appreciably in recent years, but retains an ancient hill-top church and various notable houses such as timber-framed Walsh Hall, Meriden Hall, chiefly by Francis Smith, and the early 18th-c Manor House, now a hotel. The Forest Hall is the HQ of the ancient and exclusive archery club, The Woodmen of Arden. **Packington Hall**, ¾m NW, and in Warwickshire, is a classical mansion with a Capability Brown park, fallow deer, and the Old Hall, home of Jane Lane (Lady Fisher) who helped Charles II to escape after the battle of Worcester (1651). Not open to the public.

Solihull 7J5
The heart of a Metropolitan Borough, the erstwhile village now has the inevitable shopping centre, as well as civic buildings that include a magnificent library with a theatre. Although industry is present, it is a fashionable residential district, especially favoured by **Birmingham** commuters. Historic features include the parish church (St Alphege) of 13th-c origin, with unique chapels, one above the other, the late 15th-c Manor House, in the High Street, and Malvern Hall (now a school) associated with the artist John Constable. Hillfield Hall, at present a restaurant, has a front dated 1576. Birmingham Airport, Birmingham International station (BR) and the modern National Exhibition Centre are within the Borough.

Sutton Coldfield 7J6
Mainly residential and now part of **Birmingham**, with modern shopping precincts, the Royal Town has architectural reminders of its past, including Georgian and earlier houses and Holy Trinity Church containing the tomb of Sutton's Tudor benefactor, Bishop Veysey. A modern Hall, with a golf-course, occupies the site of the mansion he built for himself at Moor Hall. Chief attraction of the town, however, is 2,400-acre Sutton Park to the W, largely preserved in its natural state. 1½m SE is the moated, medieval mansion *New Hall*, one of the oldest inhabited houses in the country.

Temple Balsall 7K5
The late 13th-c church, built by the Knights Templar, and much restored by Sir George Gilbert Scott, adjoins Lady Katherine Leveson's Hospital for aged women founded by Robert Dudley. The various buildings here form an attractive group in rural surroundings near 18th-c Springfield House. At the Old Hall, excavation has revealed an important find of late 17th- and early 18th-c glass and pottery.

Wednesbury 7J6
The prominent and very handsome St Barnabas' Church is largely Victorian with much good stained glass by C. E. Kempe, but incorporates some medieval work and has a unique, pre-Reformation lectern with fighting-cock instead of eagle. There is a Jacobean oak pulpit and a 'Descent from the Cross' by Jean Jouvenet, a 17th-c French artist. Also in the town is Sandwell Art Galley and Museum.

West Bromwich 7J6
A surprising town which seems uninteresting at first, but has extensive parkland and two historic mansions in unlikely surroundings. The 16th- and early 17th-c Oak House (open all year) has excellent period furniture and an Elizabethan-style garden. The medieval manor house at Stone Cross, embedded in tenements until recent years, retains an impressive great hall and detached kitchen, a moat (discovered and filled again with water) and a garden with bee-boles. An 18th-c gatehouse (Francis Smith) of demolished Sandwell Hall, where the Earls of Dartmouth lived, is stranded on a traffic island. Asbury Cottage (open all the year) at *Great Barr*, 3m NE from West Bromwich centre, was the home of Francis Asbury, first Bishop of the American Methodist Church.

Wightwick Manor 7I6
3m W of **Wolverhampton**. This is a rare example of a richly-timbered William Morris period house (NT) with Pre-Raphaelite works including Morris wallpapers, tapestry, curtains, de Morgan tiles, Kempe glass and trees planted by famous folk. Open all year except Feb. at set times.

Wolverhampton 7J6
It has been called the 'Queen of the Black Country' (some indignantly deny that it is in that region, though areas it has taken over certainly are!) and is an important industrial centre, with excellent modern shopping facilities. The fine, if much-restored, St Peter's Church (monuments) is partly medieval and adjoins a probably mid-9th-c cross and a statue by Sir Charles Wheeler of Wulfruna, who endowed a monastery around which the town grew, and which was captured by the Danes in 945.

DERBYSHIRE AND STAFFORDSHIRE

AN INTRODUCTION BY
PHIL DRABBLE

Derbyshire and Staffordshire must be two of the least publicized, least known and least appreciated counties in England – that is, apart from the Peak District. They stretch from the Pennines in the north to the industrial clamour of the Black Country in the south, and the country varies from the bleak stone-wall mountain scenery in the north of Derbyshire to some of the richest dairying country in England, in the Uttoxeter area.

The main road from West Bromwich, in the south, through Stafford and Stoke, passes through some of the dullest – but most important – industrial areas in the land. Yet only a few miles to the east, the road through Lichfield, across Needwood Forest to Sudbury and Ashbourne to Bakewell might almost be in another country: Needwood is famous for its oaks, and the whole route is well wooded until one climbs the stone-walled hills of Derbyshire.

The lovely River Dove divides the two counties, and Dovedale, shared between them, has scenery rugged and wild enough to give a wonderful sense of solitude even in this bustling, crowded age. Indeed, its characteristic mood can be very awe-inspiring. Black clouds often crown its glowering peaks; and when the thunder groans and belches and roars to crescendo, the echoes buffet from rock-face to rock-face down the valley until they magnify the difference between Nature and puny Man. This Peak District, the northern tip of Staffordshire and northwestern part of Derbyshire, is a National Park that is worth exploring times without number.

The red marls and gravels and sandstone of Staffordshire and south Derbyshire give way to the typical limes and millstone grits of Derbyshire. Beresford Dale, where Charles Cotton so often played host to his friend Izaak Walton, has been the object of pilgrimages by fishermen ever since nor is it only associations that draw them: it is the excitement of the scenery too.

Although it is such a wonderful country to explore, some of its best parts can be reached only on foot. Such as Milldale, with its little stone bridge, built for packhorses but scarcely wide enough for men, and the wild stone-wall country above, with craggy hills where nothing disturbs the peace but sheep and the soulful cries of the curlew. With the car left on the road below, there are rocks to be climbed and unforgettable views as reward for the effort. Even in the summer the breeze is drawn up the valleys, as if in a chimney-stack, giving freshness to the most sultry day. In the winter the road from Chapel-en-le-Frith through Castleton to Hope is an adventure. To leave the main road there and potter up the by-road to the north till it peters out at Edale or Upper Booth is a lesson on the superficiality of Progress.

The Cat and Fiddle Inn, just inside Cheshire on the Buxton–Macclesfield road, boasts that, at 1,690 feet, it is the highest in England. Certainly it is the coldest and bleakest – which makes the warmth and hospitality of the folk who live in these harsh hills more charming by contrast. To the south of the Peak District, where Derbyshire runs into Staffordshire, one might be in another land, though the Roaches, grim rocks tumbling down the hills outside Leek, are as wild as anything Derbyshire can show. It is still a stone-wall country of lonely farms and dewponds, the last filled by double the rainfall of the Midland Plain a few miles to the south. From the Cheshire border, in the west, across to Ashbourne in Derbyshire and down to Uttoxeter and Abbots Bromley, in Staffordshire, stretches a tract of superb dairying and stock-feeding country. Between the Stafford–Cannock and Stafford–Rugeley roads, Cannock Chase is a huge 16-square-mile lung for the teeming industrial population of the Black Country, in the south, and of Stafford and the Potteries in the north. Half of the Chase is afforested with egregious foreign conifers; but half is lovely open moorland and natural woods of silver birch and oak. There are grouse and deer to be seen by those who will park at Milford Common or Sherbrook Valley and walk a mile or so from the milling thousands who enjoy themselves there at weekends.

Customs

Staffordshire and Derbyshire are particularly rich in customs which still continue from ancient days. At Abbots Bromley, on the Lichfield–Uttoxeter road, the

A sense of solitude – stone-wall country of lonely farms and dewponds near Hathersage, Derbyshire

ancient Horn Dance is still performed in September to commemorate the hunting rights which were once enjoyed in adjacent Needwood Forest. The ceremony is a remarkable example of the way in which the church frequently took over the traditional pagan customs. In this case the process is not complete. The horns, huge reindeer horns mounted on handles, are kept in the church (where they may be seen at any time), and they must not be taken outside the parish; but there the vicar's jurisdiction over them ends. Although they are housed in the church, it is the dancers who control them. For generations the horn dancers have mostly been members of one family, and they choose their own team.

At Tissington, in Derbyshire, between the Ashbourne–Buxton and Ashbourne–Winster roads, the wells are 'dressed' on Ascension Day. Although it really perpetuates a pagan ceremony of propitiation to the gods of water, this has been absorbed into the church to a greater extent than the Horn Dance. It is thought by some to commemorate the survival of the villagers from the Black Death of 1348, in which the purity of their well may have played a part – but the real origins are possibly very much older. Several other towns and villages in Derbyshire also have well 'dressings' on various dates throughout the summer.

At Ashbourne they have a Shrovetide Football Match in which any of the inhabitants may partake, Sturston Mill and Clifton Mill, at each end of the town, being 'goals'. The players play towards the goal nearest their own homes, and the ball has to be struck against the mill-wheel after being taken up the mill-race. The player so scoring a 'goal' keeps the ball and is a hero for a year. The game is not recommended for those of a delicate constitution.

History

Derbyshire is a lucrative hunting ground for the prehistorian. Ploughing has never been practicable on the rocky uplands, and so ancient remains have been disturbed unusually little. In the Hartington area, especially, tumuli of great importance remain. High Low, Lean Low, Carder Low and, most famous of all, Arbor Low, are well worth visiting. Ditches, vallums and stones, dating from the period of Stonehenge or earlier, are still as they have always been. At Arbor Low, stones like giant figures round a sundial lie stark and lonely. It is seen at its best on a blustery spring afternoon, when the sense of solitude there is almost tangible and the curlews cry like lost souls pleading to the priests of a religion long dead.

Both counties are rich, too, in Roman remains. Ryknield Street and Watling Street cross at Wall, where the Roman town of Letocetum once stood. There were baths here for the garrison; and the hypocausts, a complicated system of flues for heating the floors, are still clearly visible – to provide food for thought for all whose modern systems of central heating may well seem less efficient. At Buxton, in Derbyshire, there was a bath heated naturally by water gushing, as it does today, hot from the belly of the earth. It may well have been thought the only warm place in 'bitter Buxton' on a winter's day.

Industry

Buxton was built on the profits of its lime industry – 100,000 tons have been dislodged in a single blasting operation. But the famous Crescent, one of the most gracefully dignified streets in England, is said to owe its existence to copper, the 5th Duke of Devonshire having built it in 1784 from the profits of one year's working of his copper-mines at Ecton. Since then the population has multiplied twentyfold to about 19,000.

The main industries of the two counties, apart from the quarrying and farming previously mentioned, and brewing at Burton, are bound up with coal and iron. There are coalfields scattered from south Staffordshire and Cannock Chase to north Staffordshire and Derbyshire. In the north of Staffordshire are the Potteries, described in many of Arnold Bennett's novels and for ever associated with the name of Josiah Wedgwood.

Derbyshire, too, spreads its interests widely. Although it is not nowadays of industrial significance, lead mining has been practised in Derbyshire at least from Roman times, and there are many old workings. As well as Buxton's lime, Derbyshire is much concerned with iron-smelting, heavy and general engineering and textile manufacture, particularly using rayon. These last two are especially centred round Derby itself, which can also claim to be the birthplace of the most famous and luxurious motorcar in the world, the Rolls-Royce (which is now no longer made here), and of many of the aero-engines which power the world's aircraft.

GAZETTEER

Abbots Bromley, Staffs   7J7
An attractive village of black-and-white houses (notably Church House and Goat's Head Inn, with a butter cross in the market place), where the Horn Dance (*see* Introduction) is still performed every September. *Blithfield Hall* is 3m SW across a large lake. The ruins of *Chartley Castle*, in its great park with an 18th-c manor house, are 5m NW.

Alton, Staffs   7J7
On a rock to one side of the Churnet Valley stand the tower of a medieval castle and a 19th-c convent (chapel by Pugin); to the other, we find Alton Towers, 19th-c Gothic, with park, amusements and splendid gardens and many attractions. Open March–Oct.

Ashbourne, Derbys   7K8
Small country town close to Dovedale and the Manifold Valley, with a handsome Church Street (16th-c grammar school, 17th c Owlfield and Pegg's Almshouses; Georgian mansion house, where Johnson and Boswell stayed with Dr John Taylor; clergymen's widows' houses and the Green Man Hotel); and one of the finest churches in the county, mainly 13th–14th-c, with 212ft spire and numerous monuments, particularly Thomas Banks' white marble Penelope Boothby. Ashbourne Football (*see* Introduction) is played in streets and stream on Shrove Tuesday and Ash Wednesday. Town noted for its gingerbread.

Ault Hucknall, Derbys   7K8
Hardly any village to speak of, but a church to shout about, early Norman, with some 14th-c alterations. Good, Italianate, monument (1627) to the wife of the 1st Earl of Devonshire, and a memorial slab to Thomas Hobbes, the philosopher, who died at near-by Hardwick in 1679.

Bakewell, Derbys   7K8
Handsome little market town on River Wye, crossed by medieval bridge, and convenient for visiting both **Haddon** and **Chatsworth**, with *Monsal Dale* 4m NW. Several stone houses of 17th and 18th c (Market and Town Halls, Catcliffe and Bath Houses, Holme Hall and others), and a 16th-c Old House Museum, open Easter–Oct. Cruciform church, typical of this county, 12th–14th-c (fine effigies in Vernon chapel, stump of Saxon Cross in churchyard, other fragments in S porch).

Betley, Staffs   7I8
Half-timbered houses beside an attractive mere. But the chief interest lies in the church. Not only is the whole supported by octagonal oak pillars, but the arches of the nave, clerestory and roof are all of finely worked timber.

Biddulph, Staffs   7I8
On the edge of its moor (1,100ft) near the source of the River Trent and the ancient Bride Stones. Spectacular views from Mow Cop. Here are the ruins of the Old Hall, destroyed during the Civil War, and a later one of the 17th and 18th c. In the church, note the Norman font, sandstone altar-rails and Flemish glass in one window. 1m S is Greenway Bank Country Park.

Bolsover, Derbys   9K2
The castle (AM), standing on a steep hill above the chimneys and pit-heads of the valley, is a Jacobean building on the site of Peveril's Norman keep, and is being restored. Open all year. Built by two generations of the Cavendishes (the younger entertained Charles I here at a cost of £15,000, which included a Ben Jonson masque), family monuments may be found in the Cavendish chapel, which survived when fire gutted the church in 1897.

Broughton, Staffs   7I7
Among the woods that still remain from Blore Forest, both church and hall were built by Thomas Broughton in mid-17th c. The first has high oak pews and period glass; the second is a gabled house with richly carved timbers.

Burton-upon-Trent, Staffs   7K7

Famous for brewing, an industry started by the monks of Burton Abbey after they had discovered that the water of Burton made beer clear and sparkling. The Abbey was founded in 1002 and became a collegiate church after the Dissolution. A few relics of the Abbey remain near St Modwen's Church, parish church of Burton. The Bass Museum of Brewing is open all year. 6m W is **Hoar Cross** Hall and church.

Buxton,★ Derbys   9I2

Standing nearly 1,000ft above sea level, a centre for exploring the Peak District, Spa waters known to Romans and Mary Queen of Scots, but developed by the 5th Duke of Devonshire, who built the Crescent, Assembly Room (now a library) and stables about 1790. These last, with 19th-c additions (including the great dome), are now the Devonshire Royal Hospital. A good viewpoint is the tower on Grin Low (1,450ft), above Poole's Cavern, a fine natural limestone cave (with stalactites and stalagmites) which is open Easter–Oct. Buxton Country Park is adjacent. From Grin Low you can see *Goyt Valley* and Reservoirs 3½m W and *Axe Edge*, with its inn, the Cat and Fiddle (1,690ft), is S. Buxton Festival held each summer. Local museum open all year, and Transport Museum April–Oct. A Natural World Exhibition at the Micrarium is open March–Nov.

Cannock, Staffs   7J6

A large mining town at the edge of *Cannock Chase* which, with 17,000 acres designated as an area of outstanding beauty, rises to 800ft at prehistoric Castle Ring. 4m SW, moated *Hilton House* stands in a fine park.

Castleton, Derbys   9I2

A magnificent situation★★ at the W end of the Hope Valley, separated from *Kinder Scout* (2,083ft) and *Kinder Low* (2,077ft), 5m NW, by Lose Hill, Back Tor, Mam Tor and the Vale of Edale. Just above the village is the Norman keep of ruined *Peveril Castle* (AM). The church has a Norman chancel arch, and box-pews. The Cavendish House Museum has one of the finest collections of Blue John in the world. Open daily. The neighbourhood abounds in caves open to the public. 1½m W, *Mam Tor*, the 'Shivering Mountain' (1,700ft) (NT), has an Iron Age hill fort on its summit. Also W is Blue John Cavern, the source of the rare stone discovered by the Romans (open all year), Peak Cavern, the largest natural cavern here (open March–Sept.), and Speedwell Cavern with underground boat journey (open daily).

Caverswall, Staffs   7J8

The castle, now a convent, is a turreted Jacobean building standing within the dried-up moat of the medieval original. In the church, the kneeling figure of Lady St Vincent is by Chantrey (1816), and there is a Jacobean altar table.

Chatsworth,★, Derbys   9J2

Near *Baslow*. With **Haddon** and **Hardwick**, one of the three great Derbyshire mansions, its grounds among the most notable in the country. Of the original Elizabethan buildings, the Hunting Tower and Queen Mary's Bower in the grounds survive, but the old house was replaced by the present one between 1687 and 1707 by the 1st Duke of Devonshire (architect, Talman), while in the early 19th-c the 6th Duke employed Sir Jeffry Wyatville to add a new NE wing. The interior is decorated with sumptuous painting, carving and plasterwork. The garden has a fine cascade and one of the highest fountains in Europe. House, grounds and farmyard exhibition open late-March–Oct.

Chatsworth: originally built by Bess of Harkwick but enlarged by her grandson the 1st Duke of Devonshire

Cheadle, Staffs   7J8

On the edge of a wild moor leading to the Weaver Hills stands a group of timbered and gabled Elizabethan houses near the 19th-c church. The other church, with its 200ft spire and rich internal decoration, is one of Pugin's masterpieces. 2m NE is the *Hawksmoor Nature Reserve* (NT), 300 acres of woodlands, moors and marshes.

Chesterfield, Derbys   9J2

Industrial and commercial centre, famous for its church's 228ft spire, warped out of the perpendicular by its lead and timber covering. Mainly 14th-c, but much restored, the church is notable for the number of chapels (once belonging to guilds) and the series, some very good, of Foljambe monuments. The Peacock, a fine medieval timber-framed building, recently restored, is now a Tourist Information and Heritage Centre. There is a museum at *Old Whittington*, about 3m N, in Revolution House. Open May–Sept. 10m NE is *Barlborough Hall* (1583) with a magnificent stone chimney piece. Now a prep school but open at stated times in the summer.

Clifton Campville, Staffs   7K6

The mainly 14th-c church, one of the finest in the county, has a spire 189ft high, with flying buttresses. Above the chapel in the N transept is a priest's chamber with fireplace and 13th-c windows. There are five screens, and carved stalls and misericords, a Rysbrack monument and a fine Tudor table-tomb of alabaster. 3m W, *Haselour Hall* is a gabled building not to be missed.

Crich, Derbys   7K8
Rugged hill-village with lead-mining and limestone-quarrying traditions. The church has a Norman N arcade and font, but the rest is mainly 14th-c, including good effigy of a bearded man thought to be Sir William de Wakebridge, who founded a chantry here, and built in stone a lectern of a type peculiar to Derbyshire. Crich Stand, a tower with beacon light, 950ft above sea level, is a war memorial to the Sherwood Foresters Regiment. In a quarry (once worked by George Stephenson) below the Stand, is the National Tramway Museum, open Easter–Oct., with rides along 1m of track.

Cromford, Derby   7K8
The Old Mill (1771) is where Richard Arkwright first used water-power to drive a cotton mill. The whole mill complex is being restored and is open April–Oct. In the village street stands the Georgian Greyhound Inn and the church built by Arkwright. The 15th-c bridge has rounded arches on one side and pointed on the other. At the S end are the remains of a bridge chapel. Willersley Castle is the house Arkwright built for himself in the late-18th-c classical manner. Horse-drawn boat trips are run from Cromford Wharf on summer Saturdays and Sundays on a restored stretch of the Cromford Canal to *Leawood Pumphouse*, 1½m SE, where a restored 1849 beam engine is operated on occasional summer weekends. There is also a small museum on Cromford Wharf (open April–Oct. on Sun.).

Croxall, Staffs   7K6
Three-storeyed Oakley farmhouse to the S, was the manor of the Stanley family 500 years ago. The gabled brick hall was for many generations the home of the Curzons, to whom there is a remarkable series of tombstones in the church. But the most interesting memorial here is to Sir Robert Wilmot-Horton and his wife: of her, Byron wrote, 'She walks in beauty like the night . . .'. Sir Robert was responsible for the decision to burn the MS of the poet's memoirs.

Croxden, Staffs   7J7
A tiny, remote village dominated by the ruins of Croxden Abbey (AM), a Cistercian house founded in 1176, which bestrides the village street. The W wall of the church and the S wall of the S transept, both with tall lancet windows, are the most impressive of the surviving remains.

Dale Abbey, Derbys   7K7
Part of the gatehouse, some vaulting in a cow-house and the great arch of the E window are all that remain of a 12th-c foundation, situated beneath sandstone cliffs in which is a medieval hermit's cave. The village church, only 26ft by 25ft and under the same roof as a dwelling house, formerly an inn, is, however, one of the most curious in the country. It is filled with box-pews, a gallery and a 1634 pulpit, and has 13th-c wall paintings. The Cat and Fiddle Windmill, an 18th-c post mill, is renovated and is open to the public by appointment.

Derby, Derbys   7K7
Britain's newest city (created 1977) was a prosperous trading town in the Middle Ages; industrialization began with the introduction of the country's first silk mill (now an industrial museum) in 1717, hence the preponderance of 18th-c domestic architecture that typifies the centre of the town (Market Place, Irongate, Queen and King Street, Wardwick and, especially, Friargate). Growth of engineering in the 19th and 20th c, including railways and Rolls-Royce, has more than doubled the population. Derby

Industrial Museum has a Rolls-Royce collection of aero engines. Open all year Tues.–Sat. The tower of All Saints (parish church, raised to cathedral in 1927) is 16th-c. The church itself, rebuilt by Gibbs (1723), the architect of **St Martin-in-the-Fields** in London, is a splendid example of its period, with numerous monuments and splendid wrought-iron screens and communion-rails by Robert Bakewell (1682–1752). The most significant municipal buildings are County Hall (1660) and the Assembly Rooms (1977). The rare, but considerably restored, Bridge Chapel is 14th-c. The Royal Crown Derby Porcelain Co. Museum (open weekdays) and the City Museum and Art Gallery (open all year except Mon.) have good collections of Derby porcelain. The Art Gallery also houses a splendid collection of works by the 18th-c artist Joseph Wright of Derby.

Dovedale, ** Derby and Staffs   7J8
A lovely stretch of the River Dove (famous trout stream); a steeply wooded limestone ravine with crags and caves, running some 7m N from *Thorpe* and continuing as Wolfscote and Beresford Dales to **Hartington**. *See also* **Ashbourne** and **Ilam**.

Elford, Staffs   7K6
Charming little village in the Tame Valley, with an old tall-chimneyed Hall, a cluster of picturesque cottages and a lime avenue leading to the church, which, much restored in the 19th c, contains a sculptured gallery, modern wood-carving and medieval alabaster tombs.

Ellastone, Staffs   7J8
Near the River Dove, at the foot of the Weaver Hills, which rise to 1,000ft, it is the 'Hayslope' of George Eliot's *Adam Bede*; her father, the model for the hero of the novel, spent his youth here in a thatched house that is still standing. 2m W, *Wootton Lodge*, splendidly situated, is a 17th-c mansion, probably by Robert Smythson, who designed **Hardwick Hall** and **Wollaton Hall** (Notts).

Elvaston, Derbys   7K7
The handsome medieval church within the 200-acre park (now a country park; open all year) of Elvaston Castle contains good monuments of the Stanhope family, Earls of Harrington. The mansion, redesigned by James Wyatt in 1812, retains a small portion of a 1633 house, but is less impressive than the gardens laid out by William Barron between 1830 and 1850. A Working Estate Museum, open Easter–Oct., recreates life as it was on the Elvaston estate around 1900.

Enville, Staffs   7I5
The tower of the church is modern, the nave-arcades Norman, the chancel (carved misericords) rebuilt in the 14th c by Roger de Birmingham, who is buried here. Near by stands the Hall (fine collection of pictures) in charming grounds designed by the poet Shenstone. *Kinver Edge* (NT), a viewpoint 2m SE, is crowned by an ancient camp, and there is a rock-dwelling known as Holy Austin Rock.

Eyam, Derbys   9J2
Some 800ft above sea level, with *White Edge* (1,156ft) 3m away to E, this is the Plague Village, whose inhabitants in 1665–6, inspired by their rector and his predecessor, stayed within the parish confines and so prevented the plague from spreading elsewhere. A private local museum is open by appointment. ½m E, *Riley Graves* (NT) contain seven members of a family who died within seven days. There is a 9th-c Saxon cross in the churchyard, which is surrounded by

Lichfield: the 'Ladies of the Vale', the cathedral's spires, built on the site consecrated by St Chad

pleasant houses, including the Georgian Rectory. The Hall is Jacobean, stone with mullioned windows. 2m N, on Eyam Moor, *Wet Withens* is a Bronze Age circle of 16 stones, still standing within a bank of earth.

Haddon Hall,★ Derbys   **7K8**
2m SE of **Bakewell** it is wonderfully sited, among trees and fields sloping to the River Wye, and one of the most romantic places in the county. Mainly constructed in the 16th and 17th c, but on the foundations of a Norman stronghold (it was not lived in between 1700 and 1900; then it was admirably restored), its beauty is the result of growth rather than design – e.g. it is typical that the Norman font in the chapel has a Jacobean cover, and that both seem in place. Charming terraced garden. Open April–Sept.

Hanbury, Staffs   **7K7**
Pleasant village on edge of Needwood Forest with superb view from churchyard N across Dove Valley. Splendid monuments in the church include probably the oldest alabaster effigy in England (thought to be of Sir John de Hanbury, d.1303). The tomb of Sir John Egerton (1662), Axe Bearer of Needwood Forest, was erected, unusually, at the E end of the N aisle by his sister so that he might be 'away from the gaze of the Puritan ladies', Mrs Agard (1628) and her daughter Mrs Woollocke (1657), who stare down disapprovingly from busts above the vicar's stall.

Hardwick Hall,★ Derbys   **7L8**
At *Doe Lea*, off the A617 5m SE of **Chesterfield**. It is 15m E of **Haddon Hall** but unlike it, far from having merely grown, it took its present shape in 1591–7, by the direction of a woman who was over 70 when she began and yet managed to live the last ten years of her life there. The formidable Bess of Hardwick, having married from the Old Hall (its ruins stand close by) at 13 and outlived four wealthy husbands, started her project at the age of 71. The result was the Elizabethan mansion (NT) that we see today, with its presence chamber and most of the original decoration, hangings and furniture. Open April–Oct.

Hartington, Derbys   **7J8**
Attractive little village near the entrance to Beresford Dale, with cottages and 19th-c town hall in the market place; gabled and mullioned 14th-c hall rebuilt 1611 and now a youth hostel; and church with two-storeyed porch.

Hathersage, Derbys   **9J2**
A Peak town 3m S of *High Neb* (1,500ft) with Carl Wark, an Iron Age hill fort, to the E, it is the 'Morton' of *Jane Eyre*. There are two early 19th-c mills and a 16th-c hall with 19th-c front; Robin Hood's Little John is by tradition buried in the

churchyard; and the church has brasses and tombs of the Eyre family, who lived at *North Lees*, 1½m N, a small but impressive 16th-c manor house. In September the Longshaw sheepdog trials are held near here.

Hoar Cross, Staffs   7J7
Off the A515 near *Newborough*. When Hugo Francis Meynell Ingram of Hoar Cross Hall died in 1871, his widow commissioned G. F. Bodley to build a church in his memory. The result is Bodley's masterpiece. The nave is dark, but the chancel light and lofty; the whole lavishly decorated. The glass and the carvings are superb. This is an astonishing church to discover in a tiny, scattered Needwood Forest hamlet. House open in the summer at set times.

Ilam, Staffs   7J8
Near the entrance to Dovedale, on the River Manifold, which is partly subterranean and has a lovely valley (ruins of Jacobean Throwley Hall; and Thor's Cave, near Wetton Mill). J. Watts Russell rebuilt the village and Tudor Hall (where Congreve wrote *The Old Bachelor*) in the 19th c. There are two Saxon crosses in the churchyard; the church contains a Norman font and an octagonal chapel and tomb designed by Chantrey. The shrine of St Bertram is in the grounds of the Hall.

Ingestre, Staffs   7J7
In a fine park bounded by the River Trent, a hamlet, with 17th-c Hall, rebuilt in Regency Gothic after a fire, and church (1677) usually ascribed to Wren.

Kedleston, Derbys   7K7
The Hall is the finest Georgian house in the county, with splendid grounds and lake. The N front is by James Paine (1761), but Robert Adam built the more elegant S front, the great hall, the rotunda, the music-room, some of the furnishings and the bridge. Open Easter–Sept. on set days. The church, 13th c cruciform, has box-pews, font and communion rails of about 1700; effigies of Curzon knights, and, as one would expect, an ambitious monument to the late Lord Curzon of Kedleston whose Indian Museum is also to be seen in the Hall. The future of the Hall is uncertain.

Leek, Staffs   7J8
An ancient town, its prosperity founded on the silk industry and situated in the upper Churnet Valley among moors and mountains; the rugged Staffordshire *Roaches*, rising to 1,500ft, are some 6m N beyond Rudyard Lake. Little remains of *Dieulacresse Abbey*, 1¼m N. In Mill Street, Brindley Mill, now restored, is open April–Oct. weekends. At *Chaddleton* is the N. Staffs Steam Railway Centre (open at set times).

Lichfield,★ Staffs   7J6
The red sandstone cathedral, with its three spires, splendid front choir and chapter house, is an outstanding example of Early English and Decorated work. Monuments and decoration were savaged during the Civil War, but restoration was carried out by Bishop Hacket (1662) and again in the 19th c, when much of the carving on the W front was done. The 16th-c Herkenrode windows in the Lady Chapel were brought from Belgium in 1803; stalls and Bishop's throne were carved in 1860 by George Eliot's uncle, Samuel Evans, the original Seth Bede. A lovely view of the Cathedral can be gained from across the 17-acre Stowe Pool. Dr Johnson was born in a house in Breadmarket Street, now a museum (open daily except Mon.); there is a well-restored timbered house in Bore Street, and a city museum. See also 13th c Hanch Hall. St Mary's Heritage Centre, in the Market Square is

open all year. At *Wall*, 2m SW on Watling Street the excavated Roman remains of Letocetum (AM) can be seen. 3m SW off the A51 is an interesting regimental museum at *Whittington* Barracks. Open Mon.–Fri.

Longnor, Staffs   7J8
A list of market tolls on a market hall of 1873 reveals the lost status of this charming gritstone village whose decline has been arrested by a Peak Park refurbishing project.

Matlock, Derbys   7K8
An inland spa, mainly developed through the 19th c, in the valley of the Derwent, with the Heights of Abraham rising to 1,100ft. At Matlock Bath the Peak District Mining Museum is open all year. Also an aquarium on site of old thermal pool. Open Easter–Sept. daily and winter weekends. At *Riber*, the 19th-c castle is now a wildlife park; the Hall and manor house of two centuries earlier stand in pleasing contrast. At South Wingfield, 5m SE, are the historic ruins of *Wingfield Manor* (note the tower and vaulted crypt), begun in 1440 and originally larger than **Haddon Hall**, where Mary Queen of Scots was long imprisoned. Open all year on request at the gatehouse. 3m SE are *Lea* Rhododendron Gardens also with azaleas, rock gardens, woodland. Open April–end July. 4m W *Winster* Market House (NT) is late 17th-c and open April–Sept. on set days.

Melbourne, Derbys   7K7
The exterior of the church is largely masked by a tithe barn, but inside we find magnificent clerestoried Norman nave and crossing. The Hall (16th-c, enlarged and considerably redesigned in the 18th) is open June–Oct, and its splendid grounds all year.

Moseley Old Hall, Staffs   7J6
Elizabethan half-timbering now under 19th-c brick. Panelled rooms served as refuge of Charles II after the battle of Worcester in 1651. Garden in 17th-c style. (NT). Open March–Nov. on set days.

Norbury, Derbys   7J7
Church and manor house form an exquisite picture in a leafy frame. The 14th-c church, one of the finest in Derbyshire, has a spacious chancel lit by large windows with much contemporary glass, and splendid Fitzherbert monuments. An early 18th-c façade masks an early Tudor manor house, behind which is a medieval hall house of *c.*1250, now restored and open in summer by written appointment.

Peak District,★ Derbys *see* Introduction,
and **Bakewell, Buxton, Castleton, Dovedale, Hathersage** and **Tideswell.**

Peveril Castle *see* Castleton

Potteries, The, Staffs   7I8
The potter's craft has been practised here from the 17th c to the present day; and Arnold Bennett's Five Towns – *Stoke, Burslem, Longton, Hanley* and *Tunstall* – were made famous, long before he wrote about them, by Wedgwood, Spode, Copeland and Minton; specimens of their work may be seen in the Gladstone Pottery Museum at Longton and the new City Museum at Stoke. Also the Chalterley Whitfield Mining Museum (including underground demonstrations); the new Minton Museum; and the Spode Museum. Visits organized at most factories. At *Trentham* 1m, SW of Longton, the 1,000-acre park with its lake and garden is now open daily.

Repton, Derbys 7K7
Remains of the ruined 12th-c priory are incorporated in the famous school, the most important being Prior Overton's Tower, now part of the Headmaster's House. The Saxon crypt of St Wystan's Church should not be missed. The chancel above is of the same period. *Foremark Hall*, now a preparatory school, 2m E, is a Palladian house of 1760; the church, a century older and externally Gothic, has kept intact its original Jacobean furnishings, box-pews, three-decker pulpit and rood-screen. Foremark Reservoir has a nature reserve, woodland walks, sailing etc.

Shardlow, Derbys 7L7
Georgian canal port on the Trent and Mersey Canal, ¾m W of its junction with the River Trent. Numerous canal buildings survive, including the Clock Warehouse of 1780 which houses a permanent Canal Exhibition (open daily all year). Shardlow Hall, now Ministry of Agriculture offices, was built by the magnate of the earlier river port in 1684.

Shugborough, Staffs 7J7
Begun in 1693 and twice enlarged in the next century, the mansion (NT) contains fine pictures, French furniture and numerous souvenirs of Admiral Lord Anson's circumnavigation of the world. It is the ancestral home of the Earl of Lichfield. The Triumphal Arch, one of several neo-Greek monuments (mainly by James 'Athenian' Stuart) in the beautiful park, also commemorates the Admiral. The stable block has been converted into a splendid museum of Staffordshire Life, which is open throughout the year. The house is open March–Oct.

Stafford, Staffs 7J7
Although more famous now for electronics, Stafford still makes boots and shoes as it did in the 18th c, when its M.P., Richard Brinsley Sheridan, said, 'May its trade be trod underfoot by all the world.' He used to stay at Chetwynd House (now the post office); and in the same Greengate Street are two Tudor houses: High House and the Swan. St Mary's has a great octagonal tower, rare in this country, a spacious 13th-c interior, a Norman font, and a bust of Izaak Walton, who was baptized here. Tucked away near by, St Chad's has a Norman nave with clerestory, and a superb chancel arch, with five orders of almost unimpaired Norman carving. The M6 motorway has encouraged industrial growth and the borough has a modern centre. There is a walk on the site of Stafford Castle. Izaak Walton's Cottage at *Shallowford*, 5m NW, is open throughout the year, except Tues. 12m N at *Barlaston* is the Josiah Wedgwood Museum and factory – open all year. 6m NE is ruined *Chartley Castle* (AM). *See also* **Stone.**

Steetley, Derbys 9K2
Small but lavish Norman chapel, with obscure history, in a field. Carefully restored by J. L. Pearson in 1880.

Stoke *see* **Potteries, The**

Stone, Staffs 7J7
Birthplace of Admiral John Jervis, Earl St Vincent, who is buried in the family mausoleum in the churchyard. His bust by Chantrey is in the very early Gothick Revival church of 1753 (with galleries and box-pews), but his old home, Meaford Hall, has been demolished. The imposing exterior of the Crown Hotel, designed by Henry Holland in 1778, the gabled, brick railway station of 1848 and the boats on the Trent and Mersey Canal hint at the importance of Stone as a communications centre. *See also* **Stafford.**

Sudbury, Derbys 7J7
A pretty brick village, with a notable inn (1671) and a 17th-c Hall (NT), containing a superb staircase and a wealth of plasterwork and carving. The Hall, and the Museum of Childhood in the stables, are open April–Oct. Wed.–Sun. The restored church has fine Vernon effigies. *Somersal Herbert Hall*, 2½ NW, has Elizabethan half-timbering.

Tamworth, Staffs 7K6
An imposing castle, with Saxon and Norman work in the keep and curtain-wall, which encloses Tudor and Jacobean domestic buildings, now a museum. It stands on a 130ft mound, raised by Alfred's daughter Ethelfleda (d.918), and overlooks the junction of the Tame and the Anker. The church has a unique feature: twin spiral stairs leading to the roof of the Norman tower. It also has windows by Ford Madox Brown and William Morris. The town hall (AM) was built in 1701 by Thomas Guy, founder of Guy's Hospital, London. 2m S at *Fazeley* is Drayton Manor Park and Zoo.

Tideswell, Derbys 9I2
This small town, with Miller's Dale 2m S and the mountains of the Peak District rising to the N, is noteworthy for one of the outstanding churches of the county, a 14th-c structure with a four-turreted tower. 2m NE are the well-known round barrows, *Tideslow* and *Tup Low*.

Tissington, Derby 7K8
Lovely limestone village with Hall (1611), and Norman church over-restored in 1854, but containing finely turned communion rail *c*.1600 and two-decker pulpit. The five village wells are dressed each Ascension Day, a custom followed in about 20 Derbyshire villages during the summer.

Tutbury, Staffs 7K7
A pleasant little town on the River Dove, with a timbered inn. On the hill below the ruins of the medieval castle in which Mary Queen of Scots was imprisoned stands the Priory church, with Norman arcades, clerestory and triforium, and the magnificent W front. Open all year. Also Glassworks open most of the year.

Weston Park *see* **Tong,** Shropshire

Winster *see* **Matlock**

Wirksworth, Derbys 7K8
The Civic Trust project, which has restored the ruggedly handsome appearance of this former lead-mining centre, the 'Snowfield' of George Eliot's *Adam Bede*, was scheduled to end in March 1984 but has been extended for another five years. An Anglo-Saxon coffin-lid of *c*.800 is the most important of numerous good monuments in the impressive medieval church standing within a miniature close. The Middleton Top Engine House has a restored steam winding engine built 1829. Open Easter–Oct. on Sun. Engine operated first Sat. each month.

Youlgreave, Derbys 7K8
The restored church contains much Norman work, including the font, and a 15th-c tower. Alabaster effigies of Cokaynes and Gylberts can be seen; the E window in the chancel is by Burne-Jones and William Morris. Old Hall Farm (1630) and Old Hall (1650) lie to the NW. *Lathkill Dale* is accessible from *Alport*, 1½m E. *Arbor Low*, 3½m W, a Bronze Age circle of recumbent stones about 250ft across, is the most famous Derbyshire antiquity; and near by is the large round barrow, *Gib Hill*.

BEDFORDSHIRE AND NORTHAMPTONSHIRE

AN INTRODUCTION BY
W.G. HOSKINS

In Northamptonshire we are in the innermost Midlands. To outsiders, this (and Bedfordshire, which lies to the southeast of it) is very indeterminate country, too often merely a country of passage, since it lies right across most of the main routes out of London to the north and northwest. To the native of either county, each is distinctive and could not be anything else; but it must be confessed that scenically their charms are not easy to see at a glance or to appreciate from a car. A Victorian guidebook summed up Northamptonshire as having 'a quiet beauty that is very refreshing', and this is still true of a good deal of the county, and of much of Bedfordshire.

But one must bring to this (on the whole) green and quiet part of England a greater measure of knowledge – of geology and landscapes, of church and domestic architecture above all, and perhaps of English history in general – than one normally carries about, if its real character is to be enjoyed. Some parts of England reveal their beauties, or appear to, flamboyantly and immediately, and in that way encourage a lazy and superficial visit. Of these two counties it would be true to say that visitors who come totally unprepared (save for the well-advertised charms of Woburn Abbey) will leave them feeling disappointed except for the occasional pleasant surprise.

Geology and Scenery

The grain of the country runs from southwest to northeast in both counties: that is, across the main lines of movement. Incidentally, one can often achieve happy results in England by noticing any obvious grain like this and deliberately travelling along it rather than across it as the unimaginative or the busy have done for centuries. It is true that this involves the slightly tiresome business of having to cut across busy roads instead of rushing along them; but apart from this minor nuisance there is a lot to be said for such gentle pottering along the line of the grain. It means some intelligent map-reading – but in return one gets a view of a little bit of England that is totally unexpected, of a small piece of country that is homogeneous because of the underlying rocks and the buildings that have come out of them.

So the main grain of Northamptonshire is the Great Oolite, the most beautiful of the limestones (usually called Cotswold stone), and it runs almost the entire 70 miles of the county from the banks of the Cherwell, not far from Oxford, right up to the edge of Peterborough in the Fens. This forms physically the so-called Northamptonshire Uplands, gently undulating country rising to 600 or 700 feet above sea level in places. Flanking this belt of good building-stone (note the Barnack and Weldon stones) all along its northwestern edge is the Middle Lias, better known as marlstone, or occasionally as ironstone since it is rich in iron ore, the quarrying of which is now one of the biggest industries in Northants. This same stone was much used for building in past centuries, ranging in colour from a rich gold in some places to a deep velvety brown in others. So one gets in rural Northants a belt of sheep-grey limestone villages, such as Geddington and Weldon, and a parallel belt of golden or warm brown villages. In some villages the two stones are intermixed in a delightful decorative way. There is another distinctive difference between the lias and the oolite, and that is that for centuries the Liassic clays have been under pasture (there are many 'lost villages' in this part of the country, depopulated when the open-field village was turned over to grass for sheep and cattle in the 15th and 16th centuries); whereas the oolite generally gives a light arable land, more open landscapes, and many pheasants. In the extreme northeast, Northants runs right into the Fens near Crowland – at first sight dull country, but those who live there grow very fond of the great skies, and dark endless fields, and the immense misty views.

Bedfordshire, too, though much smaller and with a very different geology, has a southwest northeast grain. In the south, the chalk downs continue the better-known Chilterns and give the greatest heights, usually 600 to 800 feet above the sea. These are perhaps 'the Delectable Mountains' of John Bunyan, who was born, and lived, near Bedford. Then comes a narrow belt of heavy gault clays (cf. the village named Barton-in-the-Clay), followed in turn by a timbered upland of the lower greensand, a light buff-coloured sand producing low wooded hills (but rising to just about 500 feet in one or two places) that die away towards the northeast. Except where mixed with clay, these sands are infertile; and it is no historical accident that along the entire length of the ridge from Woburn on the west to Sandy on the east we get a string of considerable parks and big houses, of which Woburn is the largest and the best known. The fine views from this ridge attracted the builders of country houses, and the stretches of natural heathland made the creation of parks easier than it would have been in a richly-cultivated country. We get the same string of great parks – but on an even grander scale – for the same reason in the so-called Dukeries of Nottinghamshire.

In the centre and north of Bedfordshire the heavy Oxford clays produce a stiff soil, chiefly under grass. It is, however, far from dull scenery: the broad valley of the Great Ouse especially gives some of the most appealing river scenery in the Midlands and much excellent fishing. Bedfordshire is small, and a summary description like this makes it seem smaller and more uniform than it really is. It has to be appreciated rather like chamber music, listened to again and again, unlike the grand and rather obvious symphonic music of counties such as Yorkshire and Devon. Explore it slowly along its various geological grains and you will be rewarded hour after hour. One sees this in the flora, for example, where the variety of soils and sudden changes of elevation produce an exceptionally interesting variety for so small an area: chalk downland, river-meadows, parks and woods, and arable hedgerows. It is also apparent in the farming, for this one small county can show a dozen distinct types of farming – almost a complete miniature of British farming as a whole, with a special emphasis on market-gardening, especially round Sandy and Biggleswade.

Architecture
The old saying about Northamptonshire is that it is a county of 'spires and squires' – in other words, of fine churches and fine country houses. Archeologically it follows the same pattern as other East Midland counties in not being visually very exciting; but its churches and country houses put it in the first rank among English counties for interest. Moreover, an exceptional number of the finest houses remain in the hands of their ancient owners – Althorp, Boughton and Castle Ashby, to name only some of them. Again, as Pevsner rightly says, the country houses of Northants are so numerous and so spread out in time that one could write the architectural history of England between 1560 and 1700 from this county alone. Among the medieval houses, Drayton (from 1328 onwards) is of the highest importance, so too are Northborough and Yardley Hastings. But it is in the Elizabethan period, when many of the great state

officials were trying to outbuild each other, that Northamptonshire becomes architecturally the most important region in England. Of these really great houses Holdenby, the largest of them all, survives only as fragments; but Kirby Hall (begun in 1570) remains perhaps the loveliest Elizabethan ruin in all England, especially when one sees it in early summer amid its flowering chestnuts and beeches. But Burghley, just across the border in Cambridgeshire, remains outwardly intact. Other great houses take the story on into the 18th century. Bedfordshire suffers by any comparison such as this; but it has good things, ducal Woburn, and Wrest Park (with its formal canal garden) among them – and, above all, Luton Hoo, the home of one of the finest private art collections in England (the Wernher collection of paintings, tapestries, ivories, etc.). It is foolish to compare, but in Northamptonshire one can think only of the pictures at Althorp as in the same class.

The churches of Northamptonshire have been the Mecca of ardent ecclesiologists (or church-crawlers) for over 100 years. Few counties if any can show so much exciting Saxon work – notably, of course, Brixworth, which has been called the finest monument of the 7th century north of the Alps. The massive chancel arch at Wittering is also something quite remarkable, and so too are the Anglo-Saxon towers of Brigstock, Barnack and Earls Barton. But how can one do justice to such a county in a page or so, beyond saying that one could write the history of English church-building, from the 7th century to the 20th, from this wonderful county alone? Still, one must mention at least the superb Warmington Church (perfectly Early English) and noble unfinished Fotheringhay (15th-century) as places of special pilgrimage. And the other thing about the churches is their spires, the broach spires especially, that are so marked a feature of every view in the eastern half of the county.

Once again Bedfordshire suffers by being grouped with Northants. Yet the Bedfordshire churches in general are very interesting, and not as well known as they ought to be. Dunstable Priory Church (1130 onwards) is famed, of course; so are the magnificent remains – not only of the church, but also of the nunnery and of Hillersden Mansion – at Elstow; so too are Leighton Buzzard Church and perhaps the delightful 13th-century church at Eaton Bray. But there are scores of others that ought to be visited by the leisurely motorist making his way, as I have suggested, along the grain of some geological formation, with a one-inch map. Perhaps the small-scale charm of deepest Bedfordshire is epitomized in the unspoiled country interiors of Chalgrave, a few miles north of busy Dunstable, and perfect little Dean, in the extreme north of the county, lost among its trees. The very name is redolent of an older, quieter England – Upper Dean.

GAZETTEER

Althorp, * Northants 5H8
6m NW of **Northampton** on the A428 near *Harlestone*, and 6m from M1 exit 16. Home of the Spencers, the Princess of Wales' family, since 1508. Queen Anne, James I's wife, stayed here on her journey S from Scotland in the wake of her husband, a masque by Ben Jonson being performed in her honour. The 16th–19th-c house was covered with grey brick by Henry Holland. Magnificent rooms with pictures of European schools, much porcelain and French furniture. An impressive long gallery and great staircase. Handsome stables contain tea-room, shop, etc. Deer park. Open all the year on set days. To the W of the park, *Great Brington* Church contains Spencer family tombs from early dates onwards, and brasses commemorating ancestors of George Washington.

Ampthill, Beds 4G7
This typical country town is at its busiest on Thurs., when people congregate at the market, which dates back to 1219. The church is of special interest to Americans because it contains a monument to Richard Nicholls (1624–72), the first English Governor of Long Island, New York. Above it is embedded the Dutch cannon-ball that was the instrument both 'of his mortality and immortality'. 17th-c Ampthill Park (not open to motor traffic) has trees planted by Lady Holland in imitation of the Almeida in Madrid. It has been a Cheshire Home in recent years.
1m N are the ruins of 17th-c *Houghton House* (AM). Possibly 'House Beautiful' in Bunyan's *Pilgrim's Progress*. Beautiful views across Vale of Bedford. 4m SE at *Silsoe* is Wrest Park House and Gardens (AM). The gardens represent the history of gardening in England and are open April–Sept. weekends.

Ashby St Ledgers, Northants 7L5
The Gunpowder conspirators are said to have met at the manor house, which was much enlarged by Lutyens, though extensive demolition has occurred in recent years. A very pleasing village with thatch and a fine church.

Aynho, Northants 7L4
It is unusual to find apricots growing on English cottage walls, but here they are. *Aynhoe Park* (the spelling differs from the village) has work ascribed to Thomas Archer and was remodelled by Sir John Soane. This former home of the Cartwrights is open May–Sept. on set days.

Bedford, Beds 4G7
The county town on the Ouse has since World War II been enlivened by an influx of Italian workers who formed a colony of their own. The river on its slow course to the Wash is ideal for boating. There are two interesting bridges – one is Georgian and designed by Wing while the other is late Victorian and for pedestrians only.
Visitors will be reminded of the town's associations with John Bunyan (1628–88) by his statue at the N end of the High Street, not far from the site of the county jail, where he was imprisoned following an indictment for 'devilishly and perniciously abstaining from coming to church to hear Divine Service....' Many of his relics are kept at the Bunyan Meeting House, built in Mill Street in his honour in 1850 on the site of the barn where he preached. The Bunyan Memorial Library Collection is attached to the public library. The Cecil Higgins Art Gallery should not be missed.

Open all year except Mon. 9m W at *Sandy* is the Lodge Reserve – owned by the Royal Society for the Protection of Birds. Open all year.

Biggleswade, Beds 4G6
The centre for market gardens supplying London with vegetables.

Boughton House, * Northants 5I7
3m NE of **Kettering**, off the A43 near **Geddington**. A ducal palace gradually evolved around seven courtyards, originally a Tudor monastic building. It has impressive 'French' work of the late 17th c. Superb French and English furniture, tapestries, 16th-c carpets and porcelain; works by El Greco, Murillo and Caracci; armoury; park with avenues and lakes. Open April–Oct. on set days.

Brackley, Northants 7L4
Magdalen College School, founded in the 16th c, uses the old chapel of St John's Hospital. Look for the statues in the niches of its tower, similar to those in the parish church. *See also* **Sulgrave Manor**.

Brigstock, Northants 5I7
A village at the centre of Rockingham Forest where the Woodland Pytchley pack of hounds are kennelled. Portions of the church date from before the Norman Conquest. Part of the manor house is Pre-Reformation.

Brixworth, * Northants 5H8
The church was built in the late 7th c and at two closely related periods afterwards. Roman bricks from a still earlier structure are in its fabric. The Pytchley Hunt's kennels are neo-Georgian buildings (1818).

Cardington, Beds 4G7
The victims of R.101, the airship which crashed in France in 1930, are buried in the churchyard of St Mary's.

Castle Ashby, Northants 5I7
8m E of **Northampton**, 1½m N of the A428. A property of the Marquess of Northampton. An Elizabethan mansion with a later front ascribed to Inigo Jones, 17th-c ceilings, staircases and panelling. There are fine pictures, beautiful gardens and a parish church within the grounds. Open April–Sept. at set times.

Church Stowe *see* **Stowe Nine Churches**

Charwelton, Northants 7L4
The Cherwell rises in the cellars of an old farmhouse and passes under a 13th-c pack-horse bridge.

Cockayne Hatley, Beds 4G6
The wood-carvings of the altar rails came from a monastery in Belgium, and the oak pulpit from Antwerp. The poet W. E. Henley is buried in the churchyard.

Collyweston, Northants 5I7
Home of the famous Collyweston tiles (still manufactured here), found on the roofs of the stone-built houses here and elsewhere. A pretty village with a manor house (1696) and dovecot. Church has fine tower and interesting 15th-c doorway, also carved pews and bench-ends.

Corby, Northants   5I7
Until recent times this was a small village, but its population was vastly increased owing to the steel industry, now sadly in recession. There has been much open-cast mining in the neighbourhood. 4½m W on the A427 is *East Carlton Country Park* with a Steel-Making Heritage Centre. Open daily.

Coton Manor Gardens, Northants   5H8
10m NW of **Northampton**, off A428 and 2m from the A50. Old English gardens with wildfowl, flamingos and tropical birds at large in water gardens. Open April–Oct. on set days.

Daventry, Northants   7L5
Best known in the 20th c for associations with wireless telegraphy. Charles I stayed here for a week in 1645 before his decisive defeat at the battle of Naseby. 8m S on the B4525 is *Canons Ashby House* (NT); part of a 13th-c priory it is an exceptional 16th c manor house modernized in Queen Anne's time. St Mary's Church is part of an Augustinian priory church. Open April–Oct., Wed.–Sun. 1m N is Daventry Country Park.

Deene Park,* Northants   5I7
5m NE of **Corby** on the A43, in *Deene*. The splendid mansion of the Brudenells has important Tudor work. The gardens are delightful. Open April–Aug. on stated days.The near-by church contains the tomb of the Earl of Cardigan who led the Charge of the Light Brigade.

Delapré Abbey, Northants   5H8
1m S of **Northampton** centre. House rebuilt or added to 16th–19th c. Now the County Record Office. Open all year.

Drayton House,* Northants   5I7
'Not a rag in it under forty, fifty or a thousand years old,' said Horace Walpole of a country house with origins and remains dating from the reign of Edward III. 'The rags' include precious china and fine furniture. The house is open by written appointment.

Dunstable, Beds   4F7
The town has found other manufacturing outlets since the decline in the straw-plait trade. The church of SS Peter and Paul, built on the site of an Augustinian priory, is partly Norman and partly Early English, and was restored over 100 years ago. From its lady chapel, Archbishop Cranmer pronounced sentence of divorce against Catherine of Aragon in 1533.

Ecton, Northants   5H8
The father of Benjamin Franklin emigrated from here to New England, U.S.A. in 1685.

Elstow, Beds   4G7
Birthplace of Bunyan and, like **Bedford**, has many associations with him: the cottage in which he lived in 1649, the Moot Hall used by his adherents as a meeting-place and now containing a collection illustrating life in the 17th c (open all year except Mon.), and the church with the font in which he was baptized. Of special note are the bells in the separate tower of the church, which Bunyan delighted to ring until deterred by scruples.

Finedon, Northants   5H7
The 14th-c church has an unusual strainer-arch in the nave. Over the porch is a theological library (18th-c). Near by is the Bell Inn (1042) oldest licensed house in England.

Fotheringhay, Northants   5I7
Mary Queen of Scots was tried and executed here. Nothing remains of the castle except a grassy mound. The church has a splendid lantern tower; the chancel was destroyed in the 16th c at the Dissolution of the chantries.

Geddington, Northants   5I7
A beautiful Eleanor Cross marks one stage of the funeral procession of Queen Eleanor of Castile, which travelled from **Harby** in Nottinghamshire to **Westminster Abbey**, London, in 1290. The other two Eleanor Crosses that still remain are at *Hardingstone* and **Waltham Cross** (Herts). *See also* **Boughton House.**

Grafton Regis, Northants   4G8
Edward IV is said to have met his bride, Elizabeth Woodville, under a great oak in Whittlebury Forest, and to have married her here.

Guilsborough Grange, Northants   5H8
10m N of **Northampton**; 10m SE of **Rugby**. There are birds and wildlife in a peaceful setting of country house and garden. Open all year.

Higham Ferrers, Northants   5H7
Archbishop Chichele (1362–1443) of Canterbury honoured his birthplace by building a school-house and bede-house in the grounds of the church, as well as a college in what is still called College Street. The double nave of the church is an interesting feature.

Holdenby House Gardens, Northants   5H8
6m NW of **Northampton**, off the A428 and A50. Charles I was arrested here. The house was rebuilt in Victorian times, but there are remains of the vast Elizabethan mansion built by Sir Christopher Hatton. Small museum. The delightful gardens are open April–Sept. and the house by appointment.

Ickwell Green, Beds   4G6
Birthplace of Thomas Tompion, the most famous English clockmaker, in 1638.

Irthlingborough, Northants   5H7
One among the churches typical of this country has a detached bell-tower surmounted by an octagon.

Islip, Northants   5H7
Pretty village on the Nene. The Perpendicular church contains a memorial to a member of the Washington family, and a chancel-screen in remembrance of Mathias Nicholl, Mayor of New York in 1671.

Kelmarsh Hall, Northants   5H8
In Kelmarsh 5m S of **Market Harborough** (Leics) and 11m N of **Northampton** on the A 508. A stately Palladian house by James Gibbs with a formal garden and old English White Park cattle. Open April–Aug. weekends.

Kettering, Northants   5H7
One of the boot- and shoe-manufacturing centres for which this county is famous, and to which have been added other industries. The church's spire makes an outstanding landmark. The Baptist Missionary Society, founded in 1792 by local worthies, met in the house still known as the Mission House. Alfred East Art Gallery and also a local museum.

Woburn: the Chinese Dairy designed by Henry Holland in the 1790s stands in the Abbey grounds. (See page 201.)

Kirby Hall *see* **Weldon**

Lamport Hall, Northants   5H8

In Lamport, 8m N of **Northampton** on the A508. The chiefly 17th- and 18th-c home of the Isham family for over 400 years from 1560 to 1976 with work by John Webb and 'Smith of Warwick' and the younger William Smith. There are family portraits, an important library and lovely gardens including England's first alpine garden. Hall, church and former rectory make an important architectural group. Open Easter–Sept. on stated days.

Leighton Buzzard, Beds   4F7

A railway timetable of 1861 records that the journey to London took 63 minutes at a fare of 7s., 1st class single. The Early English church of All Saints has a beautiful broach spire and fascinating gargoyles. *Ascott*, 2½m SW, at **Wing** in Bucks, contains Rothschild collections.

Luton, Beds   4F7

Though the hat-making industry has outstripped the straw-plait manufacture on which the prosperity of the town was founded, many other consumer goods are made, not least cars. St Mary's Church has some remarkable features, including a rather cumbersome canopied baptistery and a delicate 15th-c chapel built around the tomb of William Wenlock (d.1392), prebendary of **St Paul's Cathedral**. A visit to modern St Andrew's Church, by Sir Giles Scott, makes an interesting contrast. Also a local museum and art gallery. 2m SW is *Whipsnade Zoo*. An open-air zoo in 500-acre park which started in 1931. As the animals are mostly not behind bars cars are admitted and a minibus service runs. Open daily. *See also* **Luton Hoo** and **Ivinghoe** (Bucks).

Luton Hoo,★ Beds   4F6

30m N of London, via M1, exit 10. Exterior commenced by Robert Adam, 1767 later burned and rebuilt; the interior was remodelled in 20th c in French style. A fabulous art collection includes paintings, porcelain, Fabergé jewels and a unique Russian collection, and there are beautiful gardens and a park laid out by Capability Brown. Open April–Oct. on stated days.

Naseby, Northants   5H8

Not until 1936 was a column (correcting one raised in 1823) placed to mark the true spot where in 1645 General Fairfax and the Parliamentarians beat the Royalist forces under the command of Charles I and his nephew Prince Rupert. The earlier column still stands where it was put. Naseby Battle and Farm Museum has a commentary, relics, etc. Open Easter–Sept. weekends.

Northampton,★ Northants   5H8

Few buildings survived the fire that occurred in the town towards the end of the 17th c. This is a tragedy, since its history is full of events from Saxon and Norman times, right through the Wars of the Roses and the Civil War. Because the town had been disloyal to him, Charles II ordered the castle to be razed to the ground after the Restoration. The attractively named Marefair leads towards most points of interest. There are only four round churches in England, and St Sepulchre in Sheep Street is one of them. It was built in the early 12th c in the pattern of the Church of the Holy Sepulchre in Jerusalem. Several museums including regimental, the Central Museum with its footwear collections and a museum of leathercraft. At *Wootton*, S of the town, is Turner's Musical Merry-go-round – an unusual collection of

mechanical musical instruments. Open all year. 4m E is *Billing Aquadrome* with boating etc. and mill with museum. Open March–Oct. 2m NE is Overstone Solarium at *Sywell* – 110 acres of parkland. *See also* **Delapré Abbey**.

Old Warden, Beds   4G6

The *Swiss Garden* is 2½m W of **Biggleswade** and approximately 2m W of the A1. This is a restored early 19th-c garden with fine trees and original buildings adjoining the *Shuttleworth Collection of Historic Aeroplanes and Cars* at the aerodrome. Open all year. 1m S is *Southill Park* built by Henry Holland and home of the Whitbread family since 1795. Open occasionally.

Oundle, Northants   5I7

Home of the famous public school. Pleasant country town with good 17th- and 18th-c houses. The Talbot Inn contains an oak staircase and other detail brought from **Fotheringhay Castle** when it was dismantled. 1m NE is *Ashton* with a mill exhibiting old farm machinery, and a fish museum. Open Easter–Oct. weekends. ½m S is *Barnwell Country Park*. 5m S on the A605 is *Lilford Park* – 240 acres. Aviaries, craft centre and special events. Open Easter–Oct.

Rockingham, Northants   5I7

One of the county's stone-built villages. Rockingham Castle, originally built by William the Conqueror, and the property of the Tudor kings, has a magnificent banqueting hall from the reign of Edward I, and a fine Norman gateway and keep. The gardens and views are of much beauty, and there are Dickens' associations. It featured as Arnescote Castle in BBC TV's 'By the Sword Divided'. Open Easter–Sept. on stated days.

Rothwell, Northants   5H8

One of the traditional towns of the footwear industry. The church has interesting brasses and a most unusual ossuary in the crypt. The Market House was begun in 1577 but not completed until 1895.

Rushton Hall, Northants   5I7

This fine country house, completed in the early 17th c, has in its demesne a Triangular Lodge (AM) built (1593–5) by Sir Thomas Tresham in veneration of the Holy Trinity. Open by appointment in Aug, limited view of interior.

Slapton, Northants   4G8

Because wall paintings in English churches are less common than in other countries, the parish church here should not be overlooked.

Southill, Beds   4G6

Admiral Byng is buried in the family mausoleum of his parish church. He was executed in 1797 for his responsibility in the loss of the British colony of Minorca.

Stagsden, Beds   4G7

5m W of **Bedford**. In the Bird Gardens are many bird species and varieties; and shrub roses are a feature. Open all year.

Stoke Bruerne, Northants   4G8

An attractive village on the Grand Union Canal, with an interesting Waterways Museum (open all year) and also a Rural Life and Farm Museum (open Easter–Sept. weekends). A short walk along the towpath is the entrance to Blisworth Tunnel, over 300yd long, opened in 1805. Near by is Stoke Park Pavilions – all that remains of the first Palladian house built in England. Open certain days in summer.

Stowe Nine Churches, Northants 7L4
At *Church Stowe*. Though it is impossible to locate the sites of the other eight, the surviving church has significant monuments and a fine Saxon tower.

Sulgrave Manor, Northants 7L4
8m NE of **Banbury** (Oxon), 7m NW of **Brackley**. Home of ancestors of George Washington. A delightful small manor house and garden with thatched cottages near by. Open Feb.–Dec. except Wed.

Towcester, Northants 4G8
Like other towns with a similar suffix, Towcester has a history that goes back to Roman days. It also possesses literary associations; with Dean Swift, for instance, and as the prototype of 'Eatanswill' in the *Pickwick Papers*. At *Paulerspury* is the Sir Henry Royce Memorial Foundation with the Rolls-Royce Archives. Open all year on stated days.

Warmington, Northants 5I7
The beams and wooden groins in the construction of the Early English church are of the greatest interest.

Weldon, Northants 5I7
2m N of the village is *Kirby Hall* (AM), once the Renaissance home of the Hatton family, and said to have been altered by Inigo Jones in the 17th c. House and gardens fell into decay, but both have been restored to a limited extent, and are open to the public all year.

Kirby Hall: begun in 1570, this is a large, ruined courtyard house with a maze of classical detailing

Wellingborough, Northants 5H7
Shoemaking and ironworks are the traditional industries. People with an eye for the antique will admire the misericords in St Luke's Church, but should not neglect the church of St Mary, a modern masterpiece of ecclesiastical architecture. 2m SE is *Irchester Country Park*.

Whipsnade Zoo *see* **Luton**

Woburn Abbey,★★ Beds 4G7
The crowds who throng this most popular ducal seat are given good value for money: a tour of the house and its priceless contents, and of the park with its stately trees, Wild Animal Kingdom, boat trips, art galleries, shops, pottery, rhododendron gardens etc. The original house was founded in 1145 but rebuilt in the 18th c and remodelled by Henry Holland. Open all year. (*See also* page 199.)

Wrest Park, Beds 4G6
10m N of **Luton** on the A6. An impressive formal canal garden with notable garden buildings. Part of the 19th-c mansion is shown. Open April–Sept.

Yardley Chase, Northants 4G8/5H7
Extensive tract of woodland noted for fine oak trees, and much loved by the poet William Cowper (1731–1800).

LEICESTERSHIRE

AN INTRODUCTION BY
W. G. HOSKINS

The Midlands tend to get written off as much of a muchness and as generally pretty dull. Few people ever consider going to Leicestershire for pleasure, except those rich enough to hunt with the Quorn, the Belvoir, or the Cottesmore in winter. Yet Leicestershire has some beautiful pastoral scenery, especially in the east and south, and above all, to my mind, along the towpaths of the old canals, of which there must be 100 miles or more. It has been enriched, since 1974, by the addition of Rutland, which was the smallest of English counties and (next to Dorset) the most unspoiled. For those still capable of moving about slowly, motoring in what used to be Rutland is like what it was in England as a whole 30 years ago.

Geology and Scenery

Contrary to another general impression, held by those who know it only from speeding along the M1, Leicestershire is not flat. Much of what its inhabitants still regard as Rutland is a minor version of the Cotswolds, created out of the same oolitic limestone, and is flat only in the sense that the top of the Cotswolds is flat, that is, a country of long undulating slopes and free-flowing wind.

This is a fairly small county yet its geology and therefore its scenery covers a very wide range, from the pre-Cambrian rocks of Charnwood Forest, a landscape of crags and splintered rocks and almost moorland scenery in places, to the placid levels of the limestone country in the east.

Heart-shaped, Leicestershire is divided into halves, east and west, by the River Soar on its way to the Trent. The western half, underlain by red Triassic rocks, is generally rather dull – what most people think of as typically Midland. It has its precious little oases, of course; but on the whole it is a landscape that does not vary enough in height to be interesting, and it is dotted with too many red-brick hosiery and boot-and-shoe villages, and very ordinary little towns. The special area of Charnwood with its forest is really worth visiting for the scenery. It is very small, about 7 miles by 5, but most distinctive: wild crags and boulder-strewn slopes, rising to 912 feet at Bardon Hill; and in Bradgate Park it has an almost untouched landscape of the Middle Ages. Bradgate began as a hunting park for some medieval magnate in the 12th century, was taken over for a Tudor nobleman's house about 1500 but never landscaped in the formal sense, and now belongs jointly to the city and county of Leicester, for the use of the public for ever. 'Going out to Bradgate' is a popular excursion for motorists and pedestrians in all the towns around it. Here, in Bradgate's 850 acres and in Charnwood generally, one can still walk on the bracken-covered hills and startle the wild deer.

East of the large city of Leicester, one climbs gradually up into the Liassic uplands. These give a clay country for the most part, usually covered, as in west Leicestershire, with a thick blanket of glacial boulder-clay. On top of this clay again we find islands of sands and gravels, on which most of the villages stand. Ten miles out of Leicester the resistant marlstone breaks through the clays and stands up to some 700 feet; and this higher country rolls away about as far as Uppingham. It is lonely country; for on these uplands many villages perished when enclosures for sheep and cattle pastures were made during the 15th and 16th centuries, and such villages as survive are generally small. Yet this clay country is far from monotonous. It flows away like a green sea for miles in every direction, with little dark spinneys (fox-coverts most of them) dotted about at intervals, and sometimes larger and more ancient woodland, the scene punctuated by dark slender spires. Away from this deserted country, down in the lower levels, we find a landscape largely created by the Enclosure Commissioners of George III's time, crossed by quiet roads with broad grass verges as laid out in those days, and a church spire about every couple of miles.

Eastward we come to the broad limestone belt which crosses the whole of England diagonally from Dorset to Yorkshire, the same oolitic limestone that gives us the Cotswolds and all that that word implies – seemly stone-built villages, solid great barns that speak of long-continued arable farming – no longer the green pastures of the clays, stone walls instead of quickset hedges; and the grand towers and spires of the parish churches – loveliest of all at Ketton.

Architecture

Leicestershire is immensely rewarding for the confirmed church-crawler. Not much of the early periods, though Leicester has the 7th-century church of St Nicholas, and at Breedon are some remarkable Mercian carvings of the 8th century. In the Norman age, St Mary de Castro in Leicester, and Morcott, Tixover and Tickencote. Of secular building, the castle hall at Oakham (c.1180–90) is of national importance, a wonderful thing to find in a small country town. The finest medieval churches belong to the years between 1150 and 1350. Visually what one notices is their soaring spires in the wide, open landscapes of the East Midlands: the broach spires (mainly c.1300) which reach their summit of perfection at Market Harborough, and the later recessed spires (15th-century) such as Bottesford and Queniborough and so many others. They always seem particularly appealing in the winter months when, under the dead white sky of a Midland November afternoon, one sees these needles silently piercing the horizon all around. The Midlands in winter have a vast melancholy appeal: those utterly still days when the sky seems to press down on an empty countryside, when the water in the old canals lies leaf-strewn and idle, and the bridle-paths go gently on for mile after mile with no one in sight, past the dark spinneys, the ash-trees and the lonely spires of the deep hunting-country.

Of the Middle Ages, too, are three outstanding secular monuments: the castles of Ashby-de-la-Zouch and Kirby Muxloe, both late 15th-century fortified houses rather than true castles; and the Bede House at Lyddington, once the palace of the medieval bishops of Lincoln. And of a later age there is Staunton Harold Church, a complete survival from the Cromwellian period; Brooke Church (an Elizabethan interior); and King's Norton, mid-18th-century and deeply appealing to lovers of that age. The church monuments are also worth looking for: above all those at Bottesford, where a series of tombs of the first eight earls of Rutland is one of the finest collections in England; and at Exton, a more varied collection but equally staggering in its impact.

The country houses are generally not of the first rank. Only Burley-on-the-Hill can be put in the same class as, say, Chatsworth. Nothing vast and Elizabethan, for which one may be thankful, but many medium-sized and excellent houses, like Quenby (1620–30). The grandest pile (and pile for once describes the general effect) is Belvoir Castle, on a magnificent site and very romantic-looking at a distance (rebuilt in the early 19th century). Mostly, though, the country houses are more homely, not

The Bede House, Lyddington, once a palace, became an almshouse in 1602. Bede comes from 'biddan' – to pray

shut off in enormous parks, but visible from the village road and often in the village itself. Peasant building is also very rewarding. The red brick of 18th-century Leicestershire can be most attractive, with roofs of the rough-hewn Swithland slate from Charnwood; while on the Stone Belt one gets houses of ironstone or limestone, finished off with the velvety brown, stone slates from Colly Weston in Northamptonshire. Also one should examine in town and village churchyards the beautifully lettered and carved headstones, of Swithland slate and Ketton stone, some of them remarkable examples of popular art before it degenerated in the early 19th century.

Flora and Fauna
The characteristic trees are the ash, planted at intervals in the hedgerows, and the flowering hawthorn, which was universally used in the enclosures of the Georgian period (1760–1820) to produce a quick-growing fence, now the delight of the hunters. These quickset hedges, and the big square fields, the long, easy, exhilarating slopes, the small willow-fringed streams at the bottom – all these ingredients have produced the most famous hunting-country in England. The fox is to be found everywhere; and there are wild deer at Bradgate Park most likely descended from those brought there when the park was created some 800 years ago. Fishing in the numerous 18th-century canals is a common sport, and a characteristic sight on a Saturday afternoon.

For the Gourmet
Leicestershire has long been notable for two good things to eat: pork pies and cheese. Most people have heard of Melton pies, first created for the hunting people for whom Melton is spelt Mecca; but I myself think the best pork pies in England are made in Leicester. As for cheese, Stilton was first created in a Leicestershire country house in the early 17th century. When it was transported to the Great North Road, to the Bell Inn at Stilton, it acquired a national reputation and a new and false name. It is too late to alter that now; but in south Leicestershire an excellent red cheese is still made and named after the county. This, at its best, is one of the great regional cheeses of England.

GAZETTEER

Appleby Parva   7K6
Birthplace of Sir John Moore, who became Lord Mayor of London and contributed handsomely to the rebuilding of **St Paul's**. He then consulted Sir Christopher Wren about a village school for Appleby, and Wren's design, slightly altered, was executed in 1693–7 by Sir William Wilson. The building, standing in its own grounds like a handsome country house, is an astonishing school to find in a small village.

Ashby-de-la-Zouch   7K7
Readers of Sir Walter Scott's *Ivanhoe* will remember the scenes of pageantry in the tournament ground here. Though the chivalrous episodes are fictional, such a field exists not far away. The present fortress was built on the site of an earlier Norman stronghold, but was 'slighted' – that is, disarmed and partly demolished – in the Civil War. The most impressive portions that remain are the Great Hall and the kitchen. The chapel is ruined. Near it stands the Solar, the sun parlour occupied for a short time by Mary Queen of Scots (AM). Open all year.
The church has family tombs, an effigy of a 15th-c pilgrim, and a finger-pillory believed to have been used on those people whose behaviour was offensive in church! Local museum and information centre.

Bardon Hill   7L6
Vantage-point 912ft above sea level looking across **Charnwood Forest** towards Derbyshire and the Welsh Marches. It was a Bronze Age settlement, covered with primeval forest, but quarries have now cut into the hillside.

Belvoir Castle   5K8
7m SW of **Grantham**. Seat of the Dukes of Rutland, rebuilt in 1816 after a fire, at a period early enough to escape the worst of 19th-c taste. The view from the terraces is remarkable, and the gardens with their classical statuary are beautifully landscaped.
The galleries contain paintings by Dutch and Flemish masters – Rembrandt and Rubens among them – and portraits by great English painters. Other treasures on view include Gobelin tapestries, armour, fine furniture and relics of that Marquis of Granby who gave his name to so many English inns. Open April–Sept.

Bosworth, Field *see* **Market Bosworth**

Bottesford   5K8
A most attractive Early Perpendicular church noted for the tombs and monuments of the Manners family, the owners of **Belvoir Castle**; the inscriptions read like a history book. The spire, 210ft high, is a landmark pointing to this wealth of decoration.

Bradgate Park   7L6
Adjoining the city of **Leicester**. Lady Jane Grey, the proclaimed Queen of England for so pathetically short a time, was born in the house in 1537. Exhibition in chapel. Open April–Oct. on set days. The park covers 850 acres.

Breedon-on-the-Hill   7K7
The church incorporates in its fabric many fragments of a sculptured frieze that have survived from some building of the Saxon period. The figures – a lion, with saints and strange beasts – are surrounded by an interlaced pattern of curves and spirals.

Brooke   5I7
The interior of the church is full of beautiful Elizabethan woodwork, unrestored.

Brooksby   5J8
George Villiers, 1st Duke of Buckingham, was born in this Tudor manor house, which, despite its charms, he quickly outgrew at the Court of James I.

Buckminster   5J7
A handsome, tree-lined estate village, mainly c.1850, which has lost its big house. In the village centre by the church is a large rectangular green with splendid trees.

Burley-on-the-Hill   5J7
To a grander mansion came George, Duke of Buckingham, and here was staged a masque by Ben Jonson. The house has twice been destroyed and twice rebuilt, and now has a beautiful N front of columns and Doric capitals. The Norman church contains a 15th-c font, a carved reredos, and the alabaster figures of a knight and his lady whose dress places them as having died not later than the early 15th c.

Castle Donington   7L7
A small attractive town, with a gabled and timbered keyhouse. The stone pulpit in the church is made of memorial slabs taken from the floor. See also the brasses of Robert de Staunton and his wife with their children and pet dogs. An earlier carving, c.1320, shows a monk laid out in elaborate vestments. Near by, *Donington Park* has a museum of single-seater racing cars, the world's largest collection (open daily), adjoining the motor-racing circuit; the East Midlands Airport has a visitor centre and aircraft museum of interest, and *King's Mills* on the Trent is most picturesque, with weirs, water-wheel and cottages.

Charnwood Forest   7L7
Wild scenery on miniature scale to the NW of **Leicester**. *Mount St Bernard Abbey*, built 1835, houses a community of Cistercian monks of Strict Observance. The church and grounds are open to visitors.

Clipsham   5J7
From local quarries came much of the stone that makes this district's little-known villages as delightful as those of the Cotswolds. It can be seen at its best in Clipsham Hall, which also has a fine yew hedge.

Cottesmore   5J7
The chapel on the N side of the church is a memorial to the men of the British and American Air Forces who were stationed here in World War II. Bronze Age and subsequent early burial-places have been excavated near by.

Donington-le-Heath   7K6
The manor house is the oldest house in Leicestershire and one of the oldest in England. Dating from about 1280, with 16th- and 17th-c alterations, it was a farmhouse for centuries, its ground-floor ultimately a piggery. Now splendidly restored, with its original timber roof-frames intact, it is open from Easter–Sept.

Exton   5J7
The church stands in parkland, and contains a noteworthy collection of monuments, mostly of the Noel and Harington families, from the 14th c to the present day. The angel seated at the organ on the tower screen should not be missed.

Foxton   5I8
Spectacular flight of ten locks arranged in two tiers – each with five locks – connected by a pool. The water is raised 75ft – on the *Grand Union Canal*, ½m W towards *Gumley*.

Foxton Locks: this 'staircase' of ten locks raises the Grand Union Canal by 75 feet

Great Casterton   5J7
In addition to the Roman remains visitors should see the church for an example of 13th-c architecture untouched by restorers. The square Norman font, decorated roughly in diamond pattern, is quite exceptional. Note too the Elizabethan pulpit, the ironwork on the door of the church and, of course, the Norman arches.

Hallaton   5I8
Bottle-kicking is the name of the game here. It takes place each Easter Monday; a strange form of football with 'bottles' (wooden casks) as balls. It follows a scramble for hare-pies on Hare Pie Bank. The origin and age of both customs is obscure. The village, once a market town, is attractive, with several buildings from the 17th and 18th c, an unusual butter cross and a handsome church rebuilt in the 13th and 14th c, but with some surviving Norman features. Local museum open May–Oct. at weekends.

Kegworth   7L7
This town on the River Soar has a beautiful church of the Late Decorated period, with two aisles, carved figures in the roof and stone angels supporting the chancel. The stained glass, some of it 600 years old, is set in tracery and finely matches the general design.

Ketton   5I7
The 14th-c church with earlier tower does not allow itself to be dwarfed by the cement works or by the factory chimneys

that make a landmark in this flattish countryside. Ketton was once famous for the stone that forms part of many important buildings far afield.

Kirby Muxloe 7L6

5¾m W of **Leicester**. Ruins of a moated and fortified country house built in the late 15th c. The stone gatehouse and brick façade survive, though the interior has crumbled (AM). Open all year.

Langton Hall *see* Market Harborough

Leicester* 7L6

Industrial city still following the traditional manufacture of hosiery and footwear, while having expanded in other directions, especially in engineering.

At the Roman period the city was fortified. Remains of that occupation are preserved in the Jewry Wall, a mass of masonry demonstrating the brick courses used by the Romans, and retaining four arched alcoves. This adjoins the Forum, near which are Roman baths of a slightly later date. Most of the preserved pieces of Roman pavement are exhibited at the museum on the site. Open all year.

In the 13th c, Simon de Montfort was Earl of Leicester, and despite his political interests he became concerned for the welfare of the town. His statue takes pride of place among three others in the 19th-c clock tower at the city's centre, where the main streets cross.

The event that has had perhaps the greatest effect on Leicester was the discovery of the stocking-frame in the late 17th c. Modern travellers will also remember that Thomas Cook inaugurated his tours in 1841 by a railway excursion from Leicester to **Loughborough** and back.

St Nicholas is the most ancient of the city churches and adjoining the Castle to which it belongs, stands the church of St Mary de Castro. Its unusual design is due to the addition of a chancel in the 12th c and later still a wide nave and a tower.

The façade of the Castle Hall, where the Judge of Assize sits, with the river and the surrounding lawns, make a perfect setting at the heart of the city. On the way out through the gateway into the Newarke, and beyond Trinity Hospital, some famous houses have been formed into the Newarke Houses Museum; they contain collections that illustrate graphically the industrial history of Leicestershire. Open all year except Fri.

St Martin's Church, near the Guildhall, has been the Cathedral since 1926. The bishop's throne is particularly fine, and shows carved birds and animals as amusing as those on a chair in the sanctuary, which enact a hunting misadventure that could take place at any time in the shires. The Guildhall is a 14th-c hall used as the Town Hall from the 15th c until 1876. Open daily except Fri.

Other museums include the county museum and art gallery and Jewry Wall Archeology Museum, a regimental museum, a museum of costume at Wygston's House in Applegate, and a museum of technology. The Haymarket is one of the finest new repertory theatres to be built in the provinces. The University of Leicester Botanic Gardens at *Oadby*, 2m SE, cover 16 acres. Open all year on weekdays. 2m N on the A6 is *Belgrave Hall*, a small Queen Anne house. Open from Easter, gardens all year. See also **Bradgate Park** and **Kirby Muxloe**.

Lindley Hall 7K6

3m NW of *Hinckley*. Birthplace of Robert Burton, author of *The Anatomy of Melancholy*, in 1577. Best known nowadays as a testing centre for motor-industry research.

Loughborough 7L7

Another of the traditional towns of the hosiery trade that have added engineering to their occupations. It has an important university. The War Memorial Tower,* built in 1923 to commemorate the dead of World War I, is memorable for the carillon from which bell-music was broadcast for the first time (open April–Sept.). Bells have been part of Loughborough since the arrival of John Taylor in the 19th c. He came to recast the bells of the parish church, and stayed, setting up a bell-foundry that has become world-famous. Great Paul of **St Paul's Cathedral** was cast here – the biggest bell in England, 9ft tall and over 16 tons in weight. The Great Central Railway has steam trains to **Rothley**, open most days. The Midlands Steam Centre has over 500 exhibits and is open all year Fri.–Sun. In the Old Rectory local archeological finds are displayed. Open April–Oct. on Sat. 3m E, *Prestwold Hall* (1840) is open by appointment. 4m NW, *Whatton Gardens* (25 acres) are open Easter–Sept.

Lutterworth 7L5

John Wycliffe was rector here for 20 years until his death in 1384. Thirty years later his writings were condemned by the Council of Constance, and his remains were disinterred, burned and scattered into the Swift – by which, according to his doctrine, they were dispersed across the world. He is now chiefly remembered for having promoted the first translation of the Bible into the common tongue. St Mary's Church contains relics that are of interest through their age, though they cannot with any certainty be attributed to the great reformer. 6m S off the B5414 is *Stanford Hall*, built in the 1690s and seat of the Cave family. Fine collection of paintings and furniture. Motor-cycle and car museum, gardens, nature trail, etc. Open Easter–Sept.

Lyddington 5I7

Thomas Cecil, son of Queen Elizabeth I's Lord Burghley, transformed a medieval archiepiscopal palace into a verandahed bede house for 12 men and two women. The upper floor keeps some of its panel-work, a fine ceiling and handsome windows in what was originally the banqueting hall, though the whole structure has been restored (AM). Open April–Sept. (*See* page 203.) St Andrew's Church has circular altar rails.

Market Bosworth 7K6

It may be difficult to imagine Dr Johnson as a humble usher at Market Bosworth Grammar School. But the defeat and death in 1485 of Richard III on *Bosworth Field*, 2m S, at *Sutton Cheney*, is readily visualized through film, models, exhibition and a battle trail at the Battlefield Centre, open Easter–Oct. Market Bosworth Park on the SE outskirts has an arboretum. Open all year.

Market Harborough 5I8

A neighbourhood famous in fox-hunting tradition for the Pytchley, Quorn and Fernie hounds. The early 17th-c Grammar School (restored 1868 and 1977) in the market place and the spire of St Dionysius, are worthy of attention. Also the local museum which includes a collection of corsetry. 4m N, *Langton Hall* is a splendid stone house dating from 1550 to 1620, but remnants survive from an early medieval house. Chinese classical furniture. Gardens, bird sanctuary and animal park. Open Easter–Sept.

Market Overton 5J7

Roman and Saxon treasure has been found near here, including a primitive clock run on a principle, known to the Egyptians, by which a pierced vessel sinks in water.

Melton Mowbray* 5J8

Fox-hunting again, but now more in retrospect after the day's chase, at inns where Melton Mowbray pork pies and Stilton cheese are served near their place of origin. Special displays on them and local life in the Melton Carnegie Museum. Open all year. The church of St Mary is remarkable for its W porch and a clerestory of 48 windows added to the nave and transepts in the 16th c. 4m E, *Stapleford Park* dates from 1500, but was much altered and enlarged in the 17th c, with further alterations on the S side in the 1890s. Only a churchyard cross remains of the village, but a church of 1783 in a restrained Gothic style with magnificent interior stands in the grounds of the house. 6m S is *Burrough Hill* the site of an Iron Age hill fort. Fine views.

Oakham 5J7

The former county town of Rutland epitomized the old county; settled, beautiful, unhurried. Its social and economic life is vividly recalled in the Rutland County Museum (open all year). The Norman banqueting hall of the Castle, in reality a manor house on the grand scale, is handsome and beautifully ornamented. On its walls, in accordance with a custom that goes back beyond memory, hang horseshoes nailed there by visiting royalty and the nobility. These shoes range from the tiny to the enormous, and most are inscribed with historic names. Castle open all year. Above the church perches Cock Peter, one of the oldest weather-vanes in England. Inside is kept the Oakham Bible, contemporary with Magna Carta. The Grammar School, founded in the 16th c, and sharing its founder with **Uppingham**, has outgrown its original buildings, but these still stand. The butter cross and the town stock are in the square. Titus Oates (1649–1705), who was responsible for the Popish Plot, was born here; so was Jeffery Hudson, the dwarf knighted by Charles II. He hopped out of a piping hot pie and amused his royal master. At Catmose Farm is the Rutland Farm Park, a working farm with rare and commercial breeds, 18 acres of park. Open May–Sept. except Mon.

Quorn 7L7

The hounds of the famous Quorn Hunt (whose kennels are now at Barrow-on-Soar) take their name from the village that was once known as Quorndon. The church has two unusual stone screens, and a 14th-c chapel full of memorials to the Farnham family; one of these was an Elizabethan gentleman who, 'descended of an ancient house, with honours led his life', to the extent of winning a pension from his Queen.

Rothley 7L6

Lord Thomas Babington Macaulay was born at Rothley Temple founded as a perceptory for the Knights Templar in the 13th c and home of the Babington family. It is part of an Elizabethan house which is now a hotel.

Rutland Water 5I7/J7

At Whitwell off the A606. England's largest manmade lake covers 3,200 acres in a pleasantly undulating landscape. There are facilities for sailing, windsurfing, trout-fishing etc.; and a 350-acre wildfowl nature reserve.

Shawell 7L5

After the death of his friend Arthur Hallam, Lord Tennyson wrote *In Memoriam* while he was staying at the Rectory.

Stanford Hall *see* Lutterworth

Staunton Harold 7K7

One of the rare churches built in the Commonwealth period; hence its inscriptions are worthy of note. For instance, over the doorway appears the record that 'In the year 1653, when all things sacred were throughout the nation either demolished or profaned, Sir Robert Shirley, Baronet, founded this church, whose singular praise it is to have done the best things in the worst times and hoped them in the most calamitous' (NT). Open April–Oct.

Stoke Golding 7K6

The detail in the village church is very beautiful, especially the tracery of the windows and the clustered pillars with elaborate capitals.

Swithland 7L6

Among much modern housing in this elongated village, many buildings survive in the traditional vernacular styles, using local materials. The mainly 13th-c church has fine Swithland slate wall monuments; the churchyard has slate headstones. The slate came from two vast quarries, now disused, in Swithland Wood, the remnant of an ancient oakwood, which has become a country park.

Tickencote 5J7

The church has a late Norman arch over the chancel, in five curved patterns, some of them unique. The vaulting of the roof over the choir resembles that of **Canterbury**. Note also the square 13th-c font.

Uppingham 5I7

The school founded towards the end of the 16th c has become one of England's most famous institutions. It is based on a very attractive town.

Waltham-on-the-Wolds 5J8

At the centre of Leicestershire's little-known Wolds.

Wanlip 7L6

Site of a Roman villa. Admirers of brasses should not miss that of Sir Thomas Walsh, the church's founder; he has a lion at his feet, while his wife obviously prefers the two dogs at hers. Dated 1393, this piece presents the earliest English prose inscription on brass known in England.

Woodhouse Eaves 7L7

A growing **Charnwood Forest** village with a Victorian church dramatically perched on the summit of a granite hill On N edge of village on the B591, *Broombriggs Farm* (130 acres) is a typical Charnwood farm with a good farm trail open April–Oct., and a system of paths for walkers and riders throughout the year. ½m W on the same road, *Beacon Hill* affords superb views from its rocky summit at 818ft, and has the remains of a Bronze Age settlement on its slopes.

CAMBRIDGESHIRE

AN INTRODUCTION BY
J. WENTWORTH DAY

Cambridgeshire, the Isle of Ely and, since the 1974 reorganization of local government, the former county of Huntingdonshire, are an odd, indivisible trinity. They share one unique natural feature. Today it is their fount of riches – the Great Fen. That once savage, trackless land of shining meres, stinking bogs, half-drowned rough-grazings, waterways and endless rustling reed-beds covered 680,000 acres. It was 60–70 miles long from Lincoln to Cambridge, and 20–30 miles wide from Huntingdon to Soham. Today it is some of the richest, blackest land in England, worth several thousands of pounds an acre.

Cambridgeshire, the Isle of Ely and Huntingdonshire produce corn, endless potatoes, carrots, celery, a great deal of canned and fresh fruit, jams, beef, sheep, pigs, bloodstock and, industrially, bricks, cement, artificial manures, electronics, beer, light engineering and a few lesser industries. Agriculture is by far the biggest producer. The Fens proper are a peat topsoil, lying mainly on blue clay, with a rich belt of siltland to the east. This area of some 2,000 square miles has been won from swamp, bog and tidal floods by centuries of hard work, ingenuity and ceaseless vigilance. Once it was little more than a continuation of the Wash, into which the rivers Welland, Witham, Glen, Nene, Cam, Great Ouse and Little Ouse emptied the autumn and winter floods of half central England.

The Romans dreamed of draining it. They built the great Car Dyke to keep out the sea. The Saxons neglected it. The Danes raided it. The Normans forgot it. Elizabeth I made plans to reclaim it. The Stuart kings started the work. Francis, 4th Earl of Bedford and his band of 'Gentlemen Adventurers' shouldered the burden in 1630 and broke the back of the sullen swamp, which men had said could never be drained.

When one considers Cambridgeshire, one regards a county of two utter contrasts. To the south lie the chalk downs and gently rolling hills, bright with corn, rimmed with thin belts of fir trees, the land of the partridge, the extinct great bustard, of barley and rye, beechwoods and cloud-topped elms. Northward lies the black, black, treeless prairie of the endless Fens. Dyke-seamed with roads straight as swords,

here and there a lonely farmhouse islanded among willows or whispering poplars. It is a land of sharp winds, autumn fogs, endless horizons, breathtaking sunsets – and black monotony. A farmer's paradise – an aesthete's earthly hell.

Two remnants of the Old Fen survive: Wicken Fen, where this scribe spent an enchanted boyhood, and Wood Walton Fen in old Huntingdonshire. We will deal with them later.

First, south Cambridgeshire. Its unique features are the three great defensive earthworks or dykes, Fleam Dyke near Balsham, Bran Ditch by Fowlmere and the mighty Devil's Dyke, $7\frac{1}{2}$ miles long, from Reach, a Roman inland port, to Wood Ditton. It lies over the Icknield Way and is bisected by the Street Way. Bank and fosse are 40 yards wide and the ditch is 15 feet deep. The dyke is 60 feet high. These three early Anglo-Saxon dykes were probably raised by the East Angles to keep out the Middle Angles or Mercians in the 6th, 7th or 8th centuries.

South Cambridgeshire villages, churches, manor houses and farmhouses all have borrowed something from the architectural characteristics of neighbouring Essex, Hertfordshire, Suffolk and Bedfordshire. Old Cambridgeshire covered no more than 550,000 acres. It is not surprising that it has little definite architectural character of its own, apart from the few remaining lath-and-plaster cottages and farmhouses on the Fen 'islands', still thatched with reed or, more rarely, sedge. The outstanding mansions are Burghley House and Wimpole. They are the most splendid great houses in a county notably deficient in the kind. Here and there one will find old farmhouses, small manor houses, rectories and villages which preserve something of the atmosphere and architectural beauty of earlier centuries. For the most part the county is not blessed with good houses.

Cambridge

The pride and glory of Cambridgeshire is, quite naturally, the University and its superb colleges, churches, chapels, libraries, courtyards, bridges – and that enchanting example of riverside landscaping, the Backs. Cambridge, to my mind, is the loveliest city in England. It is obviously impossible in this short guide to detail its glory and enchantments. Neither a week nor a year is enough in which to appreciate, discover and fall in love with it.

No visitor should miss Trinity, with its superb Great Gate, Great Court, Nevile's Court, the Hall and the rest of this stately college. King's Chapel, a dream of architecture, is without peer. An organ recital or Sunday Service in this chapel, whose foundation stone was laid on 25 July 1446, is an unforgettable experience. Less obvious are the beauties of the older parts of Queen's; the Library of St John's and the Combination Room in the same college; the Library at Trinity Hall; the inner courts of Corpus Christi; the grey simple dignity of Peterhouse, oldest of all Cambridge colleges; the Old Court of Pembroke; the cosily charming Hall of Magdalene. Jesus preserves a splendid gatehouse (c.1500) and parts of the old nunnery of St Rhadegund, suppressed by Bishop Alcock of Ely in 1497, who replaced it with the College. The Nunnery at that time had only two nuns.

In addition to its medieval buildings, Cambridge is splendid with classic architecture: Pembroke Chapel by Wren; Peterhouse Chapel, consecrated in 1632; the Gate of Virtue at Caius, and Trinity College Library, another Wren masterpiece. The Senate House and Fellows' Building at King's, both by James Gibbs (1722–30), are superb examples of the grace and taste of 17th- and 18th-century England. The Fitzwilliam Museum (1837–41); Pembroke New Building; New Court, St John's, heavily Gothic; and Downing College – all preserve canons of good taste.

Ely

The Isle of Ely, for long a Liberty and almost a County Palatine, in which the Bishop had almost the authority of the King, was and still is the heart and centre of Fenland. The Isle became a division of Cambridgeshire as recently as 1826 and rose to the rank of an administrative county in 1888. The glory of Ely is, of course, the magnificent Norman cathedral, one of the most splendid in England. It dominates the flat fenland for miles around. St Etheldreda began to build a minster in Ely in 673. The Danes sacked it in 870. It was reconsecrated 100 years later. In the last Saxon century it was as mighty as Canterbury or Glastonbury.

Hereward the Wake, Lord of Bourn, 'the Last of the English', held out in the Isle of Ely against William the Conqueror long after the rest of England had surrendered to the Norman power. Today, the great Norman cathedral with its unforgettable nave, its early 14th-century Octagon, the mid-14th-century Lady Chapel and the 13th-century Retrochoir are among the best examples of their style in England. Thus, ironically, Norman work utterly dominates that isle which held out longest and last against the armed might of Norman William.

Ely was once an island. Its cathedral was built in 1043 – but the West Front with Galilee Porch in 1174–89

Bishop Alcock's Palace (1486–1501) is notable, as are a few other houses in Ely, including the great South Gatehouse. For the rest, Ely is a bright little city of rather more than 10,000 people. Cambridge requires a week or longer; Ely deserves at least a day.

Wicken Fen is the chief and, indeed, unique natural attraction of Cambridgeshire. It is the last of the old Fen – still undrained. Still a place of dense reed-beds, of sedge jungles, of forests of sallow-bushes and creamy oceans of meadowsweet. But the old village proprietors, the fen owners, who had each their few acres of the wild fen, where they cut their reeds, mowed their sedge, and speared their eels, have sold out. The National Trust owns the fen today, almost to the last acre. (See page 215.)

But on Wicken and in a small stranded corner of Burwell Fen there are still butterflies and moths which are rare elsewhere, and which draw, like summer lodestars, entomologists from the four corners of Britain. There are sometimes, in summer, Montagu's harriers, which nest deep among the reeds, hid in the heart of the Fen. The Fenmen call them by their old English name, 'blue hawks'. There is still, sometimes, in the quiet dusk of a June night, the ghostly note of a bittern. There are grasshopper-warblers, which reel their unending songs through the small hours of the summer nights, when the white sheets and gleaming lamps of the entomologists make ghostly patches of light over pools and sedgy paths where, half a century ago, the will-o'-the-wisp lit his 'corpse candle' and danced his deathly dance. There are little owls on the Fen and barn-owls which float like huge lemon-coloured moths, and kestrels which hover and swing on the summer air-currents under high blue skies, and sparrow-hawks who take the pheasant poults.

There are the wild duck, and teal, and sometimes tufted duck, and, in winter, the wild geese come sparingly on the flooded 'washes' of the Cam – grey-lag, and pink-foot, and white-front. There are the redshank, which nest by the brown dykes and on the cattle pastures of Spinney Fen, and ring their million bells in the green days of spring.

Huntingdonshire
The old county of Huntingdonshire is a shy, demure place which likes to be left alone. A place of squires and yeomen. It was busy when the coaches ran. Huntingdon and Godmanchester with their lovely houses, Tudor, Stuart, Queen Anne and Georgian, have all the grace and beauty of the older England.

Apart from its memories of Cromwell and Pepys, Huntingdon possessed, until 1851, the largest natural lake in southern England, Whittlesey Mere. One remnant of a lovely wilderness is Wood Walton Fen, now a nature reserve. From the demure Georgian loveliness of Huntingdon, you go over to corn-bright uplands, down a narrow lane, over a 'cock-up bridge' above lily-starred waters where a pike swirls, and suddenly you find – the English jungle.

An old barge up-ended and thatched. A turf-barrow, such as peat-diggers used 300 years ago. A pile of spits and brotches for thatching. A scythe stuck in a bush. The old tools of the Fen greet one. Ahead, a green path runs by the dyke through man-high reeds, sallow-bushes, over-arching oaks and willows. The air is heavy with the scent of meadowsweet. Over all, that ineluctable Fen smell of water and wet reeds, fish

and damp peat. The old smell of Saxon England. Wood Walton is unique for its insects. The marsh moth (*hydrillula palustris*), practically unknown elsewhere in Britain, is taken every year. The list of rare plants is botanically mouth-watering. Marsh thistles grow 12 feet high and grass snakes are nearly 4 feet long!

Holme Wood, once a fen and now a forest, and that great relic of the great Huntingdon Forest, Monk's Wood, are two other outstanding places of natural beauty and both are nature reserves. In either, a man alone could lose himself. They say that the last kites in England nested in Monk's Wood.

There are other, enduring pictures of the Englishness of this shy shire. The broad, sunny High Street of Kimbolton, one of the loveliest villages in England – dominated by the Palladian castle of the Dukes of Manchester. Hounds trotting off across the park to draw Tilbrook Bushes. Houghton Mill, of a splendid homely stateliness, presiding over foam-flecked swirl of waters, a merganser diving in the pool. The winter ring of steel on ice as fen skaters flee over the flooded Port Holme meadows, with swinging strokes, arms going like windmills. Brampton, where Pepys's father lived for several years and walked beside the 'plenteous Ouse'. Cromwellian memories at Hinchingbrooke. The ghost of Charles I being led by John Ferrar of Little Gidding to spend Sunday and sleep a night in that white, thatched farmhouse at Coppingford near Hamerton – this was the King's lodging on 2 May 1646, when he went privily across country from Oxford to Stamford and so to join his army at Newark.

Nearly every village has its thatched and plastered cottages, gardens bright with flowers, its moated manor house or manor farm. You can catch great chub, murderous pike, slab-sided bream, highly pugnacious perch and dace, swift as silver arrows, at those happily named river villages, Offord Cluny and Offord D'Arcy. If Izaak Walton looks over your shoulder at Hemingford Grey, you may even land a Pomeranian bream, found in few English rivers.

GAZETTEER

Alconbury   5H6
Large, attractive village with a stream running through its green; the Manor Farm, behind its glowing brick wall, lies alongside the church, 13th-c with broached spire. Two nature reserves, *Monk's Wood* and *Wood Walton Fen*, lie NE: permits needed for visitors.

Balsham   4G5
Thatched cottages, duckponds and squat-towered brick-and-flint church, remarkable for elaborately carved chancel-stalls and screen. Two magnificent brasses on the chancel floor, with that rarity, an original 13th-c rood-loft

and stairs. Near the village is an important section of Fleam Dyke. *Westley Waterless*, 5m NNE, has a splendid brass of a knight and his lady, 1325.

Bottisham   5H5
Fine clerestoried church with exceptional 14th-c work, including oak parclose, and stone chancel and screens. Also 17th- and 18th-c tombs, one to Sir Roger Jenyns, whose family owned the Hall (rebuilt 1797). Village College (1937) by S. E. Unwin. 1½m NW, *Anglesey Abbey* (NT) is 13th-c, with a Tudor house: interesting contents, outstanding gardens of 100 acres. Open April–Oct.

Cambridge: on Christmas Eve the famous Festival of Carols and Nine Lessons is held in King's College Chapel

Bourn 5H6

Its post windmill, possibly the oldest in the country, still stands. The Hall, lovely red-brick Jacobean, is on the site of a Norman castle, with part of the moat still to be seen in the park; and there is considerable Norman work in the church, which has a fine 13th-c tower, beneath which is a maze set in the floor. Chancel screen and roof-timbers are 15th-c, but the angels looking down are modern.

Brampton *see* Buckden

Buckden 5H6

Charming village, where for centuries the Bishops of Lincoln made their home. Impressive remains of their palace, now incorporated in a school (open Sun. in Aug. and Sept.). Great Tower, and gatehouse with diapered brickwork. The adjacent church has 16th-c woodwork and interesting monuments. Laurence Sterne was ordained here, 1736. At *Brampton*, 3m NE, on a loop of the Ouse, is Pepys House, where the diarist spent some time. Open weekdays. His sister, Mrs Jackson, is commemorated in the church, 1689.

Burghley House* 5I7

1m SE of **Stamford** (Lincs). Splendid Elizabethan house, built for William Cecil, Lord Burghley, with later state apartments, including the fabulous 'Heaven Room' painted by Verrio. Paintings in great profusion, furniture and tapestries. Capability Brown park. Open April–Oct.

Burwell 5H5

Of the once commanding castle, only the earthworks of moat and keep remain, but the great tower of the church still looks out across the Fens. Inside, the nave and chancel roofs are rich with timber-carving. 2m SW, *Swaffham Prior* has

two churches in one churchyard: St Mary's with octagonal tower, St Cyriac's now redundant. Two windmills, one preserved, the other decayed, and Windmill Hill offers splendid views. 5m SW, at Waterbeach, *Denny Abbey* (AM) has 12th-c remains.

Cambridge** 5H5

Nowhere else in England, perhaps, is there so much of beauty and interest in so small an area. From Emmanuel College to the foot of Castle Hill is barely $\frac{3}{4}$m; turn left into Queen's Road, with the trees and lawns and gardens of the Backs on one side and Clare's new building and the University Library on the other, and 1m will bring you to the corner of Silver Street; turn left again, and $\frac{1}{2}$m more brings you back to Emmanuel. Except for the lovely Tudor brickwork of Jesus and the stone classicism of Downing (begun in 1807), practically the whole of historic Cambridge lies within that oblong. Two other thoroughfares traverse it: King's Parade, continuous with Trinity and St John's Streets; and, best of all, the river, idling between tree-shaded banks and under half-a-dozen bridges – notably Clare and the 1960 footbridge at Garret Hostel Lane, each of which is a starting-point for closer exploration. To catalogue what can be found there is impossible: the 20 or more colleges, each with its library, chapel, hall, its courts and gateways and master's lodge, have been built and pulled down and rebuilt over the centuries, sometimes with noble imagination, sometimes imitatively or meanly. The great thing is to wander, and look, as visitors may do, through the colleges' grounds and courts. The Introduction makes some suggestions. One could add 'And don't neglect the lovely symmetry of Clare, and St Mary the Great, and the Round Church of St

Sepulchre (though over-restored), and . . .' But perhaps more helpfully, as a reminder that what you are looking at is a living and growing community, observe what has been achieved at the Sidgwick site, opposite Newnham; or Sir Basil Spence's new building at Queens'; or Churchill College, out on the Madingley Road, the first post-war college to be built. Of all the new works, the most recent, Robinson College (1981) in Grange Road, is perhaps the most successful. *Wandlebury Ring* on the crest of the Gog Magog Hills is a hill fort. *See also* **Bottisham** and **Grantchester**.

Castor, Cambs   5I6
The 12th-c church has a magnificently decorated church tower, and a 14th-c wall painting of St Catherine.

Elsworth   5H6
A biggish village, with farms and thatched cottages, clustering round a brook, and a beautiful 14th-c church on the wooded slopes above it; a fine building, with clerestory and pinnacled tower, and poppy-head stalls, with linenfold backs and curious locker book-rests. 3m SE, *Childerley Hall*, retains Jacobean panelling in the chamber where Charles I spent a night in captivity in 1647.

Elton   5I7
Two streets of stone-built cottages by the River Nene, with almshouses (1663) and a gabled parsonage a century earlier. Elton Hall, in a 200-acre park, is a later rebuilding of a Tudor house, with a fine collection of furniture, paintings and books. Open May–Aug. The church, with impressive tower, has two Anglo-Danish wheel-headed crosses in the church-yard. 3m N is an earlier Jacobean hall, finely preserved among other old houses in the village of *Stibbington*.

Ely★★   5I5
From a wooded bluff, above the Ouse and mile upon mile of Fenland, rise the great W tower of the cathedral and Alan of Walsingham's octagonal lantern, supported by eight 63ft oaks, built to replace the Norman tower that collapsed in 1322. Inside we see a majestic Norman nave, the light from the octagon streaming down on the crossing of the transepts, and beyond it the rich Perpendicular work of the choir and apse; and all around a wealth of carved stalls, chantry chapels and tombs. The N triforium has a museum of stained glass. The King's School (Henry VIII) stands near by, incorporating part of the original monastic buildings, notably Prior Crauden's Chapel and the Ely Porta. Across the street called the Gallery stands the diapered Bishop's Palace (15th-c, partly rebuilt in the 18th), and behind it St Mary's Church, with its timbered vicarage, where Cromwell and his family lived, 1636–47. Apart from this cluster of superb buildings, the town holds little interest, though a pleasant riverside walk has been made, and, to the N, there are nature trails at Roswell Pits. To the SW, *Haddenham* has a farmland museum, and *Stretham* the famous 1831 beam-engine which drained 6,000 acres of fens. The village of *Stuntney*, 1m SE, where Cromwell once owned a farm, provides a splendid view of Ely cathedral (*see page 209*).

Godmanchester   5H6
Meeting-place of several Roman roads, including the so-called Via Devana to **Cambridge**; Ermine Street; and another, visible only from the air. It was a small Roman station: recent excavation has revealed two gates and a bath-suite. Today a place of timbered-and-plastered houses, an Elizabethan grammar school and a large church that contains a set of 15th-c stalls, with carvings of birds and animals, said to come from **Ramsey** Abbey.

Grantchester   5H5
A delightful and still relatively unspoiled village 2m up-stream from **Cambridge**, with thatched cottages, Rupert Brooke's vicarage, and Mill Pool, and a church notable for its singularly perfect Decorated chancel. You *can* go by road, but you *should* go by river. The bridge over the Cam leads to *Trumpington*, another attractive village, though its closeness to Cambridge has encouraged some recent suburban building. The Green Man is a 16th-c inn, and Anstey Hall was built *c*.1700. The restored church is best known for the 7ft brass to Roger de Trumpington, 1289, the second oldest in the country.

Guilden Morden   4G6
Here among the meadows and orchards on the Hertfordshire border is one of the county's noblest churches, its spire rising above the pinnacles of a great stepped tower. In the light from 10 clerestory windows angels look down from the hammer-beam roof. The double rood-screen has, on either side of the entrance, small enclosed chapels, later used as private pews. 2m E, *Abington Pigotts*, on the upper reaches of the Cam, has good new cottages, and an Iron Age site at *Bellus Hill*, NW of the church.

Haslingfield   5H5
A pretty village on a bend of the Cam, grouped round the handsome church and the manor house built by Henry VIII's physician. Chapel Hill, though scarcely 200ft high, is a magnificent viewpoint in the flat landscape, with **Ely** gleaming from 20m away on a clear day, the towers and spires of **Cambridge**, and dozens of parish churches peeping out among the trees. 2m S, *Barrington* has a large village green, and the great quarries and chimneys of a cement-works. Good woodwork in the church. 1m further S, Docwra's Manor at *Shepreth* has a walled garden with unusual wild flowers. Open March–Oct.

Hemingfords, The   5H6
Hemingford Abbots and *Hemingford Grey* are two enchanting villages, lying along a loop of the River Ouse, an ideal spot for exploring this stretch of the river by boat or punt. Hemingford Abbots has a heronry, two lakes, a splendid spire, and angels and figures with musical instruments in the painted roof of the church. Hemingford Grey lost its spire in a hurricane, 1741. The manor house, moated on three sides and of great interest, is built round a 12th-c upper hall and has a vast chimneypiece. The village has suffered from recent building development.

Hinchingbrooke House   5H6
Just S of **Huntingdon**. 'Old, spacious, irregular, yet not vast or forlorn' (Horace Walpole). The Cromwell family obtained a 13th-c nunnery at the Dissolution and began to rebuild on a grand scale, incorporating part of the church and chapter house, and bringing the gatehouse from **Ramsey** Abbey. The impoverished Sir Oliver (the Protector's uncle) sold it, in 1627, to Sir Sidney Montagu, whose son (Pepys's cousin) became Viscount Hinchingbrooke and Earl of Sandwich. There were 17th-c extensions, and more after a fire in 1830. The house is now part of a school, but still has the Sandwich family paintings and is open on Sun. in summer. The HQ of the Cambridge Constabulary is in the park close by.

Houghton-cum-Wyton   5H6
Undistinguished but pretty villages and boating-centres, between **Godmanchester** and **St Ives**, with some attractive thatched houses. The Three Jolly Butchers, 1622, at Wyton has wall paintings.

Huntingdon   5H6

Massive earthworks, the only remains of the Norman castle, stand in a meadow by one of the finest surviving medieval bridges, linking Huntingdon and **Godmanchester**. A graceful pedestrian bridge was recently built, and the town was bypassed, so that it has been rescued from most of the traffic hazards. Cromwell, born here 1599, attended the school that is now the Cromwell Museum. Many buildings of the 16th, 17th and 18th c including two interesting inns, a town hall of 1745, and Cowper House, home of the poet for two years. Two notable churches, St Mary's having Norman remains and 17th-c inscriptions. 5m SW, *Graffham Water* is a new reservoir, 2½sq. m, a favourite spot for fishing and sailing, and with a bird sanctuary. The Sailing Club won a Civic Trust Award, 1968. *See also* **Hinchingbrooke House**; and for the environs see under **Godmanchester, Hemingfords** and **St Ives**.

Impington   5H5

Now practically swallowed by **Cambridge** and the A45 loop. The Victorianized Hall, now a 'factory farm', was once the home of the Pepys family. Church opposite well-cared-for: interesting wall paintings and a brass of 1504. The Village College (Gropius and Fry, 1938), set among trees, is considered one of the best buildings of its time.

Kimbolton   5H6/7

Small town with attractive houses flanking its High Street. The church, at one end, has a fine tower and spire, and interesting monuments and inscriptions to the Manchester family. The 4th Earl engaged Vanbrugh to remodel the Tudor castle (where Catherine of Aragon spent her last years). Now a school, it has fine painted walls and ceilings by the Venetian, Pellegrini, and a gatehouse by Robert Adam. Open at certain times in the summer.

Kirtling   5H4

In finely wooded country, with thatched barns, a duckpond, and the dried moat of the vast Tudor mansion where Elizabeth I and her whole court were entertained in 1578. Only Kirtling Towers, the turreted gatehouse, remains. Its builder, Lord North, Henry VIII's Chancellor, had done well out of monastic lands at the Dissolution. He lies in a marble tomb (1564) in the partly Norman church.

Leighton Bromswold   5H6

In 1625, the poet George Herbert was appointed prebendary here and undertook the rebuilding of the ruined church: to him are due the perfect Jacobean furnishings, which include a twin lectern and pulpit. The curious four-turreted building to the E of the church was once a moated gateway for a 16th-c castle, never finished. *See also* **Little Gidding**.

Linton   4G5

This attractive village, straddling the River Granta, has a long street (now happily bypassed) with a variety of ancient houses including the timber-framed Guildhall (1523). The church, much restored, has interesting monuments. There is a village college, 1938. Linton Zoological Gardens, in 10 acres, has a good wildlife collection. Open all year.

Little Gidding   5I6

The house where Nicholas Ferrar, friend of George Herbert, set up the 17th-c religious community has disappeared, but the little church, somewhat altered, contains a unique brass font, and other handsome furnishings. The village recalls T. S. Eliot's poem of the same name. **Leighton Bromswold** is some 5m S.

March*   5I5

One of the Isle of Ely's largest towns, since the last large-scale drainage scheme brought the 1,500-acre Whittlesey Mere, 12m SW, under cultivation, and so made possible a railway network, more than a century ago. The old town lies S of the bridge across the former course of the River Nene (the new river now runs in a straight line to the N, taking most of the water), and is chiefly remarkable for the church of St Wendreda. A few houses cluster round it, including a thatched farmhouse, 1658, and it is approached by a fine avenue, though its churchyard has been 'tidied up', cleared of headstones, and so robbed of much character. However, nothing can detract from the splendour of the church itself. The tower is built on two open arches, thus preserving an ancient processional way, and is crowned by a fine spire. The clerestory windows, set in the flint fabric, scarcely prepare one for the glorious double hammer-beam roof, with a host of nearly 200 angels spreading their wings from every vantage point. Early 16th-c brasses probably commemorate contributors to the work. 7m SE, *Purls Bridge* Nature Reserve is especially interesting in early spring, when the marshes are flooded. The *Welney Wildfowl Refuge*, 6m E, has public hides, and an observatory.

Peterborough   5I6

The town grew up round a Saxon monastery which was founded *c.*650 on the site later occupied by the cathedral. Destroyed by the Danes, rebuilt, burned, the cathedral as we know it was begun in the 12th c and added to in the 13th and at the turn of the 14th, was sacked by Cromwell, was refurnished in the 19th c and given the modern figures of the Apostles on the W front in 1949. This history can be traced from the Saxon foundations, through the Monk's Stone in the choir-aisle (which commemorates those massacred by the Danes); the effigies of 12th-c Benedictine abbots; the first burial-place of Mary Queen of Scots before her translation to **Westminster Abbey**; and the grave of Catherine of Aragon, showing traces of desecration by the Puritans; down to the figures added in modern times.

The city itself has, in modern days, become an industrial town, with an accent on railways and brickfields, and plans for further growth in the 1980s. The museum in Priestgate (where the best Georgian houses are) has a good collection of local exhibits, and needlework of Mary Queen of Scots. The legal profession shows much interest in the 16th-c portrait of a judge, the earliest to be painted in traditional robes. Peterborough's expansion has encouraged the provision of leisure amenities in the neighbourhood. To the W, *Ferry Meadows Country Park* has sailing, fishing, riding, etc., and at Thorpe Wood a nature trail. 7m N, the *Peakirk Wildfowl Trust* has many species in 17 acres of water gardens. *Longthorpe Tower* at the city's W edge, *c.*1300, has the most extensive series of contemporary wall paintings in England. *Whittlesey*, a few miles E, has a museum of natural history and local industry.

Ramsey   5I6

Perhaps the oldest of the 7th-c foundations that arose along the Fen borders. Of the Norman abbey, the 13th-c Lady Chapel now forms part of the Abbey Grammar School. The ruined gatehouse (NT) is 15th-c. Several fires have devastated the town. The church, originally the monastery's guest house, was converted to its present use in the 13th c. It is largely late 12th-c, but the tower is post-Reformation. The town is an agricultural centre in an intensively cultivated area of fenland growing vegetables. *Warboys*, 4m S, is a large fenland village, scene of a celebrated witch trial, 1593, ending in executions.

St Ives 5H6
A busy market town, approached by a fine 15th-c bridge, whose little chapel is one of only three such chapels in England: key at the local museum. Oliver Cromwell once farmed here: his statue stands in the market place. Pretty riverside walks, and attractive buildings, including Clare Court, a new development which won a Civic Trust Award. To the E, the Ouse flows past *Holywell* and *Earith* in a lovely 10m stretch. *See also* **Hemingfords**.

St Neots 5H6
Like **St Ives**, it owes its origins to a now-vanished monastery. Its ancient bridge, leading into Bedfordshire, was replaced by a concrete one in the 1960s. The fine broad market square, with Georgian buildings, leads towards the church, one of the county's largest. The Longsands Museum of local history is open during school term-time. *Eynesbury*, the mother-parish of St Neots, adjoins on the S and has a noteworthy church with 17th-c tower. Paper-making is an old industry: the first machine-made paper was produced here in 1798. The mill still stands on the river.

Sawston 4G5
The first of the county's celebrated village colleges was built here in 1930. Sawston Hall, occupied by one family for four centuries, was rebuilt with stone from **Cambridge** Castle, incorporating a priest's hole, in the late 16th c. It had been burned by a Protestant mob after Bloody Mary had spent a night there at the moment of her accession, 1553. Open occasionally. 2m SW, at *Duxford*, a former airfield is an exciting annexe of London's **Imperial War Museum**.

Soham 5H5
Felix of Burgundy founded an abbey here, just before Etheldreda established hers at **Ely**, 5m NW across the causeway. The Danes destroyed both, but hers was rebuilt. The church has Norman work, but the handsome tower, screen and hammer-beam roof are later. Tablet commemorates a railwayman who saved Soham from disaster from a blazing ammunition train in 1944. Downfield Windmill (1726) is once more operating, when the wind allows. 2m E, *Isleham Priory* (AM) has the remains of a Norman chapel. At *Wicken Fen*, 1m SW, the NT preserves 730 acres to show how the Fens looked before being drained, and is especially interesting for plant and bird life.

Swaffham Prior *see* Burwell

Thorney 5I6
Northernmost of the Fen islands, and the site of one of Hereward the Wake's last stands against William the Conqueror. Its trees form a contrast with the flat surrounding countryside. This was another 7th-c monastic foundation, destroyed by the Danes, resurrected in 972, and rebuilt after 1066. Its final demise came at the Dissolution, when much stone was removed to **Cambridge**, for the chapel of Corpus Christi College, and the Russells, Dukes of Bedford, acquired Thorney's lands. They gave their name to the Dutchman Vermuyden's 17th-c drainage schemes. The duke in the 19th c provided model housing for his tenants.

Tilbrook 5H7
Small village, 2m from **Kimbolton**, whose church has a fine rood-screen (15th-c), still with vaulted loft and faded medieval colouring. There are brasses, *c*.1400, to a man and wife, each with a dog, the man wearing a long dagger.

Wicken Fen *see* Introduction and **Soham**

Wimpole 4G6
8m SW of **Cambridge**. The central block of Wimpole Hall, a spectacular great brick mansion at the end of a 2m avenue, was built *c*.1640 for Sir Thomas Chicheley. The Earl of Hardwick, Lord Chancellor, made additions a century later, leaving the place in much its present form. It was bequeathed to the NT in 1976, together with its contents and 3,000 acres, by Mrs Bambridge, Rudyard Kipling's daughter, and is now open to the public: magnificent rooms, and a chapel painted by Sir James Thornhill. The gardens with a Gothick folly were landscaped by Capability Brown and Humphry Repton. The church has 16th-c heraldic glass and many monuments by notable sculptors, including Scheemakers and Westmacott. Open April–Oct.

Wisbech   5J5

Once 4m but – since river-works of the 1770s – now almost 12m from the sea, which, however, can still do harm, as in January 1978 when gales whipped up an already swollen river, flooding a large area of the town. Still active as a port, Wisbech is the centre of the bulb, flower, and fruit-growing trade of the Fens, much visited when the surrounding fields are heavy with spring flowers. There has been unhappy demolition and building-work, but Wisbech still has much to admire. North and South Brinks, facing the river and quays, have fine Georgian houses, including Peckover House (NT) with decorative wood and plasterwork, and a romantic garden: rare trees, grotto, cemetery of cats. In Museum Square, the museum itself (on the site of the Norman castle)

Soham: Wicken Fen Nature Reserve consists of 730 acres of sedge and reed fen, dense scrubland and an open mere

is one of the earliest examples of a purpose-built museum. Its collection illustrates Fenland and natural history, as well as the career of Thomas Clarkson, hero of the anti-slavery movement, whose father was headmaster here, and whose memorial by Sir George Gilbert Scott stands near the bridge. St Peter's Church has a 16th-c tower-porch and guild chapel, reminder of Wisbech's medieval trade guilds. Fine royal arms, 1605, large brass, and interesting monuments. 5m NNW, *Tydd St Giles'* church has a detached tower and good headstones in the churchyard. Nicholas Breakspear, the only English pope (Adrian IV), was once curate here.

SUFFOLK

AN INTRODUCTION BY
ADRIAN BELL

On one border of Suffolk they plant belts of conifers to stop the soil blowing away; on the other side they plant marram-grass to stop the sea washing the soil away. Erosion is constantly at work. Suffolk is a county of contrasting soils: there are sandy heaths along the coast, and heathlands again in the north-west area around Brandon, called Breckland. But the middle region consists of fertile glacial clay, retentive of water, and this is known as 'high Suffolk'. This is the country of wheat and of oak trees, of thatched and timbered houses, framed with the oak and roofed with the straw of the wheat.

The fertility of high Suffolk depends on a system of pipe-drains and ditches to carry off the winter's rains. The stability of the Breckland soil depends on the afforestation carried out by the Forestry Commission. The battle of the sea-coast is in perpetual crisis: every material has been used, from concrete to marram, to keep the sea at bay. Thus Suffolk as we see it today is a creation of the hand of man, and the face of the county is domestic: you may say it represents a marriage of husbandry and housewifery. The carved and plastered farmhouses speak of a substantial comfort supported by the fields of corn around them. Pastures are few, save in the river valleys. The Stour Valley and the Waveney Valley bound the county to the south and northeast respectively. Here, in contrast to the marram-grass of the east and the conifers of the western areas, you find yourself in a pastoral landscape of willows and green levels full of cattle. The Stour Valley is still the land of Constable's pictures.

But all across Suffolk itself, between Stour and Waveney, are lesser pastoral valleys, dividing the rolling cornland: valleys of streams which for much of their length a horse could jump – the Brett, the Lark, the Blyth and even the Deben. Every small town has its stream or mill brook, as Eye, Framlingham and Lavenham. Windmills were once a feature of every ridge of higher ground, as one would expect in a country of corn. Even 60 years ago mill-sails turned in Suffolk without being much remarked on. A few mills have been preserved: a post mill at Saxtead Green, near Framlingham, now restored and in the care of the Department of the Environment, is one of the finest examples of its kind. Another at Thorpeness houses a permanent exhibition about the Heritage Coast of Suffolk.

Before it was subdued by man, the corn-growing region of high Suffolk was a great oak forest. Even today, if you walk across the late stubble you may see a host of embryo oak-trees sprouting up, twin leaves from acorns dropped from the hedgerow oaks or carried by birds. You realize that in a generation or more, if men were no more, the oak forest would be well on its way again to resume possession of the land in this now fertile agricultural area.

Farm and Village

The nature of the farming has determined the shape of the villages. Comparatively few compact villages remain – those are the ones which formerly approximated to small towns – Laxfield, Stradbroke, Debenham. These villages included men of every trade required for the amenities of life, from miller and saddler to chemist and glover. The whereabouts of the old compact villages of the open-field system of agriculture may be conjectured from the siting of churches, which are now often some way from the nearest house, and in a number of instances approachable only by a footpath over a cornfield, or across a meadow or through a farmyard.

When high Suffolk was enclosed, a village resolved itself into groups of cottages around the nuclei of the big farms, whose tenants worked on them. The pattern of many of these farmsteads is a house which is Elizabethan at the back, with a Georgian addition in brick of a dining and drawing room, the two best bedrooms above them. Flanking the farmyard are cottages which were for horseman and stockman, who needed to be close to their charges. With its barns and yards, a large farm whose layout belonged to the early 19th century approximated almost to a village itself. There would be several of these farms in a parish, with the lonely church as the only focal point for its population. Footpaths formerly linked these scattered farming hamlets; but with the coming of tarmac and the bicycle, the footpaths have fallen into disuse. To compensate for this, Suffolk has many narrow and winding byways. The few motor-roads crossing the county siphon off the fast traffic; so you may walk or cycle these lanes (which is the only way really to see the country) in peace through the still remote-seeming parishes.

Although the visitor may be unable to discover anything he could call a hill in Suffolk, the county is not flat, but undulating from valley to valley of the small streams that drain it. From a spot on the Cambridgeshire border you can see Ely cathedral like a crumb on the horizon, 20 miles away in the Fens. From the same spot you can also see King's College Chapel in Cambridge, 13 miles away, when a sunbeam lights it up. For there you stand on that chalk ridge which becomes Newmarket Heath – no heath in the sense that Breckland is heath or the country behind Dunwich, but really the eastern end of the Chiltern Hills, which reach here across Bedfordshire and Hertfordshire.

The work of Suffolk is agriculture. It is still the least industrialized of the English counties. Formerly it was the most industrialized. Its prosperity was based on overspill: refugees from religious oppression on the Continent settled here and wove the wool from the great flocks of sheep which the county supported. (Silk-weaving is still a staple industry of Sudbury.) Hence the richly carved houses of Lavenham, a wool-weaving town, and the churches of even smaller villages like Worlingworth, whose font-cover reaches almost to the roof. The same power of money and wealth which later was to build the cities of Manchester and Birmingham, in an earlier century created lovely little towns like Clare, and embellished churches.

Buildings
Apart from two small regions of crag and limestone near the coast, Suffolk's only stone for building is flint. One of the most impressive examples of this is Bungay Castle, on the River Waveney. The remains of the 12th-century square keep, and twin-towered gate-house, illustrate well the qualities of this often underrated building material. Rough flints and mortar were used to build the round towers of small 11th-century churches, and the effect is a sort of petrified pudding. But dressed flintwork later became a fine art, and was used in chequer designs, interspersed with freestone, or in a series of cuspidal forms around church walls, as at Covehithe. The dark flint cores catch the light flickeringly, like black glass. The nature of Suffolk's chief building materials, wood and plaster, begot a galaxy of talent in carving, in embossing designs on plaster, known as pargeting, and in thatching. The outstanding example of pargeting is the Ancient House at Ipswich, which is a plasterer's fantasy. Barn-building was a trade allied to house-building in this country of abundant corn

harvests. Suffolk also abounded once in small brickyards – hence the numerous 'Brick Kiln Farms' in the county. The thatcher's art still flourishes, both in reed and straw.

Great lords lie in effigy in Suffolk's country churches, the Dukes of Suffolk sleeping remote in Wingfield Church on a hillside with only two houses near. Lord Bardolph who fought at Agincourt lies in Dennington and the Dukes of Norfolk with their ladies are supine on lofty tombs in Framlingham. It was from Framlingham Castle that Mary marched on London to claim the throne. Blythburgh Church, another beauty from the wealth of the wool trade, rides the surrounding heathland like an ark. From here you can walk to Blyford along the bank of the Blyth river, on which the barges used to ply to Halesworth. Wenhaston Church near by contains a famous Doom – a posse of nude lovelies being received into the Devil's maw, their blonde hair and flesh-tints still fresh. You can't help wondering how the monk who painted this warning to his flock knew so accurately the graces of the female figure.

Industry Old and New
The Suffolk boundary lies close to the source of man's first tools – flints from the Neolithic workings known as Grime's Graves near Brandon. For centuries flints for flintlocks have been knapped in Brandon. Ipswich produces the implements, as well as the fertilizers, for the mechanized farming of today. Sizewell's nuclear power station completes the gamut of man as a tool-using animal.

Not far from Sizewell is Aldeburgh, which drains London of its art critics for its festival, where Benjamin Britten's operas have had their premières. Architecturally Aldeburgh lacks charm, save for its Moot Hall, once in the town's centre, but now almost on the beach. Southwold, a little to the north of the drowned city of Dunwich, is prettier than Aldeburgh. It is still essentially a cluster of fishermen's white-washed cottages around a lighthouse, backed by a heath – but cottages which now look as if they were lived in by the ladies of Cranford. There are also some painted ladies in Southwold; but they are figureheads from old ships, refurbished and gazing down from the walls of the Sailors' Reading Room. The winter weather is bitter on the east coast: it would kill a West Countryman; but it stimulates the inhabitants to live almost for ever.

Behind Aldeburgh lies heathland which the poet Crabbe described. Now people play golf where in Crabbe's day gypsies huddled and starved. To read Suffolk's two poets, the Reverend George Crabbe and Robert Bloomfield, is to realize what different feelings the windswept heath of the coast and the rich farmlands of mid-Suffolk could evoke. Crabbe had bitter memories of his boyhood home; Bloomfield had fond ones, although he worked hard as a farmer's boy at Sapiston, and was not strong physically. Crabbe, where he lived at Slaughden, saw:

Small black-legged sheep devour with hunger keen
The meagre herbage, fleshless, lank and lean.

But in Bloomfield's country, shepherds and their boys:

Boast their pastures and the healthful show
Of well-grown lambs, the glory of the spring.

Owing to the unstable coastline, there is no continuous coast road in Suffolk. Orford, Aldeburgh, Dunwich, Southwold are all a few miles to the east of the main north–south road, which runs from Ipswich to Lowestoft. The only waterside town that lay on it, Woodbridge, has been bypassed. Woodbridge today is lively, painted and preserved, a place of youth in sailcloth trousers. The Deben estuary is bright with white and blue sails, and glitters at high tide before a background of fields and woods.

Suffolk is a county above all of detail. Unless you travel slowly, you miss many charming glimpses of this domesticated countryside. The fields are nearly always busy: new shapes appear in them, which the machine makes in dealing with the immemorial stuff of harvest. You will see a modern combine-harvester at work, and then perhaps an old harvest wagon, with grass sprouting from its joints, dragged into use once more at need. At Abbot's Hall, Stowmarket, there is the Museum of East Anglian Life. The tools of the horse age are being collected, just before it is too late, and preserved. The collection is continually expanding and is the Folk Museum of the county. Ipswich has in Christchurch Mansion a museum of Suffolk social history, building and personalities. There is also a museum devoted to natural history and archeology. Although industry and overspill are enlarging the areas of the big towns, Suffolk is still a community that lives chiefly by and on the land – and that is what it still looks like.

GAZETTEER

Aldeburgh 5H2
Attractive seaside town, once an important harbour in 15th–17th c. Moot Hall, two-storeyed timber-framed building, early 16th-c, restored 1854, now a museum of local history (open Easter–Sept.). Birthplace of Crabbe (1754), and home of Benjamin Britten until his death (1976) – his opera *Peter Grimes* was based on Crabbe's tales in *The Borough*. Annual music festival held here and at **Snape** in June.

Beccles 5I2
Well-placed above the River Waveney, with streets of Georgian houses sloping to the quay, and yachting centre with annual regatta. The 14th-c church has fine porch and detached campanile. SW of the town, Elizabethan Roos Hall and Leman House, in Ballygate, are both worth seeing. Small museum of local history.

Blythburgh 5H2
One of E. Anglia's finest churches, 15th-c flint flushwork and stone, and tower 200 years earlier. The spaciousness of the interior is enhanced by a painted roof with beautifully carved angels.

Bungay 5I2
Market town, with boating on the River Waveney, and ruins of Earl Bigod's 12th-c castle. A disastrous fire in 1688 accounts for the number of 18th-c red-brick houses. We also find an octagonal butter cross, and Georgian monuments in Holy Trinity. *Mettingham*, 2m SE, has the flintwork gatehouse of a 14th-c castle, and a moated hall with Dutch gables, *c*.1660.

Bury St Edmunds* 5H4
Acquired its present distinctive appearance 1750–1850, though many existing Georgian façades conceal earlier structures. Two of the oldest buildings are in Churchgate Street: at one end, Norman House; at the other, the Cemetery Gate, serving as bell-tower to St James's, now the Cathedral of St Edmundsbury. Near by is St Mary's, early 15th-c, with a beautiful roof and fine chancel monuments. Of the medieval abbey only scant ruins in Abbey Gardens and the splendid gateway (1347) remain (AM). Outstanding examples of Georgian architecture are the Unitarian Chapel (1711); Angel Corner (1711), now belonging to the NT and open all year; the Athenaeum Subscription Rooms (1804); the Guildhall (1809) with its 13th-c doorway; the Art Gallery, originally designed by Robert Adam as a theatre; and the Theatre Royal, which replaced it in 1819, now restored and in use again. Museum of local history in Moyse's Hall, a rare 12th-c house.

Clare 4G4
Beautiful little town on the River Stour, many of the houses with exceptional pargeting; among the best are Nethergate and the 15th-c priest's house by the church which has fine windows in choir and aisle, a 17th-c gallery pew and heraldic glass in the E window of the same period. Priory Gardens open daily. Country Park of 25 acres. The villages of *Cavendish*, 3m E, and *Stoke-by-Clare*, 2m SW, are both attractive; the first for its colour-washed cottages round the church; the second for its lovely 15th-c pulpit (only 28in in diameter) and the Queen Anne house (now a school) incorporating parts of a Benedictine monastery.

Debenham 5H3
Near the source of the River Deben. The church at the head of the village street has a fine nave roof and arcade, and a Lady Chapel over W porch. There is a windmill and a moated Elizabethan house, Crowes Hall.

Dennington 5H2
The restored church is memorable for the beauty of its contents: delicately carved screens and lofts, alabaster tomb of the Lord Bardolph who fought at Agincourt, pyx-canopy before the altar, painted font-cover, and some of the best 15th-c carved benches in the county.

Clare: a 15th-century priest's house, displays elaborate ornamental plasterwork known as pargeting

Denston 5H4
Noble 15th-c flint-and-stone church, with impressive nave windows and clerestory, containing medieval tiles and glass, carved chancel-stalls and nave-benches, and box-pews from the 18th c in the aisles. The rear wing of the Hall is Tudor; the front, fine 18th-c.

Dunwich 5H2
The 13th-c port with its nine churches lies at the bottom of the sea, which still encroaches. All that remains today is a hamlet, an early 19th-c church beside the chapel of the ruined leper hospital, and fragments of a 13th-c priory. The small museum, and still-crumbling cliffs complete the story. Neighbouring *Minsmere* (RSPB) has public hides for bird-watching. 2m S is the nature reserve of *Westleton Heath*.

East Bergholt 4G3
The birthplace (1776) of Constable, and much painted by him, it has Tudor houses, and Stour Gardens, home of the late Randolph Churchill: open all year. Church bells hang, upside down, in an external bell-cage. *Flatford Mill*, 1½m S, owned by Constable's father, subject of 'The Hay Wain', is now NT: used by the Council for the Promotion of Field Studies. At *Little Wenham*, 4m N, the 13th-c Hall is one of the best-preserved brick houses of the period. Interesting church (now redundant) and fine barn near by.

Euston 5I4
In the NW of the county, Euston Hall, in beautiful parkland (William Kent and Capability Brown) has a remarkable collection of pictures: Van Dyck, Lely, Stubbs. Open at certain times through summer. Church in park has wood-carvings after, perhaps even by, Grinling Gibbons.

Felixstowe 4G2
Seaside resort, with golf, 2m promenade and good bathing. A passenger ferry connects with **Harwich** in Essex, across the estuaries of Stour and Orwell. Since 1966, the port of Felixstowe has expanded enormously for trade with Europe and the Middle East, and there are daily passenger ferry services to Zeebrugge.

Flatford Mill *see* East Bergholt

Framlingham   5H2

Attractive market town, with fine domestic architecture, particularly in Market Hill and Castle Street. Castle (AM) has curtain walls and 13 flanking towers, late 12th–early 13th-c. The Tudor brick chimneys were added by the Howards, Dukes of Norfolk, whose tombs are in the splendid church near by. *Saxtead Green*, 2m W, has an 18th-c post mill (AM), open April–Sept. except Sun. 2½m SE, *Parham*, has romantic 16th-c Moat Hall, now a farmhouse. Further S, *Letheringham* watermill, and gardens, is open Easter–Sept.

Fressingfield   5H2

Well worth visiting for the charm of the carved bench-ends in the church, the Queen Anne rectory, and the plaster-and-timber Fox and Goose inn. Whittingham Hall, with Dutch gables, dates from mid-17th c.

Hadleigh   4G3

Market town on a tributary of the Stour, crossed by a medieval bridge. The church (Early English, with screen, brasses, lead-covered spire and bench-end illustrating the legend of King Edmund and the wolf) is one of a group of almost contemporaneous buildings, such as the three-storeyed, timbered Guildhall (*see* page 10), and the Deanery Tower with its elaborate brickwork. Excellent Tudor and Georgian buildings, some with pargeting.

Helmingham   5H3

The quadrangular Tudor Hall, often modified and with 18th-c crenellation added by Nash, is surrounded by a moat (the drawbridge still raised each night) and deer park. Built by the Tollemache family whose monuments, handsomely restored, are in the church. Deer park and fine gardens. Open in summer on Sun.

Hengrave   5H4

Sir Thomas Kitson's handsome early Tudor Hall, now a Roman Catholic Ecumenical Centre, may be visited by appointment. Beautiful Renaissance carving over main entrance, 16th-c glass in chapel. Elizabeth I was entertained here in 1578. The little church, with round pre-Conquest tower, stands in the park alongside the mansion.

Herringfleet   5I2

The church has an early Norman round tower and thatched roof. Some brick vaulting remains from the 14th c in the ruins of St Olave's Priory (AM). Near by is last complete smock windpump on Broads in working order: occasional demonstrations. 1m SE, *Somerleyton Hall* was rebuilt 1844 in the Italian style. House and gardens, with maze and miniature railway, are open in summer.

Heveningham   5H2

The Hall is the outstanding Palladian building in Suffolk, with internal decoration by Wyatt, and park laid out by Capability Brown. The gardens have an orangery and ribbon wall. The Hall was sold in 1981, but it is open to the public for one month in the summer. The church has a 14th-c Heveningham effigy in wood.

Ickworth House   5H4

The house, with its 200yd curved stucco front and central rotunda (144ft high), was begun for an Earl of Bristol, who was also Bishop of Derry, but not completed till after his death in 1803. It contains notable silver and pictures, including Gainsboroughs, and was acquired by the NT in 1956, along with the park of nearly 2,000 acres. The house is open April–Sept. on set days, the park at all times.

Heveningham Hall: the house has fine examples of James Wyatt's work, particularly in the entrance hall

Ipswich   4G3

Industrial town at the head of Orwell estuary (being spanned by a fine new bridge in 1982), the largest port between Thames and Humber, its wet dock and handsome Custom House built in the 1840s. Twelve medieval churches remain, some redundant or put to other use. The civic church, St Mary-le-Tower, rebuilt in Victorian Gothic, has interesting brasses and a fine pulpit, but the best ecclesiastical building is the Unitarian Meeting House (1699) standing beside the spectacular offices, in black glass, of Willis Faber and Dumas (1976). Wolsey's Gate, red brick with royal coat of arms, is the only relic of the Cardinal's project for a college in his birthplace, though his name survives in the modern theatre (1979). Ancient House, a remarkably intact specimen of Jacobean building, with sumptuous pargeting, is now a bookshop. Ipswich Museum has replicas of Sutton Hoo (*see* **Woodbridge**) and **Mildenhall**. Christchurch

Mansion, in its fine park, is a museum of local history, with furnished period rooms, 16th–19th-c, and a picture collection including works by Constable and Gainsborough. There is a Town Trail starting in Cornhill. At *Westerfield*, 2m N, the Hall, with formal gardens and Dutch gables, is late 17th-c; and the fine hammer-beam roof of the little church is carved with 36 angels.

Kedington   4G4
The church is full of fine monuments of the Barnardiston family (leading Puritans). The best of the woodwork includes the family pew, the screen (1619) and the three-decker pulpit, complete with canopy, wig-pole and hour-glass.

Kersey   4G3
Unspoiled village street, intercepted by water-splash and lined with half-timbered cottages. The church, well-sited, with flint tower and S porch, has suffered restoration.

Kessingland   5I1
Fishing village, much swollen by caravans. The church's 96ft tower serves as a landmark for sailors. The Suffolk Wildlife and Country Park has several acres of woods and a large bird and animal collection.

Lakenheath   5I4
Overlooking a great stretch of Fenland, now occupied by one of the largest U.S. air bases in Britain. Lovely church, of limestone and brick, with a chantry over the W porch. Inside, brick floor, Norman chancel-arch, 14th-c wall paintings and carved bench-ends.

Lavenham*   4G4
Medieval clothing town, rich in timbered houses and dominated by the church, with splendid tower and fine woodwork in its two chantry-chapels. 1520s Guildhall (NT), now a museum, open March–Nov. Alongside, Little Hall, now appropriately home of the Suffolk Preservation Society, may be visited. 1½m walk along former railway-track is well-managed.

Laxfield   5H2
Dowsing's Farm, now at peace with its moat, was the birthplace of the Puritan iconoclast, William Dowsing, who did untold damage to the county's churches in the Civil War. The Seven Sacrament font and carved bench-ends in his own church were spared. The restored 15th-c Guildhall is now an interesting museum of local history.

Leiston   5H2
Until recently home of 19th-c ironworks, whose site is under development as a museum. Ruins of 14th-c abbey (AM) now home of music school but are open to visitors. *Sizewell*, on coast near by, has a nuclear power station.

Long Melford*   4G4
A spacious village green, 16th-c inn and almshouse (both much restored) and two great Elizabethan houses. Melford Hall (NT) in turreted brick, with 18th-c additions, contains furniture, pictures and porcelain: open April–Sept. on set days. Kentwell Hall, moated and approached through a lime avenue, was long neglected but has been restored. Now open regularly, and with interesting special events. The church is considered Suffolk's best being late 15th c, with much contemporary stained glass. It also has fine monuments and brasses. The Lady Chapel retains evidence of its former use as a schoolroom. Rodbridge Picnic area, to S of village, is a pleasant site

Lowestoft   5I1
Important harbour and centre of fishing industry, connected by swing-bridge with *South Town*, a resort with bathing and the usual holiday amenities. *Lowestoft Ness* is Britain's most easterly point. Spacious 15th-c parish church, its tower and spire earlier. Lake Lothing connects with *Oulton Broad*, holiday centre with lively boating industry.

Mildenhall   5H4
Market town on the River Lark at the edge of the Fen country. Some Georgian buildings, including an almshouse; and an old market cross. A very fine church, with Lady Chapel and beautiful N porch; but its glory is the roof which is elaborately carved with Biblical scenes. The 4th-c Roman Mildenhall Treasure, discovered 1946, is now in the **British Museum** in London.

Minsmere *see* **Dunwich**

Nayland-with-Wissington   4G3
Attractive villages, facing each other across the upper reaches of the River Stour, both with noteworthy churches: the first for carving of roof and gallery, eight painted panels of the 15th c, and Constable reredos; the second for Norman nave and chancel, and 13th-c wall paintings. At Wissington, near the church, stands a fine mill and the Hall, enlarged at the end of the 18th c. Alston Court is an early Tudor building, with richly carved timberwork.

Newmarket   5I15
Scene of the first recorded horse race in 1619, and famous ever since for racing, blood-stock sales, the Jockey Club and the National Stud. Apart from the Rutland Arms and a few houses of the same period, the Georgian atmosphere is fast disappearing. The impressive earthwork, *Devil's Dyke*, which stretches 7m across the heath, is actually over the Cambridgeshire border.

Orford   5H2
A fishing and holiday village on the long arm of the River Ore within the Ness. Henry II's castle (AM) has a splendid view from its roof. Church, 14th-c, has brasses, and a plaque commemorating the first performances, there, of Britten's church operas.

Snape*   5I12
Fine Victorian maltings alongside quay now house a magnificent concert-hall and music school, the latter a memorial to Benjamin Britten. Both may be visited during the summer. Numerous musical events, Easter–Christmas, and a major Antiques Fair in May.

Southwold   5H1/I1
Attractive little resort and residential town on cliff top, grouped around greens, from one of which surprisingly springs a lighthouse. There is a little Dutch-gabled museum. The church, 15th-c, is another example of sparkling flint flushwork, with a noble tower, hammer-beam roof, screens with much original colouring, and a Seven Sacrament font.

Stoke-by-Nayland   4G3
Behind a group of half-timbered cottages rises the 120ft tower of the church Constable so often painted, with its admirable brasses and alabaster monuments, and a notable 17th-c library over the S porch. 2m NE, *Giffords Hall*, Tudor, quadrangular, with a gatehouse, contains a fine hammer-beamed hall. 2m SE, 17th-c *Thorington Hall* (NT) has a fine chimney-stack.

Sudbury: cottages at Brundon Mill. A very ancient borough, formerly an important cloth and market town

Stowmarket 5H3

Market and industrial town, with much new development. Church has a rare wig-stand, monuments, and a portrait of Milton's tutor, Dr Young, whom he visited here. Close to the town centre, the Museum of East Anglian Life has an extensive collection and reconstructed buildings, including a smithy and watermill. Craft demonstrations each summer weekend. Museum open April–Oct.

Sudbury 4G4

The Eatanswill of *Pickwick Papers*, and Gainsborough's birthplace, 1727. His statue stands on Market Hill; his charming house, near by, with Georgian façade and 'Strawberry Hill Gothic' rooms, is a museum and art centre (open all year): furniture, paintings and exhibitions. Victorian Corn Exchange has become the library, most successfully. Three medieval churches, one of them redundant.

Ufford 5H2

Outside the church, stocks and whipping-post still stand. Inside is the superbly-carved 18ft font-cover (1480), once gilded. Some of the original colour can be seen in the roof. There are painted saints on the S side of the rood-screen. The bench-ends are admirably carved.

Wingfield 5H2

The only inhabited castle in Suffolk (but not open to the public), mostly Tudor, but the original 14th-c S front is complete, with central gatehouse and corner turrets protected by a moat. Wingfield College, with medieval buildings behind its Palladian front, has interesting concerts and recitals throughout the year. The church, with chantry chapels adjoining the chancel, is famous for the wood and alabaster tombs of the Wingfields and de la Poles.

Woodbridge 4G2

On high ground above the Deben estuary, looking across to *Sutton Hoo*, Woodbridge is one of Suffolk's most attractive towns: Tudor and Georgian houses, a splendid Dutch-gabled Shire Hall, and handsome early 19th-c almshouses. At the quay, the 18th-c Tide Mill has been finely restored and is open, Easter–Oct. *Kyson Hill* (NT), $\frac{3}{4}$m S, is a charming stretch of parkland of some 4 acres along the river bank. 7m NW at *Wickham Market* is Easton Farm Park (open in summer).

Woolpit 5H3

A village (happily now bypassed by the A45) of half-timbered and red-brick houses, whose church has a hammer-beam roof famous for its angels. We find also traceried bench-ends and rood-screens, 17th-c chancel-gates and fine monuments.

Yoxford 5H2

A village of charming houses, some timbered and oversailing, some with bow-windows and balconies, surrounded by the parkland of three country houses. Of these, Cockfield Hall is the most beautiful, with its red-brick N wing, stables and gatehouse dating back to the time of Henry VIII, and with a restored central Jacobean block.

NORFOLK

AN INTRODUCTION BY
J. WENTWORTH DAY

Charles II had no use for Norfolk. He said it was fit only to be dug up to make roads for the rest of England. Horace Walpole shuddered when obliged, for family estate reasons, to journey into 'the wilds of Norfolk'. As for Holkham, home of Coke of Norfolk, Earl of Leicester and 'Father of English Farming', that 40,000-acre estate when he inherited it in 1776 was so barren 'that two rabbits might often be seen fighting for one blade of grass'.

These are unseemly libels. Norfolk is a county unique. A broad, bright land of high heath and great fir forests; of green marshes and shining broads; of vast barley stubbles that run on to the sky; or moorland purple with heather; of saltings just as purple with sea lavender, and, for contrast, a great city of antiquity, Norwich, proud in ancient beauty yet pulsing with industrial life.

Norfolk has probably the bluest skies in England, the clearest visibility and the least rainfall. Its blue skies, clear distances and that blend of heath and marsh, woodland and stubble, ancient manor house and reed-thatched cottage gave birth to the greatest school of landscape painters in England – the Norwich School. Crome, Cotman, Stark, Stannard, Henry Bright, the Ladbrookes, Lound, Short and, in our day, Munnings, are among its immortals.

The Rocks
The geology of Norfolk is fascinating. Chalk underlies most of it, from the Cambridgeshire Gog Magog Hills through west Norfolk from Thetford to Castle Acre and on to Holme-next-the-Sea. Breckland, that unique wild country of heath, sandy rabbit-warrens and lonely wastes, was the armoury of prehistoric man. Here Neolithic man quarried his flints in at least 366 pits and underground workings, of which Grime's Graves, northwest of Thetford, are the classic example. His flint axes, arrow-heads, skinning-knives and scrapers were exported all over eastern and midland England.

At Hunstanton one finds carstone, a dark brown, gritty, rather soft 'gingerbread' stone, much of it lying below Red Chalk. There is also much gault clay. Flint pebbles and cobbles are a ubiquitous material.

Faced flints are common as building material. Hence the thousands of flint-built farmhouses, cottages, barns, walls and other buildings.

Links with the Past
Many prehistoric barrows exist and finds of metals, weapons, ornaments, urns, pottery and other relics of man, dating from 400,000 BC to 500 BC have been made, the earliest, consisting of pear-shaped axe-handles of the so-called Acheulian type, from the Great Inter-Glacial Period. These have been found at riverside knapping-sites such as Whitlingham.

In Breckland, in the centre of Mickle Mere, are remains of lake-dwellings similar to those of the Somerset lake-villages. Bronze Age swords, gold dress-fasteners and other objects have been found at Caistor St Edmund, Downham Market, in Norwich itself, at Caister-on-Sea and in a few other places. An interesting early Iron Age settlement was excavated in 1935 at West Harling and its complete plan revealed.

At Brancaster the Romans built the northernmost of their so-called forts of the Saxon Shore, which extended as far south as Dover. Although this covered $6\frac{1}{2}$ acres, and once commanded the approaches to the Wash, little remains of it today. Burgh, near Great Yarmouth, is a more impressive example, its great walls and bastions enclosing 4 acres. Little more can be seen of the once-walled town of Venta Icenorum at Caistor St Edmund, which enclosed 34 acres of streets, houses, baths, temples and places of business.

The outstanding survivals of the Anglo-Saxon period are the remains of a Saxon cathedral at North Elmham, and the round church towers which are a distinctive feature of the Norfolk scene. There are just under 180 such towers in England, of which Norfolk has 119. About 20 of them are Anglo-Saxon, the rest probably Norman. But a unique feature of the Saxon period are the Norfolk Broads themselves, many of which are believed to have been formed by extensive peat-digging in Saxon times.

The most splendid example of Norman architecture in the county is Norwich Cathedral. The Normans also built three great abbey churches at Binham, Wymondham and Thetford. Castle Acre, a Cluniac priory, is a poem of gaunt majestic splendour.

Towns

Norwich is still a city of splendid houses, dominated by the white Norman keep of the castle, called charmingly in medieval times 'Blanche-Flower'. Where there is so much of outstanding interest and beauty it is hard to pick out individual items; but the following cry out for mention: the Cathedral, its close and cloisters, approached through two magnificent gateways, the churches of St Peter Mancroft and St George, Tombland (there are more than 30 old parish churches, many of note), Suckling House, the Guildhall and the Bridewell (miraculous squared flintwork), Elm Hill (for its old houses) and the Maddermarket Theatre. Among its many old inns, the Maid's Head was where Robert Kett kept open house during his rebellion, and the Dolphin was once a Bishop's palace. Picture-lovers cannot afford to miss the collection of paintings by the members of the Norwich School (Crome, Cotman and the rest), while the collection of civic plate is second only to London's. In short, Norwich preserves more of beauty from the past than almost any other city in England. Its famous citizens have included Sir Thomas Browne, George Borrow, Archbishop Parker, Harriet

Beside the River Wensum in Norwich is Pull's Ferry, a house at the ancient watergate to the Cathedral

Martineau and Elizabeth Fry. Today it thrives on the production of mustard, beer, shoes and machinery, and on baking and insurance, among a host of other goods and services.

King's Lynn is an ancient, Dutch-like port on the Wash, with the remote yet bustling air of a provincial capital. Its architecture is quite outstanding – a lot of good Georgian brick (and older), especially in the Tuesday and Saturday market places, the old Guildhall, with a fine front of chequered flint and stone, the 17th-century Customs House and the Greenland Fishery Building, with early 17th-century wall paintings. Much of the ancient town-wall survives, with parts of the Greyfriars Monastery and other medieval buildings. Red Mount Chapel, a pilgrim's chapel (c.1485), is one of the most remarkable Gothic churches in England. St Nicholas' Church, from the late 14th and early 15th centuries, is fine. The secular plate, including King John's Cup (mid-14th-century) in the Guildhall, is superb, and among other treasures is an almost complete set of Charters signed by Canute and later monarchs. In short, you can spend two days in Lynn and find beauty in every hour of them – and it has some of the finest port-wine cellars in England.

When Defoe described Lynn in the 18th century as having 'more gentry and gaiety' than Norwich or Great Yarmouth, it was still a busy port, whose ships, quays and warehouses supplied nine counties. It is busy still – with fruit and vegetable canning, the making of beet sugar and fertilizers, malting barley

and brewing beer, in addition to mussel, whelk and shrimp fishing and other maritime activities.

The Broads
The Broads, which include some 5,000 acres of water and many miles of rivers, are unique. Annually they attract more than 100,000 visitors. In summer they are overcrowded, noisy and vulgarized. In spring, autumn and winter, this land of marshes and windmills reverts to its old secret beauty. The peace of slow waters. Wind in the reeds. High clouds sailing like galleons. The chattering of sedge-warblers. Wild duck quacking in the reed-beds. Wild geese chanting under the moon. The bittern booming on indigo nights of spring. Great pike plunging. The sibilant whistle of an otter. Herons fishing like grey ghosts in the shallows. Reed-cutters' barges stacked high with Norfolk reeds – the finest thatching material in England. These are the sounds and faces of beauty.

In spring, a riot of marsh flowers from the rare orchids to kingcups, brassy by the dyke-sides, water-lilies glimmering moonlike, meadowsweet in waves of sweet sickliness, watermint sharp on the air. A botanist's paradise.

Some of the rarest birds in England are found on the Broads. The bittern, once thought extinct, has returned. The rare bearded tits or 'reed-pheasants', climbing like feathered mice through the reeds, ring their tiny bells of song.

The osprey is an occasional splendid visitor. Almost every rare duck on the British list has been recorded and most of the rare waders.

On the coast, with its marching miles of hairy, crested sandhills, miles of shining sands with, at Wells-next-the-Sea and elsewhere, thousands of acres of wigeon-haunted saltings, the sense of lonely, other-worldly beauty persists. That same sense of strange, ineluctable beauty broods over Breckland, the ancient heaths that knew the Ancient Briton and the last of the British great bustards, birds as large as turkeys. Today, some 40,000 acres of dense black, unimaginative Forestry Commission plantations cover these once wild heaths.

Norfolk as a county has produced more than its share of great men: Lord Nelson, Coke of Norfolk, 'Turnip' Townshend, Prime Minister Walpole. It is full of good and splendid houses, Holkham, Houghton, Raynham, Ryston, Rainthorpe, Elsing, Kirstead, Breckles, Morley Old Hall, Blickling, Hunstanton Hall, Oxburgh, East Barsham, Great Cressingham, and a host of others. Castle Rising and Castle Acre are noble ruins. The Peddars Way and the Icknield Way are highroads of prehistory. Today, the rabbit and the homing farm-hand use the ancient trackways of Neolithic man. Many of its old families still survive, and it is heartening that so many of them live on their ancient lands, maintaining the best traditions of good landlordism and 'high farming'. Pre-eminent among private landowners is Her Majesty the Queen at Sandringham. There she owns some 15,000 acres or more, which include heathery moorland, rolling farmland, cattle-dotted marshes, great woodlands and model villages. The Sandringham estate was bought in 1861 by Edward VII, as Prince of Wales. It was then only 7,000 acres. It has been steadily enlarged. Today, more than Buckingham Palace or Windsor, it is 'home' to the Royal Family – their own private beloved country estate. Norfolk could receive no more splendid compliment. Sandringham House, a modified Jacobean residence, was built in the 1870s.

No man wrote greater truth than old Thomas Fuller, who said of this bold, independent land of the North Folk, which shoulders itself into the North Sea: 'All England may be carved out of Norfolk, represented therein not only to the kind but degree thereof. Here are fens and heaths and light and deep and sand and clay ground and meadow and pasture and arable and woody, and (generally) woodless land, so grateful to this shire in the variety thereof. Thus, as in many men, though perchance this or that part may justly be cavilled at, yet all put together complete a proper person; so Norfolk, collectively taken, hath a sufficient result of pleasure and profit, that being supplied in one part, which is defective in another.'

GAZETTEER

Aylsham   5J3
On the River Bure. The church has a gallery, an admirable font (probably a 19th-c restoration) and the monument of Bishop Jegon, who built the manor house in 1608. Abbot's Hall, of the same period, occupies the site of the older house that belonged to the Abbots of **Bury St Edmunds**. 1½m NW is *Blickling Hall*, a Jacobean brick mansion whose gabled and turreted façade conceals a splendid interior; handsome state rooms, and plaster ceilings of great beauty. Once the home of the Boleyn family, now the seat of the NT in East Anglia. The park has a fine lake and the gardens were laid out by Humphry Repton, whose grave is in Aylsham churchyard. Open April–Sept.

Binham   5K3
The nave of the Benedictine priory (AM), whose excavated remains can be seen near by, is now the parish church. Mainly Norman, with notable Early English W front and doorway, it contains an octagonal font. *Stiffkey*, a village overlooking saltmarshes, lies in a valley 3½m N under *Warborough Hill* (excellent views). The Elizabethan Hall, built by Francis Bacon's brother, is by the churchyard.

Blakeney   5K3
A favourite yachting and wildfowling centre, with neighbouring *Cley*, where the Dick Bagnall-Oakley Memorial Centre has displays and magnificent views. Both villages were ancient seaports, now separated from the sea by saltmarshes, much of them belonging to the NT. Blakeney Point and *Salthouse Broad*, 2m E, are both famous for their variety of bird life. There has been a ternery at Blakeney since 1839. Some 256 species have been seen here while 190 varieties of flowering plants have been recorded. Blakeney's fine church has two towers, one built as a beacon and its Guildhall is *c*.15th-c. Cley's is memorable for its S porch, with chamber above. 2m S, *Glandford* has a famous Shell Museum, open in summer.

Bressingham   5I3
Notable gardens and a collection of steam engines. Visitors can tour the gardens by narrow-gauge railway!

Broads, The *see* Introduction
and **Potter Heigham, Ranworth** and **Wroxham**

Burnhams, The   5K4
Domesday Book noted seven Burnhams within a radius of 2m, all 'by Sea' and all with churches, three of which have disappeared, while the sea has receded beyond the marshes. *B. Thorpe* is notable as Nelson's birthplace (church restored 1890 as a memorial); *B. Overy* (Norman church tower, with Jacobean cupola) is a good point from which to visit *Scolt Head*, with its bird sanctuary; *B. Norton*, Norman font, round flint tower and six-sided painted pulpit (1450); *B. Deepdale*, Saxon tower and an exceptional carved Norman font. ¼m NE of *B. Market* are the remains of a Carmelite Friary; 2m S at *North Creake* the church has the 12 Apostles as well as splendid angels in its roof.

Caistor St Edmund   5J2
Originally the Roman town, Venta Icenorum. Materials from its old walls have been used in the medieval church (beautiful font and wall paintings) and in Caistor Old Hall.

Castle Acre   5J4
3½m N of **Swaffham**. The earthworks (among the finest in England, and with a splendid view of the Nar valley from the top) have been successively occupied by British, Romans, Saxons and Normans. Of the Norman castle (AM) the 13th-c gateway remains, overshadowing a village shop. Past the church (painted pulpit panels, fine font-cover) are the most impressive monastic ruins in the county, the 11th-c Cluniac priory (AM). Note the Tudor gateway and, especially, the W front, magnificent Norman work. Below is a natural bathing pool in the River Nar, celebrated for trout fishing.

Castle Rising   5J5
This tiny village once returned two members to Parliament. The Norman keep (AM), one of the largest in England, and earthworks, are impressive. Trinity Hospital (1614) is an almshouse and may be visited: the inmates wear red cloaks and black hats to church on Sundays.

Cawston   5J3
Mellow brick and curved gables add to its other attractions, such as a tree that bears oak, beech and hornbeam leaves, and the 'Duel Stone' (1698), both at the Woodrow Arms; and its remarkable church (graceful tower, painted rood-screen, font-cover and a very fine hammer-beam roof with carved angels dating from 1460). 4m SW at *Great Witchingham* is the Norfolk Wild Life Park. Open all year.

Blakeney: one of the prettiest villages in Norfolk – a paradise for yachtsmen, birdwatchers and botanists

Cromer   5K3
Fishing village, justifiably famous for its crabs, grown to an agreeable resort, with cliffs (fossils), bathing beaches, pier, lighthouse and interesting lifeboat museum. 3m S, *Felbrigg Hall* (NT), a fine Jacobean mansion, has 18th-c furniture and pictures. The grounds were laid out by Humphry Repton. There is a nature trail. Open April–end Sept. on set days.

Dereham   5J3
Ancient market town, with 18th-c buildings and modern industrial ones. House of Bishop Bonner (Wolsey's chaplain) with excellent pargeting now houses the local museum. The large church, with detached bell-tower, has fine Seven Sacrament font, and Flaxman's monument to the poet Cowper, who died (1800) in a house on a site now occupied by the Congregational church. *Dumpling Green*, 1½m S, is the birthplace of George Borrow (1803). At *Gressenhall*, 2m NW, the Norfolk Rural Life Museum occupies the former workhouse. Open summer months. 7m NW is *Beeston Hall*, a Gothic-Georgian house. Open April–Sept.

Diss
5I3

An attractive town with Georgian buildings. 4m W are **Bressingham** *Gardens* and Steam Museum.

Elsing
5J3

On the edge of heathland, a charming village from which to explore the Wensum valley. St Mary's Church has 'the most sumptuous of all English church brasses' (Pevsner), 1347. Elsing Hall is a 15th-c moated manor house. At *Morley*, 2m W, the Angel Inn was once the home of Abraham Lincoln's ancestors. Parson Woodforde (*Diary of a Country Parson*) held the living of *Weston Longville*, 4m SE, at the end of the 18th c.

Fakenham
5J4

Little market town at the junction of seven roads. 2½m NE, *East Barsham Manor* is one of the best examples of Tudor brick and terracotta work in England, and has a notable gatehouse. 3m SW is the main entrance to *Raynham Hall*, once the home of the great agriculturist 'Turnip' Townshend, Robert Walpole's brother-in-law. *Thursford*, 6m NE, has the world's largest collection of steam engines and organs. Concerts throughout the year.

Great Yarmouth
5J1

At the mouth of Breydon Water, the confluence of three rivers, combines a historic fishing-port and a holiday resort: 5m of sea-front, bathing beaches, gardens and (new in 1981) a vast Marine Leisure Centre. St Nicholas' Church, restored after damage in World War II, is the largest parish church in England. Several museums of local, domestic and maritime history and also wax figures display (open Easter–Sept.) and a permanent circus building with a summer season. Off S Quay is the Old Merchant's House (AM) open April–Sept. The castle at *Caister-on-Sea*, 2m N, was owned by the Paston family (of the Paston Letters). It now incorporates an extensive motor museum (open May–Oct.). 5m SW of Yarmouth, *Fritton Lake* and Country Park is a popular summer attraction and also *Somerleyton Hall* (*see* **Herringfleet**, Suffolk).

Gresham
5K3

Here are a church (round Norman tower and well-preserved Seven Sacrament font), and the moated site of a manor held by Margaret Paston in 1450. 1½m SW, at *North Barningham*, the church has Palgrave monuments; and farther on, in a fine park, are the nave of a church and *Barningham Hall*, built for Sir Edward Paston, 1612, with dormers, crow-stepped gables and fine brickwork – the S front was remodelled by Repton in 1805.

Grime's Graves *see* **Methwold**

Harpley   **5J4**
The village church on Massingham Heath has an angel roof, carved pews and 14th-c screen. *Houghton Hall*, 2m N, was built for Sir Robert Walpole in 1721. Much of the original furnishing by William Kent remains, and decoration by Rysbrack and Grinling Gibbons. Open Easter–Sept.

Hingham   **5I3**
Picturesque market town with 18th-c houses. In the church is Abraham Lincoln's bust and the tomb of his ancestor, Richard (*see* **Elsing**), whose grandson Samuel sailed to America in 1627.

Holkham Hall★   **5K4**
In Holkham, 1m W of **Wells-next-the-Sea**. The Palladian mansion, in its park by Capability Brown, was built 1734–60 for Thomas Coke, Earl of Leicester, by William Kent. It was later the home of another Thomas, 'Coke of Norfolk' (1754–1842), the agricultural reformer, whose 120ft monument stands in the park. The house is open in summer.

Holt   **5K3**
Largely 18th-c rural town, with market place and copies of the original buildings of Gresham's School (founded 1555), rebuilt in 1858. 1m S is Holt Lowes Country Park: 200 acres of wood and heathland, with nature trail.

Houghton Hall *see* **Harpley**

Hunstanton   **5K5**
Pleasant resort with golf, bathing, famous red and white striped cliffs, and lavender fields close by. St Mary's Church has brasses of the Le Strange family. 3m NE, *Holme* has a nature reserve and bird observatory: visitors welcome.

King's Lynn★   **5J5**
A busy town, port and agricultural centre, still having one of its medieval gates and, in the octagonal Greyfriars Tower, a reminder of the dozen monastic institutions Lynn once had. St Margaret's Church, in Saturday Market, has two justifiably famous brasses. The town has undergone some unhappy redevelopment but in the various streets between Saturday and Tuesday Markets, and especially between King Street and the quay, are several splendid buildings and merchants' houses, Tudor and Georgian. One, now the Museum of Social History, is also a brass-rubbing centre. Another, St George's Guildhall, has become the Fermoy Centre and Art Gallery, home of the King's Lynn Festival (July). Another Guildhall (1421) in striking chequered flint, houses the town regalia including the so-called King John's Cup. Henry Bell's 17th-c Custom House is perhaps Lynn's most distinguished building.

Knapton   **5K2**
Situated on rising ground, the fine church tower (vane designed by Cotman) is a well-known landmark. The double hammer-beam roof (1504), carved with 160 figures of saints and angels, is unsurpassed, and the octagonal Purbeck marble font has an early 18th-c cover. At *Trunch*, 1m W, the clerestoried church has another magnificent roof, one of the finest painted screens in Norfolk and one of the three carved and crocketed font-covers of their type in England.

Kings Lynn: the chequered flintwork of a Tudor porch matches that of the neighbouring Guildhall built in 1421

Methwold   **5I4**
Lonely among the heaths, forests and airfields of Breckland, it is a good place from which to visit (via Mundford or Weeting) *Grime's Graves* (AM), the prehistoric flint mines, 4,000 years old. Of the 300-odd pits, one is open for inspection: old clothes advisable!

North Elmham   **5J3**
In the meadow adjoining the rectory gardens are the excavated ruins of a Saxon church, probably the cathedral of East Anglia's oldest bishopric (673–1075); and on a farm beyond the King's Head is the site of a Saxon cemetery.

North Walsham   **5K3**
Octagonal market-cross, with clock, cupola and weathervane. The church has a painted screen, tall font-cover and 17th-c Paston monument. Nelson was a pupil at the Grammar School here. 3m NW, *Gunton Park* is open to motorists: the Hall is now a romantic ruin. The little classical church was rebuilt in 1769, by Robert Adam. At *Dilham*, 5m SE, the Norfolk Wildfowl Conservation Centre, 17 acres of water, is open Easter–Dec.

Norwich★★   **5J2/3**
This historic city, now with some of its oldest streets paved and pedestrianized, centres round the cathedral and castle, whose keep houses the museum and art gallery (fine collection of the Norwich School of Painters). Other notable museums are Strangers' Hall and the Bridewell. The cathedral, with 315ft spire, shares its close with the Erpingham and Ethelbert gateways, and with King Edward's School. Norwich Cathedral is, after **Durham**, the most notable example of Norman work in England, particularly the nave,

S transept and apse. Note the bishop's throne, the 15th-c stalls and misericords in the choir, and the vaulted and embossed roof. In the cloisters, these roof-bosses, newly coloured, are easier to see in detail. Thirty-odd medieval churches survive, several put to other uses. Elm Hill still has the atmosphere of a medieval street. Some of the city's notable individual buildings are Suckling House, Music House, St Andrew's and Blackfriars Halls, Samson and Hercules House and the 1754 Assembly House. The 15th-c flint-and-flushwork Guildhall was the seat of local government until 1938 when the new City Hall was completed. Earlham Hall, on the W outskirts, has the University of East Anglia, with buildings by Denys Lasdun. The Sainsbury Centre for Visual Arts (1978), also there, houses a famous art collection in a remarkable building. (*See also* page 224.)

Oxburgh Hall   5I4
7m SW of **Swaffham**. The castellated mansion (NT), surrounded by a moat, was built at the end of the 15th c and is still the home of the Bedingfield family. Open April–Sept, on set days. The brick gatehouse is especially fine. The near-by church was badly damaged when its tower collapsed in 1948, but the Bedingfield chapel and monuments remain unharmed.

Peddar's Way   5J4/K4
A prehistoric trackway, later used by Romans, partly metalled, running from a point on the Wash 2½m NE of **Hunstanton**, through **Castle Acre**, to about 4m E of **Thetford**, but now interrupted by battle-training area.

Potter Heigham   5J2
With its celebrated bridge, this is one of the most popular cruising-centres in the **Broads**. Upstream, the River Thurne gives access to Martham, Horsey and Hickling Broads. Downstream, it flows into the River Bure, and thence either SE via Breydon Water and the Waveney to **Lowestoft**, or W through a number of Broads to **Wroxham**. 2m E, *Martham* has the Countryside Collection, with special craft demonstrations in summer.

Ranworth   5J2
The village church contains some of the county's finest treasures, particularly the 15th-c painted screen. Ranworth Broad has the Broadland Conservation Centre, with floating observation gallery and displays: essential visit for understanding and appreciating the Norfolk **Broads**. At *South Walsham*, 1½m SE, the Fairhaven Garden Trust, with many rare species, is open in summer.

Sandringham   5J4
Country home of the Royal Family since 1861, and certain parts are open in summer when no members are in residence, along with the park and motor museum. The church has souvenirs of, and gifts from, several kings and queens.

Saxthorpe   5K3
On the River Bure. 2m NE is *Mannington Hall*, built of flint, haunted and with fine gardens; and, 1m farther on, *Wolterton Hall*, early 18th-c. At *Heydon*, 2m SW, is the Elizabethan Hall where Bulwer-Lytton wrote many of his novels.

Sheringham   5K3
Seaside resort with celebrated golf-course. Sheringham Hall's park and rhododendron woods (and the house occasionally) are open in summer. From Sheringham station, the N Norfolk Railway runs a steam-train service in summer.

Swaffham   5J4
Pleasant little town of red-brick 18th-c houses on open heathland; market-cross erected 1783. In the church, note the angels in the roof and the unique 'Black Book' and very rare Book of Hours in the priest's chamber. 3m SW, *Cockley Cley* has a popular folk museum and reconstructed Iceni village. Open Easter–Sept. *See also* **Castle Acre** and **Oxburgh Hall**.

Tasburgh   5I3
The church, inside Roman earthworks, has a round tower, wall paintings and the tomb of Elizabeth Baxter, who lived at the lovely old Rainthorpe Hall, 1½m N.

Terrington St Clement   5J5
Among the many marshland churches (*Tilney All Saints*, 3m SE, and especially *Walpole St Peter*, 3m SW, are also outstanding), here is 'the Cathedral of the Marshes': a cruciform building, with clerestory and 81 glazed windows, its tower standing apart from the church. Near by is the lovely stone and brick mansion, Lovell's Hall.

Thetford   5I4
Small market town until expanded by GLC overspill in 1950s–60s. In the 11th c it was one of the major cities of England. The castle mound survives, three of the 20 churches, and the priory (AM). But the Guildhall, Bell Inn, King's House and Ancient House (museum) are reminders of the earlier greatness. Tom Paine ('Rights of Man') born here, 1737. Thetford Chase, planted 1919, is Britain's second largest forest. 1m NE is *Kilverstone Wildlife Park*, in 50 acres of parkland, specializing in S. American animals and birds. Open all year.

Walsingham   5K4
Of the two Walsinghams, *Little Walsingham* is the more important. Set among parks and woodlands, this village of Georgian and medieval houses is among the most beautiful in the country. Until the Reformation, the pilgrimage to the shrine of Our Lady (recently revived and the shrine rebuilt) was of such fame that men called the Milky Way the 'Walsingham Way'. The ruins of the priory, with its 15th-c gateway, stand in the grounds of the modern abbey. The 18th-c Court Room contains the Shirehall Museum. In *Great Walsingham* the church has fine bench ends. 1m SW is the Slipper Chapel at *Houghton St Giles*, where all pilgrims had to leave their shoes before approaching the shrine.

Wells-next-the-Sea   5K4
Georgian houses round the green, and the quay busy with whelk and shrimp boats, and pleasure craft. NT nature reserves at *Scolt Head*, to the W. *See also* **Holkham Hall**.

Wroxham   5J2
On the River Bure, another popular centre for the *Broads*, with access to Hoveton, Ranworth and S. Walsham Broads; then N by the River Ant to Barton Broad, or E to join the River Bure (*see* **Potter Heigham**).

Wymondham   5I3
With narrow alleys and old houses clustering round the 17th-c two-storey timbered market cross, the central splendour of this town is the church, with its two towers. The choir of the original abbey church was destroyed at the Dissolution; and what remains is the superb nave, its Norman arches and triforium surmounted by a 15th-c roof of great delicacy. Kett's rebellion started here on the Common, and he was hanged from the W tower after his defeat.

LINCOLNSHIRE

AN INTRODUCTION BY
M. W. BARLEY

Some people are faddy about food, others about scenery. Lincolnshire is an acquired taste. Those who do not already know it would be sensible to try it. One of the largest counties in England, it is probably the least known and one of the least regarded. Yet it has scenery and a coastline as distinctive as any; as grand a collection of churches as any, set in villages of great variety; woodland, open upland and marsh; and a county town distinguished by one of the most impressive cathedrals in England.

The Rock Beneath
The scale of the scenery is Lincolnshire's most distinctive characteristic, containing on the west the River Trent at its widest; holding, on the east and southeast, the largest expanse of absolutely flat (and immensely fertile) agricultural land in England; giving, from its vantage points, the widest views of earth and sky.

The rock frame is a simple one. Layers tilted up to the west and gently down to the east provide a succession of steps or scarps. The most pronounced, a ridge of limestone, runs all the way from the Humber to the Leicestershire boundary. This ridge known as the Cliff broadens south of Lincoln into a plateau called the Heath, wide enough for airfields. The next step to the east is of chalk, known as the Wolds.

A prehistoric ridgeway follows the scarp of the Wolds and from the high points on it there are more immense views, with Lincoln Minster and Boston Stump as their farthest landmarks. The smooth curves of the chalk landscape and the limestone Cliff are to be seen everywhere under the plough so that, in Tennyson's words, the summer corn 'clothes the Wold and meets the sky'.

Fen and Marsh
The Fen is a wide band of low ground surrounding the Wash, which persistent effort, spread over 1,000 years, has reclaimed from the sea and protected from river floods. It is criss-crossed by flood-banks and water-channels of every age from Saxon times to the present day. Its safety has long depended on pumping – first windmills then beam-engines driven by steam and now electric pumps, such as that at the mouth of the Black Sluice at Boston. The fine silty soil is as rich as any in England.

The marshland lies between the Wolds and the sea. It, too, has been reclaimed over the past 1,000 years from saltmarsh. Behind the seaside resorts lies a band of rich grazing land which is used for the famous Lincoln red cattle.

The Past
The Roman conquest left very distinctive traces. Lincoln was the Roman city of Lindum Colonia, a centre for retired soldiers; the market towns of Caistor and Horncastle have traces of their Roman walls, and at Ancaster, the line of the wall and ditch can be clearly seen. The motorist can enjoy, driving along Ermine Street both south and north of Lincoln, the most impressive stretches of Roman road in Britain. The Foss Dyke, the canal joining the Trent at Torksey with the Witham at Brayford, now carries pleasure boats, not barge-loads of corn, as it did in Roman times. Salt was made on the coast at Ingoldmells. Nor does archeology end with the departure of the Roman armies: one of the county's most distinctive types of monument is the deserted village, of which there are scores of examples. Most of these villages died between 400 and 500 years ago. Now all that remains are banks and mounds in grass fields, showing where lanes once ran and farmhouses stood. Several Norman castles have left impressive earthworks behind them, as at Castle Bytham, Old Bolingbroke and Owston Ferry on the Trent.

Coast and River
People from Midland towns hurry through the county to get to the coast, because it really is 'so bracing', as the old Skegness poster said. There is room for all of them, and more, on the immense stretches of firm sand, sheltered by sand-dunes covered with sea buckthorn and marram-grass. Behind the sandhills one sees, inevitably, a spread of bungalows and caravans; but once on the beach one ceases to be aware of anything but the great expanse of sea, sand and sky.

At any weekend in the season, the waterways of Lincolnshire are lined with fishermen. The Trent and the Roman Foss Dyke, and more especially the Witham, the Ancholme, the Welland and the South Forty Foot provide the most comfortable fishing in England for those who like a day out with the family. The Witham is the main centre for match angling.

Local Industry
The oldest Lincolnshire industry and certainly the most highly developed is agriculture. Wherever you look you cannot see an acre unused. The large farmstead now has a lofty glasshouse or an artificial light barn, for bringing on seed potatoes in the spring; a corn drier, running for 24 hours daily in harvest time; perhaps a short-wave radio station for communicating with neighbouring farms under the same management; even a landing ground for the farmer's light aircraft. From farming stems the canning industry – vegetable and fruit at Boston and Spalding. One industry is now a matter of history – or indeed of archeology: salt-making, using brine from salt-impregnated clay from the marsh, preparing a solution and evaporating it in clay pans over turf fires. The waste product was soil washed free of salt. It was stacked round the kilns; and you may still see, both in the Marshland and in the Fens, mounds which might appear natural but are really as artificial as the tip-heads round a coalmine. Pottery and other debris of the salt industry of Roman times can sometimes be found at low tide at Ingoldmells, and the mounds are particularly obvious near Bicker.

One unique industry draws each year thousands of visitors in April and May: the growing of spring flowers, tulips in particular, round Spalding. Only the richest soil can be used for such a crop. Fields with stripes of the most brilliant colours are spread over many miles; but the most unusual sight is the Spalding Flower Parade, where the huge floats are decorated with millions of tulip heads, or an arranged carpet, perhaps outside a farmhouse, made of heads of tulips cut off because it is the bulbs that are wanted and not the blooms.

The fenland around Spalding, in the area of the county called Holland, is the centre of Britain's bulb industry

Lincoln Cathedral's West Towers (206 feet high) and West Front seen from the Observatory Tower of the Castle

Tennyson's Lincolnshire

Visitors to Lincoln itself will see the bronze statue of the Lincolnshire poet standing by the Minster; but his home was many miles away, in the southern Wolds. He was born in the rectory at Somersby, and he knew the country round and the people well enough for them to leave a strong mark on his poetry. If you explore Tennyson's country, you are bound to notice the strange names of near-by villages – Salmonby, Bag Enderby, Fulletby, Skendleby and the like. Names ending in *-by* were given by the Danes, who settled 1,000 years ago. They also bequeathed to us Hogsthorpe and all the other names ending in *-thorpe*. In Lincolnshire towns you may find street-names like Kirk Gate, which is simply the Danish version of Church Street. Most counties have place-names of distinctive character; here that character is Danish.

Wild Life

Lincolnshire naturalists have had great success in preserving remnants of the once extensive tracts of wild country. Over 90 acres of washland on the River Glen was acquired some years ago for the purpose of developing a winter wildfowl refuge. The biggest nature reserve in the county is the splendid expanse of sand-dunes and saltmarsh between Skegness and Gibraltar Point. A field station, bird observatory and visitor centre are maintained there. There are also reserves in the sandhills and marshes at Saltfleetby and Theddlethorpe. Linwood Warren, near Market Rasen is a reserve of heathland with birch, pine, heather and rare birds.

GAZETTEER

Alford   5L5

This small town springs to life on market days (Tues.). Its thatched manor house of 1540, altered in the 17th c, houses a lively folk museum. Open May–Sept., Mon.–Fri. Alford Windmill, a five-sailed, six-storey working tower mill, built in 1813, is occasionally open to the public.

Ancaster   5K7

A hoard of coins and other remains uncovered on the 9-acre site of the Roman camp on Ermine Street is shown in **Grantham** Museum. The famous Ancaster stone has the quality of hardening immediately after being quarried and has been used since medieval times especially for churches.

Ashby Puerorum 5L6
So called because a local bequest contributes to the support of the choirboys of **Lincoln** Cathedral.

Aubourn 5L7
On the outskirts of this village on the River Witham are two disused churches. Aubourn Hall is a 16th-c red-brick house, with panelled rooms and a fine carved oak staircase open only on a few stated summer days.

Bardney 5L7
The great Benedictine abbey N of the town is believed to have been founded by Ethelred, King of Mercia, in the 7th c. The foundations of its church have been excavated, and stonework from the ruins is preserved in the Parish Church of St Lawrence. The local museum has an exhibition of the history of IX Squadron RAF. Open by appointment.

Belton House 5K7
In Belton, 2½m NE of **Grantham**. Generations of the Brownlow and Cust families have devoted themselves to enriching their home, in 600 acres of parkland (NT). The H-shaped house dates from 1685, with some alterations by James Wyatt in 1777. Some of the rooms, and the private chapel, are festooned with carvings by Grinling Gibbons, and there are splendid collections of paintings, porcelain and tapestries. The house and formal gardens are open April–early Oct. The church is filled with Brownlow memorials, and has a Norman font. The model estate village, grouped round a cross, was laid out about 1850.

Blyton 5M8
The chancel of the church is hung with flags of the Allies, donated by kings, heads of government and famous men of World War I – a collection initiated by a mother whose son died in France.

Bolingbroke Castle see Old Bolingbroke

Boston* 5K6
Merchants built the church of St Botolph in the 14th–15th c when this was one of Britain's chief ports. In the 17th c the Corporation petitioned that their borough 'might be put among the decayed towns'. The famous church tower known as the Boston Stump has for centuries shown a guiding light for travellers on land and sea.

Boston, Massachusetts, was founded by men who sailed from here to New England in 1630 in the wake of the Pilgrim Fathers. The link has been perpetuated. Fydell House (1726), occupied by a Pilgrim College, sets aside a room for transatlantic Bostonians (open in term time by appointment). St Mary's Guildhall (museum open all year) contains the Court to which Brewster and others who later embarked on the *Mayflower* were brought from the cells below. The SW chapel of St Botolph was restored in the middle of the 19th c by New Englanders in memory of John Cotton, who was vicar here before leaving for America in 1633. The lower section of the church tower has a tablet inscribed with the names of five men who became Governors of Massachusetts.

Bourne 5J7
Birthplace of Robert Manning (1288–1338), the Gilbertine monk who pioneered writing in language that could be understood by the common people. Also of William Cecil (Lord Burghley), Lord High Treasurer to Elizabeth I, and Worth, the costumier, but probably not, despite local tradition, the birthplace of Hereward the Wake. White Bread Meadow is auctioned annually for charity during the time

taken by schoolboys racing over a measured distance. Five old inns are among many listed buildings. The Red Hall is an Elizabethan gentleman's residence containing contemporary furniture. Open all year, Mon.–Fri.

Brant Broughton 5K7
An elegant 14th-c spire presides over a comely Georgian village, with some earlier houses, notably the Tudor manor house with 17th-c alterations, and the Priory of 1658. The church is enriched by stained glass designed and fired in the village by a former rector, and by ironwork produced by a village family of smiths.

Burgh-le-Marsh 5L5
Mesolithic, Roman and Anglo-Saxon finds indicate the historic importance of the raised site above the marshes of this little market town. Its 15th-c church contains good contemporary and Jacobean woodwork. The five-sailed, tower windmill (built 1833; last worked 1947) has been restored to working order and is open daily.

Caistor 5M7
A well in the citadel of the Roman camp on the site of an ancient British hill fort is still used. It is near the church, which has evidence of Norman, Saxon and medieval building in its tower.

Canwick 5L7
For a superb view over **Lincoln** and to refute ideas that the county is entirely flat, the hill is worth the climb. The Norman nave arcade and chancel arch in the church are additional attractions.

Castle Bytham 5J7
The cruciform church treasures an 18th-c sundial inscribed with the pun 'Bee in Thyme'; a brass candelabra of the early 19th c; and the village maypole, which was later used as a ladder to the belfry. The earthworks of the Norman castle are across the stream that flows into the River Glen.

Coningsby 5L6
The dial of the clock in the church tower measures 16½ft and has a single hand, typical of the early 17th-c clocks. The mechanism includes a pendulum suspended independently in the tower wall, and clockweights of stone.

Corby Glen 5J7
Beautiful medieval wall paintings were discovered in 1939 under the plastered and whitewashed interior of the church. An annual sheep fair reminds us that this picturesque stone-belt village was once a market town. Its former grammar school of 1673 is now an exhibition centre.

Crowland 5J6
The Benedictine abbey was built in the 8th c by King Ethelbald over the hermitage of St Guthlac, whose wisdom had attracted numerous followers. The monastic buildings were partly destroyed and rebuilt many times, but the N aisle (used now as the parish church) survives; so does the tower at the W end, to which has been added a two-storeyed porch and a blunt spire. The remainder of the ruined but still magnificent W front has five tiers of statues representing saints, apostles and personages associated with the early history of the Abbey. A statue of Christ holding the World, believed to have come from the missing W gable, surmounts the extraordinary triangular bridge in the centre of the town. This bridge of three semicircles meeting at an apex was built in the 13th c when the streets were waterways.

Doddington Hall 5L7

5m W of **Lincoln**, Doddington Hall is one of the few Elizabethan houses in the county. It was built of brick and stone in the 1590s for the Recorder to the Bishop of Lincoln, probably by Robert Smythson, architect of **Longleat** (Wilts), **Wollaton Hall** (Notts) and **Hardwick Hall** (Derbys). Georgian interior of the 1760s, executed by Thomas Lumby, a Lincoln carpenter, whose superb staircase is surprisingly plain for its period. The Delaval family portraits are outstanding. The house, and its charming walled garden, are open May–Sept. on set days.

Donington 5K6

Formerly a centre for flax and hemp; it still has an important horse and cattle fair. The church contains a memorial to Matthew Flinders (b.1774), who surveyed the unknown coasts of Australia.

Dunston 5L7

A pillar 92ft high was set up on the Heath in 1751 by the eccentric Francis Dashwood of the Hellfire Club, to act as a land lighthouse for travellers. To commemorate his Jubilee, the lantern was replaced by a statue of George III, but it had to be removed when it became a danger to low-flying aircraft and is now in the grounds of **Lincoln** Castle.

Edenham 5J7

The church has effigies of 14th-c knights, and an arcaded 12th-c font on shafts of Purbeck marble. The monuments of the Bertie family, Earls of Lindsey and Dukes of Ancaster, show an unbroken line since the time of Charles I. The

Gainsborough: the Old Hall has the best surviving example of a medieval kitchen in Britain

family seat, *Grimsthorpe Castle*, is palatial, with a 13th-c tower, Elizabethan wings and N front built in 1722 by Vanbrugh. Its rooms contain treasures, such as the clothes worn by Charles I when sitting to Van Dyck for his portrait; this painting itself is there too, and a collection of coronation robes, furniture and ceremonial plate – the perquisites of successive Lord Great Chamberlains. Open in summer.

Gainsborough 5M8

The descriptive passages in *The Mill on the Floss* by George Eliot, who used this town as a prototype for her St Ogg's, are still identifiable. King Alfred was married here in 868, and Sweyne, King of the Danes and father of Canute, died at his camp at Thonock Park in 1014. Many years later the town was a frequent battleground between Royalist and Parliamentarian troops. The Old Hall (AM), part of a medieval manor rebuilt in the late 15th c, has a fine roof, a stone oriel window, a kitchen with great ovens and fireplaces and a collection of dolls and period dresses. Open all year. The quayside has fine 18th-c warehouses.

Grantham★ 5K7

A perfect view of St Wulfram's magnificent church is obtained from Swinegate. Above the S porch, in a room formerly occupied by the priest, is kept the library (some of the books still chained), which was left to the church in 1598. The 14th-c crypts are remarkable. Grantham House (NT) has a 14th-c hall used in 1503 by Princess Margaret, daughter of Henry VII, on her journey N for her wedding to James IV of Scotland. Open April–Sept. on set days. The statue opposite the Guildhall honours Sir Isaac Newton (1642–1727), a pupil of the Grammar School. An 18th-c landlord of the Angel Inn, the medieval hostelry established by the Knights Templar, bequeathed an annual sum for the preaching of a sermon against drunkenness. Local museum has a collection of Sir Isaac Newton material. *Fulbeck Hall*, 11m N, has 18th-c interiors and collections of textiles, porcelain, etc. Terraced gardens. Open on set days. *Harlaxton Manor*, 2m SW, has the largest conservatory in the E. Midlands. Open by appointment.

Gunby Hall   5L5
The Hall (NT), Tennyson's 'haunt of ancient peace', was built of brick with stone facings in 1700 in the Wren style for Sir William Massingberd. The house (NT) with its contemporary wainscoting and Reynolds portraits, has much charm. Open April–Sept. Thurs. afternoons.

Harrington Hall   5L6
9m N of **Spilsby**, off the A158. Its terrace is, traditionally, the 'high Hall gardens' which Tennyson's 'Maud' was invited to enter. Neither garden nor house has changed much since the poet was in love with Rosa Baring, who lived at the Hall. The setting is romantic. The house, long but deceptively narrow, presents a warm, rose-pink front to the charming gardens. It was rebuilt, 1678–81, on a medieval stone base, but retains from the older house a tall, projecting Elizabethan porch. House open Easter Sept. on stated days; gardens and garden centre April–Oct.

Heckington   5K6
The eight-sailed windmill is restored and open daily, except Sun. The former pea-sorting warehouse is a fine craft and heritage centre. The third church on the site was built in the 14th c by the Abbey of Bardney. Richness is expressed in its design and decoration, notably in the Easter Sepulchre of Richard de Potesgrave, vicar of this church and chaplain to Edward III.

Holbeach   5J6
Market town mentioned in Domesday Book, and now the centre of a bulb-growing district. Birthplace of Susannah Centlivre, wife of Queen Anne's cook, who wrote 18 comedies, in one of which David Garrick played the lead. The Late Decorated and Early Perpendicular N porch of the church has a traceried arch.

Horncastle   5L6
Site of the Roman fort, Banovallum. The town's horse fair is described by George Borrow in *The Romany Rye*. The church has a brass depicting the King's Champion of 1519 (*see* **Scrivelsby**), an inscription to Sir Ingram Hopton who 'paid his debt to nature' at Winceby in 1643, and a collection of scythes said to have been used as weapons at that battle.

Kingerby   5M7
The 19th c Hall stands on a circular mound surrounded by fosse and embankment, where Stone Age implements and skeletons of early Britons have been discovered below Roman works.

Kirkstead   5L6
The beautiful chapel of St Leonard, erected for the use of lay persons, has survived the Cistercian abbey to which it was attached. Note the 13th-c timber screens, the second oldest in England.

Knaith   5L8
Thomas Sutton, founder of Charterhouse School and Hospital in London, was born at the Hall in 1532.

Lincoln**   5L7
The Norman bishop Remigius built his church on rising ground to be 'as strong as the place was strong and as fair as the place was fair'. It developed after fire and earthquake into the present triple-towered cathedral. The Early English work of Bishop Hugh of Avalon (d.1200) is the aisled choir, apse and transept was continued by his successors, resulting in one of the most magnificent of the English cathedrals. Lincoln's copy of Magna Carta is preserved in the chantry of Bishop Longland. Stephen Langton, the Archbishop of Canterbury who played a leading part in the struggle with King John, was born in the county. In Minster Yard are the remains of the Bishop's Palace (AM), dating from 13th c. (*See also* page 232.)

Among many remarkable sights, the city has a castle (open all year) founded by William the Conqueror, two well-preserved Norman domestic buildings (the Jew's House and another misleadingly known as 'The House of Aaron the Jew'), a gateway that has been in use since Roman times (Newport Arch), the High Bridge with medieval houses built over the arch, the Guildhall with open timber roof and bosses of 15th and 16th c., and a river frontage at Brayford Pool. There are several museums and also the Usher Gallery which has a Peter de Wint collection. 4m SW is *Hartsholme Country Park*.

Louth   5M6
The crocketed spire of the 15th-c church is attached to the tower by flying buttresses. The grammar school founded by Edward VI existed as an endowed school 300 years earlier. Its scholars include Governor Eyre of Jamaica, Sir John Franklin, Captain John Smith (first President of Virginia) and Alfred, Lord Tennyson. The Naturalists, Antiquarian and Literary Society Museum has a fine display of moths and butterflies.

Mablethorpe   5M5
Now a pleasant seaside resort, this, in Tennyson's boyhood, was a village with lonely sand-dunes where he and Charles played and read their joint masterpiece *Poems of Two Brothers*, published by a Louth bookseller.

Markby   5L5
The tiny, thatched church, unique in the county, stands within a moat which once encircled an Austin priory. The interior contains an Elizabethan double-decker pulpit, an ancient strap-hinged chest, a 17th-c altar-table and box-pews.

Marston   5K7
A Purbeck marble, canopied tomb of William Thorold (1569) is the oldest of many monuments in the medieval church to the Thorold family, who have owned land here since the early 14th c. Their Tudor manor house, Marston Hall, which has changed little since the 18th c, is sometimes opened to the public. In its ancient gardens are what may be the oldest laburnum tree in England (about 400 years old), and perhaps the largest girthed wych elm.

Old Bolingbroke   5L6
Bolingbroke Castle (AM), which was owned by John of Gaunt and was the birthplace of Henry IV in 1367, suffered demolition by the Parliamentarians in 1643. Undergoing reconstruction. Open all year.

Pickworth 5K7
Bomb damage in World War II led to the discovery of 14th-c wall paintings in the church.

Revesby 5L6
Sir Joseph Banks (1743–1820), the naturalist who sailed with Captain Cook, was born on the site of what is now the derelict Victorian building of Revesby Abbey. His forestry and drainage work in the district are a lasting memorial.

Scrivelsby 5L6
Home of the Dymoke family, traditional holders of the title of King's Champion, conferred on an ancestor by William the Conqueror. Their privilege was to ride in full armour into **Westminster Hall**, London, at the time of the Coronation, challenging to single combat all who denied the King's sovereignty. This demonstration of chivalry was last performed at the coronation of George IV.

Sibsey 5K6
The trader mill, the only six-sailed windmill (AM) in England dates from 1877 but has been restored. Open daily April–Sept.

Skegness 5L5
Holiday resort with bracing air and all manner of entertainments. Church Farm Museum in 19th-c farm buildings is open May–Sept. 4m S, *Gibraltar Point* Nature Reserve and Visitor Centre extends over 1,500 acres of dunes, saltmarsh and foreshore. Open all year.

Skirbeck 5K6
The old mill, the last in England to grind woad, ceased work in 1932. One of the treasures in the church of St Nicholas is an Elizabethan pulpit with a desk supported by six strange birds carved in wood.

Sleaford 5K7
Market town that owes its prosperity to road and rail communications. In the cathedral-like church of St Denis, note particularly the tracery of the windows, the oak roodscreen (early 15th-c), a tapestry pulpit-cushion worked in Warwickshire, and the needlework altar-carpet (framed). The last two are of the 17th c.

Somersby 5L6
Alfred, Lord Tennyson (1809–92), was born at the old rectory (not open to visitors). He wrote of it: 'The well-beloved place, where first we gazed upon the sky'.

Somerton Castle 5K7/L7
2m W of *Boothby Graffoe*. Two ruined towers (one attached to an Elizabethan farmhouse), and a moat full of water, are part of the great fortified manor house where the captive King John of France was entertained in 1360. Open by appointment only.

Spalding 5J6
Fenland town, a centre for agriculture and bulb production. A visit in springtime is delightful, when a tulip festival is held in early May at the height of the bulb season at *Springfields*, 1m E. Open April–Sept. daily. (*See* page 231.) Ayscoughfee Hall, restored in the 18th c, was the home of Maurice Johnson, who in 1710 founded the still extant 'Gentlemen's Society of Spalding' to which Newton, Addison, Pope, Sir Hans Sloane and other men of letters and science belonged. Exhibitions in Hall Museum, open April–Oct; gardens daily.

Spilsby 5L6
A statue of Sir John Franklin, born here in 1786, stands in the market place. Memorials in the 14th-c church and in **Westminster Abbey**, London, commemorate the explorer. 9m NW is **Harrington Hall**. 3m W is *Wheelabout Wood* and Arboretum.

Stamford★ 5J7
An archway known as Brasenose Gateway recalls the students who seceded from **Oxford** and in the 14th c set up a rival seat of learning. The town is celebrated for its architecture; examples are Browne's Hospital (open daily), built by a wealthy merchant in the reign of Henry VII, the Town Hall, Stamford School (founded in 1532), the ruined chapel of St Leonard's Priory and six ancient churches. Sir Malcolm Sargent was a pupil at Stamford School. The Brewery Museum is open April–Sept. on set days. *See also* **Burghley House** (Cambs).

Stow 5L7
The cruciform church, built *c.*1040 under the patronage of Leofric of Mercia and his wife Lady Godiva, is remarkable for being mainly of that century except for the 15th-c tower and minor architectural detail.

Swineshead 5K6
A farmhouse has absorbed the materials of the 12th-c Cistercian abbey where King John lodged in 1216 after the incident when he lost his baggage in the Wash. The battlemented tower of the parish church, the stocks in the war memorial garden and the tolling curfew in winter months are unusual survivals.

Tattershall Castle★ 5K6
After Agincourt, Ralph Cromwell transformed an old Norman castle into a home of medieval brickwork, with a quadrangular tower standing over the moat, and four storeys topped by octagonal turrets, from which there is a remarkable view. The guard house is a museum, and the property belongs to the NT. Open all year. A row of 17th-c almshouses of the church was restored in 1967. In Tattershall in the Old Railway Yard an aviation museum is open Easter–Oct. on Sun. Leisure Park also near by. 1m W, *Dogdyke Pumping Station* has a beam-engine of 1855 operating perhaps the only surviving land-drainage scheme of this kind in Britain. Open May–Oct. on stated Suns.

Wainfleet 5L5
Birthplace of William of Waynflete, the Bishop of Winchester who founded Magdalen College, **Oxford**, and in 1484 gave Magdalen College School to this town.

Willoughby 5L5
Boyhood home of John Smith (1579–1631), the penniless local boy who became President of Virginia and Admiral of New England, and whose life was saved by Pocahontas, the Red Indian princess, who died at **Gravesend** (Kent) in 1617.

Woodhall Spa 5L6
Health-giving bromo-iodine springs were discovered accidentally during an unsuccessful attempt to find coal. A championship golf-course and pinewood walks make this a popular inland resort.

Woolsthorpe 5K8
The stone-built manor house (NT) was the birthplace of Sir Isaac Newton in 1642; adjoining it is the orchard where he is said to have discovered the law of gravity. Open April–Oct.

NOTTINGHAMSHIRE

AN INTRODUCTION BY

M. W. BARLEY

In this motor-car age, many people know England well enough to pick out a coastal county by its resorts and scenery, but would find it much more difficult to signalize the character of a midland county. Yet Nottinghamshire has its own pattern of scenery, distinct and attractive, if the traveller has the eye and patience to find it.

The Rock Beneath

In this county more than in most the scenery grows out of the rock. The bony structure, as it were, is a fairly simple one. Successive layers of sedimentary rock were later tilted down to the east, so that as one drives from Mansfield through Newark towards the east coast, one crosses first the sandstones of Sherwood Forest, then clays beginning at Ollerton, and eventually (east of the Trent) the lias limestone. In the west the narrow band of magnesian limestone, hard and very good for building, has the hilliest scenery of the county. In the gently rolling country of the sandstones, the fields are sometimes covered with pebbles, and the soil is so sandy and poor that the area was royal forest, reserved for hunting. The sandstone soaks up water like a sponge, so that while farmers are short of it on the surface, the lower levels have great supplies, which are pumped up to supply Nottingham, Newark and other towns. The rock is easily cut, and underneath Nottingham's buildings there is a fantastic honeycomb of caves, wells and passages, some of which may be 1,000 years old; Mansfield's rock-dwellings were inhabited until relatively recently.

The clays form a plateau in the centre of the county, its edges cut by valleys and 'dumbles' in the Southwell Farnsfield area; the steep slopes of red soil and tree-lined valleys are as attractive as any part of the county.

It is easy for the traveller to tell where he passes from one formation to another, because each western edge forms a pronounced scarp. The road from Nottingham through Ollerton runs on the sandstone (because it is dry) and the clay scarp of the Keuper Marl lies in view to the east. Going from Ollerton to Tuxford, the short hill in Kirton takes the road up on

to the Keuper Marl plateau; so does the road from Retford to Gainsborough at Clarborough. The next pronounced step, going eastwards, lies just outside the county boundary but frames its scenery: the Belvoir Hills to the southeast and the limestone ridge of south Lincolnshire.

Overlying this simple pattern, and complicating it somewhat, are rivers, geologically new, and deposits made during or since the Ice Age. The River Trent, which once flowed east from Nottingham, now curves north past Newark; it has cut its way through the red clays of the Keuper Marl (Radcliffe on Trent, Clifton) so that at Gunthorpe and Hazelford there are steep, tree-covered bluffs visible on the other bank. The Trent has also laid down a wide band of gravel and other alluvial deposits all the way from Attenborough to the Lincolnshire boundary. In the southeast, the Nottinghamshire Wolds consist of boulder-clays laid down during the Ice Age; they were once wooded (hence *wolds*), but are now mostly under grass.

To someone attached to, say, the Yorkshire Dales or the Lake District, the Vale of Trent and the Vale of Belvoir may seem undistinguished; but, seen from vantage points like East Bridgford, the high ground north of Tuxford, or Broughton Hill on the Melton Mowbray road, the immense sweeps of wood and field with silver rivers, church spires and power-stations seen through a misty air have a strong charm of their own.

Local Industry

For 2,000 years man has been busy taking what he needed from these soils and changing the landscape. On the western boundary the River Erewash cuts through the coal measures, which must have been worked in Roman times, judging from the coal on Roman sites in the East Midlands. Wollaton Hall, one of the grandest Elizabethan mansions in England, now within the boundaries of Nottingham, was built in 1588 from the profits of coal. Between the scatter of mining, old and new and the villages which it has created are untouched pockets of beautiful country: the winding lanes, deep valleys and small woods round Teversal, or the more open but very secluded farmland round the site of Beauvale Priory. New mines have been sunk to greater depths and farther east, including the first south of the Trent, at Cotgrave.

The gypsum found in the Keuper Marl also created an old industry – quarrying alabaster for church monuments, which were made up in Nottingham, and, more recently, working its softer forms to make plaster for floors and walls. All the older houses in the county have plaster floors; quarries and mines at Staunton near Newark and at Gotham south of Nottingham produce plaster-board in great quantities. At Barnstone, at the foot of the Belvoir hills, the lias limestone is quarried for cement.

Modern industry has an immense appetite for gravel and concrete; and great lagoons have been created in the Trent Valley, at Attenborough, Hoveringham and north of Newark. They have added a new element to the scene – water sports and also some form nature reserves. The newest industry of all is electricity. Power-stations line the Trent and the Soar (Wilford, Staythorpe, High Marnham, West Burton and Ratcliffe-on-Soar), using local coal and river-water for cooling. The great cooling-towers are strikingly impressive at a distance; but near at hand the acres of railway sidings and the power-lines crossing every field make a mess of the landscape.

One local industry has altered villages and created towns without directly affecting the landscape. William Lee, an Elizabethan parson born at Calverton, invented a machine for knitting stockings. Eventually Nottingham and near-by villages became famous for their stockings. The frames were usually in an upstairs room and lighted by a long window, examples of which can still occasionally be seen.

Sherwood Forest
First legends, then facts. Legends about Robin Hood and his fellow outlaws were popular even in the Middle Ages; but no historian has been able to prove that he actually existed. Nevertheless, the stories are a valid commentary on the rich and the poor of medieval England, and on the unpopularity of laws with a class bias. Now facts. The poor, sandy land of central Nottinghamshire was used for hunting by the men of the Shire (Shire-wood). Then Norman kings took it over as a royal forest; special courts administered special laws, to preserve the beasts of chase and the forest and the undergrowth in which they flourished. Land was cleared only by royal concession. Most of Nottinghamshire's medieval monasteries – Welbeck, Newstead, Rufford, etc. – were planted within its bounds by feudal landowners, who alone had the land to give – land not already settled and farmed – and could get the necessary licences.

There is little left of what children imagine as Sherwood Forest. It must always have been a region

of glades and open tracts, rather than dense woodland. Most of the oak has gone, for building castles, abbeys, churches and ships, or for charcoal. The Forestry Commission's plantations surround the new mining villages such as Clipstone. The glades of oak and silver birch near Ollerton and Edwinstowe (Bilhaugh and Birklands) give the best impression of a medieval forest, and some giant oaks still stand.

The Dukeries
When the monasteries disappeared, in 1536–40, dukes took back what their ancestors had given. Great aristocratic mansions were created at Worksop, Welbeck, Rufford and Newstead out of monastic buildings, and a new site was developed at Thoresby. The old roads through the forest became private drives, flanked by ornamental planting and entered by monumental gateways. Streams were dammed to make lakes, or monastic waterworks improved; derelict woods were replanted and fields improved. Now, the peers have gone; only Welbeck and Thoresby remain of the mansions although the fine parks of Clumber and Rufford can be visited.

The room in which D. H. Lawrence was born at 8A Victoria Street. Eastwood, now a museum

Byron and Lawrence

Newstead Abbey, the home of the Byron family from 1539, was the poet's residence for a short time, but Greece meant more to him, just as his grave at Hucknall near by is a place of pilgrimage for Greeks.

D. H. Lawrence was, in a much more real sense, a Nottinghamshire man. Though he left the county early in life, his first novels, stories and poems are set in the mixed mining and farm land round Eastwood, northwest of Nottingham, where he was born, and whose essential flavour he could convey.

Why Come to Nottinghamshire?

For views – from the Belvoir Hills or the Trent Hills. For scenery of great variety: the sweeping woodland of Sherwood Forest, or the secluded valleys round it; the great sweep of the Trent Valley or the fascinating marshland on the northern fringe of the county, now reclaimed and drained. For churches – rich town churches (Nottingham and Newark), a great minster (Southwell) and good village churches. For castles (Nottingham, Newark), country houses, abbeys and charming villages built of red brick with pantiled roofs. For sailing, on the Trent or the gravel-lagoons; for coarse fishing, again in the Trent, in old canals and lagoons. Even for birds – especially for lapwings – and Nottingham sewage works at Stoke Bardolph are well known to ornithologists. The pleasures and rewards of the county, if not flamboyant, are very real and remarkably varied.

GAZETTEER

Annesley 7L8

Mary Chaworth, who inherited Annesley Hall, was the first love of Lord Byron; both were in their 'teens. She, however, married Jack Musters, thus uniting two local land-owning families.

Arnold 7L8

A village now almost swallowed up by **Nottingham**, but at one time closely associated with the Luddites, the weavers who fought the Industrial Revolution by smashing the machines that threatened their livelihood. Richard Parkes Bonington (1802–28), the landscape painter, was born at 79 High Street, but did most of his work in France. He died when 26 from 'brain fever' caused by exposure to the sun while sketching.

Aslockton 5K8

Archbishop Cranmer was born in a manor house that no longer exists. He was able to spend only the shortest periods at home between his 14th year and his martyrdom, but from the earthwork known as Cranmer's Mound he 'surveyed the face of the country and listened to the tuneable bells of Whatton'.

Attenborough 7L7

The church, in which Cromwell's horses were stabled, has one of the oldest doors in England, grotesque carvings and beautiful glass. The baptism of Henry Ireton is recorded in the parish register for 1611. He fought on the Parliamentary side at Edgehill and Marston Moor, married Cromwell's daughter, died of plague and was buried in **Westminster Abbey**. After the Restoration his body was exhumed and hanged at Tyburn.

Beauvale Priory 7L8

NW of **Hucknall**. Agricultural buildings have assimilated the remains of the 14th-c Carthusian priory that fell victim to Henry VIII's dissolution of the monasteries.

Beeston 7L7

Centre for the manufacture of drugs and toilet preparations which grew from the business genius of Jesse Boot, 1st Lord Trent, who started work at the age of 14 in his mother's small herbal shop in **Nottingham**.

Bingham 5K8

The Early English and Perpendicular-style church of All Saints has a notable lancet window set into the thickness of the wall at the W end, carvings of the Seven Deadly Sins, and a sequence of memorials dating from every century since the church's foundation and culminating in the wooden figure of Ann Harrison, the fish-seller who died in 1928 when 99 years old and who gave most of her earnings to the church where her photograph is displayed in a book.

Blyth 9K2

Part of the church has early Norman work similar to that done on the Continent before the Conquest. Much of this has been crowded out by Early English and Perpendicular additions.

Budby 9K2

The 1st Earl Manvers built this model neo-Gothic village in 1807 for workers on his Thoresby estate.

Bunny 7L7

With the exception of the 14th-c church, everything in this village bears the stamp of Sir Thomas Parkyns, who was known as the Wrestling Baronet. The Hall was designed by him, and took on much of his eccentricity; he commissioned a school and an almshouse, which fared rather better. He wrote a treatise on wrestling, *The Cornish Hugg*, which he dedicated to George I; he also designed his own monument in the church, which depicts a tiny figure laid low by Time.

Calverton 7L8

Believed to be the birthplace of William Lee, the Elizabethan parson who invented a stocking-frame. The Queen was disappointed that it could not make silk stockings, and the frame was eventually developed in France. Nevertheless it is due to Lee's invention that the hosiery industry flourishes in this county. Folk Museum open by appointment.

Car Colston 5K8

In a county where village greens are rare, there are two here, the larger having a cricket pitch, stocks and a fringe of attractive buildings. The church is notable for its splendid 14th-c chancel.

Clipstone   7L8
Very little remains of what is known as King John's Palace
but that part which dates from before his reign. It continued
to be the royal hunting lodge of the Tudors before passing to
the nobility. The eccentric 5th Duke of Portland built a
gatehouse on the way to **Edwinstowe**. It is similar to the
one at **Worksop** Priory, and is embellished with representations of Robin Hood and his band.

Clumber   9K2
4½m SE of **Worksop**. This great seat (NT) of the Dukes of
Newcastle was built in 1770 and demolished in 1937, except
for the stable block, but the 3,500-acre park, with its pleasure
gardens, woodlands, lake, Georgian classical bridge and the
longest double lime avenue in Europe, is always open.
Bodley's Victorian Gothic Revival chapel, which the 7th
Duke of Newcastle called 'a cathedral in miniature', has
recently been restored and was rededicated in 1979.

Cossall   7L8
D. H. Lawrence was once engaged to Louie Burrows, who
lived at Church Cottage, one of several 18th-c cottages in
this village which he called Cossethay in *The Rainbow*. The
Willoughby almshouses of 1685 set an architectural pattern
that was followed giving the village its homogeneity.

Creswell Crags   9J2/K2
5m SW of **Worksop**. Caves in a limestone ravine on the
Derbyshire boundary have yielded some of the earliest
artefacts by man in Britain. The finds are interpreted in a
new visitor centre. Open all year.

East Leake   7L7
In addition to noteworthy architectural detail, the church
has a 'shawn' or tin trumpet which measures 10ft when
extended. This was used by the bass singer until mid-19th c,
and is one of the six surviving in England.

East Stoke   5K8
Where Lambert Simnel having been 'crowned King of
England' in Dublin, was captured by Henry VII in 1487.

Eastwood   7L8
The birthplace of D. H. Lawrence (1885–1930) at 8A Victoria
Street is a Lawrence Museum (*see page 238*). Open all the
year as is the adjacent Craft Centre in renovated cottages.
Eastwood Library has a Lawrence Study Room with a
collection of books and other Lawrentian material. The
town figures memorably as Bestwood in *Sons and Lovers*. In
Garden Road is the D. H. Lawrence 'Breach' House which
was the home of his family during 1887–91. Open all year on
Sun. afternoons.

Edwinstowe   7L8
Centre for *Birklands* and *Bilhaugh,* two stretches of **Sherwood Forest**. Some trees are so striking that they have been
given individual names. The hollow Major Oak is said to be
several hundred years old. Another tradition is that Robin
Hood married Maid Marian in Edwinstowe Church. Sherwood Forest Visitor Centre and Country Park, including
Robin Hood exhibition, is open all year.

Gotham   7L7
Though mining and plaster works are the village's industries, a more lasting product may be the medieval Merry
Tales, in which the Wise Men of Gotham did various idiotic
things, such as building a hedge around a cuckoo to prevent
it from flying away.

Harby   5L7
Eleanor of Castile, wife of Edward I, died here in 1290.
Beautiful Eleanor Crosses were erected at every stage
where her funeral procession halted on its journey to
Westminster Abbey, London.

Hawton   5K8
The church is visited chiefly for its magnificent Easter
Sepulchre on which is carved the story of the Resurrection.
From Good Friday until Easter Sunday the church's crucifix
was placed in a niche and guarded by watchers dressed as
Pilate's soldiers.

Holme   5K8
John Barton, who made a fortune out of the wool trade with
Calais, rebuilt the church in the late 15th c. Above the porch
is a room known as Nanny Scott's Chamber, where an old
woman immured herself against the plague, but died from
sorrow at having to witness the burial of her friends.

Holme Pierrepont   7L7
The National Water Sports Centre, with adjacent country
park, has emerged around disused gravel pits by the River
Trent. 1m W, Hall and church form a striking group. Behind
the Hall's early Tudor brick front, with Gothic Revival
crenellations, survives a 15th-c roof, rediscovered in recent
restorations, and a noble late 17th-c staircase. The Hall,
frequently open in summer, has undergone many alterations
in nearly 700 years of occupation by Pierreponts, whose fine
tombs are a feature of the 13th- and 17th-c church.

Hucknall Torkard   7L8
Lord Byron's body was brought here from Greece when his
relatives found that permission for burial in Poet's Corner at
Westminster Abbey was unlikely to be granted. His bust is
in the chancel, a lamp burns in his name, and a brass wreath
of laurels is set into stone sent to England by the King of
Greece. Eric Coates (1886–1957), the composer, was born
here. *See also* **Beauvale Priory** and **Newstead Abbey**.

Kelham   5K8
The Hall, now local government offices, was built mid-19th c
by Sir George Gilbert Scott in the neo-Gothic style. It has a
new chapel with sculptures by Charles Jagger.

Kingston-on-Soar   7L7
Rebuilding the church of St Wilfred in 1900 employed as far
as possible the materials from the earlier structure, and
preserved within it the Babington Chantry (*c*.1550). This is
one of the most important church monuments in the county,
and has been described by Sacheverell Sitwell as being
'somewhat of Portuguese-Indian influence'. It has columns
covered with a hexagonal pattern, and a wealth of other
decoration including some 200 figures of infants in barrels –
a 'pun' on the family name of Babington.

Langar   5K8
The recumbent figures of Thomas, Lord Scroope and his wife
Philadelphia are watched over by the smaller alabaster
effigy of their son in the family chapel within the church.
The detail of their robes is worth studying. Admiral Howe
(d.1799) is buried in the churchyard, and Samuel Butler
(1835–1902), author of *The Way of All Flesh*, was born in the
rectory adjoining the church.

Laxton   5L8
The pre-Enclosure open-field farming system survives here,
uniquely. The farms, with crofts behind, line the village

street, with the three open fields beyond. The mound alone remains of a Norman motte-and-bailey castle, but the mainly 13th-c church has the only wooden medieval effigy in the county, as well as a stepped sedilia and miniature Easter Sepulchre.

Linby 7L8

One of the two crosses in the village has a very old medieval base. But Linby is best known for Castle Mill, a battlemented building where James Watt set up his first machine for the spinning of cotton and flax. The toll of young lives is chronicled in the churchyard by 42 graves of child apprentices. *See also* **Newstead Abbey**.

Mansfield 7L8

The market town adjoining **Sherwood Forest** has grown into an industrial centre. It was the legendary Miller of Mansfield who dared to entertain Henry II with venison poached from his own preserves. In the museum and art gallery is a recent natural history display about the town. Also a good collection of Wedgwood, Rockingham, etc.

Mattersey 5M8

The meagre remains of a late 12th-c priory of the Gilbertine Order (AM) stand in isolation 1¼m E of the village.

Newark* 5K8

Long before the town's prosperity was founded on wool shipped down the Trent to the merchants of Calais and Flanders, it was a stronghold on the way to the N. The castle, in which King John died in 1216, was dismantled in 1646 on the collapse of the Royalist cause, and is a splendid ruin but now partly repaired.

The church of St Mary Magdalene has unusual proportions, its spire being 22ft higher than the length of the church. The oldest parts are four central piers and the crypt. The wide nave dates from the reign of Edward II. Because of their slight stonework, the windows in the transepts are especially noteworthy. See also Robert Markham's chantry chapel, which has a peephole and a crudely painted Dance of Death.

The town has a wealth of fine old buildings, especially around the market place, which Pevsner found 'a joy to examine', where a magnificent 14th-c timber-framed former inn has been restored. There are several museums – on local and folk life, on history, the Vina Cooke Collection of Dolls and Costumes (open all year by appointment), and the Air Museum at the airfield (open all year).

Newstead Abbey* 7L8

11m N of **Nottingham** at *Kirkby in Ashfield*. Byron and his mother were too poor to live at Newstead when he inherited the property, but after he left **Cambridge** he moved in, despite heavy debts, until obliged to sell six years later. The house was originally a 12th-c Augustinian priory. It was

Newstead Abbey: after the Dissolution it became the Byron family's home in 1540 until 1817

Nottingham: a statue of Robin Hood at the castle. Sherwood Forest, his legendary home, is near the city

converted by an ancestor of Byron in 1539 and presented to the City of Nottingham by Sir Julian Cahn in 1931. It has a beautiful W front, and romantically landscaped gardens. The magnificent rooms contain the poet's possessions, including furniture, portraits and rare editions of his work. SE wing now refurbished. Open Easter–Sept., and gardens all year. *See also* **Hucknall Torkard**.

Nottingham*   7L8

Though not lacking in history, this town, because of its good planning, appears to be modern. The proud civic buildings include a Council House (1929) designed with a dome and pediment that derive from **St Paul's Cathedral**.

The town of Snotingaham was occupied by the Danes in 868, and the imposing castle was built on its present rock site after the Norman Conquest. A Royal Charter was granted by Henry II. Having been held by the Royalists, the castle was demolished in 1651, but rebuilt in an Italianate style by the 1st Duke of Newcastle, only to be burned by Luddite rioters in the 19th c. In 1878 it was converted into a museum and now also has an art gallery. Bronzes of Robin Hood and his men by a local sculptor have been set out below the castle wall, and at Castle Gate House is a Robin Hood Exhibition of his life and times (open all year). At the foot of Castle Rock are five 17th-c cottages with exhibitions showing daily life in the city at that time. The council has also acquired

Elizabethan **Wollaton Hall** as well as Byron's home at **Newstead Abbey**. Other interesting old buildings have been preserved and converted into museums of social history, costume, canals and industry.

The famous annual Goose Fair, traditionally held in the market place, now spreads its stalls and amusements over a less restricted site at the edge of 'The Forest' in the city centre. The market place has been planted with trees and flowers, and the market itself put under cover.

Though Nottingham was originally celebrated for lace curtains and carvings in alabaster, both now out of fashion, the city has kept up with the times, aided undoubtedly by its central position and by the navigable Trent on which it stands. It boasts a R.C. Cathedral designed by Pugin and the fine Victorian Theatre Royal, recently restored, as well as an excellent modern repertory theatre. The history of the lace industry can be traced at the Lace Centre in Castle Road and at the Museum of Costume and Textiles with its new lace room. Both open all year. 6m S at *Ruddington* in St Peter's Room is an exhibition of the village's story on illustrative panels (open by appointment); also a village museum and a Framework Knitter's Museum (open on Weds.). 2m E is *Colwick Park* with nature reserve, boating, fishing, etc. Also E is Greens Mill (recently restored) at *Sneinton* with its new museum (1984). *See also* **Strelley**.

Owthorpe   5J8

The aisleless church in the fields was reduced in size in 1705, but retains its Jacobean pulpit, screen and altar-rails.

Papplewick   7L8

Relics of the early cotton industry lie S of this handsome village. The church to the NW in the grounds of Papplewick Hall (1787, attributed to the Adam brothers, but not open), despite the apparently Gothic exterior, dates only from 1795, but it is worth finding for the squire's pew, with fireplace, at the E end of the long N gallery, and for two incised slabs to foresters of Sherwood – one with sling, bow and arrow, and the other with a knife. 2m E, Papplewick Pumping Station has two beam-engines in ornate engine-house within landscaped park. Open Easter–Oct., Sun. afternoon.

Retford   5L8

The two parts – West and East Retford – of this mainly Victorian town are joined by a bridge across the River Idle. The cruciform church of St Swithun is largely 15th-c, though the central tower collapsed in 1651 and was rebuilt on its four 13th-c arches. The Wetlands Waterfowl Reserve off the A638 is open daily. 4m E is *North Leverton* Windmill built in 1813. Open all year.

Rufford Abbey   5L8

The home of Arabella Stuart, who came to a tragic end because she was close in succession to James I. The ruins of the Elizabethan house are closed to the public, but its parkland and 25 acre lake are always accessible. A craft centre in the stables is open. Gardens and sculpture gardens. Open all year.

Scrooby   9K2

From this inland village on the small River Ryton the *Mayflower* was launched. William Brewster, one of the two leaders of the Pilgrim Fathers, worshipped in the church, which contains a pew known as Brewster's Pew. It has handsome wood carvings and a 15th-c bench-end.

Sherwood Forest*   9K2

Largely between *Ollerton* and **Worksop**. Whether or not Robin Hood is mythical, this area was once a strictly preserved royal forest. Including the Dukeries, which have formed three great enclosures, it still measures 20m by 5–10m. Much of it is heath but there are many fine trees – oaks as well as birches – in *Birklands* and *Bilhaugh*. *See also* **Edwinstowe**, where there is a visitor centre.

Southwell*   5K8

Charles I stayed at the Saracen's Head (at that time the King's Head) in 1646 before being taken into the captivity that ended in his execution.

The Minster, though possibly the least visited of English cathedrals, makes Southwell notable. The town itself is also less seen than it deserves. The Minster was begun in the early 12th c; yet the transepts and nave of the first building period are still standing. Of the three Norman towers, two have the pyramidal roofs of their original design, despite rebuilding after fire in 1711, and further work in 1880. The glass in the E window was brought from the Chapel of the Knights Templar in Paris, where Marie Antoinette worshipped. The brass lectern was reclaimed from the lake at **Newstead Abbey**, where it had been thrown at the time of the Dissolution of the Monasteries. The chapter house, built at the end of the 13th c, is exceptionally graceful, owing much to its construction without the usual central pillar. Its door, which has a centre shaft, is one of the most beautiful in England. Throughout the Minster, carved foliage, with every leaf different and never stylized, appears over doorways, around seats and on the capitals of pillars. At least a dozen different types of leaves are represented.

Strelley   7L7

A surprisingly rural *cul-de-sac* village on the W edge of **Nottingham**, with an almost totally 14th-c church, notable for its superb chancel, rood-screen and medieval monuments to the Strelley family, who owned the predecessor of the adjacent late 18th-c Hall.

Teversal   7L8

An unexpected oasis in a desert formed by colliery workings. Lime avenues lead from pretty village to charming group of 18th-c manor house, earlier rectory and church with Norman S door and complete 17th-c furnishings, including combined pulpit and reading desk, a W gallery, box-pews and a sumptuous squire's pew looking like a four-poster bed with tall windows. The monuments are impressive, too, especially those to the Molyneux family.

Thoresby Hall   9K2

4m N of *Ollerton*. The seat of Earl Manvers, lacking the long history of **Welbeck** and **Rufford Abbey**. It was enclosed out of the Forest in 1683. The present residence dates from 1864–75, and has all the impressive qualities of that period. It is set in a splendid park through which runs a public road, and the damming of the River Meden has produced beautiful ornamental waters. Open at certain times of the year.

Thrumpton   7L7

A leafy village street slopes down to the Hall and the River Trent. The Hall dates basically from 1607, but a priest's hole at the foot of a secret staircase survives from an earlier house. A richly carved cantilever staircase was a 1660s' addition, and further alterations followed in the 1820s. The house is open to parties by appointment.

Welbeck   9K2

Though the history of the abbey goes back to a 12th-c Premonstratensian monastery, the existing structure is architecturally mixed. It combines mainly 18th-c work linked with restorations that followed a fire in 1900. Its chief fame is the complex of underground buildings constructed for the eccentric 5th Duke of Portland. These included a ballroom and an extraordinary glass-roofed riding school known as the Tan Gallop. The many rooms were linked by tunnels and served by a miniature underground railway. The Tan Gallop has been demolished, but alongside it is a giant covered riding school in cast iron. The house and grounds are an army school and not open to the public.

Wollaton Hall   7L8

2½m W of **Nottingham** city centre on the A609. One of the most grandiose though not the most beautiful of Elizabethan houses, now the property of the City of Nottingham, and containing a natural history museum, and an industrial museum in the stables. The fine early 19th-c Camellia House has been restored in the grounds where a high standard of horticulture is maintained. Open all year.

Worksop   9K2

The 12th-c priory church originally resembled **Southwell** Minster, having twin Norman towers with wooden spires and mouldings of foliage in the interior. But only the shell remained until between the two world wars, when the church and lady chapel were restored and civic buildings were grouped around them. The gatehouse S of the Priory was originally the entrance to the monastic buildings. Local museum is at the library. 3m N is the Old Mill Museum at *Carlton* Mill (open by appointment in summer). *See also* **Clumber** and **Creswell Crags**.

CHESHIRE

AN INTRODUCTION BY
FRANK SINGLETON AND ALAN BRACK

Despite its strong identity, Cheshire is one of those regions which tend to be thought of, superficially, as 'the gateway to . . .' – whether the north or the south depends quite literally on the point of view. It is not like Lancashire, with which, for many purposes, it has so often been popularly associated. Cheshire is urbane, smart; and lots of lovely Manchester money has surrounded the pretty meres in the north with expensive, attractive modern houses, their beautiful gardens in settings of woodland and water.

The county is a hollow plain, lying between the uplands of the Pennines and of North Wales. Here, as everywhere, the scenery and buildings indicate the nature of what lies beneath the surface of the earth. It is the varieties of red sandstone that make Cheshire a plain, not uniformly flat, but diversified by gently rolling country, a rural, warm, red landscape in contrast to the greys and browns of Lancashire, as is its domestic architecture, black and white, in contrast to brick or stone.

Landscape

Between the mouths of the Dee and Mersey, there thrusts out, northwestwards into the Irish Sea, the wedge of the Wirral Peninsula, the top half of which has been hived off to the Metropolitan County of Merseyside. What remains is typical Cheshire landscape of grass, arable, heath and mixed-farming country with distant views of the Welsh hills, though, increasingly in recent years, commuters have discovered the delights of this part of the world and the house-building trade has been only too eager to cater for them. Wirral, beloved by bird-watchers, ends just short of Chester, greatest and most beautiful of the county's towns. Along southern Merseyside and hugging the conurbation of Greater Manchester are Cheshire's chief suburban centres. The heart of the county is mainly rural and agricultural. Potatoes and milk are the main products. The pastures are carefully tended; the grazing season for high-yielding cows is long. Farm buildings are well planned and constructed.

The traveller sees the evidence of this from the train, as the green, grassy landscape, and the rich pastures for the grazing cattle, roll gently up the first slopes of the Pennines on the east. 'How lush and lusty the grass looks – how green!'

Industry

Cheshire has beneath its soil a source of wealth peculiar to her – salt. Under the rich grasslands run the salt deposits, liable to subside at times. Here and there a church spire leaning at some strange angle is a reminder. The ancient industry of salt-mining is responsible for some of Cheshire's most characteristic features. All around Nantwich are little meres, caused by the subsidence of stretches of land which have been mined below. Here, and at Middlewich and Northwich, conveniently placed for distributing their products to the many businesses who use them so widely, are the famous alkali works where Sir John Brunner and Dr Ludwig Mond established a thriving concern from which grew Imperial Chemical Industries.

Not far away is Crewe, a paradise for train-spotters and all interested in railways, which were the sole begetters of this home of 50,000 people, many connected in some way with the great locomotive works. Widnes and Runcorn are centres of the chemical industry and, generally speaking, do not lift the heart. But at both places, brave attempts have been made to relieve the workaday gloom, especially at Runcorn where a brand new town, carefully landscaped and generously treescaped, has been centred on Halton.

Mirror of the Plain

Alderley Edge is a woodland district on the western side of the ridge which runs through mid-Cheshire and which, like any ground that presumes to rise in a plain, enjoys disproportionate advantages.

The plain and the rich variety of what it contains can be seen, as well as anywhere, from the heights which, by contrast, seem to rise abruptly. On a summer day you look over a changing scene of green fields, black-and-white farms and houses, woodlands, the meres gleaming through the trees, and rivulets and little rivers winding across the rich meadows.

This Cheshire plain has mirrored the changing history of the county since earliest times, through Cheshire's part in each chapter of the island story. The crowning glory of Cheshire is Chester, which is indeed one of the glories of England.

History of Chester

Castra – a camp. And what a camp! – guarding the coastal gate of the road into England that avoided the mountains of Wales, and the sea-gate through which invaders from the River Dee came, until in the 15th century the sands, so ruinous in other ways, in this case provided protection. Today Chester is full of beguiling black-and-white houses and other buildings and you can still obtain a novel view by perambulating the ancient walls (part Roman, part medieval) which encircle the city. Famous and unique are the Rows which convert the pathways into shadowed corridors along their length – another medieval legacy designed to afford the pedestrian some refuge from the noisy traffic. The castle looms up on its height. The cathedral glows rosily in sandstone. Grey and slender church pinnacles, big doll's house structures with bulging windows, the old

Chester's Rows are medieval balustraded arcades above and beside the shops reached by steps from the street

bridge spanning the slow river, make the place a sort of magic, fairytale setting for all the events of the crowded past, not always so gentle as it may seem, including in the story, war, plague and scarcity.

At Domesday, Cheshire included the parts of Lancashire between Mersey and Ribble, as well as parts of what is now called Clwyd, and was raised to the status of county palatine, a dignity much diminished by Henry III. Prince Edward (later Edward I) was, however, created Earl of Chester, a title which is borne by the Prince of Wales. The Middle Ages are epitomized in Chester and its cathedral, the Tudor period in the many examples of black-and-white architecture – some, such as Moreton Old Hall and Gawsworth Rectory, among the finest to be seen anywhere in the country.

Food

Dairy farming enabled Cheshire to produce a famous cheese, less crumbly than Lancashire, not so hard as Double Gloucester. George Borrow's dictum that if you would enjoy the famous Cheshire cheese do not look for it in Chester is no longer true.

Cheshire is a good place for eating out, often in picturesque surroundings in country villages, with pleasant inns which are often good for the salmon which the Dee very acceptably yields.

GAZETTEER

Adlington Hall   9H2
5m N of **Macclesfield**. One wing of this half-timbered house was built in 1581, but the Legh family lived here before then. The Great Hall contains a 17th-c Bernard Smith organ (restored 1959) which Handel is said to have played. It was a Royalist garrison during the Civil War. Open April–end Sept.

Alderley Edge   9H2
The Edge (NT) is a lofty, wooded escarpment providing extensive views. Alderley Old Mill, 1½m S, is NT property.

Arley Hall   9H2
5m N of **Northwich**. Opened for first time in 1982. Warburton family and descendants have lived at Arley for over 500 years. Present Hall is styled 'Victorian Jacobean'. Interesting pictures, furniture and historical exhibitions, including a doll exhibition. Award-winning gardens. Open April–mid-Oct. (*See* facing page.)

Beeston Castle   7H8
3m SW of *Tarporley*. The ruins of a 13th-c castle stand on a rocky outcrop which gives a remarkable view extending to the Pennines in the E and Wales to the W. There is an exhibition on the history of the castle in the museum.

Burton   8F2
The Wirral Peninsula's prettiest village, birthplace in 1663 of Thomas Wilson, Bishop of Sodor and Man for 58 years. Burton Manor, now used as an adult education centre, formerly belonged to a son of William Gladstone. St Nicholas Church, and its tower with one-handed clock, dates from 1721. In unconsecrated ground in the wood behind the church are two Quaker graves of 1663.

Capesthorne Hall   9H2
7m S of *Wilmslow*, 7m N of **Congleton** off A34. The Bromley-Davenports and their ancestors have lived here since Domesday times. Large Jacobean-style mansion, partly rebuilt after disastrous fire in 1861, contains fine treasures. Beautiful Georgian chapel. The gardens and lake surrounding the mansion have wild fowl, fishing, nature trails. Open on certain days April–Sept.

Chester★★   7H8
Though they follow the line of the Roman fortifications on two sides, the town walls which encircle the city and provide an interesting walk, are mainly medieval. From King Charles's Tower in 1645, the king watched his forces defeated at the battle of Rowton Moor. Of the Roman remains above ground, the amphitheatre, one of the largest of its kind, is the most remarkable and a park near by has a selection of Roman stonework, including a reconstructed hypocaust.
The cathedral is built of the same red sandstone as the city walls. It began as a college for canons and then became a Benedictine abbey. A large amount of rebuilding was done in the 14th and 15th c, but not until after the Reformation did the abbey church become a cathedral. Comprehensive restoration work was undertaken in the last half of the 19th c. The 14th-c stalls repay close scrutiny. The Spanish ironwork of the gates into the choir aisles is exceptional; so too are the Early English Lady Chapel and the reconstructed shrine of St Werburgh.

Cheshire Military Museum has interesting regimental exhibits from the Cheshire Regiment, Cheshire Yeomanry and the Carabineers.
The bridge over the Dee, built in the 13th and 14th c is unusually picturesque through the lack of symmetry in its seven arches. The Rows (*see* page 245) and the old houses, inns, alleys and churches give Chester its unique character. At the British Heritage Exhibition in Vicars Lane, 2,000 years of the city's history are vividly depicted; in the Grosvenor Museum, Grosvenor Street, the displays include Roman archeological finds. Behind the Town Hall, Chester Market (open Mon.–Sat.) sells antique jewelry, art, bric à brac etc.
2m N is Chester Zoo – *see* **Upton-by-Chester**.

Cholmondeley Castle   7H8
Home of the Marquess of Cholmondeley. Gardens and farm with rare breeds of farm animals only open Sun. and public holidays, Easter–Sept.

Congleton   7I8
Ancient town on the River Dane once noted for silk-weaving. 18th-c St Peter's Church has box-pews, galleries and a handsome brass chandelier dated 1748. There are three 17th-c hostelries and some black-and-white timbered houses. The Bridestone near by is a Megalithic burial chamber dating from 3000 BC. Cigars were formerly made at the adjoining village of *Havanna*. 4m SE is ruined *Biddulph Hall*, a Tudor mansion destroyed during the Civil War.

Daresbury   8G2
Birthplace of Rev. C. L. Dodgson (Lewis Carroll), author of *Alice in Wonderland*. All Saints' Church has a striking memorial window based on Tenniel's original illustrations for the book.

Ellesmere Port   8G2
Now a modern industrial town it developed as Britain's first and biggest canal port. The Boat Museum (the National Waterways Museum) located in Thomas Telford's canal basin alongside the Manchester Ship Canal has Europe's largest collection of inland waterways vessels some of which may be boarded by visitors. A large exhibition hall contains a full-size narrowboat, artefacts and *memorabilia* of canal life. Lecture theatre with audio-visual presentation, souvenir shop and café. Other special exhibitions, including an Energy Exhibition, and temporary exhibitions of widely varying nature. Craft workshops also on site. Canal boat trips in summer months. Open daily.

Farndon   7H8
Riverside village of ancient half-timbered houses, the birthplace in 1552 of John Speed, cartographer and historian. Fine 14th-c bridge over the River Dee has nine arches and joins England to Wales. Noted for its strawberry farms. The Shelton Mill near by has a water-powered corn mill dating from 17th c and restored to working order. Open April–Sept. Demonstrations daily.

Gawsworth★   7I8
Beautifully situated picturesque village with 15th-c Old Rectory and 15th–16th-c church grouped round three ancient fish-ponds. In *Maggoty's Wood* (NT) is the grave of Samuel (Maggoty) Johnson (d.1773) said to be the last

Arley Hall Gardens: these are extensive and well-established gardens dating from Henry VIII's time

professional jester. Gawsworth Hall is a 16th-c half-timbered manor house in a superb setting. Dining- and drawing-rooms virtually unchanged since Tudor times. Carriage museum. Open mid-March–Oct.

Great Budworth   8G2
Picturesque Tudor village with brick and timber houses with twisted chimneys and notable church from the same period. Sometimes used as a ready-made set for films and television.

Jodrell Bank   9H2
Between *Holmes Chapel* and *Chelford*. The Mark 1A 250ft radio telescope is one of the largest fully steerable radio telescopes in the world, controlled by computer. The Concourse Building which was opened in 1966 has radio-astronomy exhibitions. Display models can be operated and there is a planetarium. Open daily March–Oct.; weekends Nov.–March.

Knutsford   9H2
Attractive old market town immortalized by Mrs Gaskell as *Cranford*. She worshipped at Brook Street Unitarian Chapel, built 1698, and is buried in the churchyard. Gaskell Memorial Tower, with the adjoining King's Coffee House in King Street, the Ruskin Rooms and some houses in Legh Road are the work of the wealthy eccentric Richard Harding Watt (1842–1913). They defy architectural classification but lean towards the 'Italianate'. The May Day celebrations –

where no mechanical vehicles are allowed to take part – are among the oldest in the country. Near by Caldwell's Nursery Garden Centre, established by William Caldwell over 200 years ago, is still on the original site.

Little Moreton Hall★   7I8
4m SW of **Congleton**. This is the most famous of all black-and-white half-timbered houses (NT). Surrounded by a moat with access across a stone bridge, Little Moreton Hall is the best-known example of 15th-c half-timbered construction with bold black-and-white patterns. The house is a complex of overhangs, irregular lines and seemingly dangerous though picturesque angles. The wainscoted Long Gallery well represents Elizabethan England. Open March–Oct.

Lyme Hall and Park   9I2
(NT leased to Stockport and Greater Manchester Councils.) At *Disley* 7m SE of Stockport off the A6. Elizabethan, with 18th- and 19th-c addditions, Palladian façade, Jacobean rooms, pictures and furnishings, noted for its tapestries, period furniture and Grinling Gibbons carvings. Mary Queen of Scots stayed here when, though in captivity, she was allowed to take the waters at Buxton as a cure for rheumatism. Largest of all Cheshire's great houses, its 1,320 acres of parkland, including an Italian garden, is home for a herd of indigenous red deer which have been bred here for centuries by the Legh family.

Lymm   9H2
The age of the market-cross, which stands on a sandstone dais, has baffled experts. It is surmounted by a weathercock and has two stocks at its foot.

Macclesfield 9H2

Home of the British silk industry for over 200 years. First charter granted in 1261, its medieval past is discernible from street names – Jordansgate, Chestergate and Backwallgate. St Michael's Church (founded in 1278 by Queen Eleanor) has been twice restored but the Savage Chapel (1501–7) and the Legh Chapel (1620) are original. Among the multifarious monuments is the curious 'Pardon' Brass of Roger Legh who died in 1506.

Mow Cop 7I8

1,000ft-high rocky outcrop (NT) crowned by Mow Cop 'Castle', an 18th-c mock ruin. Primitive Methodists held their first camp meeting here in 1807.

Nantwich 7I8

Market town, rich in black-and-white architecture, notably Churche's Mansion, completed, we are told precisely, on 4 May 1577. *Dorfold Hall*, 1m W, is a Jacobean house built in 1616 with notable plaster ceilings, especially in the Great Chamber. Open April–Oct. Nantwich Parish Church, 14th-c, often called 'the Cathedral of S. Cheshire', with interesting architectural features, stone and medieval wood carvings. Bridgemere Nurseries, near by, is a garden centre and a tourist attraction with more than 250 acres of plants, flowers, shrubs and trees of every description.

At *Poole*, near Nantwich is the Nantwich Pottery, one of the largest craft potteries in England, where pots can be seen being made by hand. Open daily.

1m S are the *Stapeley Water Gardens*, Europe's largest water-garden centre, extending over 30 acres, 6 acres of which are open to the public. Open daily.

Northwich 8G2/9H2

The Anderton Lift is a unique 19th-c boat-lift linking the Trent and Mersey Canal with the River Weaver. Boats are raised and lowered in water-filled tanks. The Salt Museum, unique in Britain, tells the story of Cheshire salt from Roman times with, as exhibits, authentic equipment and detailed models. Part of the Salt Works is AM.

Parkgate 8F2

Packet port for Ireland in the 18th c. After silting of the Dee and the rise of **Liverpool** brought shipping to an end (c.1820) it flourished for a time as a fashionable resort. Some houses and cottages from its heyday are still to be seen along The Parade which now fronts vast acres of green salt marsh, a haven for sea birds which attract the bird-watchers. From Mostyn House School came Sir Wilfrid Grenfell (1865–1940), famous as 'Grenfell of Labrador' for his work as a doctor and missionary among the Eskimos.

Peover Hall 9H2

4m S of **Knutsford**. Brick-built house dating from 1585. Famous Caroline Stables with Tuscan columns and ornate ceiling. Open May–Sept. (except public holidays); Thurs., stables and gardens only. The 13th-c church of *Lower Peover*, 2m W, is a rare black-and-white timbered church, built of oak and plaster, except for the stone tower.

Runcorn 8G2

A port and busy chemical manufacturing town. The bridge over the Mersey to *Widnes* which was opened in 1961, replacing the well-known Transporter bridge, has a span of 1,082ft, the largest in Europe, third largest in the world. The Norton Priory Museum displays the remains which have been excavated and conserved of the medieval priory. Set in woodland gardens.

Sandbach 7I8

In the market place are the Sandbach Crosses (7th-c) which were rescued and reconstructed as far as possible in 1816 after being broken up in the 17th c.

Shotwick 8F2

An important military port of the Middle Ages until the Dee silted up, now a quiet hamlet. St Michael's Church has a Norman doorway, 16th-c tower, 19th-c three-decker pulpit and box-pews. Shotwick Hall dates from 1662.

Styal Mill and Country Park 9H2

Museum of the cotton industry in the northwest set in 18th-c textile mill (NT). It has demonstrations of working machinery with displays illustrating its social impact. The Georgian mill, village and Apprentice House are in 250 acres of Country Park.

Tatton Park* 9H2

This most visited, and one of the most complete, of all NT houses is maintained, financed and administered by Cheshire County Council. Set in a 1,000-acre deer park containing two meres, the house and estate came to NT when the 4th Earl of Egerton, last of the line, died in 1958. The Egertons had lived here since 1598. The magnificent Georgian Hall (1788–91) is beautifully furnished and has been authentically redecorated. Gillow furniture, much china, glass, paintings by Canaletto and Van Dyck. Tenants' Hall built to house the 4th Earl's hunting trophies – hundreds of animal heads line the walls of this extraordinary display with other exhibits such as his veteran vehicles and historical artefacts. 15th-c Old Hall has been restored. The Home Farm is run as it was in its 1930's heyday. House open Easter–Oct.; park and gardens open all year.

Upton-by-Chester* 7H8

Chester Zoo is now one of the world's foremost zoos, extending over 110 acres of parkland. The majority of animals are in large outdoor enclosures amid superb gardens, which can be toured on foot or by boat on an encircling canal. The Cheshire Workshops offer visitors a personal demonstration in candlemaking and the making of hand-crafted glass.

Warrington 8G2

Warrington Academy once boasted among its tutors such intellectual giants as Joseph Priestley who discovered oxygen, Gilbert Wakefield, the classical scholar, and Jean-Paul Murat, the French revolutionary murdered in his bath by Charlotte Corday. The 18th-c Town Hall (formerly Bank Hall) was bought from Lord Winmarleigh in 1872. The magnificent cast-iron gates, 25ft high, 54ft broad, were the gift of Frederick Monks in 1893. Warrington Museum has a display of natural history, geology, ethnology, Egyptology, small arms as well as local history.

Widnes *see* Runcorn

MERSEYSIDE

AN INTRODUCTION BY
ALAN BRACK

The Metropolitan County of Merseyside – to give it its full and august title – was carved out of southwest Lancashire and the Wirral Peninsula of Cheshire by the Local Boundaries Commission in 1974. With the great city of Liverpool as the focal point, the Commission simply added to it those conurbations which they deemed had much in common – that is to say, its immediate neighbours and the main dormitory areas for the city's workers. That is why a length of Deeside is included and why Southport – seemingly out on a limb if you look at the revised map – has been gathered in. It has produced an administrative entity of five Districts with a total area of 250 square miles and a population of 1,630,000 – only half the size and less than half the number of people of its metropolitan neighbour, Greater Manchester.

For all that, it is a county with as nicely a varied spectrum of people, jobs, housing and terrain as can be found anywhere and with a kindly climate that many people who come from other parts find to be an unexpected bonus.

Natural Amenities
Consider, too, its natural amenities: the many delights of the Wirral Peninsula, which still exist despite the galloping consumption of land for houses over the last 25 years, coupled with the pleasures of the 15-mile sandy stretch northwards along the Irish Sea coast from Crosby to Crossens; splendid sea-washed beaches a long line of golf-links (in the county as a whole there are no less than 30 golf-courses, including two of the most famous in the land – Royal Liverpool at Hoylake and Royal Birkdale at Southport); a nature reserve at Ainsdale and away-from-it-all dormitory areas.

This new county also includes postwar 'overspill' towns at Kirkby and Knowsley (where the Earl of Derby has given over 360 acres of his vast estate to a safari park), as well as age-old Prescot, once famous for its clocks and watches, now known for its electric cables; and the town which continues to bring light into the world, the glassmaking town of St Helens. It also includes Newton-le-Willows where leviathan steam locomotives were once produced, as well as

little Billinge, a delightful village at the foot of a hill, the summit of which offers magnificent views of several counties and the Irish Sea.

Rise of Liverpool
We know precisely to the day when Liverpool was elevated from being a muddy creek inhabited by a few hardy fisherfolk to being a borough and a port. King John signed his name to Letters Patent bestowing the title on 28 August 1207 and he offered a 2-acre plot of land, together with 'all the liberties and free customs which any free borough upon the sea has within our land' to anyone who would come and settle in the place. It was no act of simple benefaction; he needed a base hereabouts from where he could ship his troops to Ireland. He was Lord of Ireland but the intransigent Irish sought not to recognize his authority and he had to keep an army there to exercise his will.

But it was a long time before Liverpool really emerged as a port – another 300 years, in fact, when the shipping trade began in a small way with the carrying of Cheshire's salt to the Isle of Man and ports along the northwest coast. As trade grew, bigger ships were built to sail into foreign waters and by the end of the 17th century Liverpool ships were trading with America and the West Indies. It reached its heyday as a port when the British Empire was at its height in the latter half of the 19th century and the pre-World War I years of the 20th. This was the era when many of its finest buildings were erected, the era when it became a diocese and a city, founded a university, and set out to build not one, but two, cathedrals. In the event, the vast Roman Catholic cathedral, to a design of Sir Edwin Lutyens, made only slow progress so that by the time World War II broke out only the crypt had been built. In 1953, Cardinal Heenan, the then Archbishop, grasped the nettle and promoted a competition to design a building, using modern methods and modern materials, which could be finished in less than a lifetime. Incorporating the Lutyens crypt, Sir Frederick Gibberd's conical, concrete structure – alien to many a person's idea of what a cathedral building should look like – was completed in less than five years. Sir

Giles Gilbert Scott's Anglican Cathedral – bigger than any other in Britain, fifth largest in the world – was completed in 1978, 74 years after the foundation stone was laid.

Maritime Fortunes

In the last 20 years Liverpool's maritime fortunes have suffered a decline, exacerbated by our entry into the Common Market which favours the east-coast ports. Air travel put paid to those great Atlantic liners which sailed with such grace and style into Liverpool for so many years and made the Pier Head such an exciting place. The strictly functional container ships do not rouse the emotions in quite the same way and, in any case, they nip into and out of the docks in Bootle nearer the mouth of the Mersey estuary so that the water where the river is widest, between the Pier Head and Birkenhead and Wallasey, is often as devoid of shipping as the Arctic Ocean save for the valiant criss-crossing ferry-boats keeping up a service begun 800 years ago. But a trip on the Mersey ferry is still exciting and provides the best possible view of that fine trinity of buildings which together constitute one of the world's most famous waterfronts – the Royal Liver with its famous Liver Birds, Cunard Building, inspired by a Roman palace (but no longer the home of Cunard), and the Port of Liverpool Building incorporating domes from a design originally submitted for the Anglican cathedral competition.

Advent of Railways

In the rest of the county, history, generally speaking, is comparatively recent. Elegant Southport dates only from early years of the 19th century when a small hotel was established there to cater for the new-fangled craze for sea-bathing and it only grew into a sizeable town after the railways came, as did all the other desirable residential areas along the foreshore between it and Bootle. Bootle itself was also a sea-bathing resort and a rural dormitory for the Liverpool gentry at the same time and only grew with the advent of steam propulsion for ships and the building of the northern line of docks.

The Wirral Peninsula, for the main part, was inhabited by fishermen and farmers until the ferry-boats became steam-driven, so providing a regular, reliable service which allowed the better-off to move over the river from Liverpool and 'commute'. The coming of the railways put the area within reach of all and the motorcar age caused the building of *two* Mersey road tunnels – like the under-river rail tunnel of 1886, all engineering marvels of their time.

St Helens owes its origins to its situation in the Lancashire coalfield and its best-known product to the fact that there was also on hand an abundant supply of the right kind of sand for glass-making.

Kirkby and Knowsley are of this generation. Both tiny villages before the outbreak of World War II, they owe their existence today to the postwar planners' notion that people born and brought up in the inner cities which had been bombed or otherwise fallen into decay would be better off living in the countryside beyond the boundaries. Whether they are has been a matter of great debate ever since.

What else is there to say about Merseyside that is not universally known? Its particular sense of humour which has turned up so many famous comedians is as legendary as the exploits of its footballers. As a cultural centre it is second to none. The Royal Liverpool Philharmonic Society is one of Europe's oldest and its famous orchestra – spoken of everywhere as 'the Phil' – has an international reputation, while the city boasts two famous repertory theatres which have nurtured many a star name. I could go on and on. As a county, Merseyside may not be all that big, but like a Christmas hamper, it is packed with good things.

GAZETTEER

Aintree   8F3

6m N of **Liverpool**, the site of the Grand National steeplechase. The course is 4m 856yd and includes 30 jumps. Although frequently threatened in recent years for housing developments, the famous course has so far been preserved for horse racing.

Billinge   8G3

Billinge Beacon, 18th-c landmark, 589ft above sea level, provides extensive views.

Bidston   8F2

Church Farm (with 13 floor levels giving an irregular pattern to its mullioned windows), The Lilacs and Yew Tree Farm are all 17th-c. Stone Farm was once the Ring o' Bells inn whose last landlord, Simon Croft, is the subject of the song, 'Simon the Cellarer'. Bidston Hall (16th–17th-c), former seat of the Earls of Derby, was restored in the 1960s. Bidston Hill has a late 18th-c (restored) windmill, a disused lighthouse (rebuilt 1972–3), an Observatory (1866) – now the Institute of Oceanographic Science's researching tides and making tidal predictions for world's major ports – and the rebuilt 'Tam O' Shanter Cottage' (original c.16th c) is a field study centre.

Birkenhead   8F2

Birkenhead Priory was founded about AD 1150. A Benedictine prior and 16 monks farmed a large part of N.W. Wirral and provided lodgings and ferry service for travellers. Ferry rights confirmed by Royal charter in 1330 have ensured service ever since. Priory closed at the Dissolution of the monasteries and became ruinous but the Norman chapter house – the oldest place of worship on Merseyside – is still in use for Sunday morning services. The town grew rapidly following establishment of a shipyard by William Laird and the steam ferry service. The shipbuilding yards of Cammell Laird's have built many famous vessels including aircraft carriers, battleships, nuclear submarines and transatlantic liners. Hamilton Square (1826–46) rates as one of the finest squares in Europe. The Williamson Art Gallery and Museum houses watercolours, the Knowles Boney Collection of Liverpool and other porcelain. Birkenhead Park, 180 acres in area – Britain's first municipal park and a model for Central Park, New York – has an impressive Grand Entrance and was laid out by Sir Joseph Paxton in 1843–7. Birkenhead had Europe's first tram service, using horse-drawn trams, in 1860.

Bootle   8F3
Most of the Port of **Liverpool**'s docks are located here. Much bombed during World War II, the town centre has been rebuilt as an extensive office complex. The Royal Seaforth Dock (1973) is one of the world's largest. Bootle Museum and Art Gallery is a small museum noted for its collection of English pottery and porcelain. Open daily.

Bromborough Pool   8F2
Model industrial village (1853–1910) built for the employees of Price's Patent Candle Company (now Unichema Chemicals Ltd) predating by more than 30 years the more famous **Port Sunlight**.

Croxteth Hall   8G2
5m NE of **Liverpool** city centre. Former seat of the Molyneux family, Earls of Sefton, set in 500-acre estate developed by the present owners, Merseyside County Council, as a country park. Victorian walled garden, farmyard with rare breeds, miniature railway. Open April–Sept.

Formby   8F3
Extensive sandhills to the W are NT. 18th-c church. Fine golf-course. 1½ E is *Altcar* (Lancs) with its large rifle range where in 1860 Colonel Adam Stuart Gladstone, a cousin of the Prime Minister, founded the National Rifle Association.

Hoylake   8F2
Residential and seaside resort containing the famous links of the Royal Liverpool Golf Club. Hilbre group of islands, once known as a telegraph station in the Dee estuary, famous among ornithologists, can be reached on foot at certain states of the tide. (Landing permit required from local authority offices, Riversdale Road, West Kirby.)

Knowsley   8G3
The Stanley family, the Earls of Derby, have occupied their Knowsley estates since the 14th c. Knowsley Hall (c.1500 but much altered over the years) is not now used as a residence. Merseyside Police occupy most of it; the rest is used only on rare formal occasions. The Earl lives in a modern, less grandiose house near by. At the *Prescot* end of the estate is the 360-acre Knowsley Safari Park, open Easter–end Sept.

Liverpool**   8F2
Although shipping trade has declined the city has many fine buildings and, generally speaking, the best hail from Liverpool's heyday in the 19th c. St George's Hall (1841–56), which has been described as 'the finest neo-classical building in Europe', with the famous Walker Art Gallery (1874–7) housing paintings and exhibitions from the Gothic to Pop Art, Sessions House (1882–4), Picton Reading Room (1875–9)

Liverpool's Royal Liver building has towers 295 feet high topped by the mythical Liver birds

and William Brown Library and Museum (1857–60), make a remarkably impressive group of buildings devoted to the pursuit of learning and the law. There is also the Sudley Art Gallery where English paintings collected by Liverpool merchant George Holt are shown in his own house. Liverpool Town Hall was reconstructed by James Wyatt and has one of the finest civic suites in the country. The Council chambers and Lord Mayor's Parlour are open to the public for two weeks every year (usually August). The Bluecoat Chambers are also particularly fine. Formerly Bluecoat School (1717–1906) now studios, galleries, offices mainly devoted to the arts. Queen Anne building set round three sides of attractive cobbled forecourt, garden to the rear. Also outstanding is the world-famous waterfront at the Pier Head with the Royal Liver Building (1910, topped with the largest clock in Britain and the legendary Liver birds), Cunard Building (1915) and the Port of Liverpool Building (1907). The Anglican Cathedral, designed by architect Sir Giles Gilbert Scott (largest in Britain, fifth in the world), was completed in 1978 after 74 years' building, the foundation stone having been laid by Edward VII. Linked to it by Hope Street is the Roman Catholic Metropolitan Cathedral of Christ the King on Mount Pleasant, a circular, glass and concrete cathedral designed by Sir Frederick Gibberd on a crypt of brick vaults previously designed by Sir Edwin Lutyens; using modern methods and materials it was built within five years and consecrated in 1976. The University of Liverpool, in the city centre – the original building on Brownlow Hill gave rise to the expression 'red-brick university' – was established in 1881 and has expanded greatly in the postwar years. Three tunnels run under the River Mersey – the Mersey Railway tunnel opened in 1886, the first road tunnel (the longest in the UK) between Liverpool and **Birkenhead** in 1934 and a second twin-tube tunnel between Liverpool and **Wallasey** opened in 1971. At the Pier Head is the Merseyside Maritime Museum. Open April–Nov. The Merseyside County Museum includes displays on land transport, Liverpool history, archeology etc., a space gallery and planetarium. Open daily. The sound of the Beatles is recaptured in Beatle City, with museums and exhibitions of Beatles' *memorabilia*, their instruments, clothes and tours.

Liverpool Botanic Gardens are at Calderstones Park/ Harthill Estate 4m S of the city centre. Largest and most comprehensive collection of plants in the North. 100 acres includes 1½ acres of glasshouses with tropical plants, ferns and the largest collection of orchids in the country.

Lydiate 8F3
The Scotch Piper Inn (*c*.1320) is built round the base of a tree. Near by are the ruins of Lydiate Abbey (15th-c).

Maghull 8F3
Frank Hornby, inventor of 'Meccano' and Hornby model trains, lived here and is buried in the churchyard.

Ness Gardens 8F2
1m S of *Neston*, Wirral. University of Liverpool Botanic Gardens. 60 acres of sweeping lawns, flower beds, specimen trees and shrubs, water gardens, heather and terrace gardens, rose collection in a superb setting affording views across the Dee estuary to N. Wales. Visitor centre.

New Brighton 8F2
Some of the villas built by James Atherton in the 1830s as part of his plan for a fashionable watering-place still remain in Wellington Road and Montpellier Crescent. Fort Perch Rock (1826–9) was built to guard the Mersey approaches, open to the public April–Oct. Perch Rock Lighthouse (1827–30) is no longer in use. There is an all-purpose entertainments centre called New Palace Amusement Park.

Port Sunlight★ 8F2
Famous garden city of 1st Viscount Leverhulme for the employees of his adjacent soap works. Highly regarded Lady Lever Art Gallery (1914–22) has very fine collection of furniture, paintings and *objets d'art* mostly collected by Leverhulme himself. Especially fine collection of Wedgwood ware. Impressive village war memorial by Sir W. Goscombe John (1919–21). Information and display centre in Greendale Road. The whole village of 130 acres is 'listed'.

Raby 8F2
The thatched Wheatsheaf Inn dates from 1611.

Rainhill 8G2
Famous for the Rainhill Trials of 1829 on the world's first passenger railway line when Stephenson's 'Rocket' proved an easy winner, and for its 'skew' bridge, believed to be the first ever built.

St Helens 8G2
The ruined Windleshaw Abbey near the East Lancashire Road was built in 1423 as a chantry chapel. The Sankey Navigation from St Helens to **Warrington** (completed in 1762) was Britain's first artificial waterway. The head office of Pilkington's glassworks designed by Maxwell Fry (1964) ranks among the finest industrial buildings in Europe. Adjacent is the Pilkington Glass Museum which records the history of glassmaking from Phoenician times to the present. Open daily.

Sefton 8F3
The parish church of St Helen, dating from early 16th c, has an impressively rich interior with handsome screens, a canopied pulpit and carved oak pews among its many impressive features. Memorial to John Sadler who invented the art of printing from engraved copper plates.

Southport★ 8F3
A beautiful resort by the Irish Sea with a great expanse of sand and tree-shaded streets, the chief of which, Lord Street, with gardens, broad pavements, fashionable shops, is regarded as one of the finest thoroughfares in the world. Southport has the largest artificial boating lake in the country. It was the earliest garden city in the country and is famous for its annual flower show – the Chelsea of the North – and the Royal Birkdale Golf Course which frequently stages the British Open Championship. In Rotten Row, alongside Victoria Park (site of the famous flower show in August every year), is a ½m long herbaceous border, at its best May–Sept. Botanic Gardens at Churchtown. There is also a 2-acre model village, containing perfect copies of houses, trains and miniature shrubs and an amusement park, Pleasureland. The Atkinson Art Gallery has a collection of British art of the 18th, 19th and 20th c, oils, watercolours, sculptures, contemporary prints, and old English glass.

Speke Hall 8G2
On the edge of **Liverpool** Airport, this ancestral home (NT) of the Norris family is one of the finest black-and-white, half-timbered houses in the country. Fully furnished in the style of four centuries, famous for its priestholes, it has spacious grounds. Open daily.

Sudley 8G2
Mossley Hill Road, Aigburth, 4m S of **Liverpool** city centre. Early 19th-c house and grounds, former home of George Holt, founder of Lamport and Holt shipping line, bequeathed to City of Liverpool by his daughter, along with comprehensive collection of paintings, including works by Turner, Gainsborough, Reynolds and Romney.

Thornton Hough 8F2
One-time country village archetypally rebuilt by Joseph Hirst, retired Yorkshire woollen manufacturer, and (for the most part) the 1st Viscount Leverhulme, with large village green, black-and-white cottages and a smithy beneath a spreading chestnut tree.

Wallasey 8F2
Originally a number of separate villages strung out along the Mersey. With the advent of steam ferries and the Mersey railway it developed rapidly as a dormitory for **Liverpool**'s white-collar workers. Impressive Town Hall (1914–20) is on the promenade which stretches for 5m from Seacombe Ferry to Harrison Drive, **New Brighton**.

GREATER MANCHESTER

AN INTRODUCTION BY
ALAN BRACK

I suppose that, in devising this new county, the Local Boundaries Commission genuinely believed that they were doing no more than giving expression to what had become a general habit. Politicians, bureaucrats, commentators and 'the media' had talked for years about 'Greater Manchester' as a convenient way of referring to this most densely populated area in Europe. But exactly what that implied depended on who was using the term and in what circumstances. Most people, if asked, would have unhesitatingly said that it included places like Salford and Stretford and Sale, Eccles and Swinton, and Ashton-under-Lyne and Oldham and Rochdale, and sundry smaller urban areas round the city's rim. Few would have said that it included such bedrock Lancashire towns as Bolton, Bury, Wigan and Leigh. And yet, when the Boundaries Commission had finished their work, it was as though the City of Manchester had been taken up to a great height and dropped so that it landed like a huge blob of ice cream on a hot pavement and spread as it melted to cover an area nearly 15 times its size. Places like Ramsbottom, Turton and Tottington on the edge of the moors, and Wardle and Littleborough at the foot of the Pennines, not to mention little Marple in the valley of the Goyt and Lowry's Mottram-in-Longdendale, both deep-rooted in Cheshire, found themselves under the same gargantuan umbrella as Ancoats and Ardwick, Moss Side and Miles Platting. *That*, said the Boundaries Commission, is Greater Manchester. An area of 500 square miles with a population of $2\frac{3}{4}$ million.

Not surprisingly, the subsequent mass marriage in April 1974 was something of a shotgun affair. Many of these old character-full towns did not feel they had all that much in common with Manchester or Mancunians. They had long enjoyed a splendid independence and it suited them. Manchester was the place where some of them went to work or for a day's shopping, the theatre or a football match — nothing more. In the case of Bury, Rochdale, Oldham and Stockport there was some boundary sharing with the big city but Wigan and Bolton had Salford in between as a sort of buffer state and, as all Salfordians will tell you, Salford is a city in its own right, with its own university and the River Irwell in between. The areas to the south, round Stockport and Sale, and Altrincham, Bowdon and Sale, were deeply entrenched in the lush pastures of Cheshire but they relied to a greater extent upon Manchester for a living and few would dispute that over the years they had increasingly become suburbs of the city.

Common Thread
For all that, there is a common thread which tied this big municipal family together for many years – a thread of cotton. When cotton was king, Manchester was its capital and all these towns were textile towns. King Cotton's palace, the Royal Exchange in Cross Street, was once the greatest cotton market in the world and the city was known as 'Cottonopolis'.

What happened to the cotton industry is too recent a story to need retelling here. Many a mill has been demolished and scores of chimneys have been felled like diseased elms. The old cotton towns have diversified as best they can into a wide variety of other industries and, in many cases, the best of the old mill buildings have been adapted to meet the new needs.

It was from these towns, too, that banner-carrying workers in their thousands marched to Manchester in August 1819, to St Peter's Field, to hear local leaders address them on the subject of Parliamentary reform. Official misjudgment turned what was intended to be a peaceful demonstration into a disaster. The crowd, charged without good cause by a contingent of half-trained, sabre-wielding soldiery, panicked. In the ensuing mêlée a dozen died and hundreds were injured. So the former textile towns which now make up Great Manchester are also joined by the memory of 'Peterloo'.

A couple of decades later, the tie was further strengthened by the activities of the Anti-Corn Law League and the campaigning speeches of Richard Cobden and John Bright in the Free Trade Hall, built on the site of 'Peterloo'

Music and Theatre
The Free Trade Hall (badly damaged by wartime bombing and largely rebuilt) is today still used for

meetings and functions of all kinds but has become best known as the home of Manchester's world-famous Hallé Orchestra while – who would ever have thought it? – the Royal Exchange has had a curious, tubular-framed, theatre-in-the-round built on its main floor, looking like a spacecraft come to rest. But it is highly successful and regularly attracts productions and performers of the highest calibre.

Manchester itself, of course, provides entertainment of all kinds in boundless variety, sport in profusion, and endless opportunities for the pursuit of all things cultural. In the outer districts it is often left to the enthusiastic amateur to provide the entertainment although the Octagon Theatre in Bolton and the Oldham Coliseum are established centres for professional productions. But the amateurs have for a very long time reached a professional level of competence in one sphere – brass bands. Besses o' th' Barn, Fairey's, Wingate's, Mirrlee's, CWS Manchester and others have blown themselves into musical history. It is a form of music-making which seems so evocative of the life and times of this part of the world. Amateur orchestras, choral societies and light operatic societies abound but the authentic sound of the northwest is the sound of brass. It has lifted the spirit in hard times, and been heard in defiance, in sorrow and in celebration.

Environment

Environmentally, this new metropolitan county may not be able to boast the scenic splendours of its neighbours; the industrial revolution took a great toll of areas of natural beauty although, it must be said, in many places great efforts have been made to remove all traces of man's despoiling years and turn the blighted acres into recreation grounds and country parks. The city, and all the component towns, have many splendid municipal parks and open spaces and to the north and the east there are attractive little villages nestling at the foot of the hills or at the gateway to the moors. To the south and west there is some very attractive countryside and, since Manchester is at the centre of the most comprehensive network of motorways and railways in the land, the peace and quiet of the pastoral scene is never more than just a few miles up or down the road.

GAZETTEER

Ashton-under-Lyne   9I3
Fine 15th-c glass in the church pictures Sir John Ashton and his family, and five other beautiful windows give the history of St Helena and her discovery of the True Cross. Park Bridge Museum, in part of an old Victorian stable block, traces the industrial, natural and social history of the Medlock Valley.

Blackstone Edge   9I3
Hill-ridge crossed by remarkable (some say Roman) road leading into Yorkshire, with pavement and curbstone and a shallow groove running down the centre, the exact purpose of which is not known. Conjectured to have been made for brake or guide attached to vehicles descending the slope. Fine views from the summit (1,553ft).

Bolton   9H3
Birthplace of Samuel Compton who invented the spinning-mule in 1779 while living in rooms in the decayed Hall i' th' Wood. The half-timbered house, built in 1483 with later additions, was eventually rescued and restored by another famous son of Bolton, the 1st Viscount Leverhulme, who gave it to Bolton Corporation in 1902. Refurnished in true period fashion as a museum. The Bolton Steam Museum exhibits four working examples of Victorian engineering and other displays. The Textile Machinery Museum houses Hargreaves's spinning-jenny and others. Behind the impressive Town Hall (1873) is the non-profit-making Octagon Theatre (1967), designed with a stage capable of being used in any of three ways: open, thrust, or in-the-round. The British Marathon takes place in Bolton every year.

Bramhall   9H2
Bramall Hall (note the spelling!) is one of the country's finest examples of 16th-c, black-and-white, half-timbered architecture in a magnificent parkland setting. Built in 1350 with Elizabethan additions and home of the Davenports for nearly 500 years. Open mornings for schools and organized parties, afternoons for guided tours.

Bromley Cross   9H3
On the N side of **Bolton**, the derelict farm buildings of 18th-c Orellfold Farm have been cleverly transformed into a mock 18th-c village called 'The Last Drop', with cottages, traditional pub, workshops, restaurant, residential hotel and conference facilities. 'Olde Englishe' outside but all mod. con. within. Also, annual craft fair, Sunday morning antique 'flea' market.

Bury   9H3
Birthplace of Sir Robert Peel (1788–1850), twice Prime Minister, who, when Home Secretary, founded the modern police force. His bronze statue is in the Market Place. Kay Gardens has a statue of another son of Bury, John Kay, who invented the fly-shuttle. There is a transport museum and Fusiliers' Museum. The art gallery and museum contains the Wrigley Collection of 19th-c paintings, watercolours and engravings.

Denton   9H3
Parts of this unusual black-and-white church are at least 400 years old.

Dunham Massey Hall   9H2
3m SW of *Altrincham*. 18th-c Dunham Massey Hall (NT), former seat of the Earls of Stamford, descendants of Lady Jane Grey, contains much 18th-c furniture, Huguenot silver and series of family portraits. Famous deer park with avenue of beeches reputedly 250 years old. There is a renovated Elizabethan mill still in operation. Open April–Oct.

Foxdenton Hall   **9H3**
At *Chadderton*, 4m NE of **Manchester** city centre. Late
17th-c brick manor house, former home of the de Traffords.

Heaton Hall   **9H3**
At *Prestwich*, 5m N of **Manchester** city centre. Former
home of the Earls of Wilton; 18th-c, described as 'the finest
neo-classical house in the northwest'. Furniture, paintings,
etc., 18th-c organ, still working. Open April–Sept.

Last Drop Village★ *see* **Bromley Cross**

Manchester★★   **9H3**
The centre of Manchester has changed dramatically in
recent years and there is little left which predates the 19th c
but there are still some old buildings to be seen in the city, in
particular in King Street and St Anne's Square, and in
Shambles Square are an old half-timbered pub now restored
and called the Old Wellington and Sinclair's Oyster Bar also

*Manchester: the Town Hall – there are many statues of
historic figures including Gladstone and Sir Charles Hallé*

in the square is restored. The Cathedral, now also a brass-
rubbing centre, formerly the parish church, was built
between 1422 and 1520 and Chetham's Hospital and Library
– now a school of music for gifted musicians – was founded
with a bequest of Humphrey Chetham in 1653. Parts of the
building are 13th c and the library is the oldest in Europe
still in use. The library is open to the public; the school can
be visited only with prior permission of the Bursar. The
city's glory is its Gothic Town Hall (1868–77), designed by
Alfred Waterhouse, with its 281ft-high clock tower and bell
chamber with 23 bells. The Great Hall is decorated with 12
vast murals by Ford Madox Brown depicting scenes from the
city's history. The Sculpture Hall contains an exhibition of
the City's silver collection. The Free Trade Hall, the interior
of which was destroyed by wartime bombing, was rebuilt
(1951) retaining the façade and is now the home of the Hallé

Orchestra. John Rylands University Library (1900) contains rare books and manuscripts, including 3,000 books printed before 1501. Peter Mark Roget of *Thesaurus* fame was the first secretary of the Portico Library (1802–6), a private library with more than 40,000 scholarly volumes. The Central Library, adjoining the Town Hall, has a stock of over 800,000 books.

The City Art Gallery (1824–35) was designed by Sir Charles Barry who also designed the **Houses of Parliament**. The Whitworth Gallery is also remarkable for its English watercolours, including many by J. M. W. Turner. In the Royal Exchange (closed in 1968), the original 19th-c cotton exchange, a 700-seat theatre-in-the-round has been devised. The Arndale Centre is the largest covered shopping centre in Europe. The Manchester Education Precinct, 3m from city centre, is the site of the University of Manchester Institute of Science and Technology (better known as UMIST), Manchester Polytechnic, The Royal Northern College of Music and the Manchester Business School, with some 20,000 students. Manchester Museum and the Whitworth Art Gallery are part of the university.

In *Castlefield* near by there is an Urban Heritage Park with Roman fort, Air and Space Museum and the Greater Manchester Museum of Science and Industry, situated on the oldest railway station in the world.

1m N of the city centre, the Museum of Transport displays over 50 buses and other vehicles relating to the history of public transport in Greater Manchester.

Monks Hall   9H3

At *Eccles* 6m W of **Manchester** city centre. Owned by the City of **Salford**, this 16th- and 17th-c house is now a small museum. Permanent exhibitions include early engineering machinery and a toy room featuring interesting collections of dolls and games.

Oldham   9H3

The Industrial Revolution made it the most important of the cotton-spinning towns. Most of its important buildings are 19th-c though the town centre has been rebuilt. Tommyfield Market is among the largest open markets in Britain. Open Mon., Fri., Sat. with second-hand market Wed.

Old Parsonage   9H2

At *Didsbury* 5m S of **Manchester**. 19th-c parsonage in the Gothic style, now the Fletcher Moss Art Gallery and Museum featuring art and architecture of the Northwest. Walled gardens with orchid house. Open April–Sept.

Platt Hall   9H2

At *Rusholme* 2m S of **Manchester**. Mansion built in 1764 now houses important collection of English costume from 17th c to, inter alia, Mary Quant. Open each day April–Oct.; rest of year by appointment.

Ramsbottom   9H3

Grant's Tower is a memorial to two Scottish brothers who brought prosperity to the area through their printing works and were great benefactors. Hard-working and of a constantly happy disposition, they were immortalized by Dickens in *Nicholas Nickleby* as the Cheeryble Brothers.

Rochdale   9H3

Well known for its blankets, calicoes and flannels. Birthplace of John Bright MP (1811–89), the Quaker reformer who is buried in the graveyard of the Friends Meeting House, Edwin Waugh, the Lancashire dialect poet, Gracie Fields, the singing star, and, at 31 Toad Lane the Co-operative movement. In 1844, the Rochdale Society of Equitable Pioneers opened a shop here paying a dividend to members. The shop is now a 'Co-op' museum. The impressive Town Hall has a 90ft-long Great Hall with hammerbeam roof and a 35ft-long mural painted by Henry Holiday. 2m E is the Roman road, **Blackstone Edge**.

Salford   9H3

Though separated from **Manchester** by the Irwell the two cities are so closely joined that they appear as one. But Salford is over 750 years old and has its own University (1967) and R.C. Cathedral (1855). Sacred Trinity, the parish church, was founded in 1635 but all except the tower was rebuilt in 1732 with Victorian restorations. The City Art Gallery boasts the largest public collection of L. S. Lowry paintings. In Peel Park there is the public library (the first free municipal library) and museum, the latter containing 'Lark Hill Place', a street of reconstructed houses and shops from the past. Salford Museum of Mining has a replica of a coal mine.

Stockport   9H2

Until the 1974 boundary changes, this was Cheshire's most populous town. Once the centre of hat manufacturing the trade declined as the wearing of hats declined. There is now a wide variety of industries and a very good shopping centre. The story of Stockport's heritage is told in Bramall Hall (*see* **Bramhall**) and **Lyme Hall and Park** (Cheshire). The parish church (1814) still has its 13-c chancel. A viaduct of 26 arches carries the railway through the town over the River Mersey. The undenominational Sunday School in Duke Street, built by public subscription in 1805, is reputed to be the largest and oldest in the world and once boasted 5,000 pupils. There is a War Memorial Art Gallery, and a Municipal Museum in Vernon Park.

Wigan   8G3

Prosperous manufacturing town: plastics, coach-building and canning. The parish church of All Saints is, with the exception of the tower which is original, a faithful reproduction of the medieval church. The remnant of Mab's Cross at Standishgate is associated with the 14th-c legend of Dame Mabel Bradshaigh who, as a penance, walked barefooted once a week for a year from her home in Haigh Hall 2m away. 19th-c *Haigh Hall*, former home of the Earl of Crawford and Balcarres, and its 244-acre estate were bought by Wigan Corporation in 1947. Elizabethan *Winstanley Hall* has been in the possession of the Bankes family for nearly 400 years.

Worsley   9H3

In 1759–61 the 3rd Duke of Bridgewater built a canal to transport coal directly out of his mine to **Manchester**. The canal basin and landing steps (with the water orange-brown from the iron deposits) can be seen and, N of Worsley Road, the tunnel entrance to the mine. Educational trips are available on a traditional narrow boat.

Wythenshawe   9H2

Baguley Hall is a 14th-c timber-framed building, recently restored. Wythenshawe Hall standing in a beautiful park, dates from the 16th c and is half-timbered and restored. Presented to Manchester's Council by Lord and Lady Simon in 1926. The estate previously the seat of the Tatton family for 550 years. 17th-c furniture, paintings, arms and armour, oriental prints. Wythenshawe was laid out in 1931 as a garden city by Manchester City Council. It has two outstanding churches: St Michael's and the William Temple Memorial Church.

LANCASHIRE

AN INTRODUCTION BY
FRANK SINGLETON AND ALAN BRACK

As much as England itself, the Red Rose county provides within its boundaries the most remarkable contrasts – lovely mountains, picturesque villages, industrial towns, rich farmlands, bare moorlands and beautiful rivers. The bewildering variety may, however, be broken down into some broad categories. The industrial and agricultural plain is an extension northwards of the New Red Sandstone of Cheshire. It grows narrower but is discernible around the coast, broadening out again to the north where, meeting the eruption of the limestone, which has come down from the Yorkshire Dales and the Pennines, it contributes to the beautiful and contrasting scenery around the great sweep of Morecambe Bay.

Rock and Soil

Scenery and, to some extent, buildings are always conditioned by the nature of the crust of the earth beneath. The plain to the west of a line drawn from Lancaster to Skelmersdale is mainly agricultural, with the peaty mosslands given over to market gardens whose owners are now as likely to sell most of their produce to the passing motorist as to the wholesale market. Further south, towards Ormskirk, there are farms operating on a much larger scale growing crops against the stop-watch for the food-processing factories. Between the Ribble and the Lune, and behind Blackpool, the plain is known as the Fylde. Vast acres of glass soak up the sun's warmth and they grow food for the holidaymakers of Lytham St Annes and Blackpool and for Preston market.

To the east of this line is a moorland district with more rain, poor soil and, particularly south of the Ribble, manufacturers. Here are the great industrial towns like Preston, Blackburn, Accrington and Burnley where once King Cotton reigned supreme – today they manufacture everything and anything.

Architecture

Lancashire has not a good record for caring for its old buildings. It avails not to bewail what has gone. Much still remains. Throughout the northern area peel towers, and the general architecture of fortified houses, farms and even churches are constant reminders of the persistence after the Norman settlement of the marauding Scot. The grim stone castles kept watch through Plantagenet and feudal times. Some, like Clitheroe, are romantic ruins. Lancaster Castle still lives, dominating the town, an imposing setting for the Crown Court and the pageantry of law. With the Renaissance came fine houses such as Hoghton Tower and many smaller houses.

The Gothic revival and the Victorian church-building era left their mark. Pugin, Street, Waterhouse, and later, Sir Ninian Comper and Sir Giles Scott, did their best and their worst. Gothic, Gothic, everywhere and in the grand house at Scarisbrick the maddest fantasia of all.

Food

The human qualities which make most southerners pronounce enthusiastically for the friendliness of the people, are found everywhere. The gourmet, however, will do best who can rid himself of prejudice in the matter of food. The traditional Lancashire offerings live on. It has long been a land of cakes. Nelson and Eccles cram them with currants. From near Preston comes an over-sweet but popular confection, Goosnargh cake. From Bury come Simnel cakes and Bury puddings — delicious kidney-shaped concoctions that can vie with any haggis for flavour, and are utterly superior to the fatless hoops of insipid filling known in the south as 'black puddings'.

There is a great consumption, too, of what, during World War II, Government off-puttingly referred to as 'edible offals'. Tripe here is already cooked, not, as in the south, requiring several hours' preparation. Cowheels, lambs' trotters, pigs' feet and chitterlings do not reach the table of the genteel, except the more discriminating. To sample them you should ask for them in France where they are offered as delicacies. Those who shrink from the delicious nutrition of a pig's nose will enjoy it as a *museau* in a dish of *hors d'oeuvres* in Paris. Greatest of all is a well-made Lancashire hot-pot. Lancashire cheese is good and best of all cooking cheeses. Morecambe Bay shrimps are famous.

GAZETTEER

Altcar *see* **Formby**, Merseyside

Blackburn 9H4
Birthplace of James Hargreaves (1745), inventor of the spinning jenny. With the decline in textile manufacture there is now a wide variety of modern manufacturing industries. The Lewis Taylor Textile Museum tells the story of the industry by means of working models. In 1926 the parish church of St Mary the Virgin was elevated to cathedral status. Blackburn Cathedral is the only Anglican cathedral in Lancashire.

Blackpool 8F4
Britain's most popular holiday resort attracts up to 6 million visitors each year. Every form of entertainment is provided in a season extended into October with its famous illuminations. Extensive beaches, 7m promenade with electric tramway service, zoo park, three piers and the famous 518ft-high Blackpool Tower, which includes the most beautiful permanent circus building in Europe. To the S *Lytham St Anne's* is a more genteel neighbour.

Bleasdale 8G4
Remarkable circle of wooden posts similar to Woodhenge, which preceded **Stonehenge** (Wilts) in antiquity. When exposure to air threatened them with disintegration, they were removed to the Harris Museum in **Preston** and concrete posts substituted. Fascinating site.

Burnley 9H4
Former cotton-manufacturing town now with diversified industries. The ancestral fortified home of the Towneley family, Towneley Hall, dates from 14th c with later additions, and combines beauty of house and grounds of 210 acres (a public park) with a museum of local crafts and industries and art gallery. It is now owned by the Borough of Burnley. Edmund Spenser lived at *Hurstwood*, 3¼m N.

Carnforth 8G5
Steam Town is a railway museum containing a large collection of railway locomotives from Britain (including the *Flying Scotsman*), France and Germany, many of which have been restored to full working order and frequently haul special excursion trains on main British Rail lines. Open daily. *Leighton Hall*, 3m N, is a beautifully-situated 18th-c house and former home of the Gillow family. Gillow furniture, paintings, antique 12ft-long American doll's house. Flying eagles display in the grounds. Open May–Sept.

Chorley 8G3
Industrialized market town and part of the Central Lancashire New Town. Also birthplace of Henry Tate in 1819. He founded a sugar empire and endowed the **Tate Gallery** in London. Miles Standish (1584–1656) of *Mayflower* fame was born at Duxbury Hall, 1½m S, now demolished. *Astley Hall*, ¾m NW, an Elizabethan mansion reconstructed in 1666, contains fine pottery, furniture, tapestries and pictures. Grounds are a public park. Open daily.

Clitheroe 9H4
The castle, ancient stronghold of the de Laceys, is perched high on a limestone crag and dominates the town. It witnessed bitter fighting in the Civil War. Little remains but the Norman keep, the smallest in England. The Castle

Museum has an important collection of fossils. Superb views of Ribble Valley. 7m N is *Sawley Abbey* (AM), near *Gisburn*. A Cistercian abbey founded in 1147. It has a long choir and tiny nave.

Colne 9H4
At 2 Sun Street is the British in India Museum displaying photographs, coins, model railways, and dioramas – all connected with the British rule in India. Open May–Sept. weekends.

Downham 9H4
Picturesque estate village belonging to the Assheton family who have lived at Downham Hall continuously from 1559.

Fleetwood 8F4
Fishing port and seaside resort at the mouth of the Wyre. It was developed in the 19th c by Sir Peter Fleetwood-Hesketh, founder of Rossall School, whose buildings overlook Morecambe Bay 2m S.

Gawthorpe Hall 9H4
Off the A671 near *Padiham* is the 17th-c ancestral home of the Shuttleworth family, restored in 1850s (NT). Remarkable collection of lace and embroidery and good early European furniture. Open mid-March–Oct. on set days. Gawthorpe is now part of a College of Further Education.

Heysham 8F5
Linked with **Morecambe** as a popular holiday resort. Originally a very old village Heysham Harbour is now a passenger port for Ireland and the Isle of Man. St Patrick's Chapel, a ruined Celtic church, stands on a cliff top. Near the later (12th–14th-c) church there is a good example of a Viking hogback tombstone and the shaft of a 9th-c cross. Heysham Head Entertainments Centre is a major attraction with a zoo, go-kart racing, marineland, bird house etc.

Hoghton Tower 8G4
5m E of **Preston**. Hill-top residence of the de Hoghton family since 12th c where it is said James I 'knighted' the loin of beef and made it 'sirloin' in 1617. Open Easter–end Oct. on Sun.

Lancaster* 8G5
The place that has given its name to a dynasty, an energetic county and a royal duchy remains the county town although **Preston** is the administrative capital. In 1322 Robert Bruce burned the castle and town to the ground, but both were rebuilt by John of Gaunt and enlarged and restored by Elizabeth I as a defence against the Spanish Armada. John of Gaunt's Gateway Tower is one of the finest in England. The castle is partly used as a Crown Court and a prison but the Shire Hall with its collection of coats of arms from the 12th c may be visited (open Easter–end Sept.). The 15th-c church of St Mary has beautiful choir stalls that originated in Cockersand Abbey. The Old Town Hall (18th-c) now houses the City Museum of Local Antiquities and the Museum of King's Own Royal Regiment. The old Custom House (1764) was built by Robert Gillow and the University of Lancaster (founded 1964) on the southern edge of the town

Blackpool Tower, at 518 feet high, forms the spectacular centrepiece of the promenade's autumn illuminations

was built on the site of the original Waring & Gillow furniture factory. Dominating the southern approaches, like a scaled-down Taj Mahal, is the Ashton Memorial in Williamson Park. Judges' Lodgings, a 17th-c town house, used by assize judges 1826–1975, containing Gillow and Town House Museum and the Museum of Childhood (over 1,000 dolls) (open summer months). Furniture by local-born Gillow and others in period settings. Open Easter–end Sept. 2m SE the *Hornsea Pottery Leisure Centre* has guided tours and is open daily.

Martin Mere 8G3
Just outside *Burscough*, this reserve of the Wildfowl Trust covers 360 acres of which 40 acres are given over to wildfowl gardens with captive birds, the rest left for the flocks of migratory birds which may be viewed from hides. Open to the public throughout the year but best seen in the winter months.

Morecambe 8G5
Holiday resort on Morecambe Bay, the town originated the idea of autumn illuminations as a means of extending the holiday season, the first 'lights' being made from candles in glass jars. Any blown out by the breeze were speedily re-lit by a watchful team of fleet-footed boys. Famous fairground, marineland and a leisure centre. *See also* **Heysham**.

Ormskirk 8G3
Ancient and busy market. Famous for Ormskirk Gingerbread and its parish church (*c*.13th- or 14th-c). *See also* **Rufford Old Hall**.

Pendle Hill 9H4
At 1,831ft high, it has been the source of much witchcraft lore which formed the background for, *inter alia*, Harrison Ainsworth's *The Lancashire Witches*. Good views★.

Preston 8G4
Seat of Lancashire County Council. One of the oldest towns in the country with its first Royal Charter granted by Henry II in 1179 who authorized holding of the famous Guild Merchant once every 20 years (hence the phrase 'once every Preston Guild' meaning at very long intervals). Last held in 1972. Birthplace of Sir Richard Arkwright (1732–92), inventor of the spinning-frame and other mechanical aids which greatly speeded up cotton manufacturing process. Eggrolling festival (thought to be of pagan origin) takes place on the slopes of Avenham Park every Easter Mon. The Harris Public Library, Art Gallery and Museum is outstanding, both architecturally and for their contents (*see* **Bleasdale**). The town centre has undergone extensive redevelopment since World War II. The Guildhall (1972) is impressive and the modern bus station is Europe's largest. *See also* **Hoghton Tower**.

Rawtenstall 9H4
Weaver's cottage at Fall Barn Fold is one of the few remaining examples of a purpose-built 18th-c loom shop. Open at weekends.

Ribchester 8G4
Picturesque old village where the Romans had an important fort, Bremetannacum. One of the largest in the country, covering nearly 6 acres, it is now owned by the NT. Part of the fort has been exposed to reveal foundations of two granaries near the church and the rectory. Museum of excavated Roman antiquities open throughout the year. Early English church. Several 17th-c and 18th-c houses and a 17th-c bridge.

Rivington 8G3
Rivington Pike (1,190ft) and beautiful 400-acre Lever Park, with the 18-c Rivington Hall, barn and replica castle.

Rufford Old Hall★ 8G3
7m N of **Ormskirk**. Former seat of the Hesketh family for 400 years it is one of the finest medieval half-timbered houses (NT) in the country. The banqueting hall has a very rare 15th-c movable screen and a hammer-beam roof. The Hall also houses the Philip Ashcroft Folk Museum. Open April–end Sept.

Samlesbury 8G4
The Higher Hall (2m outside village) which succeeded a fortified mansion destroyed by the Scots after Bannockburn, dates from 15th and 16th c with the west wing dating from 1835. Once owned by the family of Blessed John Southworth (1592–1654), the Jesuit martyr. Open all year.

Sawley Abbey *see* **Clitheroe**

Scarisbrick Hall 8G3
3m SE of **Southport** (Merseyside). The Hall, built by August Pugin and his son, is an excellent example of Victorian taste. It is now a private school not open to the public.

Stonyhurst College 8G4
Famous Roman Catholic public school in a 2,000-acre estate. Imposing buildings (containing library with many rare books and manuscripts) are partly Elizabethan. Grounds are open to the public. Tour of the college only on prior written application to the secretary.

Tunstall 8G5
Riverside village which became the Brocklebridge of Charlotte Brontë's *Jane Eyre*. Here, in real life, the sisters walked to the church from the Clergy Daughters' School (Lowood in the book) which they attended at *Cowan Bridge* 2m away.

Turton 9H3
A 15th-c pele tower. The church has a library of 52 chained books. The Ashworth Museum is in a 15th-c tower.

Whalley 9H4
The 14th-c gateway, part of the chapter house, kitchen and refectory are all that remain of a once-famous Cistercian abbey (AM) founded 700 years ago, though foundations and ground plan can be seen. Parish church, partly Norman though mainly 13th-c, contains impressive carved woodwork and a rare Hepplewhite altar table. There are three Saxon crosses in the churchyard. First Lancs. v. Yorks. cricket match was played at Whalley cricket ground.

Wycoller 9H4
Picturesque village alongside a stream crossed by several quaint and ancient bridges, one of them a 13th-c pack-horse bridge. Ruined Wycoller Hall is the Ferndean Manor of Charlotte Brontë's *Jane Eyre*.

WEST YORKSHIRE AND SOUTH YORKSHIRE

AN INTRODUCTION BY
PHYLLIS BENTLEY AND ELLEN WILSON

The historic West Riding lost some of its northern beauty spots and was divided into the two counties of West Yorkshire and South Yorkshire in the county boundaries reorganization in 1974. Since then they have formed the most heavily industrialized part of the region and these two counties today contain a surprising diversity of landscape and lack only a sea-coast to complete their variety.

A glance at history shows first invasion and then frequent rebellion. Britons, Romans, Angles, Danes, Normans – the list of invaders is familiar in English history. After the Norman Conquest the North rebelled, and William the Conqueror put the rebellion down with fire and sword; the terrible results appear in Domesday Book (1086) where entry upon entry shows the severe drop in value of lands after the Conquest. The Norman barons built castles – the ruins of Pontefract and Conisbrough still remain – here as elsewhere, but did not penetrate into the wild hilly west. During the Wars of the Roses in the 15th century the local barons were actively engaged on both sides; the Yorkist white rose and the Lancastrian red rose became identified later as the emblems of the two counties. In the Civil War of the 17th century what was the West Riding was divided in opinion; the west was for Parliament, the east for the King, and not only political but religious differences tore the region in half. Later John Wesley (1703–91) preached frequently in the western part of the counties, and the population has remained largely Nonconformist, as the numerous chapels show. The coming of the Industrial Revolution caused riots and even murder on the part of the textile operatives, particularly in Huddersfield and Halifax. Some of the rebellious 'Luddites' were betrayed by one of their number, tried at York Castle and hanged.

There are four great physical facts which have made West and South Yorkshire what they are today: the Pennine Chain; the innumerable streams flowing down eastwards from its heights; a great coalfield; and a deposit of iron ore.

The Pennine Chain is not a long thin ridge of mountains, but a turbulent mass of interlocking hills spreading from the west. As they roll east these hills gradually diminish in height until they sink into the Vale of York, where two minor gravel ridges are to be found.

In the millstone-grit landscape of the Pennines in West and South Yorkshire, the hills show dark, very hard rock covered with moors of purple heather and stretches of bracken and long, rough grass; the streams tumble briskly down, limeless. Here the fields are divided by dry walls, but their stones are less spiky and less elaborately arranged than in the more northerly country. Many large reservoirs feeding neighbouring towns lie high up in these hills, ruffled into waves like mountain tarns. These millstone-grit hills are perhaps bare, bleak and wild but they have a sombre, massive beauty very dear to Yorkshire hearts. Both limestone and millstone-grit hills afford pasture to sheep, but on the millstone hills, with their scantier pasture, the breeding of sheep is no longer the important occupation it has remained on the limestone landscape of North Yorkshire.

Neither county is at present well forested. The Pennine summits are above the tree line, and industrial smoke has bared many hill slopes. Oak and ash were the indigenous trees, to which other deciduous trees (not very tall) and sometimes firs and larches have been added. The flora and fauna differ little from those of other counties, but purple heather and ling, bilberries and white-bolled cotton grass are found on the moors, while the mauve-blue harebell brings its delicate colouring and slender stem to the grass. In the wilder parts curlew with their long pointed beaks and melancholy cry are to be seen and heard by the rivers, the acrobatic peewit loops above the grass, the grouse calls *go-back go-back* on the moors.

Coal, Wool and Steel

A considerable coalfield, fringing the hills, lies beneath the surface of the millstone grit, north to south from Castleford to Sheffield, west to east from Barnsley to Doncaster and on under the North Sea.

A deposit of iron ore, now exhausted, originally lay under the hilly country around Sheffield.

The southern part of the plain of York, once long ago a marsh, is now from the silt of the rivers fertile

High up on Ilkley Moor, southeast of the spa town, are Cow and Calf Rocks. A popular spot for rock climbers

farming country, growing barley and oats and affording ample pasture to milk-cows and cattle.

These physical facts made possible the steel and wool-textile industries.

Sheep and limeless streams provide wool and soft water kind to fabric, both essential features in wool-textile manufacture; tumbling water provides easy water-power; iron provides the material for machinery and steam-engine boilers; coal provides the steam. The wool-textile trade has a well-documented history of at least 600 years, for contemporary tax records show that 974 pieces of woollen cloth were manufactured in 1396 in the West Riding, and from then onwards historical records are abundant. First located chiefly in York, the hand cloth industry presently took great hold in the Pennines, where it supplemented the produce of the infertile land as a livelihood. When water-power, machinery and steam-power were one by one invented, the Pennines had the materials necessary for these close at hand. The area roughly enclosed between Bradford, Leeds, Batley, Huddersfield and Halifax is a major producer of textiles but the historic dependence on the wool trade has given way to diversified industries. The landscape of these industrial towns was once a dramatic if 'satanic' landscape of interlocking hills, forested by

innumerable mill chimneys springing from various levels, with rows of small houses clinging, at times it seemed precariously, to the hillside slopes, and the Pennines looming close around. But today buildings have been cleared and there are smokeless zones.

Combined with neighbouring supplies of coal, some other necessary ingredients and (again) water, the deposit of iron ore led to the great steel industry of Sheffield. The city's history of cutlery-manufacture goes back for at least 600 years. Chaucer in his *Canterbury Tales* (*c.*1387) says of the Miller of Trumpington: 'A Sheffeld thwitel baar he in his hose' – a thwitel or whittle being an ancestor of our small knife. Begun as a domestic industry, Sheffield steel now occupies many huge forges and rolling-mills; the tipping of a molten cauldron and the rolling of the red-hot steel provide superb though alarming spectacles. The Sheffield mark is known worldwide as indicating excellence, and standards are regulated by the Cutlers' Company.

Architecture

A wealth of old parish churches, Norman castles, and fine nobility houses exists. Of special local interest are the yeoman clothiers' houses of the 17th century and the old weavers' cottages with their long row of windows in the 'loom-chamber' in the second storey, which are to be found in numbers in the upland folds of the hills round Halifax and Huddersfield.

Recreations

No county has a more glorious record on the cricket field than Yorkshire, which in the past century has won the county championship 27 times outright, and to this result West and South Yorkshire players have largely contributed. To football also, especially Rugby Union and Rugby League, the area is devoted. The St Leger Race at Doncaster in September is widely known. Pigeon-racing and whippet-racing, especially by miners, are popular sports.

Associated with the recent expansion of tourism is the development of long-distance footpaths, of which the most important is the Calderdale Way, opened in 1978. It follows a 50-mile circle in the southern Pennines, starting at the 17th-century Clay House, Greetland, and taking in scenic valleys, farms and communities around Halifax.

Of intellectual recreations, music is West Yorkshire's prime interest. The many choral societies are justly famed, and Huddersfield's yearly performance of Handel's *Messiah* has gained a nation-wide reputation on radio and television. Musical societies of all kinds flourish, including those for the amateur performance of musical comedies. The brass band is a homelier but very genuine witness to the popular love of music. Leeds, Sheffield and Bradford have outstanding provincial theatres; and Leeds, the most atmospheric music hall surviving in Britain.

Food

Yorkshire pudding, a delicious fluffy batter baked in the oven till it achieves a crisp, light-brown surface, often served before the roast beef it traditionally accompanies and eaten with gravy as a course by itself, is strongly to be recommended, as is the rich, brown treacly parkin. 'High tea', a 'knife and fork' meal which is eaten between five-thirty and six-thirty in the afternoon, usually comprises ham, with every possible variety of bread, scone, teacake, sweet cake, parkin and pastry. Yorkshire women are good providers and expect their guests to make a hearty meal.

Character

The Yorkshire character is robust, shrewd, stubborn, sardonically cheerful though not optimistic, plain-spoken when speaking at all, warm-hearted and extremely independent. Perhaps because of their long history as earners in skilled industries, the people are accustomed to regard themselves as everyone's equal; indeed they think so well of themselves that a stranger has to prove his worth before he is considered an equal. Once he is admitted to friendship, however, he is a friend for life. Tenacity of feeling is preferred to expressiveness, and any affectation of effusiveness or superior manners is despised. A broad humour, laconically uttered, a considerable respect for that formidable and competent housewife the Yorkshirewoman, a slightly excessive interest in 'brass'; and, again – and again – obstinacy: these complete the portrait.

The number of celebrated persons born in this region is so considerable that no account of them can be given here: reference should be made to the appropriate volumes. The three Brontë sisters, of Irish and Cornish parents, are the most famous writers; their home in Haworth near Keighley, now the Brontë Parsonage Museum, should certainly be visited. In the 20th century two strong groups of novelists have given vigorous if rather sardonic pictures of the life of their native counties.

GAZETTEER

Austerfield, South Yorks   9K3

William Bradford, eventual Governor of Plymouth, New England, who kept a log of the *Mayflower* on her 1620 voyage to the New World, lived in the modest yeoman's house, Austerfield Manor, preserved in his memory. *Mayflower* descendants rebuilt the N aisle of the church.

Barnsley, South Yorks   9J3

With its impressive civic buildings and a new town centre it is a centre for the iron and coal industries. 40-acre Locke Park was presented to the town in memory of Joseph Locke, a railway builder apprenticed to George Stephenson. Cannon Hall, now a museum of decorative arts, was built by John Carr. The Cooper Gallery occupies a 17th-c grammar school. A thrice-weekly market is a regional attraction. At *Monk Bretton Priory* (AM) on the outskirts 2m NE, the plan of the ruined Cluniac house is clearly visible. 2½m S is the *Worsbrough Mill Museum* which has two corn mills (one 17th- and the other 19th-c) both in working order in a county council park.

Birstall, West Yorks   9J4

Charlotte Brontë, who came here on visits to her friend Ellen Nussey, describes Elizabethan Oakwell Hall – 'Fieldhead' – in *Shirley*. The house is now restored as a museum in a new country park with crafts centre and other facilities. Open daily.

Bradford, West Yorks   9I4

Historic hub of the worsted trade where the city centre has been brashly rebuilt and surviving Victorian buildings (especially the City Hall) scrubbed to their natural beige. St Peter's Cathedral, mainly of the 14th and 15th c, has good Victorian glass by William Morris. Cartwright Hall, erected as an Art Gallery in 1904 to honour the inventor of the power loom, stands in Lister Park. A museum of domestic and social life fills Bolling Hall which consists of a pele tower, c.1330, with 17th- and 18th-c additions. A redundant spinning mill has been converted into a museum of the worsted industry on Moorside Road, *Eccleshill*. The manager's house is also on view. Also in the city is the National Museum of

Photography, Film and Television – everything from the camera obscura to satellites. All museums open daily except Mon.

Bramham, West Yorks   **9J4**
Bramham Park is a Queen Anne House, partly destroyed by fire in 1828 and restored in 1907 when a horseshoe staircase modelled on the one at the Palace of Fontainebleau was added to the W front. A collection of paintings hangs in splendid rooms. The house was designed and built by the first Lord Bingley and has been home to his descendants since. The stable block and an oratory overlooking the lake were designed by James Paine. The French gardens, with their ingenious use of running water, make this estate unique. Bramham village surrounds a square with limestone cottages and an early 12th-c church.

Conisbrough,★ South Yorks   **9K3**
A magnificent white, stone cylindrical keep (AM) supported by six massive buttresses stands high above the Don, the best castle of its kind in the country. Sir Walter Scott set a scene in *Ivanhoe* here. A park connects the castle to the Priory, now council offices. Elsewhere in the industrial town, St Peter's Church dates from Saxon times.

Doncaster, South Yorks   **9K3**
The town on the site of a Roman station was chartered in 1194 by Richard Coeur de Lion. Roman relics are exhibited in the Museum and Art Gallery. Since the railway arrived in 1848, Doncaster has developed as an industrial focus of the Yorkshire coalfield. Although buildings are mainly modern, with a rebuilt shopping centre, the pretty 1748 Mansion House by James Paine and the 19th-c St George's Church by Sir George Gilbert Scott, its 170ft tower of almost cathedral proportions, recall the past. The St Leger, the last of the year's racing classics and senior to the Derby by four years, is run on Town Moor. The South Yorkshire Industrial Museum occupies Cusworth Hall, nicely set in a country park. *See also* **Conisbrough**.

Guiseley, West Yorks   **9I4**
A pageant to depict the life of the saint is staged in August to celebrate St Oswald's Day, in the grounds of the delightful Elizabethan Rectory. The parents of the talented Brontës were married here.

Halifax, West Yorks   **9I4**
Early industrial town built on the cloth trade and still producing carpets and yarns. The great 18th-c Piece Hall, splendidly restored, is the only cloth hall to be seen now in the Yorkshire textile region. Cottage weavers displayed their woollen 'pieces' in its 315 small rooms off colonnaded galleries around a grassy square. Crafts, antiques and bookshops, a textile museum, art gallery and restaurant fill it now, with open markets twice a week. The Italianate Town Hall is by Sir Charles Barry. Bankfield Museum in the old home of Edward Akroyd, beneficent mill owner, shows textiles and costumes. Shibden Hall, a half-timbered house with later additions, contains period furniture and a folk museum in its outbuildings. St John's Church near the station is mainly 15th- and 16th-c with fine woodwork and Commonwealth glass. The boldest spire tops All Souls, closed for safety, completed by Sir George Gilbert Scott in 1859. To the SW *Hebden Bridge* and *Heptonstall*, within easy reach, are picturesque woollen mill towns and important centres in the Pennines. A visit can take in the NT's beautiful *Hardcastle Crags Valley*. There are many walks and trails including the 50m-long *Calderdale Way*.

Harewood House,★ West Yorks   **9J4**
9m N of **Leeds** at *Harewood*. The Earl of Harewood's seat, standing in a landscape planned by Capability Brown, was begun by John Carr in 1759 and decorated by Robert Adam. In the 1840s Sir Charles Barry added a third storey and pompous terrace. Adam designed much of the furniture (made by Chippendale) to harmonize with the elegant plasterwork and murals executed by such craftsmen and artists as Turner, Rose, Collins, Rebecca, Kauffmann and Zucchi. In the ornate rooms are 18th–19th-c furniture and a rare collection of Sèvres and Chinese porcelain. A Bird Garden is the latest addition. All this is reached through monumental gates in the millstone-grit village with its neat terraces of cottages. Open April–end Sept.; in winter, house closed but Bird Garden open at set times.

Haworth, West Yorks   **9I4**
The old weaving village is a modern literary shrine and a steep main street leads to the bleak Parsonage where the Brontës moved in 1820. Now an evocative museum of the Brontë Society, it contains the sofa upon which Emily died, Charlotte's work-basket just as she left it, and the books, barely an inch square, that the children wrote in secret. Open daily except in Dec. Outside a graveyard slopes to the church. A rear path leads to the moors and 'Brontë Falls'. The steam-powered Worth Valley Railway runs regularly between **Keighley** and *Oxenhope*, with a stop at Haworth.

Hebden Bridge *see* **Halifax**

Holmfirth *see* **Huddersfield**

Huddersfield, West Yorks   **9I3**
Fine worsted, manufactured first in cottages and later in mills, built this Calder Valley town. The centre has been redeveloped, but confident Victorian buildings, including the railway station and town hall, survive. The Tolson Memorial Museum in Ravensknowle Hall exhibits looms and relics of the Luddite riots. 6m S is *Holmfirth*, a tourist centre made famous by TV's 'Last of the Summer Wine' series. Beautiful countryside in the Holme Valley.

Ilkley, West Yorks   **9I4**
A former spa with an elegant shopping centre, it is ideal for touring *Wharfedale* or walking over Ilkley Moor (*see* page 262) seeking traces of Ancient Britons in carved stones and rocks. The 16th-c Manor House, built on foundations of Roman Olicana, is a museum of prehistoric and Roman relics, also displays by regional artists in the art gallery. There are three Saxon crosses in the church which also has a 13th-c S doorway.

Keighley, West Yorks   **9I4**
Cliffe Castle, the town's museum and art gallery, has a display of life in mid-Airedale from the beginning of time until the coming of man. *East Riddlesden Hall*, 1m NE, is a 17th-c manor house (NT) with one of the best medieval tithe barns in the North. House offers fine panelling and plasterwork, furniture, pictures and pewter. Open Easter–end Sept.

Kirkstall Abbey, West Yorks   **9J4**
2m NW of **Leeds**. Founded in 1152 by monks from **Fountains Abbey** – Kirkstall is second only to Fountains for its entirety; see especially chapter house, cloisters and abbot's lodging. Iron forging began here in 1200. The Abbey House Folk Museum is housed in the gatehouse of this Cistercian abbey – it has streets, shops, collections of pottery, costumes, toys and games. Open daily.

Leeds, West Yorks   **9J4**
Once the country's ready-to-wear capital, this manufacturing centre has a noted Classical Revival Town Hall near the City Art Gallery which has added a wing for works of Henry Moore (open daily). The rebuilt shopping centre is largely pedestrianized and keeps its charming covered arcades. The Grand Theatre is an imposing Victorian playhouse. Polytechnic and University cover a hillside with Parkinson Hall at the top. Beyond is *Headingley* cricket ground. Roundhay Park has woodlands, tropical gardens, aquarium, sports facilities etc. Open all year. Another Corporation prize is Edwardian *Lotherton Hall*, 10m E at *Aberford*, noted for Oriental porcelain and exhibitions of costumes from the 18th c to the 1980s. Open all year. In Leeds' NW suburbia, St John's Church, once in the village of Adel, is rich in Norman carving. 6m NW is *Golden Acre Park* on the A660 – 76 acres of gardens, woodland and lake. Open daily. The 'Museum of Leeds Trail' is a 6m-long footpath linking the city centre with over 40 historic sites along the valley of the Aire.

Monk Bretton Priory *see* **Barnsley**

Near Keighley: East Riddlesden Hall has an unusual two-storeyed porch with a circular window of eight lights

Nostell Priory *see* **Wragby**

Otley, West Yorks   **9I4**
The cosy market town where Thomas Chippendale was born in 1718 lies in *Wharfedale* below 900ft Chevin Hill. J. M. W. Turner, frequent visitor to near-by Farnley Hall, painted many views hereabouts. All Saints' Church has a Norman N doorway and 17 fragments of four Anglo-Saxon crosses. Many antique shops. Annual Agricultural Show.

Pontefract, West Yorks   **9J4**
The castle where Richard II was murdered or starved to death in 1400 was 'slighted' in 1649, and nothing remains but ruins on a splendid site. The church of All Saints below the castle is restored. Pontefract cakes are lozenges flavoured with liquorice, a Mediterranean plant which may have been imported by the Romans. In 1760 George Dunhill, a chemist, began making liquorice sweets here.

*Roche Abbey: its beautiful setting was enhanced by
Capability Brown who landscaped the grounds near by*

Roche Abbey, South Yorks   9K2
8m E of **Rotherham**. 12th-c Cistercian ruins (AM) in a
lovely valley. Excellent gatehouse and transept walls reaching
to nearly full height of the abbey. Open April–Sept.

Rotherham, South Yorks   9J2/3
Coal and iron town possessing a fine Perpendicular-style
church with a crocketed spire. The chantry is built into the
15th-c bridge over the Don. Roman relics and Rockingham
china are in Clifton House Museum. 8m E is **Roche Abbey**.

Sheffield, South Yorks   9J2
The prosperous and modern industrial city celebrated
throughout the world for cutlery. It was made here in
Chaucer's day. In 1720 a Lincolnshire clockmaker, Benjamin
Huntsman, started a series of experiments that resulted
in the discovery of crucible steel, on which the present
industry's reputation was founded. The cruciform cathedral
of St Peter and St Paul, dating from the 14th c, is greatly
altered with a glass and steel entrance added. Graves Art
Gallery at the Central Library has Constables, Cotmans and
Turners, plus Chinese ivories. The popular Crucible Theatre
is near by. Mappin Art Gallery and the City Museum with its
unique collection of cutlery and Sheffield plate are at
Weston Park near the University. The city is within easy
reach of the Peak District. Not to be missed is the *Abbeydale
Industrial Hamlet*, 4m SW of the centre, a restored 18th-c
scythe and steel works in the valley where metal was first
worked by the Beauchief Abbey monks.

Temple Newsam,★ West Yorks   9J4
4m SE of **Leeds**. Built by Thomas, Lord Darcy c.1521, and
enlarged in the 17th and 18th c, it is a splendid mansion with
a suite of fine Georgian rooms. It has one of the country's
best collections of house furnishings illustrating decorative
arts with excellent porcelain and ceramics. Gardens have
magnificent rhododendrons and azaleas in spring. Farm
museum in grounds. Open daily.

Wakefield, West Yorks   9J3
An old weaving and dyeing centre, whose economy is
underpinned by coal. The highest of many towers is the 247ft
crocketed spire of All Saints' Cathedral added in 1861 to an
ancient fabric. A restored medieval chantry chapel stands
on the old bridge. At Wakefield's museum are artefacts from
Sandal Castle. The site can be visited. Barbara Hepworth,
born here, is represented in the Art Gallery and by sculptures
in Castrop-Rauxel Square. The Yorkshire Sculpture
Park opened in 1980 at Bretton Hall College, *West Bretton*.
Heath Hall, 2m E, is a restored John Carr house of 1753 with
fine wood and plasterwork. Deer-shed in the park.

Wragby, West Yorks   9J3
The Perpendicular church with its hundreds of panels of
16th–18th-c Swiss glass stands surrounded by yews in the
park of *Nostell Priory*, ancestral home of the Winn family
now in the hands of the NT. The splendid façade of the
Palladian house was built by 19-year-old James Paine in
1733, and a wing was added by Robert Adam. It is celebrated
for a collection of Chippendale furniture and a remarkable
portrait gallery. Garden, lake, motorcycle and aviation
museum. Open Easter–end Sept. at set times.

North Yorkshire and Humberside

AN INTRODUCTION BY
MARIE HARTLEY AND JOAN INGILBY

A peace and quiet that have been lost to many parts of England are to be enjoyed in both North Yorkshire and Humberside, the new counties which replace the North and East Ridings of old Yorkshire. North Yorkshire alone is the largest English county, and contains two National Parks, the North York Moors and the Yorkshire Dales. Humberside, combining the old East Riding with North Lincolnshire and now connected by the Humber Bridge, has important industries especially in Hull, Immingham and Grimsby. A major coalfield is developing around Selby in North Yorkshire. But these counties remain for the most part relatively unspoiled, characterized by villages tucked under hillsides, farms covering the plains, mansions sheltered by woodlands and headlands overlooking bays.

Besides the western dales and the northeastern moorlands (the latter alone cover 1,000 square miles) there are the Yorkshire Wolds, the Howardian Hills, the great Plain of York, many miles wide, and other vales such as those of Pickering and Mowbray.

The coast runs for almost 100 miles, from north of the highest cliffs in England, at Boulby, to the low-lying shore of Holderness and across the Humber estuary to Cleethorpes. Large holiday resorts, quiet seaside towns and former fishing villages, preserving their individual charms, face lovely bays and firm extensive sands.

The Shape of the Land

As would be true elsewhere, the different underlying rocks have affected the scene and also the way of life of the people. The region falls geologically into three principal divisions: the rocks of the Carboniferous age in the Yorkshire Dales, those of the Jurassic system in the North York Moors and chalk in Humberside.

The various strata of the Carboniferous series – the limestones, shales and sandstones, which weather differently – have given the characteristic stepped shapes to the hills of the Yorkshire Dales. Swift powerful rivers spanned by graceful bridges flow down the main dales – Wensleydale, Swaledale and Wharfedale – and cleave the Pennines, which rise to well above 2,000 feet. Waterfalls offer grand spectacles. Hardraw Force, 2 miles from Hawes, is the highest single-drop waterfall in the country. The hard water, resulting from the limestone, discouraged the establishment of industries such as textiles; so that these dales remain sparsely populated, green and pastoral, where sheep and cattle are reared, and where grey-stone villages, linked by stone walls, merge into a scene that is harmonious from valley bottom to fell top.

From this hilly country we must traverse the Plain of York to reach the North York Moors. The great vale, almost wholly devoted to farming, forms the link between the different regions of Yorkshire. Up it a narrow strip of magnesian limestone makes a ridge along which the Roman legions tramped towards Hadrian's Wall and where now modern traffic ceaselessly roars on the double trackway of the A1 trunk road.

Across the vale rises the escarpment of the Hambleton Hills, with beyond them the Cleveland Hills – in other words the area known as the North York Moors. Here we find the same rock-system, the Jurassic, that underlies the Cotswolds; so that, as there, a fine durable limestone has been quarried to build castles, abbeys, mansions, houses in village streets and piers of harbours. Also, the presence of clays encouraged the making of tiles and bricks. Buildings are characterized by the warm hue of limestone and the mellow tone of red pantile roofs.

Rivers and valleys, chief of which are Bilsdale and Ryedale, are numerous and small in scale. Patches of arable land, and, in places, bosky dells in deep-set dales adjoin the flat tabular hills, clad with mile after mile of heather. Parkland and some of the most delightful villages in England stretch from the moors to the Howardian Hills, so named after the family at Castle Howard. Around Whitby, in the Lias, the lower strata of the Jurassic rocks, are found the well-known fossils, ammonites and belemnites.

The third geological division, the chalk, underlies most of north Humberside. Although of a harder nature, it is part of the same chalk belt that runs up England from Dorset and the Channel. It has given us

Flamborough Head with ocean-washed caves, pillars and white-cliffed bays with pebbly beaches.

The main chalk mass, the Yorkshire Wolds, rises to 800 feet. Dry uplands, intersected by steep-sided dales, swept by fierce winds and covered with a thin soil, they were once a huge sheep-walk. Reclaimed gradually by local landlords in the 18th century, they have been converted into fruitful cornlands, planted with trees and laid out with roads. Here the landscape is in an altogether lighter key than those of the two other regions. Besides the white chalk, exposed in cliffs, quarries and old lanes, the bright light from the sea is reflected from windy skies on to a land that in August and September surges away to distant horizons – an expanse of waving corn.

Farther south, east of Hull, lies another division of Humberside, Holderness, where chalk, much lower, has been overlaid by alluvial soil left after the Ice Age, and is now some of the richest land in Britain. The low cliffs of boulder-clay offer little resistance to the tides that wear them away at a rate of over four feet a year. They end at Spurn Head, a spit of sand three miles long.

Early Man and the Romans

For those who wish to study prehistory, visits to the British Museum and to museums at Hull, Scarborough, Whitby and York are essential. If the Romans interest you most, Yorkshire, where many forts, stations and roads were required for subduing the fierce Brigantes, offers a wealth of material. Especially at the County Museum, in York, may be seen inscribed stones, tombstones and tessellated pavements. In 1959, Catterick, the Roman capital of North Yorkshire, was excavated before the A1 trunk road was driven across it; and the fort at Bainbridge in Wensleydale has been explored by archeologists from Leeds University. From Roman Malton, next in importance to York as a road centre, the road northwards, passing through Cawthorn Camps, now extensive bracken-covered earthworks, is well seen near Pickering. Another feature of Roman Yorkshire are the signal stations spaced along the coast.

Castles, Abbeys, Churches and Great Houses

For a fine summer's day we can think of no more rewarding sightseeing than to visit a ruined abbey or castle; and nowhere in the country is there to be found a greater wealth of medieval building in a similar area. If, for instance, from a point half-way between Leyburn and Richmond we describe a circle only 8 miles in diameter, we take in three castles – Richmond, Middleham and Bolton, and three abbeys – Easby, Jervaulx and Coverham.

In these wild and remote regions the Norman earls built castles from which to protect their lands, and the Cistercians founded their abbeys, which, gradually enlarged and beautified, stood in splendid settings by the rivers. The ruins of Rievaulx and Byland at the edge of the North York Moors, are no more than 6 miles from each other, while Fountains is of unrivalled beauty. In them history and architecture unite in a unique appeal. Whitby reminds us of religion in Saxon times and the first English poet Caedmon. The first monastery was linked with others at Hackness and Lastingham in the North York Moors and at Kirkdale Church in the same region is to be seen a famous Saxon sundial. Goodmanham Church, in Humberside, is connected with the conversion of King Edwin of Northumbria. Almost every village church is worth visiting for some architectural feature – especially the elaborate Norman doorways at Riccall, Kirkburn, North Newbald and elsewhere. If we had to pick out two, the Early English church at Skelton near York and the Decorated at Patrington in Holderness would be our choice. York is, of course, the gem of North Yorkshire, a visually exciting city whose compact centre is embraced by white magnesian limestone walls with four superb medieval gates, here called bars. The street pattern of the Middle Ages is not greatly changed and the principal places of interest, crowned by York Minster and spanning periods from the Roman occupation to the 20th century are within easy reach. At Beverley in Humberside another Minster shows us the perfection of medieval building.

As well as two architectural treasures – Castle Howard and Burton Agnes Hall – several of the great houses of the two counties are regularly on view.

For those who like to make literary pilgrimages, there are Wood End, the home of the Sitwells, now partially a natural history museum, at Scarborough, and Shandy Hall, at Coxwold, where Laurence Sterne wrote part of *Tristram Shandy*. But nothing except the village itself, Winestead in Holderness, reminds us of the birthplace of Andrew Marvell.

Industries Past and Present

In the Yorkshire Dales, lead-bearing veins gave rise to an industry that began with the Romans and faded away, because of the imports of cheap foreign lead, at the end of the 19th century. Ruined smelt-mills and spoil-heaps, long grassed over, lend an interest, if but a sad one, to remote dales. Similarly, alum and jet were once mined along the coast and on the Cleveland Hills. The jet gave rise to Whitby jet ornaments and carvings, which, developed by skilled craftsmen, flourished in Victorian times. The craft is now carried on by only one or two men. Development of potash deposits is taking place near Whitby. The industrial area round Hull and Grimsby consists largely of docks, engineering works and other light industries. Scunthorpe developed as a major steel producer and the Selby coalfield is steadily expanding. Elsewhere farming is all important. The horned Swaledale sheep and Cleveland bays (bought for the Royal Mews) are

York Minster is famed for its medieval stained-glass windows; the east window is one of the finest

specialities. It is a commentary on the times that the Fylingdales ballistic missile early-warning station has been built within the confines of the North York Moors National Park.

Flowers and Woodland

Naturally, with such a diversity of rock and geographical features, the flora to be found in the two counties is very varied. Perhaps the wild daffodils in Farndale make the finest botanical sight, for they stretch for nine golden miles along the banks of the River Dove. Along the coast grow plants such as sea-holly. In the Yorkshire Dales, the meadows easily rival those in the Alps for profusion of flowers, and especially in Upper Swaledale the pastures are sprinkled with mountain pansies. On the moors and in the gills many mosses and ferns occur.

Here and there, as in Upper Swaledale, hazel woods are remains of the forest that once covered the dales, while in Swaledale juniper claims only a fraction of the acreage of former times. Magnificent trees grace many parks, and large tracts of the North York Moors have been taken over and planted with conifers by the Forestry Commission.

Sport and Food

When every kind of sporting facility abounds in the county, small wonder that Yorkshiremen are regarded as great sportsmen. Many are the famous Yorkshire packs in the annals of hunting. Every river, from the Ure in the west to the Whitby Esk in the east, provides excellent trout fishing, and the Driffield Beck is a nationally known chalk-stream. As for grouse moors, North Yorkshire possesses some of the best shoots in Britain. Winners of races from the Derby to the Grand National have been trained at Malton and Middleham and racing in Yorkshire is at Thirsk, Catterick Bridge, Pontefract, Wetherby, Doncaster, Beverley, Ripon and York. Not only are there miles of glorious walking country, but Scarborough has a cricket and a lawn-tennis week, and Ganton a famous golf-course. At Sutton Bank is the headquarters of the Yorkshire Gliding Club. Whitby Marina is a centre for sea sports.

Sport and food are, not surprisingly, linked together: grouse and trout may be had at the appropriate seasons. Yorkshire pudding, light as a feather, cheesecakes, a speciality of farmhouses all over the area, tasty York ham, tender moorland lamb and most kinds of fish freshly caught, make mouth-watering dishes, not to mention the Wensleydale cheese, made from the milk of cows pastured in the dales.

GAZETTEER

Aldborough, North Yorks 9J5
¾m E of **Boroughbridge**. The former capital of the Brigantes and later site of the Roman 9th legion's Isurium Brigantum, where the rulers of **York** built their villas, this quiet village holds a small museum (AM) exhibiting Roman coins, utensils and jewelry. Two superb tessellated pavements were excavated. In the 14th-c church, where the Temple of Mercury stood, is a worn statue of the god. Open April–Sept.

Alkborough, Humb 9L4
York Minster is visible from this height above the confluence of the Ouse, Trent and Humber. In addition to the 11th-c church, there are two unusual sights: a Roman camp, incongruously named the Countess Close after Countess Lucy, wife of Ivo Tailbois, Norman Lord of the Manor; and, cut in the turf, a maze. Of this last, a plan in black and white stone is set into the floor of the S porch of the church.

Ampleforth, North Yorks 9K6
English Benedictines, exiled to France, returned in 1793 as refugees of the French Revolution and founded the Abbey and College at the E end of the Hambleton Hills village. Their Romanesque-style church by Sir Giles Scott was completed in 1961 just after his death. The parish church is Norman with Early English doorways.

Aysgarth, North Yorks 9I6
A single-arched Elizabethan bridge spans the Ure, which is famous for its cataracts that pour over limestone terraces. A Yorkshire Museum of Carriages and Horse Drawn Vehicles is at Yore Mill. Open April–Oct. *Bolton Castle*, 4m NE, is a 14th-c bastion in Wensleydale built by the 1st Lord Scrope. There are a folk museum and restaurant in this former prison of Mary Queen of Scots. Open daily except Mon.

Barton-upon-Humber, Humb 9M4
A once-important river port now looking to the Humber Bridge, which vaults the river from here to Hessle, to revive its declining fortunes. Baysgarth Hall, one of a few outstanding houses, is a museum. The lower part of the Saxon tower of redundant St Peter's Church has beautiful arcading, round-headed below and triangular above. Near by the parish church of St Mary's is a striking 13th-c structure. *See also* **Thornton Abbey**.

Bedale, North Yorks 9J6
The tower of the church of St Gregory in this market town at the centre of hunting-country was used as a defensive position against Scottish raiders, with access through a portcullis. Note the arcading in the church and the fresco of St George and the Dragon. Georgian Bedale Hall (now council offices) across the street has extraordinary plasterwork and a 'flying' staircase. *Snape Castle*, 3m S, a medieval stronghold, was the home of Catherine Parr, who outlived Henry VIII.

Beningbrough Hall, North Yorks 9K5
5½m NW of **York**. The NT's showpiece restoration is a charming early Georgian red-brick house with Baroque features built in 1716 on the River Ouse. A window above the porch is a copy of a window by Bernini in Rome. Outstanding great staircase and two-storeyed hall. The woodcarving throughout is exceptional especially in the State Bedroom

with its William and Mary bed. The corner fireplaces in several rooms display Delft and Oriental porcelain. Some 102 paintings loaned by the **National Portrait Gallery**, London, in 1978 hang in the splendid rooms and an exhibit on 18th-c portraiture occupies the servants' quarters. A Victorian laundry and the stable block are also restored. Gardens. Open April–Oct. at set times.

Beverley, Humb 9M4
A delightful, spacious market town between the Wolds and **Hull** with two ecclesiastical buildings of national importance: the Minster, dating from 1220, with twin pinnacled towers, and St Mary's parish church, originally a chapel to the Minster, with its soaring tower, painted ceilings and minstrels' pillar. The Minster, built in the form of a double cross, holds treasures of wood and stone carving, notably its 68 misericords and the Percy shrine, with its superb 14th-c canopy. The Minster and parish church contain one of the largest collections of carvings in the world. There is also a Snetzler organ of 1767 in the Minster. The brick North Bar is the only survivor of five medieval gates. The market-cross of 1714 is a domed and open octagon. The Georgian Guildhall displays pewter plate in the magistrates' room. Council meetings are held in Lairgate Hall, *c*.1700 (open Mon.–Fri.). *Skidby Windmill*, 4m S, was built in 1821 and recently restored to its white-capped, full-sailed self by the borough council.

Bolton Abbey, North Yorks 9I5
Beautiful ruins where the Wharfe spreads out into a valley. The priory was founded in the early 12th c for Black Canons of the Augustinian Order who, unlike monks, came under the jurisdiction of bishops. The nave of their church was spared during the Dissolution of the Monasteries, and is to this day used for services. Stepping stones and a footbridge cross the river here. N is the *Strid*, where the River Wharfe is forced into a narrow chasm.

Boroughbridge, North Yorks 9J5
Where Edward II won his victory over the Duke of Lancaster in 1322. The *Devil's Arrows*, W of the town, so-called in the belief that they were bolts which were 'shot at ancient cities and therewith overthrew them', are three megaliths comparable with those at **Stonehenge** (Wilts) – the largest being 30ft high. Over 3,000 years old, they may have influenced the Romans when they chose a site for Isurium (*see* **Aldborough**). Long an important coaching stop, the town was bypassed by the A1 and suffers neglect but many good buildings remain as well as the cobbled square and pretty market-cross. *See also* **Newby Hall**.

Bridlington, Humb 9M5
A popular resort that combines new and old, the old exemplified by the fine priory church founded in the reign of Henry I, and the great Bayle Gate, dating from about 1388, which is now a museum. When Queen Henrietta Maria, wife of Charles I, landed in 1643 with arms purchased from the proceeds of the Crown Jewels, the harbour was bombarded and she retreated to Boynton Hall (*c*.1550). This arrival embarrassed the owner, a Parliamentarian. *Sewerby Hall*, NE on the cliffs, is an art gallery and museum with the Amy Johnson Trophy Room, gardens and a variety of amusements including a miniature zoo and aviary. Hall open Easter–end Sept., grounds daily.

Brimham Rocks, North Yorks   9I5
Outcrops of millstone grit weathered into grotesque shapes. They have descriptive names such as Yoke of Oxen, Baboon Rock, the Dancing Bear, etc. The 200-ton Idol Rock balances on a stalk 12in in diameter. The loneliness of their situation on Brimham Moor makes them a weird sight. Owned by the NT with 387 wild acres.

Burton Agnes, Humb   9M5
'We enter under a Gate house built with 4 large towers into a Court, which is large, in the middle is a Bowling green palisado'd round' – so wrote a visitor in 1697, and it is the first impression on arriving today at this late Elizabethan manor house. The plasterwork and overmantels, the oak staircase and the current owner's French Impressionist paintings are special features. The house's Norman forerunner, to the W, was re-faced in Elizabethan brick.

Burton Constable Hall, Humb   9M4
8m NE of **Hull**. Paintings and Chippendale in a great house dating from 1570. Country park, zoo and adventure playground. Open Easter–Sept. on regular stated days.

Byland Abbey see **Coxwold**

Carlton Towers, North Yorks   9K4
6m S of **Selby**. Yorkshire home of Duke of Norfolk. Victorian Gothic house with fine furnishings and family robes. Open at stated times.

Castle Howard, ★ North Yorks   9K5
Home of the Howard family, begun by Vanbrugh in 1702 and continued while he was working on Blenheim Palace (see **Woodstock,** Oxon). Magnificent rooms at the ends of corridors flanked by hidden staircases contain a wealth of art treasures. The grounds, set off by ornamental water, the Temple of the Four Winds by Vanbrugh and the mausoleum by Nicholas Hawksmoor complete the splendour of the place. Costume Galleries and exquisite rose gardens are recently added attractions. Location of the TV series 'Brideshead Revisited'. Open Easter–end Sept. daily.

Catterick, North Yorks   9I6
The village with its Perpendicular church and placid green is bypassed by the A1. A Roman camp was sited here. *Kiplin Hall* at Scorton, 2m E, was built in 1620 for Lord Baltimore, founder of Maryland, U.S.A. Open at advertised times. There is also a racecourse and Catterick Camp near by is the 'Aldershot of the North'.

Cawood, North Yorks   9K4
Site of the palace to which Cardinal Wolsey retired in 1530, vainly hoping to end his life enlarging and enriching it to rival **Hampton Court** (London), which he had given to Henry VIII. Though the palace was demolished in 1646, the graceful 15th-c gatehouse was spared, complete with oriel window and the vaulted archway through which many royal personages rode. Battered by time, it now connects a barn and a house. A Norman church stands on the brink of the Ouse, crossed by a swing bridge.

Clapham, North Yorks   9H5
Centre for walking, climbing and pot-holing, convenient for waterfalls, an ascent of *Ingleborough* (2,373ft) and a maze of limestone caves crowded with stalactites and stalagmites deep in the mountain. The grounds (with nature trail) of Ingleborough Hall were laid out by botanist Reginald Farrer when he lived here.

Cleethorpes, Humb   5M6
Popular resort which developed from a fishing hamlet, with miles of sandy beaches, pier pleasures, golf, and a new leisure centre with swimming pool.

Coverham Abbey, North Yorks   9I6
Most of the 12th-c foundation of Helewisia de Glanville has been enclosed in a private garden in one of the smaller of the Yorkshire dales. Two arches and part of the transept survive, also sculptured coffin-lids and the effigies in stone of two knights, believed to be the foundress's son and grandson.

Coxwold, North Yorks   9K6
The church where Laurence Sterne preached (1760–8) has a rare octagonal tower. In the gabled house which he named *Shandy Hall* he wrote *A Sentimental Journey* and *Tristram Shandy*. It has been faithfully restored and is open at designated times for visitors to this dreamy buff-stone village. So is *Newburgh Priory*, ½m SE, an Elizabethan mansion with 12th-c priory ruins, where a bricked-up attic room is thought to contain the body (or just the heart) of Oliver Cromwell brought here secretly by his daughter Mary. *Byland Abbey*, 1m NE, founded 1177, is notable for a rose window and S transept to the ruined abbey church, and fine medieval floor tiles (AM).

Craven   9H5
An area of fells and peaks in the Western Dales, noted for climbing and caving. See **Malham, Settle,** and **Skipton.**

Easby Abbey see **Richmond**

Epworth, Humb   5M8
John Wesley (1703–91) and his brother Charles (1707–88) grew up in the 1709 Rectory, built to replace their birthplace which was burned by a mob opposed to their father's politics. Owned by the World Methodist Council, it can be visited. Wesley Memorial Church (1889) commemorates the brothers. An 1860 chapel, now a youth centre, honours the dissident Methodist Alexander Kilham.

Filey, North Yorks   9M6
The seashore is characterized by Filey Brigg, a 1m-long reef of oolite rock which juts into the sea. The receding tide exposes hundreds of rock pools. St Oswald's Church, overlooking a ravine, belonged to Augustinian canons until the Dissolution. The old fishing village here has turned into a modern holiday resort and claims 6m of sands.

Flamborough Head, Humb   9M5
Chalk headland (215ft), which caused innumerable wrecks until the lighthouse was built in 1818 to replace an octagonal tower. Fine observation-point for shipping, birds and stack rocks, within reach of many caves. A nature trail follows the Iron Age earthworks known as *Dane's Dyke* W of the village. *Bempton Cliffs* (350ft) only nesting place for the gannet on the mainland in England.

Fountains Abbey, ★★ North Yorks   9J5
4m W of **Ripon**. The loveliest of England's ruins (NT) was founded by Archbishop Thurstan in the early 12th c for 12 Benedictine monks who decided to embrace the Cistercian rule. The abbey grew in size and wealth through the wool trade and ownership of land, but in 1539 the treasure was scattered and the roofs dismantled. The nave with 11 bays, and the Chapel of the Nine Altars at the end, are special features. Note also the chapter house, the double avenue of

Fountains Abbey: the most impressive cellarer's range in Europe – 300 feet long and vaulted in 22 double arches

arches in the cellarium, and the foundations of the infirmary, which was built in part over the Skell. Near by Fountains Hall (*c*.1610) was constructed of stones taken from the Abbey. The best approach is on foot from **Studley Royal** – the abbey ruins are part of these gardens.

Gilling Castle, North Yorks   9K6
This lovely house, built in the 16th and 18th c, was acquired in 1929 for use as a preparatory school to **Ampleforth** College. The Elizabethan dining-room known as the Great Chamber has pendentive ceilings. The original frieze, oak-panelling and stained glass, which had been sold in 1929, were salvaged from the estate of William Randolph Hearst, the American publisher, who had removed them to a London warehouse, and were reinstalled. The Long Gallery, also sold in 1929, is at Bowes Museum, **Barnard Castle** (Durham). The terraced gardens below are open to the public, and the house can be seen by arrangement.

Goodmanham, Humb   9L4
The 12th-c church is believed to occupy the site of a pagan temple destroyed by Coifi, its high priest, when he was converted in 627, as was King Edwin.

Goole, Humb   9L4
Port with extensive docks, though situated 50m from the sea. The Don meets the Yorkshire Ouse via the Dutch River, a canal cut by Vermuyden, a Dutch engineer employed by Charles I.

Grassington, North Yorks   9I5
Where visitors are spoiled for choice, this is an attractive and useful centre for exploring *Wharfedale*, one of the most beautiful valleys in England, with peaceful villages and wild landscapes. It became a tourist centre in the 19th c

when lead mining was the chief occupation. It has a cobbled market square and pretty back alleys, with an increasing variety of shops and accommodation. Upper Wharfedale Museum exhibits tools for many trades. 1m N are Grass Wood and Bastow Wood, botanists' delights.

Great Ayton, North Yorks   9K7
Picturesque village at the foot of the Cleveland Hills. Captain Cook attended the Old School and the upper room contains relics (open afternoons) but the major Cook museum is at **Marton** 6m NE in Cleveland. The Cooks' cottage site is marked but the building went to Australia in 1834. Of the Cleveland Hills roundabout *Roseberry Topping* (1,057ft) is the chief landmark and an ancient beacon site.

Grimsby, Humb   9N4
The 14th-c *Lay of Havelock the Dane* tells us how Grim the Fisherman rescued the King's son and landed with him at what was to become the foremost fishing port in Europe. The docks and the fish market are still busy. The port operates in conjunction with *Immingham*'s, a 20th-c development for deep-water vessels and bulk cargo. It was from Immingham that the Pilgrims sailed for Holland in 1608.

Harrogate,★ North Yorks   9J5
Brawton in James Herriot's books. It is an inland watering place, an ideal centre for tourists and much favoured for conferences. The properties of the waters were discovered in the 16th c when William Slingsby noticed their resemblance to those of continental spas. A small temple covers the original Tewit well on the Stray. At the Royal Pump Room, now a museum, you can sample the sulphurous water. From the Harlow Hill observatory there is a grand view of this hilly, dignified town of hotels, fine houses and beautiful gardens. An Art Nouveau theatre and Baroque Royal Hall are centres for entertainment including the annual August festival of arts and sciences. The town's new International Centre is the most modern landmark.

Hedon, Humb   9M4
Port superseded by **Hull**. A beautiful mace of the reign of Henry V, believed to be the oldest in England, may be seen at the town hall. The church known as the King of Holderness (begun c.1180) has a glorious N front, two tiers of traceried windows and a magnificent tower.

Helmsley, North Yorks   9K6
The 12th-c castle (AM), once owned by George Villiers, 1st Duke of Buckingham, fell into disuse when Sir Charles Duncombe, a London banker, commissioned Vanbrugh to build the great house known as Duncombe Park and now occupied by a girls' school. A delightful small market town of red roofs and warm stone buildings, nestled in the Rye valley. *See also* **Nunnington Hall, Rievaulx Abbey.**

Hornsea Mere, Humb   9M5
Largest freshwater lake in the region, 12ft above sea level, ¾m from the sea and originally formed by glacial deposits. It has fishing, sailing, a sanctuary for birds and a breeding spot for herons. Attractions of Hornsea village, a small resort, include the cobblestone church, North Holderness Museum of Village Life and pottery.

Howden, Humb   9L4
A market town possessing a medieval church with a dominating tower and W front. The ruined choir and chapter house, best seen at first from the market place, are particularly beautiful.

Hull, Humb   9M4
Properly Kingston-upon-Hull, a major seaport laid out by Edward I in the late 13th c. Container traffic and North Sea ferries operate from the docks which stretch 5m along the Humber, but the trawler fleet is much depleted. Fish from foreign vessels are now processed here. The bombed-out town centre was rebuilt with shopping precincts and flower beds. In the Old Town are such historic buildings as Trinity House (1753), home of the 600-year-old Guild of Seafarers; 14th-c Holy Trinity Church, St Mary's, whose tower arches over a street, and Wilberforce House, the birthplace in 1759 of the emancipator. It is now a museum with collections including relics of the slave trade and period rooms, with many Wilberforce mementoes. The Transport and Archeological Museum, near by in the High Street, contains prehistoric, Saxon and Roman remains, including the Mortimer collection. Ferens Art Gallery exhibits British and Dutch paintings.

Humber Bridge, Humb   9M4
Since 1981, the Humber River has been crossed by the longest single-span suspension bridge in the world, a spectacular sight from the flat banks of the broad estuary. For the first time the important centres of **Hull** and **Grimsby,** on opposite shores, were conveniently linked. The Romans crossed by ferry from the S bank to *Brough* W of Hull. Considerably later, British Rail operated a toll ferry between Hull and New Holland. Construction of the toll bridge, its S foot near **Barton-upon-Humber** and its N at *Hessle* on Hull's W outskirts, began in 1972. The reinforced concrete piers rise 510ft; the main span is 4,626ft long and about 44,000m of wire hold it up.

Hutton-le-Hole, North Yorks   9K6
Picturesque village built round a green and watered by a stream crossed by foot-bridges. The Ryedale Folk Museum in 18th-c farm buildings and reconstructed cruck cottages illuminates rural history, superstitions, work and crafts.

Ingleton, North Yorks   8G5
The ravines down which plunge the Doe and the Twiss form a chain of waterfalls that can be followed on foot. Thornton Force and Beezley Falls are most impressive after rain. *White Scar Caves,* discovered in 1923, present a complication of rock chambers. This paradise for potholers also takes in *Gaping Ghyll Hole,* the most spacious in Britain, on the S flanks of *Ingleborough* (2,373ft).

Jervaulx Abbey, North Yorks   9I6
The destruction of this great Cistercian abbey at the Dissolution was thorough, but the ground plan can be sufficiently well traced to give an impression of the day-to-day life in a monastic house. The first Wensleydale cheese was made by monks here.

Kilburn, North Yorks   9K6
The great White Horse on Roulston Scar was cut by the village schoolmaster and a band of helpers in 1857. Robert Thompson (d.1955), who was famous for woodwork that rivalled medieval craftsmanship (he signed it with the carving of a mouse), had his workshop in a timbered house on the green where oak furnishings are still handmade.

Kirkbymoorside, North Yorks   9K6
The parish register records the death of Charles II's favourite, 'Georges Viluas, Lord Dooke of Bookingham', who died here in 1687 after a fall with the Sinnington Hunt which still meets here.

Kirkdale, North Yorks   9K6
The church combines Saxon, Norman and Early English architecture and is crowned with a 19th-c tower. A Saxon sundial over the porch records that Orm the son of Gamal bought St Gregory's Church when it was 'all to brocan and to falan' and caused it to be made anew from the ground in the days of Edward the King and Earl Tosti (the Confessor and the brother of King Harold); in other words, 1060.

Kirkham Priory, North Yorks   9K5
5m SW of **Malton**. Religious house (AM) endowed by Walter l'Espec c.1130 after a fatal accident to his son. It is beautifully situated by the River Derwent. The Norman doorway to the refectory, the cloister lavatorium where the monks washed before meals, and the fine 13th-c sculptured gatehouse still stand erect.

Knaresborough, North Yorks   9J5
Attractive town on the River Nidd, possessing many 18th-c houses. The 14th-c keep is the best-preserved part of John of Gaunt's castle, where Richard II was held captive in 1399. Two famous local sights are the Dropping Well, a waterfall that trickles as if through a giant sieve, and has petrifying properties, and the Wishing Well of Mother Shipton, the Yorkshire prophetess. The manor house, with its chequerboard walls, was presented by James I to his son Charles as a fishing lodge.

Lastingham, North Yorks   9K6
The early Norman crypt built in 1078 over the grave of St Cedd is reached by steps inside the present church. It has its own chancel, nave, aisles, vaulted roof of squat pillars and an ancient altar stone. The village lies in a hollow of the moors between *Rosedale* and *Farndale.*

Malham, North Yorks   9H5
The River Aire emerges from underground into Malham Cove. 2m beyond this limestone cliff (over 300ft) lies

Malham Tarn (NT) and Tarn House where Charles Kingsley wrote *The Water Babies* (now a Field Centre). *Gordale Scar* to the E is part of the same geological fault, and produces a ravine with a magnificent succession of waterfalls.

Malton, North Yorks   9L5
Market town on the Derwent for cattle and corn country. St Michael's is late Norman with a Perpendicular tower and 19th-c additions. The Roman Museum, Market Place, has relics from the camp in Orchard Field. N of this site is *Old Malton* with quaint stone houses and fragments of a 12th-c priory. Malton and adjacent *Norton* are known for racing stables and studs. *See also* **Kirkham Priory**.

Markenfield Hall, North Yorks   9J5
3m S of **Ripon**. Early 14th-c moated manor house. The drawbridge has been replaced by a stone structure.

Marston Moor, North Yorks   9J5
Scene of Cromwell's decisive victory over the Royalists in 1644. An obelisk on the road between *Long Marston* and *Tockwith* marks the field where 4,300 died in three hours.

Middleham, North Yorks   9I6
The ancient stronghold of the Neville family was taken over by the Crown after the battle of Barnet in 1471. It was dismantled in 1646 and became a source of building material for the *Wensleydale* village but the splendid keep and walls (AM) of what was one of the greatest castles in the N remain imposing. Richard III grew up and married here and his son Edward, who died an infant, was born here. The Swine Cross in the town, the Well of St Alkelda – the Saxon princess who shares the dedication of the church – and the church itself should be visited, and a watchful eye kept for horses in training in this Newmarket of the N.

Mount Grace Priory, North Yorks   9J6
7m NE of **Northallerton**. Most complete of Carthusian priories in England, founded by Thomas Holland in 1397 for 20 monks, who lived in separate small terrace houses around a cloister, according to their strict rule. Though sharing the common fate of monasteries under Henry VIII, part was made habitable as a private house in 1654, and it was enlarged in 1901. It now belongs to the NT and is managed as an AM.

Newby Hall, North Yorks   9J5
4m SE of **Ripon**. Set in a beautiful garden this is an Adam house with tapestry room, Chippendale furniture and Adam sculpture. Gardens, miniature railway, restaurant. House open Easter–end Sept. at stated times. Gardens daily.

Northallerton, North Yorks   9J6
The improbable county town of England's largest county, with much sprawling growth. Its history as a coaching stop accounts for the many inns along the broad High Street which also serves as a twice-weekly market. Dickens stayed at the Fleece. The mid-Victorian Town Hall fits nicely with its mainly Georgian neighbours. All Saints' on a shady triangular green has a Perpendicular tower. A bronze shield on an obelisk 2m N commemorates the battle of the Standard where 12,000 Scots were killed. *See also* **Mount Grace Priory**.

Norton Conyers, North Yorks   9J5
This Jacobean house N of **Ripon**, near *Melmerby*, is reputed to be the model for Thornfield in Charlotte Brontë's *Jane Eyre*. The mansion with its distinctive Dutch gables and

Great Hall has housed Grahams since 1624. It contains a Brontë collection and interesting family paintings, furnishings, costumes and manuscripts. An 18th-c walled garden is still cultivated. Open by appointment.

Nunnington Hall, North Yorks   9K6
4½m SE of **Helmsley**. NT's riverside manor house of Tudor and late Stuart construction. Carlisle collection of miniature rooms. Open May–Sept. at stated times.

Patrington, Humb   9N4
The church known as the Queen of Holderness, a fine example of the Decorated period, has a 189ft spire incorporating an arcaded belfry. The S transept, the Easter Sepulchre and the modern gilded reredos are features of a cathedral-like church. Built chiefly 1310–49, when the Black Death stopped work, it was completed in 1410 in the new Perpendicular style.

Pickering, North Yorks   9L6
Market town in a prosperous valley and tourist centre for Pickering Vale and the North York Moors. Of the moat-and-bailey castle with its two courts (AM), some outer wall, three towers, the shell keep and chapel survive. Lovely mural paintings of the 15th c were discovered in the nave of the church under a coat of whitewash. Beck Isle, a late Georgian house, is a museum of rural life on murmuring Pickering Beck. The North Yorkshire Moors Railway starts here for a scenic run 18m over the moors to *Grosmont*. Both steam and diesel locomotives are used. The line was built by George Stephenson in the 1830s, closed by British Rail in 1965, and re-opened as a private venture in 1973.

Richmond, North Yorks   9I6
An ancient town on a dramatic site at the entrance to *Swaledale*, with a spacious market place and alleys known as wynds. The 11th-c castle (AM), never finished and never attacked, overlooks all. A splendid view can be had from the top of the keep. Redundant Holy Trinity Church is a Green Howards Regimental Museum. Down Friar's Wynd is the Theatre Royal of 1788, closed in 1848 and now restored to use in virtually its original intimate state. A riverside footpath leads 1m E to *Easby Abbey* (AM) founded c.1155. Parts of the infirmary, refectory and cloister survive. Open April–Sept.

Rievaulx Abbey, ★ North Yorks   9K6
3m N of **Helmsley**. Second only to **Fountains** in splendour, this rich Cistercian monastery (now AM) was almost completed by the end of the 12th c on a romantic site in the secluded Rye valley. Substantial remains of the church and living quarters illustrate the transition from a Romanesque style to pointed arches. The choir is an Early English masterpiece. Lovely views of the great ruin are part of the Georgian plan of Rievaulx Terrace (NT), a picturesque ½m grassy walk, with classical temples overlooking the valley.

Ripley, North Yorks   9J5
The Ingilbys who have occupied Ripley Castle since 1350 remodelled the village in Alsatian style in the 1820s, complete with Hôtel de Ville. Thoroughly English stocks and market-cross are in the square, off which stands the 15th-c gate of the castle, a Tudor tower joined to an 18th-c hall. Chandeliers, portraits, Civil War armour and a priest's hole are among noteworthy contents. Grounds on the River Nidd were planned by Capability Brown. Cromwell slept here after battle of **Marston Moor** and the execution of several Royalist prisoners. Castle open April–Sept. In the churchyard is the base of a 'weeping cross'.

Ripon, North Yorks **9J5**
Ripon received its charter from Alfred the Great in 886. The cathedral's Saxon crypt is a perfect setting for the church treasures. The late 15th-c carved screen and choir stalls with misericords are exceptionally fine and the W front an unusually beautiful example of Early English stonework. Many old buildings including the Tudor Wakeman's House on the bustling market square which is a museum and information centre. The City Hornblower in traditional dress sounds the 'setting of the watch' nightly at 9 p.m. at the obelisk in the market square commemorating William Aislabie who kept his parliamentary seat 60 years. *See also* **Markenfield Hall, Newby Hall, Norton Conyers, Fountains Abbey, Studley Royal.**

Robin Hood's Bay, North Yorks **9L7**
Picturesque fishing village once notorious as the haunt of smugglers. A magnet for artists with its huddle of cottages, shops and inns down a steep ravine. **Leeds** University has established the Wellcome Marine Biology Station in the village.

Scarborough, North Yorks **9M6**
'Scarthaborg' was burned by Harald Hardrada in 1066 and rebuilt below the 12th-c castle (AM) whose ruins stand on a Roman signal station site E of the town centre. Britain's first holiday resort with the discovery of spa waters in 1626. Still enjoyed as a resort or year-round residence, with the old fishing harbour, beaches S, a breezy promenade and long

Robin Hood's Bay: the sea has often threatened houses in the lower streets of this popular village

sands N of the cliff-top castle. Scarborough offers theatre-in-the-round and many gardens along with traditional seaside amusements. It is seen best from Oliver's Mount, 500ft above sea level. Anne Brontë is buried in the graveyard of St Mary's Church, badly damaged in the Civil War. The Sitwell family's holiday home, Woodend, is a natural history museum. A good centre for visiting the North York Moors National Park.

Scunthorpe, Humb **9L3**
This modern steel town which swallowed up five old villages has a bold new civic centre with theatre, museum, art gallery and park. Older buildings which still stand have new uses: Brumby Hall is a student hostel and *Normanby Park*, 2m N, built by Smirke in 1825–9, is a Regency museum with public gardens.

Selby, North Yorks **9K4**
Believed to be the birthplace of Henry I (1068–1135), the only English-born son of the Conqueror. Navigation of the Ouse so far inland is possible by small steamers. The Abbey Church of St Mary and St Germaine is considered one of the most splendid monastic churches in England. It was damaged by fire in 1906, but has been well restored. In the 110sq m around the town, the world's biggest and deepest coal mine is developing. The first coal emerged in 1980.

Settle, North Yorks 9H5
Old-world town high in the valley of the Ribble surrounded by fells, it is characterized by gabled houses with oriel windows and turrets. The local museum contains bones and artefacts found in Victoria Cave (reached from *Langcliffe*), some of which date from the Ice Age. The Knoll of Castleberg (500ft), reached from the market place, dominates the town.

Skipton, North Yorks 9I5
Sizeable market town in the centre of **Craven**, it is a gateway to the Yorkshire Dales. The castle, founded by Robert de Romillé in Norman times, came into the hands of the Clifford family in 1269. Their motto 'Désormais' is sculptured in great letters on the parapet over the gateway. The castle, including the dungeon, is open to the public. Craven Museum holds relics of the Iron Age, Roman and local lead mining. High Corn Mill has been restored.

Sledmere, Humb 9L5
The tidy village and great house belong to the Sykes family which in the 18th c transformed bleak and barren Wolds into rich farmland. A classical temple commemorates Sir Christopher Sykes's achievements. Opposite the church is a copy of **Northampton's** Eleanor Cross converted into a 1914–18 war memorial. Still another monument pays tribute to the local Waggoners' Reserve. The House dates from 1751 and suffered badly in a 1911 fire, but all contents including doors and banisters were saved and its restoration was accomplished from paintings, original designs, and plaster moulds. Furnishings, statuary, porcelain and the tiled Turkish Room are all notable but the exquisite long, vaulted library tops all. On alternate Sun. visitors hear organ recitals. Open May–Sept. at set times.

Stamford Bridge, Humb 9K5
Scene of the last great Saxon victory, when in 1066 Harold defeated his brother Tostig and Harald Hardrada, King of Norway, after they sailed up the Humber. The narrow 1727 bridge over the Derwent is near the battlefield.

Studley Royal, North Yorks 9J5
The deer park and pleasure gardens (NT) make a perfect approach on foot to **Fountains Abbey** past avenues and hedges, temples and statuary and Italian and Dutch gardens that have brought the River Skell into ponds and fountains. St Mary's Church (AM) is an extraordinary product of 1871 in the style of the 14th c, decorated with carvings, glass and ironwork, walls of Egyptian alabaster and a painted roof.

Sutton Park, North Yorks 9K5
8m N of **York**, in *Sutton-on-the-Forest*. A Georgian house built in 1730 with period furniture, fan collection. Gardens with terraces, trails and a Georgian ice-house. Tea room. Open Easter–end Sept. at set times.

Thirsk, North Yorks 9J6
Market town with an attractive square that once contained a bull ring. The market-cross can be seen at 18th-c Thirsk Hall. The 15th-c church has an impressive oak roof and fine glass in the E window. In Thomas Lord's House (1755) is a folk museum – Lord founded Lord's Cricket Ground in London. Good centre for touring the Hambleton Hills. This is James Herriot's Darrowby.

Thornton Abbey, Humb 9M4
4m SE of **Barton-upon-Humber**. Remains include magnificent 14th-c gateway and part of the chapter house of an Augustinian moated monastery. Open April–Sept.

Wensley, North Yorks 9I6
This attractive village gives its name to one of Yorkshire's largest, most peaceful dales, drained by the River Ure. It was decimated by plague in 1563. The church (1245) has wall paintings, box-pews and a tablet to Dr Peter Goldsmith who attended the dying Nelson.

Wharfedale *see* **Bolton Abbey** and **Grassington**

Whitby, North Yorks 9L7
The Esk divides the old and new parts of this small port and picturesque holiday centre. A synod held in Whitby in 664 consolidated Christianity in the land, besides settling the date of Easter. Whitby Abbey, founded in 657, was destroyed a century later by the Danes. The remains (AM) are Early English. Captain Cook served his apprenticeship in a house in Grape Lane – his ships were built in the town. The W front was bombarded during the 1914 War. Once a great whaling station, the port is still busy with fishing, and the local jet that found favour with Queen Victoria continues to be polished by a few remaining craftsmen. Near *Sleights*, 2m W, the first enemy aircraft was brought down during World War II. A plaque records the event.

York, ** North Yorks 9K5
The capital of the North, unique for the completeness of its walls and a townscape which blends medieval with later architecture. Of late it has enjoyed a tourist boom, greatly encouraged by the superb restoration of York Minster and the coming of the National Railway Museum. Caer Ebrauc to the British, Eboracum to the Romans, Jorvik to the Danes – the titles are an illustration of early history. William the Conqueror built two castles here, facing each other across the Ouse. The survivor is Clifford's Tower (AM), built in the 13th c by Henry III in a quatrefoil plan high on a mound. It was saved centuries later from demolition by pleas of the citizens of York. Three excellent 18th-c buildings face it across Castle Yard: the Assize Courts and two prisons which make up the famous Castle Museum with its period rooms and streets and an immense collection of bygones.
  The Minster is the largest cathedral built in England in the Middle Ages (60,952sq ft). It grew on the site of four earlier churches, taking two and a half centuries to complete after a beginning in 1220; thus it combines the best of the Early English, Decorated and Perpendicular periods. By the orders of Sir Thomas Fairfax after the battle of Marston Moor, the fabric was spared destruction at the hands of the victorious Parliamentarians. The Norman crypt adjoins the new Undercroft Museum which exhibits remains of earlier buildings back to the Romans, as well as the cathedral's treasures. But it is for medieval glass that the Minster is justly world-famous, its sole rival being Chartres. Of the 125 windows, the E window and the Five Sisters window are the best known, but throughout the cathedral are superb examples of the local glassmakers' art. All of the glass has been cleaned and releaded. *See also* page 269. In 1984 the roof of the S transcept was destroyed by fire.
  The city deserves to be explored on foot and at leisure, taking in the great medieval walls and 'bars' or gates, the Assembly Rooms and the medieval Shambles, where shops lean precariously across a narrow street. The Art Gallery, medieval guildhalls and Yorkshire Museum, set in beautiful gardens with a restored observatory and free-ranging peacocks, are other places to linger in. To the plethora of museums is added a Jorvik Viking Centre, fruit of a spectacular dig on Coppergate, opened in 1984 by Prince Charles. A full-size reconstruction of the Viking town which can be visited in special electric time-cars. Open daily.

NORTHUMBRIA: NORTHUMBERLAND, TYNE AND WEAR, DURHAM AND CLEVELAND

AN INTRODUCTION BY

SID CHAPLIN

The four counties of Northumberland, Durham, Tyne and Wear, and Cleveland cover much of the Anglo-Saxon kingdom of Northumbria and stretch from the Scottish border south to Teeside and North Yorkshire, from the Cheviot Hills and North Pennine range on the west to the North Sea on the east. This is a land of marked contrasts. Ships and coal were the basis of Tyneside's growth while giant petrochemical industries have overtaken coal as the chief business of Teeside, the other large industrial conurbation. Inland, Roman roads and settlements bonded the region together, and the warm, wide dales of the Tees, Wear, Tyne and Coquet are united in more than the rich arable land and pastures of their 'bottoms', or great sheep-runs where sheep are not counted to the acre, but acres to the sheep. From the old priory of Lindisfarne we can trace that Celtic Christianity which drew its piety and strength from St Cuthbert, its love of learning from the Venerable Bede, and which flowered again in the Methodism that conquered the mining villages and penetrated to every valley head. Here is a splendour of language as well as of landscape and architecture. The border ballads are no longer sung but a love of good conversation prevails.

The Rocks Beneath

The record of the rocks makes relatively easy reading. The land is built, essentially, of those rocks of the Carboniferous age which form the rolling moors of the north and the extensive heather-clad fells of the Pennines.

Eastwards, these rocks pass beneath the Coal Measures, which in their turn disappear beneath the newer Permian rocks, of which the most important member provides those unlikely hills, cliffs, caverns and sea-shore sculptures of the Durham coastline. Marsden offers the treat of a descent by lift down into the dining-room or bar of an inn excavated from the cliffs, and there the visitor can view (and hear) the turbulent colonies of fulmar petrels, kittiwakes and cormorants on the splendid Gothic pinnacle of Marsden Rock with its sea-worn arches.

The Romans

In the Museum of Antiquities, University of Newcastle upon Tyne, there is a superb reconstruction of a temple of Mithras, the Persian sun-god worshipped by the legions. It is rich in colour and decoration. On the altar lie the implements used to carry and kindle the specially-imported fir-cones. At Corstopitum, that Roman city within the Wall near Corbridge, we can see in plan the foundations of their granaries, temples, military quarters, aqueducts and drains. The garrison strong room, as deep and narrow as a mausoleum, is now open to the sky. In the museum we can see coins, tools, fragments of armour, pottery, jewelry – treasure and trivia of which the sum total has less power to move than the grooves made by wagon wheels at Housesteads, or a piece of coal recovered from the abandoned coal-hole of a Roman-British settlement at Bolam Lake.

The Wall

From Newcastle westwards, the Roman Wall may be easily discovered from the Military Road (the B6318). Much of the Military Road was constructed by General Wade, after the Rebellion of 1745, from the demolished stones of the Wall and often built over its foundations or those of the road that ran within it. Hence the story of an encounter with the apparition of a Roman officer on horseback, lopped short because he was riding along the *old* road below! In its final form the Wall was of stone 10 feet broad and too high to be scaled by one man on another man's shoulders. It was protected by a ditch. Within the

Wall ran a road, and, some distance behind it, a great flat-bottomed ditch known as the Vallum, used to delimit the military zone when the Wall was built by Hadrian about AD 122.

The Wall was pierced by gateways, called mile-castles because they are one Roman mile apart, with watch-towers at intervals, and further strengthened by 17 fortresses, like Housesteads and Chesters, each manned by auxiliary regiments.

If you would see the Wall at its best, go to Housesteads. There is a car park on the Military Road, and an uphill climb over pasture land leads to the southern gateway of the fortress. Outside the gateway is a cluster of buildings which may have been shops or taverns, or the posts of traders who dealt with the people of the country beyond the Wall. Within the fortress itself are the foundations of the commandant's house, the regimental shrine and latrine, and the inevitable granaries. The clifftop camp was built for 1,000 infantry.

Near Housesteads the Wall overlooks a cluster of little lakes, the Northumbrian loughs, and undulates like a snake of stone over rolling hills, to crown sheer cliffs and plunge headlong down steep ravines – in Camden's words, 'riding over the high pitches and steep descents, wonderfully rising and falling'. The feel of the country can only come from walking to Twice Brewed where there is a marvellous view (for motorists there is a car park near by). Or better still, if you are in good heart and can spare the time, to the Nine Nicks of Thirlwall, so-named because here the tribes once breached or 'thirled' the Wall.

Birds, Beasts and Flowers

St Cuthbert, it is said, loved the birds and beasts. The grey seals, which still inhabit the outer Farnes, kept vigil with him. Legend has it that he once gave his breakfast to an eagle, and that he taught the eider-ducks their gentle ways. They may still be seen riding the waves near Dunstanburgh, their brood following in a single line. The Lindisfarne Gospels are full of wild creatures and seabirds, perhaps a better guide to the Celtic imagination than to the living creatures. Thomas Bewick, in his illustrations and tailpieces to *British Birds and Quadrupeds*, is true to life, and adds affection to accuracy. He worked all his life in Newcastle, but he always retained his roots in the countryside.

His walks must often have taken him past the cottage at Wylam where George Stephenson was born. There is every opportunity to compare Bewick's art (many of his woodcuts and superb watercolours are collected together and displayed in the Newcastle Central Library and the Hancock Museum of Natural History) with the life of his native countryside; but one must go farther afield to see his raven ranging the Cheviot hilltops, or his wild white bull and surviving herd of wild white cattle in the park at Chillingham

Castle. Of all the gibbets which so obsessed him there remains only one, Stang Cross, on the moors at Elsdon. As one would expect in a region where at any given time the sheep will outnumber the human population, many birds – nearly two-thirds of those recorded in Britain – are to be found, and so are most of the British beasts. The Tweed and Coquet are great salmon rivers in the season that opens with a riot of rowan berries: the troutfisher's line still cuts the crystal air in these and the remainder of the streams and rivers of the region.

In Teesdale, on Widdybank Fell, with its bell-heather and juniper, are such rarities as the spring gentian, the bog-sandwort and the mealy primrose. In the Cheviot valleys, I am told, there are to be found star saxifrage, the dwarf cornel and *pyrola secunda*. But most of us will be content with the purple spread of heather over hills and fells; the cuckoo-pints and bluebells of Castle Eden and other denes; the waterside array of mint and kingcup along the waters of the Tyne. Or with the pansies of Weardale, the red and gold of butcher's broom on the Derwent slopes, and sand-dune treasure in harebells, campion, valerian and thyme.

A Choice of Buildings

I admit a preference for the odd and unconsidered works of man: the web of dry-stone walling, for instance, with its variations in technique and patterns of lichen, or those tiny chain-factories of Winlaton with their double hearths and stone water-troughs. There is nothing much of architectural interest, I suppose, in Heighington, in Durham, but the village with its watch-dog of a church and succession of greens is all of a piece, and there is pleasure in 'tasting', first Belsay, then Bywell, in Northumberland, one for its Italianate arcades and quiet dignity and the other for its unexpected riches of two churches, a castle and a market-cross in a meadow. The visitor who calls at the Palace of Bishop Auckland would be lacking in enterprise if he failed to deviate a mile or two to see the Saxon Church of Escomb, tall and narrow with some of the original floor of naked cobble still intact, before continuing to Durham and the Romanesque splendour which surrounds the shrine of St Cuthbert. He should look at the pele towers of Corbridge and Doddington as well as the castle of Alnwick, and walk a colliery wagonway as well as a Roman road. At Causey Arch, East Tanfield, in Durham, is a bridge built in 1727 to carry the wooden rails of one of those early railways over a deep ravine – a forerunner of Robert Stephenson's two-tier High Level Bridge built in 1849 at Newcastle upon Tyne and Royal Border Bridge at Berwick-upon-Tweed.

Durham Cathedral, high above the River Wear, has many magnificent features including its early vaulting

The Flavour of the Land

Castle, minster and ancient church – these are listed in the Gazetteer which follows. But there is much else. The gourmet will remember to sample 'caller herrin'' baked in rolls, and Craster kippers, as well as fresh salmon, but he will have to make friends with mining folk to enjoy 'singin' hinnies', spice loaf and stotty cake. The cult of the giant leek is followed from Bishop Auckland to Amble: on a September evening the visitor might do worse than call at a leek show, and sample a free bowl of soup with local ale.

If he should wish to return with other souvenirs than violet crystals of fluorspar, or a handful of barytes fragments in green, yellow, white and blue, there are casts of a Roman blacksmith or Celtic god to be had at Corstopitum or paintings of the Border school from the Stone and other Newcastle galleries.

With these would go memories and impressions, indelible pictures in the mind – of sheep flowing like a stream by the abandoned smelt-mill at Ramshaw, or folk gossiping in the square at near-by Blanchland. There would be the velvet lawns and jackdaws of Durham – or that token of cruel times, the grotesque, foliated face of the Sanctuary door knocker. There would be herdsmen driving cattle through the streets of Alnwick and Hexham, miners marching with banners and brass bands to their Durham 'Big Meeting', and an immaculate and dazzling ship passing on her first trial through Tynemouth piers into the open sea. Above all there would be the ring of voices, voices of shepherds, miners and ship-builders, farm-hands and steel-workers, different in shades of dialect but full of that warmth, that feeling for the 'hyam', or home, which lies between Tees and Tweed.

GAZETTEER

Alnwick, Nthmb   11M4
Attractive stone town, dominated by Alnwick Castle (Norman, but restored in the 14th, 18th and 19th c). Fortress home of the Duke of Northumberland where visitors can see keep, dungeon, museum, fine furnishings and old masters. The poker-tailed Percy lion gazes across town from an 83ft column raised by loyal tenants. Entrance to the broad cobbled market place, with its 1774 town hall, is through the sole surviving gateway, 15th-c Hotspur Tower. Howick Gardens (open April–Sept.) have flowers, shrubs and rhododendrons. St Michael's Church (mainly 15th-c) is unusually wide, with fine tombs and stone carving. The 13th–15th-c ruins of *Hulne Priory* overlook the Aln 3m NW, beyond the gatehouse remains of White Canons Abbey. At *Glanton*, 6m W, is the World Bird Research Station (open June–Sept. daily). *Alnmouth*, 4m SE, is a pretty estuary resort, popular for sand and dunes, golf and boating. *See also* **Dunstanburgh Castle.**

Bamburgh, Nthmb   11M5
Unspoiled seaside village clustered beneath a feudal red sandstone fortress jutting 150ft above the waters. Once a seat of kings, restored for domestic uses in later times, the castle admits visitors (April–Oct.) and offers them spectacular views of the *Farne Islands*, NT bird sanctuary. St Aidan's Church has 13th-c crypt and chancel and a churchyard monument to 19th-c lifeboat heroine Grace Darling. RNLI's museum opposite bears her name and illustrates her life. Trips to the Farne Islands begin at *Seahouses*, 1½m SE, a herring port now mainly devoted to holidaymakers. Further S is little *Beadnell* with dry-stone walled harbour and old lime kilns (NT). Broad sands and smooth sailing on Beadnell Bay. Remains of ancient St Ebba's Chapel. SW of Beadnell at Chathill is *Preston Pele* (AM) (1415). Open April–Sept.

Barnard Castle, Durham   9I7
Pleasant centre for Teesdale. Great Hall and the round keep remain of a 13th-c castle (AM) rising in lofty grounds. In the market place is an octagonal 1747 market-cross. Blagrave's House, a restaurant now, is Elizabethan. Charles Dickens stayed at the King's Head. Magnificent *Bowes Museum★* and gardens are remarkable civic treasures. 1½m SE are the

romantic riverside ruins of *Egglestone Abbey* (AM). St Mary's Church, *Staindrop*, 5m NE, dates from Saxon times and is crowned with Neville effigies. Their splendid moated **Raby Castle** near by boasts nine towers.

Beamish North of England Open Air Museum
see **Stanley** and page 21

Berwick-upon-Tweed, Nthmb   11L5
After changing hands 13 times, this picturesque border town has been English since 1482. Three bridges were flung across the salmon-filled river here, a handsome stone one of 15 arches in 1634, the towering Royal Border of 28 arches for the railway in 1850 and the less exciting Royal Tweed in 1928 for road traffic. There are ruins of the castle wall (AM), whose site is taken by the station. Elizabethan town walls (AM), well worth walking, were built to Italian design, unique in Britain and best-preserved in Europe. The 18th-c barracks contain a military museum. Within the walls is the town's Conservation Area. Good 18th-c buildings line the Quay Walls. The bells of the classical Guildhall (1754) ring for towerless Holy Trinity Church (erected 1648–52) and proclaim the 8 p.m. curfew. *Tweedmouth* and *Spittal*, S of the Tweed, have good beaches.

Blanchland,★ Nthmb   11L2
Exquisitely sheltered by moorland rising to 1,170ft at Dukesfield Fell N and Hangman's Hill, over 1,400ft to the W, this endearing village was created from mellow stones of the Abbey in the 18th c. A monastery gatehouse leads into the gravelled square. The church is basically the 13th-c Abbey chancel. Near by Derwent Reservoir offers sailing (to members of the club only), bird watching and a country park, *Pow Hill.*

Bowes, Durham   9I7
Sweeping views from the massive Norman keep (AM) within the one-time Roman hill fort here. Dickens's Dotheboys Hall is thought to have been modelled on the local school which closed after *Nicholas Nickleby* was published. St Giles' Church has a Roman dedication stone of about 204 as well as one Norman and one 13th-c font.

Brancepeth, Durham   9I8
In the grounds of the castle (largely 19th-c) is St Brandon's Church, a treasure house of the 17th-c Gothic Revival carving for which Bishop Cosin's restorations in County Durham are famous.

Brinkburn Priory *see* **Rothbury**

Bywell,★ Nthmb   11M2
Secluded on the Tyne are the dreamy reminders of a bustling medieval village serving two manors: a market-cross, a lifeless castle, a hall rebuilt by James Paine and two companionable churches – redundant St Andrew's with fine Anglo-Saxon tower and St Peter's with traces of that period. Thomas Bewick was born at Mickley Bank in *Ovingham*, 3m NE. His monument is in the 13th-c church, which retains its Saxon tower. 3m further NW is George Stephenson's Cottage (NT) at *Wylam*. Open April–end Oct. at set times. There is also a railway museum in the village. Across the Tyne from Bywell is *Prudhoe Castle* (AM) which dates from the 12th c. Notable for barbican, curtain wall and gatehouse.

Callaly Castle *see* **Whittingham**

Chester-le-Street, Durham   11M2
The Romans first built a fort here on the River Wear. In 882 the monks built a wooden church to house the body of St Cuthbert. The present church (11th–14th-c) displays 14 Lumley effigies jammed on to a bench. *Lumley Castle*, 1m E, a splendid quadrangle with crenellated towers only slightly altered since the late 14th c, is a hotel, offering Elizabethan banquets. *Lambton Castle*, 1½m NE, is essentially a 19th-c reproduction. *See also* **Finchale**.

Chesters *see* **Chollerford**

Chillingham, Nthmb   11L4
A village of neat cottages by the great park in which stands the 14th-c Chillingham Castle, ancestral home of the Earls of Tankerville. The famous herd (once depleted but now on the increase) of completely white cattle roams, as it has for 700 years, over 365 acres of the park. Open April–Oct. except Tues. *See also* **Wooler**.

Chollerford, Nthmb   11L2
On the North Tyne river, and near the Roman Wall (*see* Introduction) that runs through Chesters Park where a cavalry fort of the 2nd c (Cilurnum) has been expertly excavated on a 5-acre site (AM). Well-preserved bath house and an excellent museum. Chesters House (1771) has a stable block by James Paine.

Corbridge, Nthmb   11L2
A small picturesque town: the bridge is 17th-c, the church has a Saxon tower and the vicar's pele tower alongside is an information centre and art gallery. ½m NW, at *Corstopitum*

Chollerford: the Roman bath house and changing rooms at Fort Chesters – there were hot, cold, dry and steam baths

was a 3rd–4th-c military supply depot for the Roman wall. Here are the best preserved Roman granaries in Britain and an enlightening new museum. 1½m NE, *Aydon* has an unusually fine 13th-c fortified house (AM). To the SW, the Devil's Water flows through lovely woods, past ruined *Dilston Castle*, 1½m away. *See also* **Hunday National Tractor and Farm Museum**.

Cragside *see* **Rothbury**

Darlington, Durham   9J7
A busy Victorian market town, the western terminus of the world's first railway passenger line. Stephenson's *Locomotion No. 1* (1825) and the *Derwent* (1845) are exhibited at the North Road Station (1842) Railway Museum along with other railway relics. Also of interest is the Early English Collegiate Church of St Cuthbert, now hemmed in, but of great beauty (note the stone rood-screen, carved misericords and stalls, and spectacular font-cover). Good civic theatre and arts centre. The Tees Cottage Pumping Station shows the full range of motive power. Open April–Oct.

Dunstanburgh Castle, Nthmb   11M4
Superbly situated on the crags of the Whin Sill 8m NE of **Alnwick** at the S end of Embleton Bay, this great castle (AM), built in the 14th c, has been decaying since the 16th, but is still magnificent. *Embleton* village, standing back from the sea, has a fine church, and the pele tower of the vicarage is 15th-c. 2m S is the fishing village of *Craster* which gives its name to excellent oak-smoked kippers and 2m farther still, beyond *Cullernose*, is the village of *Howick*, with its harbour and 18th-c Hall, gardens and woods.

Durham,** Durham   9J8
The old city of Durham was originally confined to the rocky peninsula that is almost enclosed within a loop of the Wear, and was dominated by its cathedral and castle. Today it is essentially unchanged. In 1832 the University took over the castle but the superb 12th-c buildings remain, scarcely changed in appearance. It is one of the grandest sights in the country. The best view is from 18th-c Prebend's Bridge.

A good view of the cathedral can be seen from the gardens of St Aidan's College (designed by Sir Basil Spence). The cathedral's splendour is attributable to the fact that its basic structure – nave, chancel and transepts – was created in a single period, roughly 1093–1140. After that, the two principal additions were Bishop Pudsey's Galilee Chapel, about 1170, and, 60 years later, the Chapel of the Nine Altars behind the high altar. Neither of them detracts from the majesty of Bishop Flambard's nave. The Galilee Chapel contains the tomb of the Venerable Bede and the Chapel of Nine Altars that of St Cuthbert.

The same two bishops played a major part in the construction of the castle, whose Great Hall can, and should, be visited. The monks' dormitory attached to the cathedral contains Anglo-Saxon carvings and in the cathedral treasury museum, near the Undercroft Restaurant, is St Cuthbert's pectoral cross, the sanctuary knocker, plate and illuminated manuscripts. Palace Green, with its mainly 17th-c buildings, is delightful, while N and S Bailey, with attractive old houses, remind us by their name that these were once part of the city's fortifications. Durham has several other museums, notably the unique (in Britain) University of Durham's Museum of Oriental Art, the Heritage Centre, the Durham Light Infantry Museum and Arts centre and the Old Fulling Mill Museum of Local Archeology. The Regatta in June is claimed to be Britain's oldest rowing event.

Escomb, Durham   9I7
2½m from *Bishop Auckland*. St John the Evangelist is a nearly perfect Anglo-Saxon church which is made of Roman stones. Sundial over porch may be the oldest in the country still in its original position.

Finchale, Durham   9J8
Here, 2m NE of the village of *Pity Me*, are the ruins of a 13th-c priory (AM) (open April–Sept.). Not only are these the most important remains in the county, but they lie in a lovely curve of the River Wear, with a background formed by trees. A bridge across the river leads to Cocken Wood. *See also* **Chester-le-Street**.

Ford,* Nthmb   11J5
Ford and neighbouring *Etal,** both charming villages on the River Till, with the Cheviots rising 5m to the S, and both with castles of the 14th c. Ford was Gothicized by Robert Adam in the 18th and modified in the 19th c; the other is a picturesque ruin. The village of Ford was remodelled in the 19th c by the Marchioness of Waterford whose Biblical paintings line the former village schoolroom. At Etal there is also an 18th-c manor. *Duddo*, some 3m N, has a group of prehistoric standing stones.

Gainford, Durham   9I7
A greystone village above the River Tees, with an attractive green. The beautiful 13th-c church (Jacobean font-cover and monument to John Middleton) stands close by the river, and the Hall is Elizabethan, well restored in 19th c. Gainford Hall, with its 11 chimneys, was built *c.*1600. At *Winston*, 2m W, is another Teesside village, with a fine single-span bridge built in 1762–3 to carry coal into Yorkshire.

Gibside, Tyne and Wear   11M2
Here, on the Derwent, 3m SW of *Whickham*, is a once notable 18th-c estate. In the landscaped grounds is a mausoleum designed by James Paine *c.*1760 (converted into a church 50 years later, now restored by the NT), which is perfectly furnished with period three-decker pulpit and sounding board, and box-pews. Open April–Oct. at stated times.

Guisborough, Cleveland   9K7
The ruins of the great Augustinian priory (AM) founded by Robert the Bruce in 1119 stand in the grounds of the 19th-c Guisborough Hall, but the monument known as Bruce Cenotaph, rescued from the priory at the Dissolution of the Monasteries, is in St Nicholas's Church in the old town. An attractive dormitory for industrial Teesside and a good centre for visiting the near-by moors and dales.

Hadrian's Wall *see* Introduction, **Chester-le-Street, Chollerford, Corbridge, Hexham, Housesteads** and also entry in Cumbria

Haltwhistle, Nthmb   11K2
A country town wonderfully situated in the S Tyne valley, where the Caw Burn flows down from Greenlee Lough, beyond the Roman Wall (*see* Introduction). Just outside the town are the ruins of *Bellister Castle*; *Blenkinsopp Castle* (1339) is 3m W, and 1m farther on are the ruins of *Thirlwall Castle*, itself built with stones robbed from the Wall. Most attractive of all is *Featherstone*, a Jacobean rebuilding of a medieval castle, 3½m SW, in its wooded park above the river.

Hexham,* Nthmb   11L2
Perhaps the most romantic of all Northumbrian towns still sturdily withstanding some blatant modernization. Seen

from the Tyne bridge, the priory ruins and church, the 15th-c moot hall and still earlier manor office (or jail) stand out against a distant background of trees. There are parts of an Elizabethan grammar school; and the curious market covered with piazzas (1766). But the chief building is the Priory Church of St Andrew (only fragments of the monastic buildings remain). Here we find the finest surviving Saxon crypt in England, the remnant of the first church on the site, built with stones from the Roman base near **Corbridge**. In the church look at the Early English choir, rood-screen (1491–1524) and transepts, the unique broad and worn night stair, three Saxon treasures – a frith stool, font bowl and the Acca cross – and the medieval misericords. Middle March Centre for Border History is open April–Nov. 14m SW is *Allerdale*, famed for its Baal Fire on 31 December. *See also* **Chollerford**.

Holy Island *see* **Lindisfarne**

Houghton-le-Spring, Tyne and Wear   11N2
A one-time mining town, now an area shopping centre, where at the 13th-c St Michael and All Angels' Church, Bernard Gilpin, the Apostle of the North, is buried in a tomb chest. The Kepier Grammar School buildings (1574) and 17th-c Davenport almshouses face the churchyard.

Housesteads,* Nthmb   11K2
The most visited site on the Roman Wall and best preserved of its forts, AM cared for by the NT. Housesteads is a major NT/National Park Information Centre. ½m uphill from the car park is the infantry garrison (Verovicium) with its hospital, baths and flush-latrine. From here visitors can walk the best-preserved section of the Wall, rewarded by breath-taking views. 8m W is the Carvoran Roman Army Museum at *Greenhead*, where the life of the Roman army of occupation is documented.

Hunday National Tractor and Farm Museum,
Nthmb   11L2
At *Newton*, Stocksfield, 6m E of **Corbridge**. Unique agricultural and farm museum of vintage tractors, engines and hand tools, plus a farm kitchen and dairy showing evolution of farm work 1880–1950. Narrow-gauge railway. Open daily.

Hylton Castle *see* **Sunderland**

Ingram, Nthmb   11L4
An angler's village on the Breamish, where it comes tumbling down from Cushat Law, Comb Fell and Hedgehope Hill, all over 2,000ft (with Cheviot itself, 2,676ft, just behind them). In *Breamish Valley* is a Northumberland National Park information centre and camp site. Near the waterfall of Linhope Spout, is the prehistoric village of *Greaves Ash*.

Jarrow, Tyne and Wear   11N2
The shipbuilding town made famous by the 1936 'Jarrow Hunger March' was the 'cradle of English learning' when the Venerable Bede lived and worked in the monastery (AM) founded in 681. The chancel of St Paul's Church is the Saxon nave of the church Bede knew. A Victorian nave was added in 1866. The monastic ruins lie beside it. A green separates the church from the 18th-c Jarrow Hall, preserved as the Bede Monastery Museum. Modern shopping precinct.

Kielder Water, Nthmb   11K3
This vast reservoir, created by damming the North Tyne, has a maximum depth of 170ft and has added new recreational possibilities to the Border Forest National Park. Fishing, sailing, pony trekking, nature trails, picnic areas, camping and caravan sites are provided for. The largest manmade lake in Europe, it extends for 7m with 27½m of shoreline. Fine views from the Victorian railway duct. An information centre and Forestry Commission Centre are maintained at Kielder Castle, once the shooting lodge of the Dukes of Northumberland, ½m N of *Bakethin*. A 12m forest drive leads from there to *Byrness*.

Lanchester, Durham   9I8
A Norman and 13th-c church, with fine carving in chancel (tympanum and corbel heads), and three pieces of 13th-c stained glass. In the porch is a Roman altar to the goddess Garmangabis, probably from the Roman fort of Longovicium, ½m SW, which was in use till the end of the 4th c. The former **Durham** to Consett line through Lanchester is being reclaimed as a 12m countryside walk.

Lindisfarne, Nthmb   11M5
Or *Holy Island* (as St Aidan came here from **Iona**, Strathclyde, at the invitation of St Oswald to teach the new faith in the 7th c) is less than 2m by 2m in extent, yet it has a village, a public house, a 16th-c castle (NT) converted to a residence by Sir Edwin Lutyens in 1903, and the ruins of an 11th-c Benedictine monastery (AM), plundered by the Vikings. At low tide, the island can be reached on foot or by car across the causeway (see tide tables) from *Beal*, a small seaside and golfing resort.

Marton in Cleveland, Cleveland   9K7
A suburb of **Middlesbrough** but a village when Captain James Cook was born in 1728 to a farm labourer and his wife. The Captain Cook Birthplace Museum stands close to the site (marked by a granite vase) in Stewart Park. Here are a model of the *Endeavour*, a life-size effigy of Cook and displays tracing the life of the great navigator. A Cook monument stands high on Easby Moor.

Middlesbrough, Cleveland   9J7
Port on the S of the Tees estuary, noted for pig iron, steel and petrochemical industries, and for having produced the material for some of the world's most famous engineering structures, such as Sydney Harbour Bridge and the Storstroem Bridge in Denmark. The town's own remarkable bridges, the Transporter, which can carry nine vehicles and 600 persons, and the Tees (Newport) Bridge, which operates on a vertical lift and can rise 100ft in 45 seconds, are reminders of this town's achievements. The centre has been rebuilt with covered shopping and pedestrian precincts. 3m SE is 18th-c *Ormesby Hall* and Gardens (NT) (open April–Sept. at set times). *See also* **Marton in Cleveland**.

Middleton-in-Teesdale, Durham   9H7
An attractive village in the SW corner of the county where the River Lune, flowing down from Outberry Plain (2,143ft), joins the Tees, continuing over the Yorkshire boundary into Lune Dale. 5m NW is the impressive *High Force* waterfall, where the Tees drops 70ft. The snug terraces were built when lead mining flourished. Middleton House was the headquarters of the London Lead Co. Near by also are Bowlees and Hanging Shaw (waterfalls and cliffs) on the B6277. On the *Pennine Way* and a good centre for exploring *Teesdale*.

Morpeth, Nthmb   11M3
An ancient town situated in the lovely Wansbeck Valley. The clock tower, once a prison, still nightly sounds the curfew. The church, largely 14th-c, has some fine glass, and there are ruins of a castle, but most of the town dates from

the fire in the 17th c, including Vanbrugh's modified town hall (1714). *Mitford*, 1m W, is a village with an ancient church, a pretty vicarage and a ruined castle, sited on a rocky hill. Near by, on the right bank of the Wansbeck, are the ruins of *Newminster Abbey*. 3m downstream, *Bothal* has a 14th-c gateway to its castle, and a church with an angel roof and the fine Ogle tomb. 6m W is *Meldon Park* built by John Dobson in 1832. Fine rhododendrons. Open in summer.

Newbiggin-by-the-Sea, Nthmb   11M3
Originally an old fishing village and mining centre but now a seaside resort. The church (13th-c) has a fine spire. Leisure facilities include the Wansbeck Riverside Park. 1m S at *Ashington* is 11th-c Woodhorn Church now a museum.

Newcastle upon Tyne,★ Tyne and Wear   11M2
Once a Roman fort and settlement, Saxon monastery, medieval borough, Norman stronghold and now the capital and industrial hub of Tyneside. The city has altered dramatically with motorways and developments such as the huge Eldon Square covered shopping centre (one of the largest in Europe), but some 19th-c achievements, including dignified Grey Street with the Theatre Royal and the Grey Monument, recall the rebuilding of the centre by Richard Grainger and John Dobson 1835–40. Dobson also designed the fine Central Station. From earlier periods, examples are the well-preserved Norman keep of the castle, which, with the adjoining Black Gate, now houses Roman antiquities and the world's first Bagpipe Museum; surviving sections of the turreted town walls; and the cathedral, with its crypt and rare 'crown' spire. The most noteworthy of the other churches is perhaps the (now redundant) elliptical All Saints', rebuilt in classical style in the 18th c. The Guildhall,

Newcastle upon Tyne: the oldest bridge is the two-tier High Level Bridge beyond the arched New Tyne Bridge

given a new front in 1796, retains its 17th-c interior; and the Holy Jesus Hospital (17th-c), recently renovated, houses the John George Joicey Museum depicting local history and period furniture and a regimental museum. The Laing Art Gallery has an excellent collection of British art, local ceramics, and glass. The Hancock Museum of Natural History has major new displays of John Hancock's famous collection of birds. There is also an excellent museum of science and engineering near the Central Station with motive power and maritime galleries. The *Turbinia*, the world's fastest ship in the 1890s, can be viewed at Exhibition Park. Sandhill, by the quayside, has 17th-c domestic architecture, notably the fine Surtees House; and the city is remarkable for its open spaces, among them the 927-acre Town Moor and picturesque Jesmond Dene Park. In the N the new buildings of the University and the Civic Centre (Civic Trust Award) dominate the skyline. The University houses the Hatton Art Gallery, Greek museum and Museum of Antiquities. Blackfriars, a 13th-c Dominican friary, now restored, is a tourist information centre with crafts workshops and a useful exhibition of the city's growth. Six bridges and the Tyne Tunnel connect the city to the S bank. The coastline to the N is designated an area of outstanding natural beauty – *see* **Bamburgh, Dunstanburgh** and **Warkworth**.

Norham, Nthmb   11L5
A grey little village on the Tweed, with a pleasant vicarage beside the church (fine Norman chancel) at one end and, on high ground at the other, the keep of the Norman castle (AM), associated with Scott's *Marmion*. Norham Station was closed in 1965 and is now a railway museum (open weekday afternoons).

Prudhoe Castle *see* **Bywell**

Raby Castle, Durham   9I7
1m N of *Staindrop* which has a lovely village green. Moated seat of Lord Barnard. Rising of the North was plotted in 1569 in Barons' Hall. Victorian drawing-room, medieval kitchen, portraits, coachhouse, stables tea-room and deer park. *See also* **Barnard Castle**.

Rothbury, Nthmb   11L3
A charming village in the heart of Coquetdale with Simonside (1,409ft) towering up to the S. Excellent fishing, touring and walking centre. *Cragside*, now owned by the NT, the ebullient Victorian mansion built for the 1st Lord Armstrong, the arms maker, by Richard Norman Shaw is just outside Rothbury. The first house to be lit by electricity, it holds a series of interesting rooms with Shaw-designed furniture climaxed by a great drawing-room with 10-ton marble chimneypiece and inglenook. The famous rock gardens and woodlands, long open to the public, now form a 900-acre country park. NW are the ruins of *Cartington Castle*; and 4m downstream stands *Brinkburn Priory* (AM), wonderfully situated by the river, its church very well restored in the 19th c. 7m W is Lady's Well (NT) at *Holystone*.

Ryton, Tyne and Wear   11M2
Most attractive of Tyneside villages, with its green, its 18th-c houses and cottages and the broach spire of Holy Cross (17th-c screen and stalls) rising from the trees.

Seaton Delaval,★ Nthmb   11N2
The Hall, Vanbrugh's masterpiece and one of the outstanding secular buildings in the county, with its gardens, orangery, obelisks and statues, is now the scene of medieval

banquets. Seaton Sluice, a curious harbour built in 1670 by a Delaval for the growing coal trade, has gates operated by the tides. Open May–Sept. at set times.

Sedgefield, Durham   **9J7**
Grouped around the green are the early 18th-c almshouses, rectory and manor (now council offices), and the notable Early English church (fine stone carving in chancel, and 17th-c woodwork). The grounds of *Hardwick Hall*, 1m W, form a country park around an 18th-c lake and arboretum.

Stanhope, Durham   **9I8**
An attractive little Weardale town, 700ft up and with fells all around, rising to over 2,000ft in the SW. There is a medieval church, with Flemish carved oak inside and a petrified tree stump without. The old rectory (Stone House) was built in 1697 and rebuilt in 1821. The castle on the market place was rebuilt in 1798 in medieval fashion. In *Stanhope Dene* are remains of lead and iron mines and from there the South Beck leads to Heathery Burn Cave, 500ft long, where Bronze Age tools, weapons and ornaments were found and are now displayed in the **British Museum**.

Stanley, Durham   **11M2**
The North of England Open Air Museum on the old *Beamish* estate was created by four county councils to illustrate the region's past. A reconstituted colliery and pit village, a railway and station and a farm can be examined here. *See also* page 21. The period rooms and collections in Beamish Hall include a schoolroom, chemist's shop, tea room and pub, all Victorian. Open Easter–Sept. daily, winter daily except Mon. 1m N is Causey Arch, the oldest railway bridge in the world.

Sunderland, Tyne and Wear   **11N2**
An ancient settlement and an industrial town for centuries, latterly concentrating on shipbuilding, engineering and glassmaking. It is also a seaside resort with 2m of sandy beaches. The Museum and Art Gallery exhibits pottery, glass and silver; Grindon Museum has Edwardian period rooms (post office etc.); the North East Aircraft Museum at the airport is open on Sun. The Town Hall and Civic Centre is an impressive modern building. The town's Crowtree Leisure Centre is one of the largest in Europe. Souter Lighthouse, with the largest lamp now in use, gives climbers a fine view of the coast. Monkwearmouth on the N bank of the Wear was the site of a large monastery established in 674, seven years before **Jarrow**. St Peter's Church was part of it, the first English church to use window glass. Victorian Monkwearmouth Railway Station is now a Museum of Land Transport. Also of the same period are Ryhope Pumping Station, now an engine and water museum, and Fulwell Mill. On Penshaw Hill SW of the town is the *Penshaw Monument* (NT), a notable 19th-c landmark. 3¾m W is *Hylton Castle* (AM), a ruined 15th-c gatehouse, keep and chapel guarding a ford on the Wear. *See also* **Washington** and **Houghton-le-Spring.**

Tynemouth, Tyne and Wear   **11N2**
An old, still-popular resort with good beaches made special by the ruins of a wealthy priory and castle (AM) on the cliffs. Prior's Haven is a sandy cove for water sports of all kinds and a statue of Admiral Collingwood overlooks the harbour.

The Volunteer Life Brigade Museum is worth a visit. N are *Cullercoats*, once a fishing port and artists' colony, and *Whitley Bay* with its wide range of seaside amusements.

Wallington Hall, Nthmb   **11L3**
Near the village of *Cambo*, 12m W of **Morpeth**. This Hall (NT), is distinguished as much by its public-spirited former occupants, from Sir Walter Blackett to the Trevelyans, as by its architecture, though it is surely one of the finest stately homes in the county. Dating from 1688, it was much altered in the 1740s. Fine rococo plasterwork, furniture (including Lord Macaulay's writing desk), porcelain, paintings, and dolls' houses are among the contents. There are also a museum of coaches, a walled garden with notable fuchsias and roses and 100 acres of woods and lakes to enjoy. Open April–Oct. at stated times.

Wark-on-Tyne, Nthmb   **11L2**
Charmingly situated on the North Tyne river, with picturesque *Chipchase Castle* (Jacobean additions to an ancient pele tower); 2m SE. Wark was the seat of Scottish rule in Tynedale until the 14th c.

Warkworth, Nthmb   **11M4**
A magnificent ruined 12th–15th-c castle (AM) of multi-coloured stone, spectacular even on this coast bristling with castles, dominates the village. A fortified bridge (1379; pedestrians only) crosses the Coquet and a steep street of 18th-c houses leads up to the castle keep (open to the public). The Norman church with its stone spire has been well restored. The *Hermitage* (AM) dug into the riverbank is upstream and is open April–Sept.; in the other direction, is a beach, 1m away.

Washington, Tyne and Wear   **11M2**
Washington Old Hall, in Washington New Town District 4, 5m W of **Sunderland**, is the home of the ancestors of the first president of the U.S.A. George Washington 1183–1613. It has been restored with American help by the NT. Beamed rooms with period furnishings and Washington mementoes. Open March–Oct. daily except Wed., Nov.–Feb. weekend afternoons. Washington has a large waterfowl wildlife park (District 15) designed by Sir Peter Scott (open daily). There is also an Arts Centre at Biddick Farm, and an industrial museum.

Whittingham, Nthmb   **11L4**
A pretty village on the Aln. It has a modernized pele tower, and a pre-Conquest church, whose size testifies to the importance of the place when the main western route to Scotland crossed the river here, before it was diverted to Coldstream. A Saxon tower was replaced in 1840. *Callaly Castle* (NT), 2m away, is a 17th-c mansion incorporating a 13th-c pele tower and Georgian and Victorian additions. Italian stucco artists from **Wallington Hall** worked on the drawing-room. Open April–Sept. weekends.

Wooler, Nthmb   **11L4**
An excellent centre for walking enthusiasts, close to the *Cheviot Hills*. Various walks are organized and there are Forestry Commission trails. The Cheviot Field Centre and Museum is open daily. NW near *Branxton* is the site of the battle of Flodden (1513).

CUMBRIA

AN INTRODUCTION BY
MARGUERITE STEEN

This county comprises the territory of the former Cumberland and Westmorland, plus a small area from Lancashire north of Morecambe Bay. The new name was, in fact, in general use long before the official boundary changes gave it the stamp of authority.

The unifying feature of this area is the beauty of the scene, the purity of the light and the dramatic variations of colour and contour, which become progressively exciting as one penetrates inland, leaving the flat coastal strip with the river-mouths of Kent, Leven, Duddon, Esk and Derwent for the mountains, purple with heather and flaming with bracken in autumn, bejewelled with lakes and tarns, each holding its own colouring of purple, blue, green or near-black.

Rock and Rain

Over millions of years volcanic eruptions, floods, frosts, snows and rains shaped what today is known as the Lake District. The traces of glaciers are left on its rocks, its milder contours indicate what once were moraines, its small, savage screes are survivals of the Ice, Stone, Bronze and Iron Ages. Glaciated igneous rocks form its core, with small outcrops of limestone, printed with fossils. At Kentmere lie the post-glacial deposits known as diatomite. Fault lines have influenced the pattern of its valleys, winds and warfare its dark, uncompromising architecture.

The climate (admitted, even by residents, to be a little formidable) is largely responsible for the notable beauty of the region, which receives the western, rain-bearing winds direct from the sea; the hills enjoy the heaviest rainfall in England – hence the soft air, the delicacy of the colouring, the luxuriance of trees and herbage. Lakelanders say with truth that to know the full glory of their country is to visit during the winter months, when the mountain tops are lost in low-rolling cloud, when the lakes overflow (on rare occasions Bassenthwaite and Derwentwater, Buttermere and Crummock, become two instead of four), and fearsome sunrises are succeeded by no less fearsome sunsets. It is under these conditions that the traveller may come closest to appreciation of the local character, with its toughness and resilience – for himself, he may be excused for preferring the mild spring and summer, or the glowing autumn.

Rural Industries

The paramount rural industry is sheep-farming. Ancestors of the little dark Herdwicks were, according to a highly dubious legend, washed ashore from the wreck of a Dutch East-Indiaman, and established themselves on the loose shale and thin turf of the hillsides. From their fleece was made the famous hodden grey, a coarse, hard-wearing tweed admirably handled by Lakeland tailors. John Peel 'with his coat so grey' is buried in Caldbeck churchyard. The Herdwick sheep tend today to be replaced by Swaledales – heavier, better mothers and economically more satisfactory.

Next to sheep, tourism is the major industry and, as such, now taken seriously. Cumbria has suffered little from the so-called progress which has invaded less-remote regions. It is expensive to drive new roads into the mountains, but very few farms are now without the benefits of electricity.

Some Tours

For the motorist, making his preliminary survey of the district, there are certain 'musts'. One is the good road from Newby Bridge, skirting Windermere, north by Ambleside, the quiet waters of Rydal and Grasmere, over Dunmail Raise, by Thirlmere to Keswick at the head of Derwentwater; thence following Bassenthwaite and the Derwent Valley to Carlisle. This route affords an inimitable panorama of the better-known lakes and, at a distance, of Helvellyn, Skiddaw and Blencathra, giants of the Lakeland mountains. From Kendal one may break off over the beautiful desolation of Shap Fell, with its eery light and eerier legends, to Penrith and the Scottish border; alternatively there is the road over Kirkstone Pass and by Ullswater, which brings one to the same destination. Westward from Kendal, skirting the Langdale Pikes which like slumbering elephants, trunk to trunk, dominate the horizon, a more adventurous driver can reach Wastwater, most

The Lake District. The largest lake in England is Lake Windermere which is over 10 miles long

dramatic of the lakes with its dark water and plunging screes. Having made these lengthy journeys, the motorist has no more than scratched the surface, unless he has at some moment abandoned his four wheels, to climb to the tarns, such as small, bleak Goats' Water. None but the walker can claim more than superficial acquaintance with the Lake District.

Flora and Fauna

Cumbria was formerly rich in wild flowers. Chemicals and agricultural mechanization have now robbed the hedgerows and accessible woodlands of many of their treasures; but in the more distant reaches may still be found such rarities as the bee orchis, pink sundew, bird's-eye primrose, bog asphodel, various saxifrages and parnassus grass. On the limestone flourishes the rock rose, in all its varieties of colour, and wild scabious.

Fauna include the usual small rodents and mammals; ermine (the white-coated, winter stoat) has been seen above Wastwater; red deer, fox and otter.

Trout and salmon, formerly free to local fishermen, now require a licence. A little game is strictly preserved. Free to the eye and camera of the naturalist are goosander and great crested grebe, winter visitors. Occasionally osprey, great grey shrike, waxwing and rock dove – even, rarely, the golden eagle. Peregrine, buzzard, woodpecker and wood-warbler breed locally. The heron is a familiar figure on the fringes of lakes and estuaries. Curlew, plover and gull nest in bogs.

The roar of the red deer, the bark of the fox, contribute to the local music of waterfall, curlew and that shy, occasional visitant, the whooper swan, while Old Brock, the badger, lumbers about his business.

The Past and Present

The Stone Age men who tamed the wild goat, grew corn and made the querns in which to grind it would be surprised today to find their troughs used as bird baths in private gardens. The Roman invasion under Agricola swept north through Cumbria and left its traces in the western terminus of Hadrian's Wall at Bowness on Solway, and in forts such as those at

Hardknott and Ravenglass. It was not until 1157 that Cumberland became part of England. After the Roman invasion and the Norman Conquest it still belonged to the Scottish kingdom of Strathclyde. Hence some of the names: Blencathra, Helvellyn, Glaramara, Skiddaw. Runic and Celtic relics in the form of fonts or crosses survived the long Border warfare, which ended in the battle of Clifton Moor, near Penrith, in 1745. During those belligerent years were built the numerous castles and fortified churches (notably Salkeld) and all the little yards and courts in which the peaceful population took refuge from the marauders. In 1745 Prince Charles Edward Stuart advanced from Carlisle with his army of Highlanders on what was to prove a disastrous expedition and was beaten back along the same track from Derby. 'Here the Pretender stabled his troops' is a common label along the line of that dolorous pilgrimage, which may be traced today in a rusted stirrup, a scrap of chain armour, or even the armoured corpse of one of Charles Edward's troopers, reclaimed (as the writer saw) from the peat which preserved it.

You may fish, swim, shoot, sail and glide. Beagling is a favoured sport. Sheep-farming and fox-hunting run together: the footpacks of the Blencathra and Melbreak hounds are strongly supported by farmers, shepherds, quarrymen and others. There is a variety of climbing, some of the climbs rated 'Vee Diff' in mountaineering vocabulary. The famous Tophet Bastion offers hazards which are regarded respectfully even by alpinists.

Of spectator sports there is endless variety. Sheepdog Trials take in Hound Trails and Terrier Shows. Sheepdogs are the leading event and attract competitors from across the Yorkshire and Scottish borders. The Hound Trail has peculiar fascination for the stranger: specially bred hounds hunt a drag of oil and aniseed and are heavily backed by the local fancy. As for the Lakeland terrier, his section of the show is invariably popular – a tough, courageous little character, equal to tackling a fox in its earth. After the Trials, Grasmere Sports is the leading event of the season, and here Cumberland wrestling takes pride of place. There are fell-racing and point-to-points. The winter visitor has fine skating or curling on the tarns and good skiing on Helvellyn.

The Mary Wakefield Westmorland Musical Festival, held biennially in Kendal, was the forerunner of many of its kind which, in the last half century, have sprung up all over the country. Fifty years ago it was attracting musicians and singers of world-wide renown to the town and it is still a notable local event.

Famous Figures

Cumbria, for all its beauty, has attracted writers rather than painters. The Lakes conspicuously lack a Constable. Of the Lakeland Poets, Wordsworth, the indigenous one, was born at Cockermouth, educated at Hawkshead, lived at Grasmere and Rydal, and is buried in Grasmere churchyard. Southey lived for 40 years at Greta Hall, near Keswick, and is buried at Crosthwaite; Thomas de Quincey lived at Nab Cottage on Rydal Water. Ruskin lived for nearly 30 years at Brantwood, near Coniston.

Of modern writers, Constance Holme rates as the Mary Webb of the Lakes; she lived at Milnthorpe, the so-called 'lost seaport' of Westmorland on the Kent estuary. After Graham Sutton's less well-known work, one turns for the Cumbrian scene to Hugh Walpole's Herries saga. The four big romantic novels, written at 'Brackenburn' on the shores of Derwentwater, range from the early 18th century to the present day. Beatrix Potter's house at Sawrey attracts an average of 70,000 visitors every year. The creator of Peter Rabbit devoted a handsome share of her royalties to the purchase of some 4,000 acres of land which she left to the National Trust.

GAZETTEER

Ambleside 8F6
A sheltered situation under Wansfell and within 1m of Lake **Windermere** provides excellent walking (to Loughrigg Terrace and Jenkin Crag for views), for ascents of Wansfell Pike (1,587ft) and Loughrigg Fell (1,101ft) and for touring the Langdales. The fascinating 17th-c Bridge House, in Chapel Hill, once a summer house surrounded by orchards, is an information centre for the NT. It is the smallest property owned by the NT. Once part of Ambleside House it became the NT's first information centre in 1926. A picturesque ceremony takes place every July when children come in procession to strew the floor of St Mary's Church (19th-c) with rushes. The extensive Roman fort of Galava (AM) at *Borrans Field* at the head of the lake, shows signs of having been rebuilt after flooding. *Stagshaw Gardens* (NT), a woodland garden with views 1m S, are open in spring.

Appleby 8G7
Its High Street rises steeply from the Eden Valley. The castle was held for Charles Stuart by the Lady Anne Clifford whose marble monument is in the church of St Lawrence. The Norman keep is surrounded by beautiful lawns. At the June Horse Fair, gypsies gather outside the town.

Arnside 8G6
A pretty little holiday resort on the E side of the Kent estuary, looking across to **Grange**, and up to the Lakeland hills. Pleasant walks over Arnside Knott (NT). Arnside Tower, SE of the Knott, belonged to the Stanleys.

Barrow-in-Furness 8F5
The red sandstone *Furness Abbey* (AM), situated in the 'Vale of Deadly Nightshade' 1½m N of this shipbuilding

town, was founded in 1127 by a small group of monks. The layout of the ruined monastic buildings is clear, and substantial portions of the church towers, walls and architectural detail have survived. Note the treasures in the chapter house, the rows of stone seats in the sanctuary, and the effigies of 12th-c knights in the Infirmary Chapel.

Bewcastle 11K2
Remote moorland village which was the site of a Roman fort with a ruined castle revealing material taken from **Hadrian's Wall**. It has also the shaft of a cross (7th–8th-c) sculptured on all four sides and standing in the churchyard.

Birdoswald 11K2
The turf continuation of **Hadrian's Wall** runs to the N of this Roman camp. Its remains include a stone wall, a corn-drying kiln, and stones showing the marks of Roman chisels have been used for building near-by farmhouses. Small discoveries can be seen in **Carlisle** Museum.

Blencathra 8F7
Mountain E of Skiddaw also known as Saddleback (2,847ft). It should be climbed from *Threlkeld* or following the ridge from *Scales*.

Bolton 8G7
Pretty church with two Norman doorways, unusual stone-work and a geometrical chancel-screen.

Borrowdale★★ 8F7
Perhaps the most beautiful of the Lakeland valleys, situated above **Derwentwater** on the road from **Keswick**. *Castle Crag*, an ancient fort between the Jaws of Borrowdale, and the arrestingly balanced *Bowder Stone* are features of note.

Bowness on Solway 11I2
Site of the Roman camp at the western extremity of **Hadrian's Wall**. The bells in the church porch were stolen from Scotland as a reprisal after a border raid in which the church's own bells were lost in Solway Firth.

Brampton 11J2
Market town within reach of **Hadrian's Wall**, a pretty lake known as Talkin Tarn, and the Written Rock above the River Gelt, where a Roman standard-bearer has carved a moving inscription. *Lanercost Priory* (AM), 2m NE, stands in the beautiful meadowland bordering the Irthing. The Early English nave is still used for worship. Note the Lanercost Cross (1214) in the aisle, the clerestory arches, and the 12th-c gatehouse where Edward I was three times received by the monks. Open April–Sept.

Brough 9H7
A strategic route centre from the earliest times. There is a Roman fort and a strongly built Norman castle (AM) which is open throughout the year. The village is divided into *Church Brough* and *Market Brough*, where the annual fair held in late Sept. is still an important occasion for gypsy families.

Brougham 8G7
Situated at a strategic crossroads, near **Penrith**. The Roman fort of Brocavum may be seen in the field S of the medieval castle, the 12th-c keep of which is particularly fine (AM). Open to the public throughout the year. Like **Brough**, the castle came into the hands of the Clifford family, and was repaired during the 17th c by the redoubtable Lady Anne Clifford.

Broughton-in-Furness 8F6
The spacious market square, with stocks and fish slabs, still has an air of the 18th c. Broughton Tower dates from the 19th c, and is built on the site of an old defensive tower, but is not open to the public.

Burgh-by-Sands 11J2
Edward I, who died within sight of Scotland on his way N against Robert the Bruce, was brought back to lie in state in this fortified church. The 12th-c tower, embattled and without ornamentation, has the appearance of a Norman keep. A monument to Edward I stands near the village. Lamonby Farm, a restored 17th-c longhouse of cruck-framed construction with clay walls, is open to the public throughout the year.

Buttermere 8F7
The village, built on a level site, is finely situated between the lakes of Buttermere and Crummock Water.

Caldbeck 8F8
John Peel lies in the graveyard surrounded by the fells where he hunted on foot with his hounds for years. The rousing song about him was written in the huntsman's lifetime by his friend J. W. Graves.

Carlisle★ 11J2
Always a border stronghold against the Scots, the town never surrendered until 1745, when the Young Pretender rode in on a white horse preceded by 100 pipers – very soon to return beaten and dispirited after the retreat from **Derby**. The cathedral suffered partial destruction in 1645 at the hands of General Leslie. Its proportions have been affected, though some Norman work of 1123 and much detail have been spared. Note the E window, which has glass as beautiful as any in **York** Minster.

The castle (AM) (open all year) founded in 1092, has in its inner ward a Norman keep, at the top of which is a windowless cell named after MacIvor, Sir Walter Scott's hero in *Waverley*; the walls and door are covered by drawings made by prisoners. Mary Queen of Scots was imprisoned in Queen Mary's Tower (now a military museum) in 1568. Tullie House Museum and Art Gallery has impressive Roman remains from **Hadrian's Wall**. Recent excavations in the city centre have revealed well-preserved Roman buildings of wood. St Cuthbert's Church is a fine 18th-c building, and has a unique movable pulpit.

Cartmel 8F5
The 12th-c priory church was unroofed at the Dissolution. Some fine bench-ends show the effect of weathering before the church was restored and it is provided with a black oak screen of Flemish workmanship – the rarest of its great possessions. Note also the tomb of Sir John Harrington (c.1380) and an umbrella used for centuries to shelter the vicar officiating at burials. Kent's Bank was the N end of the 7m route across **Morecambe** Sands (Lancs) used by coaches and horsemen before the coming of steam.

Castlerigg Circle 8F7
1½m E of **Keswick**. Ring of 48 standing stones (AM), the biggest nearly 8ft high – assumed to be Keats' 'dismal cirque of Druid stones upon a forlorn moor'. (*See* page 292.)

Cockermouth 8E7
The house where William Wordsworth (1770–1850) and his sister Dorothy were born is kept by the NT as a place of literary pilgrimage and is open to the public April–end Oct.

Coniston★ 8F6
Village made famous by John Ruskin (1819–1900), who lived at *Brantwood*, 2m SE, now with its grounds and gardens open to the public Easter–Oct. He took great interest in the museum, which has since been given his name and contains many of his possessions. Coniston Old Man (2,635ft) can be climbed in under two hours. The lake, a smaller edition of **Windermere**, to which it lies parallel, is celebrated for the water speed records of Donald Campbell. It can be best viewed from *Tarn Hows*, an area of NT land at the lake's head, some of which was bequeathed by Beatrix Potter.

Dalton-in-Furness 8F5
Birthplace of Romney (1734–1802), who is perhaps best known for his portraits of Emma, Lady Hamilton. Though his wife and children did not share his fashionable London life, he returned to them after 37 years, and is buried here. The castle (NT), a 14th-c pele tower, is open to the public throughout the year.

Debatable Land, The 11J2
Tract from the Sark to the Esk, long disputed between Scotland and England.

Dent 9H6
This old wool town has retained its cobbled streets, and contains many picturesque corners amid its higgledy-piggledy buildings. Outside the church stands a granite memorial to Adam Sedgwick, the great Victorian geologist, who was educated here.

Derwentwater★ 8F7
This lovely lake, 3m long, has scenery of wonderful variety; behind it Skiddaw rises to the N. Its islands are the property of the NT. The Falls of Lodore, extolled by Southey, are at their most impressive after heavy rain. A memorial to John Ruskin (1819–1900) stands on Friar's Crag above the E shore of the lake.

Duddon Valley 8E6/F6
Wordsworth's sonnets describe this beautiful scenery with the utmost fidelity.

Edenhall 8G7
According to Longfellow's ballad, the luck of the House of Musgrave would fail if the precious medieval 'fairy' cup in the family's possession were shattered. As it happens, the house has been demolished, and the 700-year-old cup of exquisite Syrian or Persian enamelwork is kept safely in London. The Norman church, on Saxon foundations, contains numerous Musgrave monuments.

Ennerdale Water 8E7
Stern mountains encircle the least frequented of Cumbria's lakes, and promote an individual but rather sombre atmosphere.

Eskdale 8E6
Lakeless valley noted for waterfalls and ascended by a light-gauge railway. Walkers should make for *Hardknott Pass* with its Roman fort (AM) at the W end, and tremendous view★ of *Scafell Pike see* **Scafell**).

Gilsland 11K2
Two altars, with inscriptions, are reminders of the Roman forces on this part of **Hadrian's Wall**. Sir Walter Scott, who described the village in *Guy Mannering*, met his future wife, Charlotte Charpentier, here in 1797.

Gosforth 8E6
The tall slender cross is judged to be a relic of Scandinavian settlement before the Norman Conquest. Its carving shows a combination of early Christian and Nordic pagan symbolism.

Grange-over-Sands 8F5
Steeply wooded hillsides shelter this holiday resort, noted for its mild climate. On Hampsfell, one of the limestone hills behind the town, stands the Hospice, from which there are superb panoramic views.

Grasmere★ 8F7
Wordsworth lived for ten years at Dove Cottage, near the almost circular little lake. It is open to the public March–Oct. The museum near by (open all the year) is a worthy commemoration of the poet and his circle. Wordsworth and his wife and his sister Dorothy are buried in the churchyard of St Oswald's. De Quincey (1785–1859) took on the cottage from him.

Great Salkeld 8G8
The embattled church tower is entered through a cunningly devised gate of 14th-c ironwork, and contains two vaulted rooms and a dungeon connected by a spiral staircase. The Roman altar, now in the porch, was discovered in 1890.

Hadrian's Wall 11J2/K2/L2
This is the fortified line dating back to Roman days, stretching from Wallsend to Solway Firth ($73\frac{1}{2}$m), comprising a wide ditch, the 15ft wall (built of turf W of **Gilsland**, later succeeded by stones), and the Vallum, which was intended as a southern defence. The Wall (AM), built AD 122–6 under Aulus Platorius Nepos, had regularly spaced mile-castles about 1,620yd apart with interspaced turrets, which were supplied by garrisons from 16 forts. *See also* **Hadrian's Wall** in Northumbria.

Hardknott *see* **Eskdale**

Hawkshead 8F6
Wordsworth lodged at Ann Tyson's Cottage (note its quaint outside staircase) while he was attending the grammar school (NT), where he carved his name on his desk. The Elizabethan church, together with the curious alleys and archways of the little town, are worth a leisured visit. The *Courthouse* (NT), $\frac{1}{2}$m N, is a fine medieval building reputed to have been used for the manorial courts. It contains an exhibition to illustrate Lake District domestic and working life in the past. Open May–Sept.

Helvellyn★ 8F7
Three routes from Patterdale lead to the summit of the third highest mountain (3,118ft) in the Lake District. Another popular ascent is from *Wythburn*, on the E shore of Thirlmere.

Holker Hall 8F5
Situated on the B5278, at *Cark-in-Cartmel*. This Cavendish seat dates from the 16th c. It has fine formal gardens, and many peripheral attractions, including the adjacent, but independent, *Lakeland Motor Museum*. Open to the public Easter–early Oct.

Hutton-in-the-Forest 8F7
6m NW of **Penrith**. Originally a medieval pele tower, this house has been greatly extended piecemeal from the 17th c onwards. Formal gardens. Open to the public May–Oct.

Kendal 8G6

This busy market town and administrative centre has many dignified streets built mainly of grey limestone. Some of the older 'yards' at the end of alleyways running from the main thoroughfare have also been preserved. The parish church (Holy Trinity) is a spacious building, with five aisles, dating from the 13th c, and recalling Kendal's long association with the woollen industry. Catherine Parr, the wife who outlived Henry VIII, was born in the now ruinous castle which stands above the town. Abbot Hall Art Gallery is situated next to the church in a fine Georgian house, furnished in period, and with portraits by Romney, who had close links with the town. In the stable block is the Museum of Lakeland Life and Industry, and in Station Road is the Museum of Natural History and Archeology. These galleries and museums, along with the lively Brewery Arts Centre (once a brewery) and the biennial Mary Wakefield music festival, give Kendal a foremost place among provincial towns as a cultural centre.

Keswick* 8F7

One of the best centres for Lakeland. The Fitz Park Museum contains manuscripts of the poets and Sir Hugh Walpole. Coleridge lived at Greta Hall in 1800–09, and Southey in 1803–43. *Crosthwaite* Church on a site chosen by St Kentigern in 553, has a complete set of consecration crosses. Here Canon H. D. Rawnsley (1851–1920) is buried. As one of the founders of the NT, he ensured the preservation of large tracts of country. From Lingholm Gardens (open April–end Oct.) there are exceptional views of **Borrowdale**. *See also* **Castlerigg Circle**.

Levens Hall Gardens: designed by a Frenchman in 1701–4, they are known for their yew, holly and box topiary work

Kirkby Lonsdale 8G5

In the words of John Ruskin, here are 'moorland, sweet river and English forest at their best'. The town also has Georgian houses and a 15th-c bridge across the Lune.

Kirkby Stephen 9H7

Market town among high mountains. The church, of cathedral-like proportions, has carvings and also memorials of the Musgraves and Whartons, who lived at Wharton Hall, 1¾m S, now mainly a farmhouse.

Kirkoswald 8G8

The moated castle ruins consist mainly of dungeons and one fine turret. The church has a tower set 200yd away from its main body, and a stream flowing from under its nave. The great house of the Fetherstonhaugh family, known as the College, is a private residence.

Kirkstone Pass* 8F7

The Kirkstone Pass Inn, between Caudale Moor and Red Screes on the road from **Windermere** to **Ullswater**, is the highest in the Lake District at 1,489ft. On the ascent into Patterdale, Brothers Water can be seen.

Levens Hall 8G6

The Elizabethan house grew from a pele-tower refuge against the Scots. More famous even than the house's carved fireplaces are its topiary gardens laid out in 1692. Also unique steam collection. Open Easter–end Oct.

Lindale 8F6

The first model iron ship to confute the experts completed successful trials in 1786 on a reach of the Winster bordered by country famous for iron since Roman times.

Long Meg and Her Daughters 8G8
Stone circle near *Little Salkeld*, comparable with that of
Stonehenge (Wilts). The circle at 350yd circumference is
larger than that of **Castlerigg Circle** near **Keswick**.

Lowther 8G7
The remains of the castle stand in an imposing 3,000-acre
park. Of the house, with its 500ft terrace and ramparts, only

*Castlerigg Circle: also known as the Carles and the
Druid's Circle is 100 feet in diameter (see page 289)*

a portion of one tower is 13th-c, the rest having been
destroyed and rebuilt many times, including the rooms
where Mary Queen of Scots enjoyed the hospitality of Sir
Richard Lowther. The Lowther Wildlife Adventure Park is
open Easter–Oct.

Mallerstang   9H6
Pendragon Castle, reputed to have been built by the father of King Arthur, is in a remote valley near the Yorkshire border.

Maryport   8E8
Formerly a seaport based on the coal and iron industries, this town now has a new industrial estate not centred on iron and coal. An unprecedented discovery of Roman altars at *Netherhall* was made in the 19th c, and there have also been more recent discoveries.

Millom   8F6
The castle (not open to the public) and ancient parish church are 1m outside the boom town based on 19th-c iron discoveries, now struggling to establish itself as a holiday resort. With its equable sunny climate and miles of golden beaches, it deserves to do so.

Muncaster Castle   8E6
From the terrace of the Pennington family seat there is a famous view of the mountains above **Eskdale**. Among many treasures, the family cherishes the enamelled bowl known as the 'Luck of Muncaster', presented by Henry VI when he was in flight after his defeat at Hexham, and a piece of the *Fighting Téméraire* set into panelling – a relic of the great sailing ship painted by Turner. Fine rhododendron gardens, bird garden, bear garden, nature trail. Open Easter–early Oct.

Naworth Castle   11K2
Imposing 14th-c castle built around a central courtyard. It is the private residence of the Earl of Carlisle.

Newby Bridge   8F6
Picturesque little village by the foot of **Windermere**. Lakeside is the terminus of the lake steamers and of the rescued railway which runs up the Leven valley from Haverthwaite. *Rusland Hall* near by is a Georgian manor house with a mechanical music exhibition. Open April–Sept. The rhododendron gardens at *Graythwaite Hall*, 2m N off the A592, are open April–June.

Newton Arlosh   11I2
The old church here was also a fortress. Holme Cultram Abbey, often a target for border raids, in near-by *Abbeytown*, is still used as a parish church, and is also a lively arts centre.

Penrith   8G7
Original capital of Cumbria, for centuries engaged in border strife; now has a ruined castle (AM) surrounded by a public park. Richard III slept in a wainscoted room in the Gloucester Arms. A feature of the churchyard is a group of 'hogback' stones, little houses for the dead dating from before the Conquest. *See also* **Brougham**.

Ponsonby   8E6
Here there is a moated church with 13th-c remains.

Ravenglass   8E6
Harbour of declined importance. Walls Castle, one of the greatest Roman survivals in the N, shows signs of having been a villa or bath connected with a fort at **Muncaster**. A famous breeding-place for gulls and terns may be visited by boat. Starting point for the Ravenglass and Eskdale narrow-gauge railway, which runs 7m to Dalegarth in **Eskdale** through beautiful scenery. Open all year.

Rusland Hall *see* **Newby Bridge**

Rydal★   8F6
The village on the smallest of the Lakes, is where the poet Wordsworth lived at Rydal Mount (open March–mid-Jan.) in 1813–50, and where he died. He planted Dora's Field with daffodils and gave it to his daughter, and from a rock known as Wordsworth's Seat he sat and surveyed the view that was so much part of his life and poetry. Three other famous men chose to live near: Dr Arnold of Rugby, Thomas de Quincey and Hartley Coleridge.

St Bees   8E7
A priory was built on the site of the nunnery founded by a legendary Irish princess of the 7th c, who was granted 'as much land as was covered by snow on Midsummer Day', and of which one carved stone endures. The school was founded by Archbishop Grindal in 1583.

Sawrey   8F6
Beatrix Potter (1866–1943), who has delighted generations of children with her books, lived at 17th-c Hill Top Farm, preserved by the NT. Open April–end Oct.

Scafell★   8F6
May be ascended (3,162ft) from **Wasdale Head** or, by experienced cragsmen, combined with *Scafell Pike* (3,210ft) via Mickledore Ridge. (*See also* page 22.)

Seascale   8E6
Small seaside resort making a good base for *Wastwater* and the high mountains to the E. The 19th-c church has a wealth of carved oak and fine glass.

Sedbergh   8G6
A busy little upland town, which is an ideal centre for walking in the Howgill Fells. Dominated by the presence of the famous public school.

Shap   8G7
High village famous for quarry stone, and for the remains of a 16th-c abbey (AM). *Keld Chapel*, 1m SW, is NT property.

Silloth   11I2
A planned 19th-c town, which was to have been a port for **Carlisle** and also a new holiday resort. Perhaps this section of the Solway shore was too exposed for the venture to succeed, but there is a marvellous view across the sea to southern Scotland.

Sizergh Castle   8G6
The Strickland family have enjoyed occupation of their castle since 1239. It has a 14th-c pele tower flanked by Elizabethan wings, and a room occupied by Catherine Parr after Henry VIII's death. The chapel contains a portable altar of painted Italian leather, a licence for which was granted to Sir Thomas Strickland over 500 years ago. Formal gardens. (NT). Open April–end Sept.

Temple Sowerby Manor   8G7
Acorn Bank Garden (NT) famous for spring bulbs and herbs. Open April–end Oct.

Troutbeck   8F6
Near **Windermere**. A very attractive, straggling settlement with few buildings less than 200 years old. Townend (NT) (open April–end Oct.) is a perfectly preserved statesman's, or independent farmer's, house. The old Garburn

Troutbeck: cottages are built of thick local stone to endure the long hard winters

road crosses to *Kentmere* on the other side of the valley from Troutbeck. Nearer to Windermere are the gardens of the Lakeland Horticultural Society at *Holehird*, open throughout the year, and famous for its collection of heathers.

Ullswater★★ 8F7/G7
Great lake in three reaches which increase in grandeur to the N, it is bordered by *Gowbarrow Park* (NT), associated with Wordsworth's 'Daffodils'.

Ulverston 8F5
A busy market town, the centre of which has preserved much of its late 18th-c character. An unmistakable landmark is the lighthouse-like monument on Hoad Hill to Sir John Barrow, a native of the town who became famous in the early 19th c for his share in encouraging polar exploration. Swarthmoor Hall was the home of Judge Fell, whose widow, Margaret, married George Fox, founder of the Society of Friends (Quakers). It is a fine Elizabethan house, open mid-March–mid-Oct. Conishead Priory is a Victorian Gothic stately home on the site of a medieval priory. It is now a Buddhist College, and is open Easter–end Sept.

Vale of St John 8F7
Romantic valley flanked by Wanthwaite Crags and the Dodds of Helvellyn. *Watson's Dodd*, a strange rock formation, was Scott's fairy castle in his poem 'The Bride of Triermain'.

Wasdale Head★ 8F7
Chief British centre for rock climbing. England's highest mountain, *Scafell Pike* (3,210ft) (*see* **Scafell**), towers above *Wastwater*, her deepest lake.

Whitehaven 8E7
In the 17th c, the development of coal mines and port facilities were fostered by the Lowther family, so that in 60 years a hamlet became a seaport. In 1788 Paul Jones sailed into the harbour in *Ranger*, his privateer, but failed to capture it. A fine example of 18th-c town planning, crowned by the magnificent church of St James.

Windermere★ 8F6
Town combined with the older **Bowness** on the largest English lake, which is narrow and beautiful, with wooded banks, and splendid views of the fells. There is a summer steamer service. The wooden equestrian statue of St Martin, in the church of which he is the patron saint, is of a very rare kind and may have been carved locally in the early 17th c. 1m N is *Brockhole*, the Lake District National Park's premier visitor centre, with 30 acres of gardens and grounds, open late March–end Oct. On an island in Windermere, *Belle Isle*, is a unique round Georgian house, containing Gillow furniture and Romney portraits. Boat service from Bowness. Open late May–mid-Sept. There is a steamboat museum in the town. (*See* page 287.)

Workington 8E7
A struggling industrial town. Workington Hall has been largely rebuilt since Mary Queen of Scots stayed there and wrote her letter of appeal to Elizabeth before being escorted to Bolton Castle, *see* **Aysgarth** (N. Yorks). The Helena Thompson Museum is open throughout the year.

Wreay 8G7
Sarah Losh, a wealthy 19th-c recluse, built two schools, a cemetery chapel and a church in the style of a Roman basilica, designing them herself and employing a local mason. The pulpit, lectern and reading desk are of prehistoric bog oak.

THE ISLE OF MAN

AN INTRODUCTION BY
ALAN BRACK

Most writers hold to the belief that the Isle of Man came into existence millions of years ago as the result of some great terrestrial convulsion when the earth was white-hot, followed by a cooling-down to a period of cold so intense as to defy the imagination. As a child I was told how a great giant in the northeast corner of Ireland had a quarrel with a great giant in southwest Scotland and the Ulsterman in his fury tore up a great chunk of land and hurled it with all his might at the Scot. But his trajectory was wrong and the missile fell short, landing in the sea just half way between Scotland and Ireland. There it remained and became known as the Isle of Man. Proof of this tale lies in the existence of the bizarre Giant's Causeway in County Antrim which was left after the frenzied giant had clawed the earth away.

I must admit that further education tended to shake my belief in this explanation and I could not really argue with the geologists' theories about volcanic activity and the effects of several Ice Ages and that the island was once a part of mainland Britain and even the European continent. It has several hills and a mountain, many glens and chasms, some rivers, picturesque waterfalls and a beautiful coastline as jagged in parts as – well, as though it had been savagely ripped out of a greater land mass by some gigantic hand.

Climate and Scenery

The Isle of Man's climate is usually described as 'equable'. That means that over the course of a year it can vary from quite cold to very warm, even hot, but for long periods it is nicely temperate, kept that way by the warming influence of the Gulf Stream. But winter can bring its gales. The prevailing southwest wind can blow with unbridled fury and lash the island as though taking revenge on it for some past misdemeanour. But that happens, too, in England's southwest which has a reputation for mildness and it so happens that weather records suggest that the overall weather of the Isle of Man and Cornwall is similar – though the island's weather is possibly the more prone to sudden change. But here fuchsias, veronicas, olearias and other tender shrubs grow

prolifically enough to form hedges and any visitor faced with a next-door neighbour who may have holidayed in foreign climes will not have much difficulty in finding a palm tree to include among the holiday snapshots.

Scenically, the island is a microcosm of Britain itself and in its 227 square miles one can find everything from beautiful glen and fine mountain scenery to sandy coves, steep cliffs and, in the southwest corner between Port St Mary and the Calf of Man, there are spectacular rock formations called The Chasms.

Holiday Island

Some may criticize the way the holidaymaker is increasingly being catered for with manmade attractions which can be found in any resort on the mainland, but it is by tourism that a substantial percentage of the 60,000 population earns its livelihood and, in recent years, they have had to vie with the popularity of the sun-guaranteed package holiday abroad.

One attraction which has spread the name of the Isle of Man throughout the world is the famous TT races. These motorcycle races, round a maximum of six laps of a mountain circuit, each lap being $37\frac{3}{4}$ miles long, in June (with professional riders) and the Manx Grand Prix (for amateurs) in September, stretch the holiday season at each end. But there has been a realization that one of the Isle of Man's most precious assets is, simply, being *Manx*. At times they have tended to forget this, getting rid of things which were peculiarly their own purely on economic grounds. The unique horse-tram service still clop-clops along the promenade at Douglas during the season (though someone did try to stop it), the lovely Victorian steam-hauled trains of the Isle of Man Railway were closed down in the 1960s but were rescued and while they now only run from Douglas to Port Erin in the summer months, at least they run. Happily, too, the Manx Electric Railway is still there to take you on the most spectacularly beautiful tram ride ever along the coast and through the wild glens from Douglas via Laxey to Ramsey. At Laxey you can break your journey and take a 5-mile electric mountain railway trip to the summit of the island's highest mountain, Snaefell (2,036 ft), where, as the Manx never tire of pointing out, six kingdoms can be seen: England, Northern Ireland, Scotland, Wales, Man – and the Kingdom of Heaven. On the right day you may well feel that the latter two are one and the same.

Independent Kingdom

The Isle of Man is an independent kingdom. Under its proud 'Three Legs of Man' symbol, it has its own language, its own laws, its own currency, its own postage stamps, its own taxation system, its own Customs and Excise and, of course, its own species of tailless cat. It is also now well known for having its own low rate of income-tax and, with the abolition of exchange controls, it has built up a new 'industry' as a tax haven – or, as they prefer to term it, a low tax area designed to create an international finance centre.

The Isle of Man is not part of the United Kingdom. It has no representation at Westminster and is a self-governing British possession with its own parliament (Tynwald) which owes allegiance to Her Majesty the Queen in her capacity as Lord of Man. As with other self-governing British possessions, she is represented by a resident Lieutenant-Governor.

The Manx parliamentary system goes back over 1,000 years and owes its origins to Scandinavia, not Britain. On manmade Tynwald Hill – used by the Vikings for sun worship – usually on 5 July with due pomp, procession and ceremony, summaries of the legislation enacted by the House of Keys and the Legislative Council (the upper chamber) during the previous 12 months are formally proclaimed to the people in both Manx and English. There will be few among the crowd of watchers who will understand the Manx version. A hundred years ago this derivation of Gaelic was spoken by over 10,000 people; today it is mainly kept alive by this Tynwald ceremony and the Manx Language Society and can only claim about 50 competent speakers despite evening classes, a weekly newspaper column and a weekly programme on the local radio. Bravely, and I suspect mainly as a novelty for the tourists, dual-language street signs have now appeared as in Wales and Eire. The capital is signposted as Douglas/*Doolish*, Peel is *Purt-ny-Hinshey* and Onchan is *Kiondroghad*. Not all that pleasing to the ear (although I like the island's other name of *Ellan Vannin*) but it keeps alive the notion that the Isle of Man is a place apart. Their holiday slogan a few years ago was: 'Come Abroad To The Isle of Man'. It was not an empty phrase.

GAZETTEER

The Ayres   8C6
Unspoiled coastal heath. Visitors' centre open during the summer season.

Ballasalla   8B5
Rushen Abbey (in ruins) dates from the 12th c and is now part of an inn-garden. Crossag Bridge (14th-c) is the finest example of a medieval bridge in Britain and the island. ½m along the river is *Silverdale*, **Manx National Glen**.

Braddan   8C5
1m outside **Douglas**. It has two churches. Inside the old church, restored in 1773, are five ancient Scandinavian crosses. Open-air services held in a near-by field on Sun. mornings in the holiday season attracts many visitors.

Calf of Man   8B5
Island bird-sanctuary and observatory at SW tip of the coast, presented to the NT for England and Wales in 1937 to ensure its preservation for the Manx nation. Many grey seals to be seen off and on the rocky shoreline.

Castletown   8B5
Capital of the Isle of Man until 1869, the town is dominated by Castle Rushen. This 12th–14th-c stronghold has state apartments, a Norman keep flanked by towers, and a one-hand clock reputedly given by Elizabeth I. Of great interest is the Nautical Museum in the old boathouse of the Quayle family, with its ancient occupant, the 18th-c yacht *Peggy*. Overlooking Castletown Bay is King William's College, famous boys' public school. The Buchan School is the

island's public school for girls. The Witches' Mill contains a museum of witchcraft. Scarlett Visitors' Centre along the coast open in season.

Cregneish   8B5
Picturesquely situated village containing open air National Folk Museum, with typical crofter's, fisherman's and weaver's cottages (including Harry Kelly's Cottage, a crofter who was one of the last people to speak Manx as his mother tongue). *See also* page 18. The Chasms, fissures of great depth, lie on the N side of the village. Much of the coastline here is owned by the Manx NT and is an important area for breeding seabirds.

Douglas   8C5
Supplanted **Castletown** as the island's capital in 1869 because of its superior harbour. Popular holiday resort with 2m-long promenade and wide streets, where over one-third of the island's total population live. *See* Introduction. The Legislative Buildings are where Tynwald (the Isle of Man's parliament) meets. Open each Wed. and Fri. during the summer. The Manx Museum covers all aspects of Manx archeology, history, daily life in times past, natural history, fine and applied art; also national library. Open weekdays throughout the year. Manx Electric Railway open May–Sept. *See also* **Braddan**.

Injebreck Reservoir   8B6
Built at the head of West Baldwin valley in 1905, man's handiwork has actually enhanced the valley's natural beauty. Trout fishing allowed under licence.

Douglas: a popular resort and the capital of the Isle of Man, an independent kingdom

Kirk Michael 8B6
Church with runic crosses and monuments and tombs of several Bishops of Sodor and Man. *Bishopscourt*, former seat of the bishops, lies 1m N, with Man's oldest trees, sweet chestnuts, planted by Bishop Wilson (consecrated 1698).

Laxey 8C6
King Orry's Grave and Ballanagh spiral stone on N side of valley. The Big Wheel ('Lady Isabella'), formerly used for pumping water from the lead mine and still in working order, is 72½ft in diameter, 6ft wide – the largest water-wheel in the world. Laxey Glen, a blend of manmade and natural gardens near the famous Laxey Wheel. The eucalyptus tree behind the public house is one of the island's tallest trees.

Manx National Glens
The Isle of Man is richly endowed with beautiful glens, with 17 of them managed by the IOM Forestry, Mines and Lands Board to ensure their future as beauty spots.

Maughold 8C6
In the churchyard is a Cross House containing 33 Celtic and Viking crosses. Sir Hall Caine, famous Manx novelist, is buried here. *Cashtal yn Ard* megalithic tomb is 3 m SW.

Meayll Circle 8B5
Megalithic stone monument below the summit of Mull Hill, **Cregneish**, which has six pairs of burial chambers arranged in a circular pattern. Cremated human bones and pottery were found during excavations in 1893.

Peel 8B6
The home of Manx kippers, the herrings are cured in the old smokehouses on the quayside. Peel Island (or St Patrick's Isle or Peel Holme), reached by a causeway, has been inhabited since prehistoric times; St Patrick is said to have landed here in 444. *Islet*, currently the scene of important excavations, also contains St German's Cathedral (ancient home of the Kings of Man), St Patrick's Church, the ancient parish church, with adjacent 10th-c Round Tower to protect it, and *Peel Castle*, 12m NW of **Douglas** facing Peel Bay. The 14th-c castle was captured by the Manxmen in 17th c. 2m away is **Tynwald Hill**.

Port Erin 8B5
Fishing-port and popular family holiday resort with good beach, Marine Biological Station and Aquarium (open to the public) is run by the University of Liverpool. Important mining remains and Milner Tower (monument to the safe-making philanthropist) on *Bradda Head* N of bay.

Port St Mary 8B5
Steep small town with delightful harbour. Very good bathing beach and yachting centre. Headquarters of the IOM Yacht Club.

Ramsey 8C6
Queen Victoria made an unexpected landing here in 1847 when adverse weather made landing unsafe at **Douglas** where official dignitories waited. She re-embarked and sailed away again before the official party could get there. The Albert Tower marks the spot where Prince Albert viewed the scene. A family resort with miles of golden sands, much favoured by retired people because of its sheltered aspect. Beyond harbour, is Mooragh Park with marine lake. *The Grove*, N of Ramsey, is a Victorian residence, now Rural Life Museum, with period rooms, household displays, agricultural equipment, vehicles and horse-driven threshing mill. Open mid-May–late Sept.

St John's Nurseries 8B5
S of *St John's*. 5 acres of gardens belonging to the IOM Forestry, Mines and Lands Board.

Snaefell 8C6
The highest mountain in the island. The view from the top takes in the whole of the island. On a clear day, the peaks of the Lake District, the Mull of Galloway in Scotland and the Snowdon group in Wales can be seen. Murray's Museum has an interesting collection of veteran and vintage motor-cycles as well as ancient arms and musical instruments.

Sulby Reservoir 8C6
Latest enhancement of the Manx hills. Visitors' centre open in summer season.

Tynwald Hill 8B5
At the rear of the Hill and St John's Church is *Tynwald National Park* laid out to commemorate the Millennium Year of Tynwald.

WALES

PREFACE TO WALES

A PREFACE BY

ALUN LLEWELLYN

To enter the Principality is to cross a border from the United Kingdom into a country of different speech and different historical and cultural traditions. The name 'Welsh' by which the Celtic Cymry are known was one of several used by the largely Germanic *foederati* of the decaying Roman Empire to describe their Romanized neighbours. Walloons in Belgium, Wallachs in Romania, Vlachs in the Balkans share that distinction with the Welsh. It makes an interesting footnote that the famous if defamatory rhyme 'Taffy was a Welshman' and a thief, ran originally 'Taafe wass ein tief' as used by the Flemings of the 17th century when taunting their Walloon neighbours. It is from its Romano-British descent that Wales inherited its sense of natural justice. The learned Bede of Northumbria about AD 700 recorded that after the Roman Empire assigned its defence of Britain to the native municipalities 50 years were needed for repacification after which 50 years of peace followed. This is the century associated with the name of Arthur. It is a name Wales shares with Scotland, Cornwall and Brittany; it is found even in Irish legend. In itself it records the attempt, for some time successful, to stabilize Roman civilization in the West, not in Britain alone since the legendary 'lost land of Lyonesse' which Arthur tried to gain was what is now the Lyonnaise in France. Arthur, when first mentioned, is referred to as 'Miles', a title given to a specific rank in the later Legions, roughly Captain of the Vanguard but below the rank of the Commander in Chief who was called the *Pater* or Father. The recent excavations at Wroxeter (Uronicum) confirm Bede and mark the 6th-century foundation of Powys.

When Henry Tudor became King Henry VII of England in 1485, Welsh nationalism considered it had completed the Arthurian ambition of recovering the Crown of London. But in reaction against his father's policy of fostering Welsh self-awareness, Henry VIII banned the official use of the Welsh language. Yet, he neither could nor did prevent the translation of the Bible into Welsh in 1537 during his own reign and his daughter Elizabeth I commanded the holding of an Eisteddfod at Caerwys in 1568.

This celebration of poetry and song in the Welsh language, dating from the Middle Ages has remained an annual event. As a 'sitting-down in peace' it draws all Welsh people together from all quarters including the far-off Welsh colony around Trelew in Patagonia. There is no one centre for it and the venue is changed every year. The language is that Brythonic speech Wales shares with Cornwall and Brittany and, vestigially, with the shepherds of Cumbria. A literature beginning perhaps before the 13th century with the collation of even earlier themes has continued with its own styles and images not only into the present day but has entered English literature. G. Manley Hopkins' use of 'sprung rhythm' and 'consonantal chime' was in direct imitation of the Welsh which he closely studied and tried to write. Dylan Thomas was a writer whose poetry, like that of George Meredith, reflected the intricate methods of Welsh thought-construction. The metaphysical poets of the 17th century, Donne, Vaughan, the Herberts, Traherne had long ago preceded them.

The demands of modern urban civilization have drowned areas deeply identified with Welsh tradition under reservoirs for alien cities, afforested agricultural communities which were centres of native culture, erected an atomic power station in the centre of moorlands that inspired the poetry of Hedd Wyn and, above all, brought alien standards by way of television into Welsh homes. The visitor to Wales will remember the deep-rooted national sense of the Welsh which has an ancient and vigorous culture to defend not only for its own sake but for the sake of all nationalities and the 'equal right to be different' which is the only foundation of liberty and justice.

Pronunciation of Welsh

Welsh is a phonetic language; pronunciation is always as spelt. The alphabet, however, differs from English there being no J, K, Q, V, X or Z. F is pronounced as English V. Ff represents the English F. Dd is sounded as the *th* in *that*. Ll is sounded by

Previous page: The haunting ruin of Dinas Bran, near Llangollen in Clwyd, is a reminder of more turbulent times

Caernarfon Castle, Gwynedd – a fortress built by Edward I and scene of the Prince of Wales' Investiture in 1969

placing the tongue in the cheek and blowing gently over it; *ch* as in the Scots *loch*. *Rh* is a separate letter of the Welsh alphabet – an aspirated *R*. *Si* corresponds to the English *sh*. *U* is pronounced as *ee*. *Y* when by itself means 'the' and pronounced like *uh*. *W* is spoken as *oo* which makes it difficult for a Welshman to say 'woods'. There are certain rules called 'Ignition' which alter the first consonant to make for more mellifluous speech. For example, to write 'In Gwent', the change is made to *yngh Ghwent*. But perhaps this need not concern the traveller.

The Meaning of Some Common Words

Bach: little
Bryn: hill
Bwlch: gulch
Caer: an enclosure used particularly in connection with Roman sites to mean city
Carn: heap of stones often a hill top
Dinas: a fortress
Dyfi, dyfr, dwr: water usually of a river
Gallt: a wooded hill
Glyn: a valley
Llan: a levelled place, usually the site of a church

Llyn: a lake
Mawr: large
Mynydd: a mountain
Pant: a hollow
Rhiw: a twisted ridge
Sarn: a causeway
Taren: a notched hill

Names of colours
Cethin: brown
Glas: blue
Goch: red
Gwyn: white
Llwyd: grey
Melyn: yellow

Clwyd

AN INTRODUCTION BY
ALUN LLEWELLYN AND JEAN WARE

This tract of country, formerly the counties of Denbigh and Flint, lies between Gwynedd, the fortress of Wales, and the boundary of Cheshire in England. It was inevitable that it became a borderland of intense struggle to determine the history of Wales. It is remembered as the scene of Welsh military struggle and political surrender and is remarkable for the significant reassertion of Welsh identity.

At Holt the remains were recovered of the Roman station of Bovium held by the 20th Legion which also controlled Chester and Caersws in Powys. While the sub-Roman 'kingdom' of Powys, following the tread of the 20th Legion, took Chester as its northern strongpoint for the pacification of Wales. At Bangor on Dee (Bangor-Is-y-Coed) a great monastery of monks of the Celtic Church was established. The refusal of that Church to submit in matters of doctrine to the Augustine mission from Catholic Rome led to the defeat of the British by the Northumbrian army at the battle of Chester in 615, the massacre of the monks and destruction of the monastery. This disaster separated Powys from the British of Cumbria and Strathclyde. Eliseg's Pillar near Llangollen was set up as a memorial to one of the Welsh leaders who fell in the struggle. It stood for 1,000 years till it was shattered by Cromwell's Puritans. It was re-erected in 1779 by the excellent Mr Lloyd of Trevor Hall. Perhaps an even greater calamity was suffered in the 8th century when the Saxon Offa of Mercia overthrew Welsh forces at Rhuddlan in a victory so total that he was able to lay down the lines of Offa's Dyke as a powerful barrier between what was Wales and what was England. And at Ruddlan in 1284 Edward I imposed the Treaty which proposed the subjection of Wales after the death of Llywelyn the Last. To enforce it he supplanted the Welsh castles with his own.

Clwyd has a 12-mile strip of sands on the northwest, a central peaty plateau and coal to the southeast. The uplands form a high platform rising to 2,713 feet in Moel Sych, and falling steeply to the vales of Conwy and Clwyd. Here there is rough grazing for sheep; on the lower slopes are cattle, pigs, oats, barley and potatoes. The best agricultural areas are the red sandstone, which in the vale of Clwyd overlays the older limestone. On the hills above Llanrwst the soil is either yellow loam or peat, both dry and boggy; in the valley below, it is clay. This is the only county in Wales where alpine woundwort, downy woundwort and spider orchid may be found. Hazels and ash abound, with buckthorn, hawthorn and blackthorn on the uplands. Except for the lovely basin of the Ceiriog, tipped towards Powys and the Berwyns, the southeast of Clwyd is industrial.

The Pontcysyllte Aqueduct, built by Telford in 1794–1804, carries the Llangollen Canal 121 feet above the Dee

In Llangollen in July, thousands of European dancers and singers mingle with the American and Commonwealth teams in the beflagged streets at the International Music Festival. This town of only 3,000 inhabitants has every year since 1947 entertained over 150 choirs and teams of dancers from all over the world – an enterprise of great vision.

Llangollen is as famous now as it was in the early coaching days, when the Ladies of Llangollen, two Irishwomen in masculine attire, entertained the celebrities of the day at Plas Newydd, the black-and-white house you may visit, as they passed through to or from Ireland. The ruined fort (Dinas Bran, *see* pages 298–9) and abbey (Valle Crucis) above the town were built by a 13th-century prince of Powys and later fell under the rule of a Marcher Lord.

Walkers may follow the upland path used by the Beaker folk along the slopes of the Clwydian hills from above Nannerch to Moel Fenlli behind Ruthin. There are a number of Iron Age forts in the county. At Cefn near St Asaph and Plas Heaton near Denbigh you may see good examples of Stone Age caves. Along the eastern border of both Clwyd and Powys you can follow the remains of Offa's Dyke, which runs from the estuary of the Dee near Prestatyn to the Severn estuary near Chepstow. You can see it marching south through Ardwy'r Clawdd, Ruabon and Chirk.

A tour of the ruined castles will take you to Ruthin, Holt, Chirk, Rhuddlan and Denbigh and to the sad, green mound at Sycharth, near Llansilin – all that is left of the mansion where Owain Glyndwr once spread his tables.

GAZETTEER

Abergele 8E2
Ancient market town with the little resort of *Pensarn* just to the N, and several old manor houses on the outskirts. The church, like several others in the county, has two parallel naves, and some old glass. 1m W, *Gwrych Castle*, impressively sited, is an imitation antique.

Bangor-on-Dee (Bangor-Is-y-Coed) 7H8
A place that is now the only memorial to the great monastery of the Celtic Church which in 596 was said to have 2,400 monks. Founded in 180, as legend has it, a Northumbrian army destroyed it in 615. A racecourse has replaced it.

Basingwerk Abbey 8F2
A religious house founded in 1132 for the Savigniac Order but in 1147 transferred to the Cistercians. Parts of the church and monastic buildings have survived.

Bodnant Garden 8D2
Here, near the little village of *Tal-y-Cafn*, is the seat of Lord Aberconway, who made over the gardens to the NT in 1949. More than a century old, they are admirably laid out, and can be visited all year round.

Caerwys 8F2
The original town-plan was laid out under Edward I. The rectangular grid of its streets was copied by Dr Thomas Wynne, a native of the place, to provide the pattern for William Penn's new foundation of Philadelphia in his American colony of Pennsylvania. In 1968 it celebrated the 400th year of its Eisteddfod authorized by Elizabeth I.

Cerrigydrudion 6F8
A small mountain village, bypassed by the main road, with a little church, and almshouses dated 1717. 1m SE, to the left of the **Corwen** road, are the remains of an ancient British camp crown the hill of Pen y Gaer, traditionally the spot where Caradog (Caractacus), King of the Britons, was betrayed to the Romans. The B4501 runs N past 3m-long *Alwen* and *Brenig* Reservoirs, surrounded by forest and woodland, rising to 1,200ft and then dropping down to **Denbigh**.

Chirk 6G7
Famous for its splendid castle, standing in parkland 2m W. Outside walls and towers have scarcely changed since 1310, apart from the insertion of windows; the domestic buildings (NT) in the courtyard, with their handsome furniture and decorations are open to the public. The church, with its 15th-c timbered roof and tower, contains monuments to the Myddletons and Trevors. Near by, the River Ceiriog is spanned by Telford's aqueduct, carrying the Shropshire Union Canal, surpassed only by his masterpiece – the even larger *Pontcysyllte Aqueduct* (1,000ft long and 121ft high) that carries the Llangollen Canal across the River Dee on 18 arches 1m N (*see* **Llangollen**).

Clwyd, Vale of 6F8/9
Fertile land bounded by mountains: an approach to more grandiose Welsh scenery.

Colwyn Bay★ 8E2
A traditional resort on the N coast of Wales, with a 3m promenade (unfortunately parallel to the railway), excellent sands, mixed architecture, mild climate, golf and fishing in both sea and river. The promenade is continuous from Old Colwyn on the E to *Rhos-on-Sea* on the W. Eirias Park, with its Dinosaur World, is open to visitors. Just a few miles S on the A470 is *Felin Isal*, a working flour mill, open to visitors.

Corwen 6F7
On a lovely stretch of the River Dee, situated at the N end of the Vale of Edeyrnion, this little market town was once associated with Owain Glyndwr. 2m E, beyond Carrog station, is a wooded hillock, called Glyndwr's Mount; and some 200yd farther on are the remains of a moated building known as Glyndwr's Palace. On a hill N of the river from Corwen is *Caer Drewyn*, one of the best-preserved prehistoric stone ramparts in Wales.

Denbigh 6F8
A busy little town overlooking the **Vale of Clwyd**, best seen from the ruined castle (AM), perched above the town, with the intricate structure of its gateway, between octagonal

towers (1382) impressively intact. Within the precincts, the Norman tower of St Hilary's Chapel still stands. A museum here illustrates the life and work of H. M. Stanley. The Town Hall, built by the Earl of Leicester (1572), was enlarged in the late 18th c. The church of St Marcella, 1m E, with its double nave, has fine hammer-beam roofs, chancel-screen and 14th-c glass, and alabaster. The A453 to *Pentrefoelas*, after passing *Llyn Bran*, reaches a height of 1,523ft, then crosses the shoulder of Mynydd Hiraethog between the Alwen Reservoir (*see* **Cerrigydrudion**) and *Lake Aled*.

Derwen 6F8
Tiny hillside village, whose church has one of the finest screens and rood-lofts in the county and a fine churchyard cross (AM), dating from the 15th c.

Dyserth 8F2
In the church note the Jesse window (illustrating the genealogy of Christ) and an early cross.

Ewloe 6G8
The castle was a stronghold of Llywelyn ap Gruffydd, and later witnessed the defeat of Henry II. The apsidal Welsh tower and the circular one to the W were built in the 13th c.

Flint 8F2
With its Great Tower, the plan of the castle is unique in Britain, though it has parallels in France. The English building, begun by Edward I, is a melancholy place washed by shallow tides.

Glyndyfrdwy 6G7
Part of the former estate of Owain Glyndwr, known to the English as Owen Glendower, the champion of Welsh freedom in the early 15th c. He took his name from this place, meaning the Valley of Two Rivers.

Gresford 6G8
The village (where, in 1934, 261 miners lost their lives in a tragic colliery explosion) is situated in the valley of the River Alun. The peal of 12 bells in the exquisite tower of the church is one of the so-called Seven Wonders of Wales. The carving of the stalls and the monuments in the Trevor Chapel are noteworthy; while the glass in the end windows of the aisles, and the font (both late 15th-c and perhaps brought from **Basingwerk Abbey**), are worthy of one of the finest Perpendicular churches in Wales. 4m E is **Holt**.

Hawarden 6G8
The home for 60 years of William Ewart Gladstone (1809–98) is not open to the public, but the old castle in the grounds is open during spring, summer and early autumn. The circular keep and the remains of the banqueting hall are imposing and command a fine view. The Gladstone Library – St Deiniol's – is also open to visitors and residential students. In the church is a stained-glass window by Burne-Jones to commemorate the statesman.

Holt 7H8
Its eight-arch bridge was built about 1400. It joins the village with the town of *Farndon* across the Dee. At Farndon Church pictures can be seen of the Cavalier gentry who rode out with Charles I in the Civil War. Relics of the Roman legionary station have been recovered showing it to have been a centre of great importance, set on a major highway. It was preceded by a Bronze Age settlement which may have been connected with the traffic between Ireland and the Wessex Culture represented by **Stonehenge** (Wilts).

Holywell 8F2
The well of St Winefride has been diverted by mining operations, and is now fed from a reservoir into the original bath in the crypt of a chapel built in 1480 by the mother of Henry VII. Legend proclaims that water burst out of the ground at the spot where the saint's head rolled after being severed by Prince Caradoc, whose advances she spurned. Since earliest times this has been a place of pilgrims, a hospice for whom was erected as late as 1870, and pilgrimages continue today. The architectural grouping of chapel and well forms the best-preserved medieval pilgrimage centre of its kind in Britain. At near-by *Holway*, there is a fascinating collection of old military vehicles displayed underground at the Grange Cavern Military Museum – the main tourist attraction. During World War II the cavern was used to house bombs including Barnes Wallis' bouncing bombs used by the Dambusters.

Llanarmon-Dyffryn-Ceiriog 6G7
A tiny village near the source of the River Ceiriog, backed by the Berwyn mountains, with a well-known fisherman's inn, reached by the B4500 from **Chirk**.

Llanasa 8E2
The church has windows, set up from 1501 to 1520, depicting the instruments of Christ's crucifixion: a cock and the hand of Judas grasping a bag of money.

Llanfair Talhaiarn 6F8
A small village with boating, country crafts, pony trekking, a rich farming landscape and fishing in the River Elwy. The poet Talhaiarn (John Jones), well-known to Welshmen, died here in 1869 and is buried in the churchyard.

Llangollen* 6G7
Famous for its Vale, its 'Ladies' and, since 1947, for its festival of international folk song and dance, held each summer. The Ladies of Llangollen were Eleanor Butler (d. 1829) and Sarah Ponsonby (d.1831), two eccentric recluses who for 50 years never left their home, Plas Newydd, the black-and-white house where they received most of the notabilities of the day, and which now belongs to the town and is open to the public. The 14th-c bridge (AM) across the River Dee, though one of the traditional Seven Wonders of Wales, has been somewhat spoiled by widening. The Dee is also crossed by the *Pontcysyllte Aqueduct* carrying the Llangollen Canal, a branch of the Shropshire Union Canal, which linked the town with the Midlands and is popular with canal boaters today. The aqueduct, opened in 1805, is one of the wonders of the canal system. In a former warehouse on the canal wharf there is an exhibition showing the story of canals as a transportation system in Britain. Boat trips along the canal in summer. *See also* **Chirk** and page 302. There is a working woollen mill and a pottery by the Dee. In the town the superb timber roof of St Gollen's, carved with angels, flowers and animals, is said to have been brought from **Valle Crucis**. 1m N is *Castell Dinas Bran*, a ruin crowning a hill (*see* pages 298–9); and 3m further on the manor house, Plas Uchaf. A road, 2m NW, leads to *Horseshoe Pass*, 1,300ft high.

Llanrhaiadr-yng-Nghinmeirch 6F8
The Perpendicular, double-carved church of this **Vale of Clwyd** village is remarkable. In addition to the timbered porch and lych-gate and the delicate hammer-beamed chancel roof, there is a Stem of Jesse window (1553), which was buried for 10 years during the Commonwealth in the parish chest, still kept in the church today.

Moel Fammau   6G8
The highest point (1,100ft) in the Clwyd mountains, surmounted by the remains of a tower erected on George III's Jubilee in 1820. The views towards Derbyshire and Snowdonia are magnificent.

Offa's Dyke   6G7
This great defensive earthwork, consisting of an embankment with a ditch on the Welsh side and running intermittently for 140m from the mouth of the Dee to that of the Wye, was built by Offa, king of the Mercians, at the end of the 8th c to contain the Welsh. It is accompanied for some 40m from the Dee to the Severn, by a similar fortification, Watt's Dyke, about 3m E following the 400ft contour. A footpath runs along the line of the Dyke. *See* **Montgomery** (Powys), **Ruabon** and entry in Hereford and Worcester.

Prestatyn   8E2
A popular holiday resort, favoured by visitors from the other side of the **Liverpool** inlet. *See also* **Offa's Dyke**.

Rhuddlan   8E2
A castle built in the 13th c to guard the mouth of the Clwyd and the coastal route to Wales. Richard II was imprisoned here. It was 'slighted' by the Parliamentarians in 1646.

Rhyl   8E2
Popular seaside resort, with tides that recede far across the sands. The multi-million-pound Sun Centre provides all-the-year-round warmth and recreation.

Ruabon   6G7
A small manufacturing town (chemicals and terracotta) in the coalfield of N.E. Wales. The church contains several monuments to the Wynn family, whose family mansion, Wynnstay, now a school, is near by (not open). In the large park are the Nant-y-Belan and Waterloo towers, and a section of Watt's Dyke (*see* **Offa's Dyke**).

Ruthin   6G8
Built on a hill in the **Vale of Clwyd**, its rather uninviting outskirts conceal an attractive market square. Here are old framed houses with quaint porches; the *Maen Huail* (AM), an ancient stone block on which, according to tradition the brother of Gildas the historian was beheaded by order of King Arthur; and the old collegiate church, minus its choir and with a modern spire, but still distinguished by the carved, timber roof dating back to Henry VII and its exquisite wrought-iron gates. Christ's Hospital near by, and the Grammar School, are both Elizabethan foundations; and, also close to the market square, the ruined, red sandstone drum towers and curtain-wall of the moated castle (AM), stand in the grounds of a modern mansion, now used as a hotel. The old mother church of Ruthin is 1m SE at *Llanrhydd*, where the Hall used to be the home of the novelist Stanley Weyman. On the approach to the town there is a fine craft centre, where visitors may watch a number of craftsmen at work.

St Asaph   8E2
In this 'village city' the most notable building is the small cathedral (182ft long, 65ft wide and 108ft across the transepts), venue for the North Wales Music Festival. It was destroyed by the English in 1282 and rebuilt; its woodwork was burned by Owain Glyndwr, its tower overthrown by a storm, but it has survived with many treasures, including a collection of early Bibles and prayer books kept at the chapter house.

Valle Crucis Abbey: built on simple lines in the 13th century, it has a notable entrance and lancet window

Valle Crucis Abbey★   6G8
In a remote and lovely dale 1½m NW of **Llangollen**, the ruins of this Cistercian abbey are the most impressive monastic remains in N. Wales. Begun in 1202 by Madog, Prince of Powys, the main features of the W end of the ruined church can still be distinguished – its Early English windows and, above them, the later rose-window. Of the monastery buildings there remain the 14th-c sacristy and chapter house, with the dormitory on the first floor. ¼m away, standing in a field, is the broken *Eliseg's Pillar* (AM), erected at the beginning of the 9th c by Prince Concenn, in memory of the victory of his great-grandfather Eliseg, Prince of Powys, killed at the battle of Bangor.

Wrexham   6G8
Thanks to its being the centre of an extensive coalfield, this is the largest town in N. Wales, though English in speech and appearance. Its chief attraction for the visitor is the five-storeyed tower of the 14th-c parish church, 135ft high, splendidly proportioned and richly decorated. Two of the monuments in the church are by Roubiliac; the 18th-c wrought iron gates of the churchyard, like those at **Ruthin**, are the work of the Davies brothers of *Bersham*; and W of the tower is the tomb of Elihu Yale (d.1721), the founder of Yale University, U.S.A., whose father emigrated to America from near by. At *Glyn Ceiriog* in lovely surroundings a memorial was placed to Thomas Jefferson, President of the U.S.A. in 1801. *Erddig Hall* (NT), 2m S of Wrexham, is a remarkable house of the 17th c with its original furniture and gardens restored to their 18th-c formal beauty. The outbuildings, including the laundry, sawmill, blacksmith's etc., demonstrate the workings of an 18th-c squire's country estate. There is also an agricultural museum at Felin Pulesten on the estate. At near by *Bersham*, where iron-master John Wilkinson had his ironworks, a Heritage Centre has been opened to interpret the 7m-long Bersham Industrial Trail. There is also a Geological Museum at *Bwlch Gwyn*.

GWYNEDD

AN INTRODUCTION BY
GEOFFREY BOUMPHREY

This county comprises the former counties of Caernarvonshire, Merioneth and Anglesey, with a small sliver from Denbigh, and if any excuse were needed for the new boundaries history provides it, for they follow nearly enough those of the ancient Welsh kingdom of Gwynedd.

Protected on the north and west by the sea and on the south and east by formidable mountain ranges, the whole region is a natural fortress which for centuries resisted penetration by the invader. When in 1158 the rulers of the other three kingdoms in Wales submitted to Henry II and were reduced to the status of barons, Owain ap Gwynedd, though he would do homage, insisted on bearing the title of prince. In 1267 Llywelyn II, with the acquiescence of Henry III, declared himself Prince of Wales. Not until his death in 1282 did Gwynedd fall. It was then that Edward I declared his own son Prince of Wales, creating a precedent which is still followed.

The Rocks

If traces of human warfare are not hard to find, evidence of nature's struggle is everywhere. The physical 'grain' of the land runs roughly northeast–southwest. This is the line of the north coast of Gwynedd, of the Menai Straits dividing the mainland from Anglesey, and of the Lleyn Peninsula, that long arm of Wales which bounds Cardigan Bay on the north. It is the line, too, of the three river valleys and estuaries that lead into the bay (one of them, the 'Bala fault', extending over 20 miles inland from Barmouth, on the Mawddach estuary, to Bala Lake) and of the great cleft that splits the length of the Cader Idris range from Tywyn to Tal-y-llyn and further. This noticeable grain is due to the existence of immense corrugations in the underlying Archaean rocks, the most ancient found on the earth's surface – so ancient that they contain no fossil evidence of life.

In the 600 million or more years since the formation of this Archaean sheet, it has been alternately lowered beneath the sea for long periods during which sedimentary rocks would be formed, and raised above the surface for the forces of erosion to do their work. Volcanoes have boiled up, ejecting or injecting

flows of lava on it or into it, or spreading vast quantities of volcanic ash to settle in sedimentary beds. And the whole 'club-sandwich' of variegated rocks has been raised, lowered, folded, cracked and subjected to pressures and temperatures that have, in some instances 'metamorphosed' the original sediments into quite new forms. These are the processes to which we owe the rich variety of rock in the region – the dark grey, almost greenish black of Snowdon and the adjoining ranges, the brown precipices of Aberglaslyn, the green and purple slates of the quarries, or the network of white quartz veining some of the rocks round Llanberis. One other potent force helped to mould the region. About a million years ago a great ice-sheet crept down from the north, following the depression of the Irish Sea and thrusting across the Cheshire plain. In the high mountains of North Wales, too, as the cold deepened, the local glaciers spread and merged into a Welsh ice-cap, powerful enough to deflect the thrust of the main icefield southwestward. The last of the Ice Ages ended less than 20,000 years ago – and so there still remain in Snowdonia clear and abundant traces of the glaciers' work: valleys deepened and straightened, rocks scored by the flow of ice, 'hanging valleys' gouged out high on the mountain sides (as at Nant Ffrancon); or, conversely, 'moraines' of material loosened and carried down from above, sometimes forming ridges, mounds or flat tablelands, sometimes filling or damming valleys, and even forming lakes (such as the Marchlyns, between Llanberis and Nant Ffrancon).

Snowdonia

The mountains of Snowdonia rise from sea level; and so their scale and grandeur always come as a surprise to those who know only the continental peaks. Experienced climbers rate them as 'real mountains', for their steep and jagged character, and for the difficulty of many of their ascents. To the Welsh the whole wild region was aptly known as Eryri, the Land of the Eagles. There are four main groups between the county's eastern boundary on the River Conwy and the base of the Lleyn Peninsula. First the bluff Carnedd range, rising steeply from the wide green

On Snowdon Mountain Railway steam locomotives, with rack and pinion drive, propel single coaches at 5mph

Conwy Valley and once a formidable bastion in Gwynedd's eastern defences. Between this and the narrow precipitous Glyders runs the Nant Ffrancon pass, threaded by Telford's Holyhead road, the A5, on its way from Betws-y-Coed to Bangor. Forking left off this at Capel Curig, the A4086 for Caernarfon runs through the next gap, the sombre Pass of Llanberis, with the Glyders now on the right, and on the left Snowdon itself. Viewed from almost any angle, Snowdon is a magnificent mountain, worthy of its rank as the highest peak (3,560 feet) in Wales and England. Its summit forms the apex of six long ridges which radiate from it like flying buttresses. It is these – and one almost sheer precipice – that give the climber such wide scope, from the simple to the very difficult. The view from the top on a clear day is superb. It can be reached by rack-railway from Llanberis; but for those to whom such a course would be sacrilege, there are walking ascents from the two passes mentioned, from Nant Gwynant and from Rhyd Dhu, through which runs the road from Beddgelert to Caernarfon, the A487. Beyond this lies our fourth group of mountains, the Hebogs, tapering down to the lower hills of Lleyn. Southeast of these four lie the blunt-topped Moelwyns and sharp-edged Moel Siabod.

Snowdonia is sprinkled with lakes – from Bala, the biggest, 4 miles long, to innumerable llyns set like jewels among the mountains. There is at least one beside each road through the three great Snowdon passes. High on Migneint lies Llyn Conwy, in which that most beautiful river has its source. The Dee, on the other hand, springs from a pallid marsh beneath the frowning precipice of Y Duallt (the Black Height), one of the Arenigs. It flows through Bala Lake at the start of its long course to Chester. Snowdonia boasts many 'beauty spots' – the Torrent and the Precipice Walks near Dolgellau, the Fairy

Glen and the Conwy and Swallow Falls, near Betws-y-Coed and Pont Aberglaslyn, near Beddgelert.

Merioneth
Almost the whole of south Gwynedd lies above the 600-foot contour, and where it joins with Powys and Clwyd on the Berwyn mountains its average height above sea level is about 2,000 feet. Yet everything is more genial than in former Caernarvonshire and Snowdonia. The principal range of mountains, the Rhinogs, runs southwards along the coast from Tremadog Bay, in the 'armpit' of Lleyn, to Barmouth. Flat-topped, their rolling moorland flanks are spangled with many small lakes. To the south their foothills face the stark precipices of Cader Idris across the Mawddach estuary, and in turn the southern side of this great mountain (2,927 feet) confronts the slopes of Plynlimon across the Dovey Valley, boundary alike of Gwynedd, and of North Wales. The Cader Idris range forms the southern end of what has been called 'the Ring of Fire', an S-shaped chain of clearly volcanic mountains whose upper arm is formed by the four Snowdon ranges. The next link to Cader Idris is the sharp-featured Aran range, with peaks of almost 3,000 feet. These run on into the Berwyns, which are hardly lower, though smooth and well-rounded – clearly of sedimentary origin. But before meeting the Berwyns, the volcanic chain sweeps north as the Arenigs, with Bala Lake in the cleft of the fork. Arenig Fawr (2,800 feet) is the highest of these. Northwards again (to join eventually with the Moelwyns on the county boundary) is a hilly but swampy region marked Migneint on the map. Its average height above sea level is about 1,500 feet, and since it is crossed by only one main road (the B4391) from Bala to Ffestiniog, the walker could hope for nothing better. You can go 30 miles or so north-north-eastwards from Dolgellau to Pentrefoelas, crossing only this one road, climbing six peaks averaging nearly 2,400 feet, and bathing, if you wish, in mountain lakes.

Isle of Anglesey
In contrast to the mainland, Anglesey has been almost levelled by erosion and by glacial action. The great ice sheet left behind it a deposit of boulder-clay on which sprang up a thick forest of scrub oak. As this was gradually cleared, the land proved capable of growing heavy crops of grain. The men of Gwynedd could pasture their animals in the deep mountain valleys; but they needed Anglesey as their granary. Edward I conquered Wales by first taking the island and so starving the mainland of cereals. Until the opening of Telford's fine suspension bridge in 1826, the Menai Straits had to be crossed by ferry, a passage beset with dangerous currents causing whirlpools at certain states of the tide. From the bridge today one can look down on the blue-green water far below and see it streaked viciously with white. The richly wooded banks rising high on either side and the yachts moored off Beaumaris give the scene a Riviera-like quality. Inland, the scenery of Anglesey is not spectacular. But the coastline is particularly attractive: low cliffs, indented with many small sandy bays, their headlands gay in spring with primrose, white campion, blue squill and sea-pink. Beaumaris was founded in 1295, at the same time as its castle – one of the ring of great castles (Rhuddlan, Conwy, Harlech and Caernarfon) with which Edward I encircled Gwynedd. Holyhead, the largest town, is much less picturesque. It stands on Holy Island, separated from Anglesey by a narrow estuary-like channel, noisy at low tide with the cries of wading birds. Only on Holy Island, in the cliffs near the South Stack lighthouse, is any grandeur to be found in Anglesey; but everywhere one is conscious of the magnificent backcloth of the mountains of Snowdonia beyond – seen nowhere better than from the domed summit of Holyhead Mountain (720 feet).

Industries, Towns and Recreations
Apart from the holiday trade, the main industry of the county is sheep farming, the animals being sent down from the mountains to winter in the milder climate and on the more fertile pastures of Anglesey and Lleyn. The fulling mill (or 'pandy'), still flourishes in a few places. Roofing-slates were produced at Bethesda, Llanberis, Nantlle and Blaenau Ffestiniog; slab slate for billiard tables at Aberllefenni. A considerable amount of labour is employed by the Forestry Commission, whose activities have displaced many sheep-farms. Dolgellau, formerly the county town of Merioneth, was once important for its wool market, situated as it is near the head of the lovely 8-mile Mawddach estuary and at the junction of two mountain passes and several main roads, including the A470, A487 to Caernarfon and the A494 to Chester (pioneered by the Romans). The A494 goes through Bala, another important wool market and once famous for its stocking-knitters.

On the coast, apart from the four old garrison towns of Conwy, Caernarfon, Beaumaris and Harlech, only two seaside resorts have been built to a definite plan – Llandudno and Portmeirion. The former, on a promontory just across the estuary from Conwy, is a Victorian pioneer of town-planning; the latter, the fulfilment of a 20th-century architect's dream. Italianate in style, romantic, and beautifully situated in a wide ravine leading down to the sea, it is unique in Britain. Bangor, with its cathedral and University College of North Wales, is a good shopping town and centre for exploration rather than a seaside resort. Golfers will know that the course at Trearddur Bay in Anglesey is one of the best in North Wales, and there are many others, not least that at Harlech. Climbers will stay at Llanberis, Capel

Conwy: Telford's suspension bridge, completed in 1826, has towers to match those of Conwy Castle beyond

Curig, Beddgelert, Pen-y-Gwryd or Pen-y-Pass, since all the principal climbs are in the four Snowdon ranges. Lovers of mountain scenery will add to this list such places as Dolgellau, Betws-y-Coed and many others. The archeologist will not – despite Tacitus – expect to find traces of the Druids in Anglesey.

The area is rich in wild life. In high Snowdonia the chough and the raven are to be seen, and the pied fly-catcher breeds in the old oak and birch woods. Redstart, wheatear and ring ousel are by no means uncommon. Among mammals, the beautiful pine marten is said still to exist, with the polecat, the red squirrel and the badger. Otters are plentiful in the large rivers – too plentiful to suit the salmon-fishers. There are brown trout in nearly all the mountain streams and lakes. The gwyniad, a rare member of the salmon family, is found in Llyn Padarn and Llyn Peris at Llanberis, landlocked by the Ice Age, and in Bala Lake, where he is seldom caught except by netting. Among plants, at least one, the mountain spiderwort, can be found nowhere else in Britain; while on the high, north-facing rock ledges of Snowdonia a wide variety of alpine plants grow, many of which are presumed to have survived since the last Ice Age. They include the purple and the mossy saxifrage, the moss campion and the rose-root. Here, too, though not an alpine, grows the yellow Welsh poppy. In addition to the Snowdonia National Park, there are two nature reserves on Anglesey.

GAZETTEER

Aber 6E8
¾m from a sandy beach, this unspoiled village is situated at the mouth of one of the loveliest glens* in the county, leading to the Aber Falls 2m away. At low tide it is possible to walk out across the Lavan sands to **Beaumaris**, but this can be dangerous because of the returning tides.

Aberangell 6F6
Centre for exploration of the nature trails opened in Dyfi Forest.

Abercywarch 6F6
Ancient village on the wild Cywarch stream. George Borrow assumed it to be the birthplace of Ellis Wynne who adapted a poem of the Spaniard Quevedo into the fine *Y Bardd Cwsg* ('The Sleeping Bard'). The Cywarch Valley shows rural Wales at its unspoiled best and gives the most rewarding approach to the ascent of Aran Fawddwy.

Aberdaron 6C7
A fishing village and resort, 2½m from *Braich-y-Pwll*, the westernmost extremity of the *Lleyn Peninsula*, which can be reached by a fine cliff walk. The old house of Y Gegyn Fawr was once a 14th-c hostel for pilgrims on their way to St Mary's Abbey, the sparse remains of which can still be seen on *Bardsey Island*, across the Sound. The village has 1½m of fine sandy beach.

Aberdovey 6E6
A golfing and seaside resort, with extensive sands, just inside the estuary of the River Dovey, which here forms the boundary with Dyfed.

Abersoch *see* **Llanengan**

Amlwch 8C2
In the first half of the 19th c, the copper from the Parys mines, already known to the Romans, dominated the copper market of the world. Today the old workings provide a background to this little port, which, with near-by Bull Bay, is developing as a resort, popular for fishing and bathing. The harbour, once used for the export of copper ore, is now an off-landing oil terminal. 1½m E the village church of *Llanwilian*, with its 12th-c tower and spire, has a finely-carved screen and rood-loft, and a curious chapel.

Bala 6F7
A market town, with a Norman castle mound, at the point where the River Dee issues from the largest natural lake in Wales, 3¾m long. At the far end of the lake, *Llanuwchllyn* is a favourite resort for fishermen, and a good point from which to climb the Aran peaks, 5m S, the highest of which is nearly 3,000ft. It is also the terminus of the narrow-gauge Bala Lake Railway, built on the site of the Great Western Railway route. *See also* **Llangynog** and **Lake Vyrnwy**, Powys.

Bangor
6D8
City with cathedral and university. The first was once the much-restored parish church; the second occupies modern buildings, completed in 1911, in Upper Bangor. In Ffordd Gwynedd is an art gallery and a museum of Welsh Antiquities. 2m W is **Menai Bridge**; and 1½m E is *Penrhyn Castle* (NT), a 19th-c imitation Norman fortress. Open to the public.

Barmouth
6E6
A popular resort with bathing, fishing and golf, standing on a narrow strip of land between sea and mountains. Across the lovely Mawddach estuary is the sandy resort of *Fairbourne*. The church at *Llanaber*, 2m N (the mother church of Barmouth), is architecturally the most remarkable in Gwynedd, having remained almost unaltered since its completion in 1250. Some 4m farther on, *Cors-y-Gedol* is the most impressive Tudor mansion in the district and it has a fine gateway.

Beaumaris
8D2
From this lovely old town on the Isle of Anglesey there are views★ across **Conwy Bay** to the mountains of *Snowdonia*. It is now a dignified little residential town, with yachting and bathing. The County Hall and the Old Bull Head are 17th-c, and a timbered house in Castle Street dates from 1400. The church has noteworthy monuments and some carved woodwork, but the moated castle (AM), built from 1295, dominates the town. Of its many features, the Great Hall and a little chapel in the central tower are most remarkable. *Penmon Priory* (AM), with its restored Norman church and dovecot for 1,000 birds is 4m NE, at the extremity of the island.

Beddgelert
6E8
Derives its name from the grave of the legendary hound 'Gelert', slain by the Welsh prince, Llywelyn, in error. At the foot of Moel Hebog, and with *Snowdon* only 4m to the N, the village remains delightfully picturesque despite the summer traffic due to its position at the junction of three important roads. The road to the NW climbs 500ft on its way to **Caernarfon**; a second, to the NE, follows the valley of Nant Gwynant, with its twin lakes: while the third leads to the Pass of Aberglaslyn, where the river forges its way to the S between pine-clad crags.

Betws-y-Coed★
6E8
Though much sought as a beauty spot, the 'Chapel in the Trees' in the valley of the River Conwy is still an enchanting place. The old church has a Norman font and an effigy of the grand-nephew of Llywelyn ap Gruffydd; and the bridge by which the **Llanrwst** road leaves the village has been there since the 15th c. The Betws-y-Coed Railway Museum has recently been opened here with a display of old rolling stock and railway *memorabilia*, and here also is the Interpretative Centre for the Snowdonia National Park, housed in the stables of the former coaching inn. Betws-y-Coed is also the centre for walking in the *Gwydir Forest*, which has dozens of waymarked trails, picnic sites and orienteering paths. Three of the most visited spots in the neighbourhood are the *Conwy* and *Swallow Falls* and the *Fairy Glen*. At the head of the Gwybernant Valley, leading out of the valley of the Lledr, is *Ty Mawr* (NT), the birthplace of Bishop Morgan, the first translator of the Bible into Welsh in the 16th c.The house is open to the public.

Caernarfon
6D8
The county town, but also a major touring centre; it is one of the few places in the kingdom that still retains its city walls and towers (AM) almost intact. The castle, built by Edward I on the Menai Strait and moated on its landward side, covers some 3 acres; and, though little but the outward shell of its walls remains, its towers and two gateways are impressive. To the SE, the Roman fort of *Segontium* may also be visited. In keeping with the tradition begun by Edward I, Prince Charles was invested with the title, Prince of Wales, in the castle in 1969. (*See also* page 301.)

Capel Curig
6E8
One of the best centres for exploring the mountains★★ of *Snowdonia*. 4m SW at *Pen-y-Gwryd*, and 1m farther on at the highest point of Llanberis Pass (1,169ft), is a hotel and a YHA hostel known to rock-climbers throughout the country. From Pen-y-Pass the Miners' Track, one of the best routes to the top of *Snowdon* (3,560ft), leads past the 1m-long Llyn Llydaw to the foot of the main precipices of the mountain. NW from Capel Curig the main **Holyhead** road follows the rugged Nant Ffrancon Pass, between towering mountains, passing Llyn Ogwen and its waterfalls at almost 1,000ft. Here, on the opposite side of the road, a path leads to Llyn Idwal, an eerie spot, with the inaccessible Devil's Kitchen to the S.

Clynnog Fawr
6D8
A whitewashed village between sea and mountain; the old collegiate church, rebuilt in the time of Henry VII, is notable for its porch and carved, timber roof, rood-screen and stalls. In the N transept is the chest of St Bueno, who founded a monastery here in the 7th c, and whose remains are in a little chapel connected to the church by a passage.

Conwy★
8D2
One of the most attractive of the Welsh towns, and now a popular resort. From the ramparts of Edward I's romantic castle (AM), with its eight drum towers, are the splendid views of the town and the mouth of the river. (*See* page 309.) The town walls (AM) form a circuit of more than 1m and include the three original gates, the best of which, Porth Uchaf, has both an inner and outer barbican. In close proximity to the castle, and spanning the Conwy estuary, is Thomas Telford's fine suspension bridge, now owned by the NT. Aberconwy House (NT) is a fine example of a medieval timber-framed building, now open as a Heritage Centre illustrating the history of the town. Of the many other old buildings, Plas Mawr, built in 1573 and now headquarters of the Royal Cambrian Academy, has panelling and plaster ceilings, and a picturesque screen. 4½m SE is **Bodnant Gardens** (Clwyd) (NT).

Corris Isaf or Lower Corris
6E6
To be reached off the main road by crossing the bridge by Ffridd Gate. This is the old Roman road still in its undeveloped state. It passes the striking rock formations above the River Dulas called the Gelligen Stone Chests and the Cave of the footpad Hwmffra the Red. Caravan parking has been developed on the other side of the river.

Criccieth
6D7
A sheltered seaside resort, facing across Tremadog Bay to **Harlech**. There are the ruins of a native Welsh castle (AM), later taken by Edward I. At the pretty village of *Llanystumdwy*, 2m W, Lloyd George was born, and is buried in a mausoleum designed by Clough Williams-Ellis. A Memorial Museum to Lloyd George is open to the public.

Llandudno: the largest resort in Wales, it has fine beaches and superb views of Snowdonia (see page 312)

Dinas Mawddwy   6F6
Till the time of Henry VIII the capital of the lordship of Mawddwy, this village, with its old pack-horse bridge across the Dovey, is today visited for its mountain scenery, extending to the N to the twin Aran peaks. The main road to **Dolgellau** climbs the Bwlch yr Oerddrws Pass to 1,178ft; while a rougher road, leading NE to **Bala** by way of the Bwlch-y-groes Pass, attains a height of 1,790ft with wonderful views all the way. At the Meirion Mill, on the site of the former railway station, visitors can watch the various processes in the production of Welsh tweeds and tapestries.

Dolgellau   6E7
A severe little Welsh town of stone and slate, but magnificently situated in the valley of the Wnion, near the head of the Mawddach estuary and 3m N of *Cader Idris* (2,937ft). Some idea of the splendour of the surroundings★ is obtained from the Precipice and Torrent Walks. Of the 12th-c Cistercian Abbey of *Cymmer*, little remains but the restored Norman church. 2m SW, *Gwernan Lake* lies among the mountains; and 5m N is the lovely *Ganllwyd Glen*, and the *Maesgwm Forest* Visitor Centre.

Dolwyddelan   6E8
An isolated quarrymen's village, stands on the River Ledre, to the S of Moel Siabod (2,860ft). In the unrestored 16th-c church is a notable brass; farther up the valley the tower of the castle (AM), possibly pre-Norman, matches the ruggedness of the mountain. It was a native Welsh stronghold in which Llywelyn the Great was born in 1194.

Ffestiniog   6E7
Perched above the lovely Vale of Ffestiniog, through which flows the River Dwyryd, there are a number of waterfalls in the neighbourhood of this village. The slate-quarrying for which the district became famous is mainly carried on at *Blaenau Ffestiniog*, 3m N. At *Blaenau* the Lechwedd Slate Caverns and the Gloddfa Ganol Slate Mine offer impressive records of the old industry.

Harlech   6E7
Once the capital of Merioneth, and one of the historic towns of Welsh nationalism. Yet its splendid castle (AM), built on a rocky spur ½m from the sea, is a place of lost causes. Glyndwr captured it in 1404, but its fall led to his defeat in 1409; it was the last place to hold out for the Lancastrians in 1468; and it was the last Royalist castle in Wales to be captured by the Parliamentary forces. Today Harlech is the home of the adult educational centre, Coleg Harlech, and of the Royal St David's Golf Club.

Holyhead   8B2
The largest town on the Isle of Anglesey, owing its importance to the major ferry service to Ireland, which has been the principal route since prehistoric times. The church of St Cybi has 13th-c features, and the wall of the churchyard is probably Roman. Many visitors are drawn here by the cliff scenery and bird life near South Stack lighthouse, and the views at the top of Holyhead Mountain, from which Ireland, the Isle of Man and the mountains of *Snowdonia* can be seen.

Llanallgo   8C2
An important centre for archeologists just inland from the NE coast of the Isle of Anglesey. It has a burial chamber dating from the New Stone Age with possible connections with the important axe factory sites in Ulster and **Caernarfon**. Pottery dates from the Bronze Age and probably shows connection with the copper-mining around

Parys Mountain. At *Din Lligwy* near by an ancient hut settlement was converted into a stronghold in the 5th–6th c to secure Welsh dominance over Irish settlers.

Llanberis   6D8
A quarrying town, beautifully situated along the shore of Llyn Padarn, between which and the smaller Llyn Peris, stands the solitary tower of Dolbadarn Castle (AM). At the end of the town is the station for the mountain-track railway (*see* page 307) to the top of *Snowdon*★ (3,560ft), past Nant Peris (Old Llanberis), in a picturesque cluster of houses and a church, before starting the ascent through the most awe-inspiring of all the Snowdon passes★. Llanberis now has a remarkable feature in the Welsh Slate Museum and perhaps an even greater attraction in the newly-founded Oriel Eryri, an Environmental Centre, and also the country park on the shores of Llyn Padarn. The Llanberis Lake Railway which once carried slate from a near-by quarry, runs along the lake shore. This is the site, too, of the Dinarwig hydro-electric power scheme, one of the world's most exciting and advanced engineering projects.

Llandudno★   8D2
100 years ago a mere village, today it is the largest and in some respects the most pleasant seaside resort and residential town in N. Wales. It is splendidly situated on the bay between the Great and Little Orme headlands. At the top of the first, 679ft above the sea, is the little church of St Tudno; and the Marine Drive curves round the base of the promontory. If you walk to the summit you can take the Victorian tramway or the cabin lift, the longest cable-car system in Britain. The town is well laid out with good shops, a major conference centre, the Mostyn Art Gallery, pier, Rapallo House Gallery, and Doll Museum. (*See* page 311.)

Llanengan   6C7
Overlooking the sandy beach of Porth Neigwl, or Hell's Mouth, the church is worth visiting for its finely carved screen and rood-loft. The bells are said to have been brought here from Bardsey (*see* **Aberdaron**). 1m NE is the yachting centre of *Abersoch*, with bathing and golf, and expeditions to the bird-haunted *St Tudwal's Islands*.

Llanfairfechan   8D2
A pleasant seaside resort, in a wooded valley with mountains rising above. Golf-course, and bathing from sand and shingle beach.

Llanrwst   6E8
A little market town on the River Conwy spanned by a three-arch bridge (AM), dated 1636, reputedly designed by Inigo Jones, with Tu Hwnt i'r Bont, an old court house (now NT), at its W end. The church is notable for its screen and roof-loft and the Gwydir Chapel, built by Sir Richard Wynn before the Civil War. This contains family monuments and a great stone coffin, said to be that of Llywelyn ap Iorwerth. Across the river, Gwydir Castle, a Tudor mansion burned in the 1920s, and partly restored, with its Dutch garden and clipped yews, is open daily in summer. The dower house, Gwydir Uchaf, is a youth hostel: its chapel (AM), noted for its painted ceiling, was built in 1673. Remote in the hills, 2m W, the ancient and very primitive church at *Llanrhychwyn* is known as 'Llywelyn's Old Church'.

Maentwrog   6E7
A pretty village in the Vale of **Ffestiniog**. In the yew-shaded churchyard may be seen the stone (maen) of Twrog, the 6th-c saint to whom the church is dedicated. Coed Llyn Mair

Nature Reserve is just off the main road in the direction of Rhyd Maentwrog. Plas Tanybwlch, at Maentwrog, is the *Snowdonia National Park*'s study centre, offering a variety of courses on environmental subjects within the park. Not far from the station is the Tomen-y-Mur, a castle mound, built by William Rufus within the site of a Roman camp. 3m SE, the A487 road runs along the great **Trawsfynydd** Reservoir, where there is good sport for fishermen.

Menai Bridge*   6D8
Here are two remarkable feats of engineering: Telford's suspension bridge completed in 1826 as a link in the mail-coach service to **Holyhead**, and widened 20 years ago; and the tubular Britannia Bridge, built by Robert Stephenson in 1850 to carry the railway, but now considerably adapted to carry both a new road and the railway. The 90ft column standing on a hill is to the memory of the first Marquess of Anglesey, who was second-in-command at the battle of Waterloo, where he lost a leg. *Plas Newydd*, the later 18th-c mansion presented by the present Marquess to the NT, is open to the public. In the park are two fine dolmens; and 2m farther on, to the SW, is the chambered cairn, *Bryn Celli Ddu* (AM). In Menai Bridge is a lovely museum of childhood with toys and other *memorabilia*.

Nefyn   6C7
An ancient little town (Edward I held a tournament here in 1284), and now a seaside resort with bathing and sea-fishing. 4m NE are the twin peaks of the Rivals, on the lower slopes of which the road reaches a height of nearly 700ft at the quarrying village of *Llithfaen*. The lower of the two mountains (1,591ft) is crowned by an Iron Age village of more than 100 hut-circles.

Pantperthog   6E6
A small place set in the pleasant woodlands of the upper Dyfi Valley. It is the site of the Centre for Alternative Technology which has a blacksmith forge, nature trail etc. Guided tours if booked in advance.

Penmachno   6E8
The Penmaelino Woollen Mill (open to visitors) and near-by Machno Falls are worth visiting; so too is the church for a rare, carved stone and what are regarded as the three earliest Christian tombstones.

Penmaenmawr   8D2
There is bathing and golf at this resort beneath the great quarried headland of Penmaenmawr, rising 1,500ft out of the sea. Good views of Conwy Bay with 3m of sandy beach, a marina for yachts and trips to *Puffin Island* in the bay. Near by is a Druid's circle, *Maen Hirion*, which is now part of an interesting History Trail.

Pennal   6E6
On the **Machynlleth**–Aberdyfi road. Unspoiled village prominent in the 16th–17th c with an inn and a Tudor house dating from that period. It was one of the five major Roman fortresses and was set to watch the approaches up the Dyfi Valley. At *Cefn Gaer* the squared outline of its foundation can be seen. Today it offers the best way to enter the network of Forestry roads which break into the valleys and hill slopes of the Daren Gesail range with their view into the **Tal-y-llyn** Valley and across to *Cader Idris*.

Pentraeth   8C3
At Red Wharf Bay, a little to the N, are sands and excellent bathing. 4m SW the old manor house of *Penmynydd*, with

18th-c additions (not open to the public), was the birthplace of Owen Tudor, whose grandson became Henry VII. 5m N is the unspoiled fishing village of *Moelfre*, a famous lifeboat station, where there is a memorial to the 452 lives lost when the *Royal Chester* sank off the coast here.

Porthmadog   6D7
A busy little resort, with boat-filled harbour and maritime museum. There are bathing, golf and boating at *Borth-y-Gest* 1m S. At *Tremadog*, to the N, Lawrence of Arabia was born. The house where Shelley lived for a time can also be seen. Another attraction is the voluntarily-run narrow-gauge Ffestiniog Railway, oldest of its kind in the world, which carried slate from Blaenau Ffestiniog (*see* **Festiniog**) to waiting ships in Porthmadog harbour. *Portmeirion*, on a privately owned peninsula at the head of Tremadog Bay, is a charming Italianate village resembling Portofino or Sorrento, created by the architect Sir Clough Williams-Ellis. Village open to public Easter–Oct. (entrance fee).

Portmeirion *see* Porthmadog

Pwllheli   6D7
A popular and growing resort, with golf, bathing and a small harbour, designated for development as a marina.

Rhosneigr   6D8
A quiet little resort, with rocks and coves for bathing, a golf-course, and sailing on Llyn Maelog. In a bay near *Aberffraw*, another small coastal village 3m SE, the tiny church of St Cyfan stands on an island that is accessible at low tide.

Snowdonia *see* Introduction, **Betws-y-Coed,** **Capel Curig, Llanberis** and **Maentwrog**

Tal-y-llyn   6E6
At the W end of the lake (Llyn Myngul) this is little more than a couple of fishing hostelries. Its views of the lake and the valley are striking where *Cader Idris* and the Darens face each other. The church is *c.* 15th-c and has interesting paintings and a Welsh verse which forbids anyone to enter that 'kingly place' unless his heart is pure.

Trawsfynydd   6E7
The Trawsfynydd Reservoir 2m long and Nuclear Power Station dominate the wide stretches of moor. The lake is noted for its perch and trout catches and attracts fishermen from far afield. The Roman road network known as the Sarn Helen has a branch here. Below Mynydd Bach can be seen two of its mile-posts. Along it lie the relics of the Gwynfynydd gold mine and the Roman and later Norman stronghold of Tomen y Mur. The small town has a statue of the poet Hedd Wyn crowned as Chief Bard at the Royal National Eisteddfod in **Birkenhead** (Merseyside) when he lay dead in Flanders Fields in World War I.

Tywyn   6E6
The old village is some distance from *Morfa Tywyn*, with its esplanade and miles of sands. The church, though partly modern, has a Norman nave and aisles, and a font of the same period, but its greatest pride is St Cadfan's Stone, 7ft long and inscribed on all four sides in 7th- or 8th-c Welsh. The Tal-y-llyn Narrow Gauge Railway runs from the wharf to *Abergynolwyn* some 7m NE; from which point the road, on the other side of the river, continues another 5m to the pretty lake of Tal-y-llyn. The village here is an admirable point for the ascent of *Cader Idris*★ (2,937ft), one of the grandest mountains in Wales.

Powys

AN INTRODUCTION BY
ALUN LLEWELLYN

Powys (now including the former counties of Montgomery, Radnor and Brecon) was originally a strategic structure guarding the three major points of entrance into Britain from the west sea and forming a barrier against attack through the English Midlands. Its origin was in the sub-Roman period and it built on the Roman defence system as Lhuyd's 16th-century Map of Wales makes clear.

The Normans, however, set up their system of border commands, the Marches of Wales, and Hugh the Wolf of Chester and De Braose of Abergavenny have remained in Welsh memory as archetypes of tyranny and genocide. Powys found its centre penetrated by the Norman lords of Montgomery and fell back towards the Dyfi estuary and Penegoes, protected by the bare and largely impenetrable moorlands of Plynlimon with Radnor as its outpost.

Although later administrations set Plynlimon in Cardiganshire and now therefore in Dyfed, tradition places it firmly in the Kingdom of Powys. If Powys was the strategic centre of Wales the Dyfi was the strategic centre of Powys. Its valley offers the readiest route to penetrate the English Midlands from the Irish Sea; the Roman roads that run from Talybont in Dyfed to Machynlleth in Powys and to the same place from Corris in Gwynedd, like the 17th- and 18th-century coach-roads which followed them, explain the importance of the Plynlimon upland. Its five valleys centre on Penegoes and the Five Summits from which it takes its name can be clearly distinguished there upon the motor road which passes through that village and follows the older Roman way from Machynlleth to Newtown. A land of lakes and peat-bogs that stretched to touch the Berwyns, the Breiddens, the Brecon Beacons and Radnor Forest, it was known to Giraldus Cambrensis as Ellenith. Romans first made it a centre for lead-mining. But earlier prehistoric traffic is evidenced by the discovery of a hoard of finely shaped flint arrow-heads close to Bugeilyn Lake and burial mounds which show the presence of settlement by the Bronze Age Beaker Folk of about 1000 BC. Perhaps even earlier hut-circles have been drowned beneath the reservoir at Nant y Moch constructed in the 1960s. By the early

1900s, Plynlimon had become a place of wide-ranging sheep-walks; it had been an area alive with the red foxes introduced in Roman times and still haunted by the much older grey and wolf-like fox native to Britain, hovered over by buzzard, merlin, kestrel and seagull and where the Severn, the Rheidol and the Wye found their spring-sources in open heather-cloaked moorland, but by the end of the century it has become heavily afforested with alien conifers. Its oak-filled valleys took on a new character, their deserted farmsteads standing crumbled and buried in the new growth. Whatever effect this has had on the ecology and economy of the region it has benefited the foxes, by giving them fresh and effective cover, and the tourist for whom the new forestry roads have opened up some of the most beautiful and hitherto unseen regions of Wales.

The industrialization of the south, concentrated as it was on the coal-mining, steel-production and tin-plate works mainly of Glamorgan, shifted not only the vast majority of the population of Wales away from Powys but changed the character of Wales itself in the eyes of the outside world. But Powys still remains the historic heartland of the country.

There are two centres for the exploration of this region, distinct in character and in their contrast summarizing between them the whole history of Powys.

Machynlleth stands at the neck of the Dyfi estuary. Its main street, Maengwyn, still retains much of the finely built houses which in the 17th and 18th centuries marked its importance as the centre for the stagecoach traffic of those days and for the busy shipping along the river. It was once celebrated for its 24 coaching inns; but of these only two, the Wynnstay and the White Lion, now remain. Its site is among the foothills of Plynlimon and its markets and its long-standing sheep trials show its intimate connection with the ancient pastoral community of isolated farmlands surrounding it. In and around the near-by village of Fforg (Forge) can be seen the derelict wheels of the watermills that once served the busy industry of wool-weaving. The local hunt has its kennels in Plas Machynlleth, once the seat of 16th-century gentry and later owned by the Marquess of Londonderry, but now the property of the Town Council, and at Llynlloed, its neighbour. The hunt runs a foot-pack since following by horse is impracticable among the network of irregular valleys. It is called out only when a farm has been raided by foxes in search of their fowl and operates more as a police patrol than as a blood sport. The foxes are ingenious in avoiding pursuit and seem to have no fear of being overtaken. One who has followed this hunt for 40 years can confirm that he has never seen a fox tracked to earth or killed.

Across the river the skyline is dominated by the sharp ridge-backs of the Tarens in Gwynedd, now claimed to be part of the Snowdonia Forest. These also have been knifed open by forestry roads. From their tops they look across the lake of Tal-y-llyn to Cader Idris and the humped hindquarters of the Arans. Southward from Machynlleth the roads lead past the flank of the Plynlimon massif to the wide seascapes and marshland of the estuary and the gentler land of northern Dyfed.

The second centre for exploration is Montgomery, once the seat of administration but now a reposeful country town. To the Welsh it is known as Trefaldwyn, Baldwin's Town, and so preserves the memory of the Norman Baldwin de Boller who in the days of Henry I of England raised his fortress there.

Unlike Machynlleth, which preserves in its old Parliament House the murals by Murray Urquhart that celebrate Glyndwr's victory at Mynydd Hyddgant, Montgomery looks further back to the earlier connection of Powys with the shire of Shropshire. Its native architecture is of the half-timbered style often associated with Tudor taste, but in fact, used by the Romans as a protection against a shifting soil. Its memories link it with Powis Castle at Welshpool and with Chirbury, close at hand, and John Donne, Edward Lord Herbert and his brother George the priest, all three of whom were distinguished poets not only of Welsh descent and connection but who wrote in English with the overtones of Welsh lyric tradition in their ears.

From Montgomery the way can be taken to Brecon and Radnor. From Buttington near Welshpool the English border can be followed in the track of Offa's Dyke laid out by the Saxon of that name, King of Mercia, after his victory over the Welsh at Rhuddlan (Clwyd). The hills of Kerry with their distinctive breed of sheep and still firmly part of Wales and the calm places of Clun Forest, which were once Welsh and called Colunwy, lead to Radnor Forest. Very much unpopulated this part of Powys offers wide

The Brecon Beacons form the centre of a national park created in 1957 and covering an area of 529 square miles

stretches of country unrivalled for the exercise of horseriding. Not only are its hills possessed by herds of wild free-roaming mountain ponies but at Penybont it affords the opportunity to witness or even take part in some of the most remarkable horseracing events to be found anywhere. The small town of New Radnor with streets laid out in a chessboard pattern looks back for its foundation to Harald, Earl of Hereford and the last Saxon King of England, though a more direct attribution may be made to the execrated Norman De Braose who seized on Radnor about 1200. Harald had in fact destroyed the site now known as Old Radnor where the Romans may have settled themselves. All that is left of the place is its ancient church though this is well worth a visit. Its font is reputed to be the oldest in Britain although its stone may date further back to pre-Christian times; the church itself is reputed one of the finest in Wales. Charles I of England visited it after his defeat at Naseby. Some of the most ancient pastoral traditions of Wales are to be found at Beguildy (Shepherd's House) and the small chapel at Betws y Crwyn (Chapel of Fleeces). The small church at Partrishow is of outstanding interest; it escaped the destructive intentions of the Puritan Roundhead troops during the Civil War because of its hidden remoteness among the Black Mountains. Although Tudor in style it has an 11th-century font of stone which bears a Latin inscription attributing its making to one Genlli, identified with an early ruler of Powys who held his frontiers against the Normans. Later monuments to these border wars are to be found in the castellated keeps of Norman origin at Bronllys, Tretower and Crickhowell. Heol y Gaer at Glasbury and a more recently identified camp at Clyro give evidence of the thrust of Roman power into this area at an even earlier date. The centre of Norman control was at Brecon itself where Bernard of Neufmarche set his castle. In his time the present Cathedral was founded as a Priory, a place of peculiar miracle and sanctity as Giraldus Cambrensis observed in the 12th century. Today this part of Powys is noted for its several once-famous spas, Llandrindod, Llanwrtyd, Llangammarch and Builth where the River Wye joins the Irfon, although their principal purpose today may be thought to be the opportunities they give for fishing on the rivers and in the excellent lakes rather than the quality of their waters.

GAZETTEER

Abbeycwmhir   6F5
'The abbey of the long valley' was founded in 1143, but the buildings started in the 13th c were never finished; the abbey was sacked by Glyndwr in 1402, and little more than the bases of the walls remain.

Beguildy   6G5
Its name Shepherd's House is descriptive of the area. Above it on the **Black Mountain** (*see* in Dyfed) ridge overlooking the River Teme and the River Clun is *Betws y Crwyn*, the Chapel of Fleeces. There and at *Bryn Amlwg* are ancient stone circles. About 1m S is another standing stone and a tumulus. Very beautiful countryside.

Brecon   6F3
Finely situated in the valley of the Usk where it is joined by the Honddu and the Tarell. The centre of a busy agricultural area. Many excellent Georgian houses. The 13th–14th-c red sandstone Priory Church, once administered by the Benedictine monks of **Battle** Abbey in E. Sussex, is now the Cathedral of the diocese of **Swansea** and Brecon. Remains of a 12th–13th-c castle and of old town walls. Good historical and archeological museum and a military museum in the barracks of the South Wales Borderers. Sarah Siddons (1755–1831) was born in Brecon at a house now a pub called the Siddons Vaults. 2m W is the site of a Roman fort, *Y Gaer* (AM), founded *c.*AD 75 and then abandoned in AD 140.

Brecon Beacons   6F3/G3
The highest ground in S. Wales, separated from the **Black Mountains** (*see* in Dyfed) by the valley of the Usk; on the SE is the deep Glyn Collwyn, and Glyn Tarell is on the W. From the SE the land rises to the precipitous escarpment on the N side; here are the three prominent points, the Beacons: Pen-y-Fan (2,906ft), Corn-Du and Cribyn, with tremendous views to the **Malvern Hills** (Hereford and Worcester) and across the Bristol Channel to **Exmoor** (Somerset). Another good viewpoint is at the Mountain Centre at *Libanus*, a National Park interpretative centre. The Brecon Beacons National Park now includes the largest show-cave complex in W. Europe, the Dan yr Ogof and Cathedral caves. Open daily Easter–Oct. Information at *Abercrave*, Swansea Valley. Pony-trekking and boating on Llangorse Lake and the Brecon and Abergavenny Canal. (*See* page 315.)

Bronllys   6G4
Norman church with a detached tower used as a place of refuge in troubled times, and ruins of a 13th-c castle. Near by is *Gwernyfed Hall* (15th-c) with a 12th-c door.

Builth Wells   6F4
Where the Wye is joined by the Irfon. Good fishing, and a centre of pony-trekking with hillsides above the River Wyre. The beauty of the Wye Valley is animated by a succession of rapids just above the town. Once a year, in July, Builth plays host to Wales' major agricultural show, the Royal Welsh Show, which is staged at the permanent showground at *Llanelwedd*. To the S *Mynydd Epynt* has many good walks E of the B4519 (military training grounds to the W). At *Cilmeri*, 4m W, there is a monument to Prince Llewelyn of the 13th c.

Caersws   6F6
Site of a Roman military station. It was the connecting point for Roman Chester, Wroxeter and Pennal. There is a fine old half-timbered house, Maesmawr, now a hotel, and another, Talgarth, 5m W, near *Trefeglwys* (Clwyd). 2m NW, at *Llanwnog*, we find a 15th-c rood-loft and screen in the church.

Clyro 6G4

Site of a Roman fort and Norman castle now ruined. A Tudor mansion destroyed by fire still has its battlemented gateway preserved as the entrance to a farm. Here Francis Kilvert, curate for seven years, began his famous Diary.

Craig-y-Nos 6F3

The castle belonged to Madame Patti, the famous singer, who spent enormous sums in developing and beautifying the estate, which is now a country park.

Crickhowell 6G3

Village in the Usk Valley with remains of a castle built in the 13th c on the site of an earlier building. Several Tudor and Georgian houses, and a fine 13th-c bridge over the river.

Darowen 6F6

600ft above sea level this place can be reached along the old green road from **Penegoes** over Ffridd Wyllt and Bryn Wg, Wild Forest and Rising Hill. Its medieval church is between two standing stones which bear directly on Bwlch Gwyn Peak. The one to the N is pear-shaped, that on the S is 7ft high and squared to the cardinal points. Their antiquity is much greater than that of the church. Several pretty and unspoiled villages are in the neighbourhood.

Dylife 6F6

Its name is from the Floods which describe its place on the edge of the **Plynlimon** upland. It was the centre for Roman lead-mining operations which were followed in the 17th and 18th c. The local gallows were at one time erected on the hill above. It was also the regular venue for holding the Court of Strays to decide the ownership of sheep. The *Pennant Falls*, *Clywedy Reservoir* and the *Hafren Forest* can be reached from here.

Forge 6E6

A narrow street beside a ravined stream. Once a considerable centre for the 'pandys' or fulling mills whose waterwheels can still be found in the vicinity. It is now on the best route for approach to the Hengwm Valley and the most beautiful approach to the head of **Plynlimon**, an area of great archeological interest.

Hay-on-Wye 6G4

A busy little place on the Wye amid pleasant hill country. Through the town runs the little stream which at this point separates England and Wales; most of Hay is in Wales. The market has been held since 1233. Remains of a Norman castle have been built into a private house, now part of the world's largest second-hand bookshop. Dominating the skyline to the S is the border summit of Hay Bluff (2,219ft), northern sentinel of the **Black Mountains** (*see* in Dyfed).

Kerry 6G6

On the River Mule, whence the wild mountainous sheep country of the Kerry Hills rises to the S. This may be seen from Kerry Pole (1,500ft), 1m N of the lonely Anchor inn, 5m SW of the village on the road to **Clun** (Shropshire). Note the fine Norman arcades of the church (consecrated in 1176, but rebuilt in the 15th c) and its timbered belfry.

Knighton 6G5

Pleasant little town on the Teme with wooded hills all around. There is a weekly market; thousands of ewes and lambs are sold at the autumn fairs. On both sides of the town are stretches of **Offa's Dyke** (Clwyd), the history of which is depicted in the town's Heritage Centre.

Llandrindod Wells 6F4

Benefit is still to be derived from the saline, magnesium, sulphur, lithia and chalybeate springs which first brought the town into notice. The town's Pump Room has been restored in the Rock Park Spa where you can 'take the waters'. The Victorian atmosphere has also been recreated, especially during Festival Week in Sept. when all the townsfolk don Victorian costume. Nowadays it is recognized also as a conference centre and a holiday resort, besides being the seat of government of the county. There is good fishing in the Eithon. 2m N is the site of the Roman camp *Castell Collen*.

Llanelieu 6G3

1½m E of *Talgarth*. High up on the slopes of the Black Mountains, a small remote church with a splendid double rood screen still with its original tympanum, original S door and ironwork. Note the pair of 7th–9th-c inscribed stones.

Llanfair Caereinion 6G6

A village famous for its position as terminus of the narrow-gauge Welshpool and Llanfair Light Railway, one of the great Little Trains of Wales. A single-spanned bridge crosses the River Einion, which is much frequented by fishermen; and there is a notable 14th-c effigy in the rebuilt church. 5m NW, at *Llanerfyl*, the church is remarkable, not only for its contents, but for its circular graveyard, corresponding to an earlier stone circle, and also an inscribed Romano-British gravestone.

Llanfillo 6G3

2m W of *Talgarth*. Pleasant village with a church retaining a well-restored 16th-c rood-screen, a pre-Norman font and other interesting features.

Llanfyllin 6G7

Little market town in the wooded valley of the Cain, noted for the sweetness of the bells in its 18th-c church; and, once, for its ale ('Old ale fills Llanfyllin with young widows').

Llangammarch Wells 6F4

One of the group of three spas of mid-Wales. Now just a village, beautifully situated on the Irfon with fishing.

Llangorse Lake 6G3

The discovery in the 20th c of an ancient canoe and other remains showed that men fished in this lake (the largest natural lake in S. Wales) in prehistoric times. It is now a popular venue for all kinds of watersports.

Llangynog 6F7

Small stone-quarrying village at the junction of the lovely Eirth and Tanat Valleys. 2½m W is the lonely little Norman church at *Pennant Melangell*, with early monuments, and 15th-c rood-screen (now removed to W. Gallery), carved with representations of hares, of whom St Melangell (Monacella) was the patroness. The road to **Bala** (Gwynedd) continues up the valley of the Tanat to the top of the wild *Milltir Cerrig Pass* (1,838ft).

Llanidloes 6F5

The slate and stone of this little Welsh market town are modified by the painted stucco of one or two buildings in the main street, giving a slightly Georgian impression. The half-timbered Market Hall is now occupied by a museum of local history. The church is notable for its timbered belfry, N arcade and fine hammer-beam roof, these last two brought from Cwmhir Abbey at the time of the Dissolution. The main

Aberystwyth road to Dyfed soon leaves the Severn Valley for the higher valley of the Wye, which it reaches at the pretty village of *Llangurig*, 900ft above sea level, with **Plynlimon** (2,468ft) away to the NNW. A mountain road runs N from Llanidloes past the superb Clywedy Reservoir through *Staylittle*, with its old Coach Road moorland walk, to Cemmaes Road and **Machynlleth**. The B4518 runs S through beautiful hills to **Pant-y-dwr**.

Llanwrtyd Wells 6F4

On the strength of its chalybeate and sulphur springs, Llanwrtyd Wells set itself up as a spa. But the vogue for such institutions passed, and the village is now a pleasant holiday resort, pony-trekking and activity centre, with fishing in the Irfon and the brooding heights of Mynydd Eppynt to the SE. The **Tregaron** road to Dyfed runs N up the picturesque Abergwesyn Valley.

Llyswen 6G4

In the churchyard is the raised tomb of John Macnamara who won the mansion of Llangoed in a bet, to hold as long as he was above ground. The house is splendidly situated beside the Wye. It originated in the 17th c but has been virtually rebuilt by Clough Williams-Ellis.

Machynlleth 6E6

A little town with many old houses, in the lovely valley of the River Dovey. Now bustling in summer with tourists and fishermen, it was here in 1402 that Owain Glyndwr summoned his first Parliament to proclaim himself Prince of Wales; in fact there is no question that he really acted as King of the country. The Institute named after him, with its library and interpretative centre, the Owain Glyndwr Centre, is thought to have been the Parliament House. Plas Machynlleth, formerly a residence of Lord Londonderry, standing in delightful grounds, now belongs to the town. To the N lie the 17,000 acres of Dyfi Forest, and the National Centre for Alternative Technology at **Pantperthog** (Gwynedd) and 4m SW is the picturesque Llyfnant Valley.

Meifod 6G6

A large village, charmingly situated on the River Vyrnwy, which here flows through the Vale of Meifod, famous for its beauty. The church has Norman arcading and an embattled tower; and across the river stands the fine Regency house, Pen-y-Lan.

Montgomery 6G6

County town once only in name, 1m from its railway station and on no major road, with houses of every period from Elizabethan to Georgian, but none modern, this charming little town sleeps at the foot of the Welsh mountains, almost on the border of England. Above it are the fragmentary walls and towers of the Norman castle (AM), where the poet George Herbert was born in 1593, and where his elder brother, Lord Herbert of Cherbury, lived through the Civil War. Their father's tomb is in the 14th-c church, which also has an early Norman font, carved misericords and a screen, perhaps from the demolished Abbey of Chirbury in Shropshire. Lymore is an example of black-and-white, half-timbered Jacobean architecture, and the town hall is Georgian. 2m SE the B4386 crosses **Offa's Dyke** (Clwyd and Hereford and Worcester) into England.

New Radnor 6G5

An ancient borough shorn of its privileges and shrunk to the size of a village. Earthworks of a Norman castle (destroyed during the Civil War) and remains of the old town wall. Here the Somergill river runs underground for a short distance. Radnor Forest rises NW towards the summit of Great Rhos, over 2,000ft above sea level. *Old Radnor*, 3m SE, has a fine church with an exceptional rood-screen, an organ case of Henry VIII's time, medieval tiles, and a large pre-Norman font carved from a single block of stone.

Newtown 6G6

Till the beginning of the 20th c one of the main centres of the Welsh flannel industry, this town is now, with **Welshpool**, one of the two administrative capitals of the county. There are some attractive houses, of which Upper Bryn, half-timbered and dated 1660, is the most impressive. The main interest for many people will be that Robert Owen, the socialist reformer, was born here in 1771, in the house now occupied by a bank. Opposite, in a building which housed the Co-operative Movement's free library, is a memorial museum to the 19th-c social reformer and philanthropist. When famous, he returned here to die and is buried in the old churchyard near the bridge. The A483, leading S from the town, offers a variety of mountain scenery. Rising sharply, it forks just beyond *Dolfor*, the main road to **Llandrindod Wells** rising to 1,200ft and following the course of the River Ithon for many miles. Even better, perhaps, is the left fork, which reaches a height of over 1,500ft in the Kerry Hills and continues to **Knighton**.

Offa's Dyke *see* entry in Clwyd and also Hereford and Worcester

Pant-y-dwr 6F5

A straddling village on the B4518, S of **Llanidloes**, situated high in the hills. It has many fine views.

Partrishow 6G3

Famed for its secluded church with splendid rood-loft and carved screen. Note the 11th-c font and its inscription.

Penegoes 6E6

3m W of **Machynlleth**. Birthplace of Richard Wilson the internationally famous 18th-c artist. The Rectory will show the bedroom in which he was born on reasonable request. He is buried in the churchyard at *Mold* (Clwyd). Owain Cyfeiliog, ruler of Powys in the 12th c, had his seat on the hill Gallt y Llan. The name of the village means Head of the Valley Openings and it is the best centre from which to walk the five valleys of the **Plynlimon** range.

Penybont 6G5

A village lying W of **New Radnor**. Radnor Forest is seen at its most attractive along the foot and horse trails between them. Wild ponies wander around in considerable numbers. Famous for its horseraces and, in particular, those between pony-drawn sulkies and two-wheeled vehicles.

Pen-y-Bont-Fawr 6F7

With fishing in the River Tanat, this is a good point from which to visit **Lake Vyrnwy** 6m SW, and the superb waterfall, *Pistyll Rhaeadr*, compared by George Borrow to 'the long tail of a grey courser at furious speed'. From *Llanrhaeadr-ym-Mochant*, 2½m NE, a by-road follows the River Disgynfa for 3½m NE to where the stream, descending below the Berwyn Hills, is flung over a cliff and through a natural arch from a height of 230ft.

Pistyll Rhaeadr *see* **Pen-y-Bont-Fawr**

Plynlimon Fawr *see* entry in Dyfed

Presteigne   6G5
The church is mainly 11th–15th c and the half-timbered Radnorshire Arms is early 17th-c. The curfew is still rung nightly at 8 p.m. from the church tower.

Rhayader   6F5
Set 700ft above sea level in the Upper Wye Valley, and nearest jumping-off point for the *Elan Valley Reservoirs★* which provide **Birmingham** with its water. Drive 4m along the SW road out of Rhayader; then follow the road beside the lakes as they wind among the hills for some 8m. Here is some of the finest lake scenery in Wales. When the lakes are full, the excess water spills magnificently over the great dams. These were completed just after the turn of the century. A recent extension involved the damming of the Claerwen Valley and the creation of a new lake 4m long.

Rhulen   6G4
A little 14th-c church with an attractive barn-like simplicity and surrounded by a circular churchyard. Perched high in the mountains amid beautiful scenery.

Tretower   6G3
Prettily placed village with well-restored remains of a splendid 14th-c fortified manor house, Tretower Court (AM, NT). Adjoining is the keep of the Norman castle with its central round tower (AM).

Vyrnwy, Lake   6F7
Formed by damming the River Vyrnwy 825ft above sea level to make a reservoir for **Liverpool**, this is the largest lake in Wales, 5m long and nearly 1m wide. Most easily approached from the SE and (*see* **Pen-y-Bont-Fawr**) it is encircled by a good road; while at the NE end is a rough but magnificent mountain road running over the Rhiw Hirnant Pass (1,641ft) direct to **Bala** (Gwynedd), 14m away. Trout-fishing permits

Welshpool: 13th-century Powis Castle, occupied by the Herberts since 1587, has beautiful terraces and gardens

may be obtained at the hotel in the model village of *Llanwddyn*. In a former chapel in the village the RSPB and Severn Trent Water Authority have established the Vyrnwy Visitor Centre.

Welshpool   6G6
The county town, close to the River Severn, which is here separated from England by the Long Mountain, rising to 1,338ft at Beacon Ring. Built mostly of brick, which is unusual for Wales, many of the houses are Georgian, such as the old post office in Broad Street, originally an inn; but there is a group of timber-framed houses near the castle, one of which has an inscription over the door in nails: 'G— d— old Oliver 1661'. Powis Park, with its lovely woodlands and some of the largest trees in the British Isles, is always open to the public; the castle, bequeathed to the NT by the Earl of Powis in 1952, is also open. The oldest part of the castle dates from the late 13th c, but many of the domestic apartments were added in the 16th; they now contain much fine plasterwork and carving, as well as pictures, Georgian furniture and Clive relics. The gardens, modified by Capability Brown, are remarkable. Opposite the door of the parish church (Powis tombs and a fine chancel roof), the Maen Llog, originally a Druid altar, was later used as a throne by the Abbots of Strata Marcella, only the foundations of which are now extant, 3m NW. The Powysland Museum has an admirable collection, representing the art and history of the region. Welshpool is the terminus of the Welshpool and Llanfair Light Railway; steam locomotives from Austria, Africa and the West Indies have been brought together to operate on this steeply graded track. The journey takes you through pastoral and woodland scenery on the borderlands of Powys.

DYFED

AN INTRODUCTION BY
ALUN LLEWELLYN AND R. M. LOCKLEY

The present Dyfed (formerly Cardigan-, Pembroke- and Carmarthen shires) has a larger extent than the ancient district of the Demetiae known to the Romans, or the later Welsh Dyfed which followed it and was mainly centred on Pembroke. It begins at the Dyfi where Gwynedd and Powys meet and where the partly reclaimed reed-bannered marsh of Cors Fochno and the tiny church and vicarage of Llan Cynfelin together mark the memory of Wales in the Dark Age time of saints. Near Eglwys Fach stands a tall pillar of stone, Dolmen Las, set up in days of Bronze Age traffic. Further south along the road is Taliesin where, according to legend, the grave of the eponymous poet of Arthurian Wales can be seen. Eglwys Fach or Little Church once had the important position of a river port serving the trade in ores from Plynlimon and timber and wool from the Llyfnant Valley. The coach-roads of the 17th and 18th century were busy here. But the route was also important for the Romans who had their station across the Dyfi at Pennal and stretched their communications from the lead mines of Plynlimon to the gold mines at Dolau Cothi. Here, inland from the modern Aberystwyth, the roads lead east to reach Goginan where Romans may have mined for silver, but which is better known as the home of Dafydd ap Gwilym, the 14th-century Welsh lyric poet acknowledged to be of European stature. Further still Devil's Bridge stands over the Mynach (Monk's) Stream. George Borrow, the 19th-century traveller, reached this place during his walks about Plynlimon by way of Glaspwll at the end of the Llyfnant Valley. His *Wild Wales* speaks of his fierce reception there by women to whom he spoke in Welsh. The granddaughter of one of them made it clear it was not racial hatred, as he supposed, that made them reject him, but sheer terror at his appearance and the strange utterance of speech which he, but not they, assumed to be Welsh. On the coast road the way runs to the pleasant old harbour towns of Aberarth and its supplanter Aberaeron and the 17th–18th-century foundation of New Quay (Cei Newydd). But leaving at last the west flank of the Ellennith or central moorland of Wales the roads lead towards Cardigan and Carmarthen.

Here the countryside with its haycocks built in a style more traditionally Irish than Welsh is filled with history. The Normans raised their castles, such as those at Carew, Manorbier as well as Cardigan and Carmarthen, to hold down their conquests; but, from the native Welsh stronghold of Cilgerran, a Prince of Powys, Cadwgan, carried out a campaign in the early 12th century which recovered most of Wales and even took the war into England. Early in the next century Llywelyn the Great was able to repeat the same successes and after the recapture of Cilgerran summon a Parliament for all Wales. Carreg Cennen Castle, the most isolated and romantic of Welsh castles preserves a legendary memory of the Owain, Ywaine de Galles, whom Froissart records as the champion of Welsh independence under Edward III. At Llandeilo, the Castle of Dynevor stands on the site from which Rhodri the Great succeeded in uniting Wales against the Dane and in 870 distributed the government of Wales among his three sons, one to rule Gwynedd, one Powys, one the south. At Whitland near St Clears, Rhodri's grandson Hywel managed to hold a Parliament for all Wales and lay down a code of law which Edward I recognized as effective for organizing the new Principality he had set up for his son.

Although the Viking Black Army had made a determined attempt to conquer Britain from the west by seizing the waist of Wales, Rhodri succeeded in confining them to the islands in the Bristol Channel and to trading settlements on the coast. The islands of Skokholm, Skomer, Ramsey and their neighbours had their names from Scandinavian tongues as did the towns of Fishguard and Hasguard. The isles are now inhabited by wildfowl of the sea, though in Skomer there are remains of hutments of an ancient population which was much larger than the island could have supported from its own resources. It may have been associated with the prehistoric sea traffic which brought gold from Ireland to serve the sophisticated Wessex culture and built Stonehenge from sarsen – that is 'foreign' stones – shipped from the Prescelly Hills near Newport overlooking the Bay. Stone circles following the pattern of Stonehenge, though on a considerably reduced scale, can be seen close at hand (Gors Fawr) and throughout the area. Standing stones engraved with Ogam signs, a script of incised stops and grouped lines, are to be found as much in southwest Dyfed as they are in Ireland. This script has been assumed to be Irish in origin and to be an attempt in about AD 400 to transcribe the letters of the Latin alphabet into a primitive form. Other possibilities suggest a much earlier origin and that the script was transferred into the alphabetic signs with which we are familiar. A convenient way to examine them is to visit the National Museum at Cardiff. It is possible that the school of saintly studies at St David's, on the River Alun, may have been responsible for transferring the Ogam script into Latinized texts.

The Pembroke coast has been from earliest times a point of international sea traffic. Even in Roman administration, the Bristol Channel was guarded by a naval station at Cardiff, and in the succeeding Dark Ages maritime trade was carried on between the south coast of Wales and the Mediterranean. Pembroke above Milford Haven was seized by Normans and strengthened with its castle. Flemings were settled there by Henry I and Henry II, perhaps as mercenaries to guard the place. This gave a non-Welsh character to the hinterland which, in spite of much intermarriage, is maintained to this day. But Pembroke Dock, Milford Haven and Fishguard are now modern instances of the old tradition of international traffic by sea and by modern air routes. At Fishguard in 1797 the French assaulted these shores in an invasion attempt. It ended in ignominious surrender, the only casualty being a grandfather clock shot in panic by one of a landing party which had called at the farmstead to ask for lunch.

Natural Features

The last ice sheet covered the central massif of Wales only as far as the northern half of Dyfed. As it retreated north, it left exposed ice-scarred primitive rocks 500 million years old. Earth movements had folded and upthrust these pre-Cambrian igneous rocks between the younger sedimentary series. This elevated northern part is complicated, ranging from the primary to Cambrian and Silurian exposures with shales and mudstones forming the mountain upfold. The southern coastal plain is simpler with bands of red sandstone and carboniferous limestone and the comparatively recent coal-measures. Green mountains rise to moderate elevations, to 1,760 feet (Mynydd Preseli) and 1,515 feet. Over the border the east to the westward thrust of the Brecon Beacons tops the 2,500 feet mark where Carmarthen Van and its legendary Lake, also known as Black Mountain, tower above the mining district of Ammanford. The coal-measures run from southeast along the coast westward, a thin vein of anthracite continuing under the sea near Saundersfoot crossing to St Bride's Bay. The little mines of this area are no longer worked, even the evidence in the form of tips and levels is grown over and inhabited only by wildlife.

Dyfed is rich in the number of wild species uncommon elsewhere. The rocky islands off the coast are sanctuaries for thousands of nesting sea-birds: Manx shearwaters, puffins, razorbills, guillemots, oyster-catchers and gulls. Grassholm, often inaccessible, has many breeding gannets. Skokholm is a bird observatory with a colony of storm petrels. Skomer is a national nature reserve. Ramsey is the breeding place of Atlantic seals. On the mainland buzzards are more numerous than elsewhere in Britain. The rare red-billed chough and the peregrine survive along the cliffs. Pembrey is also a centre of bird studies.

As to flowers, the hedges and lanes are spectacular from January with snowdrops, daffodils, primroses, violets, cowslips, orchids, bluebells and columbines. Rivers, today, are fished for salmon in small primitive coracles made of lath and tarred canvas, easy to carry on the back for return up river.

GAZETTEER

Aberaeron 6D5
Old fishing port on the rocky Dyfed coast, with a small harbour and shingly beach at the mouth of the Aeron River. The Sea Aquarium, on the N side of the harbour, illustrates the marine life off the W coast of Wales.

Aberystwyth 6E5
Seaside resort and university town at the mouth of the conjoined Rheidol and Ystwyth rivers and within reach of beautiful river scenery. The University College of Wales (founded 1872) at present occupies a former hotel on the front near the pier. On the hills behind the town are the modern buildings of the National Library of Wales, Aberystwyth Arts Centre, and various university departments. Pen Dinas, the site of an important prehistoric hill fort, is S of the town centre. Aberystwyth has a small harbour, a shingle and sandy beach, and the remains of a 13th-c castle.

Angle 6B2
Charmingly situated at the mouth of **Milford Haven**, between two bays, muddy Angle and sandy West Angle. There is a ruined four-storeyed tower, with a moat and pigeon-house, and a Tudor blockhouse.

Black Mountains 6E3
This range of mountains, occupying the whole E end of the county, is separated from the Black Mountains on the Hereford and Worcester border by 25m of mountainous country, culminating in **Brecon Beacons** (Powys), and the

valley of the Usk; but all three ranges are united in a magnificent National Park★. Apart from the road mentioned below (*see* **Brynamman**), much of the area is accessible only by mountain lanes and footpaths. Yet it is worth exploring, and the only large lake in the county, Llyn-y-fan Fach, is below the rise to the highest peak, Carmarthen Van (2,632ft) just over the Powys border.

Borth 6E6
Some 4m of sand extending S from the estuary of the River Dovey. Very popular holiday resort. At low tide remains of a submerged forest are exposed.

Bosherston 6B2
The main significance of this little village, with its charming lily ponds, is its proximity to the cliffs of *St Govan's Head*. 1½m S is the tiny 13th-c St Govan's Chapel in a deep hollow of the cliffs. Access when the MOD firing range to the W is open, and also to the W is Huntsman's Leap. 1m E, between St Govan's Head and Stackpole Head is *Broad Haven* with a sandy cove, not to be confused with the Broad Haven on St Bride's Bay (*see* **Haverfordwest**). 1m N of the village is **Stackpole**.

Brynamman 6E3
A small village about 6m E of *Ammanford*, from which the A4069 starts the climb over the **Black Mountains**. At the highest point on the road, 1,618ft, which here passes over the shoulder of Gareg-lwyd (2,028ft) are magnificent views to Carmarthen Van (2,632ft) 7m NE.

Caldey Island 6C2
2½m S of **Tenby**; can be visited by motor boat. There is a modern Cistercian priory, and a 12th-c Benedictine monastery can be seen. The ancient church contains a stone with an inscription in Latin and Ogam.

Cardigan 6C4
Small market town at the mouth of the River Teifi which formerly provided a harbour for larger craft than those now using it. Further N at the mouth of the estuary, enjoying sandy beaches is the modern resort of *Gwbert-on-Sea*.

Carew 6C2
Ruins of 13th-c castle (AM), later a Tudor residence, with a richly carved, 14ft Celtic cross (AM) and French tidal mill near by. The church has a fine tower, and monuments of the Carew family, with an unusual chantry chapel in the churchyard. About 1m NW, across the river, the 13th-c gateway of *Upton Castle* is still standing.

Carmarthen 6D3
County capital and market town; the remains of the Norman castle (AM) occupy the site of the Roman station Moridunum. The church contains the tomb of Sir Rhys ap Thomas, the supporter of Henry VII, and a memorial to Sir Richard Steele, the essayist, who retired to his wife's birthplace in the neighbourhood. On the outskirts of the town in the former bishop's palace at *Abergwili* there is a fine local history museum. At *Llanstephan*, 7m S at the mouth of the River Towy, where there is a sandy beach, are the gatehouse and keep of a Norman castle and a small Norman church. The Gwili Railway, a standard-gauge steam railway, runs on most summer weekends from a terminus N of the town.

Near Bosherston at St Govan's Head: the 13th-century chapel of St Govan with its holy well is hidden by the cliffs

Cenarth Falls 6C4
A famous beauty spot on the River Teifi, it has splendid waterfalls with a salmon leap and Fishing Museum near by. Local fishermen still fish for salmon from coracles. An old bridge crosses the river into Cenarth. (*See* page 326.)

Cilgerran 6C4
Impressive Norman castle (AM, NT), situated above the River Teifi, which here flows through a tree-covered gorge. 3m NW, also on the Teifi, at *St Dogmaels*, are the remains of the Benedictine abbey (AM) founded by Martin of Tours in the 11th c.

Cors Fochno 6E6
A wild track of sealand, once a deep bog covered with 6ft-high reeds, now largely drained and reclaimed. It is still in places in its original state and dangerous to explore except with care. Gull, moorhen and curlew haunt it though it has now been found necessary to set up the Penderi Nature Reserve to shield them.

Cwm Einion 6E6
The beautiful 'Artists' Valley', with waterfalls among the hills, on the S side of the Dovey estuary, about 5m E of *Aberdovey*. The name of Furnace village is a reminder of the days when there were lead-smelting furnaces in the vicinity. Near by is Bedd Taliesin, the grave of Taliesin, 'The Father of the Bards', said to have been a contemporary of King Arthur

Dale 6B2
Some 12m SW of **Haverfordwest**, at the end of the B4321, this village is a good point from which to explore the S horn of St Bride's Bay. The modern castle is built on the site of an earlier one; it was near by that Henry Tudor, soon to become Henry VII, landed in 1485. From the top of the unclassified road leading S to St Anne's Head, one can see **Milford Haven** running due E to **Pembroke**; and 4m out to sea in the opposite direction is *Skokholm Island*, now a bird sanctuary. 2m NW is the village of *Marloes*, with access to the Marloes Sands; and beyond the village, with fine cliff scenery, is *Wooltack Point*, looking across to *Skomer Island*, where hundreds of hut-circles have been found.

Devil's Bridge★ 6E5
One of the finest beauty spots in the whole of Britain. Here the River Mynach enters a deep, wooded gorge, tumbling down over a series of waterfalls. There are three bridges, almost on top of each other, the lowest and oldest of them dating from the 12th c (it was built by the monks of **Strata Florida Abbey**). This is the terminus of the Rheidol Narrow Gauge Steam Railway from **Aberystwyth**.

Fishguard 6B4
An attractive town, with a port at the foot of a hill, where a French force landed in 1797 and surrendered. 1½m W is the little resort of *Goodwick*, with its harbour for the service to Ireland. These are the only two places in Fishguard Bay where bathing is possible, since rugged cliffs extend from Dinas Head on the E to Strumble Head on the W.

Glaspwll 6E6
A small hamlet set in a beautiful valley running to connect with the **Llyfnant Valley**. When the latter was a major trade route Glaspwll was a centre of rural industry. The small chapel built about 1840 is now put to residential use. The hamlet stood on the way to the lead-mining centres in the **Plynlimon** range, dating from Roman times. George

Borrow stopped at the cottage called Ty Mawr and records the incident in his *Wild Wales*. The valley can now be reached by road but it is better to walk through the hill-track over Cae Gybi near **Machynlleth**.

Haverfordwest 6B3
Handsome market town, with 18th-c houses, on a hill above the West Cleddau River. The keep of the Norman castle remains, and sections of the old town walls. Of its three churches, the most interesting is 13th-c St Mary's with a fine oak roof and carved stalls of later date. 4½m E, in its fine park on the banks of the East Cleddau, stands *Picton Castle*, one of the few castles in Britain to have been lived in continuously from the 13th c. 6m W, on St Bride's Bay, are the attractive little resorts of *Broad Haven* and *Little Haven*, reached by picturesque lanes.

Kidwelly 6D2
Market town, with small harbour and some sand, at the head of the Gwendraeth estuary. The splendid 13th-c castle (AM) replaced an earlier fortress built in 1094 by a follower of Fitz Hammon, the first Norman conqueror of S. Wales. The church, with its fine tower, standing beside the river, was originally the chapel of a Benedictine priory.

Lampeter 6E4
Small market town where the A482 crosses the Teifi Valley. Long known for its horse fairs (in March) attended by buyers and sellers from all over Britain. St David's College founded in 1822 for Church of England students is now a constituent college of the University of Wales and is closely linked with **Oxford** and **Cambridge**. Salmon and trout fishing in the River Teifi.

Lamphey 6B2
In the grounds of Lamphey Court stand the ruins of the splendid Archbishop's Palace (AM), begun in the 13th c and completed by Bishop Gower, who also, between 1328 and 1347, built the still finer Palace of **St David's**.

Laugharne 6D3
At the mouth of the River Taf. This little township has an elegant town hall dating from 1746, and many Georgian houses. From the harbour there is a view of the castle ruins. Dylan Thomas's Boathouse is now open to the public as a museum to commemorate this great Anglo-Welsh poet.

Llancynfelyn 6E6
Little more than an old church and a Tudor rectory. The church is representative of an ancient legend: the saint it commemorates was traditionally a hermit in the depths of the **Cors Fochno**. A small island deep in the bog has been presumed to be his habitation. The legend probably dates from the earliest ages when the Dyfi estuary was a major trading route. 5m S a causeway thrusting into Cardigan Bay is named *Sarn Cynfelin*. The stretch of sealand here was where the ceremony of electing the Gwledig or chief commander of the Welsh was traditionally carried out. It is still called Traeth Maelgwn after the first known of these leaders.

Llandeilo 6E3
A market town, with fishing and golf, in the lovely valley of the Towy. 4m SE, perched on a precipitous rock 300ft above the River Cennen, are the ruins of *Carreg Cennen Castle* (AM), 'the Arthurian castle of one's dreams'; and 6m W, on the B4297, the remains of *Dryslwyn Castle* look across the River Towy to Paxton's Tower, built in honour of Nelson.

Llandovery 6E3
The name is derived from the Welsh for 'the church amid the waters', through its proximity to the junction of the rivers Towy, Bran and Gwydderig. There are some remains of a Norman castle, and the college is one of the best-known in Wales. On the right of the **Brecon** road (to Powys), some 3m E, is the Mail Coach pillar, with its long and relevant, inscription warning drivers against drunkenness. N from the town, an unclassified road, after passing through the village of *Cilycwm*, bears W under the summit of Mynydd Mallaen (1,515ft), before descending to **Pumpsaint**. Another byroad leads off the A4069, 2½m S of the town, to *Myddfai*, where there is a double-nave church, with ancient roofs and monuments, standing on the River Bran.

Llandysul 6D4
Small wool town near the junction of the Tweli and the Teifi. Several mills in the locality still flourish producing an array of traditional Welsh weaves. Incorporated in the sturdy Norman tower of the church is a 6th-c inscribed stone. A good centre for anglers.

Llanelli 6D2
A seaport and manufacturing town, the largest in the county, and owing its development to the industrial revolution in the 19th c. The town's museum has a fine collection of Llanelli pottery. Near by, at *Pembrey*, is a recently established country park and interpretative centre.

Llangadog 6E3
A pleasant little town in the Vale of Towy, with an early 19th-c mansion, Abermarlais. It is the N starting point of the road over the **Black Mountains**, described above under **Brynamman**. 3m S, *Carn Goch* is the largest prehistoric camp in Wales.

Llangranog 6D4
Coastal village in a deep narrow ravine between high cliffs. The N cliff commands fine views up and down the coast.

Llanrhystud 6D5
A stream runs down the street to a sandy beach. Prawn fishing can be rewarding. 5m inland is *Llangwyryfon*, with a little old church dedicated to St Ursula and the 11,000 Virgins.

Llanstephan Castle *see* Carmarthen

Llawhaden *see* Narberth

Llyfnant Valley 6E6
The Llyfnant, which flows into the head of the Dovey estuary, forms part of the boundary between Dyfed and Powys. There is no road up the valley, but the walk is really worthwhile. From the upper glen there is a fine view of the waterfall known as Pistyll Llyn (300ft), best seen after heavy rains have swollen the river.

Lydstep 6C2
About midway between Lydstep Haven and Sprinkle Haven. The cliffs here, with their caves and views of the coast and out to **Caldey Island**, have been acquired by the NT.

Manorbier 6C2
The moated castle ruins, still partly occupied, stand in a valley, sloping down to the sandy beach of the little bay. Here in 1146 the medieval historian, Giraldus Cambrensis, was born – he wrote *Itinerary Through Wales*.

Milford Haven 6B2

Situated on one of the finest natural harbours in Britain, the place was already important in the Middle Ages. Most of the existing town, however, dates from the improvements undertaken from the end of the 18th c onwards, though the dockyard established at that period was transferred to **Pembroke** in 1814. It is still a trawler fishing port, although a large oil refinery has been established on the opposite side of the Haven.

Narberth 6C3

An important road junction with remains of a Norman castle. *Llawhaden*, 3m NW, has remains of a 13th-c bishop's palace, with a gatehouse, and the church is remarkable for its double tower.

Nevern 6C4

A picturesquely situated village, on the slope of a hill beside a stream. The present church, though of 6th-c foundation, is partly Norman, with a battlemented tower, and the Celtic cross of St Brynach, near the S door.

Newcastle Emlyn 6D4

There are a few remains of a castle here, and fishing in the River Teifi. 3m W, are **Cenarth Falls**.

Newgale 6B3

At the N end of St Bride's Bay, it can be reached either by the winding coast road from *Broad Haven* to the S, through **Nolton Haven**, or by the main road from **Haverfordwest** to

St David's Cathedral: named after the patron saint of Wales, it was built in the 12th century (see page 327)

St David's, which passes the tower of Roch Castle. Its main attraction is the 2m or so of flat, sandy beach, backed by a pebble bank. At near-by *Crom Con* a flour mill still grinds corn in the traditional manner.

Newport 6C4

A small coastal village with a sandy beach. The bay is bounded at its W extremity by the 500ft cliffs of Dinas Head, which separates it from Fishguard Bay. Parts of the moated Norman castle have been restored as a private house, and may be visited by appointment. The cromlech of *Pentre Ifan* (AM) is 3m SE, and there are more Megalithic remains on the slope of 1,000ft Carn Ingli, S of the town.

New Quay 6D4

Small seaside resort on steep slopes overlooking Cardigan Bay. Sands, a stone pier and many boats. Magnificent views from the headland on N side of bay.

Nolton Haven 6B3

A little fishing village in the centre of St Bride's Bay, between **Newgale** to the N and *Broad Haven* to the S.

Pembroke 6B2

The town is dominated by the moated castle (AM), covering an area of 4 acres, and part of the walls (AM) that once encircled the town. Begun as a stone fortress in 1090, it was enlarged in the two succeeding centuries by the Earls Palatine of Pembroke. The circular vaulted keep, built about 1200, is 75ft high with walls 7ft thick; the Great Hall is built over the 'Wogan', a subterranean passage leading to the harbour. Opposite the castle, the medieval Monkton Priory was largely rebuilt at the end of the 19th c.

Salmon Leap Falls at Cenarth: the coracle, an ancient craft made of willow and hazel, is still used here. (See page 323.)

Penally
6C2

A small resort, between **Lydstep** and **Tenby**, with a Celtic cross in the churchyard. There are views across to **Caldey Island**, and to the E are the *Pendine Sands*, where motor-speed trials are sometimes held.

Plynlimon Fawr
6E5/6

The Welsh form of the name is Pumlumon Fawr, which means 'five beacons', the highest point being 2,468ft above sea level. The most popular walk to the top begins at Eisteddfa Gurig (1,350ft), where the A44 crosses the border into Dyfed. The mountain is an important watershed, for it is the source of the Severn, the Wye, the Rheidol and several other rivers. *See also* introduction to Powys.

Ponterwyd 6E5

In ruggedly mountainous scenery, where the A44 crosses the Rheidol on its way down from **Plynlimon**. There is a waterfall and a striking gorge. Here George Borrow wrote part of *Wild Wales*. The old Llwyernog Silver Mine is now open as a museum Easter–Sept. A guided tour shows the exploitation of silver, lead, zinc, gold, copper which has gone on since Roman times. Local place names (Arian) tell the tale of the area's richness in silver. At *Goginan* near by, the famous medieval poet Dafydd ap Gwilym spent much of his time.

Prescelly Hills 6C3

The only considerable range of hills in the county, rising to 1,760ft, this stretch of moors and streams is now a National Park. It is rich in prehistoric remains which have to be explored on foot. Only one motor road from **Haverfordwest** to **Cardigan**, the B4329, traverses the area, attaining 1,383ft at its summit.

Pumpsaint 6E4

Near this village in the wild valley of the Cothi is Dolau-Cothi, where in Roman and earlier times, mining for gold was carried on – there are still traces of the square-hewn Roman tunnels. The village is now a part of a 2,400-acre NT estate.

St Clear's 6C3

Note the fine tower of the partly Norman church. Here Owain Glyndwr was defeated in 1406; and in 1843 the little town was one of the centres of the Rebecca Riots, when men disguised as women rode about the S. Wales countryside destroying the toll-houses and gates. Though the riot was put down, it achieved its aim, the suppression of toll-gates throughout S. Wales.

St David's★ 6A3

This cathedral city of only 1,500 inhabitants stands, with its restored market-cross, on high ground, so that one's first view of the cathedral is the top of the 116ft tower. Only after passing through the S gate does the splendour of the building, built of local purplish sandstone, come into view; but then one can easily believe the story that two pilgrimages to St David's used to be reckoned the equivalent of one to Rome. The main portion of the fabric dates from the 12th c, and the Lady Chapel, rood-screen and S porch were added during the 13th–14th c. The Norman nave, with its roof of Irish oak, is noteworthy, and the interior of the cathedral is of exquisite beauty. (*See* page 325.) Near by, on the Alun river, are the ruins of St Mary's College, founded by John of Gaunt; and the 14th-c Bishop's Palace (AM), built, like **Lamphey**, by Bishop Gower. There is bathing at Caerfai Bay, 1m S, and at Whitesand Bay, 2m NW. This last is bounded to the N by St David's Head, with its prehistoric rampart, hut circles and rock-shelter. Both there and to the S, is a fine view across the sound to *Ramsey Island* (which can be visited in summer), with splendid rock scenery.

St Dogmaels *see* Cilgerran

St Govan's Head *see* Bosherston

Salmon Leap Falls *see* Cenarth

Saundersfoot 6C2

Seaside and golfing resort, on a lovely bay. 2m E is the tiny village of *Amroth*, with bathing from a sand and shingle beach, where at low tide a submerged forest is revealed.

Solva 6B3

A delightful village, perched above a winding inlet, which provides anchorage for fishing boats and yachts. The views from the cliffs on either side, S across St Bride's Bay and W to *Ramsey Island*, are remarkable. Notable sites worth visiting are the Solva Nectarium with its fine displays of butterflies and Middle Mill.

Stackpole 6B2

The site of a demolished 18th-c mansion, which was the seat of the Earl of Cawdor; it has beautiful gardens. In the church are several tombs dating from the 13th and 14th c. *See* also **Bosherston**.

Strata Florida Abbey 6E5

Among the hills near the source of the Teifi; the few remains of a once-flourishing Cistercian foundation which in the 12th–13th c was the cultural centre of Wales (AM). The ornamental doorway at the W end is notably impressive. The great medieval Welsh poet Dafydd ap Gwilym lies buried beneath the giant yew tree in the grounds.

Talley 6E3

Near this tiny hill village, in the valley of the Afon Dulais, are the remains of the Benedictine abbey (AM), founded late in the 12th c by Rhys ap Gruffydd, Prince of S. Wales; the central tower and fragments of the walls survive.

Tenby★ 6C2

The best-known resort in the county, with golf, a harbour and bathing from two separate sandy beaches. The town, with its castle and considerable remains of the town walls (both AM) on a headland overlooking the sea, dates from the 13th c, but there are many Georgian houses and two notable Tudor buildings, Merchant's House and Plantagenet House on Quay Hill, both cared for by the NT. There is a small but significant town museum. St Mary's Church has a fine chancel roof and some notable tombs, together with a raised chancel and crypt. The Manor House Wildlife and Leisure Park near by provides an interesting visit.

Tregaron 6E4

In summer this little market town among the hills is busy with sheep and cattle fairs, sheep-dog trials and pony trekkers. Fishing in the River Teifi. N of the town is the largest peat bog in Wales; in summer the moss is alight with cotton flower.

Whitland 6C3

This market town is interesting for its long association with the monastic life of S. Wales. Here, in the 10th c, an assembly was summoned to revise the laws for the country. 1m NE can still be seen some remains of the mother house of the Cistercian Order.

West, Mid and South Glamorgan and Gwent

AN INTRODUCTION BY
C. J. O. EVANS

These counties in the southeast corner of the Principality of Wales lie on the north shore of the Bristol Channel. West, Mid and South Glamorgan are mountainous in the north with deep valleys and ravines through which rivers course their way to the sea; their south is a pleasant land, largely agricultural and extremely picturesque. The westernmost part, the peninsula of Gower, open to the Atlantic Ocean and unsullied by industry, compares favourably with England's West Country. The northwest of Gwent (Monmouthshire) also has its lofty hills, which rise to 2,000 feet; but in the east it is pastoral, falling south to the low-lying lands of the Severn estuary.

Among the hilly districts of all these counties are the famous coal-mining areas of South Wales; but the south and east, fertile and pleasant to the eye are flecked with interesting towns and villages, numerous archeological remains, ruined castles and woodlands. Along the coast of the Glamorgans are popular seaside resorts with safe bathing, such as Penarth, Barry Island, Porthcawl, Aberavon and Mumbles, with many charming bays along the Gower Coast.

Among the river valleys, those of the Wye and Usk are famed for their beauty; while at Kenfig Burrows, between Bridgend and Port Talbot, is an area very different in its appeal. Here the sands have buried an ancient borough and its castle (all but part of one tower), and now support a range of plants fascinating to the botanist. On the 20-acre lake which they encircle, wildfowl are found in abundance. Not far away is the village of Merthyr Mawr, quaint and unspoiled, with thatched cottages.

Natural History

The wild cat and pine-marten ceased to exist within the last century; the polecat occasionally appears from adjoining counties where it is still common. Otter, now becoming rather rare owing to river pollution, can be seen. The fox is the quarry of several hunts. There are a few 'earths' of badger, happily not seriously worried; and the red squirrel more than holds its own. The grey squirrel is all too common. Schools of porpoise are often seen frolicking offshore in the summer.

The large birds of prey have mostly disappeared, and black grouse is very rare; but red grouse is preserved in the north, and pheasants and partridges breed well. Heronries are few, and pairs appear to be decreasing. Razorbills and guillemots breed in large numbers on the peninsula of Gower, and peregrines and raven are common. The ringed plover and oyster-catcher are seen along the coast.

In most rivers and streams fish were plentiful in early times; but industrial pollution caused severe loss. This is now being reduced and, in the main rivers, good fishing of trout and salmon, as well as of a migratory trout called sewin, is possible; Wye and Usk salmon and trout being famous beyond the county boundaries.

The flora is richer than one might expect. In the uplands coarse grass with its thin layer of earth on solid rock gives good pasturage for sheep, despite an abundance of gorse, heather and bracken. In the valleys are many varieties of fern and, occasionally, Cornish moneywort, the lesser bladderwort and green spleenwort. The lower ground is mainly rich agricultural land, arable pasture, with luxuriant hedgerows dividing field and meadow. Bluebells deck the woodlands, wild clematis and monkshood line the hedges, and on the sandy warrens and river estuaries are varieties of glasswort, sea-lavender, sea-aster, milkwort, wormwood, spurge and others. Several areas in the hills have been planted with fir, and there is a flourishing nursery of the Forestry Commission near Bonvilston.

Antiquities

Prehistory is well represented in these counties. There are many remains of the Later Stone Age in the Glamorgans – notably chambered tombs. Many Bronze Age burials and Beaker Folk interments have given us increasing knowledge of the period. The new culture which preceded the Christian era by a few hundred years, when iron supplanted bronze to a great extent, introduced a craftsmanship now known as Late Celtic Art. This reached a marvellous standard of design in decorative work, with flowing curves and scroll ornament. In the higher regions many hill-top camps of this period still survive, and several promontory camps are found on the coast. At Llyn Fawr, a pool in the north of Mid Glamorgan, was found a surprising hoard of weapons and implements of both the Bronze and Iron Ages.

At the time of the Roman invasion, Gwent was part of a large area inhabited by the Silures, a tribe whose leader was Caradoc (Caractacus). The Romans completed their dominion of South Wales by AD 90, by which time they had erected a fort, named Isca, on the side of the River Usk. This became the fortress of the 2nd Augustan Legion and is the most important Roman site in Wales. Today Caerleon, although mostly built over, is still an interesting place. It held a force of approximately 6,000 men, and outside its walls was erected a stone amphitheatre, which still remains to recall former gladiatorial combats.

The early Christian era bequeathed to us a large number of stone monuments. The Glamorgans have several with noteworthy inscriptions, such as those in the Stones Museum at Margam and in the church at Llantwit Major. In the National Museum of Wales at Cardiff are to be seen all the prehistoric finds of the area, as well as casts of inscribed stones. There is also a small Roman Museum at Caerleon.

Historical Outline
The only part of South Wales mentioned in the Domesday Survey extended to a small area west of the River Usk. The Normans came to the rest of Gwent and the Glamorgans some years later, driving the Welsh to the uplands, where they continued to be such a nuisance that the intruders had to build strongholds for defence. The powerful Norman magnates thus acquired extensive holdings which were held as 'marcher lordships'. Within their boundaries knights and vassals owed service only to the lords of the marches – even the King's writ had no authority except for treason. Castles were erected at Chepstow, Usk, Monmouth, Abergavenny, Cardiff, Neath and Swansea – to mention but a few – and lesser knights erected castles in their respective fiefs. These autocratic marcher lordships (the envy, by the way, of the English barons) continued until the Act of Union in the reign of Henry VIII.

The Welsh remained restless throughout the medieval period and many insurrections occurred, the last being that of Owain Glyndwr, who in 1403 laid in utter waste the whole of South Wales in an abortive effort to regain independence. During the Civil War, local sympathies were divided, and many leading people changed sides during the conflict. A considerable engagement was fought at St Fagan's, South Glamorgan, and the castles of Chepstow and Raglan fell to the Cromwellian troops. The Chartist movement was very violent in old Monmouthshire, the Mayor of Newport being shot and wounded in 1839 while attempting to read the Riot Act.

Architecture
Llandaff Cathedral (the only cathedral in the country not built on the plan of a cross) has little Norman work. It was badly damaged by a land-mine in January 1941. In its rebuilding an unusual addition in the modern style was made to the nave: Epstein's fine figure of Christ in unpolished aluminium and 18 feet high. Ewenny Priory Church is the finest example of Norman ecclesiastical architecture in Wales. Margam Church, also late Norman, is (except for its ruined chapter house) all that is left of a Cistercian abbey. St John's Church at Cardiff has a beautifully designed tower. The church of Llantwit Major has many unusual points, including a number of inscribed Early Christian stones.

It has been said that while Glamorgan had the largest castle in the country, it had also some of the smallest. Cardiff Castle, with its keep and imposing curtain walls, is now in the hands of the Cardiff City Council and is well worth a visit even though it has been modernized. St Donat's Castle, with its lovely terraced gardens dropping down to the sea, has been in continuous occupation since the 13th century. It was added to by its former owner, the American William Randolph Hearst, and has now become New Atlantic College. Caerphilly Castle, second only to Windsor Castle in area, has a leaning tower that has been strengthened to stand even in its ruined state for years to come. Other castles in the area are in the safe hands of the Secretary of State for Wales.

The gem of Gwent's ecclesiastical architecture – and one of the most lovely sights in Britain – is the noble ruin of the Cistercian abbey at Tintern, so beautifully situated on the banks of the Wye. Another ruin worth a visit as much for its beauty as for its associations, is Llanthony Priory, set in a secluded valley of the Black Mountains, and once a monastery of Black Canons of the Order of St Augustine. In more recent times it was for some years the home of Walter Savage Landor, the poet and author.

Gwent, too, had numerous strongpoints. Chepstow Castle, built on solid rock almost at the mouth of the Wye, is an inspiring sight as you cross into the county from Gloucestershire. Newport Castle is a mere shell, so is the one at Abergavenny; Caldicot is well preserved and used regularly to stage medieval banquets; Usk Castle stands on a commanding eminence. The 'Three Castles' (Grosmont, Skenfrith and White Castle) each have their features and are kept in good condition, as is Penhow Castle, a look-out for neighbouring Chepstow Castle; and finally, Raglan Castle, besieged by Cromwellian forces during the Civil War, is picturesque. Gwent is richer in good domestic architecture than the Glamorgans. These houses were built when the need for defence works became unnecessary. St Fagan's Castle in South Glamorgan, an Elizabethan manor house, is part of the Welsh Folk Museum (see page 18).

Industries

Until the industrial revolution at the end of the 18th century, Glamorgan and Gwent were mainly agricultural, with a few rural industries such as weaving, pottery-making and quarrying. Mining for metals had been explored by the Romans, and a little coal was dug from early days. The manufacture of iron became a profitable adventure in the 16th century; but two centuries later came the discovery that iron could be smelted with coal instead of charcoal. The northern part of the area became the great iron-producing centre of the world. From Penydarren, Merthyr, in Mid Glamorgan, the first railway locomotive in history successfully hauled a train loaded with bar iron for nearly 10 miles, settling a wager between two ironmasters. It had been built by the Cornish engineer Richard Trevithick in 1804 – 10 years before Stephenson's 'Puffing Billy'.

With the introduction of the Bessemer process, in the 19th century, steel came into its own. The Steel Company of Wales at Margam, Port Talbot, on the coast of the Bristol Channel, was one of the largest and most modern steelworks in Europe.

The docks at Newport, Cardiff, Port Talbot and Swansea continue to hold their own, though coal exports are not what they were. In 1936 the first government-sponsored trading estate was established at Treforest to the northwest of Cardiff. Ultimately in 1976, the Welsh Development Agency under State authorization became responsible for reviving the general decline of industries in the area. The recession of the 1980s has restricted its projects.

An industry which came and went during the 19th century was the manufacture of Swansea and Nantgarw china by Joseph Billingsley, a talented potter and painter. It is much prized by collectors.

GAZETTEER

Abergavenny, Gwent 6G3
'The Gateway of Wales', so called from its position on the Usk between two prominent hills. Agricultural town with cattle-markets. Good centre for exploring the valleys running up into the **Black Mountains** (Dyfed). Ruins of 12th-c castle (AM). St Mary's Church has interesting altar tombs. A museum of local history adjoins the ruins of the castle. *Llanfihangel Court*, 4m N, is an Elizabethan manor (limited opening in summer). Near by is *White Castle (see* **Skenfrith**).

Barry, South Glam 6G1
The docks were built to provide additional facilities for the export of coal. The town became a borough in 1939. Barry Island, Whitmore Bay and Porthkerry Bay are highly popular seaside beaches. Porthkerry Country Park lies to the W of the town and runs down to the sea.

Bonvilston, South Glam 6G1
Here the Forestry Commission raise seedlings for planting in the new forests (e.g. *see* **Neath**). Roman camp near by.

Caerleon,★ Gwent 6G2
The parish church stands in the centre of the site of Roman Isca, a legionary fortress with room for 6,000 men. The chief feature today is the amphitheatre (AM), and the Roman Legionary Museum. One of the many places associated with the Arthurian legends. *See also* Introduction.

Caerphilly,★ Mid Glam 6G2
The significant remains of the great 13th–14th-c castle (AM) cover 30 acres, an area exceeded only by **Windsor** (Berks) among the old castles of Britain.

Caerwent, Gwent 7H1
Small village on the site of an extensive Roman town, Venta Silurum, of which many parts have been excavated. Relics in the church and in **Newport** Museum. About 1m S is *Caldicot Castle*, small but notable for the excellence of its masonry work, now set in a country park. A local history museum is housed in part of the castle.

Cardiff, South Glam 6G1
Capital of Wales, and the first planned city centre in Britain. This is the administrative centre of the Principality, and home of the Welsh Office. Cardiff's elaborate Victorian castle sits plumb in the city centre, with an earlier Norman keep in its grounds: here too are the City Hall and Law Courts, the National Museum of Wales, and University College Cardiff. The National Stadium is well known to rugby footballers. Cardiff has hundreds of acres of parkland, extending from the central area, including Bute Park, donated by the Marquesses of Bute, and Sophia Gardens. St Fagan's Folk Museum covering an open area of 100 acres contains many reconstructed buildings to illustrate the architectural heritage of Wales (*see* **St Fagan's**). An Elizabethan manor and formal gardens, working wool and flour mills, farmhouses, cottages, a chapel, smithy, tannery, cockpit, all rescued from neglect, make a unique memorial to the past. At Cathays Park there is a significant collection of archeology, geology, botany and animal life housed in the National Museum. *Castell Coch*, 5m NW, is a folly designed by the Victorian architect, Burges, for the Marquesses of Bute, who also modernized Cardiff Castle.

Chepstow, Gwent 7H2
Here on a high rock at the lowest crossing of the Wye the Normans built an imposing castle (AM)★ which is well seen from the E bank of the river. SE of the town is the new Severn road bridge: with a central span of 3,246ft and two side spans of 1,000ft each. At *Wolvesnewtown*, 10m N, from here is a model farm of 18th-c construction. The Folk Collection is housed in unique cruciform barns and in the mill are working craft shops.

Coity, Mid Glam 6F2
Here are the well-preserved remains of a medieval castle (AM). 100yd N is a long-cairned chambered tomb probably dating from 2000 BC.

The golden sands of Rhosilli Bay on the Gower Peninsula, an area of outstanding natural beauty (see page 332)

Ebbw Vale, Gwent 6G3
This town grew up around the iron-smelting industry, and was at one time one of Britain's most important steel-making units. It now specializes in tin-plate.

Ewenny, Mid Glam 6F1
The fine Norman church is the chief remnant of the fortified priory built here in the 12th c. Note the chancel roof and the stone screen in front of the choir. The pottery near by is one of Wales' oldest.

Gower, West Glam 6D2/E2
Peninsula extending some 15m W of **Swansea** with an average width of 5m. The S and W coasts are cliff; bays and coves shelter many pleasant villages with sandy beaches that are popular holiday resorts. *Rhossili Bay*, at the W end, has nearly 3m of sand (*see* page 331). The N coast is low-lying and marshy in places. The NE verges on the industrial area of **Llanelli**. *See also* **Paviland Caves**.

Grosmont, Gwent 7H3
Old-world town on the River Monnow (good fishing) with remnants of a 13th-c castle (AM) which even in Elizabethan times was reported to be 'ruinous, time out of mind'. The Department of the Environment have done good work on what is left.

Kenfig, Mid Glam 6E2
Among the sandhills W of **Porthcawl** are a 60-acre freshwater lake and the remains of a borough and castle which were overwhelmed by a great sandstorm in the 16th c.

Llandaf, South Glam 6G1
Though now a part of **Cardiff**, Llandaff retains the air of a cathedral city, with its Bishop's Palace, Deanery and Canons' Residence. The Cathedral has Norman work, but misguided alterations in the 18th c necessitated a thorough restoration in the 19th c. The most important feature of the interior is Epstein's huge figure of Christ.

Llanthony, Gwent 6G3
Far up the narrow Honddu valley in the **Black Mountains** (Dyfed) are the beautiful remains of a 12th-c priory (AM), once the home of Walter Savage Landor. 4m farther up the valley, at *Capel-y-ffin*, are the remains of a monastery begun in 1870 but never completed.

Llantwit Major, South Glam 6F1
An unusual church, the E end being a late 13th-c addition to a former plain erection. It is traditionally claimed to be the earliest home of Christianity in Wales and was famous as a centre of learning in Celtic times. The W end of the church has many Early Christian inscribed stones.

Merthyr Tydfil, Mid Glam 6F2
Once the Welsh metropolis of the iron and steel trades, where Richard Trevethick in 1804 demonstrated the world's first steam-driven locomotive. Now a busy and prosperous town of many industries. Art gallery and museum in Cyfarthfa Park. From *Pant* the Brecon Mountain Railway runs on a narrow gauge for 2m past the Pontsticill Reservoir into the **Brecon Beacons** National Park.

Monmouth, Gwent 7H3
Quiet little market town lying in the valley where the River Monnow meets the famous Wye (both fine fishing rivers). The 13th-c fortified gatehouse on the bridge, built somewhat earlier, over the Monnow at the SW end of the town is unique in Britain. Monmouth is celebrated as the birthplace of Henry V. In the centre of the town is a statue of the Hon. C. S. Rolls (the 'Rolls' of Rolls-Royce), who was the first man to fly from England to France and back again. The Nelson Museum has a large sextant collection.

Mumbles, West Glam 6E2
On the W side of the curving Swansea Bay, a popular seaside and residential suburb which includes the village of *Oystermouth*. Bells in All Saints' Church came from Santiago Cathedral when it was burned down. In the graveyard lies Thomas Bowdler, whose expurgating of Shakespeare in the early 19th c added the word 'bowdlerize' to the English language.

Nantgarw, Mid Glam 6G2
3m SW of **Caerphilly**. In the mouth of a deep green valley is a huge coke-oven and by-products plant. Once Nantgarw Porcelain was manufactured here.

Neath, West Glam 6E2
Busy market and industrial town at the point where the River Neath emerges from its beautiful narrow valley. At Briton Ferry, now included in the borough, an 11-span viaduct carries the S. Wales road high above the docks. On the hills above Neath in 1922 the Forestry Commission planted Rheola Forest, which now supplies pit-props and sawmill timber. There are remains of a 12th-c Benedictine abbey (AM) and Norman castle. At *Aberdulais* there are a number of exciting new developments, including the Aberdulais Fall and ironworks, recently excavated, and restored sections of the Neath and Tennant Canal. At *Cilfrew*, 2m NW, is the Penscynor Wildlife Park, situated in 11 acres of grounds.

Newport, Gwent 6G2
Busy industrial town and seaport not far from the point where the Usk joins the Bristol Channel. The tidal range in this part of the Channel is among the highest in the world; this of course affects the Usk – hence the Transporter Bridge 117ft above the water. Very good museum of archeology and natural history and a small art gallery. St Woolos Church is now the cathedral of the diocese of **Monmouth**, created in 1921. Tredegar House, a fine 18th-c country house, and country park are open all year. At *High Cross* near *Rogerstone*, there is a landscaped picnic area and 14-Locks, an interpretative centre also part of the Newport canal system.

Newton Nottage, Mid Glam 6F1
1½m E of **Porthcawl**. Here is a curious freshwater spring which ebbs and flows with the rise and fall of the Bristol Channel tides.

Paviland Caves, West Glam 6D2
When Buckland discovered these limestone caves in the **Gower** peninsula in 1823 he found what he called 'The Red Lady' – the skeleton of a young man whose bones were stained red, perhaps by the action of oxide of iron percolating through the cave. Can be visited at low water.

Penarth, South Glam 6G1
Only 2m S of **Cardiff**, it is a very popular seaside resort extending S towards *Lavernock*. A walk along the cliffs, S, leads to Ranny Bay and St Mary's Well Bay. Turner House Art Gallery, part of the National Museum of Wales, has paintings by Turner, Cox, Cotman, etc. Cosmeston Lake and Country Park offer facilities for a range of outdoor pursuits.

Pontneathvaughan, West Glam   6F3
2m N of *Glyn-Neath*. Here two rivers meet in a region of
wooded hills, deep gorges and waterfalls.

Pontypool, Gwent   6G2
A historic place in the development of S. Wales industry.
Here the first hammer-mill, worked by the River Llwyd, was
opened in 1770, enabling the first tin-plate to be made. At the
stables of the Hanbury ironmaster's home the Valley
Inheritance Centre has been established, illustrating the
history and industrial heritage of Gwent's Eastern Valley.
Europe's second largest artificial ski-slope is to be found in
the grounds of Pontypool Park.

Pontypridd, Mid Glam   6G2
Busy town among the hills at the junction of the Taff and
Rhondda valleys, shopping and social centre for a wide area.
When the bridge over the Taff was built in the 18th c, the
town's original name of Newbridge was retained in the great
ironworks which made naval anchors and chains.

Porthcawl, Mid Glam   6F1
On a rocky promontory at the end of the long line of sand
dunes lining Swansea Bay. Popular seaside resort.

Port Talbot, West Glam   6E2
Busy coal and iron port S of **Neath**. SE are the great steel
works of the Steel Company of Wales on Margam Burrows.
Margam Country Park covers 850 acres. It includes the
Orangery, a major Sculpture Park, with a changing exhibi
tion of works by artists of international repute, including
Moore and Hepworth, abbey remains, Margam Castle, the
home of the Talbot family, a deer herd and a boating lake.

Raglan, Gwent   7H3
Imposing ruin of the 14th–15th-c castle (AM) with gateway
and machicolated towers.

Rhondda, Mid Glam   6F2
Once one of the 'problem' valleys of the S. Wales coalfield,
whence the population migrated owing to industrial depression. However, today many major land reclamation projects
have been completed, and Rhondda, like many other industrial valleys of S. Wales, is becoming green again. At
Blaenavon, N of the town, Big Pit, a former working coal
mine, has been opened up as a Mining Museum.

St Donat's, South Glam   6F1
One of the most perfect old baronial halls of Wales – 'a 14th-c
castle with an Elizabethan courtyard' and other anachro-
nisms. Randolph Hearst, the American newspaper magnate,
who bought the castle, brought here from Wiltshire part of
Bradenstoke Priory. It is now New Atlantic College, one of
the United World Colleges.

St Fagan's, South Glam   6G2
A small village on the River Ely, some 4m W of **Cardiff**. The
castle, an Elizabethan manor house with nearly 100 acres of
ground, was presented by the Earl of Plymouth to accommodate the Welsh National Folk Museum, well worth a
visit. Within the grounds old cottages, farmhouses, mills etc.
from all parts of Wales have been reconstructed stone by
stone. Demonstrations of traditional rural industries often
take place. *See also* page 18.

St Lythan's, South Glam   6G1
The Cromlech was a prehistoric burial chamber, though the
earth which covered the long barrow is gone (AM).

*Tintern Abbey: the nave of its majestic ruins which are set
in the scenic Wye Valley near Tintern Parva*

St Nicholas, South Glam   6G1
Near by is the remarkable Neolithic tomb at *Tinkinswood*,
with a roof capstone weighing about 40 tons (AM). At
Dyffryn House are gardens containing rare trees and plants,
including many from China.

Skenfrith, Gwent   7H3
Remains of a Norman castle (AM) built as a defence against
the Welsh, with a fine interior courtyard. One of the 'Three
Castles', the others being **Grosmont** and *White Castle*, 6m
SW. *See also* **Abergavenny.**

Swansea, West Glam   6E2
One of the major ports of Wales. Parts of the 14th-c castle
remain. The Guildhall, the Glynn Vivian Museum and Art
Gallery, and the Royal Institute of S. Wales have collections
of pictures and Swansea china. The Guildhall houses the
Empire Panels, the great murals of the artist Frank
Brangwyn. There is a Maritime and Industrial Museum, and
a multi-million-pound Leisure Centre and Marina in the
redeveloped dock area of the city.

Tintern Abbey, ★★ Gwent   7H2
One of the most beautiful Cistercian ruins in Britain, with
the wooded hills of the Wye valley all around. Dating from
the 12th c it is far more extensive than a glimpse from the
road would suggest. An exhibition illustrates the history of
the abbey and the Wye Valley. Tintern Railway Centre also
has an exhibition for walkers.

Usk, Gwent   7H2
Small town and popular fishing centre on the River Usk.
Remains of a fine Norman castle (open by appointment only)
and a Benedictine nunnery. 3m to the NE is *Cefntilla Court*,
built in 1616.

SCOTLAND

PREFACE TO SCOTLAND

PREFACE BY

J. S. GRANT

The link between Scotland and England rests on a voluntary union: a marriage, with all the complexities of mutual adjustment such a relationship implies. It was, moreover, a marriage between two fiercely independent peoples with a long history of bitter and bloody conflict. When the Scottish king became heir to the English throne in 1603 he succeeded the Queen who had beheaded his mother.

The Union of the Parliaments, which followed a century later in 1707, was one of the great reconciliations of history and an event of incalculable importance for Britain and the world. The fact that the partners were unequally yoked in population and wealth, however, inevitably sharpened the sensitivity of the weaker, while blunting the sensitivity of the stronger, so that friction did – and still does – arise from minor pinpricks, as well as from the real stresses which are inevitable in any political structure.

The visitor is most frequently reminded of Scotland's separate identity when he pays a bill. The Scottish banks have retained the right to issue their own notes, with the result that there are four different paper currencies in circulation, issued by the Bank of Scotland, the Royal Bank of Scotland and the Clydesdale Bank, as well as the standard British notes issued by the Bank of England.

The Union was not incorporative. The treaty specifically safeguards the Church of Scotland, the law courts and the legal code. These were much more important headmarks of nationhood in 1707 than they are today. Moreover they enshrine subtle but significant differences in attitudes to political power between the two partners which still to some extent persist.

Scotland did not become a region of England. In fact it has well-defined regions of its own just as England and Wales have. The difference between Lothian and the Western Isles is much the same as the difference between Kent and Wales. Shetland is further removed from Edinburgh in distance and in outlook than Cornwall is from London.

Previous page: the seat of the Clan Mackintosh is on Loch Moy. Highland clans threatened the Lowlands for centuries

These regional differences rest to some extent on geography. Travelling northwards one passes through the Southern Uplands into the Central Lowlands, from a sparsely populated area of farms into the valleys of the Clyde and Forth where industry and population are disproportionately concentrated. Around three-fifths of the Scottish population lives within 30 miles of either Glasgow or Edinburgh.

Northwards again one enters the Highlands across the mountain barrier which halted the Roman legions, a significant historical as well as physical watershed. Western civilization did not come to the Highlands through conquest by a highly organized and centralized military power but more subtly through the pervasive influence of the dispersed and egalitarian Celtic church, the ruins of whose modest structures can still be seen in the remotest islands.

Although Scotland and England came together while Ireland and England drifted apart, the legal system in the Republic is much closer to the English than the Scottish is. The Irish have retained, by and large, the system England imposed on them. The Scottish system is *sui generis*, evolved before the Treaty of Union and protected by it: an amalgam of Roman law, the feudal system, borrowings from England both deliberate and inadvertent, and behind it all an ancient Celtic legal system the traces of which can now be sensed rather than identified.

The difference between the Scottish and English legal systems is seen, for instance, in the office of the Procurator Fiscal, an official independent of the police, who prosecutes on behalf of the Crown in criminal cases; in the ease with which purchases and sales of property can be effected without waiting for the completion of legal formalities; in the feu, a form of land tenure which is neither freehold nor leasehold but has some of the qualities of both; in the 'not proven' verdict which hovers uncertainly between conviction and acquittal; and in the extraordinarily wide powers of the Sheriff Courts which exist in quite small towns throughout the country and handle everything from stairhead brawls to bankruptcy, from minor traffic offences to manslaughter or civil actions involving many thousands of pounds. The old Scottish system of marriage by consent, which made the Border village of Gretna Green so popular with English runaways (and novelettists), has been abolished but marriage by 'habit and repute' remains.

The Scottish and English legal codes, but not the structures, naturally tend to move closer together because of the shared legislature, but also, to an extent, because modern ideas on the rights of the individual have overtaken, and indeed surpassed, concepts which were indigenous to Scotland but developed only in modern times in the more rigidly hierarchical society south of the Border.

The legal differences reflect a different concept of kingship. The monarch was King of Scots, not King of Scotland. Leader of a people rather than ruler of a territory. In the early history of Scotland the Celtic system of tanistry prevailed: the heir apparent was chosen, during the lifetime of the ruler, from among the ablest of his kin – a temptation at times to the heir apparent, already a person of power, to accelerate the succession at his own hand.

The most formidable threat to the kings came from the Lords of the Isles – the great Macdonald chiefs who ruled in the area formerly dominated by the Norsemen. They were invested at a ceremony not unlike a royal coronation, maintained their own system of weights and measures, and their own legal system. It is one of the paradoxes of Scottish history that memories of the Lordship of the Isles and the old Celtic attachment to the King as a leader by consent, induced the people of the Highlands and Islands to take part in successive Jacobite rebellions in support of the Stuarts who were the arch proponents of absolute personal rule.

Many Gaelic-speaking Highlanders, of course, did not support the Jacobite rebellions, and although the Stuarts had a strong Catholic and Episcopalian base in Scotland the country was, and is, resolutely Presbyterian. The Presbyterian church, almost completely devoid of hierarchies, is the outstanding expression of Scottish egalitarianism in institutional structures, but the same spirit motivated the schools which paid no regard to wealth or social status.

Scottish egalitarianism finds its most articulate voice in the poems of Robert Burns who expressed more directly than anyone else the supremacy of character over status – 'the rank is but the guinea stamp' – and the longing of ordinary men and women for universal brotherhood, and who gave the English-speaking world its best known 'hymn' of fellowship, paradoxically written in Scots – 'Auld Lang Syne'.

The cult of Burns illustrates the almost Jekyll and Hyde dichotomy in the Scottish character, and reminds us that a church without prelates is not necessarily a church without dictators.

The great advantage which Scots derived from the Union of the Parliaments was access to English overseas markets, and the opportunity to participate in the creation of the British Empire as explorers, missionaries, traders and fighting men in numbers out of all proportion to the population.

In some respects the recrudescence of national sentiment in Scotland is a result of the loss of opportunities for the ambitious in an expanding empire. It is also, and more importantly, a reflection of the problems of all peripheral areas in an over-centralized state. In this respect memories of their ancient nationhood tend to blind Scots to the fact that their problems are regional rather than national and they have more to gain by making common cause with Cornwall, Wales and Tyneside than by trying to reverse the process of history. On the other hand, the impetus which latent nationalism gives may lead to improvements in the structure or attitudes of government which might not otherwise take place.

Diversity within a United Kingdom should be a source of strength. The fact that the periphery of the periphery, so to speak, the crofting townships of the remote northwest, so long in decay, were, in effect, an internal colony of Great Britain, enables the Highlands and Islands Development Board to establish a rapport with emergent countries of the Third World which is not possible in London, still haunted for them by the ghosts of Empire.

While this thought is perhaps too subtle for politicians the discovery of North Sea oil has fundamentally altered governmental attitudes to the Grampian Region and the Highlands and Islands. The fact that Aberdeen is now the most prosperous city in Scotland, and probably the most rapidly expanding in Britain, speaks more loudly in Whitehall than political intangibles. But, at the end of the day, it is the intangibles which persist.

NOTE

In 1973 (operative from 1975) the old Scottish counties were abolished and replaced by the present administrative regions. The arrangement of the Scottish sections of this Guide is under the new regions, but the old counties still carry many historical and sentimental associations; we have therefore given the name of the former county after each entry in the Gazetteers except for Fife, where the county and region remain the same. Similarly, burghs and royal burghs were abolished at the same time and any references to these should be understood as historical.

Although the abbreviation AM is applied to Ancient Monuments in the Scottish entries as elsewhere in this Guide, it should be noted that they are not the responsibility of the Department of the Environment but of the Scottish Development Department, 3–11 Melville Street, Edinburgh, EH3 7QD, from whom further details may be obtained. The abbreviation NTS refers to the National Trust for Scotland, 5 Charlotte Square, Edinburgh, EH2 4DU, which can supply information regarding opening hours of its properties. In general AM sites are open throughout the year except where stated; the opening hours of NTS properties vary greatly.

BORDERS REGION

AN INTRODUCTION BY
GEORGE SCOTT-MONCRIEFF

The four southeastern counties which form the Borders Region, Roxburgh, Berwick, Selkirk and Peebles, include most of the Scottish Border with England. Chiefly this is hilly country; but towards the lower reaches of the Tweed it levels down to an undulating plain in the old province of the Merse, whose early history was more closely linked with that of the rich lands of Lothian to the north. Indeed, the visitor from England, coming by way of the Cheviot Hills, is liable to feel that 'Caledonia stern and wild' is a myth when he first looks down upon the more fertile Merse. It is to the southwest, in Roxburgh and Selkirk, that we find the characteristic Border country of hills rising to well over 2,000 feet with narrow valleys and wandering mountain streams, interspersed with woods and patches of arable land. To the northwest, Upper Tweeddale, in the former county of Peebles, presents hills even more lofty and somewhat different in character to those lying nearer the English border. This area has a higher mean altitude than any of the former Highland counties, for it nowhere reaches sea level.

Industry
Visiting the peaceful, unspoiled Border countryside today, it is hard to realize that in medieval times it contained two of Scotland's four richest and busiest towns – perhaps the most flourishing of them all. They stood one at each end of the Merse, and neither exists on Scottish soil today. Roxburgh, after repeatedly falling into English hands, was razed to the ground by the Scots to prevent further enemy occupation, and leaves not a stone above the turf. An area encompassing Berwick and a few square miles on the north bank of the mouth of the Tweed is the only trophy remaining of the many bloody campaigns made by the English in their efforts to annex southern Scotland. When, long years later, the Industrial Age arrived, the Border counties were almost unaffected, since there was neither coal nor iron to exploit. In fact they might have been given over entirely to agriculture (and there were indeed some notable agricultural improvers of the 19th century among the Berwickshire farmers in particular) and to tourists brought to the countryside by Sir Walter Scott's poems and novels, had it not been for the enterprise of the men who developed weaving on a new basis.

The Border hills had long provided sheep-runs, and the weaving of tweeds had likewise a long tradition; but they now began to be produced not by single weavers working in their own cottages, but on a bigger scale, with the establishing of mills in Hawick, Galashiels, Walkerburn, Innerleithen, and the older towns themselves. None of the other native crafts of Scotland has shown itself so vigorous in maintaining quality and a sense of design within the framework of large-scale production.

The Berwickshire coast is rocky and inhospitable, with few harbours. Only Eyemouth, once a great haunt of smugglers, is sufficiently sheltered to maintain a large fishing-fleet, although St Abbs has a few boats in its picturesque harbour, and crabs and lobsters are fished from Burnmouth. Agriculture remains the chief activity of the area, but with increasing mechanization, does not prevent a steady decline in population. Shepherds from the Border, whose dogs work for them with a wisdom wonderful to see, can find employment in far parts of the world: Australia, New Zealand and South America.

The Rock
The heather-covered Border hills are formed almost entirely of brown or grey flags and shales. In fact Selkirkshire is geologically the only really homogeneous county in Scotland, a country whose great mixture of stirred-up geological formations inspired much of the pioneer work in the science. To the north of Peeblesshire, however, there is a more mixed rock that includes sandstone and a little coal on the Lothian edge. On the east of Roxburghshire there is a red sandstone, and in the richer arable land of southern Berwickshire we come into the limestone belt that continues far south into the coalfields of the North of England. St Abbs Head offers the most interesting geological study, with contorted rocks worn smooth by glacial action. Here the junction of different formations is pierced with many caves along the 300-foot high precipice of Petticowick.

The isolated peaks of the Eildon Hills form prominent landmarks in the low borderland countryside

Sandstone, both red and cream-coloured, provided the building material for the older houses in the Merse, giving place to grey whinstone in the hill-country. At Stobo in Peeblesshire a thick, dark, attractive slate was formerly worked, and may still be seen on many Border roofs.

The People

The Picts are the earliest people of Scotland of whom much is known. In the southeast some Pictish place-names survive, but more are of Brythonic origin. The Brythonic Celts, or Britons, who came into the south of Scotland, left one Arthurian romance: Lyonnesse is thought to have derived from Lothian, while the wizard Merlin is supposedly buried in a mound at Drummelzier in Peeblesshire. The great days of the Northumbrian kingdom, that at one time seemed to be achieving the consolidation of Britain with a capital in York, left Anglo-Saxon names in Berwickshire and Lothian. The collapse of Northumbria, after the Pictish victory of Nectansmere in 685, opened the way to a final settlement of the area – that of the Scottish Celts, who came originally from Ireland, bringing their own Gaelic nomenclature.

Although the northern end of Watling Street came up through Roxburghshire by Melrose, and the Romans built walls both to the north and south of the four counties, they made no important settlements here. The earlier artefacts, remains of hill fortresses, burial tumuli and occasional inarticulate standing stones, date from both before and after Roman times.

The Four Abbeys

The beginning of Scottish Border history as we know it dates from the foundation of four great abbeys whose ruins have inspired prose, poetry and painting, are still cynosures for the visitor. All four were founded during the reign of David I (1124–53). As elsewhere, the monks developed agriculture, industry and the civilized arts, despite the fact that their situation near the English frontier left them open to constant raids. Each of the abbeys was several times sacked and burned, but was constantly rebuilt until, after 400 years, the Reformation brought Nemesis. It was the monks who first established Border wool as an important export that fetched a high price on the Continental market.

The ruins of Melrose Abbey are the most substantial and interesting, retaining much finely carved detail. Dryburgh, where Sir Walter Scott chose to be buried, has the most beautiful site, set among big trees on a spur of land in a curve of the River Tweed. Jedburgh, although only the shell of the church survives, gives a fair sense of its former glory in both Romanesque and Gothic arcading. Kelso retains little more than the battered western tower in which the last monks were put to the sword by Spanish mercenaries during Hertford's raid of 1545: the tower is now surrounded by the houses of the kindly market town that grew up beside the Abbey after the obliteration of Roxburgh on the opposite bank of the Tweed.

The Border Reivers

The decline of the abbeys saw the rise of the Border reivers (or plunderers). The countryside passed into a state of anarchy in which only family loyalties held, and Scotts, Douglases, Armstrongs, Elliots and Grahams raided each other or joined forces to cross the Border and raid the English. When food grew scarce at Harden House the beautiful wife of Auld Wat Scott served a dish at table containing only a pair of spurs, implying that it was time to ride again and as the ballads tell:

> Then there was riding, riding in haste,
> And a cracking of whips out owre the lee

Jedburgh gave its name to 'Jeddart Justice', which meant hanging without the tedious preliminaries of a trial. A Scottish Act of Parliament ordered every landowner to fortify his house. In all the Border country little towers were built, often hardly more capacious than a cottage, but strongholds none the less. Most of these are in ruins today; but the survivors show a surprising and delightful architectural sense, finely matched to the countryside. Details of corbelling, machicolation and parapet seem to blossom from the austere and solid stone walls like the windswept trees and wild flowers that decorate the surrounding hillsides.

Larger castles are older: the most massive is Hermitage, whose great grim shell stands in barren country near Newcastleton. Much kindlier, Ferniehirst, south of Jedburgh, is now a youth hostel. Traquair in Tweeddale is a fairy castle breaking into history, with its memories of Mary Queen of Scots, of Montrose and Prince Charles Edward.

Of the little towers, Darnick, near Melrose, is one of the best, happily preserved. Smailholm Tower stands wonderfully austere against the background of the shapely Eildon Hills. Harden is still a Scott home, above a deep gully, 'Auld Wat's meat-safe'.

For some reason the best ballads come from north of the Border, recording in rough-hewn words the days when rough courage was a principal virtue. Even the most bloodthirsty reiver remained a hero to the Borderers, and, if he were brought to justice, was lamented in haunting rhyme. Outlaws they might be, but law was at a discount, while lawless exploits lay at the heart of Border life.

Sir Walter Scott (1771–1832)

Scotland's history was given a new gloss by Sir Walter Scott who also made its Border, home of his ancestors, the first great tourist resort of Britain. His house of Abbotsford became a place of pilgrimage in his lifetime and has remained one ever since. Architecturally it is a somewhat preposterous pastiche with none of the authenticity of his novels; but it contains many relics, in the collecting of which he was a pioneer. Besides his writings, his personality was infectious in setting value upon tradition and things old and historic.

Today

In Scott's day the ruins of the four abbeys were ivy-shrouded and tree-sprouting, fit to be romantically admired, especially by moonlight. Today they are cleaned up, their tottering walls cemented, and maintained in the care of the Scottish Development Department. But they are still interesting, and Dryburgh is beautiful in its landscape.

The little Border towns are friendly places, and the people appreciate and preserve their modest but characteristic houses. Many of these, like the rural steadings and cottages, are built of whinstone rubble, a hard, intractable stone, beautifully jointed by the handiwork of a great tradition of masons.

The Berwickshire coast has some good beaches for sunbathers but the visitor to the Border is more likely to find his way into the hills. Here there is much land lovely and remote, even secluded glens rarely seen by men, that offer the walker a refreshing solitude not readily to be found today. There are many drove roads and rights of way, and generally the wayfarer can walk where he will if he uses his discretion and his manners are good: odious only are the litter-louts, the dyke-breakers, the gate-leavers-open and the casual incendiaries.

There is excellent salmon-fishing in the Tweed, and trout to be taken from its many tributaries. The heather hills provide shooting with grouse and blackgame, and the blue mountain hare that turns white in winter; elsewhere there are common hares, partridges and pheasants. There is a little fox-hunting; but Border foxes are liable to live in wild and rocky fastnesses in the hills. Otters, badgers and roe-deer are shy creatures sometimes to be seen. The annual Common Ridings of the Border towns are loyal and lively celebrations, genuine local occasions conducted with no self-conscious eye upon the tourist. Hedgerow and moorland plants and flowers of all the usual kinds abound; but there are few alpines.

Except for the Selkirk bun, Border catering offers few specialities. It compensates with the quality of its basic ingredients: salmon and trout from clear streams, hill-fed mutton and prime beef. Homemade oatcakes, if you can get them, are better fare than any wheaten bread.

GAZETTEER

Abbey St Bathans, Berw   11K6
Small village, beautifully situated on the Whiteadder, near the Lammermuir Hills – with Heart Law (1,283ft) to NW. The church contains the tomb of a prioress from the long-vanished Abbey Church. At *Edinshall*, 2m SE, on the slopes of Cockburn Law (1,065ft), is one of the few Pictish brochs, or towers, in S. Scotland (AM).

Abbotsford House,* Selk   11J5
The mansion, built 1817–22 by Sir Walter Scott in imitation Scottish Baronial style, contains numerous historical and personal relics, a fine collection of arms and armour, and Scott's study, still much as he left it. Open March–Oct.

Bemersyde, Berw   11K5
The House, 16th-c with many later additions, was purchased by the nation in 1921 and presented to Field-Marshal Earl Haig (d.1928), the commander in World War I, thus restoring to his family their ancestral lands. He laid out the gardens to simulate those at **Hampton Court,** Outer London.

Burnmouth, Berw   11L6
Picturesque fishing village at the foot of steep cliffs, with magnificent coastal scenery on either hand.

Carlops, Peebles   11J5
This 18th-c weavers' village was the setting for Allan Ramsay's *The Gentle Shepherd* (1725) written in the old broad Scots and revived at the **Edinburgh** Festival.

Clovenfords, Selk   11J5
The present inn replaced the one in which Sir Walter Scott, as Sheriff of Selkirk, stayed before he had his own home in the Borders, first at *Ashiestiel*, which may be seen on the S bank of the Tweed, then at **Abbotsford.**

Cockburnspath, Berw   11K6
Here the A1 skirts the Lammermuirs, with glimpses of the rocky coast below. The village has a 17th-c mercat cross and a 14th-c church, though the curious round tower is considerably later. The cove contains a tiny harbour and good sands;

while at the S end of adjacent Pease Sands are remains of the Norman church of St Helen's. N of the village in the grounds of Dunglass House are substantial remains of the Collegiate Church of St Mary founded about 1450 (AM).

Coldingham, Berw   11L6
Hill-top village, near St Abbs Head (*see* **St Abbs**), where in the 7th c a church was founded by St Ebba. The 11th-c choir of the priory which replaced it is now part of the parish church (note good arcading). Near by *Coldingham Bay*, with its sandy beach, is a popular resort.

Coldstream, Berw   11L5
On N side of the Tweed, which is here spanned by Smeaton's fine 18th-c bridge leading into England. Though less popular than **Gretna Green** (Dumf), the little Toll House was the scene of many runaway marriages. From here in 1659 General Monck's Regiment of Foot Guards set out for London; having achieved the restoration of Charles II they acquired the name Coldstream Guards. Coldstream Museum in original headquarters. Open in summer.

Denholm, Roxb   11K4
An obelisk on the village green commemorates Dr John Leyden, son of a local shepherd. Poet and linguist, doctor and clergyman, he collected material for Scott's *Minstrelsy of the Scottish Borders*, and travelled abroad.

Dryburgh Abbey,** Berw   11K4
One of the loveliest ruins in Scotland, set among lawns and trees on the bank of the Tweed. Founded in 1150, the Abbey (AM) repeatedly suffered damage at the hands of the English, and from the 16th c no further attempt to repair or rebuild it was made until it was taken over by the then Ministry of Works: now cared for by the Scottish Development Department. Here Sir Walter Scott (*see* **Abbotsford House**) was buried, with other members of his family; also Field-Marshal Earl Haig (*see* **Bemersyde**).

Abbotsford House: home of Sir Walter Scott until he died in 1832 when he was buried at Dryburgh Abbey

Duns, Berw   11K5
Small market town, built after the old town on the slopes of Duns Law had been burned by the English in 1545. There is a mercat cross in a park on the S side of the town; and the Covenanters' Stone on Duns Law (713ft) recalls the encampment of Leslie's army in 1639. W of the town is the modern Duns Castle, with its 14th-c tower and fine avenue of limes in the grounds. John Duns Scotus, the 13th-c philosopher and divine, was born here in 1265 (*see also* **Uist, W.I.**).

Earlston, Berw   11K5
Formerly Ercildoune, which was closely associated with the semi-legendary 13th-c prophet and poet of Scottish folk lore, Thomas the Rhymer. A tablet in the church bears the words: 'Auld Rymer's Race Lyes in this Place'.

Eildon Hills,★ Roxb   11J4
These lovely triple peaks, the highest of them 1,385ft, command superb views of the countryside beloved of Sir Walter Scott. His *Confessions of a Justified Sinner*, ignored in his own day, is now acclaimed as the first of all 'psychological' novels. At *Newstead*, a monument marks the site of the Roman camp of Trimontium. (*See* page 339.)

Ettrick, Selk   11I4
The little church stands on the Ettrick Water, in a valley dominated by Ettrick Pen (2,270ft). James Hogg, the Ettrick Shepherd, who became well known as a poet, was baptized and buried here (1835).

Eyemouth, Berw   11L6
Fishing-port and popular resort at the head of a rock-bound bay, where the numerous caves were formerly used by smugglers. Museum open in 1981 as a memorial to the Great East Coast Fishing Disaster. There is wonderful coastal scenery near by.

Galashiels, Selk   11J5
Tweed and woollen manufacturing town in the valley of the Gala Water. Among interesting monuments are a 17th-c mercat cross and Sir R. Lorimer's War Memorial. The 17th-c Gala House, with its painted ceilings, is now an Arts Centre. The charter of 1599 is celebrated in early summer in the 'Braw Lads' Gathering' – a mounted procession round the district. The town crest on the Municipal Buildings, with its motto 'Sour Plums', commemorates the capture of some English raiders, caught robbing a plum tree in 1337.

Greenlaw, Berw   11K5
A small town on the Blackadder, with a good mercat cross (1696) and a tall-towered 17th-c church. 3m S are the ruins of *Hume Castle* (600ft), with fine views of the countryside.

Hawick, Roxb   11J4
In the heart of Teviotdale, where the Slitrig Water joins the Teviot, this is one of the most important Border towns, noted for woollen and hosiery manufactures. The Mote Hill, possibly the mound of a Norman castle, was more probably the meeting place for the town Moot or Court of the Manor. The town is noted for the picturesque 'Common Riding', held each June to commemorate a defeat of the English in 1512 at Hornshole Bridge, 2m NE. 2m SW is the massive pele tower of *Goldielands*; and, 1m further on, *Branxholm Hall*, with 16th-c tower.

Hermitage Castle,★ Roxb   11J3
Once a stronghold of the Douglases, the four towers and connecting walls of this immensely strong 13th-c fortress

(AM) are still almost perfect today; inside are the remains of an earlier tower. The scene of many grim events, the castle was visited in 1566 by Mary Queen of Scots. *See also* **Jedburgh**.

Innerleithen, Peebles   11J5
Woollen town, with golf-course and mineral springs, where the Leithen Water joins the Tweed. At St Ronan's Well, above the town, visitors may sample the waters. 5m to NE rises Windlestraw Law (2,162ft), with many hill forts in the vicinity. *Traquair House*★, 1m S, where William the Lion held court in 1209 and Mary Queen of Scots stayed with Darnley in 1566, is probably the oldest inhabited mansion in Scotland; though most of the present building dates from the 17th c (the infant James VI's cradle is one of the treasures). The old brewhouse still produces excellent ale. Open Easter–Oct.

Jedburgh,★ Roxb   11K4
One of the most attractive towns in the Lowlands, dominated by the ruins of the great red sandstone Abbey★ (AM), founded in the 12th c and frequently added to and rebuilt. The nave and the rose-window are splendid. Queen Mary's House at **Hermitage Castle**, which like the three-span bridge, was built in the 16th c, is now a museum.

Kelso,★ Roxb   11K5
One of the most beautiful towns in Scotland, on the Tweed near its junction with the Teviot. All that remains of the 12th-c Abbey (AM), once the greatest in the Borders, are the W tower and transepts of rare Norman-Transitional workmanship. The five-arch bridge built by Rennie in 1803 was the model for Waterloo Bridge, London (demolished 1934). *Floors Castle*, to the NW, seat of the Duke of Roxburghe, was designed by Vanbrugh in 1718 and added to by Playfair in 1838–49. Said to be the largest inhabited mansion in Britain, it has splendid paintings, tapestries and furniture. Open May–Sept.: closed Fri. and Sat.

Ladykirk, Berw   11L5
The little stone-vaulted church was built c.1500 by James IV as a thanks-offering for his escape from drowning in the Tweed, though the tower, with its charming cupola, was probably completed by William Adam in 1743. It was one of the last churches built before the Reformation. Across the river are the ruins of **Norham** Castle (Nthmb).

Lamberton, Berw   11L5
In the now ruined church Margaret Tudor, sister of Henry VIII, was received by the Scottish Commissioners en route to **Edinburgh** and her marriage to James IV of Scotland, whence eventually came the Union of the Crowns.

Lauder, Berw   11J5
Former royal burgh with good fishing in the Leader. Note the quaint little Tolbooth, with its flight of steps; and the 16th-c church. *Thirlestane Castle*,★ incorporating a 14th-c stronghold, contains portraits by Lely, Romney and Aikman. Privately occupied: open June–Sept. on set days. A fine road over the moors to the W reaches a height of 1,100ft, before descending to the Gala Water.

Mellerstain,★ Berw   11K5
8m NW of **Kelso**. One of the great Georgian houses, it was a property of the Earl of Haddington. Built by William and Robert Adam in 1721 and characteristic of their best work: the library is a Robert Adam masterpiece and there are many old masters. Open Easter and May–Sept.: closed Sat.

Melrose Abbey: built in 1136, it was badly ruined in Border wars and the English raids of 1543–44

Melrose,** Roxb   11J5

The finest and most beautifully situated of all the Border abbeys (AM), this Cistercian foundation of David I in 1136 suffered greatly through the centuries. It was much restored in 1822 by Sir Walter Scott with the Duke of Buccleuch's generosity and finally gifted to the nation by a later Duke in 1918. The heart of Robert the Bruce in its silver casket is buried beneath the E window (*see also* **Dunfermline**, Fife). In 1974 the NTS opened Priorwood Garden, which is adjacent to the Abbey, as a visitor centre with an apple orchard and special garden of flowers suitable for drying. Open April–Dec. Near by is a motor museum exhibiting vehicles dating from 1914 to 1940.

Morebattle, Roxb   11K4

Pleasant fishing village almost surrounded by the Kale Water. 2½m SW are the ruins of *Cessford Castle*, with its 14ft-thick walls, while across the Border rises the Cheviot (2,676ft), the highest point in the whole range.

Newstead *see* Eildon Hills

Peebles   11I5

Busy shopping centre, well known for its tweed- and knitwear mills. A good centre for fishing and touring. Queensberry Lodging, now incorporated in the Chambers Institute, which houses an interesting museum, was the birthplace of the notorious 18th-c Marquess, 'Old Q'. 1m W of the town, beautifully situated on the Tweed, is one of the most memorable of the smaller Border castles, 13th-c *Neidpath*. Open Easter–Oct.

Polwarth, Berw   11K5

A village of great antiquity 4m SW of **Duns**. It is the 'Polwarth-on-the-Green' of Allan Ramsay's famous ballad and a descendant of the Thorn Tree still flourishes. The parish church, which dates from 900, has an interesting 'Laird's pew' and the family vault of the Lairds of Polwarth. It was in this vault that Sir Patrick Hume of Polwarth hid to escape arrest for his alleged complicity in the 1684 Rye House Plot, his food being brought to him by night by his daughter Grizel from near-by Redbraes Castle. He escaped to Holland but was restored to be created Lord Polwarth (1690), Lord Chancellor of Scotland and Earl of Marchmont.

Romanno Bridge, Peebles   11I5

On the Roman road by the Lyne Water, this village has a dovecot with an inscription on the lintel recalling a battle between rival gypsies in 1677.

Roxburgh   11K4

Now a small village. The old town, which in the 13th c was one of the Court of Four Burghs (the others being **Edinburgh**, **Stirling** and **Berwick**), has completely disappeared, and little remains of the castle, some 3m NW.

St Abbs, Berw   11L6

A small sandy fishing-harbour and resort, beneath 300ft cliffs, with many caves once used for smuggling. NW from St Abbs Head (NTS), with fine views of the rocky coast, are the grim ruins of Fast Castle, the 'Wolf's Crag' of Scott's *Bride of Lammermoor*. The spectacular promontory is described as 'the most important locality for cliff-breeding sea birds in S.E. Scotland'. *See* **Coldingham**.

Selkirk   11J4

Built round a small square, on the slopes of a hill beside the Ettrick Water, the former royal burgh of Selkirk is now noted for its tweed-mills, but in the old days it was famous for its 'souters', or shoemakers. Their gallantry at Flodden Field is commemorated by a monument, and by the ceremonial 'Riding of the Marches' each June. From the 110ft spire of the Town Hall a curfew is still rung every night. Note the statue of Mungo Park, the African explorer, born near by (*see* **Yarrow**). An interesting little museum in Halliwell's Close is worth a visit. About 4m SW a Roman fort of the 1st c was discovered at *Oakwood*.

Smailholm, Roxb   11K5

The fine 16th-c pele tower (AM), romantically situated on a rock to the SW, is mentioned in *Marmion* and the *Eve of St John*; while Scott himself spent some years of his childhood at the near-by farm of Sandyknowe.

Stobo, Peebles   11I5

Norman church, with good 13th-c doorway. In the barrel-vaulted porch still hang the 'jougs', an iron collar by which wrong-doers were chained to the wall. See also the interesting 'laird's loft', or pew. On the opposite side of the Tweed, Dawyck Woods are famous for their great variety of trees, this being the first place in Britain to which the larch was introduced, in 1725.

Yarrow, Selk   11J4

This classic valley is true ballad country. Newark Castle built c.1400 was the scene for the recital of 'The Lay of the Last Minstrel' by Sir Walter Scott. The Castle may be visited by arrangement with Buccleuch Estates, Bowhill, Selkirk. Across the stream at *Foulshiels*, stands the ruined cottage where Mungo Park, the African explorer was born in 1771.

DUMFRIES AND GALLOWAY REGION

AN INTRODUCTION BY
GEORGE SCOTT-MONCRIEFF

This region comprises the southwest Lowlands, with the former counties of Wigtown, Kirkcudbright and Dumfries.

Dumfriesshire includes part of the hill-country along the English Border, then stretches north and west through more open, fertile land into the central Lowland hills, whence it may be approached by one of two dramatic entrances: the Devil's Beef Tub, whose road descends on the old spa of Moffat, or through the great green lumps of the hills flanking the Dalveen Pass. Only Kirkcudbrightshire and Wigtownshire, lying along the northern coast of the Solway Firth, have much in common, originally forming (along with Carrick, the hill-country to the south of Ayrshire) the Pictish province of Galloway, and retaining much of that earlier unity.

Industry

Industry has receded markedly from the Galloway towns. The little burgh of Gatehouse of Fleet, for example, that could once boast brewery, tannery, soapery, cotton-mills, a boat-building yard and a bobbin-factory, has now none of these. In the 18th century, after the developing laird, having built his mansion which is now a hotel, canalized the River Fleet, the port of Gatehouse even offered some rivalry to that of Glasgow. Like other Galloway harbours it no longer sees any craft bigger than the occasional yacht. Even Portpatrick, so near Ireland it once served as a Gretna Green for runaway Irish couples, is now but a fishing harbour. Only the sheltered port of Stranraer maintains a regular car-ferry service with Ireland. Tweed-mills and a distillery are virtually all the industry in the area apart from such as is directly associated with agriculture. The historic old towns of Dumfriesshire – Annan, Lochmaben, Langholm, Sanquhar, even Dumfries itself – are relatively quiet and peaceful places.

The Landscape

The Lowland belt of grey-brown shale runs right across Dumfriesshire and Galloway and provides whinstone from which most of the older houses are built. But Dumfriesshire has a good deal of sandstone,

usually of a rather dark, even liverish, red, which latterly provided a more tractable material. There is granite in Galloway, at Dalbeattie and Creetown and the hills behind, of a delicate silvery brightness, which provides finer houses. To the north, near Sanquhar, Dumfriesshire has coal-bearing rock.

Heather hills lie all the way inland from the rugged cliffs and sandy bays and wildfowl-noisy estuaries of Galloway's beautiful Solway coastline. The hills cross the border some distance into Ayrshire. They include The Merrick, at 2,764 feet the highest hill of southern Scotland, rising in fine remote country where also lies in a bare bed of granite remote Loch Enoch, itself 1,650 feet above sea level and containing an island with another loch in the middle.

The little fields of Galloway, carved out among stony outcrops and homely trees, bounded by stone dykes, rise quickly into the heather hills. It is a countryside on a wonderfully satisfying scale, small enough to be intimate, bold enough to be exciting, always with a rise and fall in the ground to lure one further.

To the north the hill-country becomes increasingly noble and rugged, with great lonely stretches by deep Glentrool, the Cauldron of the Dungeon and the Back Hill of the Bush, places that do not belie their romantic names. The wilderness overflows into the Carrick country of Ayrshire and a little way into Dumfriesshire before it gives place to the fertile fields of Nithsdale and Annandale. Dumfriesshire includes to the east the typical Border hill-country of Eskdale and Liddesdale, and to the north part of the Lowther Hills, that 'vast expanse covered with thick, short, tawny grass and moss' that stretches across the central Lowlands. All over the southwest there is a plenitude of lovely country, hill and coast, with friendly little towns and villages.

The People

While in early times Dumfriesshire became part of the kingdom of the Britons of Strathclyde, Galloway remained a Pictish province, isolated from the kingdoms of the northern and southern Picts which occupied the greater part of Scotland. The degree of

Roman penetration is disputed: it was certainly not great, but through it, indirectly, a Romanized Pict became the first Christian missionary to Scotland.

St Ninian seems actually to have spent some time in Rome before he established his *Candida Casa* on the peninsular Isle of Whithorn in about the year 393. On the coast at Glasserton is the cave he used as an oratory before building his stone chapel. It was to Whithorn Priory that the Scottish kings made their pilgrimages for many centuries: the last royal pilgrimage being that of Mary Queen of Scots in 1563.

Coastal Galloway had its share of Viking incursions, and a final overlay of Dalriadic Scots who left their Gaelic language to linger longer in the southwest than anywhere else in the Lowlands. Probably there were Galloway hill-folk of the 19th century who used Gaelic words, and there are still those who pronounce their Gaelic place-names correctly.

The Gallowegians long maintained considerable independence, sometimes siding with the English and giving Robert the Bruce a hard time in subduing them.

Stone and Lime

Inscribed stones, one in the museum at Whithorn and two in the church at Kirkmadrine, date back almost to Ninian's day and may be the oldest Christian relics of British origin. The Kirkmadrine stones have been described as menhirs christened with the Chi-Ro symbol. The famous richly carved 7th-century cross in Ruthwell Church, to the south of Dumfriesshire, is one of the finest examples of European art to survive from the Dark Ages.

The church of New Abbey, better known as Sweetheart Abbey, is, although roofless, relatively intact. At Dundrennan, further along the Solway coast, the Abbey ruins are singularly beautiful. West again, little but the fine chapter house of Glenluce Abbey survives.

Galloway was a great stronghold of the Covenanters, the Presbyterians who opposed Episcopacy in the 17th century. Tombstones of slaughtered Covenanters in the old churchyards bear epitaphs in vigorous rhyme. The little kirks of the period are of an architectural austerity and simplicity now better appreciated than they once were. There is a good example at Mochrum, with outside stairs and a carved oak pulpit surmounted by a sounding-board. The only ornament permitted was in the 'laird's loft', the gallery from which the local bigwig might listen to the sermon.

The later medieval castles of Scotland in many ways represent the most individual and characteristic examples of native architecture. Galloway has Mochrum and the cottage-size castle of Craigcaffie. Outstanding among several Dumfriesshire castles is Amisfield Tower, in which the tradition may be seen at its fullest flowering in the south, austerity

On the 7th-century Runic cross in Ruthwell Church is carved the oldest poem of the English language

enriched both in appearance and comfort by the skilful projecting of upper chambers. Dumfriesshire also has in Drumlanrig a splendid late 17th-century anachronistic castle.

Beasts and Flowers

Galloway once had its own breed of sheep, and its native ponies were famous for their hardiness and mettle. The sheep have long been replaced by the coarser-woolled blackface breed. But Galloway cattle are still much to the fore, a popular beef breed, and the 'beltie', black with a clean white cummerbund round the middle, is pleasing to see.

Moorland and shore birds are to be seen in rich variety – even, on occasion, the golden eagle. There are great stretches of grouse-moor, and Wigtownshire has some of the best partridge-shooting in Britain. There is good salmon and trout fishing in the many rivers, burns and lochs.

The mild climate of the southwest makes for a lush vegetation. It is a little surprising to see palm trees among the cabbages in cottage gardens on the Mull of Galloway. Here at Logan is a famous botanic garden with many unusual exotic and semi-tropical trees, plants and shrubs.

Men and Books

Born near Ayr and dying in Dumfries, making friends and writing poems in Galloway, Robert Burns belongs to the southwest. His first and last homes are pilgrim places. Thomas Carlyle's birthplace at Ecclefechan in Dumfriesshire, an attractive white house built by his master-mason family, is in the keeping of the National Trust for Scotland. *Guy Mannering*, one of Scott's best novels, is set in Galloway, and the cave of his smuggler villain, Dirk Hatteraick, may be found (not without difficulty) below the cliffs at Ravenshall. Robert Louis Stevenson set *The Master of Ballantrae* in Galloway.

Paul Jones, father of the U.S. Navy, was born in the gamekeeper's cottage at Arbigland, near Kirkbean. Many Galloway names are to be found in the Arctic, bequeathed by two early explorers, Sir John and James Ross, whose family home of Balsarroch deserved preservation both for its association and its architecture. Galloway also provided a background for the 'kailyaird' novelist, S. R. Crockett, for some

of John Buchan's stories and for Dorothy Sayers' thriller, *Five Red Herrings*. Langholm is the Dumfriesshire birthplace of the 20th-century poet, Hugh MacDiarmid.

The three Faed brothers from Gatehouse were Victorian artists whose remarkable virtuosity merits them some return to favour. More recently, its charming old houses and water-girt setting have made Kirkcudbright the home of many artists.

It is said that Queen Victoria once asked Carlyle what he thought was the most beautiful scenery in Scotland, to which he replied, 'The road from Gatehouse to Creetown.' She tried again, hoping he would mention her own Deeside: what did he think was the second most beautiful scenery? 'The road from Creetown to Gatehouse,' he told her firmly.

Although many people share Carlyle's feelings for the scenery of the southwest, it still remains a countryside largely unspoiled and uncluttered, where solitude – especially in the Galloway hills – is freely to be found.

GAZETTEER

Ae, Dumf   11H3
Boasting one of the shortest place names in any gazetteer. Ae was created by the Forestry Commission in 1947 for workers in their vast forests: it has its own school, shop, post office and community hall. Important cultivation experiments have been conducted and much wildlife may be seen from the marked walks.

Annan, Dumf   11I2
A 12th-c de Brus (Bruce) stronghold from whose motte the market town developed at the mouth of the River Annan. It was formerly dependent on haaf-net, stake-net and leister (salmon-spear) fishing and building tea-clippers; now shrimps are canned and there are other new industries. Thomas Carlyle taught at Annan Academy, the 'Hinterschlag Gymnasium' of *Sartor Resartus*.

Beattock, Dumf   11I3
Now a substantial village. Familiar to winter travellers for its periodically snow- and ice-bound condition as the summit (1,029ft) of the A74 main road from Scotland to the industrial NW of England. *See also* **Elvanfoot**, Strathclyde.

Caerlaverock, Dumf   11I2
Famous for its castle (13th-c) and National Nature Reserve (1,500 acres). The castle (AM) is triangular with round towers, within a double moat and heavy 15th-c machicolation; the fine 17th-c buildings were added when it became a residence rather than a fortress. The Nature Reserve between the River Nith and Lochar Water, on the Solway Firth, consists of a large area of merse (saltmarsh) and foreshore which attracts up to 10,000 barnacle, pink-footed and greylag geese, ducks and waders in late autumn and winter. It has the most northerly colony of natterjack toads (and the visitor should be warned that these are so protected that it is an offence even to pick one up). There is no admission to the merse sanctuary, towards the E.

Cairnryan, Wig   10E2
Formerly a fishing village on Loch Ryan which became an important port in World War II: part of the Mulberry Harbour used in the D-Day invasion was made here and the area is still busy with private enterprise.

Canonbie, Dumf   11J2
An angling village on a bend of the River Esk. Hollows Tower, 2m N, recalls Johnnie Armstrong, the 16th-c Border raider, feared for his exploits as far away as Newcastle.

Carsphairn, Kirk   10G3
The A713, running SE from **Ayr** (Strathclyde) to **New Galloway** and **Castle Douglas,** here reaches 800ft above sea level, making the village an excellent centre for walking. Within a radius of 6m the highest points are Corserine (2,669ft) SW and Cairnsmore (2,613ft) NE.

Castle Douglas, Kirk   11H2
A busy little town on Carlingwark Loch, a haunt of wild fowl. 1m W are **Threave Gardens**. On an island in the River Dee, 2m W, are the grim ruins of Threave Castle, once a stronghold of the Douglas family.

Castle Kennedy, Wig   10E2
3m E of **Stranraer** between the White and Black Lochs, the castle was destroyed by fire in 1716. Lochinch Castle, built 1867 to replace it, is the home of the Earl of Stair (castle not open). The grounds, famous for rhododendrons, rare shrubs and azaleas, and pinetum, are open April–Sept.

Dalbeattie, Kirk   11H2
The town, on the Urr Water, owes its origin (1780) to its impressive granite quarries. 2½m NNW is the notable Mote of Urr, an 80ft mound surrounded by a fosse. 1m W is the ruined castle of *Buittle* or Botel, once the home of John de Baliol, founder of Balliol College, **Oxford**, in the 13th c.

Dumfries: Devorgilla's Bridge dates from 1426 and was named after Lady Devorgilla of Sweetheart Abbey near by

Devil's Beef Tub, Dumf   11I4
6m N of **Moffat**, on the A701. A deep corrie at the head of Annandale used by cattle raiders to hide their animals; and by Scott in *Redgauntlet*. A monument near the summit states that 'Near the head of this burn on 1 February 1831, James McGeorge, Guard, and John Goodfellow, Driver, of the Dumfries to Edinburgh mail lost their lives in the snow after carrying the bags thus far. Erected 1931.'

Dumfries, Dumf   11H2
Historic town, the centre of a road network at the lowest crossing of the River Nith, which here ripples over a weir. The town was made a royal burgh by William the Lion and its oldest existing charter was granted by Robert II in 1395. Robert Burns ended life here (1796) in a house, now a museum, in Burns Street, and was buried at St Michael's. The museum, recently refurbished has a camera obscura and good exhibits. 1½m N are the ruins of *Lincluden Abbey* (AM), founded as a convent in the 12th c.

Dundrennan Abbey,* Kirk   11H1
Founded for the Cistercian Order by David I and Fergus, Lord of Galloway, in 1142. The Abbey (AM), now in ruins, has a late 13th-c chapter house, transept and cloisters, with many fine monuments. Mary Queen of Scots spent her last night in Scotland here on 15 May 1568, before she fled across the Solway Firth to England and captivity.

Ecclefechan, Dumf   11I2
The arched house (NTS) in which Thomas Carlyle was born (1795) contains a collection of manuscript letters, furniture from his Chelsea house and personal relics. Open Easter–Oct. He was buried in the churchyard (1881).

Eskdalemuir, Dumf   11I3
12m up the Esk from **Langholm**. Near the church, a footbridge crosses to the 2nd-c Roman fort of Raeburnfoot and up to Craik Cross (1,481ft) the Roman road leading to Trimontium (Newstead) at **Melrose** (Borders). In striking contrast, 3½m N of the church is Eskdalemuir Observatory which makes geomagnetic and meteorological observations and is the most important seismological station in Britain:

the Atomic Energy Authority also has a 'listening post' to detect nuclear explosions. A small Buddhist community has a temple at Eskdalemuir.

Gatehouse of Fleet, Kirk   10G2
This small village, 2m from the head of a narrow bay, is a good centre for exploring the Fleet Water and a number of castles in the neighbourhood. Of these, *Cardoness Castle*, 1m SW, has a good 15th-c tower.

Glenluce, Wig   10F2
The beautifully sited ruins of Glenluce Abbey (AM) (founded 1192) on the E bank of the Water of Luce consist of the S aisle and transept, with the 1470 chapter house. Michael Scott, the 13th-c wizard, is said to have lured the plague then raging to the Abbey and locked it in a vault. Castle of Park, a fine castellated mansion, was built in 1590 by the last Abbot's son. 2m NE stands *Carscreugh Castle* built 1680 by Sir John Dalrymple, 1st Lord Stair and President of the Court of Session, whose daughter Janet was the inspiration for Sir Walter Scott's tragic heroine Lucy Ashton in *The Bride of Lammermoor*.

Gretna Green, Dumf   11J2
The small River Sark is the border between Scotland and England and Gretna Green thus became famous for runaway couples who could be married there under 18th-c Scots law by a declaration before witnesses. Marriages were held at the Sark Toll Bridge (King's Head Inn) until 1826 but then moved to the Gretna Green Smithy. Pressure, particularly from the Church, was put on Parliament which led to an act passed in 1940 resulting in 'anvil weddings' being made illegal. Then the English Act of 1969, lowering the age of marriage without parental consent from 21 to 18, ended the demand at Gretna, although it remains a popular tourist attraction and many couples still wed there.

Grey Mare's Tail, Dumf   11I4
A dramatic 200ft waterfall of the Tail Burn as it drops from Loch Skene into Moffat Water, off the A708 10m NE from **Moffat**. Rare wild goats may be seen on the hills. Some 2,500 acres owned by NTS include White Coomb (2,695ft).

Kirkbean, Kirk   11H2
Birthplace of John Paul Jones (1747–92), regarded as a founder of the U.S. Navy. At one time also he was commissioned by Catherine the Great as a Russian Admiral. A memorial font was presented to the church by the U.S. Navy in 1945.

Kirkcudbright, Kirk   10G1
An old royal burgh and former county town, now Stewartry District headquarters, has good architecture and streets unchanged since the 18th c. The imposing MacLellan's Castle (AM), built 1582, dominates the harbour. The Stewartry Museum has fine local antiquities, and 18th-c Broughton House, later home of the artist E. A. Hornel, houses much of his work. At *Tongland Abbey*, 1m N, the abbot, John Damian, a charlatan and alchemist, tried to become a Scottish Icarus by flying from the ramparts of **Stirling** Castle (Central) in front of James IV.

Langholm, Dumf   11J3
Noted since 1832 for its tweed-mills. It has retained some of its cobbled streets. Further up Eskdale (the river has fine angling) at a cottage (the foundations only now visible) on Meggat Water Thomas Telford (1757–1834), the great road-and bridge-builder, was born and served apprenticeship. A

stirring event is the Common Riding, held on the last Friday of July since 1759 (originally on foot, but since 1816 on horseback).

Lochmaben, ★ Dumf   11I3
This ancient former royal burgh was the centre of Bruce family power from 1200 and Robert the Bruce is said to have been born (1274) in the ancient castle or possibly in the large motte. The existing castle (AM) was built 1503–6 but fell into decay after the Catholic rising in 1588. The Castle Loch is the only fresh water in Scotland, possibly in Britain, containing vendace (a small delicate fish, *Coregonus albula*), netted in August and said to have been introduced by Mary Queen of Scots.

Moffat, Dumf   11I3
Chalybeate springs were found in 1633 and Moffat soon became a noted spa: the Baths House (1827) remains. An interesting new museum in a bakehouse has important local items and mementoes of Air Chief Marshall Lord Dowding who was born in the town. *See also* **Devil's Beef Tub**.

Moniaive, Dumf   11H3
Three rivers and three roads meet in this attractive village, associated with Annie Laurie (immortalized by the song), whose family owned Maxwelton House, 3m SE. After her marriage, she lived in Craigdarroch, 2½m W, an 18th-c Adam house with attractive gardens, where she died.

New Galloway, Kirk   10G2
Golfing and angling village at N end of Loch Ken, through which flows the River Dee. In the churchyard at *Kells*, ½m N, are curious carvings and inscriptions. NW is Glenlee hydro-electric power station; SW are *Clatteringshaws Reservoir* and *Cairn Edward Forest*.

Newton Stewart, Wig   10F2
Attractive golfing, fishing and touring centre on the River Cree. Opposite is the village of *Minnigaff*, with ruined church and carved tombstones. 4m S is Wigtown Bay. From *Bargrennan*, 7m N, a township for foresters working in Glen Trool National Forest Park, a road leads to Loch Trool, high in the hills with fine views. A cairn near the E end commemorates the victory over the English by Robert the Bruce in 1307.

Port Logan, Wig   10E1
Small fishing-village and resort on the Rhinns of Galloway, about 7m from the *Mull of Galloway* with its lighthouse and magnificent views. In the village is a sea-water pond noted for its tame fish; and the sub-tropical gardens of *Logan House*★, 2m N, are open to visitors April–Sept.

Portpatrick, Wig   10E1
Another resort on the Rhinns of Galloway, which, prior to the development of **Stranraer**, was the port for mail-boats to N. Ireland. In the bay at the foot of the cliff are the remains of the harbour built in 1821.

Rockcliffe, Kirk   11H2
The Mote of Mark (NTS), an ancient hill fort occupied about 450–700 covering some 20 acres, yielded many treasures on excavation – moulds for interlace-decorated brooches, Frankish and sub-Roman pottery and Mediterranean ware. *Rough Island* (NTS), just offshore, is a bird sanctuary: visiting is discouraged during the May–June nesting season. Muckle Lands and Jubilee Path, rough coastline between Rockcliffe and *Kippford*, also belong to NTS.

Ruthwell,* Dumf 11I2
The church contains, in an apse specially built for it, one of the two most celebrated runic crosses of Anglo-Saxon times (the other is at **Bewcastle** in Cumbria). It stands 18ft high and probably dates from the 8th c. (*See* page 345.)

Sanquhar, Dumf 11H4
Historic little town with memories of Covenanters who renounced allegiance to Charles II in 1680 and, similarly, objected to the 'Usurpation of James VII' in 1685. Note characteristic 18th-c Tolbooth (a museum) and Britain's oldest post office (1783).

Stranraer, Wig 10E2
Situated at the head of Loch Ryan, its harbour is the starting point for the short sea route (39m) to Larne in N. Ireland. In the centre of the town are the ruins of a 15th-c castle.

Sweetheart Abbey,* Dumf 11H2
At *New Abbey* on the A710. So called because Devorgilla (the daughter of Alan, last 'king' of Galloway, and wife of John de Baliol), who founded the Cistercian Abbey (AM) here in the 13th c, ordered that her husband's heart should be buried with her before the High Altar. From the summit of Criffel (1,866ft), SW of the Abbey ruins, magnificent views extend across the Solway Firth to the fells of the Lake District. *See also* **Dumfries**.

Thornhill, Dumf 11H3
Drumlanrig*, the splendid castle home of the Duke of Buccleuch and Queensberry, 3½m NW, was much altered in 1676–89 by Sir William Bruce. It has fine rooms with Grinling Gibbons carved oak panelling, historic portraits and other treasures and a chandelier given by Charles II to the Duke of Monmouth on his marriage to the Countess (later 1st Duchess) of Buccleuch. Castle, grounds and adventure woodland open Easter then May–Aug.

Sweetheart Abbey: founded by Devorgilla, Lady of Galloway, it was built in 1273 of red sandstone

Threave Gardens, Kirk 11H2
1m W of **Castle Douglas**. The estate covers nearly 1,800 acres and is particulaly famous for its daffodils, shrub roses, heaths and alpines. It houses the NTS School of Gardening with a two-year residential course for young people leading to a widely recognized diploma. Threave Wildfowl Refuge on the River Dee, with many species of geese and duck, allows access only in Nov.–March. Threave Castle (AM) on an islet in the River Dee was a Douglas stronghold in the 14th c. It has walls 70ft high and 8ft thick.

Wanlockhead, Dumf 11H4
One of the highest villages in Britain, at the head of the Mennock Pass (1,380ft). Formerly a lead-mining centre, now home of the Museum of the Scottish Lead Mining Industry. Open April–Sept.

Whithorn, Wig 10F1
St Ninian's Priory (AM) dates from the 12th c. Its transept served as parish church as late as 1822. The ruins are approached through an archway known as the Pend. A museum contains a good collection of stone crosses. In 396 Ninian, the first Christian missionary to Scotland, landed at the so-called Isle of Whithorn to the SE, where he built a chapel.

Wigtown, Wig 10F2
Two stone crosses stand in the main street. In the churchyard are the graves of the Wigtown Martyrs, two women Covenanters who, in 1685, were bound to stakes on the shore and left to drown in the rising tide. A small monument marks the site of the crime. 3½m W is the *Torhouse Stone Circle* (AM), a perfect Bronze Age circle about 60ft in diameter consisting of 19 stones.

STRATHCLYDE REGION: THE GLASGOW LOWLANDS

AN INTRODUCTION BY
JACK HOUSE

The population of Scotland stands at more than 5,000,000. Of that number just over 2,000,000 dwell in the Strathclyde Region, which takes in the former counties of Ayr, Lanark, Renfrew, Dunbarton, most of Argyll, a small part of Stirling, and the City of Glasgow, the region's capital.

Why should Glasgow and its environs be so populous? The answer is simple. First of all, the River Clyde. Second, the deposits of coal and iron on its banks. The River Clyde is more than 100 miles long. Its source is a little spring in the Lowther Hills at the extreme south end of the County of Lanark. At its source it is known as the Daer (pronounced 'Dahr') Water, and once it flowed down the Daer Valley to Watermeetings, where it met the Little Clyde Burn and became the Clyde. But now it goes first into the Daer Dam, which provides water for much of the Glasgow Lowlands and is also noted for good fishing. Once you come to the confluence of Watermeetings, the river is known as the Clyde. Famous for salmon and trout, it runs shallow through an area of placid beauty in the English style, with soft hills, famous orchards, fertile farms and good hotels. No one, seeing the Clyde hereabouts, could imagine that on its waters the world's biggest ships have been launched. There are pleasant little villages on its banks, and only the existence of a main trunk road gives any indication that an industrial belt lies ahead. The first signs are at the Falls of Clyde, near the town of Lanark: unless there has been very heavy rain, they look only a shadow of their former selves, because they have been harnessed for a hydro-electric supply.

It is well worth taking the steep road up to Lanark, which keeps its ancient air very well. Here in June is one of the outstanding festivals of Scotland – Lanimer Day. The whole town goes *en fête* for a week, and the climax is 'The Lanimers', when an enormous fancy-dress parade of children goes through the town to the Wallace Monument (Sir William Wallace, Scottish hero, lived in Lanark), and the Lanimer Queen is crowned.

For several miles the Clyde still wanders through delightful orchard country, and then there is a sudden and dramatic change. On the heights above the glen through which the river flows are the industrial towns of Motherwell and Wishaw, and then the former royal burgh of Hamilton. We have come from vegetables and fruit into iron and coal, and although steelworks have replaced the iron, and many of the mines are now derelict, the area is still highly industrialized. But there are still many pleasant patches of countryside and Hamilton itself is full of picturesque little town scenes – to say nothing of the famous mausoleum of the Dukes of Hamilton, set in the grounds of what was once Hamilton Palace. It has one of the most remarkable echo chambers in the world.

The wandering Clyde has been harnessed here to make a loch in the centre of Strathclyde Park and it emerges again by Bothwell, passing the ruins of Bothwell Castle and the birthplace of David Livingstone, and on by Cambuslang, the 'biggest village in Scotland', to Rutherglen, which is now part of Glasgow.

Glasgow

And now the river comes to Glasgow Green, the park where Prince Charles Edward reviewed his Highland Army in 1745. In coming to the Green, the river also comes to Glasgow, the biggest, the oldest, the most maligned and best-liked town in Scotland. Perhaps I should qualify that final superlative by adding that it is best liked by Glaswegians.

Saint Mungo, patron saint of the city, settled in Glasgow in the year 543. But there was a settlement by the Clyde before that, and the place was well known to the Romans, who seldom ventured north of Glasgow because the natives were hostile. The first cathedral in the city was built in 1124. Glasgow University was established in 1451. In the 18th century Daniel Defoe described Glasgow as 'the most beautiful little city in Europe'. In the 20th century John Betjeman described Glasgow as 'the finest Victorian city in the world'.

Despite all this, Glasgow has had a bad reputation among people who have never visited it. It is, in fact, a lively, friendly place. It has historical buildings, 72 parks (one of them, Queen's, has more flowers in it than the five Royal Parks of Paris put together), nine theatres, many cinemas, more than 1,000 pubs, good restaurants and tea rooms, five senior football clubs and the Gorbals. This famous former slum has been 'modernized', and there are critics who feel that it has now lost its identity.

Glasgow is known to its inhabitants as 'a great place to get out of'. This somewhat double-edged statement really means that Glasgow is especially suitable as a tourist centre. Within one hour, by road or rail, you can be in the Highlands, or in Burns Country, or on the bonny, bonny banks of Loch Lomond, or on the breathtaking Firth of Clyde, or in Stirling, where Robert the Bruce defeated the English Army at the battle of Bannockburn in 1314. Within an hour you can even be in Edinburgh, the capital of Scotland – but you should be warned that Glaswegians consider Edinburgh rather a foreign place. Edinburghers think that Glaswegians are jealous. Glasgow's reply is that 'Edinburgh is the Capital, but Glasgow has the capital!'

The Clyde flows through Glasgow and the local saying is, 'Glasgow made the Clyde, and the Clyde made Glasgow.' But shipping has declined on the

The fine building of Glasgow's School of Art, built 1897–1909, is the work of Charles Rennie Mackintosh

Clyde, as has shipbuilding in the upper reaches. An area of the docks has been made into a great exhibition centre. John Brown's shipyard, from which the famous *Queen* liners were launched, no longer builds ships and is now devoted to heavy engineering.

One of the best ways to see the Firth of Clyde is to sail down the river from Anderston Quay, in the centre of Glasgow. You can voyage in the *Waverley*, the oldest sea-going paddle steamer in the world. As the steamer reaches Renfrew Ferry, you sail out of Glasgow and see Renfrewshire to the south and Dunbartonshire to the north. From this point on it is true to say that the east is in the Lowlands, while the west is in the Highlands. This is the case all the way down the Firth of Clyde – and some parts of the Highlands are very much lower than the Lowlands!

Renfrewshire and Dunbartonshire

Old Renfrewshire is an agricultural area with a number of industrial towns. Its capital is the former royal burgh of Renfrew, and one of the titles of the Prince of Wales is Baron Renfrew. The main town is Paisley, on the banks of the River Cart, a tributary of the Clyde. It is famous for its shawls, thread, marmalade and poets. Renfrewshire has its own group of shipbuilding yards at Port Glasgow and Greenock. Port Glasgow was built by the city of Glasgow in the 17th century to be its harbour; but the deepening of

the Clyde changed all the plans. From Port Glasgow in 1812 the *Comet*, the first practical steamship in Europe, was launched by Henry Bell. Some 150 years later a replica of the *Comet* was built and sailed on the river. Greenock has the oldest shipbuilding yard in the world, Scott's, started in 1771. From Gourock down the coast to Wemyss Bay, Renfrewshire is residential and is made for holidays.

In the distance to the north you can see Ben Lomond from the deck of the steamer; but the nearer scene is very industrial indeed, with yards, factories, oil-depots, and the world's biggest grain-distillery. The distillery is at Dumbarton, just beside Dumbarton Rock (resembling Gibraltar in miniature).

From Dumbarton onwards it is a succession of holiday places, with Helensburgh, Rhu and Garelochhead outstanding. From Dumbarton or Helensburgh it is a mere step to Loch Lomond, the largest stretch of inland water in Britain. Loch Lomond is so near to salt water that geologists consider it a freak. At Tarbet, for example, it is only a mile from Arrochar, on the sea fiord of Loch Long. When a Viking leader named Magnus sailed up Loch Long, he made his men pull the galleys across that mile and refloated them on Loch Lomond, so that he could burn and pillage the loch-side villages.

Loch Lomond is beautiful, but suffers terribly from tourist traffic. It is best seen in spring or autumn. A favourite local conundrum is, 'What piece of water in Scotland surrounds a foot?' The answer is, 'Loch Lomond, because it has 12 inches in it.' Inch is the Scottish word for island, and at the south of Loch Lomond, there is a group of islands with such names as Inchmurrin, Inchcailloch, Inchtavannach and Inchlonaig. There are 30 islands in Loch Lomond.

The west and south of the loch are in Strathclyde Region, while Ben Lomond and the east of the loch are in Central Region. Strathclyde stretches up Scotland to the north and west and this part of the Region is dealt with on pages 357–63.

Ayrshire

The *Waverley* turns south down the Firth of Clyde with the Renfrewshire part of Strathclyde on the left gradually merging with the Ayrshire area of the Region. Along the shore there is an odd mixture of holiday resorts, marinas, industrial activity and a NATO base. Behind them is mainly countryside, dotted with small industries. Wemyss Bay pier shows that we are moving into old Ayrshire, once Scotland's Klondyke, with its riches of coal and iron ore.

Much of the former Klondyke has been mined out and this part of Strathclyde is more famous for its agriculture, its Ayrshire cattle and Dunlop cheese, which is appropriate because we are now in the country of the farmer poet, Robert Burns. Some cynics say that one of the biggest industries in this part of Strathclyde is Robert Burns. Tourists come from all over the world to follow the Burns Heritage Trail, which includes the cottage at Alloway where he was born, the Brig o' Doon where Tam o' Shanter was pursued by Cutty Sark, and farms, villages and small towns where he lived.

There are so many golf-courses on the seaside that it's known as the Golf Coast, until the hills start rising in the background and the beaches are replaced by cliffs and there are castles instead of luxury hotels. The scenery becomes steadily grander at the foot of the Strathclyde Region and at Loch Doon look towards the Dumfries and Galloway Region.

GAZETTEER

Alloway *see* **Ayr** and **Kirkoswald**

Antonine Wall *see* **Roman Wall**

Ardlui, Dunb   **10F7**
N end of **Loch Lomond** with Ben Vorlich (3,092ft) SW.

Ardrossan, Ayr   **10F5**
Busy port, 1m from popular seaside resort of *Saltcoats*, car ferry to **Brodick**, on **Arran**. Fine views of the Firth of Clyde, Arran and *Ailsa Crag* from 12th-c castle ruins on hill to E.

Arrochar, Dunb   **10F7**
Busy centre at head of Loch Long 2m W of **Loch Lomond**. The A83 passes through *Glen Croe* and the Argyll Forest Park amid wonderful mountain scenery. Arboretum at *Kilmun*.

Ayr,* Ayr   **10F4**
Seaport and former county town of great historic interest, and centre of Burns Country. Wallace Tower in the High

Street (1834) replaces an earlier building. Note the 'Twa Brigs' of Burns: the Auld Brig, closed to traffic, dates from the end of the 15th c; the New Brig (1788) was swept away in 1877 and rebuilt. At *Alloway*, a suburb 2m S, the 'auld clay biggin' in which Burns was born (1759) is now a museum. The Grecian monument to the poet near by contains Thom's figures of Tam o' Shanter and Souter Johnnie. *See also* **Kirkoswald**.

Ballantrae, Ayr   **10E3**
Fishing village, with golf-links; views across the North Channel to Kintyre and Ireland.

Balloch, Dunb   **10F6**
A popular resort on **Loch Lomond**. Here the River Leven flows from the loch into the Clyde.

Blantyre, Lanark   **10G5**
Birthplace of David Livingstone (1813) in Shuttle Row, is now kept as a memorial to the explorer and is a museum. 2m N are remains of a 13th-c priory.

Bothwell, Lanark   10G5
The collegiate church, partly 14th-c, is noted for its pointed barrel vault, and contains monuments to the Douglas family. The pride of the town is the impressive Douglas stronghold, *Bothwell Castle*★ (AM), to the NW, whose great tower (begun in 13th c) took 36 years to complete.

Bowling, Dunb   10F6
Western terminus of the 38m Forth and Clyde Canal, built by Smeaton in 1790. Symington's *Charlotte Dundas*, the first working steamboat, was launched here in 1802; and, in 1812, Bell's *Comet*, first of the Clyde passenger steamers.

Carfin, Lanark   11H5
A mining village 1½m NE of **Motherwell**, where a grotto, dedicated to St Thérèse of Lisieux in 1922, attracts thousands of pilgrims every year.

Crawford, Lanark   11H4
This Clydesdale village is a good centre for the Lowland hill-country. Tower Lindsay is all that remains of a once important castle.

Crookston Castle *see* **Paisley**

Crossford, Lanark   11H5
A little village set among orchards, near the junction of the Nethan with the Clyde. 1m SW is the interesting and well-preserved 16th-c *Craignethan Castle* (AM), the 'Tillietudlem Castle' of Scott's *Old Mortality*.

Crossraguel Abbey *see* **Kirkoswald**

Culzean Castle *see* **Turnberry**

Cumbernauld, Dunb   11H6
One of the most interesting of Britain's New Towns, laid out in 1956 along a ridge W of the old village, planned to have local industries with a population of 70,000 but had not reached 50,000 by 1984.

Cumnock, Ayr   10G4
Mining town on the Lugar Water, with a good 18th-c mercat cross. James Keir Hardie, founder of the Independent Labour Party, lived here for many years, and his bust stands in front of the Town Hall. In the churchyard of the neighbouring town of *Auchinleck* is the grave of Dr Johnson's biographer, James Boswell. The inventor William Murdoch (1754–1839), was born in the same parish.

Darvel, Ayr   10G5
In the Irvine valley near Loudoun Hill and birthplace of Sir Alexander Fleming (1881–1955), pioneer of penicillin.

Douglas, Lanark   11H4
The restored chancel of St Bride's Church contains the tomb of the Earl of Angus (d.1514), known as 'Bell-the-Cat', and has Douglas tombs, and early French stained glass. All that remains of Douglas Castle is the chapel and porch. Note the two 17th-c towers in the town; one containing a clock presented by Mary Queen of Scots; the other commemorating the Cameronian Regiment.

Dumbarton, Dunb   10F6
Busy yacht-building and whisky-distilling town, dominated by the 250ft rock on which stands the castle (AM), with panoramic views.★ Mary Queen of Scots sailed hence for France in 1548; she gave the town a sundial.

Eaglesham, Renf   10G5
Interesting 18th-c village built by an Earl of Eglinton. The B764 **Kilmarnock** road climbs nearly 1,000ft to the SW, with good views of the surrounding hills. Rudolf Hess landed near here in 1941 after his flight from Germany.

East Kilbride, Lanark   10G5
This New Town, with lavish community facilities, was designed eventually to accommodate 90,000 people with local employment: by 1984 there were 71,220. The first meeting of Scottish Quakers took place here in 1653. 1m N is the restored 16th-c *Mains Castle*.

Elvanfoot, Lanark   11H4
In a setting of mountains and streams, the village is the starting point of two passes, Dalveen and Mennock, which cross the Lowther Hills to the SW. Both roads ascend to over 1,000ft; another SE passes **Beattock** Summit (Dumf).

Garelochhead, Dunb   10F6
Well-known resort and yachting centre. A stiff climb takes the road from sea level to *Whistlefield*, at the foot of Beinn Chaorach (2,338ft), with extensive views of both Loch Long and Loch Goil.

Gartocharn, Dunb   10F6
A quiet village from which to explore the SE of **Loch Lomond** and its wooded islands. NW is *Ross Priory* in lovely parkland.

Glasgow,★ Lanark   10G6
'Glasgow made the Clyde and the Clyde made Glasgow'; and the consequent generations of shipbuilders, merchants and manufacturers made the handsome streets and squares of 18th–19th-c houses – but were also responsible for the Gorbals. Indeed, though its cathedral dates from the 12th c, Glasgow is mainly a product of the past 200 years, when the dredging of the Clyde improved navigation. Prior to this, the city covered only a small area at the E end of the present vast conurbation, and it is here that the most ancient buildings are to be found. The Cathedral★ is the finest unmutilated Gothic church in Scotland: note particularly the 12th-c crypt and 13th-c choir and tower. The oldest house in Glasgow is near-by Provand's Lordship (1471), built as a hospital but now a museum. (*See also* **Provan Hall**.) Note the Merchants' Hall, Crown and Tron steeples, all of the 16th c. The University, founded in 1451, is partly housed in Victorian Gothic buildings in Kelvingrove Park, designed by Sir George Gilbert Scott. Near by are the important art gallery and museum with a comprehensive collection of Dutch, French and Scottish paintings and an interesting reconstruction of the home of Charles Rennie Mackintosh, the Art Nouveau architect (*see also* page 351). The Mitchell Library, a modern building in North Street, is the largest reference library in Scotland, with an important collection of Burnsiana. In the grounds of Pollok House in SW suburbs, the fine William Adam house with its own notable paintings, is the new museum/gallery opened in 1983 to house the huge Burrell Collection which languished mostly in storage for 40 years.

Gourock, Renf   10F6
A well-known resort and yachting centre on the great bend of the Clyde, with far-spreading views of Cowal, Loch Long and the Argyll Hills. There is a car ferry to **Dunoon**, and trips to all parts of the Firth and the **Kyles of Bute**. 2½m SW, near the Cloch Lighthouse, the ruins of *Levan Castle* stand among woods.

Greenock, Renf   10F6

Important industrial and shipbuilding town on the Clyde. On the waterfront near the W Pier is the old West Kirk (1591), the first to be built after the Reformation, and removed hither from its original site. James Watt (1736–1819), the famous engineer, was born here, and Chantrey's statue of him now stands in the Watt Library and Institute.

Hamilton, Lanark   10G5

Centre of important mining district. Owing to subsidence, Hamilton Palace had to be demolished, but the mausoleum still stands in Low Parks. Most interesting building in the town is the octagonal parish church, built by William Adam in 1732, in front of which stands the Celtic Netherton Cross. Good museum with extensive section on transport. To the S are the ruins of *Cadzow Castle*, with its unique herd of wild, white cattle. On the opposite side of the River Avon is Chatelherault Lodge, designed by William Adam. Barncluith with its Dutch gardens, constructed on a series of terraces overlooking the Avon, was planned in 1583.

Helensburgh, Dunb   10F6

Holiday and residential resort at mouth of the Gare Loch, with views across the Clyde to the Renfrew Hills. J. Logie Baird, the television inventor, was born here, and Henry Bell was Provost at the time when he launched the *Comet* (*see* **Bowling**), the fly-wheel of which is preserved in Hermitage Park. Hill House, the Charles Rennie Mackintosh masterpiece (*see also* **Glasgow**) was handed over to the NTS in 1982. Open April–Oct.

Irvine, Ayr   10F5

One of the oldest former royal burghs of Scotland, and at one time the port for **Glasgow**. Now Scotland's newest New Town (designated 1966) expected to double its 54,000 population (1984), it is Britain's only 'New Town by the sea'. The ruined *Seagate Castle* dates from the 14th c.

Kilmacolm, Renf   10F6

Small inland residential and golfing resort. 2m SE are the ruined church and holy well of St Fillan and the rock on which he is said to have sat while he was baptizing children.

Kilmarnock, Ayr   10F5

A busy manufacturing town. In Kay Park the Burns Museum contains many important manuscripts of the poet. The first edition of his poems was published here in 1786.

Kilwinning, Ayr   10F5

By tradition the cradle of Freemasonry in Scotland. A curious local festival is celebrated annually on the first Saturday of July, when the Kilwinning Archers shoot at the 'papingo' or popinjay suspended from the steeple of the ruined 12th-c abbey (see Scott's *Old Mortality*).

Kirkintilloch, Dunb   10G6

Originally known as Caerpentulach, one of the forts on the **Roman Wall**.

Kirkoswald, Ayr   10F3

Here Robert Burns attended the school, and his characters, Tam o' Shanter and Souter Johnnie (whose real names were Douglas Graham and John Davidson), are buried in the churchyard. Davidson's cottage (NTS) is open April–Sept. *See also* **Ayr**. 2m E is *Crossraguel Abbey* (founded 13th c), with an imposing gatehouse, a dovecot, and several buildings in a good state of preservation (AM). Open summer months.

Lanark, Lanark   11H5

The parish church has a conspicuous tower with a statue of Wallace over the doorway. The walls of the 12th-c church of St Kentigern can still be seen. S of the town are the textile mills of *New Lanark*, the model town founded by the great socialist reformer Robert Owen in 1784. Beyond are the Cora Linn Falls, 90ft high, and the remains of *Corehouse Castle*.

Largs, Ayr   10E5

Attractive seaside resort, with fine beach and lovely views across to **Bute**. Skelmorlie Aisle, with its painted roof, is all that remains of the old parish church of St Columba; it was

Loch Lomond: Scotland's largest loch. The famous song was written by a follower of Prince Charles Edward

converted into a mausoleum in 1636. Near by a mound covers remains, perhaps of Norwegians killed in battle (1263). *See also* **The Cumbraes.**

Leadhills, Lanark   11H4
The height of this attractive village, 1,350ft, is exceeded only by that of neighbouring *Wanlockhead* (1,380ft). These are the two highest villages in Scotland. Now a walking resort, the district was until recently noted for its lead, though in the 12th c there was also extensive gold and silver mining. Allan Ramsay, the poet, in 1741 gave the village Britain's first circulating library, with his own valuable collection.

Loch Lomond, ✶✶ Dunb   10F6
The 'Queen of Scottish Lochs' is the largest in Britain: 24m long, 5m at its widest point. At the S end are a number of islands, on one of which, *Inchmurrin,* stands ruined *Lennox Castle.* The Nature Conservancy Council which owns *Inchcailloch* as part of the National Nature Reserve (five islands and some mainland) has a well-marked nature trail and guide for geologists and prehistorians. On the A82 is a wildlife park open April–Oct. A fine road runs the whole

length of the W shore, beneath a range of mountains over 2,000ft high; across the loch, Ben Lomond towers to a height of 3,192ft (*see also* **Balloch, Luss** and **Tarbet**).

Luss, Dunb   10F6/7
Pretty village, facing the beautiful islands of **Loch Lomond**. Coleridge, Wordsworth and his sister stayed here in 1803.

Mauchline, Ayr   10G4
Many associations with Robert Burns. Here, in the house of Gavin Hamilton, still standing, he married Jean Armour. 'Poosie Nansie's', where the 'Jolly Beggars' met, though much altered, is still an inn; the churchyard was the scene of the 'Holy Fair'; and 'Holy Willie' was an Elder of the Kirk.

Maybole, Ayr   10F4
The former 'capital' of Carrick, the southernmost division of Ayrshire. The Castle*, the home of the Kennedies of the Cassillis and Ailsa family, is one of the strongest and finest of its class. The roofless collegiate church dates from 15th c.

Motherwell, Lanark   10G5
Famous for its coal, steel and engineering. Here, in 1871, David Colville founded the Dalzell Works. To the N is the ancient tower of *Jerviston House*, and SE 17th-c *Dalzell House* incorporates a much older tower.

Paisley, Renf   10F5
Once famous for its shawls (see display in local museum), it is now the biggest thread-producing centre in the world. The parish church, largely restored in the 15th c, was once the nave of a great Cluniac abbey, part of which, the Place of Paisley, has been restored as a War Memorial. 2m S are the Braes of Gleniffer, and 3m E 14th-c *Crookston Castle*.

Port Glasgow, Renf   10F6
The main port for **Glasgow** until the 18th-c dredging of the Clyde. *Newark Castle* (AM), with its courtyard, hall and stepped gables, is a fine example of 16th-c building.

Prestwick, Ayr   10F4
Possibly best known for its international airport. In World War II it became the main base for vital trans-Atlantic military and civilian traffic. Prestwick has been a Mecca for golfers since the first British Open championship was held here in 1860, but golf had been played on its links since the 16th c: it now has three courses.

Provan Hall,* Lanark   10G6
4m E of **Glasgow** in Auchinlea Park on the B806. Probably the most perfect pre-Reformation mansion (NTS) in Scotland, standing in acres of woodland.

Renfrew   10G6
Industrial and shipbuilding centre, with a tunnel under the Clyde to *Yoker*. **Glasgow** airport lies S of the town, off the **Paisley** road.

Roman Wall   10F6/G6/11H6
Usually known as the Antonine Wall (or as Graham's or Grime's Dyke), this was constructed in AD 140 as the N frontier of Roman Britain – a function it fulfilled for less than half a century. Consisting of a turf rampart with a ditch in front and a military road behind, it spanned the waist of Scotland from **Bowling** on the Clyde to **Bo'ness** (Central) on the Forth, linking a line of forts built by Agricola 60 years earlier. Little of it remains today. The best-preserved forts are **Kirkintilloch** and *Rough Castle* near **Falkirk** (Central); and sections of the wall can be seen at *Callendar House* and NW and NE of *Bearsden*.

Rosneath, Dunb   10F6
Resort and yachting centre on Gare Loch, with the quiet waterside villages of *Kilcreggan* and *Cove* near by. N of the latter, built over the dungeons of an old tower, is *Knockderry Castle*, the 'Knock Dunder' of Scott's *Heart of Midlothian*.

Symington, Ayr   10F4
An attractive village with a Norman church founded in 1163. Also good churches near by in *Culter*, 2m E, and *Libberton*, 4m N.

Tarbet, Dunb   10F7
A busy road junction with a pier on the W shore of **Loch Lomond**, and only 1½m from **Arrochar** on Loch Long. Some 4m N is the power station of the Loch Sloy hydro-electric scheme.

Troon, Ayr   10F4
Holiday and residential resort, with good sands and well-known golf-courses. *Lady Isle*, 3m offshore in the Firth of Clyde, is now a bird sanctuary.

Turnberry, Ayr   10F3
Robert the Bruce spent his childhood in the ancient Turnberry Castle and returned there after his self-exile to start his liberation campaign culminating at **Bannockburn** (Central) in 1314. But better known now for its great hotel and two golf-courses, turned into airfields in World Wars I and II but restored to host the Open championship in 1977. 2m NE is *Culzean Castle* (NTS) built by Robert Adam on a wooded cliff, with a remarkable oval staircase and round drawing room; fine farm buildings also. Open April–Oct. The 560 acres of grounds became, in 1970, Scotland's first country park. Open all year.

STRATHCLYDE REGION: ARGYLL, BUTE AND ARRAN

AN INTRODUCTION BY
ANGUS MacVICAR

When God had finished making Britain, some fragments of earth and stone were left in His ample apron. With a smile He flicked them out, and they fell into the western sea to form Argyll and Bute. So runs an old Gaelic legend.

A more modern legend has it that the coastlines of the district stretch for 3,000 miles, approximately the distance between Glasgow and New York. This sounds less surprising when you consider that the area includes about 100 islands, ranging in extent from giants like Mull, Islay, Jura and Arran to tiny skerries like Glunemore, off Sanda, and Pladda with its lighthouse in the Firth of Clyde. It comes even more into perspective when you discover that by air the journey from Glasgow to Campbeltown is one of only 60 miles, while by road – a magic road cavorting through mountains and around blue sea-lochs – it is double that distance: 134 miles, to be exact.

Legend and statistics, however, supply no more than the background to a picture of land and sea inextricably mingled – a picture encompassing bleak moorlands in North Lorn and lush green pastures in Kintyre; bare, sand-blown *machars* in western Islay and sheltered glens in Arran pink with rhododendrons; limpid Loch Awe, south of Dalmally, fringed with woods of pastel green; sombre pagan stones at Dunadd in mid-Argyll and a host of bright and hospitable little towns – Dunoon, Campbeltown and Oban on the mainland, Rothesay in Bute, Brodick in Arran, Port Ellen in Islay, Tobermory in Mull. But the heights of Bidean nam Bian in Glencoe to the north and a small strip of the old county of Argyll now fall in Highland Region.

But everywhere – in this district of 2,000,000 acres, which supports only 68,834 people but some 900,000 sheep and cattle – you are aware of the sea, calmly dreaming in Loch Etive and Loch Long, but turbulent where the seven tides meet off the Mull of Kintyre.

Geology

Such dramatic scenic contrasts are due in part to a complicated variety of rock formations; and, in general terms, the area can be divided geologically into three parts.

In Mull and North Argyll igneous basalt and lava beds predominate, with some intrusions of granite and felsite, notably on the Moor of Rannoch and at Crarae, southwest of Inveraray.

A central strip running southwest to northeast, which takes in Islay, Jura, North Kintyre, mid-Argyll, Cowal, the Isle of Bute and North Arran, contains rocks that are mainly metamorphic, quartzite alternating with softer schists and limestone. Hereabouts the soil produces protein-laden grass; consequently the milk is rich and mutton plentiful and sweet.

In South Kintyre and South Arran there occur considerable areas of sedimentary Old Red Sandstone. Here, for the artist, the cliffs glow red during a summer sunset. The practical farmer finds the dry soil ideal for potatoes.

But this story of successive periods of eruption, submergence and erosion has four interesting subplots. First, the raised glacial beaches – one at 25 feet, another at 100 feet – traceable throughout the area but most clearly visible along the western and southern coasts of Kintyre. Second, the whinstone (dolerite) dykes converging on Mull from the Clyde coasts – black intrusions in the ancient lava marking the volcanic pipes of more recent eruptions. Third, the disused coalmine at Machrihanish near Campbeltown, oddly situated in a region of rich farmland and gorgeous yellow beaches, which betrays the presence at considerable depth of carboniferous sediment. And fourth, the bed of white sandstone, 18 feet thick, near Lochaline in Morvon, which has supplied material for the manufacture of high-quality glass.

Flora and Fauna

The weather in Argyll and Bute is mild and temperate, owing, it has been said, to the near presence of the Gulf Stream. Snow rarely falls before January; and though rain often drifts across the mountainous interior, the common impression that the whole area is perpetually damp and depressing can, without difficulty, be proved false. Statistically, the average annual hours of sunshine compare favourably with those in any other part of Britain.

Arran is 'Scotland in miniature'. Lamlash, a sailing centre, is protected by Holy Island, a crag 1,030 feet high

As a result of this clement weather, all the common Scottish wild flowers grow in profusion, while rare species like Norwegian sandwort and thyme broom-rape are native in the area. Colourful palms and fuchsias are cultivated in gardens open to the public; and strawberries from Bute have been sold in the Glasgow shops at Easter.

State forests of pine, fir and larch blanket the lower slopes of the mountains. In older woodlands, alder and ash rub branches with beech and birch. Elm and hazel grow alongside poplar, sycamore and yew. If you can, acquire some of the local rowan and crab-apple jelly. It gives a royal flavour to soda scones.

Every second person in Argyll and Bute is an enthusiastic bird-watcher, which may be due to the fact that Kintyre and Arran provide a flight line for comparatively rare south-bound migrants in autumn. But the golden eagle, the ptarmigan, the red grouse and the divers are all indigenous, while the only choughs now nesting in Scotland are to be found in the islands. Famed for its woodcock shooting, Islay also winters large flocks of barnacle geese.

Besides the native red and roe deer, fallow and sika deer are also fairly numerous. Hares have become more common since the rabbit population was reduced by myxomatosis. Otters, foxes, stoats and weasels, badgers and wild-cats still roam the lonelier parts of Argyll. When walking on the high moors, be wary of adders: they are quick and poisonous.

My own favourite local animals are the grey Atlantic seals. At sunrise on a cold, calm winter's morning they come up on the sea-rocks, sprawling and puffing. The professional salmon-fisher hates the sight of them, because 80 per cent of their food consists of salmon. But they are friendly in a way that is almost human. When there is talk of killing, a picture comes to my mind of a white-furred calf playing alone in a sea-pool, curiously turning over stones and shells.

For the amateur fisherman, Argyll and Bute are paradise. The number of lochs and streams is beyond reckoning, and salmon, sea-trout and brown trout are abundant. Loch Eck nurtures not only the salmonid powan – elsewhere found only in Loch Lomond and sometimes mistakenly called 'the freshwater herring' – but also its own distinct sub-species of charr.

Archeology and History

After the last Ice Age, the first human beings to see the torn and tortured land of Scotland probably settled in Argyll and Bute about 6000 BC – Mesolithic men from Ireland, with flint arrows and flint tools stuck in their reindeer belts. They were followed by men of the Neolithic, Bronze and Iron Ages, and some of their arrow-heads, drinking utensils and primitive tools can be seen in the Campbeltown Museum.

The first Scots kingdom of Dalriada, founded in the 3rd century AD, had its headquarters at Dunadd where tall stones commemorate a pagan power.

There is a legend in Kintyre – which cannot be proved or disproved – that before going to Iona, St Columba and his disciples first landed on the shore at Keil, 6 miles east of the Mull of Kintyre. There, on a grassy knoll above the kirkyard, you will find a flat stone bearing the prints of two right feet. One was carved out originally – probably in the first millennium BC – to mark a place where pre-Christian chiefs took their tribal vows; but they are called locally 'St Columba's footprints'. It is significant that only 100 yards away stands a Druid altar. Columba, 'strong in stature, voice and spirit', built his new faith on the foundation of the old.

Iona itself – which you must surely visit (by ferry from Oban or across Mull to Fionnphort), to mingle with the pilgrims from every corner of the world and to see the Abbey, magnificently restored by devoted hands – Iona itself provides proof of this. Before Columba made it the base for his Christian mission in Scotland, it had been a stronghold of Druidism.

Thereafter the history of Argyll and Bute merges with that of Scotland. Four centuries of Norse occupation were followed by the reign of the Macdonalds – the Lords of the Isles – whose ruined castles are strewn across the countryside. The breaking of their independent power coincided with the Union of the Crowns in 1603. In the post-Jacobite period there began the slow decline of the old Gaelic civilization.

Local Industries

Farming is – and always has been – the paramount industry of the district. In view of the high proportion of rough grazings (94 per cent), the agricultural economy is based on livestock rather than on crop production. Sheep, mainly blackface, outnumber beef and milking cattle in the proportion of 12 to one. The chief dairying region is South Kintyre, where a creamery manufactures delicious cheese.

For centuries fishing was second in importance only to agriculture, which can be deduced from Inveraray's burghal motto: *Semper tibi pendeat halec* ('May you always have a catch of herring'). It continues to play an important part in the economy, but more local people are now employed in forestry. To some extent this is due to the disappearance of the fat Loch Fyne herring. But you can still buy wonderful kippers in Tarbert, Campbeltown and Oban, and the white fishing remains brisk. The catching of clams and prawns is a lucrative business.

There is a busy shipbuilding yard in Campbeltown and smaller yards at Sandbank, Tarbert and Tighnabruaich. Islay has a world-renowned gurgle of distilleries. Other industrial activities include sawmilling at Strachur, microprocessing in Rothesay and the manufacture of clothing and ropes in Campbeltown. One firm in Lochgilphead makes fine embroidery, another assembles carburettors. Fishfarms are numerous throughout the district.

Roads to the Isles

After farming, today's main industry concerns the care and comfort of visitors.

By road from Glasgow you come into Argyll past Arrochar and Loch Long. Then you drive over the long steep hill appropriately called Rest and Be Thankful down through the woods to Inveraray. This is the ancient capital, a little town of white houses elbowing each other around a pier. Its turreted castle (open to visitors) is owned by the Duke of Argyll – *MacCailein Mor* – whose family name is Campbell. One day, from beneath the sand and silt in Tobermory Bay, the present Duke hopes to salvage the treasure of the lost Armada galleon *Florencia*.

Another historic building is the old Inveraray courthouse where James Stewart of the Glen was condemned to death in 1752 for the murder in Appin of Colin Campbell of Glenure (the 'Red Fox'). James Stewart was almost certainly innocent, but the presiding judge and 11 of the 15 jurors were Campbells. It was a notable trial, providing Robert Louis Stevenson with the inspiration for *Kidnapped*.

From Inveraray you can double back to sail boats, catch fish or play golf in Cowal and Dunoon; you can strike west to climb mountains or to experience the thrill of Oban's water-skiing and island sunsets; you can drive south to the administrative capital of Lochgilphead – pausing perhaps to admire its ancient pagan stones and modern marina – then on to Campbeltown with its astonishing cave picture of the crucified Christ. West of Campbeltown you can play golf on the championship links at Machrihanish – birthplace of William MacTaggart, the artist – and in Southend (where there is also golf) study the whole history of Scottish civilization in easily accessible chambered cairns, duns and Columban remains.

By air from Glasgow you may travel to Kintyre and Islay in a matter of minutes. You take a steamer to Rothesay, whose fairy lights in summer make it the best illuminated town on the Clyde. There you can again savour history in its mighty castle, built in 1098 as a Macdonald stronghold against the Norse invaders. In Arran you may rest on the shoulder of Goatfell and experience for yourself the scenes and emotions described by Robert McLellan in *Sweet Largie Bay*.

People

How am I to convey to you in short the essential spirit of Argyll and Bute – the spirit of the people?

We are of mixed stock – Highland, Lowland and Irish. We are clannish, but sociable, and we like to sing and act and go to church. At the Mod – Gaelic equivalent of the Welsh Eisteddfod – the Campbeltown Gaelic Choir has won the premier trophy 13 times. Our drama clubs are legion. Our kirks are legion, too, and mostly well filled. But perhaps by joining us at one of our *ceilidhs* you'll get to know us best. There you may find that under the influence of song and story – and 'a wee dram' – our gloss of modernity flakes off a little, revealing a Celtic heritage of humour and hospitality and an independence as rugged as our history and sea girt coasts.

GAZETTEER

Ardchattan Priory *see* **Connel Ferry**

Ardgoil, Argyll 10E7

Loch Goil and Loch Long are on either side of this peninsula, known as Argyll's Bowling Green because of its rugged nature. With the neighbouring estate of Ardgartan it forms part of Argyll Forest Park.

Ardrishaig, Argyll 10D6

Village at end of the Crinan Canal is now mainly used by small craft. The canal was built in 1801 and connects the Sound of Jura to Loch Fyne. It has 15 locks in 5m, but superb scenery compensates for the effort involved in getting through them. The village and port were once important for herrings.

Arran, Bute   10D4/5/E4/5
The main industry of this exceptionally mild 56m-circuit
island is accommodating thousands of visitors enjoying its
mountains, glens and beaches, but NTS and local organizations have provided excellent amenities and craft industries
have developed. NTS owns Goatfell (2,866ft) with its magnificent views from the Clyde coast to the Hebrides and
Northern Ireland, and Glen Rosa and Cir Mhor (2,618ft), and
Brodick Castle and grounds. At *Lochranza* on the N coast
Robert the Bruce landed from Rathlin in 1307 to start his
campaign: the castle (AM) is 13th–14th c with later additions. On the W coast near *Blackwaterfoot* is the King's Cave
occupied allegedly by Finn MacCoul and later by The Bruce.
There is also a Bronze Age cairn and stone circle (AM) and
standing stones 15ft high at Machrie Moor (AM). Access to
Arran is by car ferry from **Ardrossan** to Brodick and
Claonaig, on Kintyre, to Lochranza, with excursions from
Brodick to the **Kyles of Bute** and **Ayr**. Arran has seven golf-
courses. Trips to *Holy Island* from *Lamlash Bay*. (*See* page
358.)

Ben Cruachan, Argyll   10E8
Within this mountain (3,689ft) the North of Scotland Hydro-
Electric Board created a vast cavern 300ft long and 120ft
high to contain a power station fed by water from a dam
1,315ft up the mountain to which it is pumped from Loch
Awe: it is one of the most advanced of its type in the world.
Open Easter–Oct., with visitor centre and mini-bus tour. Off
the A85 14m E of **Oban**. *See* **Dalmally**.

Bridge of Orchy, Argyll   10F8
After passing the watershed between the North Sea and the
Atlantic, the road from **Glasgow** to **Fort William** (High-
land) drops to Glen Orchy, haunt of fishermen.

Brodick, Bute   10E4
The capital of **Arran**, pleasant and busy, has 1½m N the
ancient seat of the Dukes of Hamilton and occupied more
recently by Mary Duchess of Montrose and her family and
now NTS. Part of Brodick Castle dates from 13th c with
extensions in the 17th and 19th c. It has superb silver,
porcelain and paintings, with sporting prints and trophies:
the formal garden dates from 1710, the woodland garden
created by the Duchess in 1923 has one of Europe's finest
rhododendron displays. In 1980 the gardens became a
country park. Castle open May–Sept.; park and garden all
year: bus connects with **Ardrossan** ferry.

Bute   10E5
Less spectacular than **Arran**, this island has a wide range of
scenery and the former royal burgh of **Rothesay** is much
frequented. Car and passenger ferries from Wemyss Bay and
Colintraive. Fine rough country at N and S, with good
sandy beaches at Ettrick Bay, Scalpsie Bay and Kilchattan
Bay. Depends on agriculture, tourism and boatbuilding (at
Ardmaleish and *Port Bannatyne*). The chapel of St Blain,
and remains of a Celtic monastery, are in the SW, as is
Dunagoil vitrified fort.

Campbeltown, Argyll   10D4
Former royal burgh near S end of Kintyre, dependent on
agriculture, tourism, marine sports and fishing. The Old
Quay Head is notable for an elaborate carved 15th-c cross.

Carradale, Argyll   10D4
Fishing village in sheltered bay, with lovely sands and good
boating facilities. Remains of fort on an island S of the
harbour. Gardens at Carradale House open April–Sept.

Carrick Castle, Argyll   10E7
Romantic 14th-c ruin of a stronghold of the Campbell clan on
the shores of Loch Goil, burned down by men of Atholl in the
17th c.

Colintraive, Argyll   10E6
Car ferry to **Bute** across the scenic **Kyles of Bute**, at a place
where drovers years ago swam their cattle from the island.

Coll, Argyll   12C1
Island of small crofts reached by steamer from **Oban**. A
ruined castle, lovely bays, good bathing and fishing. *See also*
Tiree.

Colonsay, Argyll   10B6/7
Island connected with **Oronsay** at low tide. Reached by car
ferry from **Oban**. The gardens at *Kiloran* are open all year,
with azaleas and rhododendrons.

Connel Ferry, Argyll   10D8
A bridge now carries road travellers over the rapids made
famous by Ossian as 'The Falls of Lora'. At very low tides the
roar is deafening and daunting. 5m to the N the twin-peaked
hill of Benderloch may have been a Pictish capital, but a
raised way between the peaks suggests early Christian
construction. Whichever it is, the summit gives a fine view.
E of *North Connel* is 13th-c *Ardchattan Priory* (AM) where in
1308 Bruce's Parliament was one of the last to conduct
business in Gaelic. The fine gardens of *Ardchattan House*
near by are open April–Sept.

The Cumbraes, Bute   10E5
Two small islands off the Ayrshire coast. A Marine Biological Station combining Aquarium and Museum is on *Great
Cumbrae*, near Keppel Pier. At *Millport*, on a beautiful
sandy bay, stands the 'Cathedral of the Isles'. Car and
passenger ferries from **Largs**.

Dalmally, Argyll   10E8
Situated on the River Orchy in delightful touring country.
To the W the waters of Loch Awe rush headlong to Loch
Etive and the sea. **Ben Cruachan** (3,689ft) looms above the
Pass of Brander, where the MacDougals of Lorn were almost
destroyed by Robert the Bruce.

Dunoon, Argyll   10E6
Deservedly popular resort, lively centre for road and
steamer trips. Car ferry from **Gourock**. Holy Loch, famous
nuclear submarine base, lies to the N opposite *Sandbank*.
The botanic gardens of *Benmore House*, the Forestry Training School 7m N at *Kilmun*, are open to the public.

Dunstaffnage Castle,★ Argyll   10D8
4m N of **Oban**. Magnificently placed on a sheer rock
guarding the entrance to Loch Etive. The three round
towers and 10ft-thick walls of this rectangular stronghold
(AM) are of the 13th c, but tradition ascribes greater age to
the ruins. A brass cannon salvaged from an Armada galleon
sunk in Tobermory Bay is mounted on the ramparts. Robert
the Bruce stormed the castle and Flora Macdonald was
imprisoned here for a short time.

Gigha, Argyll   10C5
This small, very fertile island W of Kintyre is notable for the
gardens and valuable plants, including rhododendron hy-
brids at *Achamore House* (NTS). Many of the plants have
been propagated for the Trust's other gardens. Open daily
April–Oct. Access is by ferry from *Kennacraig*, **Tarbert**.

Inveraray Castle: seat of the Dukes of Argyll and centre of the Campbell Clan, it was restored after a fire in 1975

Inveraray,★ Argyll   10E7
Small but historic former royal burgh situated on Loch Fyne and surrounded by beautiful woodlands. The massive castle greatly admired by Sir Walter Scott, and partly decorated by two of the Adam brothers, is built on the site of an earlier stronghold, and contains family portraits of the Argylls by old masters, historic relics, plate and tapestry. Open April–Oct. A 17th-c dovecot at *Carlunan*, 1m walk through the Castle grounds, is attractive, and so are the Falls of Aray, 3¼m. Sir Walter Scott, R. L. Stevenson and the local novelist, Neil Munro, are among the writers who have used Inveraray as background for stirring tales.

Iona,★ Argyll   10B7/8
This tiny isle (NTS) off the SW corner of **Mull** (passenger ferry from *Fionnphort* and cruises from **Oban** in summer) was sacred to the Druids long before the missionary landing of St Columba in 563. Even Dr Johnson, never notably a lover of Scotland, remarked that 'the man is little to be envied . . . whose piety would not grow warmer among the ruins of Iona', Norsemen continually pillaged the monastery, but it was later restored by the Scottish Queen Margaret, and early in the 13th c the Lord of the Isles founded a Benedictine abbey. This building was restored by the Church of Scotland in *c.*1905. The Chapel of St Oran on the supposed site of St Columba's cell has also been restored, and the nunnery priory is well preserved. Since 1938 the Iona Community, a religious brotherhood for the training of students, has excavated and restored sites and buildings. Reilig Odhrain is believed to contain the remains of over 60 monarchs, but their monuments were thrown into the sea during the Reformation. Of 360 fine crosses known to have stood here, three remain: St John's Cross (9th-c), St Martin's Cross (10th-c) and Maclean's Cross (15th-c).

Islay,★ Argyll   10B5/6/C5
The most southerly island of the Hebrides, reached by air (from **Glasgow**), and car ferries to *Port Ellen* and *Port Askaig* from *Kennacraig* (West Loch **Tarbert**). From Port Ellen a good road system serves the island famous for its malt whiskies. A deep indentation almost divides the Rhinns district from Oa Peninsula, named after a legendary Danish princess, and shelters *Bowmore*, a fascinating fishing village with a curious round church (18th-c) at the head of the main street. U.S. troops lost from the *Tuscania* and the *Otranto* in 1918 are commemorated at *Port Charlotte* and Machir Bay. *See* **Jura**

Jura, Argyll   10C5/6/7
An island of great scenic beauty but poor in roads and tourist accommodation. It was to this island that George Orwell retreated to work on his novel *Nineteen Eighty-four*. Passenger ferry from adjacent **Islay**. The conspicuous breast-like Paps are all over 2,400ft high. To the N, though not easily accessible, the thunderous *Corryvreckan* whirlpool is a notorious menace to ships at certain tides.

Kilmartin, Argyll   10D7
Picturesque village with a badly mutilated Celtic cross and medieval sculptured stones in the churchyard. The ruins of 16th-c *Carnassarie Castle* lie 1½m to the N (AM). The *Hill of Dunadd* (*c.*500–850), 4m S, was the site of Dalriada, capital of an ancient kingdom, designated by carvings of a boar and a footprint at the summit. Many prehistoric and medieval relics N of village. Fine view of **Jura** across the Sound.

Kyles of Bute★   10E5/6
The narrow straits between former Argyll and **Bute**, with some of the most enchanting scenery of the Firth of Clyde. The 10m stretch of water is best seen from the A8003 where there are view indicators E and W. *See also* **Colintraive** and **Tighnabruaich**.

Oban: founded 200 years ago, it is a tourist resort today overlooked by MacCaig's Folly built in 1897

Lismore, Argyll   10D8
A long, flat island in the centre of Loch Linnhe, reached by car ferry from **Oban**. The 18th-c parish church incorporates part of an early cathedral. Excavations have exposed the nave and site of its W tower. The ruins of the episcopal castle of Auchindown perch on the rocky W coast.

Lochgilphead, Argyll   10D6
The administrative capital of Argyll and Bute District. Situated at the head of Loch Gilp near *Dunadd* (see **Kilmartin**).

Machrihanish, Argyll   10C4
Towards SW tip of the *Mull of Kintyre*. Famous golf-course on sand dunes facing open Atlantic and $3\frac{1}{2}$m of beautiful beach. Airport on **Campbeltown** road.

Mull,★ Argyll   10B7/C8
Island of sea lochs and scenery rising to Ben More (3,169ft). Reached by car ferry from **Oban**. Beloved of many, though Dr Johnson considered it 'worse than Skye'! Stevenson chose it for the escape of David Balfour in *Kidnapped*. 100 m of roads maintain touch with a fascinatingly indented coast culminating in the S with the granite cliffs of the Ross of Mull. Access by boat to **Iona**. The Forestry Commission has 35,000 acres with excellent facilities for visitors: wildlife abounds, including red and fallow deer. At *Dervaig* is the smallest professional theatre in the world: it seats 45. *See also* **Tobermory** and **Lochaline** (Highland).

Oban,★ Argyll   10D8
Centre of a network of car-ferry services linking the islands with the mainland, so that the comings and goings of islanders with provisions, crops and livestock create fascinating movement in this busy fishing-port. Headquarters of the Royal Highland Yacht Club. Other sports well catered for. The ivy-clad keep of ruined *Dunollie Castle* stands above

Loch Linnhe; the key is obtainable at Dunollie House, which proudly cherishes the Brooch of Lorne wrested from Bruce in a fight, and later returned to the MacDougalls. A little further N is **Dunstaffnage Castle** (AM). The cathedral (1932) was designed by Sir Giles Scott. The pseudo-Greek or Roman structure overtopping Oban is MacCaig's Tower or Folly, started in 1897 but abandoned on his death, in 1900. The town has famous glass-works specializing in paperweights. Open on weekdays. *See also* **Coll, Colonsay, Iona, Lismore, Mull, Staffa, Tiree,** and **Lochaline** (Highland).

Oronsay, Argyll   10B6
A small island at the S of **Colonsay**, separated from it except at low tide. Remains of Augustinian priory of obscure origin, with cloisters similar to those in Saxon foundations in England. Finely executed 16th-c cross with relief of Crucifixion. Prior's House contains a collection of interesting tomb slabs.

Rest and Be Thankful, Argyll   10F7
Highest point (860ft) marked by a stone seat on the old road from Loch Long which climbs through *Glen Croe*'s wild scenery overlooked by 'The Cobbler' or Ben Arthur (2,891ft). The modern road (the A83) has ironed out the worst of the bends and gradients. *See* **Arrochar**.

Rothesay,★ Bute   10E5
Former capital of **Bute**, Scotland's first royal burgh (1401), and popular Clyde summer resort. The moated Castle (AM), conquered by Norsemen in the 13th c, was originally circular in plan, with four towers. Worth seeing are Bute Museum, the 17th-c Mansion House and the ancient church of St Mary containing two 14th-c canopied tombs. Within easy access are the fine sandy beaches of Etterick Bay and Kilchattan Bay. In 1398 Robert III created his eldest son Duke of Rothesay and this is the senior Scottish title borne by the heir to the throne (the Prince of Wales): he is correctly so styled in Scotland. He is also Earl of Carrick, Baron Renfrew, Lord of the Isles and Great Steward of Scotland.

Saddell, Argyll   10D4
Early 16th-c castle, and remains of a Cistercian monastery founded in the 12th c.

Seil, Argyll   10D7
Small island separated from the mainland by a narrow sound the width of a small river, and connected with it by the hump-backed Clachan Bridge 'over the Atlantic', built by Telford in 1791, $2\frac{1}{2}$m NE of *Balvicar*.

Skipness, Argyll   10D5
Panoramic views of **Arran**, **Bute** and Kilbrannan Sound. Remains of ruined church of St Columba and castle.

Southend, Argyll   10D3
Near the tip of Kintyre, traditional landing-place of St Columba, within sight of Ireland. The golf-course is near ruined *Dunaverty Castle*, where in 1647 Macdonald forces were butchered by Campbells.

Staffa,★ Argyll   10B8
Uninhabited island with perpendicular cliffs S and W. Can be visited from **Oban**; landings may be made in calm weather to explore the basalt rocks which match those of Antrim's Giant's Causeway. *Fingal's Cave*, the most imposing of many, is 227ft long and high, with grotesque formations which inspired Mendelssohn's *The Hebrides* overture.

Mull: its main town is Tobermory, founded in 1788 by the British Fisheries Society, and a popular yachting centre

Tarbert, Argyll   10D6
The E and W Lochs are separated by a mile of isthmus across which King Magnus (11th c) dragged his galley. East Loch Tarbert is overlooked by a ruined castle once inhabited by James II of Scotland. Centre for car-ferry services to **Harris** (W.I.), **Islay, Jura, Gigha** and **Colonsay.**

Tighnabruaich, Argyll   10E6
Small, delightful holiday resort and yachting centre on the **Kyles of Bute** (on the A8003 off the A886).

Tiree, Argyll   10A8
The ancients said this was a kingdom whose 'summits were lower than the waves'. Windswept but fertile, specializing in bulb-growing. Quarries of unusual marble, pink spotted with green. Golf-course and airport. Access by air from **Glasgow,** or by ferry from **Oban.** *See also* **Coll.**

Tobermory, Argyll   12D1
Sheltered quayside resort, yachting centre and chief town of **Mull.** Many attempts have been made to recover the supposed treasure from the hold of the Spanish galleon sunk in the bay by a Scottish hostage in 1588. Golf-course. Local folklore museum in an old church.

CENTRAL REGION

AN INTRODUCTION BY
JACK HOUSE

It is sometimes difficult to work out how the Powers-That-Be decided on the shape of the various regions in Scotland, but doubtless they had their good reasons. One that is generally considered successful is the Central Region, which incorporates the former counties of Clackmannan, most of Stirling, part of Perth and the old burgh of Bo'ness in West Lothian. And the reason for this success is that the centre of the Central Region is Stirling.

Stirling has a rival, of course, in the busy, industrial town of Falkirk, where much of the new region's administration is settled. But Stirling is the ideal centre because of its old name, still used, of the Gateway to the Highlands. The Gateway to the Highlands must, of course, be also the Gateway to the Lowlands from the Highlanders' point of view. And this is just what Stirling is. It looks to the mountains and the wild lands of the north and also to the fertile and productive lands of the south.

In the old days, when Scotland seemed to be always at war, Stirling Castle was the keypoint. Whoever controlled it was able to control Scotland: at the battle of Bannockburn in 1314, when Robert the Bruce led a Scottish army against the invading Edward II of England, the Scots were outnumbered three to one but they were the victors. Stirling Castle looks over the field of Bannockburn.

South of Bannockburn the River Forth winds, at times crazily, to Edinburgh. On a clear day you can see the two Forth Bridges and Edinburgh Castle from the battlements of Stirling Castle. The land you see in front of you is mainly industrial and agricultural. It includes Alloa, where much of the tangy Scottish beer is brewed and Magnus Pyke served his apprenticeship. There is Grangemouth, now one of the main ports of Scotland and famed for its big oil-related industries. There is Falkirk, whose proud boast is 'Wha dare meddle wi' the bairns o' Fa'kirk?' It is to Stirling what Glasgow is to Edinburgh – not, perhaps, a beautiful town, though it has its beauties, but one with verve, excitement and purpose.

In the middle of this area is the small town of Clackmannan, mainly a suburb for the other centres of the region, but with the ancient Stone of Mannan

in the middle of the place. Nobody knows how old the Stone is, but it may well be as old as the Stone of Destiny on which, traditionally, the Kings of Scotland were crowned.

Look north from Stirling and you look into Rob Roy country, which might also be called Sir Walter Scott country. From Stirling you enter South Perthshire by way of Bridge of Allan and Dunblane, which has a fine cathedral. You can continue up to Doune, where famous pistols were made, and to Callander, where

Stirling Castle's strategic position at the Gateway to the North has influenced much of Scotland's history

'Dr Finlay's Casebook' was made. (More tourists go to Callander than Doune!) Callander is the way to the fabled Trossachs, where Rob Roy held sway and Sir Walter Scott chronicled his doings – fairly faithfully.

This is South Perthshire at its best. You will never forget a sail in the *Sir Walter Scott* on Loch Katrine, scene of Scott's poem 'Lady of the Lake', and all around are memories of Rob Roy, culminating as you cross the mountains to Aberfoyle, where you will see the poker with which Bailie Nicol Jarvie defended himself in the Clachan of Aberfoyle. The Bailie, of course, was an invention of Sir Walter's, but there on a tree in front of the Bailie Nicol Jarvie Hotel is a poker chained to the trunk.

You can also see one of the only two lakes in Scotland, the Lake of Menteith. All our other pieces of inland water are called lochs. This is where, if the ice is bearing, you will see the Grand Match, the great event of the Scottish curling year. By the way, I have not attempted to describe the marvellous scenery. You must see it for yourself.

GAZETTEER

Aberfoyle, Perth **10G7**
An important centre for the **Trossachs** and the Queen Elizabeth Forest Park which covers nearly 50,000 acres. The Forestry Commission is responsible not only for the David Marshall Lodge with a resident warden, many marked walks, picnic and caravan sites, but also for the Achray Forest Drive for cars (open Easter–Sept.).

Airth, Stirling **11H6**
1m N of the road bridge over the Forth to **Kincardine** (Fife). Note mercat cross with two sundials; and Wallace's Tower (14th-c). Near by is the extraordinary Pineapple structure (45ft high) built in 1761 as the centrepiece of hothouses in which pineapples were grown by a remarkable system of heating by furnaces and double walls (NTS).

Alloa, Clack **11H7**
Important for its breweries for 200 years but with distilling, woollen, engineering and diversified industries, the former port is now a District administrative centre. It has a 15th-c tower, 17th-c ruined church and a 17th-c house in Kirkgate with an interesting sundial.

Balquhidder, Perth **10G8**
At the E end of Loch Voil off the A84 amid the lovely Braes of Balquhidder. At the roofless church (1631) are the graves of Rob Roy MacGregor, Chieftain of the Clan Gregor, (1671–1734), 'out' in the 1715 Rising and a rebel against the Establishment, his wife Helen and two of their sons.

Bannockburn, Stirling **11H6**
The NTS was responsible for rescuing a large part of the 1314 battle site and in 1964 the Queen opened the Rotunda, which contains the Borestone, Robert the Bruce's command post before the battle, and unveiled the impressive equestrian statue by Pilkington Jackson. The Centre presents an audiovisual picture of the battle and is open March–Oct. Situated off the M80/M9 at junction 9, 2m S of **Stirling**. Heritage Centre open March–Oct.; site all year.

Bo'ness (Borrowstounness), W. Lothian **11H6**
Industrial town and port, where James Watt experimented with his steam engine in 1764. In Kinneil House (AM) note 16th c wall paintings.

Bridge of Allan, Stirling **11H7**
Quiet inland resort of *Allan Water*, near its junction with the Forth. Chopin stayed at Keir House, whose woods shelter the village, in 1848; and R. L. Stevenson was a frequent visitor. Gardens open April–Oct.

Callander, Perth **10G7**
In proportion to its size has more good hotels than any other Scottish town. Centre for the **Trossachs** and the wonderful country of Sir Walter Scott's poem 'The Lady of the Lake'.

Cambuskenneth Abbey, Stirling **11H7**
1m NE of **Stirling** are the remains of the 12th-c Abbey (AM) where, in 1326, Robert the Bruce held his Parliament, and where James III and his queen were buried in 1488.

Campsie Glen, Stirling **10G6**
Village at the foot of the glen, from which the road crosses the Campsie Fells to **Fintry**. Splendid views from the top of the road (1,064ft).

Clackmannan **11H7**
Outside the old Tolbooth, note the town cross with its steps; also the ancient Clach (or stone) of Mannan, from which the town derives its name. W is the fine 15th-c Clackmannan Tower (AM) traditionally built by Robert the Bruce.

Crianlarich, Perth **10F8**
Rail and road junction amid spectacular mountain scenery. St Fillan's Pool, 3m NW, provided old-time kill-or-cure treatment for the mentally deranged. The A82 S to **Loch Lomond** (Strathclyde) (7m) leads through the beautiful Glen Falloch.

Dollar, Clack **11H7**
On the River Devon, at the foot of the Ochils, the town is famous for its Academy, built by Playfair in 1819. 1m N, in a romantic setting between the Burn of Sorrow and the Burn of Care, stand the ruins of *Castle Campbell* (AM and NTS) while, behind, King's Seat rises to 2,111ft.

Doune Castle*, Perth **10G7**
Almost impregnable 15th-c stronghold protected by two rivers and a moat. Entrance to courtyard through the great tower. Splendid example of Scottish medieval architecture. The old stables house an interesting motor museum. Open April–Oct.

Dunblane,* Perth **11H7**
The Cathedral (12th–15th-c) is on the site of the Celtic church of St Blane, after which the town takes it name. Note

especially the Celtic stone (*c*.900) in the N aisle, the effigies of the 5th Earl of Strathearn and his Countess (1271) and the W window (to be seen only from outside) which was greatly praised by John Ruskin, and six carved stalls in the nave. The Cathedral Museum, in the Dean's House, and Bishop Leighton's Library, with 17th-c fittings and books, are well worth a visit.

Falkirk, Stirling   11H6
Important industrial centre. Well-preserved sections of the **Roman Wall** (Strathclyde) can be seen in the grounds of *Callendar House* E of the town; while 2m W is the best-preserved of the Roman forts, known as *Rough Castle* (AM). On the retreat from Derby Prince Charles Edward Stuart defeated the Hanoverians here, for the last time.

Fintry, Stirling   10G6
In the Lennox country between Campsie Fells and Fintry Hills. 3m E is the Loup of Fintry, a 100ft waterfall, and beyond this Carron Reservoir. Culcreuch Tower lies N.

Grangemouth, Stirling   11H6
Busy port, container terminal and oil refinery on the estuary of the Forth; the E terminus of the long-disused Forth and Clyde Canal parts of which have been restored for use by pleasure craft.

Inversnaid, Stirling   10F7
Pleasant hamlet on E shore of **Loch Lomond** (Strathclyde), at the end of the **Aberfoyle** road. The waterfall caused by the outfall from Loch Arklet is associated with Wordsworth's 'Highland Girl'; and a road to N leads to Rob Roy's Cave, mentioned in Dorothy Wordsworth's Journal. Surrounding mountain scenery is magnificent.

Killin, Perth   10G8
Village near the head of Loch Tay, not far from the junction of the Dochart and the Lochay. Sailing, and winter sports. Stronaclachich (1,708ft) rewards walkers with a magnificent view, but Ben Lawers (3,984ft) presents a greater challenge. Much of this country is NTS property; the rare alpine plants found here should not be uprooted. The area is a National Nature Reserve and the NTS has a visitor centre (open April–Sept.).

Kippen, Stirling   10G7
An attractive village in the Forth Valley at the foot of the Fintry Hills, off the A811 from **Stirling**. The church beautifully renovated under Sir D. Y. Cameron R.A. in 1925 has rich interior furnishings.

Loch Katrine *see* **The Trossachs**

Mentieth, Lake of, Perth   10G7
One of the only two 'lakes' in Scotland. Mary Queen of Scots spent part of her childhood on *Inchmahome*, the largest of the three islands in the lake. The ruins of 13th-c Inchmahome Priory (AM) are still to be seen. The 'lake' is a corruption of *laicht* meaning 'low-lying land'; Port of Mentieth from *poirt* or ferry, to the islands.

Rowardennan, Stirling   10F7
Terminus of road on E side of **Loch Lomond** (Strathclyde) and starting point of one route up Ben Lomond (3,192ft). This is a stopping point, with a youth hostel and hotel, on the new *West Highland Way*, the 95m signposted footpath from Milngavie to **Fort William** (Highland), created by the Countryside Commission in 1980.

Stirling★   11H7
Here the Old Bridge, dating from 1400, was once the Gateway to the Highlands. The town is dominated by its fine castle★ (AM), alternately fortress and royal residence. Built between the 13th and 17th c, it contains a splendid Parliament Hall, the Chapel Royal (James VI was crowned here), with 17th-c wall paintings, and the Douglas Room, containing many interesting relics. (*See* page 364.) The approach to the castle passes the church of the Holy Rood, in which Mary was crowned Queen of Scots at the age of nine months; and an incomplete house, Mar's Wark, begun by the Regent

Mar in 1570. Argyll's Lodging, a splendid 17th-c house, is now a hospital. Stirling University (1967) on the beautiful Airthrey estate, has a 23-acre loch in its campus, much enjoyed by its 3,000 students. 1m E the *Wallace Monument*, 220ft high and standing on Abbey Craig (362ft), provides stupendous views.

Strathblane, Stirling 10G8
Resort at the foot of Strathblane Hills and Campsie Fells – an area of great geological interest. 1m NE is the waterfall, Spout of Ballagan. *Duntreath Castle* is 2m NW.

The Trossachs: one of the most romantic spots in Britain, these hills have inspired many poets and writers

The Trossachs,★★ Perth 10F7
A wild, beautiful and tangled region, as shown by translation of its name: 'the bristly country'. The gorge leads from Loch Achray to beautiful Loch Katrine. This is the heart of the Queen Elizabeth Forest Park covering 42,000 acres from Loch Venachar over Ben Lomond to **Loch Lomond** (Strathclyde). The Forestry Commission has provided Forest Trails, walks, car parks, caravan sites and viewpoints.

LOTHIAN REGION

AN INTRODUCTION BY
MORAY McLAREN

This area covers the previous counties of East and West Lothian and Midlothian, with the exception of the southeast corner of Midlothian and a tiny corner of the north of West Lothian. It is, of course, centred upon the Scottish capital Edinburgh.

Edinburgh

For half a millennium Edinburgh has been the capital (I hesitate to say the chief town) of Scotland. She has been praised as 'the Athens of the North', and abused, not so much for her smoke ('Auld Reekie') as for her greyness. The precipitate tumbling and climbing quality of Edinburgh is the first thing visitors notice about her. She is built around a central rock, and from that castellated rock she steps down to the sea or, elsewhere, upwards towards her surrounding hills, the Pentlands. So large and upstanding is 'Arthur's Seat', a huge rocky projection in the centre of the city, that you might justly call it (though not so high as the Pentlands) a mountain.

Edinburgh's chief glory lies in her dramatic contrasts of appearance. There is a great greyness – and a sudden profusion of colour; there is height – and yet vista; above all, there is the contrast of romantic and classical building. The romantic, in the Castle and Old Town, is obvious. But the visitor is implored not to neglect the finest example of neo-Georgian town-planning in Europe, the late 18th- and early 19th-century New Town, lying between the splendour of Charlotte Square to the southwest and the gracious amplitude of Drummond Place to the northeast.

There is not much danger of the visitor neglecting the romantic side of Edinburgh. The 1,000-year-old Castle stands upon its rock in the very heart of the city, visible from every quarter of Edinburgh. On one side the rock is sheer, and has been scaled only three times in history. To the east the Castle Rock slopes down more gradually, and on it is built the Old Town and 'Royal Mile', through which has flowed the stream of Scottish history – Mary Stuart, John Knox, Montrose, Boswell, all the Stuart kings and innumerable others. In the centre of it there is the High Kirk of St Giles, sometimes called a cathedral – which it never was.

The Palace of Holyroodhouse lies at the foot of the Royal Mile and at the other end from the Castle. Partly French in style, it has been added to by Scottish sovereigns for the last 500 years before and since the Union of Crowns. It is still a Royal Residence; but you can make a tour of its interior when the Royal Family is not in residence. Before Holyrood became a palace it was an abbey. You may see the delicate tracery of the Abbey Church beside the Palace. The rage of the Reformers and the neglect of the ensuing centuries have not destroyed all its beauty.

Princes Street is one of the most famous thoroughfares in Europe. North of Princes Street Gardens (once a loch), it runs parallel to the Royal Mile. It has only one side; but from that side you can look south up into the Old Town and the sun – one of the most romantic prospects in Europe. Apart from its incomparable view, it has the merit of being a fine street although, alas, recent changes have greatly eroded its architectural dignity. In the neo-Gothic Walter Scott monument it can boast the largest memorial to a man of letters in the world.

This hard core of the essential Edinburgh (the Old and the New Town) is built out of satisfyingly massive stone. On any fine day this greyness makes a superb foil for the colours in the wide and spacious gardens, the wide, long vistas to the sea and to the hills. Edinburgh is a city, above all, of space and height and varying polychrome set on a noble architectural frame of delicate grey. It must be one of the finest settings for a city in the world. It most certainly is a superb setting for the famous International Festival of Music and Drama and the Arts which takes place annually in the last two weeks of August and the first week of September. This Festival, first held in 1947, goes from strength to strength.

The Lothians

Edinburgh is the chief town of the old province, now region, of Lothian, as well as being the capital of Scotland. Lothian, which once stretched down to Berwick and the English border, is now reduced and divided into three Districts, East Lothian, Mid-

Edinburgh, Scotland's capital, is dominated by its castle. The annual Military Tattoo is held on its Esplanade

lothian and West Lothian. Of these, the last is mainly industrial; while Midlothian, a partly agricultural, partly mining District under the shadow of the hills, is chiefly distinguished by the fact that nearly half of its area is taken up by Edinburgh. Of the three, the most distinctive is East Lothian. This rich agricultural District seems to mark out its own borders for itself by the immediate presence of red soil and the red-sandstone buildings. When Cromwell's soldiers came there they found 'the greatest quantity of corn they ever saw'.

Its former county town is Haddington, which is one of the most interesting and charming towns in Scotland. Its charm lies in its beautiful, wide 18th-century streets; its interest in the fact that the Town Council has wisely preserved its character.

To the south of it there rise the beautifully rounded contours of the Lammermuir Hills. Though not 'grand' in the accepted Scottish scenic sense, they are wild moorland, filled with grouse and with small trout streams where most of the fishing is free.

In the Lammermuirs East Lothian presents the full wild moorland effect, in its lower stretches a rich farming land (one of the richest in Scotland), and on its coastline a grim determined outlook facing north-east. The Bass Rock stands severely sentinel out to sea just beyond North Berwick. By North Berwick is Tantallon Castle, also built of red sandstone, once a stronghold of the Douglases. Gullane, Muirfield, North Berwick – all these are associated with some of the finest golf-links in the world.

GAZETTEER

Craigmillar Castle, Midlothian   11I6
2m SE of **Edinburgh**, this impressive ruined castle (AM) was a favourite home of Mary Queen of Scots. From the massive 14th-c tower the view is especially fine.

Crichton, Midlothian   11J6
The small 15th-c collegiate church, standing on the steep bank above Tyne Water, is remarkable for its squat tower and barrel vaulting. To the S the splendid Castle (AM), originally a single tower, has a unique Italianate N wing added in the 16th c.

Dalkeith, Midlothian   11J6
Market town between the North and South Esk Rivers. The Palace was rebuilt by Vanbrugh c.1700 for the Duchess of Buccleuch, widow of the Duke of Monmouth (executed in 1685). Wooded walks in grounds. SW is *Newbattle Abbey*, in fine parkland, the crypt and basement of which survive beneath an 18th-c mansion, now a college.

Dalmeny,* W. Lothian   11I6
Undoubtedly one of the finest small Norman churches in Scotland, with exceptionally rich carvings. Dalmeny House, seat of the Earls of Rosebery, has fine treasures and a hammer-beam hall. Open May–Sept. Near by, overlooking the Firth of Forth, is restored Barnbougle Castle.

Dirleton, E. Lothian   11J6
Mid-way between the famous golf-courses of **North Berwick** and *Gullane*, this attractive village has the beautiful remains of a massive 13th-c castle★ (AM), with its three-storey Renaissance additions and an old bowling green set in lovely gardens and still in use.

Dunbar, E. Lothian   11K6
Fishing-port and resort at the foot of the Lammermuirs. The Town House has an interesting six-sided tower; and in the parish church, with its 108ft tower, is the notable tomb of the 1st Earl of Dunbar (1610). On a rock above the harbour are the scanty remains of the Castle, and near by is the battlefield where Cromwell defeated the Covenanters under Leslie in 1650.

East Linton,* E. Lothian   11K6
Picturesque village on the Tyne, which flows through a small gorge, crossed by a 16th-c bridge. There is a monument to the great bridge-builder, John Rennie, who was born in the near-by mansion of Phantassie in 1761. Note dovecot too. *Preston Mill* (NTS), a water-mill still in working order, is open all year. 2m SW is *Hailes Castle* (AM), with original 13th-c watergate and dungeons; behind which rises Traprain Law (724ft), where in 1919 a hoard of 4th-c Christian and pagan silver was excavated.

Edinburgh,★★   11I6
Finely situated and famous for its University and schools, as well as being the focus of the historical, political and cultural life of Scotland for centuries; any selection of the City's interesting features is bound to be invidious. The heart of the Old Town is the 'Royal Mile', the succession of streets amid many-storeyed old houses and quaint Wynds, that follows the ridge E from the Castle to Holyroodhouse. The Castle★ (AM) is the centre of a group of notable buildings: the restored chapel of St Margaret dates from

1093; the Old Palace contains the Crown Room, with the Scottish regalia, the Royal Apartments and the Old Parliament Hall; while on the N side is the impressive National War Memorial (1927). (*See* page 369.) In the High Street is the fine church of St Giles★, the 'High Kirk', with its 'Crown' steeple, and Parliament House; and, within a stone's throw, the University, designed by Robert Adam in 1789 and completed by Playfair in 1827. Continuing down the Royal Mile, note John Knox's House, the splendid Canongate Tolbooth (1591), and White Horse Close and Inn (1791). In the Palace of Holyroodhouse★, dating from 1500, are interesting relics and portraits of the Kings and Queens of Scotland, but of the Royal Chapel, once part of the adjoining Abbey, only part of the nave and W front are still standing. Very different in character is the 18th- and 19th-c New Town, extending N from the famous thoroughfare Princes Street. Its handsome streets and stately squares contain some of the most characteristic work of Robert Adam. Particularly outstanding are Drummond Place and Charlotte Square, while among individual buildings, the Register House containing the Scottish Archives, is a great beauty. The annual Edinburgh Festival of the Arts, the largest arts festival in the world, with its international programme attracts thousands. *See* Introduction.

Forth Bridges *see* **South Queensferry**

Gifford, E. Lothian   11J6
A charming village, on the Gifford Water, from which to explore the Lammermuirs (4m S is Lammer Law, 1,733ft). A lime avenue leads to Yester House, a fine Adam mansion. Beyond are the remains of Yester Castle, with the curious underground chamber, 'Goblin Ha', referred to in Scott's *Marmion*. Church dates from 1708 and has a medieval bell.

Haddington,* E. Lothian   11J6
On the River Tyne, spanned by two fine 16th-c bridges, this little town has been carefully preserved by the District Council. The restored church (AM), known as the 'Lamp of Lothian', retains the original 15th-c central tower, nave and W front. The Town House was designed by William Adam; and there are three notable 17th-c buildings, Haddington House, Bothwell Castle and Moat House. 2m N stands ruined *Barnes Castle*.

Kirkliston, W. Lothian   11I6
Notable for its partly 12th-c church, with fine W tower and saddleback roof. Across the River Almond is Edinburgh Airport. 2m W is *Niddry Castle*, to which Mary Queen of Scots escaped from **Loch Leven** (Tayside) and 2m SW is a fine Adam house, *Newliston*.

Lasswade, Midlothian   11I6
In the valley of the Esk River, this village is notable for its literary associations. Sir Walter Scott lived here 1798–1804, during which time he was visited by Wordsworth. Outside the ruined Norman church is the grave of William Drummond, the poet, who was born at *Hawthornden House*, 2½m SW, in the grounds of which stands a tree commemorating Ben Jonson's visit to him in 1618–19. And near by is Mavisbush, the cottage where De Quincey lived 1840–59.

Forth Road Bridge: opened by the Queen in 1964, its 8,244 feet span the Firth at South Queensferry

Linlithgow Palace: birthplace of Mary Queen of Scots in 1542, it was damaged by fire in 1424 and again in 1746

Linlithgow,★ W. Lothian
11H6

In the precincts, on the edge of the small loch, are the famous Palace★ (AM), where Mary Queen of Scots was born, and St Michael's Church. The chapel and hall of the former are 15th-c work, and in the courtyard formed by the Royal Apartments of the W wing is a notable 16th-c fountain. St Michael's is one of the finest 15th-c churches in Scotland. Note especially the nave and choir, and the flamboyant window tracery in the Katherine's aisle. There are a number of 16th-c houses in the town for which the NTS is responsible and the curious Cross Well, with its 13 water jets, is a careful reproduction of an earlier structure.

Musselburgh, Midlothian
11J6

The second largest burgh in Midlothian, with many historical associations (dating back to Roman times), industrial interests and sporting facilities (horse-racing, golf, archery, etc.). The mussels which gave the town its name, though still to be found, are now contaminated and unfit for human consumption. Loretto School, now in Pinkie House (famous for its painted ceiling), formerly occupied a building on the site of a chapel of Our Lady of Loretto whose stones were used in the construction of the present Tolbooth in the late 16th c.

North Berwick, E. Lothian
11J6

Well-known resort famous for its golf-course. 3m NE the Bass Rock, notable for its gannetry, rises 350ft out of the sea with a powerful lighthouse and remains of 17th-c fortifications. 1m S is North Berwick Law, a 613ft volcanic rock with a watch tower dating from Napoleonic times. 3m E beyond Canty Bay, moated *Tantallon Castle★* (AM) is magnificently situated on a rocky headland.

Pathhead, Midlothian
11J6

On the steep banks of Tyne Water, at the foot of the Moorfoot Hills. N across the river is *Oxenfoord Castle*, now a school, in its fine park, while close to the village are two attractive old houses, Preston Hall and Ford House. The

B636 to S, after passing through **Crichton**, reaches a height of 900ft, but about 1m before the summit the tiny village of *Tynehead* stands midway between the romantic *Borthwick* and *Cakemuir Castles★*. From the former massive stronghold, where Mary Queen of Scots lived after her marriage to Bothwell in 1566, she later escaped across the hills to Cakemuir, disguised as a page.

Pencaitland, E. Lothian
11J6

Picturesque village astride the Tyne Water. In the much earlier church are a good W doorway and tower of the 17th c, with three sundials and a laird's loft. Across the river to N is the fine 1620 mansion, *Winton House*, with impressive entrance lodge, fine chimneys and decorated plaster ceilings. 1½m SW is *Penkaet*, a beautiful house of the same period, with two dovecots and contemporary woodwork.

Preston Mill *see* East Linton

Prestonpans, E. Lothian
11J6

Here salt-panning was introduced by the monks in the 12th c, and Prince Charles Edward Stuart won his one major battle over the English in the 1745 Rising. An exceptionally fine 17th-c mercat cross (AM) stands opposite Northfield House, of the same period. 1m E, *Hamilton House*, restored by the NTS, can be seen by arrangement. Near by is a cairn commemorating at the battle of Prestonpans (1745).

Queensferry *see* South Queensferry

Rosslyn Chapel,★★ Midlothian
11I6

At *Roslin*, 7½m S of **Edinburgh**. Founded in 1446 by the St Clair (and last Prince of Orkney) progenitor of the Earls of Rosslyn, has been described as 'one of those architectural wonders whose intricate beauties and peculiarities extort our admiration while they baffle description'. Extensively restored in the 1950s, it is particularly noted for the unique Prentice Pillar with its astonishing detail. Open April–Oct. and used regularly on Sundays. *Rosslyn Castle*, on a cliff overlooking the River Esk, was built between the 13th and 15th c, much ravaged, burned and restored in the 16th and 17th c, but part is still used by the family.

South Queensferry,★ W. Lothian
11I6

The inn at Hawes Ferry has been described in both Scott's *The Antiquary* and R. L. Stevenson's *Kidnapped*. St Mary's, founded in 1330, and still possessing its 16th-c tower and barrel vaulting, is the only Carmelite chapel still functioning as such in Britain. Overshadowing the town are the two great bridges★: the famous 19th-c engineering feat, the Forth Railway Bridge, 2,765yds long and 361ft above the water, and the magnificent new suspension bridge for road traffic, with its central span of 3,330ft, completed 1964. 1½m S is the modernized 15th-c Dundas Castle. 3m W, *Hopetoun House★*, seat of the Marquess of Linlithgow, begun in 1699 by Sir William Bruce and completed by Robert Adam, is a splendid mansion, with interesting museum. Open May–Sept.

Torphichen, W. Lothian
11H6

High on the edge of the Bathgate Hills (the 1,017ft Knock provides a good viewpoint) the village is famous for its church (AM) and preceptory which once belonged to the Knights of St John of Jerusalem. In appearance more like a fortress than a church, the tower with its saddleback roof was once part of the domestic buildings; and its original nave is incorporated in the 16th-c parish church. 2m E, at *Cairnpapple Hill*, a fine Bronze Age burial mound (AM) has been excavated, revealing an earlier Neolithic site.

FIFE REGION

AN INTRODUCTION BY
MORAY McLAREN

This is the only one of the new Scottish regions to correspond exactly with a previous county.

Fife has been called 'A beggar's mantle fringed with gold'. The beggar's mantle part of it is Central and West Fife, given over to a rather severe form of agriculture in the minor uplands and to coal-mining. The fringe of gold is that lovely sandy coastline which stretches eastwards from Aberdour right up to St Andrews, with Crail, Pittenweem, Anstruther and St Monance in between. The 'Scottish Riviera' it has been called, and the claim is not too fanciful. It is just as beautiful a coastline as its *vis-à-vis* in East Lothian, and it has one great advantage: it faces south, displaying in the clear sunshine its colours of blue, green and gold.

Fife, bounded on the north by the wide estuary of the River Tay, on the south by the even wider Firth of Forth and on the east by the North Sea, is three parts an island. It is one of the chief boasts of Scotland that it encourages individuality in its children and in its own scenery. Fife has always kept up its individuality; and it is even said that some of the older folk there, when asked for their nationality, will say 'Fifer' rather than Scottish – and, most certainly, rather than 'British'.

St Andrews, all in all, is an entrancing little city. It has the most famous golf-links in the world. There are some fine 18th-century and neo-Georgian architecture, some spacious streets, some exhilarating if rather austerely cold bathing, and many attractions for the holiday-maker and the scholar of antiquities. It is the seat of the oldest University in Scotland founded in 1412.

It is difficult to imagine that this was once the setting for martyrdom and assassination – until we see the bottle dungeons from which no prisoner ever escaped. St Andrews is a haunted town of delicate and intimate beauty; but the ghosts who haunt it come from a time too remote to affect, still less frighten us. There is nothing in Britain to compare with this small city of gaunt bare ruins, gracious little Regency streets, wide golf-links and golden sands, grey and blue sea, and the scarlet gowns of the students to remind us of the blood that was shed here.

Fife also contains the almost perfectly preserved little 16th-century town of Culross, delicate in its grey stone (silver almost) and pink pantile roofs. In Fife, too, is the historic town of Dunfermline where St Margaret, Queen of Scotland, lies buried and where Robert the Bruce was also interred. Grey, green and proud Dunfermline is one of the many places in Scotland which has historic claims to be the capital. Falkland Palace, with its memories of Mary Queen of Scots, is very well worth a visit. So too is Cupar, the county town of Fife.

Prosperous ports like Culross built houses with harled walls, crow-stepped gables and pantiled roofs in the 1500s

GAZETTEER

Aberdour 11I6
A popular resort 5m NE from Forth Road Bridge on Firth of Forth, notable for silver sands, has 14th–17th-c ruined castle and dovecot (AM). On *Inchcolm Island*, 1½m offshore, the 12th-c Augustinian Abbey (AM) has some of the most complete monastic remains in Scotland: access is by boat (summer only) from Hawkcraig Point or **South Queensferry** (Lothian). Near by towards *Dalgety Bay* is 13th-c St Bridget's Church (AM), well preserved.

Anstruther 11J7
Formerly the main herring port with extensive harbours, it has in St Ayles buildings the important Scottish Fisheries Museum. The *Isle of May*, 6m offshore and reached by boat from Anstruther, has remains of 13th-c chapel dedicated to St Adrian, killed here by Danes in 870. The isle has a Nature Conservancy Council bird observatory and field station.

Auchtermuchty 11I7
Has very old thatched cottages, a rarity in Scotland (the reeds being from the River Tay near **Newburgh**, whence they are also exported to England), an Old Town House and Tolbooth, off the A91.

Burntisland 11I6
Has Rossend Castle (12th-c and later) where Mary Queen of Scots was staying in 1563 when she had her admirer Chastellard arrested. The castle was bought and greatly restored for private use: it may be viewed by arrangement.

Ceres 11J7
An attractive village with a green, a humpback bridge, a stone carving (1578) of the then Provost, and Fife Folk Museum based on the old Weigh House and 17th-c Tolbooth, which has exhibits of trades, crafts and rural life in the past.

Crail 11K7
Golf, and the number of old crow-stepped houses near the harbour, make this fishing-village a popular resort. There is a good Tolbooth, and an interesting 13th-c collegiate church. 2m SW are the *Caiplie Caves*.

Culross,** 11H6
Through the work of NTS and others, Culross has become a showpiece of 16th- and 17th-c domestic architecture (*see* page 373). The NTS owns the Town House (open April–Oct.) and the Study (open Oct.–March); The Ark, Bishop Leighton's House and properties privately occupied. The Trust has an audio-visual presentation. The ruined St Mungo's Chapel was built in 1503 by Archbishop Blackadder on the traditional site of the saint's birth (NTS). The Abbey (AM), a Cistercian monastery founded 1217, has later additions and the Palace, early 17th-c, has fine decorative painted woodwork and ceilings.

Dunfermline 11I6
The magnificent Abbey,* (AM) founded by St Margaret in the 11th c, has the finest Norman nave in Scotland (1150): Robert the Bruce was buried here (1329). Through the Abbey and the Palace, of which only a 200ft-long and 60ft-high wall and an oriel window remain, Dunfermline has a remarkable regal connection: seven kings (including Charles I), one empress, one queen, one queen mother, four princes were born, and nine kings, five queens, six princes and two

princesses are buried here. Charles II in 1650 was the last royal occupant of the vast Palace. The cottage where Andrew Carnegie was born (1835) is a museum and the first of his many public libraries was founded in Abbot Street; he also gave the town Pittencrieff Glen, with fine flower beds, a museum and other amenities.

Falkland,** 11I7
The Palace built by James IV and James V in 1501–41 on an older site was greatly restored by the 3rd Marquess of Bute. In the restored and beautiful gardens is the Royal or 'real' tennis court, one of the few in Britain and still in use, and the 'lang butts' for archery. Charles II created the Scots Guards here in 1650. Open April–Oct.

Hill of Tarvit 11J7
Off the A916, 2½m S of *Cupar*. The mansion house (NTS) was rebuilt from its 1696 remains in 1906 to create a setting for a splendid collection of furniture, paintings by Raeburn, Ramsay and the Dutch school and fine tapestries and Chinese porcelain. Open Easter, May–Sept.; gardens and grounds all year. ¾m W is *Scotstarvit Tower* (1579) (AM). Open May–Sept., keys from mansion house.

Kellie Castle 11J7
Dating from 1360 but mainly 16th- and early 17th-c the Castle was rescued from total abandonment by Professor James Lorimer. His son Sir Robert, the famous architect, and grandson Hew, the sculptor, continued the work and in 1970 with the splendid gardens and land it was bought by NTS. Castle open April–Oct.; gardens all year.

Kincardine-on-Forth 11H6
In 1936 acquired in its new bridge the only crossing of the Forth between **Stirling** (Central) and the then ferry at **South Queensferry** (Lothian): near by is Longannet coal-fired power station, the largest in Britain, fed from several mines by an 11m-long underground conveyor belt, the longest in the world.

Kirkcaldy 11I7
Famous for its linoleum factories, Kirkcaldy now has more sophisticated industries but owes much to benefactions of the lino pioneers. The Industrial Museum is open May–Aug. Ravenscraig Castle (AM) to the N, begun in 1460, was the first British castle designed to resist cannon shot and firearms. The Old Kirk has a 16th-c tower with later church attached. Its three parks, Ravenscraig, Beveridge and Dunnikier, are notable and there is a fine library, museum and art gallery and the John McDouall Stuart Museum, birthplace of the explorer who crossed Australia in 1861. Restored by NTS and open June–Aug.

Largo 11J7
Holiday resort on the Firth of Forth with a small harbour, it has a 16th-c chancel and tower in its parish church and was the birthplace of Alexander Selkirk (1676) whose real-life adventures were used by Defoe in *Robinson Crusoe*. There is a statue of him in the town.

Leuchars* 11J8
Notable for its very fine Norman church, with its interesting bell turret above the apse, added in the 17th c. To the E the ancient and picturesque house, Earlshall, has been

admirably restored. The RAF base near by is one of the most important operational stations in Britain.

Markinch 11I7
A town familiar to whisky connoisseurs with a partly 12th-c church dedicated to St Drostan, a nephew of St Columba. 1½m SE is *Balgonie Castle* with a 15th-c tower (not open) and 2m SE *Balfour House* where Cardinal Beaton was born: he was slain at **St Andrews** Castle in 1546.

Newburgh 11I8
Outside this harbour on the Firth of Tay is the *Island of Mugdrum*; the Mugdrum Cross in the town is more than 1,000 years old. To the E are the remains of *Lindores Abbey*; and 3m NE, ruined *Ballanbreich Castle* overlooks the Firth.

Pittenweem 11J7
Old houses surround this picturesque harbour. Near by is the cave-shrine of St Fillan. The church has an impressive square tower dated 1592. 2m NW *Balcaskie House* with its terraced gardens was designed by Sir William Bruce; and 1m further on is the turreted, 16th-c *Kellie Castle*, with its notable interior and pictures.

St Andrews** 11J7
This fascinating city and resort, standing on a promontory above long stretches of sand, has many claims to fame besides being the headquarters of golf (it has four courses,

St Andrews: the view from St Rule's Church tower of the cathedral ruins, the cliff-top castle, and the city

with the Royal and Ancient Club, founded in 1754). Its cathedral (AM), though now largely ruined, was once the largest in the country, and still includes extensive monastic remains; while close by the choir and high tower of 12th-c St Rule's (AM) are still standing. Its University is the oldest in Scotland, having been founded in 1412, and today has more than 3,600 students. The College Chapel, once the church of St Salvator, contains John Knox's pulpit, brought here from the Town Church, where he preached his first sermons; and in the quadrangle of St Mary's College a thorn tree, planted by Mary Queen of Scots, still flourishes. Interesting local relics are to be found in the Sessions House (including two repentance stools and a scold's bridle) and in the Town Hall (portraits and a headsman's axe). In the ancient ruined Castle (AM), standing on a rock above the sea, note the 'bottle dungeon' and underground passage; while 2m SE are the curious basalt pillars, the 'Rock and Spindle'.

St Monance 11J7
Old and delightful little fishing-port, with ancient St David's Church standing on the foreshore. Its shipyard, which once built the 'Fifie' trawlers, now builds yachts. 3m W along the coast road that passes the ruins of *Ardross Castle*, are the twin resorts of *Elie* and *Earlsferry*, standing at the extremities of a bay with good beaches and bathing.

TAYSIDE REGION

AN INTRODUCTION BY
WILFRED TAYLOR

This area covers the greater part of the old counties of Perth and Angus, with the exception of the southwest corner of Perth which is now in Central Region. It can well be described as the South Highlands, which may be defined as that part of Scotland (except for Caithness and the Buchan peninsula in Aberdeenshire) lying north of a line drawn from Helensburgh on the Clyde to Stonehaven on the North Sea, a few miles south of Aberdeen. This Highland line runs southwest to northeast, and almost three-quarters of it is in either Perthshire or Angus, the greater part of each of these former counties lying north of it, where the Grampian Mountains sweep up to heights of 3,500 feet or more.

The Highland line is followed through Angus and much of Perthshire by the low-lying valley of Strathmore. This valley swells southeastward to the Ochil Hills on the county boundary and in Angus to the Sidlaw Hills. These (which extend some way into Perthshire also) are separated from the Firth of Tay by another low-lying fertile strip, the Carse of Gowrie. Except for this area, and the clay in the vales and the coastal strip of Angus, much of the soil in both counties is poor and suitable only for heather, bracken, silver birch and conifers – though often enough the scenery is magnificent, especially by loch or river side.

Perthshire

Perthshire, one of the largest of the old Scottish counties, was roughly circular in shape and it offers an astonishing variety of scenery, from the bleak mountains in the north to the gentle and sweetly flowing Allan Water in the south. It is an entirely inland county except for 20 miles or so on the Tay estuary; it is a county of lofty mountains, rushing rivers, woodlands and romantic lochs. With, in its heartland, the incomparable Loch Tay, Loch Earn and Loch Tummel, it offers the nearest thing in Scotland to a Lake District. And through it flows the longest, most handsome and most majestic of Scottish rivers, the Tay, which as it approaches its estuary under craggy ramparts to the east of Perth has reminded many a visitor of the Rhine.

Perth, the former county town and the setting of Scott's *Fair Maid of Perth*, has all the appearance of a miniature capital. Lying mostly to the west of the Tay, which rolls under a number of graceful bridges, the town is fortunate in the possession of two vast green meadows, the North and the South Inch. It was on the North Inch that the last clan battle took place in Scotland in 1396. Here the Clan Kay and the Clan Chattan engaged in bitter and annihilating conflict, from which it is said only one man of Clan Kay escaped, by swimming the river, and less than a dozen of Clan Chattan – which was therefore awarded the victory.

Although its church spires and Georgian houses remind one of the antiquity of Perth, there is also a modern and harmonious town centre. As the centre of an agricultural area Perth is an important market for farmers, and its winter bull sales, which attract buyers from far overseas, add to the social life of the town, as do the Perth Hunt races.

Apart from Perth itself, there are a number of interesting little towns like Aberfeldy and Crieff. Of these the best known is Pitlochry, about 27 miles north of Perth on the A9 to Inverness. Lying in the richly wooded valley of the River Tummel, with the shapely peak of Ben Vrackie (2,757 feet) towering behind it, Pitlochry is an excellent touring-centre for such sights as the Queen's View (Victoria, it was), the Falls of Tummel or the Black Spout waterfall, the Pass of Killiecrankie and, indeed, for much of the best part of Perthshire. Its own attractions have been increased in recent years by two local developments. As part of a hydro-electric scheme, the waters of the Tummel have been harnessed by the construction of a dam on the outskirts of the town, creating the new Loch Faskally, which stretches up into the wooded hills. A big salmon-ladder has also been built, with a glass-sided observation-chamber underneath one of its steps, from which visitors can watch the salmon pausing on their climb up to the spawning-beds. And secondly, the 'Theatre in the Hills', founded shortly after World War II by Mr John Stewart, who spent his entire fortune on it, now attracts thousands of visitors to Pitlochry every summer with its repertory

The region has many historic buildings. Blair Castle, circa *1269, was the last to be besieged in 1746*

of plays. The original tented building has now been replaced by a magnificent permanent structure, called Pitlochry Festival Theatre, across the river, and just off the new bypass road to the north.

The district abounds in historic buildings, and whether it is Blair Castle or the unexpected little public library on a loop of the River Earn at Innerpeffray, there is always something to fascinate the student of antiquity. Ecclesiastical architecture is to be found in great variety, from the cathedral church at Dunkeld to the simple little churches at Kenmore or Struan.

With its abundance of lochs, rivers and burns, Perthshire is a favourite county for fishermen, who can take the choice of slipping up to some lonely little lochan in the hills or of renting one of the most expensive beats on the Tay near Stanley. In recent years sailing and water-skiing have become popular, especially on Loch Earn, where the Scottish water-skiing championships are held. In winter and spring, crowds of sportsmen flock to Ben Lawers at the weekend to ski. In all, it is a county of extraordinary richness and contrast – a county that wears its beauty serenely and enchantingly.

Angus

Angus, a square and lumpish county, is contiguous with Perthshire on its western frontiers, but is totally different in atmosphere. Although it penetrates deep into the southern Grampians, former Angus is a maritime county. After its secluded passage through Perthshire, the River Tay, before it finally contracts between Dundee and Newport, to burst into the North Sea, puffs out its chest and in its tidal pride claims a breadth of about 4 miles or so to the opposite shore of Fife.

This is one of the most beautiful parts of Scotland, although Dundee, with its metropolis, is the country's fourth city in terms of population. Despite the fact that it is the portal to some of the finest scenery in Scotland, Dundee does little to lure the tourist. In some ways, with its compressed centre and undistinguished High Street, it is a glorified market town. In other ways it is a commercial and financial centre of the utmost importance. In the past, astute Dundee financiers did a great deal to open up the cattle lands of the American southwest.

Largely dependent on jute which originated as a by-product from the 18th-century whaling industry, the city was badly hit during the early 1930s. After World War II it lifted itself out of the rut largely by strenuous local effort, and American industry was attracted to the industrial estates on the Kingsway. The young jute men sponsored great modernization projects; and now the new University, with its miniature skyscraper tower, dominates the intellectual life of Dundee in a brisk and ambitious way.

But Dundee is not Angus. Angus is an area of little towns like Forfar, Kirriemuir, Brechin, Arbroath and Edzell, a county of pretty little villages like Cortachy and rock-bound Auchmithie. It has rich and fertile farming country, traversed by the broad vale of Strathmore, with its fat farms and enchanting vistas of the Grampian rim. In its fields you will see the black, hornless Aberdeen-Angus cattle, which give, in the opinion of many good judges, the best beef in the world. It is, too, a land of romantic castles. Best known of these is Glamis, where Princess Margaret was born. Angus people are forthright and straightforward in their speech. They are men who love the soil and brook no nonsense. And Angus has its poets, writing in the rich vernacular, like Violet Jacob, Marion Angus and Sir Alexander Gray; and its authors, like Lewis Grassic Gibbon, whose prose runs to the lilt of the spoken Scots.

Angus abounds in golden beaches and links – its golf-courses are legendary, from the inland courses at Brechin, Blairgowrie and Forfar, to the seaside Carnoustie course, where the Open Championship has frequently taken place. But, best of all, Angus is the county of lovely, lonely glens. Their names make music – Glenisla, Glen Prosen, Glen Clova, Glen Doll, Glenogil, Glenesk. These glens wind deeply into the hills (the famous Braes of Angus), and with their little farmhouses, their kirks, their inns, and their charming mansion houses and castles they are an invitation to peace of mind. To those who want to feel sunburned with contentment there is nothing like those green, pastoral, mountain-walled valleys. Go up Glenesk, for instance, as this writer did, and stop at the little schoolhouse at Tarfside to watch the children, in their soft voices, rehearsing a poetic play written for them by the Angus poet, Helen Cruickshank, about the animals they know. Or, if you are a geologist, the rocks and glacial valleys of Angus will keep you busy. An antiquarian? Visit the little local folk museums and see how Angus folk in the past lived, worked and amused themselves. A lover of landscape? Drive up Glen Clova on a summer evening, up one side of the river and back by the other, and you will experience a wonderful uplift of the spirit.

GAZETTEER

Aberfeldy, Perth 13I1
A charming town on the Tay at the junction of the A827 and A826; notable for General Wade's bridge built to quell the Highlands after the 1715 Rising. At the S end is a cairn commemorating the raising of 'the Watch' in 1667 by Highlanders to guard the Highlands; in 1739 they became the Black Watch, the 42nd Regiment, the name coming from their dark tartan. There is golf, excellent fishing, nature trails and forest walks.

Abernethy, Perth 11I7
One (AM) of the two 'Irish' round towers of Scotland (see **Brechin**) survives from a history which goes far back to Pictish and monastic community life.

Alyth, Perth 13K1
Busy small town at the foot of the Braes of Angus, with a burn running down the main street. Folk Museum open May–Sept. Iron Age camp on *Barry Hill*, 2m E. *Airlie Castle*, 4m NE, incorporates remains of the 'Bonnie House o' Airlie' burned by Argyll in 1640 and avenged by Montrose.

Arbroath, Angus 11K8
A busy fishing-port, noted for 'Arbroath smokies' (haddock) and kippers, resort and industrial town. In the fine 12th–13th-c Abbey (AM) the Declaration of Independence achieved by Robert the Bruce was signed. Here on the High Altar in April 1951 the young Scots who had stolen the Stone of Destiny from the Coronation Chair in **Westminster Abbey** 'returned' it, and informed the authorities. The Bell Rock lighthouse and its Signal Tower (now a museum) were built by Robert Stevenson, grandfather of R.L.S, in 1811.

Ardoch, Perth 11K8
Extensive Roman encampment capable of accommodating over 30,000 men and the most perfect and clear example of Roman earthworks in Britain.

Birnam, Perth 11H8
In the NTS wooded gorge above River Braan is a picturesque folly, The Hermitage, built 1758. It was with branches from Birnam Woods that Malcolm camouflaged his troops on their march to Dunsinane in Shakespeare's *Macbeth*.

Blair Atholl,★ Perth 13J2
This popular resort amid beautiful scenery is dominated by white, turreted Blair Castle, seat of the Duke of Atholl, with parts dating from 1269 in Comyn's Tower. Visitors have included Mary Queen of Scots and Prince Charles Edward Stuart and his troops in 1745. The Duke is the only person in Britain allowed to maintain a private army, the Atholl Highlanders. The Castle, with its fine collection of portraits and Jacobite mementoes, is open Easter–Oct. (*See* page 377.)

Blairgowrie, Perth 11I8
Though on the edge of the Highlands, this sheltered district is famous for soft fruit – raspberries in particular. Painting by Caravaggio in the Episcopal Church. There is an unusually beautiful golf-course at *Rosemount*, 1m SE.

Brechin, Angus 13L2
Restoration work in 1901 has done much to atone for the barbarous demolition of the transepts of the Cathedral nearly 100 years earlier. An 'Irish' round tower (AM) attached to the masonry of the Cathedral tapers to a conical roof added in the 14th c (*see also* **Abernethy**). Two prehistoric forts, the *Brown* and *White Caterthuns*, 5½m NW, give a splendid view of the Grampians.

Cairnwell Pass, Perth 13J2
The highest point on any main road in Britain (2,199ft) lies between mountains 1,000ft higher. The *Devil's Elbow* to the S has severe gradients and sharp hairpin turns. *See also* **Glen Shee** and **Cairnwell** (Grampian).

Carnoustie, Angus 11J8
Famous golf-links and seaside resort. The sandbanks at Buddon Ness, at the mouth of the Tay, are a haunt of wildfowl. Ever since the flight of the Earl to France in 1715 the gates of Panmure House, 1½m, have remained closed.

Comrie, Perth 10G8
Stands at the junction of two glens over the geological fault between the Highlands and the Lowlands, from which the rumble of harmless earthquakes is frequently heard. The beautiful castellated steeple of the old parish church remains unaffected by these subterranean disturbances. The tartan museum is worth visiting.

Coupar Angus, Perth 11I8
Named thus to distinguish it from Cupar in Fife. Traces of Cistercian abbey in churchyard. Very interesting earthhouse at *Pitcur*, 2m S – key at Hallyburton House.

Craigower, Perth 13J2
A beacon hill 1½m N of **Pitlochry** with splendid views of the town, Tummel Valley and Loch Faskally. NTS has created the Dunmore Trail in memory of the 9th Earl, an active member of Council, and his father, Viscount Fincastle, killed in action, 1940. (*See* facing page.)

Crieff, Perth 11H8
Pleasant town with good hotel accommodation, at junction of two scenic roads. Antiquities include a fine mercat cross with runic carving, and cup and ring stones on the golf-course. *Drummond Castle*, 3m S, has formal terraced gardens and a multiple sundial (1630) . Open April–Oct.

Pitlochry: in a peaceful setting beside loch and forested mountains, best seen from Craigower

Dundee, Angus   11J8

Headquarters of Tayside Region suffered from the jute industry decline but prosperity was restored by electronics and oil-related developments. Its jute boom period is reflected in fine civic buildings, notably Caird Hall, which covers 2 acres. The 156ft Old Steeple, near the single roof of the three city churches, is the one antiquity of importance. Queen's College in 1967 became the independent University of Dundee with 3,600 students. At Victoria Dock, the frigate *Unicorn* has been restored – displays, etc. A public astronomical observatory is at Balgay Hill. Whaling relics in Broughty Ferry Castle Museum, 4m E of centre. For a good view of the city, docks and estuary of the Tay, go to the War Memorial on Dundee Law (571ft) 5m W, off the A85, is 15th c *Castle Huntly.* 3m NW is *Camperdown House,* c.1829, with Spalding Golf Museum and extensive parkland. *See also* **Tay Bridges.**

Dunkeld, Perth   11H8

Peacefully bypassed by a new bridge carrying the busy A9 this delightful town may now be fully enjoyed. The old bridge was built by Telford in 1809. The beautiful cathedral started in 1318 and completed with the great NW tower in 1501, was much damaged by the Reformers but the choir

(now the parish church) and much else has been restored. NTS owns and has restored 17th-c houses in Cathedral Street and High Street. It also owns Stanley Hill, the wooded background to the town.

Edzell Castle, Angus   13L2

The Bower in Stirling Tower of the castle (AM) was frequented by Mary Queen of Scots. The Renaissance formal garden below the keep has walls showing allegorical subjects in low relief, and a turreted garden house in one corner.

Forfar,★ Angus   13L1

Former capital of the county, and now District headquarters. An octagonal turret marks the site of the castle in which the Parliament of 1057 conferred surnames on Scottish noblemen. The Town Hall exhibits a specimen of the 'Forfar Bridle', a gag for the witches who were so prevalent in this region. *Restenneth Priory* (AM), 1½m E, is notable for having an 18th-c spire built over a 12th-c upper storey, itself in turn built over the remains of an 8th-c tower.

Fortingall, Perth   13I1

Off the B846 at the foot of Glen Lyon. In the churchyard stands a yew tree said to be 3,000 years old. In 1772 it had a girth of 57ft and is now well protected. Local legend says that Pontius Pilate, son of a Roman ambassador, was born here. There are Iron and Bronze Age relics.

Glamis Castle: the Queen Mother's Sitting Room at the ancestral home of her father, the Earl of Strathmore

Fowlis Easter,* Angus   11I8
6m W of **Dundee** and 2m off the A85. St Marnan's Church, built on 12th-c foundations is one of the oldest in Scotland still in regular use. It is famed for 15th- and early 16th-c oak panel paintings, the largest being 16ft by 6ft 6in; they were skilfully cleaned some years ago. Other ancient relics include the jougs used, round the neck, to punish wrongdoers.

Glamis Castle,** Angus   13K1
Probably the most attractive and evocative inhabited castle in Scotland. It is mainly 17th-c baronial style, but goes back 1,000 years in history. It is the seat of the Earls of Strathmore, forebears of the Queen Mother, and birthplace of Princess Margaret. Sir Walter Scott is chiefly responsible for perpetuating the story of a secret room known only to each heir. Armour, portraits, tapestries and fine furniture, as well as picturesque gardens. The view from the battlements is superb. Open Easter, May–Oct. The Angus Folk Museum (NTS) in the village has an interesting collection of domestic and agricultural implements. Open May–Sept.

Glen Shee, Perth   13J2
A principal skiing resort, with a chairlift from the summit of the highest main-road pass in Britain (2,199ft) up the **Cairnwell** mountain (3,059ft): in summer it is a scenic route to Deeside.

Huntingtower Castle, Perth   11I8
3m NW of **Perth** (A85), this castle (AM) was named Ruthven until all mention of that family was proscribed as a result of the Gowrie Conspiracy in 1600. The two 15th-c towers are joined by a later building which includes a great hall notable for wall and ceiling painting. The gap between the towers is the 'Maiden's Leap' of legend.

Kenmore, Perth   10G8
At the NE end of Loch Tay, this popular holiday resort had its beauty immortalized by Robert Burns in lines written over the parlour fireplace at the inn. *Taymouth Castle*, to the NE, was built in 1801 on a 16th-c foundation with a W wing added for Queen Victoria's visit in 1842. The seat of the Earls of Breadalbane, it has elaborate carved panels, a vast entrance hall with remarkable staircase rising from it, and the grounds (in which there is a golf-course) are notable for the magnificent trees. The Earl in 1847 introduced the Swedish capercailzie, a large game bird, which has spread extensively mainly N. 2m E at *Croft Moraig* is a fine group of standing stones.

Killiecrankie, Perth   13J2
The wooded pass, much admired by Queen Victoria, is near the scene of the battle in 1689 when the Jacobites under 'Bonnie Dundee' (Graham of Claverhouse) routed William III's forces. The Soldier's Leap, a great jump across the river said to have been cleared by a Royalist trooper, is below the NTS visitor centre (exhibition etc. open April–Oct.). NTS owns 54 acres and provides walks and ranger services.

Kinloch Rannoch, Perth   13I1
Fishing centre at E end of Loch Rannoch. In the Black Wood of Rannoch near *Dall* (the house is a public school) the Forestry Commission is encouraging the regeneration of Scots pines of the ancient Caledonian forest of which a number remain.

Kinross   11I7
To the W of **Loch Leven**, this resort is well known for its fishing, golf, skating and curling. Kinross House, with its beautiful gardens, is a fine achievement by the 17th-c architect, Sir William Bruce. Note the town cross, and the Tolbooth, with Robert Adam's decoration.

Kirriemuir, Angus   13K1
Probably more people have heard of Sir James Barrie's Thrums than of Kirriemuir, though it is decidedly a place in its own right. No. 9 Brechin Road (NTS; open May–Sept.), where Barrie was born, his grave, and many corners of the town made famous by him, are places of interest to lovers of his works.

Loch Leven,★ Kinross   11I7
This very attractive loch (*see also* **Kinross** and **Milnathort**), famous among fishermen for its pink-fleshed trout, is of great historical interest. From the Castle (AM) on the smaller of its two islands, William Douglas helped Mary Queen of Scots to escape after she had been imprisoned there for almost a year. On the other island are the remains of St Serf's Priory. The loch and adjacent land is a National Nature Reserve and important wintering and breeding area for great numbers of geese and duck. The RSPB centre at Vane Farm, on the B9097 off the M90, has good facilities.

Meigle, Perth   11I8
A small local museum (AM) contains over 20 interesting carved Celtic stones found in or near the old churchyard.

Meikleour, Perth   11I8
The famous beech hedge bordering the A93, planted 1746, is over 600yd long and 90ft high.

Milnathort, Kinross   11I7
Besides being one of the two towns from which **Loch Leven** is easily accessible, this little wool town is near the ruined *Burleigh Castle* (AM), once a Balfour fortress; a short distance SE are the interesting standing stones of *Orwell*.

Montrose, Angus   13M2
Former royal burgh from which Sir James Douglas embarked for the Holy Land carrying the heart of Bruce (*see* **Dunfermline**, Fife); where John Erskine of Dun established the first school in Scotland for the teaching of Greek (1534); where the great Marquess, James Graham, was born in 1612; and whence the Old Pretender fled by sea in 1716 at the collapse of the rebellion of the Earl of Mar. Now very popular as golfing and seaside resort, and of increasing importance as a port and oil-associated base.

Perth★   11I8
'The Fair City', once the Scottish capital, and the scene of numerous historic events, is now prosperously occupied in dyeing, distilling and the marketing of cattle. The city has grown greatly and is a major tourist and business centre for a wide area. Old Perth was built on the Tay between two green spaces, the North and South Inches, one famous for the contest described in Scott's *Fair Maid*, and the other for those three great medieval sports: golf, archery and witch-burning. John Knox preached his famous inflammatory sermon in the church of St John in 1559, with the result that many of the churches of Scotland were 'purged of idolatry' – and of works of art beyond reclaim. St John's was splendidly restored as a War Memorial to its parishioners. Visitors will wish to see the Fair Maid's House in Curfew Row, now a crafts shop, with its quaint upstairs rooms. The Art Gallery and Museum in North Street contain paintings, antiques, geological, zoological and botanical collections. An excellent nature trail is at Kinnoull Hill.

Pitlochry,★ Perth   13J1
Claims to be the geographical centre of Scotland. Very lively resort, with Highland Games, sheepdog trials, golf, tennis, water sports and the Festival Theatre (April–Oct.). Hydro-electric works have produced Loch Faskally with an underwater observation-chamber★ opening on to the Fish Ladder which thousands of salmon negotiate every year. Open Easter–Sept. *See also* Introduction, **Craigower** and page 379.

Rumbling Bridge, Kinross   11H7
A famous beauty spot, where two adjacent bridges span the River Devon. Devil's Mill and Caldron Linn are the finest falls, to the NE and SW respectively.

Scone Palace,★ Perth   11I8
2m N of **Perth**. Home of the Earl of Mansfield. Enlarged and embellished in 1803 on 16th-c and earlier foundations, the Palace has a magnificent collection of porcelain, furniture, ivories, 18th-c clocks and 16th-c needlework. Open Easter–Oct. The Mote Hill was the site of the Coronation Stone of Scone taken there, probably from **Iona** (Strathclyde), by Kenneth MacAlpine, 9th-c King of Scots, and stolen by Edward I of England in 1296 and installed in the Coronation Chair in **Westminster Abbey**, London.

Sma' Glen, Perth   11H8
Stony gorge 2m long on the road N from **Crieff** on the A822. An enormous flat stone (8ft by 5ft) near the head of the glen is taken to mark the burial place of Ossian, the legendary Gaelic bard.

Tay Bridges, Angus   11J8
The railway bridge built in 1883–8 to replace that destroyed in a gale in 1879 when a train plunged into the River Tay killing 90 passengers, is one of the world's longest (2m): it is supported on 73 pairs of piers. The toll road bridge was opened in 1966 and is 1½m long. *See also* **Dundee**.

Tullibardine, Perth   11H7
A district 6m SE of **Crieff**, which has a collegiate church founded by Sir David Murray in 1446 and enlarged by his successor: it is cruciform with a small tower (AM).

Weem, Perth   13I1
Castle Menzies is a good example of the Scottish baronial mansion (open May–Oct.). The village inn is associated with General Wade, the great soldier-cum-engineer of the 18th c who was responsible for much of Scotland's road system and many beautiful bridges.

GRAMPIAN REGION

AN INTRODUCTION BY
JOHN R. ALLAN AND CUTHBERT GRAHAM

The former counties of Moray, Banff, Aberdeen and Kincardine (often known as the Mearns) have many local differences but a common character: they lie between the sea and the mountains. There is a continuous strip of ploughland, from a few to more than 30 miles wide, of the lowland sort which rises and thins away into sheep grazings and grouse moors. Then there is a steep ascent into the Grampians and the Cairngorms where the high tops are over 4,000 feet. Lying far into the moors and the lower slopes of the mountains there are the glens carved out by the rivers – the Findhorn, the Lossie, the noble Spey and its tributary the Avon, the Deveron, the Ugie, the Ythan, the Don, the Dee and the North Esk – glens that become narrower and emptier of people till they end in highland solitudes or remote uplands.

Looked at on the map the region lies along the southern flank of the great inlet called the Moray Firth, with a bulging green knuckle of land pushing eastwards into the North Sea and tapering southwards and southwestwards towards the major seaport of Aberdeen, the largest in the north of Scotland. This circumstance has given the region great importance in the new economic strategy brought about by the exploitation of North Sea oil and has resulted in unprecedented prosperity and the highest average of employment in Scotland.

The main geological divisions are the Caledonian granites, mostly in Aberdeenshire, Dalradian schists in Aberdeenshire and Banff, and the Old Red Sandstone in the Howe of the Mearns, in some patches of Aberdeenshire and Banff, and in the coastal plain (the Laigh) of Moray. The upper glens of the Findhorn, the Spey and the North Esk are highly picturesque but in two respects the River Dee is unique: it has the greatest altitudinal range of any river system in Britain, with its source at over 4,000 feet where it bubbles through the gravel and the summit of Braeriach, and it must be among the very few European rivers which are virtually unpolluted from source to mouth – a flow of pure, clear mountain water even where its banks are lined with houses. Since 1852, when Queen Victoria acquired the estate of Balmoral, the Dee has been a Royal valley,

although its glen was used as a hunting reserve by the early Scottish kings from the 11th century. The river provides the water supply of the city of Aberdeen.

Flora and Fauna
In the high Cairngorms and Upper Glen Dee and Glen Derry there is a Nature Conservancy of about 60 square miles. Lower down the Dee Valley there is the Muir of Dinnet Nature Reserve while there is another reserve along several miles of coast at St Cyrus in Kincardineshire and a third at the Sands of Forvie immediately north of the mouth of the River Ythan. This has notable colonies of terns, shelduck and eider duck, while across the water at Newburgh, the University of Aberdeen has its own natural history laboratories and bird sanctuary. Where the coastlands of the region are not defended by beetling and rugged cliffs they are opened up to a landscape of long sandy bays and often shifting sand dunes. At Culbin near Forres the Forestry Commission has established a forest on a vast area of drifting sand that smothered the farmlands. This miracle of reclamation may now be visited by the public, who find it an attractive picnic site.

In autumn miles of heather on the carefully managed grouse-moors spread a purple flush over the uplands. The forests suffered greatly in the two World Wars, but the Forestry Commission has planted thousands of acres, mostly pines. There is also much private forestry, notably on the Queen's estate at Balmoral and at Glentanar, lower down Deeside, where pride is taken in the success with which the Scots pines of the ancient Caledonian Forest have been induced to regenerate themselves. Mixed hardwoods survive in many Deeside estates and it is a river famous for the graceful silver birch.

Red deer live on the hills and come to the low ground in winter – but even in summer they can be seen along the banks of the Dee between Balmoral Castle and Braemar. The birds of the high ground are ptarmigan, golden eagles, black game, capercailzie,

Balmoral Castle, the Royal Family's holiday home, was largely designed by Prince Albert in the 19th century

grouse, crossbill, siskin and the great spotted woodpecker. Oyster-catchers are becoming more common on the low ground and even nest on the gravel spread along the roofs of tower blocks in the city of Aberdeen. Woodpigeons and rooks are a trial to farmers. At Hatton, near Turriff in Aberdeenshire, the rookery has about 6,000 nests and is the largest in Britain.

The Climate
The comparative dryness of the climate was the reason why Queen Victoria was first persuaded to settle on Deeside. Over the whole area the rainfall is low, about 32 inches a year. It is rather a windy corner and the east winds are cold, but the great delight is the clarity of the air, in which all the world seems to have been swept clean. Moray is a favoured province, always a little milder than the rest. The sunsets along the Moray Firth are magnificent as the sun goes down beyond the Ross-shire hills. It is a measure of the clemency of the climate that crops ripen to the highest quality and inhabitants live to a good age.

Industries
Although hundreds of small new businesses have been attracted into the region by the North Sea oil boom, the chief industry is still farming. It has been brought up to a high standard, in many places on land that was the despair of early observers. Farms of 300 acres and more are to be found in the Howe of the Mearns, in central Aberdeenshire, in Banff and Moray. But still common on poorer land is the 'family place' of say 50 acres worked by the farmer and his family. There are smaller holdings also, the crofts which do not give a full-time job, so that the farmer works out. Mechanization is virtually complete and the horse has disappeared. Chief grain crops are barley, oats and wheat. On the best lands the yields are high, over 2 tons an acre. The best of the barley goes to make the best of whisky. Grampian farms are famous for their stock – particularly the local breeds, Aberdeen-Angus and Shorthorn, with their crosses and other breeds. On the hill farms there are thousands of sheep. Pigs are kept by the hundreds and hens by the thousands.

Fishing is the second industry. All round the coast there are the fisher villages and towns, in coves with shelter and some with none. Fishermen still live in the villages huddled against the wind by the open beaches, as at Inverallochy, or at the foot of great cliffs, as at Pennan, but they fish out of the big ports: Lossiemouth, Buckie, Peterhead, Fraserburgh and Aberdeen. Aberdeen since 1880 has been a major trawling port; the others first came into prominence as herring centres but have now mainly transferred their attention to white fish, and indeed it is one of the wonders of the new oil era that while Aberdeen has declined as a trawling port, Peterhead has begun to supplant it as the chief white fishing port. It is one of

the great pleasures of exploring Grampian Region that the colourful old fishing havens offer a very striking contrast to the scenic splendours of the glens and the mountains.

Industries survive in these parts by skill, perseverance and high quality. There are famous textile-mills at Grandholm near Aberdeen, at Huntly, Keith, Elgin and Peterhead, producing tweeds and knitwear renowned in many parts of the world. Aberdeen carried the cachet 'the Granite City' because of its skill in working the intensely hard building stone quarried at Rubislaw and other quarries, now largely worked out. Banffshire and Moray are the great whisky-making areas, pursuing the art of making malt out of barley, using peat for firing, of brewing the malt in soft hill water, and then distilling the spirit. The Grampian distilleries produce millions of gallons of whisky and tens of millions of revenue. It can seldom be that so much is earned by so few.

History: Castles and Great Houses
Grampian has its full share of prehistoric antiquities. On Bennachie (the Mountain of Light) in central Aberdeenshire, on Tap o' Noth and Dunnideer, in the same county, there were hill forts and there are traces of Neolithic villages at Sands of Forvie and elsewhere. The Moray Firth coast has its promontory forts and over the whole area there are henges and recumbent stone circles. Outstanding examples of such circles are to be found at Daviot, Midmar, Sunhoney of Echt and Tomnaverie at Tarland. Recent aerial survey has identified a major Roman camp at Crichie just north of Bennachie, lending credence to the idea that the great battle of Mons Graupius described by Tacitus was fought here. In the Dark Ages the Picts carved within the region a wonderful range of sculptured stones with animal symbols, followed by battle scenes and finally elaborate Christian crosses. The Maiden Stone near Chapel of Garioch and Sueno's Stone near Forres are famous examples.

Of medieval castles the most impressive must have been Kildrummy on the Don and Dunnottar on its stupendous cliff south of Stonehaven. Both are now breathtaking even in ruin, but of castles that survive, the 16th- and early 17th-century tower houses, collectively known as the Castles of Mar, are quite outstanding as works of art. The very best of them now belong to the National Trust for Scotland and are the work of a single master-mason – John Bell of Midmar. Crathes Castle, Craigievar and Castle Fraser are all within easy reach of Aberdeen and should on no account be missed. Another NTS property of somewhat earlier period is Drum Castle which combines a sturdy 13th-century tower with battlemented wall walk to which a gracious Jacobean mansion was later attached. The Trust also owns Haddo House, an early 18th-century country house of particular charm built for the 2nd Earl of Aberdeen. The fine wooded grounds of Haddo are now a country park. The Marchioness of Aberdeen still lives at Haddo and leads a well-known choral society which gives famous concerts in Haddo House Chapel. The only NTS property in the Moray district is Brodie Castle, which combines medieval and 18th-century features and houses a fine collection of modern paintings.

But the Moray area has also much architectural distinction ranging from the stately ruins of Elgin Cathedral and the arcaded street building of the town itself to Pluscarden Abbey, and Gordonstoun, a public school attended by members of the Royal Family.

The former county town of Banff is renowned for a splendid range of surviving 17th- and 18th-century domestic buildings. Aberdeen, beginning with its medieval treasures – the Cathedral of St Machar, the Crown Tower and Chapel of King's College, the Brig o' Balgownie and the Bridge of Dee – has charming 18th-century buildings, lovingly restored, in Old Aberdeen, and numerous noble granite buildings of the 19th century. The chief architect of these was Archibald Simpson (1790–1847) whose country houses, churches and civic offices are to be found throughout the whole region.

There are many fine gardens, both private and public in Grampian. Outstanding is the Great Garden of Pitmedden near Tarves, a 17th-century formal garden restored by the NTS. The gardens of Balmoral Castle are open to the public in May, June and July, when the Queen is not in residence. The public is also admitted to the Ballroom of the castle with a fascinating small exhibition of Victoriana.

Recreation and Sport

Sandy beaches, excellent public golf-courses and pleasure parks abound in Aberdeen and elsewhere in the region. Football, cricket, tennis and squash are available too.

Hill-walking, rock-climbing and skiing are increasingly popular in the Grampians and Cairngorms.

There are ski-lifts at Spittal of Glenshee, south of Braemar, and on the western side of the Cairngorms at Aviemore, while there is a new ski run at the Lecht, the high pass between Cock Bridge and Tomintoul.

In the summer the cattle shows bring out all the country people. So do the Highland Games where men compete in throwing hammers, tossing cabers (dressed tree trunks), putting weights, running, jumping, dancing and bagpipe music. The biggest of these events are the Aboyne Games in August and the Braemar Gathering on the first Saturday of September. The Queen and her guests at Balmoral attend Braemar, which draws enormous crowds.

The fishing is good – in the sea with the line or in the rivers with the rod for salmon, sea–trout and brown trout. Grouse are shot from 12 August, and partridges, pheasants and deer later in the year.

Food and Drink

It is fair to say that the people are good plain cooks. It is unwise to expect anything fancy to turn out well, though it often does. But the cooks understand the native foods – the salmon, the trout, the game, the poultry and the prime beef. Fish, fresh out of the sea, can be a revelation to those accustomed to fish that tastes of mortality. The finnan, the smoked haddock, is a delicacy, either grilled or cooked in milk. Oatcakes, thin oatcakes, are another delicacy, with plenty of fresh butter. Porridge is usually taken with salt, but those who wish may have sugar instead. The home baking is often very good. The coffee is weak, but the tea is virile. And in all these parts one can study the whisky. It is possible to get the single (unblended) whiskies of the local distilleries and balance a Glenlivet against a Glendronach, with a Macallan on the side for reference. That can become quite a hobby and even a life's work.

One last thing – never hesitate to ask a native for information. Either he will say: 'Och, I daena ken,' or else he will tell you perhaps more than you wish to know, which is one of the better risks of travel.

GAZETTEER

Aberdeen*   13M3/N3
Since the early 1970s this long-thriving University and Cathedral city, major fishing-port and centre for the beef and cattle trades, has become the oil 'capital' of Europe as the base for manning and servicing North Sea oil rigs and exploration platforms: new hotels, office blocks, massive housing estates have arisen and it has the world's busiest heliport and the busiest airport in Scotland. But the heart of the city, built of its famous locally quarried granite and set between two salmon rivers, the Dee and the Don, remains largely unspoiled. The seven-arch Bridge of Dee was imaginatively widened over 100 years ago without losing its medieval face. The 14th c Gothic arched Brig o' Balgownie over the Don is the oldest important bridge in Scotland still

in use. In Castle Street is the splendid 17th-c City Cross. The University is represented in Broad Street by Marischal College, with frontage in imposing Perpendicular-Gothic, and Mitchell Tower (233ft) which provides a fine view of the City. Old Aberdeen is the academic quarter centred on King's College* (founded 1495). The lovely lantern tower of the chapel was rebuilt in the 17th c; note the carving of the stalls and pulpit, the University War Memorial behind the former rood-screen, and seven fine windows. The Cathedral of St Machar* is chiefly 15th-c although founded in 1157; the flat oak ceiling, painted with emblems of spiritual and temporal monarchs, was added in 1530. The Harbour and Fish Market at the mouth of the Dee are full of busy activity; to the N are fine sandy beaches and golf-links.

Aboyne, Aberdeen   13L3
Deeside fishing, golf and touring centre built around an attractive village green. The Highland Gathering in August is one of the principal events of the Highland season.

Alford, Aberdeen   13L4
Stands in hill-ringed farming land. *Balfluig Castle* (16th-c) was originally inhabited by the Lords Forbes, who have now removed to *Castle Forbes* (19th-c), 4m NE. In Murray Park is a narrow-gauge railway.

Ballater, Aberdeen   13K3
Popular holiday town on Deeside, surrounded by beautiful woods and moorlands. Some mountain walks restricted in the shooting season. Close to *Abergeldie* skiing slopes.

Ballindalloch, Banff   13J4
Fine castle keep near the junction of Avon and Spey in a district world-famous for the waters which produce the whisky and fish.

Balmoral Castle,★ Aberdeen   13K3
The Sovereign's Highland residence, built in Scottish baronial style and modified by direction of the Prince Consort who bought the castle and estate in 1852 for £31,500. The grounds, including Queen Victoria's cottage and Queen Mary's sunken garden, are open May–July when the Royal Family is not in residence. *Crathie* Church, 1m E, contains the royal pew and memorials. *See also* Introduction, **Braemar** and page 383.

Banchory, Kinc   13M3
Attractive village where the Feugh joins the Dee. 2m NE, 16th-c *Crathes Castle* has treasures which include an oak-panelled ceiling unique in Scotland, allegorical paintings, and a jewelled ivory horn presented to a Burnett by Robert Bruce, as well as a beautifully laid-out 18th-c garden with a yew hedge dating from 1702 and extensive grounds. NTS visitor centre. Castle open April–Sept.; grounds all year.

Banff   13L5
Former royal burgh and seaport at mouth of River Deveron, with a few 17th-c houses on High Shore, vestiges of a royal castle and many interesting remains. Duff House (AM) by William Adam was modelled on the Villa Borghese for an Earl of Fife, and later presented to the town. Greatly restored since World War II. The museum has a fine bird display. An excellent golf-course is near by.

Braemar,★ Aberdeen   13J3
Famous Highland resort in magnificent scenery, 1,100ft above sea level, about 9m W of **Balmoral Castle**. The Earl of Mar raised his standard here in the 1715 rebellion. Most popular nowadays during the famous Braemar Gathering in September, usually attended by a royal party, but it is also a good centre for winter sports. 17th-c Braemar Castle by the River Dee has a round central tower, spiral stair and barrel-vaulted ceilings. Open May–Oct. *Son et Lumière*, Aug. and Sept. *See also* **Cairngorm Mountains**.

Brodie, Moray   13J5
4½m W of **Forres**. The castle (NTS), seat of the Brodie of Brodie since the 11th c, is based on a 16th-c Z plan with 17th- and 19th-c additions: it contains fine furniture, porcelain and a major collection of paintings, and there are splendid gardens and grounds with a 4-acre lake. Castle open Easter and May–Sept.; grounds all year. There are facilities for the disabled.

Burghead, Moray   15J5
Fishing village built on a headland fortified by Picts and Danes. The Roman Well inside an Iron Age fort (AM) may be an early Christian baptistery.

Cairngorm Mountains★   13I3/J3
Some of the grandest mountain scenery in Scotland. Recognized ascents from **Aviemore** (Highland) and **Braemar** avoid conflict with shooting interests and give splendid views of mountain lochs and peat streams, with golden eagles, the quartz known as 'cairngorms', and even reindeer moss at times. Pony-trekking and winter sports. Chairlift from Loch Morlich rises to 3,500ft. 3m E of Aviemore at Cairngorm ski slope is a Pine Forest interpretation centre (open all year). The Cairngorms National Nature Reserve covers 62,000 acres and restrictions on access may be imposed on some parts at particular times of year for bird and deer protection. *See also* Highland (south) Introduction.

Cairnwell, Aberdeen 13J2
The A93 road from **Braemar** to **Blairgowrie** (Tayside) rises
to 2,199ft, the highest 'A' road in Britain. The area is
paradise for skiers and hill-walkers who should set out well-
equipped in this area. *See also* **Cairnwell** (Tayside).

Craigievar Castle *see* **Lumphanan**

Cruden Bay, Aberdeen 13N4
Pleasant, quiet holiday resort with good golf-course and
sandy beach. The situation of Slains Castle, now ruined, was
according to Dr Johnson the 'noblest he had ever seen'. He
was equally impressed by the Bullers of Buchan, a deep, wide
'pot' with narrow opening to the sea, or, as he put it, 'a rock
perpendicularly tubulated' – an awesome sight in rough
weather. Now well known to the oil industry as the landfall
for the pipeline from the Forties Field, whence it flows to
Grangemouth (Central), with landscaped installations.

*The Cairngorms: view of the Pass of Rynoan. Skiing is
now a major sport with snow lying from November to May*

Culbin Sands, Moray 13I5/J5
Fertile cornland until engulfed by a sandstorm in 1694. The
drifts (100ft high) have been known to shift and reveal traces
of buildings. Afforestation has reclaimed much land; Forestry Commission walks. Near by *Hardmuir* is said to be the
heath of Macbeth's witches.

Cullen, Banff 13L5
Former royal burgh, now picturesque fishing-port and
holiday town. The older town was demolished in 1822 to
make room for improvements to Cullen House, dating from
1543 with later additions. The original mercat cross stands
in the town square. The church founded by Bruce is notable
for the tomb of Alexander Ogilvy of Findlater, a tabernacle
in the N wall of the chancel, and the carved Seafield pew.

Dufftown, Banff 13K4
A whisky-distilling centre. Mortlach Church (12th-c) has ancient tombstones (relics in local museum). *Balvenie Castle* (AM), has the Atholl family motto carved on the 15th–16th-c front.

Duffus, Moray 13J5
Gordonstoun School, founded in 1934 by Kurt Hahn and attended by the Duke of Edinburgh and later by the three Royal Princes, occupies the mansion built by Sir Robert Gordon (1647–1704), later known as the 'warlock of Gordonstoun'. Moated Duffus Castle, where David I of Scotland stayed, is in ruins (AM).

Elgin,* Moray 13K5
Prince Charles Edward Stuart stayed here before the battle of Culloden (*see* entry). The ruined 13th-c cathedral* (AM) was known as the 'Lanthorn of the North', and in spite of a history of calamity and destruction the buildings retain a luminous beauty in the northern light. The W front and the chapter house are magnificent. The town boasts good modern architecture as well as beautiful market crosses and a High Street in which a few arcaded houses survive. *Spynie Palace*, 2¾m N, the castle of the Bishops of Moray, has a tower once six storeys high, and fortifications (AM) and the graceful Bow Brig (1630) across the Lossie.

Fettercairn, Kinc 13L2
The old town cross of Kincardine forms part of the market cross in this pretty village. Stone arch (1861) commemorates a visit by Queen Victoria. The ruins of *Kincardine Castle*, 3m NE, are the sole remains of a historic town and royal residence.

Findhorn, Moray 13J5
A former village was overwhelmed by drifting sand, its successor by flood. The present village is the third of that name. Good sailing in Findhorn Bay. Remains of 12th-c Cistercian foundation, *Kinloss Abbey* are 2m SE.

Fochabers, Moray 13K5
The old market-cross near the site of Gordon Castle, now substantially demolished, is sole survivor of the removal of the village in the 18th c to its present position S of the park.

Forres, Moray 13J5
Ancient little former royal burgh proud of a mention in *Macbeth*. Angling and touring centre. Sueno's Stone (AM), in sandstone 23ft high with elaborate carvings in the Celtic tradition, may mark an 11th-c Norse victory. A granite stone marks the spot where the witches of Forres were burned.

Fraserburgh, Aberdeen 13N5
Fishing-port, with a good harbour founded in the 16th c by Sir Alexander Fraser, who built a square watchtower, later surmounted by a lighthouse, on Kinnaird's Head. Below is the Sealch's Hole, a 100ft cave. Note the fine 18th-c mercat cross at the top of the High Street.

Fyvie Castle, Aberdeen 13M4
Beautifully preserved fortified mansion. The gardens show traces of entrenchments thrown up by Montrose when pursued by Argyll in 1644. NTS plan to open castle to the public in 1986. Attractive church in village.

Garmouth, Moray 13K5
This former port, where Charles II landed from Holland on 23 June 1650, is 1m from the sea and disused through changes in the river channel. Near by *Kingston* was named by two timber merchants from Kingston-upon-Hull who pioneered an important shipbuilding centre in 1784, which flourished until sail gave way to steam, and wooden hulls to steel.

Huntly, Aberdeen 13L4
The town has acquired 22½m of fishing on the rivers Deveron and Bogie. Huntly Castle (AM), once the home of the Gordons, is well worth visiting. Built between 1597 and 1602 by the 1st Marquess of Huntly, it has been roofless for a great many years but is remarkably complete and notable for its grand doorway and carved fireplaces.

Insch, Aberdeen 13L4
Important village in agricultural district. Dunnideer, a conical hill, is surmounted by an early vitrified fort and remains of a 16th-c castle.

Inverbervie, Kinc 13M2
Sometimes known as Bervie. *Arbuthnott* Church (13th-c), 2½m W, has two-storeyed 16th-c chapel. Arbuthnott House, has attractive plaster ceilings which may be viewed by arrangement. *Allardyce Castle*, small 'fairy castle' of the early 17th c, lies 1m NW.

Inverey, Aberdeen 13J3
The end of the road up Deeside into the heart of the **Cairngorm Mountains**. Walks in the glens and on the moors with wonderful views, including a strenuous one to **Aviemore** through the Lairig Ghru. (Take local advice before setting out.)

Inverurie, Aberdeen 13M4
Prosperous town in agricultural district abounding in archeological remains. The Bass, a mound S of the town, was the site of a Norman motte-and-bailey castle. The great battle fought at *Harlaw*, 3m NW, in 1411 determined the course of Scottish history; this check to the Highland forces is described by Scott in a ballad in *The Antiquary*. *Bennachie*, a prominent hill 8m W, has an extensive Iron Age hill fort on the summit. 16th-c *Kinkell* Church (AM) has ornate details and a rich sacrament house dated 1524.

Keith, Banff 13K5
Well-planned agricultural town. The Roman Catholic Church has giant statues of SS Peter and Paul incorporated in its façade, and an altarpiece presented by Charles X of France. The Milton Tower dates from 1480 and the attractive Auld Brig over the Isla was built in 1690.

Kildrummy Castle,* Aberdeen 13L4
Most imposing of the many historic remains of the Don Valley, and so ancient that it had to be *rebuilt* in 1306 for Edward I of England, after he besieged and captured it. After much spoliation throughout its history, the Castle (AM) has been rescued in the 19th and 20th c.

Kintore, Aberdeen 13M4
A former royal burgh, though with a small population, having a delightful 18th-c Town House, and a church with 'sacrament house'. A stone in the churchyard combines pagan and Christian emblems.

Laurencekirk, Kinc 13M2
Centre of the fertile Howe of the Mearns, with linen-mills. Charles Stiven's snuff boxes made here have become collectors' pieces. The Johnston Tower, a splendid viewpoint on the Garvock Hill, has an indicator installed by NTS.

Loch Indorb, Moray 13J4
On this small loch on the Dava Moor at 969ft is the grim, off-the-beaten-track island-fortress once occupied by Edward I of England and later the stronghold of the Wolf of Badenoch.

Lossiemouth, Moray 13K5
Fishing-town serving as the port of **Elgin**, and catering for visitors. Birthplace of Ramsay MacDonald (1866–1937), first Labour Prime Minister – the cottage is marked by a plaque.

Lumphanan, Aberdeen 13L3
Village close to traditional site of Macbeth's death. Neighbouring villages are *Torphins*, a pleasant summer resort, and *Kincardine O'Neil*, with its ancient ruined church and hospital. *Craigievar Castle★*, 4m N, has seven-storeyed keep of the early 17th c. Unique Renaissance ceiling and fireplace exhortation 'Doe not vaiken sleiping dogs'. Open May–Sept., except Fri.; grounds all year.

Macduff, Banff 13M5
Large fishing-harbour and town, known as Down until renamed by the 1st Earl of Fife who, with his successors, rebuilt it in the 18th c. Splendid view from the 70ft War Memorial Tower on Hill of Down. There is a fine golf-course and open-air swimming pool.

Midmar Castle, Aberdeen 13M3
Fine turreted early 17th-c castle below the Hill of Fare, to the S of the A974.

Muchalls, Kinc 13M3
One of several picturesque villages on the coast S of **Aberdeen**. Red sandstone cliffs. The 17th-c castle mansion★ has very fine plasterwork ceilings and remarkable overmantels. This private house is open May–Sept. at set times.

Newburgh, Aberdeen 13N4
Opposite a village overwhelmed by sand-drift at the mouth of the Ythan, whose freshwater mussels yield pearls – one of which is set in the Scottish Crown (in **Edinburgh** Castle). *Ellon*, 5m NW, has a Norman mote hill where in medieval times justice was administered.

Old Deer, Aberdeen 13N5
Village notable for the ruins of a 13th-c Cistercian abbey (AM) with 14th-c refectory and abbot's lodge. Open in summer. From an earlier (7th-c) monastery here came the famous Book of Deer now in **Cambridge** University Library. It is the earliest Scottish Gaelic writing in existence.

Oldmeldrum, Aberdeen 13M4
Robert Bruce fought a battle on the site of the prehistoric fort on Barra Hill in 1307. 4m W is the *Loanhead of Daviot*, a prehistoric stone circle.

Peterhead, Aberdeen 13N5
Grey seaport near Scotland's furthest easterly point. Shipbuilding yards and busy harbours formerly the whaling and later the herring 'capital'; now of major importance in the North Sea oil and gas activities. The famous pink Peterhead granite is quarried at *Boddam*. Interesting fishing exhibits at Peterhead Arbuthnot Museum.

Pitmedden House, Aberdeen 13M4
Here are 17th-c gardens★ with pavilions, sundials and fountains reconstructed by the NTS. On the 100-acre estate the Trust has a fascinating Museum of Farming Life, artefacts, woodland and farmland walks, rare breeds of

Pitmedden House: the Great Garden, based on designs from Holyroodhouse and the 1st baronet's coat-of-arms

livestock and a visitor centre. Open May–Sept.; garden and grounds all year; facilities for disabled.

Pluscarden Abbey,★ Moray 13J5
The 13th-c monastic buildings were partially restored by the Marquess of Bute and presented to the Benedictine Order. Since 1948 the labours of the monks from **Prinknash Abbey**, Gloucester, have been so successful that in 1974 Pluscarden was restored to the rank of Abbey and its Prior became Abbot. Visitors are welcome.

Portsoy, Banff 13L5
Attractive holiday resort with excellent harbour, now a sailing centre. Notable for the distinctive rock formation, known as 'Portsoy marble'. This vein of serpentine, used by Louis XIV for two Versailles chimney-pieces, may be seen near the open-air swimming pool amid the rock to W.

Stonehaven, Kinc 13M3
Former county town, now District headquarters, busy harbour and holiday resort with fine cliff walks. The early 17th-c Tolbooth now a museum was formerly a storehouse. *Dunnottar Castle★*, 1½m S, stands on its rocky perch above the sea. It was besieged unsuccessfully by Montrose, who ravaged the country and burned Stonehaven. In 1652 the Scottish regalia and Charles II's private papers were smuggled out through the besieging Commonwealth lines. The Castle is open all year, except Sat. in winter.

Tolquhon Castle, Aberdeen 13M4
2m S of *Tarves*. Built in 15th c in a beautiful wooded dell, it has a strong rectangular keep, the Preston Tower, with a paved courtyard, ornate gun-loops and gatehouse. (AM).

Tomintoul, Banff 13K4
The highest village of the Highlands (1,160ft). Summer and winter-sporting resort surrounded by sparsely populated moors. At junction of the A939 and B9008. Local museum.

Turriff, Aberdeen 13M5
Country town above the Idoch Water. The first engagement of the Civil War, in which Forbes was routed by the royalist Gordons, was known as the 'Trot of Turriff'. Delgatie Castle, a tower house dating back to the 13th c, and former home of the Hays of Errol, has beautiful painted ceilings, and beams carved with Scottish proverbs. The Castle, now a Clan Hay Centre, is open by appointment only.

HIGHLAND REGION (SOUTH) AND WESTERN ISLES

AN INTRODUCTION BY
J.S. GRANT

The Countryside Commission has identified 40 areas in Scotland 'of unsurpassed attractiveness' which should be conserved 'as part of the national heritage'. Sixteen of them, almost as great in aggregate extent as Lancashire and Cheshire combined, lie in the southern part of Highland Region and in Western Isles. They offer a great variety of scenic forms.

The flat sandy machairs on the Atlantic coast of Uist, carpeted with wild flowers, contrast with the birch and pine woods of the Cromarty Firth which is an arm of the North Sea. The rounded summits of the Cairngorms are vastly different from the white sands of Morar or the jagged Cuillins of Skye or magnificent Glencoe in the north of the old county of Argyll.

One area of 'national scenic significance' extending to over 247,000 acres includes the mountainous southwest corner of Lewis, the whole of Harris and the little gem of Berneray, as well as much of North Uist with its astonishing profusion of fresh and salt-water lochs.

In Harris alone there is a contrast to delight the connoisseur. On the west, long sandy beaches and the open ocean. On the east a moonscape of bare weathered gneiss which, despite its bleakness, offers one of the loveliest prospects in Scotland on a summer's day when everything is glistening after a shower of rain and the Cuillins are blue along the southern horizon.

Although rich in scenery the area is not well endowed with urban sprawl which is, perhaps, another of its attractions. Even the largest town, Inverness, the rapidly growing Highland capital, has a population of only some 30,000. Inverness is an important administrative centre, housing the headquarters of the Highland Regional Council, the Health Board, the Police and Fire services, the regional offices of a number of government departments, and the head offices of two unique quangos, the Crofters Commission and the Highlands and Islands Development Board. Other towns in the area include Nairn, a very popular place to retire to because of its dry sunny climate, Dingwall, Fort William, Invergordon and Tain.

The largest town in the islands, with a population around 5,000, is Stornoway which has become a capital in its own right since the Western Isles became a local government area with a one-tier authority under the recent reform of Local Government.

The fact that the Western Isles Islands Council has chosen to call itself Comhairle nan Eilean underlines the difference between the Gaelic-speaking islands of the west and the English-speaking east.

Rock and Soil

It is impossible to write of the geology of the area without using superlatives. In Inverness-shire alone there are more than 50 peaks over 3,000 feet. On the northeast face of Ben Nevis we have the highest mountain cliff in Britain, in St Kilda the highest sea cliffs, and on the Shiant islands the finest example of columnar basalt.

At Ardivachar Point in Uist one can see the oldest rocks exposed in Britain. In Skye we have some of the youngest. The fantastic castle-like towers known as the Quirang and the Old Man of Storr are the remains of an eroded terrace of lava, and Dr Fraser Darling has claimed that the glacier-scored Cuillins provide some of the most spectacular scenery not only in Britain but the world.

A geological fault reaching across the Scottish mainland from coast to coast has given us the Great Glen through which the road winds in and out among a succession of sparkling lochs of which Loch Ness, with its reputed monster, is the largest and best known.

At Roineabhal in Harris one can see an anorthosite intrusion unique in Britain which matches similar rocks in North America with which it was once joined. The Nature Conservancy Council, in fact, has identified 113 sites of geological or geomorphological interest in the Western Isles alone, six of them 'of the highest international importance'.

At Knockan Cliff on the border between Ross and Sutherland the Conservancy has created a Nature Trail to explain to the interested layman how the unusual distribution of the strata there provided the key 'to the understanding of the origin of mountain chains throughout the world'.

This peaceful scene in Glen Affric typifies the serenity of the many beautiful areas in Highland Region

Flora and Fauna

The Highlands and Islands are remarkably rich in birds and animals not found generally in Britain. In winter hundreds of red deer can be seen quite close to the road and railway in Drumochter Pass. Loch Druidibeg in South Uist is the principal breeding place of greylag geese in Britain. St Kilda has the largest gannetry in the world, the unique St Kilda wren, and the most primitive breed of sheep surviving in Europe. North Rona is the largest breeding place in the world of the grey Atlantic seal, and the neighbouring islet of Sulisgeir is home for Leech's fork-tailed petrel which comes ashore only at night.

In the Cairngorms the osprey has been re-established as a breeding species. On the Shiant islands there is the largest puffinry in Britain, and in the wilder parts of the area the golden eagle, the peregrine falcon and the wild-cat can still be seen.

To these one must add dotterels, ptarmigan and snow bunting in the mountains, capercailzie and black cock in the pine forests, the rare Slavonian grebe on lochs near Inverness, the red-necked phalarope in the Western Isles and the mountain shearwater on Rhum.

The flora of the area is equally varied, ranging from the lush farmlands of the east, and the machairs, through the very different flora of the heather moors to the mountain tops where there are relic communities of the last glacial epoch.

In sharp contrast to all these are the sub-tropical shrubs, including forget-me-nots from the South Pacific which flourish in the NTS Garden at Inverewe in the same latitude as Perm in Siberia or Lake Athabasca in northern Canada.

Sport and Recreation

The South Highlands and Islands provide a great and growing variety of sport and recreation. Aviemore, in the Spey Valley, has been transformed from a sleepy

Highland village into an international ski centre. In many parts of the area there is fishing for trout and salmon, deer stalking and golf. There is excellent sea angling at places like Ullapool and Stornoway, and sailing both on the Minch and North Sea coasts. There are cabin cruisers on the Caledonian Canal, pony-trekking in a number of centres (including Newtonmore where it first began), curling in Aviemore and Inverness, and every grade of hill-climbing from gentle walks to severe tests of mountaineering skill.

Shinty, the most strenuous of team games, is still played quite extensively, and for those who take their leisure more passively, Inverness now boasts one of the finest theatres in Britain.

Architecture

The architectural interest of the area lies in the castles, often picturesquely situated. Among them are Eilean Donan, defended by the Spanish against the British navy in 1719; Kismul on its island site in Castlebay; Cawdor, associated in name at least with Macbeth; Dunvegan, one of the oldest homes in Scotland still occupied by the original family, and whose 'fairy flag' provides a link with the Crusades; and Urquhart of which even the ruins still dominate Loch Ness.

The Wade Bridge at Dulsie near Nairn is well worth a visit and in an age preoccupied with conservation the old Highland 'black house', primitive though it is, is of particular interest. Built with great economy of materials, it was streamlined against the wind, heat was conserved with remarkable efficiency and even the smoke-laden thatch was recycled as a fertilizer. The social life of the community centred round the peat fire in the middle of the floor, and it was there, at informal *ceilidhs*, that the ordinary people of the Highlands kept their oral tradition alive for 300 years after the proscription of the storytellers and bards. Black houses have been preserved as museums in several parts of the area.

History

There is a sense in which the Highlands are still possessed by the Jacobites. At Glenfinnan a monument, looking like a lighthouse incongruously come ashore, commemorates the raising of the standard by Prince Charles Edward. At Culloden, the battlefield is a place of pilgrimage for thousands. In Fort William a 'secret' portrait of the Prince can be seen in the West Highland Museum.

The indigenous Highlander, however, sees things differently. He is less concerned with the Jacobite adventures than the Clearances of the 18th and 19th centuries which have left few memorials but have given rise to a literature in prose and verse, and have burned themselves into the folk memory.

Local Products

The fact that the long decline in the Highland economy is at an end is testified by the fact that three of the largest graving docks in Europe are now located in this area, at Ardersier and Nigg on the North Sea coast and at Kishorn in the west. All three, and a large fabrication yard at Stornoway, are engaged in building massive structures for the oil industry in this country and abroad.

Farming, fishing, distilling, knitwear and textiles are still important. Skis are made in the Spey Valley, and there is a growing variety of other new products ranging from pottery to minute transducers, made in Skye, which are used in hospitals all over the world. Highland Craftpoint at Beauly was set up to raise the standard of craft products throughout Scotland.

The area produces an abundance of salmon, trout, venison, game birds, prime beef and mutton, while the surrounding seas provide excellent white fish, lobster, crab, scampi and scallops. Salmon, trout, eels and shellfish (including oysters) are now farmed as well as fished on a considerable and growing scale.

The well-matured single malt whiskies of Talisker, Dalmore, Glen Morangie and Tomatin are fit to rank with the finest Cognac.

Gazetteer

Acharacle, Argyll   12E2
Excellent angling headquarters at foot of fresh-water Loch Shiel with boat service to **Glenfinnan**. A road follows the stream from Shiel Bridge to the sea at *Dorlin* near romantically situated 14th-c *Castle Tioram*, the ancient seat of the Macdonalds of Clan Ranald. Fine views of Loch Moidart from the castle. Prince Charles Edward Stuart stayed at *Kinlochmoidart* to the N before the 1745 Rising.

Achnasheen, Ross & Cr   12G5
Fine views of mountains, glens and lochs which have been deepened and lengthened by hydro-electric schemes without impairing their beauty.

Alness, Ross & Cr   13I5
One-time village on N side of Cromarty Firth, expanded to accommodate workers in oil and other industries. The Black Rock of Novar, a ravine 2m long, is cut by the Allt Graat, 'the ugly burn', reached from *Evanton*.

Applecross, Ross & Cr   12E4
Remote sea village used to be reached with a sense of achievement and a storehouse of panoramic memories after negotiating the steep Bealachnam-Ba Pass (2,054ft) but a new coast road to *Shieldaig* has greatly improved access. An ancient carved stone stands near the ruined church founded by Maelrubba, the Irish monk, in the 7th c.

Ardgay, Ross & Cr   13H6
Near the junction of beautiful, wild Strath Carron and
Dornoch Firth, where **Bonar Bridge** led into Sutherland.
Carbisdale Castle, 3½m NW, now a youth hostel, stands high
above the River Oykel, where Montrose made his last stand
against the Parliamentarians in 1650.

Arisaig, Inverness   12E2
The romantic Road to the Isles from **Fort William** reaches
the sea at a bay studded with islets frequented by seals, with
Rhum and **Eigg** and the **Cuillins** of **Skye** in the distance.

Aviemore,★ Inverness   13I3
Excellent touring, fishing, winter sports and all-year recreation centre on the Spey between the **Cairngorms** (*see* in
Grampian) and the Monadhliath Mountains. Unlimited
range of expeditions: from echoing Loch-an-Eilean (3m) on
whose island the 'Wolf of Badenoch' had a stronghold, to the
strenuous walk over the mountaintops to **Braemar**
(Grampian) via Lairig Ghru or Lairig Laiogh. Imported
reindeer flourish at *Glenmore National Park* (12,500 acres)
and may be seen by arrangement. On near-by Loch Garten
well-guarded ospreys nest and may be seen from hides.

Ballachulish, Argyll   12G1
Loch Leven flows towards Loch Linnhe at great speed, but
the famous car ferry has been replaced by a bridge opened in
1975. To the NE the *Corran* Ferry takes cars across to
Ardgour on the opposite side of Loch Linnhe.

Barra,★ Inverness (W.I.)   12A3
At the southern tip of the Outer Hebrides; famed for having
the only airport in Britain, probably in the world, where
services are timed by the tides: it is on a magnificent shell
beach, *Tràigh Mhór*, at the N and handles scheduled
Loganair flights to **Glasgow** and **Tiree** in Strathclyde,
Benbecula and **Stornoway**. 12th-c *Kisimul Castle*, an
island fortress off *Castlebay*, greatly restored in the 20th c is
reached by small boat. Open May–Sept. Wed. and Sat. p.m.

Barvas, Ross & Cr (W.I.)   12D8
12m NW from **Stornoway** has near by the *Trushel Stone*, a
20ft high monolith, probably the highest in Scotland and the
Steinacleit cairn and stone circle dated at *c.*2000 BC (AM).

Beauly, Inverness   13H5
This *beau lieu* of our ancestors was named in praise of the
setting of the now-ruined priory built by French monks in
the 13th c, of which the triangular windows and the W
doorway are the most notable features. This is Lovat
country. Splendid *Beaufort Castle* (1880), residence of the
Lords Lovat, replaced Castle Dounie destroyed by Cumberland after the battle of Culloden (*see* entry) in revenge for the
Lovat support of Prince Charles Edward Stuart.

Benbecula, Inverness (W.I.)   12B4/5
It may be said, unusually, that this was an island: thanks to
World War II military activity it is now joined to N. **Uist** by a
bridge, making it possible to drive (A865) from *Newton*
(N. Uist) through Benbecula to *Ludag* (S. Uist): there is an
airport with flights to **Glasgow** (Strathclyde), **Stornoway**
and **Barra**, and excellent trout fishing in small lochs.

Ben Nevis *see* **Fort William**

Boat of Garten, Inverness   13J4
The ferry which earned this village its name has been
superseded by a bridge across the Spey. Strathspey is as

*Fort William: Ben Nevis towers over the Caledonian Canal
which crosses Scotland from Inverness to Corpach*

famous for dance tunes (in slower tempo than the reel) as for
whisky and fishing. The osprey has returned to Loch Garten
as a breeding species. The golf-course is amid glorious
scenery and there are extensive skiing facilities.

Cairngorms *see* entry in Grampian Region

Caledonian Canal, Inverness   12G2/3/13H3/4
The 'longest short-cut' in Britain, running in a straight
diagonal for over 60m from *Corpach* to the Moray Firth,
passing through 29 locks and Lochs Lochy, Oich and Ness.
Designed by Telford and built 1803–22 to enable fishing and
other vessels to avoid the dangers of the Pentland Firth
passage, it rises to 106ft above sea level. Increasingly used
by pleasure craft and seekers of the **Loch Ness** Monster.

Callanish,★ Ross & Cr (W.I.)   12C7
The standing stones (AM), dated between 2000 and 1500 BC,
16m W from **Stornoway**, are second in importance, with the
Ring of Brodgar at **Stenness** (Orkney), in Britain only to
Stonehenge (Wilts). An avenue of 19 monoliths 300yd long
leads to a circle of 13 stones round a chambered cairn
probably an altar for human sacrifice: three lines of stones
fan out E, W and S giving the impression of a cross. The huge
stones had partly sunk into the peat but in the mid-19th c Sir
James Matheson, who built Stornoway Castle, had the peat
dug away down to the bases.

Canna, Inverness (W.I.)   12C3
Island of the Inner Hebrides NW of **Rhum**. The rich iron
deposits in Compass Hill affect the magnetic compasses of
passing ships. Access is by passenger ferry from **Mallaig**.

Carrbridge, Inverness   13J4
Village which caters for winter sports. The arch of the 18th-c
bridge over the Dulnain survives alongside its successor.
General Wade's *Sluggan Bridge* is 2¼m W.

Cawdor Castle, Nairn　　　13I5
Familiar from *Macbeth* the Castle has been a family home for 600 years (Earl Cawdor). The central keep fortified in 1454 is surrounded by 16th-c buildings later remodelled: the gardens are notable. Open May–Sept. *See also* **Nairn**.

Corrieshalloch Gorge, Ross & Cr　　　12G6
This spectacular geological fault, 12m SSE of **Ullapool**, on the A835, contains the beautiful Falls of Measach 150ft high, with a suspension bridge viewpoint (NTS).

Corrieyairack Pass★, Inverness　　　13H3
Superb vantage-point (2,507ft), reached by foot on 25m mountain track from *Laggan* to **Fort Augustus**. The suspension bridge above Glen Tarff was built by **Edinburgh** University students in 1932.

Cromarty, Ross & Cr　　　13I5
At NE point of so-called Black Isle at the mouth of Cromarty Firth. Once famous for herring fisheries. Birthplace of Hugh Miller, the mason-geologist (1802–56), whose thatched cottage is kept as a museum (NTS). Open May–Sept. Passenger ferry across the Firth to *Nigg* and **Invergordon** operates mainly for industrial workers.

Cuillin Hills, Inverness　　　12D3
Famous among mountaineers, geologists and botanists, these hills on the Isle of **Skye** are the most precipitous in the British Isles with 15 peaks of more than 3,000ft. Impressively scenic themselves they afford prodigious views from their tops. Recognized base is at *Sligachan* (on the A850 19m from *Kyleakin*). There is also salmon and sea-trout angling. (*See also* pages 2–3.)

Culloden Moor,★ Inverness　　　13I4
The battle here in 1746 spelled doom to Prince Charles Edward's rising. It is commemorated by a cairn and stones marking the graves of the fallen clansmen. 'Butcher' Cumberland is said to have directed the fight from a near by boulder. NTS has in its care the graves, the Well of the Dead, the Memorial Cairn, the Cumberland Stone, Old Leanach farmhouse (restored as a Battle Museum) and a large part of the battlefield, with a visitor centre (open April–Aug., site all year) and audio-visual presentations. Near the River Nairn the *Stones of Clava★* consist of three Bronze Age cairns ringed by standing stones and containing mysterious inner chambers (AM).

Dingwall, Ross & Cr　　　13H5
A former royal burgh (1226) and county town at head of Cromarty Firth. Interesting Town House in the town centre (containing good museum of local history) dates from 1730 and was restored in 1984. Near the church is an obelisk to the 1st Earl of Cromartie, who chose his resting-place in order to frustrate his wife's avowed intention of dancing on his grave. Tenure of *Foulis Castle*, 5m NE, is subject to an annual rent of a snowball at midsummer – a condition difficult to fulfil in olden days. The town is happily bypassed by a new section of the A9.

Dornie, Ross & Cr　　　12F4
Village at junction of Lochs Long, Duich and Alsh. The 13th-c stronghold of the Mackenzies (Earls of Seaforth) on little *Eilean Donan★* was shelled by English warships in the 18th c, but has been well restored. Open Easter–Sept. The romantic *Falls of Glomach★*, reached via the N shore of Loch Long, have a 370ft drop over the spectacular black cliffs above Glen Elchaig – one of the highest falls in Britain.

Drumnadrochit, Inverness　　　13H4
Vantage-point for monster-spotters on NW shore of **Loch Ness** and home of the Loch Ness Monster Exhibition Centre. *Urquhart Castle* (AM) stands above the loch, well equipped for the repulse of rival clansmen. S of Divach Falls stands the monument to John Cobb, killed in 1952 when attempting the world water-speed record.

Dunvegan Castle, Inverness　　　12C4
At the head of Loch Dunvegan to the NW of the **Isle of Skye** (the A850 and A863). Parts date from 9th c and most from the 15th–19th c. It has been the home of the Chiefs of MacLeod for 700 years and is the oldest castle in continuous occupation by the same family in Scotland. The massive four-square stronghold was once unapproachable by land. Among the many treasures are the 'fairy flag' captured from the Saracens on a Crusade, the two-handed sword of Rory Mor, the 12th Chief, his drinking-horn, letters from Dr Johnson and Sir Walter Scott, and many portraits including that of Dame Flora MacLeod of MacLeod who died in 1976 aged 99 and was known world-wide for her clan visits. Boat trips to seal colony. Open Easter–Oct., closed Sun.

Eigg, Inverness (W.I.)　　　12D2
Small island reached from **Mallaig**, with several guest houses. Vengeful MacLeods from **Skye** suffocated 200 Macdonalds in a cave on the SE coast not far from the weird volcanic mass of the Sgurr of Eigg (1,289ft).

Eilean Donan Castle★ *see* **Dornie**

Eriskay, Inverness (W.I.)　　　12B3
S off S. **Uist** and reached by ferry from *Ludag*. Familiar world-wide through the Gaelic melody of the 'Love Lilt', this was where Prince Charles Edward Stuart first set foot in Scotland *en route* from France for the 1745 Rising. It also gained fame through the wreck of the SS *Politician* and its 20,000 cases of whisky in 1941 in the Sound, an 'incident' much publicized by Compton Mackenzie's *Whisky Galore* and the subsequent film.

Fearn, Ross & Cr　　　13I6
Centre of fertile Easter Ross. The roof of the Premonstratensian Abbey collapsed during a Sunday service in 1742 killing 44 people, and has been tastelessly restored. Peter Fraser, Prime Minister of New Zealand 1940–9, was born and educated at Hill of Fearn ½m away.

Fort Augustus,★ Inverness　　　13H3
Perfect centre for touring and fishing at S end of **Loch Ness**. The fort was built as a result of the 1715 Rising, taken by the Highlanders in 1745, and lost after the battle of Culloden (*see* entry). In the 19th c the site was presented to the Benedictine Order, who built their Abbey with a cloister and tower by Pugin, and college in 1876.

Fort George, Inverness　　　13I5
Off the A96, 8m W of **Nairn**. One of the finest late artillery fortifications in Europe, this irregular polygon (AM) was built by Robert Adam in 1748–63 to replace an earlier fort, in **Inverness**, blown up by the Jacobites. Covering 12 acres, it could hold 2,500 men. It was the depot of the Seaforth Highlanders until they amalgamated with the Camerons in 1963 to become the Queen's Own Highlanders but the Regimental Museum remains.

Dornie: Eilean Donan Castle, once a chieftain's castle and Jacobite stronghold, sits on an island in Loch Duich

Fortrose, Ross & Cr   13I5
Formed in the 16th c by the amalgamation of the towns of *Chanonry* and *Rosemarkie*, which still preserves its own name. Once an important port, but now visited mainly for golf and bathing. The ruins of the 14th-c cathedral include the S aisle with fine vaulting.

Fort William,★ Inverness   12G2
The advent of the railway brought rapid development to this town at the S end of the **Caledonian Canal** so that the fortifications built to restrain the Highlanders became obsolete and were superseded. The West Highland Museum in Cameron Square preserves relics of Scottish traditions, and historical mementoes of Prince Charles Edward Stuart and Flora Macdonald. The 'easy' route to the summit of *Ben Nevis*★, 4,406ft, highest mountain in the British Isles, begins through Glen Nevis, NE of the town. (4hrs up, 3 down – no guide necessary, but good weather essential.) The Ben Nevis Centre in the High Street has an exhibition and video show – open all year. Opposite the aluminium works to the N are the ruins of 15th-c *Inverlochy Castle*. The stretch of railway between Fort William and **Mallaig** is one of the loveliest in Britain and the journey is often made by tourists for its scenery alone – steam train several days a week started in July 1984.

Gairloch, Ross & Cr   12E5
Village on sea loch near mouth of attractively named Flowerdale. Award-winning Heritage Museum open Easter–Sept. Splendid views of **Skye** and the mountains.

Glen Affric, Inverness   12G3
Now made more accessible by the work of the hydro-electric authority, which has taken great pains to preserve the natural beauty of this untameable glen. (*See* page 391.)

Glencoe,★★ Argyll   12G1
Something of the massacre of 1692 seems to linger in this historic glen and yet contributes to its magnificence. Notices mark the site of the destroyed Macdonald homesteads. To the N a wall of rock, to the S 'naked crests fight to achieve the skies', and waters drop in cascades from the heights. The old winding route through the glen has been replaced by a good new road, which climbs beyond the watershed and over Rannoch Moor. NTS has 14,200 acres in Glencoe and *Dalness*, and an area at the Signal Rock W of Loch Achtriochtan, with a visitor centre (open April–Oct.) at *Clachaig*, and the Leishman Memorial mountain safety research laboratory at *Achnacon*. Glencoe is an important climbing and winter-sports centre. Folk Museum in village has many historic relics.

Glenelg, Inverness   12E3
Car ferry to **Skye** across Kyle Rhea in summer. Remains of two brochs – Dun Telve and Dun Troddan – with walls up to 30ft and 13ft thick (AM).

Glenfinnan, Inverness   12F2
Angling resort at head of Loch Shiel. A monument marks the historic spot where Prince Charles Edward Stuart raised his standard at the gathering of the Clans in 1745. NTS visitor centre has an exhibit of the campaign. Open April–Oct.

Grantown-on-Spey, Moray   13J4
The village, with tree-lined main street and woodland surroundings, makes an excellent centre for exploration of the mountainous countryside, with skiing and golf. Salmon fishing in the River Spey.

Gruinard Bay, Ross & Cr   12F6
Memorable both for its sands and for the first dramatic view as the road from the S tops a rise and prepares for a 1-in-4 descent to the shore. Landing on Gruinard Island is absolutely forbidden, as it was used as a testing ground for anthrax in World War II and is still contaminated.

Harris, Inverness (W.I.)   12B6/C6
The S part of the major island with **Lewis** (although each was known as 'an island' with the further anomaly that they were in different counties until they became part of the Western Isles Area) is mountainous (Clisham, 2,622ft, the highest peak in the Isles) and wild, splendid for walking and climbing but with delightful beaches and good angling. S at *Rodel* 16th-c St Clement's Church (AM) has rich decoration and sculptured slabs. Access is by car ferry from Uig, on **Skye**, and road (A859) from **Stornoway**; from **Tarbert** (Strathclyde) and *Leverburgh* there are ferry and boat services to the smaller near-by islands – *Scalpay, Pabbay, Berneray*, the *Shiant Isles* and N. **Uist**.

Invergarry, Inverness   12G3
A road to **Skye** swings W through the mountains from Loch Oich. Prince Charles Edward Stuart visited Invergarry Castle before and after Culloden (*see* entry): 'Butcher' Cumberland burned it down in revenge. N of the hamlet the Well of Seven Heads recalls one of the most gruesome episodes in Highland history: a monument at the well erected by MacDonnell of Glengarry in 1812 tells the story in Gaelic, Latin, French and English. The Glengarry headgear is named after this MacDonnell because he wore it during the Royal visit to **Edinburgh** in 1822.

Invergordon, Ross & Cr   13I5
Ancient town on N side of landlocked Cromarty Firth. Its fine harbour was an important naval base in both World Wars, and in 1931 was the scene of a mutiny against reductions in service pay. There are large distilleries and much oil-related and other industries.

Inverness★★, Inverness   13I5
The 'capital' of the Highlands, full of life independent of the tourist season. Known for the sweetness of the air, the purity of the English language spoken by the inhabitants, and for a beautiful situation astride the River Ness, with mountains to E and W, two great firths to the N, and **Loch Ness** and the **Caledonian Canal** to the SW. The cream of the world's pipers meet in competition at the Northern Meeting which is followed by the Northern Meeting Balls, sometimes graced by royalty.

Castles have come and gone since before the days of Macbeth. The terrace of the most modern (which houses the Highland Region offices and law courts) has a statue of Flora Macdonald. 19th-c St Andrew's Cathedral is well-designed and impressive, with an interesting chapter house and a copy of the famous angel font in Copenhagen. Note the many town houses of the 18th-c gentry, and the collection of Jacobite relics in the museum. Queen Mary's House, where she stayed in 1562, is sadly overshadowed by development. Inverness now has its own excellent theatre complex.

Inverpolly, Ross & Cr   12G7
An important National Nature Reserve of 26,827 acres with a wide variety of habitats including three hills over 2,000ft, marine islands, lochs, rivers and ancient birch woodland; wildlife includes wild-cat, pine marten, golden eagles, and the unique Knockan Cliff with a section of the Moine schists. The Conservancy Council has an information

centre at Knockan Cliff (on the A835 at *Ledmore* 12m N of **Ullapool**), nature trails and a motor trail.

Kingussie, Inverness 13I3
Healthy resort on the Spey 745ft above sea level, surrounded by high mountains. Fishing, golf and wonderful walks when these do not conflict with shooting and stalking interests. There is a fascinating Highland Folk Museum. Ruthven Barracks (AM) across the River Spey were built to suppress the Jacobites after the 1715 Rising but were captured by Prince Charles Edward Stuart's forces in 1746 and used as a rallying point after the battle of Culloden (*see* entry) when they disbanded and blew them up.

Kinlochewe,★★ Ross & Cr 12F5
Near the head of Loch Maree and surrounded by mountains, the most spectacular being Beinn Eighe, formed of red sandstone powdered with white quartzite. The Nature Conservancy Council established Britain's first National Nature Reserve at *Beinn Eighe* in 1951. It covers some 12,000 acres including the natural pinewood on the S shore of Loch Maree containing one of the few remaining fragments of the Caledonian Forest dating back 8,000 years. The Nature Conservancy Council mountain trail begins and ends 2½m W of Kinlochewe, covers 4m well defined by cairns and reaches about 1,700ft: wildlife includes pine marten, wild-cat, otter, fox, roe and red deer, with golden eagles, falcons and buzzards, ptarmigan and ravens. In care of NTS: open June–Sept. with visitor centre and deer museum on A896.

Kyle of Lochalsh,★ Ross & Cr 12E4
Road and rail terminus for **Skye**, giving a taste of magnificent sea-loch scenery. The wife of a Macdonald living across the Kyle earned the name of 'Saucy Mary' for stretching a chain across the channel in the hope of extorting toll money from ships. Good view of the **Cuillins** from the loch. Car ferry to *Kyleakin* (*see* page 398) in **Skye**.

Lewis, Ross & Cr (W.I.) 12C7/D8
The northernmost of the Western Isles, flatter than the others rising to 800ft. At *Arnol* is a traditional Hebridean black house. *See* **Barvas, Callanish, Stornoway.**

Lochaline, Argyll 10C8
On the Morven coast, facing **Mull**. *Ardtornish Castle*★, ancient home of the Lords of the Isles, overhangs the sea and is backed by cliffs and waterfalls which captured Sir Walter Scott's imagination. Silica sands for the making of optical glass have brought local employment. Car ferries from **Oban** and **Mull**, Strathclyde.

Lochalsh, Ross & Cr 12E4
On Balmacara estate NTS has 5,616 acres of woodlands and gardens with exotic plants from Tasmania, China, Chile, the Himalayas and other remote places. Open all year.

Loch Leven, Argyll 12G1
Should not be confused with the **Loch Leven** of Mary Queen of Scots' flight from captivity (which is in Tayside). Beautiful mountain scenery from lakeside road. At the head of the loch stands *Kinlochleven's* aluminium works.

Loch Ness, Inverness 13H3/4
This loch in the Great Glen is 24m long and forms part of the **Caledonian Canal**. Boat trips from **Inverness** notably to look for the 'monster' reputed to live in the loch. Monster Exhibition Centre at **Drumnadrochit** on the A82. Sitings often reported from *Urquhart Castle* near by.

Mallaig, Inverness 12E3
Terminus of the scenic West Highland rail route (*see also* **Fort William**) and an important port now equipped with freezing plant and lobster ponds: car ferry and sea services to **Skye**, other islands (**Canna, Eigg, Rhum**) and points on the mainland. 3m E from Carn a'Ghobhair (1,794ft) there is a magnificent panorama.

Morar, Inverness 12E3
The deepest of all lochs empties into the sea through a well-disguised hydro-electric station. Highland Home Industries overlook famous white sands.

Muir of Ord, Ross & Cr 13H5
Centre of fertile farmland. The 'muir' on which livestock markets were held is now a golf-course. Students are admitted to library and museum of Tarradale House, near the Beauly Firth.

Nairn 13I5
Three golf-courses, bathing, fishing, and a share of the Gulf Stream. The attractive fishermen's quarter, Fishertown, has streets or 'mains' leading to the harbour. Moated **Cawdor Castle**, 5¾m S, was adopted by Shakespeare as the scene of Duncan's murder (Macbeth was Thane of Cawdor).

Poolewe, Ross & Cr 12F6
At head of Loch Ewe at the 'pool' famous for fishing where the waters from Loch Maree enter the sea. The gardens of *Inverewe*★ (NTS) have a superb collection of sub-tropical plants and shrubs. Garden open all year; visitor centre April–Oct. NTS also has fishing on five lochs and caravan and camping site – open April–Sept.

Loch Ness: Urquhart Castle has endured a stormy and war-battered existence

Rhum, Inverness (W.I.)   12D2/3
This volcanic island, 8m S of **Skye**, belongs to the Nature Conservancy Council and it is a National Nature Reserve. The inhabitants are all Nature Conservancy Council workers and their families. The island covers 38sq m and rises to 2,664ft at the peak of Askival; it is of great interest to geologists and naturalists. Kinloch Castle, built in 1902, is now a museum and hostel for educational and research parties; Rhum has been designated a Biosphere Reserve by UNESCO. Access is by day trips from **Mallaig** or **Arisaig**. Limited accommodation – for permission to stay contact the Chief Warden, at White House, Kinloch in advance.

Roybridge, Inverness   12G2
Village at foot of Glen Roy, which has strange 'parallel roads' or terraces formed by lakes of the Ice Age.

St Kilda (W.I.)   *Inset* 12
This archipelago, consisting of *Hirta*, *Soay*, *Boreray* and *Dun*, was bequeathed to NTS by the 5th Marquess of Bute in 1957: the islanders were evacuated in 1930. Its remoteness, 110m W of mainland, ensures lack of access but NTS sends out working parties each summer to help in restoring the community which existed round Village Bay on Hirta. The cliffs are spectacular, those at Conachair (1,397ft) being the highest in Britain, there are countless seabirds, the world's largest gannetry and some of the wildlife – Soay sheep and St Kilda mouse and wren – is unique: because of its scientific natural history interest St Kilda has been leased to the Nature Conservancy Council.

Skye, Isle of,★★ Inverness   12D4/5
Reached by car ferry from **Mallaig, Glenelg** (May–Sept. only) or **Kyle of Lochalsh**; from *Uig* to the N services to *Tarbert* (**Harris**) and *Lochmaddy* (N. **Uist**). The coast is broken by many sea lochs, so that no inland point is more than 5m from the sea, and some of the wildest places are best reached by boat. *Portree*, the chief town, sits on a platform of rock above its busy harbour. There are many hotels on the island and many of the villages and outlying crofts welcome summer visitors. *See* **Cuillin Hills** *and* **Dunvegan Castle**.

Spean Bridge, Inverness   12G2
11m NE of **Fort William**, off the A82. The memorial to the Commandos surveys the rugged terrain which was their training ground during World War II. Here also occurred the first skirmish in August 1745 three days before Prince Charles Edward Stuart raised his standard at **Glenfinnan**.

Stornoway, Ross & Cr (W.I.)   12D7
Capital of the Western Isles Islands Authority, Stornoway has been much affected by its new status, by oil and associated industrial developments and by the Ministry of Defence decision to extend greatly the local airport as a vital NATO RAF base. The former great herring fleets have been replaced by efficient local boats supplying fish- and prawn-processing plants and lobster ponds. The handsome 19th-c castle and its extensive park were given to the town by Lord Leverhulme: the castle is now a technical college (not open). There is a golf-course, swimming pool and many

other amenities: access is by car ferry from **Ullapool**, from *Uig* on **Skye**, via *Tarbert* (**Harris**) or by air from **Glasgow** (Strathclyde), **Aberdeen** (Grampian) and **Inverness**.

Strathpeffer, Ross & Cr   13H5
The one-time spa town has remained popular for golf, fishing and expeditions in a sheltered and wooded valley which contrasts strangely with neighbouring mountain wildness. Ben Wyvis (3,429ft), 10m distant, can be climbed by the inexperienced if adequate time is allowed.

Summer Isles *see* **Ullapool**

Tain, Ross & Cr   13I6
A former royal burgh which derives its name from the Norse 'Thing', meaning an assembly. Sandy beach on Dornoch Firth, golf and water sports. The Tolbooth with its conical spire is near the 14th-c church of St Duthus. The earlier chapel of the same saint was a place of pilgrimage and penance for two Scottish kings.

Tomdoun, Inverness   12G3
Hydro-electric works have deepened and lengthened Lochs Garry and Quoich, but fishing amenities are preserved.

Uist, North and South, Inverness (W.I.)   12B4/5
Joined via **Benbecula** by bridge and causeway, are reached by car ferry to *Lochmaddy* (N) from Uig, on **Skye**, or to *Lochboisdale* (S) from **Oban** (Strathclyde) and by air to Benbecula from **Glasgow** (Strathclyde) and **Stornoway**. 8m SW of Lochmaddy are ruins of a medieval college and monastery said to have been founded in the 13th c by Beathag, daughter of Somerled, where John Duns Scotus (*see* **Duns**, Borders) studied, and of a chapel with ancient cup and ring marks. The S island has at the N a Folk Museum in a traditional thatched house, the Loch Druidibeg National Nature Reserve, a breeding ground for greylag geese, Flora Macdonald's birthplace (1722) near *Milton*, N from Lochboisdale, and the place where Prince Charles Edward hid for a month from the Hanoverians.

Ullapool,★ Ross & Cr   12G6
Most attractive lime-washed town with excellent harbour and sea-bathing in Loch Broom. Good centre for exploring the wild island-studded coast to the NW. The *Summer Isles* are to be recommended. Car ferry to **Stornoway**, excursions by other vessels.

Western Isles   12A2/D9
Under the Local Government (Scotland) Act 1973 (which came into effect in 1975) three new Islands Area Authorities were created – Orkney, Shetland and the Western Isles, each being autonomous for all services except fire and police for which they come under Highland Region. Western Isles covers the Outer Hebrides, **Lewis, Harris**, North and South **Uist, Benbecula, Barra** and several small islands, including **St Kilda** and *Rockall*: it thus covers some 1,120sq m with a population of about 31,000. The area was formerly administered by the County Councils (now defunct) of Ross and Cromarty and Inverness. **Stornoway** is the capital of the Western Islands Authority.

Isle of Skye: crofts at Kyleakin, the village the ferry sails to from the Kyle of Lochalsh on the mainland

Highland Region (North), Orkney and Shetland

AN INTRODUCTION BY
ROBERT KEMP

Is any quality held in common by the northern part of Highland Region consisting of the former counties of Caithness and Sutherland, and the two northern groups of islands, Orkney and Shetland? Sutherland, built up from ancient rocks that still seem to record some tortured spasm of the earth's crust, presents a wild and grandly mountainous aspect, whereas Caithness, with fields and moors resting on the Old Red Sandstone, is mainly flat, and seems to be swept still flatter by every wind. So too with the islands. The Orkneys, separated from Caithness by the Pentland Firth, share the geological basis of their mainland neighbour and astonish by the unexpected richness of their agriculture, while Shetland, much farther north, partakes to some extent in the geological formations of Sutherland and in appearance is altogether fiercer and more spectacular than the gentle Orkneys.

Yet these four units might be said to compose 'Viking Scotland'. True, in days long past, the long ships with their raven-helmed crews thrust far down the west coast and imposed Norse rule on the Hebrides; but it is in our chosen territory that their influence most strongly persists. Sutherland, occupying the northwest corner of the Scottish mainland, is so called because it was 'southern land' to the Norsemen. The 'ness' in Caithness, the northeastern county, is simply the Norse word for headland. And in Orkney and Shetland the signature may be read even more clearly. Both were added to the Scottish Crown in a somewhat casual way – in 1468 they were pledged by the King of Denmark in payment of the dowry of his daughter on her marriage to King James III of Scotland. But the pledge was never redeemed.

Sutherland

Former Sutherland has one other distinction, it is the only part of the Highland Region which one thinks of as truly 'Highland'. For one thing, it contains many splendid mountains. Ben More Assynt (3,273 feet) is the highest; but such summits as those of Ben Loyal, Ben Hope, Foinaven, Quinag and Suilven are very noble – in fact, many who should know maintain that the county encloses the best mountain scenery in

Scotland. This is clan country and birthplace of Rob Donn, the Gaelic poet. Most of the inhabitants are 'crofters' and follow the way of life that is still general in the Highlands and Islands.

The Norse were dominant here from 1034, when Jarl Thorfinn colonized 'Sudrland', until the early 13th century, when they were driven out by the Scottish king. They have left traces in the place names but no other visible remains. Their prehistoric predecessors, on the other hand, are remembered by 'brochs' (or round towers), 'Picts' houses', mounds, cairns and hut-circles, the best being Dun Dornadilla, in the parish of Durness. Historically, the strongest as well as the most tragic memory is of the notorious 'Clearances' in the 19th century, when the crofters were driven from their holdings in such parts as Strathnaver. For this act the 1st Duke of Sutherland is never likely to receive forgiveness in popular memory, however his apologists may attempt to defend his policy.

The area can boast no town of any size. The main centres are Dornoch in the east, architecturally the most interesting, and with a fine golf-course; Lairg in the centre, an important sheep market; and Lochinver, a fishing and tourist resort in the west, and the unexpected location of a modern and successful pottery.

Caithness

Caithness was the smallish triangular county in the extreme northeast of Scotland. Alongside its western neighbour one thinks of the area as flat and undramatic. But this is to forget that its southern corner is filled by a remarkable plateau at a level of 1,000 feet, and that three of the hills rising from this, Morven, Scaraben and Maiden's Pap, are conspicuous landmarks from afar. From these the county reaches to the north in a low-lying plain. There are two small towns – Wick, a former royal burgh, and Thurso, both giving their name to rivers not large in volume but excellent for fishing, as are the inland lochs. Prehistoric man has left his signs here, in the brochs, cairns, forts and standing stones. There are many traces of early Christian chapels, and the delightful kirks at Dunnet, Canisbay and Reay all have histories going back beyond the Reformation. Medieval times have bequeathed on us a number of stout castles, built by the independent and often lawless barons for their own survival. Survival in the present day may depend in large part on the future of Dounreay, Britain's first atomic power station which is still engaged in pioneering work at the frontiers of modern technology.

Despite wide tracts of moorland suitable only for game or grazing, old Caithness offers more promise to the farmer than does former Sutherland, which was given over to sheep and deer after the Clearances. On fertile ground cattle are bred for milk or for market.

Between Caithness and Orkney is the Pentland Firth, one of the most perilous stretches of water round the shores of Britain. Through it races the tide from the Atlantic to the North Sea and back again, at rates of from 6 to 12 knots. Many ships have met their end on the dangerous Skerries or reefs, and the local fishermen know they must avoid a number of boiling whirlpools with such picturesque names as the Swelkie, the Boars of Duncansby, the Merry Men o' Mey and the Wells of Swona. Many a ship has been wrecked on the Pentland Skerries or the cliffs of Hoy, and it is then that the world hears of the courage and seamanship of the crew of the Longhope lifeboat, which has its station in the south of Hoy.

Fishermen's houses in Stromness, on Mainland in Orkney, built with gable ends to the sea and with their own jetties

Orkney

Across the Firth, only a little more than 6 miles broad at its narrowest point, the south isles of Orkney seem to beckon us. Orkney may be reached by air from Aberdeen or Wick or by steamer from Scrabster. And here we are truly in the old Norse earldom, although the history of the Orkneys is so ancient that sometimes even this can seem to be no more than a brief episode. These were the Orcades of the ancients and gave their name to the stirring *Orkneyinga Saga*. But in far earlier times their unknown inhabitants built at Stenness a stone circle which is worthy of comparison with Stonehenge. The tomb at Maeshowe and the underground village of Skara Brae, both on the largest island (which is usually called Mainland), suggest to us strange, remote and primitive ways of life, when man seemed to be struggling for admittance on the very threshold of civilization. Orkney abounds with evidence of very old settlement by man, as far back as the Stone and Bronze Ages. But it was the Norsemen, coming in the 9th century, who contributed the chief glory of these islands: the cathedral of St Magnus in Kirkwall, once under the archdiocese of Trondheim, and now a parish church under the Presbyterian rule of the Scottish Kirk. This little masterpiece in the Norman style was begun in the 12th century and has been proudly preserved – unlike its neighbour, the ruined Bishop's Palace, still a reminder of the grandeur of the Norse period.

There are more than 70 islands in the Orkney group, but fewer and fewer are populated today – the number is under 20. The largest islands, and those of the greatest importance, are grouped round an anchorage that bears a name known to naval men everywhere – Scapa Flow.

During World War II, as part of the Navy's defences against submarines, a barrier, now known as the Churchill Causeway, was built to link all the islands between Mainland and South Ronaldsay. The Italian prisoners of war who did the work left behind them also a little chapel made from an army hut and decorated with loving care. Kirkwall and Stromness are both towns of character, huddled together about their narrow streets, with schools, newspapers and many other marks of lively communities.

Both Orkney and Shetland are virtually without trees; but in Orkney the soil is fertile and intensively farmed by a race of ingenious and up-to-date farmers, famous chiefly for their beef cattle and cheese. Whisky is distilled and the high-backed straw-plaited Orkney chairs are much sought after.

Shetland

Sailing or flying from Orkney across the stormy Atlantic waters to Shetland, the visitor passes halfway Fair Isle, a bird sanctuary now owned by the National Trust for Scotland. Its vivid traditionally patterned knitwear is world famous.

Then, still further north, he reaches Sumburgh Head, the southern tip of Shetland, a group of islands so rich in their appeal that it is hard to know how to begin. When he first sees them, the newcomer is probably struck by such features as the towering cliffs of Bressay and of Fitful Head or, in the north Mainland, of Ronas Hill. If he is somewhat appalled by the stern, naked moors, he will be delighted with the capital, Lerwick, where the narrow principal street is all paved, and from it steep lanes lead up the hill from the harbour. If his interests are archeological, he will want to spend days at Sumburgh. Here, at Jarlshof, the evidence of several layers of civilization may be studied. There is, for example, a very fine 'broch' (another may be seen on Mousa) as well as the traces of Viking dwellings and underground houses. If he is interested in animals, he may watch the Shetland ponies running wild on the northernmost island of Unst. If he comes at midsummer, he will realize that he is truly in a 'land of the midnight sun' and may watch the blazing orb descend to the horizon, rest there for a moment, as it seems, then begin to ascend the heavens again for another day. If he is an ornithologist, he will be out to study, in particular, the sea-birds which abound in such a sanctuary as Noss. If a fisherman, and at the right time of year, he may find himself fishing for sea-trout in the 'voes' or narrow arms of the sea. And perhaps he will revisit the islands in late January to participate in the festival of Up-Helly-Aa, during which a complete Norse galley is hauled through the streets of Lerwick and finally consumed in a bonfire made by the torches of its hundreds of attendants.

The Shetlanders, unlike the Orcadians, are as much seamen as crofters. Fishing plays an important, if often unreliable, part in their economy, and that simple old man to whom you talk will very likely have sailed half a dozen times round the world. In his conversation he will use many words of Norse origin. He may bear a name that is sturdy Norse and if he goes fishing he will sail a boat of the shapeliest Norse lines. He may talk of such things as 'scattald' – the common grazing on the hill – and 'udal' law, the Norse system so different from the feudal. We have passed through a region where the Vikings left many writings, but here one often feels they have never left.

In recent years the Shetland way of life has been under heavy pressure because of the discovery of North Sea oil. Almost overnight the once desolate Sullom Voe has become the largest oil port in Europe handling a greater tonnage than Rotterdam. The Shetlanders took a firm and early grip of the changing situation and obtained Parliamentary powers to control the development of oil companies. As a result they succeeded in limiting the impact on the environment and negotiated generous compensation to help restore basic industries as the oil boom passes.

Shetland is an exciting place to live in today with a tenacious and distinctive island culture and the brash levelling pressure of the multinationals.

Orkney has felt the same pressure although not quite to the same degree. It has an eloquent interpreter of the island way of life in George Mackay Brown who like his predecessors Eric Linklater and Edwin Muir has the island sense of timelessness in the midst of change.

GAZETTEER

Altnacealgach, Suth   12G7
With one of the oldest fishing hotels in Scotland is noted for its views, and climbing, of *Ben More*, Cul Mor, Cul Beag and magnificent Suilven, and for its trout fishing in lochs and streams, especially Loch Veyatie.

Altnaharra, Suth   13H8
Fishing centre at W end of Loch Naver with good hill-walking country all around with brochs and hut-circles.

Ardvreck Castle, Suth   12G7
This picturesque ruined 16th-c castle on Loch Assynt (off the A837, 11m E of **Lochinver**) was the stronghold of the MacLeods of Assynt: here James Graham, Marquess of Montrose, was captured after losing the battle of Carbisdale, ending his remarkable military career and leading to his execution.

Armadale, Suth   13I9
Farming and fishing village at the head of a pretty bay. Noted for its sheep. 6m NE is *Strathy Point* where the coastline is riddled with caves. In 1958 a lighthouse was built here with keepers' houses near by.

Ben More Assynt *see* Introduction, **Altnacealgach** and **Inchnadamph**

Berriedale, Caith   13J7
Its hairpin bends and frightening gradients were formerly a challenge to motorists: by brilliant engineering it is now just a long climb – for the benefit of commercial 'heavies'. Near *Braemore*, 5m inland, is a monument to H.R.H. the Duke of Kent, youngest son of George V, who was killed in an air crash while on active service with the RAF during World War II.

Bettyhill, Suth   13I9
Coastal village with fine sands at a point where the River Naver flows into sea. Rocky scenery; mountains well seen from Strath Naver.

Bonar Bridge, Suth   13H6
The gateway by road to former Sutherland and Caithness. Telford's 1812 bridge was necessarily replaced in 1973 by a steel bow-string bridge to cope with vastly increased traffic on the A9. The Forestry Commission has provided walks on both sides of the Kyle of Sutherland.

Ben More Assynt: its peak (3,273 feet) seen from the River Traligill in Inchnadamph Forest

Brora, Suth   13I7
Angling and holiday centre with fine sands, an excellent golf-course and good hotels, at the mouth of Strath Brora. On W side of Loch Brora, the Carrol Rock is 650ft high. There are several brochs in the neighbourhood. Clynelcish whisky is highly regarded, as are tweeds from the local mill.

Brough of Birsay,* Ork   *Inset* **13**
This small tidal island at NW tip of Mainland has 8th-c Christian, Norse, Celtic and Viking relics, these including remains of Earl Thorfinn's Hall, his cathedral church where St Magnus was originally buried (*see* **Kirkwall**) and Viking longhouses. Earl Robert Stewart's palace (AM), built 1580

on lines of **Falkland** Palace (Fife) is well preserved, and is situated adjacent to the island on Mainland.

Burra Isle, Shet   *Inset* **13**
Now joined to Mainland at **Scalloway** by bridges through Trondra. Has important early Celtic church remains: of its rare sculptured stones the Papil Stone is in the National Museum of Antiquities, **Edinburgh** (Lothian), and the Monk's Stone in **Lerwick** Museum.

Cape Wrath, Suth   12G9
Britain's NW corner, where the Atlantic hurls boulders at the 500ft. cliffs. Ferry across the Kyle of Durness (in summer), and then a 10m walk over the moors. Tough walkers can follow a route up the shore from *Sheigra*, past Sandwood Bay. *See* **Durness** and **Rhiconich**.

Castle of Mey, Caith 13K9

Formerly the Barrogill Castle, an ancient fortified grange acquired by the 4th Earl of Caithness in 1556 and converted to a castle. Since then much altered, it was purchased in 1952 by Queen Elizabeth the Queen Mother as her holiday home: it overlooks the Pentland Firth to Orkney.

Copinsay, Ork Inset 13

A 210-acre island SE off *Deerness,* noted for its sea-bird colonies. It was bought by the World Wildlife Fund in 1972 as a memorial to James Fisher, the naturalist and broadcaster, with funds raised by organizations with which he had been associated, and is administered by the RSPB.

Dornoch,★ Suth 13I6

Happily at the end of a 2m branch away from the A9 traffic Dornoch has a beautiful cathedral (now the parish church) built in the 13th c on a much earlier Culdee site: the nave was rebuilt in 1837 and the whole building finely restored in 1924. A stone marking the spot of the last burning of a witch in Scotland is in a garden towards the lower links. Golf has been played here since 1616 and its lovely links have been the nursery for many famous players: it has two courses, one of championship standard. There are vast sandy beaches on the Dornoch Firth. W from the town Andrew Carnegie built *Skibo Castle* as a holiday residence.

Dounreay, Caith 13J9

The experimental fast reactor of the U.K. Atomic Energy Authority was erected here in 1955 to test the feasibility of deriving power from uranium instead of from coal (1 ton uranium = 3 million tons of coal), and the 135ft-diameter steel sphere containing it is a familiar landmark. The Establishment has been greatly enlarged for associated developments; this is reflected in the growth of **Thurso**. The Dounreay Exhibition in the control tower of the former airfield gives visitors a general idea of the Establishment's activities. Open April–Sept.: free. Step back a few years to contemplate the little old church at *Reay,* with its external staircase.

Dunbeath, Caith 13J8

Fishing-village with a notable broch and a 15th-c castle. Picts' houses beside Dunbeath Water stand some 3m NW.

Dunnet Head, Caith 13J9

The most northerly point on the Scottish mainland, with views of Orkney (the Old Man of **Hoy** is conspicuous) across the swirling waters of Pentland Firth. Sandy beach and an ancient church with saddleback tower.

Durness, Suth 12G9

A village some 10m from **Cape Wrath**. Fine sands on Balnakill Bay. In *Balnakill,* ½m W, is Durness Old Church (1619), now a ruin. In another bay in the cliffs, 2m E, are the three *Caves of Smoo,* of which the outer one can be entered at low tide.

Egilsay, Ork Inset 13

The small island N from **Kirkwall** has the fine 12th-c St Magnus Church, walls and high round tower almost intact, in which Jarl Magnus is thought to have spent the night in prayer before his ritual murder by Jarl Haakon, in 1117.

Esha Ness, Shet Inset 13

At extreme NW of Mainland and noted for remarkable cliff formations: near by at *Hamnavoe* lived John Williamson or 'Johnnie Notions' who during a smallpox epidemic *c.*1770

Dunnet Head: the lighthouse stands on mainland Scotland's most northerly point

created and administered his own vaccine, curing several thousand people with no fatalities.

Fair Isle,★ Shet (NTS) Inset 13

Midway between Shetland and Orkney. Famous for its colourful homespun and home-dyed knitting and also has an outstanding bird observatory for the study of more than 300 species of migrating birds and breeding colonies of many sea birds. NTS has greatly improved facilities, stemming depopulation: access is by twice-weekly mail-boat and air from **Lerwick** and **Kirkwall** (Orkney) and its hostel, accommodating 24, is open 1 March–30 Nov.

Fetlar Isle, Shet Inset 13

Of interest to geologists for its varied rock types and to ornithologists as the only known haunt in Britain of the splendid snowy owl: there is an observation post and resident RSPB summer warden. Limited access only.

Flotta, Ork Inset 13

The island at S entrance to **Scapa Flow**, the vital naval base in World War I and II, became in the 1970s a major oil and gas terminal handling in 1983, 106,496,000 barrels of oil and 34,420,000 barrels of liquified petroleum gas. Particular attention has been given to the protection of the environment.

Golspie, Suth 13I6

Seaside village with excellent golf and sands. The church has notable Sutherland loft or gallery (1738) and pulpit. 1m E is *Dunrobin Castle* embodying a 13th-c keep, and with fine paintings. Open May–Sept.

Halkirk, Caith 13J9

Angling centre on Thurso river, with Loch Calder to W. Brawl Castle (14th-c) has walls 10ft thick (*see* **Watten**).

Helmsdale, Suth   13J7
Fishing village with harbour. Bathing, golf, sea and river
fishing. Remains of 15th-c castle. 7m S is a fine broch; others
lie N near Ord of Caithness, with good views.

Hoy, Ork   *Inset* **13**
Second largest island with the highest point Ward Hill
(1,570ft), a botanist's paradise, and some of Britain's finest
cliff scenery. The *Old Man of Hoy,* an isolated stack of red
sandstone, rises 450ft from the sea. Near *Rackwick,* a beach
on SW coast, is the *Dwarfie Stone,* a Neolithic burial
chamber hollowed out of a block of sandstone 26ft by 13ft,
and mentioned in Sir Walter Scott's *The Pirate.*

Inchnadamph,★ Suth   12G7
Long-established angling resort at SE end of Loch Assynt,
with rare Gillaroo trout in Loch Maoloch. Geologists have
found Archaean gneiss rock to NW, botanists and archeologists rare plants and ferns, and the Allt nan Uamh bone
caves show early occupation, in extensive Nature Reserve.
Views of *Ben More* (*see* Introduction, **Altnacealgach** and
page 403).

Inverkirkaig, Suth   12F7
Scattered crofting village at head of the bay where the
Kirkaig river rushes out to sea. There is a riverside path to
the Falls of Kirkaig, 2m away, from which the river drops
into a chasm. To the S, a narrow winding road runs among
lochs and hills to **Ullapool.**

Jarlshof,★★ Shet   *Inset* **13**
Near *Sumburgh* 28m S of **Lerwick.** One of the most
important archeological sites (AM) in Britain showing
occupation from early 2000 BC, the Bronze Age, the Iron Age,
and later structures including an aisled roundhouse and
wheel-house. After visiting Jarlshof in 1816 Sir Walter Scott
named the medieval farmhouse in *The Pirate* after it.

John o' Groats, Caith   13K9
The name is romantic, but the scene is not typically Scottish
Highland. John's house was demolished years ago; his grave
is at Canisbay Church. The northernmost point on the
mainland is **Dunnet Head.** *Duncansby Head,* 1½m E, with its
detached rocks, has a finer viewpoint.

Kildonan, Suth   13I7
On the A897 8m NW from **Helmsdale.** There is gold in its hill
burns: there was a minor 'gold rush' around 1868 and in the
1970s a Government scheme encouraged prospectors.

Kirkwall,★ Ork   *Inset* **13**
Capital of Orkney since the 9th c and notable for St Magnus
Cathedral, 234ft long and 101ft across the transepts, built by
Earl Rognvald in the 12th c to commemorate his martyred
uncle, Magnus, whose remains are preserved here, with
many other memorials. The Cathedral has been splendidly
restored and is fully used for worship. Near by are ruins of
the Bishop's and Earl's Palaces with an interesting museum
in Tankerness House. Kirkwall has grown in size and
business with the advent of North Sea oil activity at **Flotta.**
It has an 18-hole golf-course and indoor swimming pool. *See*
Egilsay, Fair Isle and **Wyre.**

Kylesku, Suth   12G8
The new bridge across the junction of Lochs Glendu and
Glencoil with Loch Cairnbawn on the A894 was opened by
the Queen in 1984. Near the head of Loch Glencoil is *Eas
Coul Aulin,* the highest waterfall in Britain (some 658ft).

*Jarlshof: the remarkable remains of three Shetland
settlements dating from the Bronze Age to the Viking era*

Lairg, Suth   13H7
Village where miscellaneous supplies brought up by rail are
transferred to road vehicles for further transport to crofts
and villages all over Sutherland. Very good centre, with
boating and fishing. Loch Shin, 15m long, is used by the
North of Scotland Hydro-Electricity Board.

Latheron, Caith   13J8
Sights include a whalebone arch, an ancient standing stone
and an old tower. 2m N is *Forse,* with ruined castle and
primitive stone dwellings.

Laxford Bridge, Suth   12G8
Where the Laxford river (noted for salmon) enters Loch
Laxford amid a glorious tangle of rocks and lochs.

Lerwick, Shet   *Inset* **13**
This, the administrative and commercial centre of Shetland
and most northerly town in Britain, shows Norse influences:
its natural sheltered harbour has been used by seafarers of
many nations for centuries, notably King Haakon of Norway who revictualled his fleet *en route* to defeat at the battle
of Largs (*see* **Largs,** Strathclyde) in 1263, and it is now much
used by oil-related vessels and the fishing industry. The
winter visitor may observe the 'Up-Helly-Aa' festival, a
parade of torch bearing guizers and the burning of a 'Norse'
longship on the last Tues. of January welcomes the strength-
ening sun. *See* **Fair Isle, Noss Isle,** **St Ninian's Isle,** and
Unst.

Lochinver, Suth   12F7
Amphibious parish containing nearly 300 named lochs and
many without names. It is strung out beside the final ½m or so
of the River Inver. Small pier, excellent fishing, both sea and
freshwater. SE, *Suilven* (2,399ft) rises as a rounded height,
seemingly inaccessible.

Scapa Flow: an area of deep water enclosed by Orkney's Mainland, Birsay, South Ronaldsay, Flotta and Hoy

Loth, Suth   13J7
Between **Brora** and **Helmsdale** on the A9. At the foot of Glen Loth is a stone marking the killing of the last wolf in Sutherland in about 1700. 2m S is an excavated broch.

Maeshowe, ⋆⋆ Ork   *Inset* **13**
3½m NE from **Stromness** with relics from 2000 BC and the finest chambered tomb in Europe. The chamber, 16ft square and high is entered by a passage 39ft long and the whole covered by a mound 26ft high and 115ft in diameter: there is fine corbelling and remarkable masonry. Pillaged by Vikings, Norse invaders left a rich collection of runic inscriptions, well preserved.

Muckle Flugga, Shet   *Inset* **13**
A large rock N of *Hermaness* on **Unst** is Britain's Ultima Thule as the most northerly habitation, the important lighthouse being manned by its keepers.

North Ronaldsay, Ork   *Inset* **13**
Most northerly of the Orkney islands, it is surrounded by a low, stone dyke outside which its peculiarly indigenous sheep graze on seaweed: there are many prehistoric sites.

Noss Isle, Shet   *Inset* **13**
This tiny island with towering sandstone cliffs, just separated E from *Bressay* (access from **Lerwick**), covering less than 1½sq m is a National Nature Reserve occupied by 400 sheep and more than 80,000 nesting sea-birds: the only habitation, 15th-c *Gungstie House* at the W tip, is used by Nature Conservancy Council wardens. The birds include great skuas, Arctic skuas, kittiwakes, tern, eider duck,

fulmars, gannets and guillemots. From The Noup (200ft) the whole of Shetland may be viewed. A walk round the island takes two to three hours: visitors are asked to avoid the central part.

Papa Westray, Ork   *Inset* **13**
The second most northerly of the islands, 4m long and 1m wide, has the *Knap of Howar*, two houses lived in 5,000 years ago and known as the 'earliest standing houses in NW Europe', ruins of St Tredwell's chapel and the 12th-c church and graveyard of St Boniface where a 7th-c Celtic stone cross was found.

Rhiconich, Suth   12G8
Here a narrow road goes NW by *Kinlochbervie* (a fishing-village) to *Sheigra*, the northernmost village on the W coast. Primitive scenery. A rough 4m walk leads N to Sandwood Bay and strong walkers can continue to **Cape Wrath**.

St Ninian's Isle, ⋆ Shet   *Inset* **13**
Joined to Mainland by a beautiful spit of white sand 6m NW from *Sumburgh* off the **Lerwick** road. In 1958 a dig by students revealed under an ancient chapel a medieval church, a Bronze Age and a pre-Norse burial site and the magnificent St Ninian's Treasure of silver bowls, brooches, and a fine Communion spoon: the treasure, now in National Museum of Antiquities, **Edinburgh** (Lothian), with replicas in Lerwick Museum, is believed to have been buried by monks wiped out by Vikings.

Scalloway, Shet   *Inset* **13**
The former capital of Shetland with its notable ruined 17th-c castle (AM) was the base for the famous World War II 'Shetland bus' when small fishing boats sailed to Nazi-occupied Norway with saboteurs and secret agents and brought back important refugees: a bronze plaque commemorates the exploit. This is a busy fishing, fish-processing and ship-repair centre. *See* **Weisdale**.

Scapa Flow, Ork   *Inset* **13**
The vast natural harbour, up to 10m wide, of deep water was a vital Royal Navy base in World War I and II. The E entrances were closed with huge concrete blocks – the Churchill Barriers – after a Nazi U-boat penetrated the defences and sank HMS *Royal Oak* on 14 October 1939. The Barriers also give access by road to the small islands of *Glims Holm* and *Lamb Holm* and to *Burray* and *South Ronaldsay*. *See also* Introduction, **Flotta** and **Stromness**.

Scourie, Suth   12G8
Village on a small bay in the rocky coast. Offshore 2m N is *Handa Island*, with great cliffs and raucous sea birds.

Scrabster, Caith   13J9
The sheltered harbour 1½m NW from Thurso is the base for car ferries and steamers to Orkney and Shetland.

Skara Brae, Ork   *Inset* **13**
On the W of Mainland with important Neolithic relics in 10 one-roomed houses occupied about 2000 BC. The remarkable state of preservation revealing simple domestic arrangements. Tools and animal bones found are in the National Museum of Antiquities, **Edinburgh** (Lothian), copies are in the small museum at the site.

Stenness,★ Ork   *Inset* **13**
N from **Stromness**, the standing stones of Stenness, dated *c*.1800 BC, and the famous Bronze Age Ring of Brodgar with 36 stones of the original 60 remaining, the tallest 15ft high. After **Stonehenge** (Wilts) this is said to be the finest megalithic henge monument in Britain with **Callanish**.

Stoer, Suth   12F7
Crofting village on rocky indented coast extending to the Point of Stoer, where cliffs are 300ft high. The views are remarkable. *Clachtoll*, 1m S, has white sands and rugged rocks. 2m S is *Achmelvich*, a township on a fine sandy bay.

Stromness, Ork   *Inset* **13**
The second town in Orkney and an important well-sheltered harbour. It was a trading port with the Baltic in the 17th c and Hudson's Bay Company's ships from 1670 to 1891. The town was built in Norse style with paved thoroughfares and many of the houses, gable-ended to the sea, have their own jetties. There is a fine natural history museum also with ship models and a feature on **Scapa Flow**, Arts Centre, heated swimming pool and 18-hole golf-course. *See* Introduction and page 401.

Sullom Voe, Shet   *Inset* **13**
An exceptionally deep and sheltered inlet of the sea penetrating nearly 8m from Yell Sound into Mainland, familiar in World War II as a Naval and RAF Coastal Command

flyingboat base, is now Europe's biggest oil terminal, storing crude by pipelines from several fields and loading the world's largest tankers. In 1983 52,220,183 net metric tonnes of oil were handled and more than 1,211,000 tonnes of liquified petroleum gas.

Thurso, Caith   13J9
Town at head of the bay sheltered by **Dunnet Head** which has increased in size in recent years with housing, schools and full-scale amenities necessitated by the workers and their families at near-by **Dounreay**. For long it was the centre of the Caithness paving-stone industry and the stones are still much in evidence. The museum contains the collection of the geologist Robert Dick (1811–66). On the W side of the bay are the ruins of the Bishop's Palace (13th-c), E of the town stands ruined Thurso Castle. Near by, Harold's Tower marks where the Earl of Caithness was killed in 1136.

Tongue, Suth   13H9
Picturesque village on the Kyle of Tongue, with bathing, fishing, boating and some circular routes through wonderful mountain and loch scenery. Nobody knows the age of Castle Varrick, now in ruins. To the S are stately Ben Loyal (2,504ft) and Ben Hope (3,040ft).

Unst, Shet   *Inset* **13**
The smallest of Shetland's three main islands has Britain's northernmost post office at *Haroldswick* and a nature reserve noted as the breeding ground of the relatively rare great skua, Arctic skuas and red-throated divers, with colonies of gannets, kittiwakes and puffins in its cliffs. The reserve includes **Muckle Flugga** and the *Outstack*: no restrictions on access but the Nature Conservancy Council has an officer at Alexandra Wharf, **Lerwick**.

Watten, Caith   13K8
Village headquarters for those who fish for trout in the neighbouring loch. *See* **Halkirk**.

Weisdale, Shet   *Inset* **13**
In the centre of Mainland 6m N of **Scalloway**, this was the birthplace of John Clunies Ross (1786–1854) who, after an adventurous career in sailing ships settled in the Cocos Islands which flourished under his reign as 'king', a position recognized by Queen Victoria.

Wick,★ Caith   13K8
Ancient town, former important herring port with a harbour in a rocky coast sprinkled with castles. Prize-winning exhibition of herring industry at the Heritage Centre. To the S are the ruined castle of Old Wick and a rock arch known as Brig o' Tram. N, precariously placed on a cliff edge, stand the ruins of *Girnigoe* and *Sinclair Castles* and Ackergill Tower. N of *Keiss* is *Bucholie Castle*, with brochs near by. Wick airport handles services to Orkney, Shetland and the South.

Wyre, Ork   *Inset* **13**
A small island N from **Kirkwall** has 12th-c *Cubbie Roo's Castle* and chapel built by Kolbein Hruga (described in the Haakon Saga as 'a mighty man from Norway') whose son Bjarni became Bishop of Orkney and composed the noted *Jomsvikingudrupa*.

USEFUL ADDRESSES

TOURIST BOARDS
British Tourist Authority
64 St James's Street, London SW1A 1NF
English Tourist Board
4 Grosvenor Gardens, London SW1 0DU
Scottish Tourist Board
23 Ravelston Terrace, Edinburgh EH4 3EU
Wales Tourist Board
Brunel House, 2 Fitzalan Road, Cardiff CF2 1UY
Isle of Man Tourist Board
13 Victoria Street, Douglas, Isle of Man
London Tourist Board
26 Grosvenor Gardens, London SW1 0DU

OTHER ORGANIZATIONS
British Waterways Board
Melbury House, Melbury Terrace, London NW1 6JX
Council for National Parks
4 Hobart Place, London SW1 0HY

Council for the Protection of Rural England (CPRE)
4 Hobart Place, London SW1 0HY
Countryside Commission
Headquarters, John Dower House, Crescent Place,
Cheltenham, Gloucestershire GL50 3RA
National Trust
42 Queen Anne's Gate, London SW1H 9AS
National Trust for Scotland
5 Charlotte Square, Edinburgh EH2 4DU
Nature Conservancy Council
19 Belgrave Square, London SW1X 8PY
Ramblers' Association
1–5 Wandsworth Road, London SW8
The Royal Society for the Protection of Birds
The Lodge, Sandy, Bedfordshire SG19 2DL
Society for the Protection of Ancient Buildings
55 Great Ormond Street, London WC1 N3J
Zoological Society of London
Regents Park, London NW1

ILLUSTRATION ACKNOWLEDGMENTS

Aerofilms endpapers, 151
Malcolm Aird 302
The J. Allan Cash Photolibrary, 37, 40, 153, 241, 265, 281, 311, 341, 345, 364, 401, 405
Heather Angel 26
Peter Baker/Photobank 43, 51, 55, 62, 69, 81, 99, 155, 160, 326, 347, 371, 395, 397, 398, 404; Photos Adrian Baker 362, 363, 369, 393
John Bethell 10, 30, 34–5, 46, 58–9, 61, 77, 96, 101, 107, 108, 115, 123, 126–7, 128, 131, 137, 139, 147, 149, 159, 167, 171, 173, 180–1, 190, 199, 201, 211, 219, 220, 222, 226–7, 232, 234, 266, 269, 272, 279, 291, 298–9, 307, 309, 319, 349, 372
British Tourist Authority 203, 238, 247, 251, 255
John Cleare/Mountain Camera 386–7
Robert Estall 214–15
Images Colour Library/Photo Derry Brabbs 322
Ironbridge Museum Trust 16
A. F. Kersting 143, 297, 305, 333, 361
S. & O. Mathews 18–19

Derek McDougall 339, 354–5, 366–7
Gunnie Moberg 406
Colin Molyneux 325, 331
The National Theatre of Great Britain 119
National Trust for Scotland 389
The Photo Source/Colour Library International 22, 334–5, 379, 391
Picturepoint 375, 403
Rainbird/Drawings Richard Reid 12–15
Kenneth Scowen 39, 49, 53, 56, 60, 65, 67, 70, 72, 74, 85, 87, 89, 90, 93, 95, 103, 110, 113, 116, 129, 132, 135, 162, 164, 168, 177, 182, 185, 205, 209, 224, 228, 242, 245, 284, 287, 292, 294, 301, 343, 373
Tony Stone Photolibrary 283
Topham Picture Library 377
Derek G. Widdicombe 28, 79, 120, 188, 192, 259, 262, 275, 358; Photos **Noel Habgood** 2–3, 231, 315
Woodmansterne 351 (Photo Clive Friend); 380 (Photo Jeremy Marks)

INDEX

MAPS

KEY

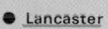	motorway
	primary route
	'A' road
	'B' road
	unclassified
	country boundary
	county boundary
	ferry port

● **Lancaster** a place of special interest or of outstanding importance
● OAKHAM

○ **Kilmarnock** other places
○ HALESOWEN

▣ Lamport Hall a site of special interest or of outstanding importance

▣ Cessford Castle other sites

Scale 1:1 000 000

0 5 10 15 20 Miles

0 10 20 30 Kilometres

SHETLAND ISLANDS

ORKNEY ISLANDS

ST KILDA

WESTERN ISLES

12 HIGHLAND

13 GRAMPIAN

TAYSIDE

FIFE

CENTRAL LOTHIAN

10 STRATHCLYDE BORDERS

SCOTLAND **11**

DUMFRIES AND GALLOWAY NORTHUMBERLAND

TYNE AND WEAR

CUMBRIA DURHAM CLEVELAND

NORTH YORKSHIRE

8 **9**

LANCASHIRE WEST YORKSHIRE HUMBERSIDE

GREATER MANCHESTER SOUTH YORKSHIRE

MERSEYSIDE CHESHIRE DERBYSHIRE NOTTINGHAMSHIRE LINCOLNSHIRE

ENGLAND

GWYNEDD CLWYD

STAFFORDSHIRE

SHROPSHIRE LEICESTERSHIRE NORFOLK **5**

WALES **6** **7** WEST MIDLANDS

POWYS HEREFORD AND WORCESTER WARWICKSHIRE NORTHAMPTONSHIRE CAMBRIDGESHIRE SUFFOLK

DYFED GLOUCESTERSHIRE OXFORDSHIRE BUCKINGHAMSHIRE HERTFORDSHIRE ESSEX

WEST GLAM MID GLAM GWENT GREATER LONDON **14-15**

SOUTH GLAM AVON WILTSHIRE BERKSHIRE SURREY **4** KENT

2 SOMERSET **3** HAMPSHIRE WEST SUSSEX EAST SUSSEX

DEVON DORSET ISLE OF WIGHT

CORNWALL

ISLES OF SCILLY

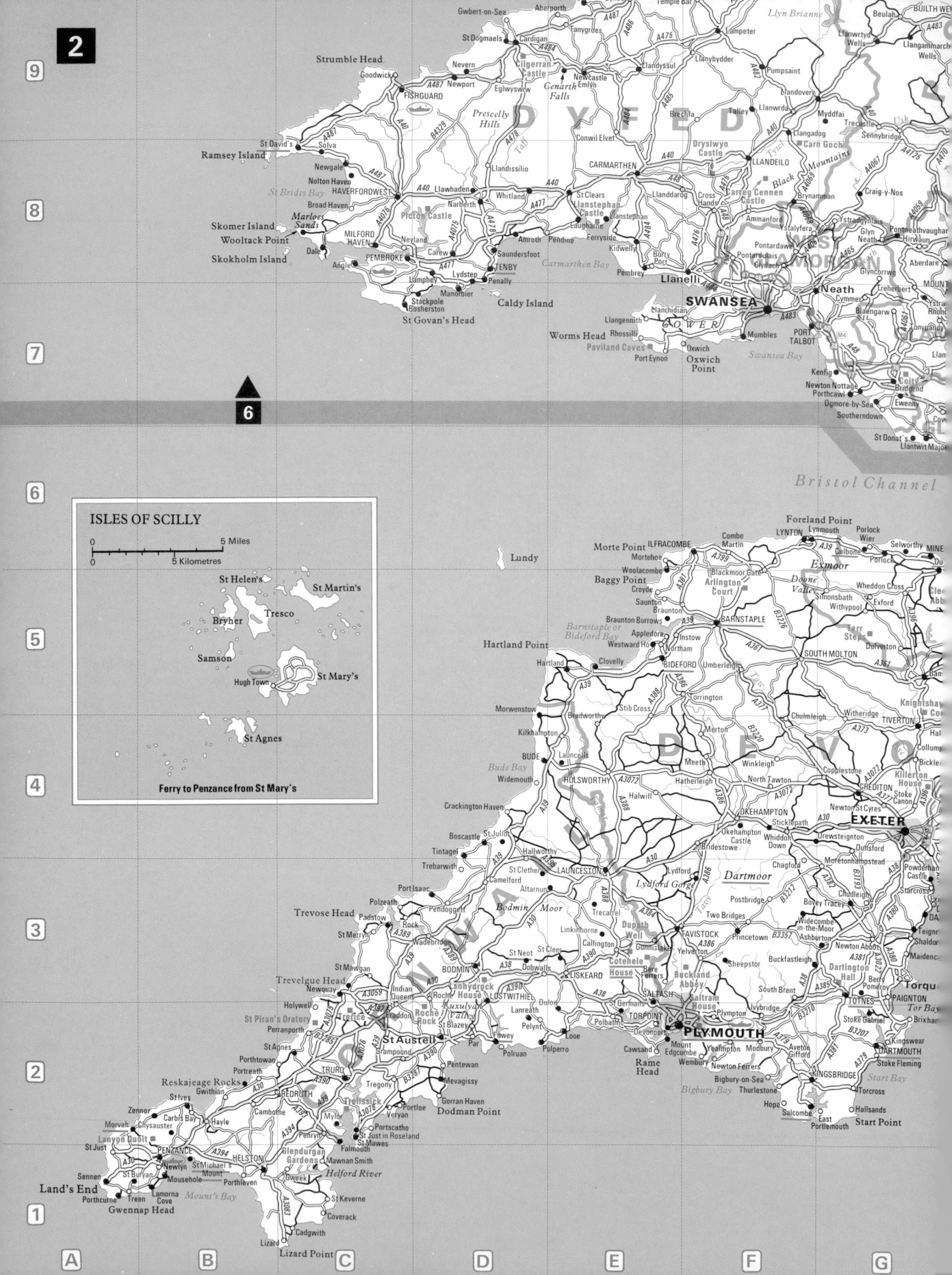

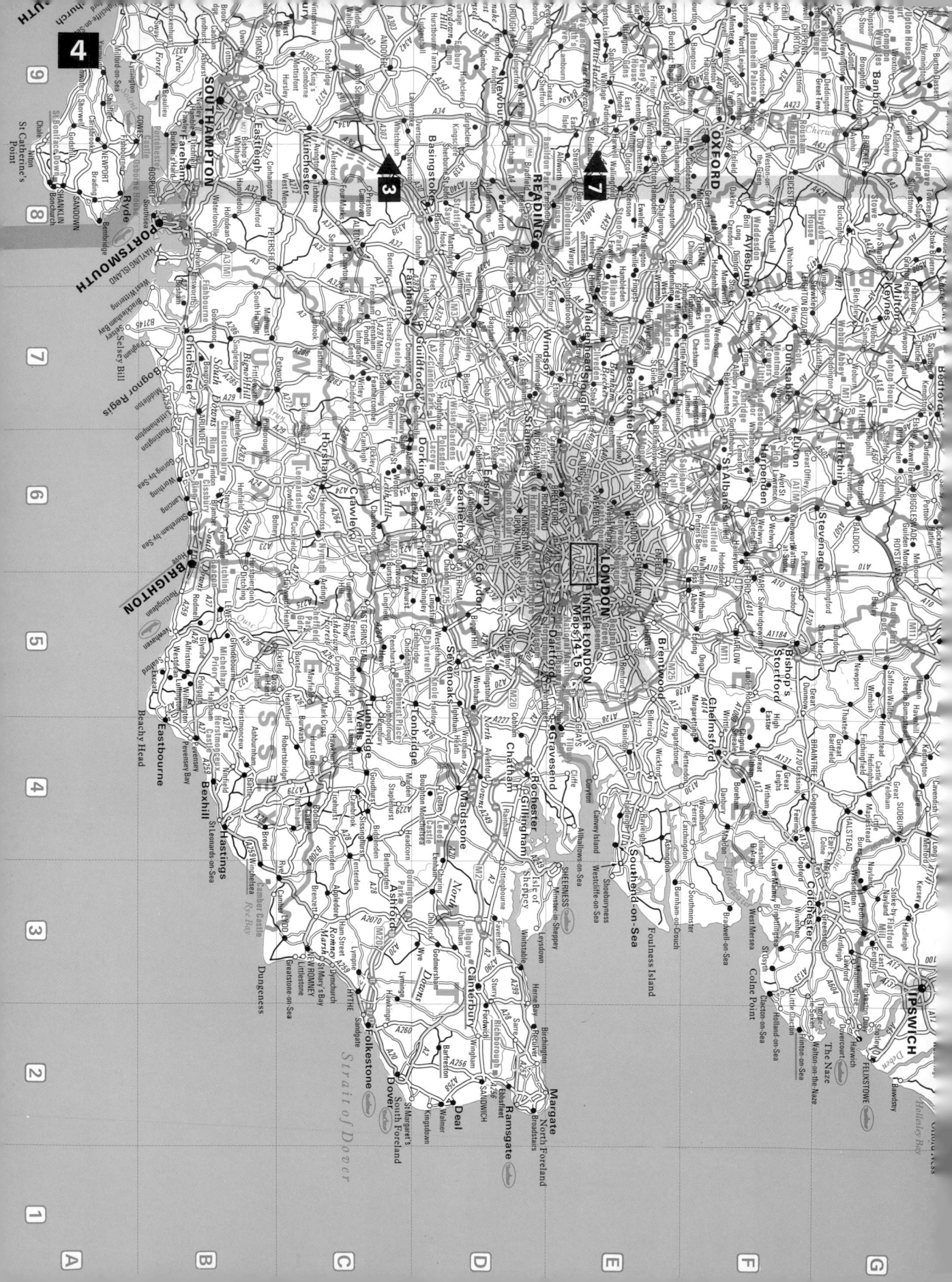

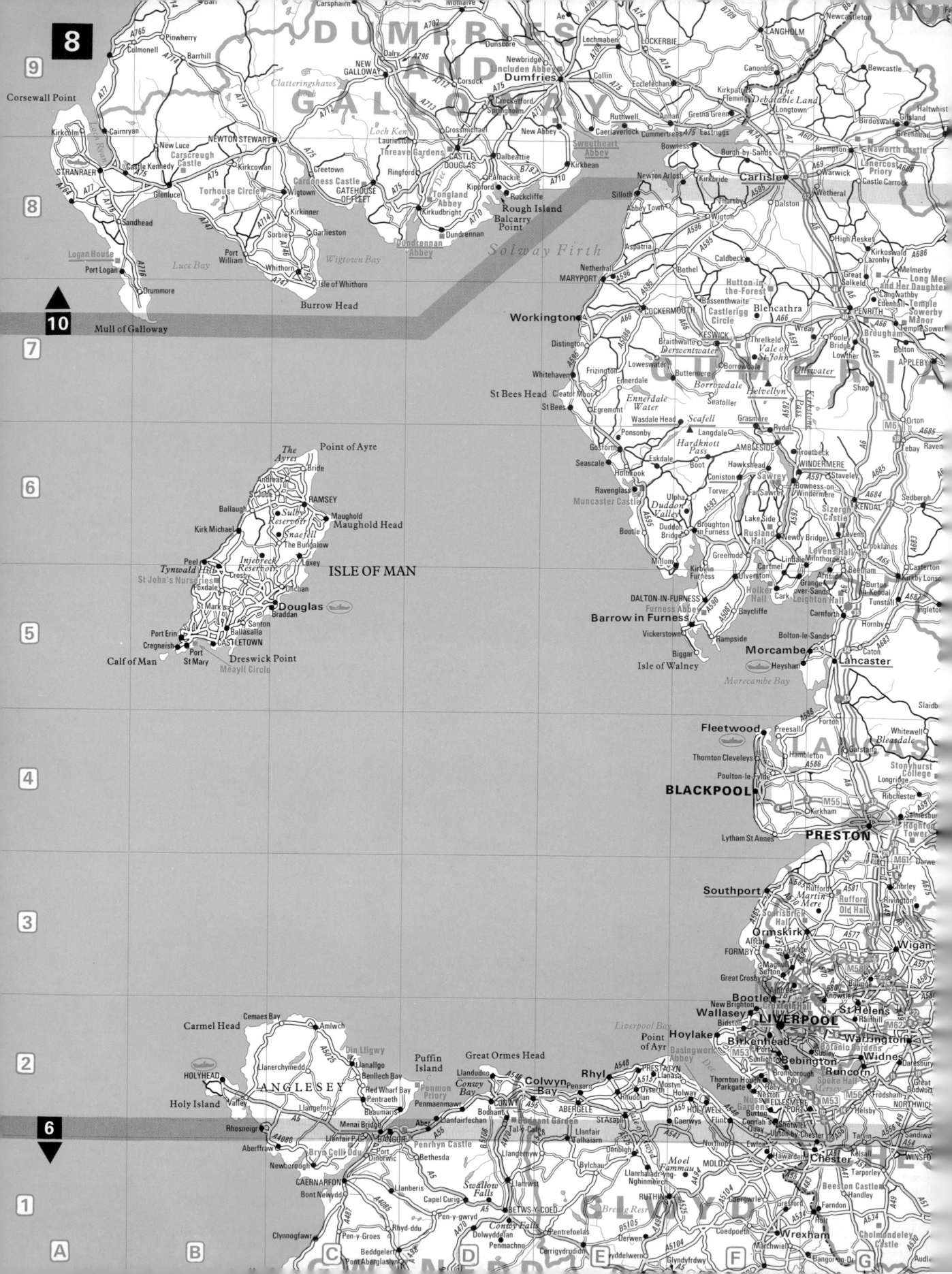

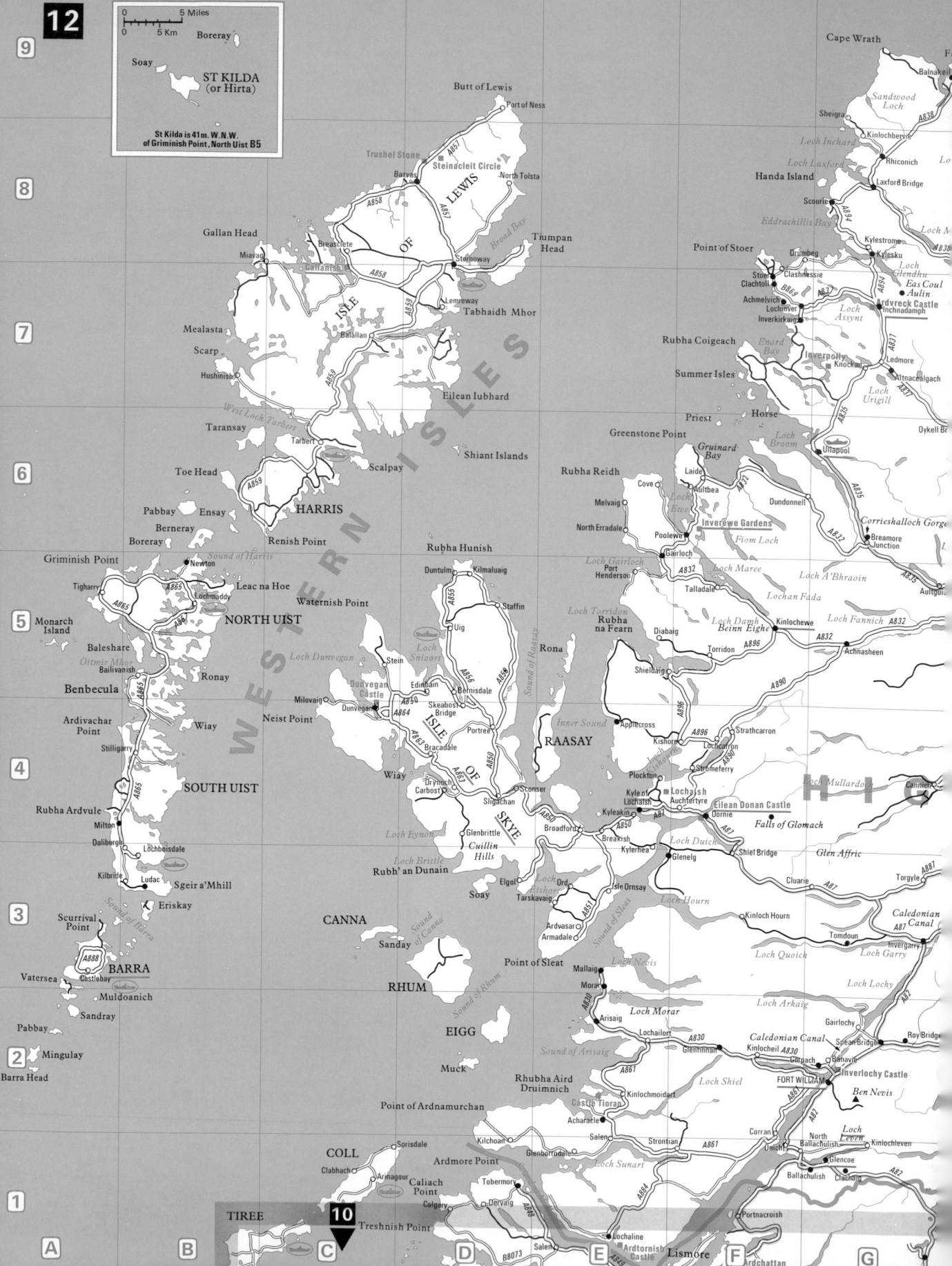

A DAY OUT IN BRITAIN

KEY

- Areas of Natural Beauty and National Parks
- *Dawlish* — Outstanding beaches
- .... Stretches of good beaches
- —·—·— Walks

Scotland has many areas of outstanding beauty which are not marked on this map because it has not yet become necessary for them to be preserved by legislation.

OPEN AIR MUSEUMS

1. Cregneish Folk Museum, Isle of Man
2. Welsh Folk Museum, St. Fagan's, near Cardiff
3. Auchindrain Museum of Country Life, near Inveraray, Strathclyde
4. Acton Scott, near Church Stretton, Shropshire
5. Shugborough Park Farm, Staffordshire
6. Manor Farm Museum, Cogges, Oxfordshire
7. Easton Farm Park, Wickham Market, Suffolk
8. Norfolk Rural Life Museum, Gressenhall, Norfolk
9. Weald & Downland Open Air Museum, Singleton, West Sussex
10. Avoncroft Museum of Buildings, Hereford & Worcester
11. North of England Open Air Museum, Beamish, Co. Durham
12. Black Country Museum, Dudley, West Midlands
13. Ironbridge Gorge Museum, Telford, Shropshire
14. Blists Hill Open Air Museum, Telford, Shropshire

WALKS

1. Leith Hill, Surrey Hills
2. Cleeve Hill, The Cotswold Way
3. Pen y Fan, Brecon Beacons
4. Dunkery Beacon, Exmoor National Park
5. Coastal Path, Pembrokeshire in West Dyfed
6. The Pennine Way, Malham, North Yorks, to Pen-y-Ghent
7. Farndale, North Yorks Moors National Park
8. Ennerdale to Buttermere, Lake District
9. Goat Fell above Brodick, Isle of Arran
10. Fort William to Ben Nevis

Map labels

Orkney Islands
Shetland Islands
Dunnet Bay
Melness
Sinclair's Bay
Highlands
Big Sand
Dornoch Sands
Fort George to Burghead
Lossiemouth
Fraserburgh to Peterhead
Lewis
North Uist
Benbecula
South Uist
Barra
Glen Affric
Glen More
Cairngorms
Cruden Bay
Balmedie
Morar
Garvan
FORT WILLIAM
Ben Nevis
Grampians
St. Cyrus
Lunan Bay
Trossachs
Argyll
Queen Elizabeth Forest Park
GLASGOW
Largo Bay
White Sands
Drum Sands
EDINBURGH
Tentsmuir Sands
Berwick-upon-Tweed
Kilberry
Catradale
Lendalfoot to Saltcoats
Northumberland Coast
Northumberland
Cheviot Hills
Amble-by-the-Sea
Druridge Bay
Cresswell
Newbiggin-by-the-Sea
Whitley Bay
The Border
Glen Trool
CARLISLE
Skiddaw
Solway Coast
Sandhead
Southerness
Redcar
Lake District
Helvellyn
Scafell
Whitby
Robin Hood's Bay
Isle of Man
North York Moors
Duddon Sands
Ingleborough
Arnside & Silverdale
Morecombe Bay
Yorkshire Dales
Flamborough Head
Bridlington to Hornsea
Forest of Bowland
Fleetwood to Blackpool
Pennine Way
Southport
MANCHESTER
Cleethorpes
Mablethorpe
Anglesey
Colwyn Bay to Prestatyn
Cheshire Plain
Peak District
Lincolnshire Wolds
Church Bay to Llanddwyn Bay
Snowdon
Snowdonia
Norfolk Coast
Skegness
Holkham Bay
Wells next the Sea
Cromer
Lleyn
Offa's Dyke Path
Wrekin
Cannock Chase
Hunstanton
The Fens
Norfolk Broads
Winterton-on-Sea
Aberdaron Bay
Porth Neigwl Bay
Barmouth
NORWICH
Great Yarmouth
Barth
Shropshire Hills
BIRMINGHAM
Suffolk Coast & Heaths
Southwold
Dunwich
Cambrian Mts
Black Mts
Malvern Hills
Dedham Vale
Pembrokeshire Coast
Whitesand Bay
St. Brides Bay to Sandy Haven
Brecon Beacons
Dean Forest
Cotswold Hills
Chiltern Hills
Clacton
Broadhaven to Pendine Sands
Gower
Porteynon Bay
Rhossili Bay
Margam Sands to Nash Point
Wye Valley
Ridgeway
LONDON
North Wessex Downs
Morte Bay
Braunton Burrows
CARDIFF
BRISTOL
Surrey Hills
Pilgrims Way
North Downs
Sandwich
Deal
DOVER
Mendip Hills
East Hampshire
The Weald
Exmoor
Quantock Hills
Salisbury Plain
SOUTHAMPTON
New Forest
South Downs
South Downs Way
Romney Sands
Littlestone-on-Sea
Camber Sands
North Devon
EXETER
East Devon
Dorset
Hampshire coast
Isle of Wight
Chichester Harbour
East Point
Bude Bay
Trebarwith
Newquay Bay
Dartmoor
Branscombe
Dawlish
Studland Bay
Chesil Beach
Durdle Door
Perran Bay
Tor Bay to Babbacombe Bay
Cornwall
South Devon
St. Ives Bay
Whitesand Bay
Gerrans Bay
Bigbury-on-Sea
Slapton
Lands End
Mount's Bay
Maen Porth
Kennack Sands
Isles of Scilly

0 — 50 miles
0 — 50 kilometres